Programmer's Guide to Microsoft® Windows® 95

Key Topics on Programming for Windows from the Microsoft Windows Development Team

PUBLISHED BY
Microsoft Press
A Division of Microsoft Corporation
One Microsoft Way
Redmond, Washington 98052-6399

Library of Congress Cataloging-in-Publication Data
Programmer's guide to Microsoft Windows 95 / by Microsoft Corporation.
       p.   cm.
  Includes index.
  ISBN 1-55615-834-3
  1. Operating systems (Computers) 2. Microsoft Windows 95.
I. Microsoft Corporation.
QA76.76.O63P7677 1995
005.265--dc20   95-13785
                                  CIP

Printed and bound in the United States of America.

1 2 3 4 5 6 7 8 9 MLML 0 9 8 7 6 5

Distributed to the book trade in Canada by Macmillan of Canada, a division of Canada Publishing
Corporation.

A CIP catalogue record for this book is available from the British Library.

Microsoft Press books are available through booksellers and distributors worldwide. For further
information about international editions, contact your local Microsoft Corporation office. Or
contact Microsoft Press International directly at fax (206) 936-7329.

Contents

Part 1   Understanding Windows 95

Part 3   Extending the Windows 95 Shell

Part 4   Using Windows 95 Features

Part 5   Using Microsoft MS-DOS Extensions

Part 6   Applications for International Markets

Part 7   Advanced Programming

Introduction

The *Programmer's Guide to Microsoft® Windows® 95* presents a series of articles covering programming issues specific to the Windows 95 operating system. This guide provides conceptual and reference information that is not available in any other document. Topics range widely from issues regarding the Win32® application programming interface (API) to how to take advantage of Windows 95 features to extend existing MS-DOS®–based applications. To better focus this range of topics, the guide has been divided into these seven parts:

- Part 1, "Understanding Windows 95," discusses the Windows 95 architecture and the API differences between version 3.*x*–based and Windows 95–based applications.

- Part 2, "Developing Applications for Windows 95," discusses common controls and dialog boxes, the registry, and dragging and dropping. This part also discusses how to create applications for multimedia and pen, and it provides an overview about installing applications.

- Part 3, "Extending the Windows 95 Shell," discusses the shell's namespace, shell extensions, application desktop toolbars, shell links, and the taskbar notification area.

- Part 4, "Using Windows 95 Features," discusses file viewers, file parsers, briefcase reconcilers, the Passwords Control Panel, device I/O control, system policies, and tool help functions.

- Part 5, "Using Microsoft MS-DOS Extensions," discusses MS-DOS extensions, long filenames, exclusive volume locking, program information file (PIF) management, and virtual machine services.

- Part 6, "Applications for International Markets," discusses guidelines for developing international applications. This part also covers the use of double-byte characters and input method editors (IMEs), and it outlines how to write Middle-Eastern applications.

- Part 7, "Advanced Programming," discusses the Thunk Compiler, a tool that assists developers in porting existing applications to the Win32 API.

Conventions

The following terms, text formats, and symbols are used throughout the printed documentation for Windows 95.

Convention	Meaning
Bold	Indicates the commands, words, or characters that you type in a dialog box or at the command prompt.
Italic	Indicates a placeholder for information or parameters that you must provide. For example, if a procedure asks you to type a filename, you must type the name of the file.
ALL UPPERCASE	Indicates a directory, filename, or acronym. You can use lowercase letters when you type directory names or filenames in a dialog box or at the command prompt, unless otherwise indicated for a specific application or utility.
`Monospace`	Represents examples of screen text or entries that you might type at the command line or in initialization files.
Windows directory	Refers to the Windows 95 system directory tree. This can be \WINDOWS or whatever directory name you specified when installing Windows 95.

Acknowledgments

Certain articles in this guide are based on white papers published originally in *Microsoft Systems Journal*, *Microsoft Developer Network News*, and the Microsoft Developer Network Development Library. These papers have been updated and appear here courtesy of their original authors.

P A R T   1

Understanding Windows 95

A R T I C L E   1

Windows 95 Architecture

About Windows 95 Architecture

This article introduces the types of software components that you can build for Microsoft® Windows® 95, and it briefly describes the features of Windows 95 that those components can use.

Software Components

The operating environment for Windows 95 consists of a computer's hardware devices and the following software components:

- Virtual machine manager (VMM).
- Virtual devices (VxDs).
- Read-only memory (ROM) basic input and output system (BIOS).
- Installable device drivers and terminate-and-stay-resident (TSR) programs.
- 16- and 32-bit Windows dynamic-link libraries (DLLs).
- Microsoft® MS-DOS®–based applications.
- 16- and 32-bit Windows-based applications.

Virtual Machine Manager

The virtual machine manager (VMM) is the 32-bit protected-mode operating system at the core of Windows 95. Its primary responsibility is to create, run, monitor, and terminate virtual machines. The VMM provides services that manage memory, processes, interrupts, and exceptions such as general protection faults. The VMM works with virtual devices, 32-bit protected-mode modules, to allow the virtual devices to intercept interrupts and faults to control the access that an application has to hardware devices and installed software.

Both the VMM and virtual devices run in a single, 32-bit, flat model address space at privilege level 0 (also called ring 0). The system creates two global descriptor table (GDT) selectors, one for code and the other for data, and uses the selectors in the CS, DS, SS, and ES segment registers. Both selectors have a base address of zero and a limit of 4 gigabytes (GBs), so all the segment registers point to the same range of addresses. The VMM and virtual devices never change these registers.

The VMM provides multiple-threaded, preemptive multitasking. It runs multiple applications simultaneously by sharing CPU (central processing unit) time between the virtual machines in which the applications run. The VMM is also nonreentrant. This means that virtual devices must synchronize access to the VMM services. The VMM provides services, such as semaphores and events, to help virtual devices prevent reentering the VMM.

For more information about the VMM, including descriptions of the services that it provides to virtual devices, see the documentation included in the Microsoft Windows 95 Device Driver Kit (DDK).

Virtual Devices

Virtual devices (VxDs) are 32-bit programs that support the device-independent VMM by managing the computer's hardware devices and supporting software. VxDs support all hardware devices for a typical computer, including the programmable interrupt controller (PIC), timer, direct memory access (DMA) device, disk controller, serial ports, parallel ports, keyboard, and display adapter. A VxD is required for any hardware device that has settable operating modes or retains data over any period of time. In other words, if the state of the hardware device can be disrupted by switching between multiple virtual machines or applications, the device must have a corresponding VxD.

Some VxDs support software, but no corresponding hardware device. In general, a VxD can provide any kind of services for the VMM and other virtual devices. Windows 95 allows the user to install new virtual device drivers to support an add-on hardware device or provide some system-wide software service.

A VxD can also provide application programming interface (API) functions for applications running in virtual 8086 mode or protected mode. These functions can give applications direct access to the features of the VxD.

Windows 95 includes a device input and output control (IOCTL) interface that allows Microsoft® Win32®–based applications to communicate directly with VxDs. Applications typically use this interface to carry out selected MS-DOS system functions, to obtain information about a device, or to carry out input and output (I/O) operations that are not available through standard Win32 functions. For more information about the device IOCTL interface, see Article 20, "Device I/O Control."

For more information about virtual devices, see the documentation included in the Windows 95 DDK.

Device Drivers

A Windows device driver is a DLL that Windows uses to interact with a hardware device, such as a display or keyboard. Rather than access devices directly, Windows loads device drivers and calls functions in the drivers to carry out actions on the device. Each device driver exports a set of functions; Windows calls these functions to complete an action, such as drawing a circle or translating a keyboard scan code. The driver functions also contain the device-specific code needed to carry out actions on the device.

Windows requires device drivers for the display, keyboard, and communication ports. Other drivers may also be required if the user adds optional devices to the system.

The Windows 95 DDK provides independent hardware and software vendors (IHVs and ISVs) with the resources to build device drivers and VxDs that are compatible with the Windows 95 operating system. The resources include a configurable development environment, documentation, tools, and header files and libraries for several device types. The Windows 95 DDK contains the following components:

- Header files and libraries for building device drivers and VxDs.
- Sample source code for device drivers and VxDs.
- 16- and 32-bit versions of the driver development tools.

Dynamic-Link Libraries

Dynamic linking provides a mechanism for linking applications to libraries of functions at run time. The libraries reside in their own executable files and are not copied into an application's executable file as with static linking. These libraries are "dynamically linked" because they are linked to an application when it is loaded and executed rather than when it is linked. When an application uses a DLL, the operating system loads the DLL into memory, resolves references to functions in the DLL so that they can be called by the application, and unloads the DLL when it is no longer needed. Dynamic linking can be performed explicitly by applications or implicitly by the operating system.

DLLs are designed to provide resources to applications. Many applications can use the code in a DLL, meaning that only one copy of the code is resident in the system. Also, it is possible to update a DLL without changing applications that use the DLL as long as the interface to the functions in the DLL does not change.

Software developers can extend the Windows environment by creating a DLL that contains routines for performing operations and then making the DLL available to other Windows-based applications (in addition to internal Windows routines). DLLs most often appear as files with a .DLL filename extension; however, they may also have an .EXE or other filename extension.

Windows 95 supports 32-bit DLLs as well as 16-bit DLLs that were written for Windows version 3.*x*. For a discussion of the issues involved in mixing 16- and 32-bit components in the Windows 95 environment, see Article 32, "Thunk Compiler."

For more information about dynamic-link libraries, see the documentation included in the Microsoft Win32 Software Development Kit (SDK).

MS-DOS – Based Applications

Windows 95 supports applications written for MS-DOS. Each MS-DOS–based application can run as a full-screen application, or it can run in a window on the Windows 95 desktop.

The system can run multiple MS-DOS–based applications at the same time. To do so, it creates a separate virtual machine (VM) for each MS-DOS–based application and shares the microprocessor among the MS-DOS VMs and the system VM (which contains all Windows-based applications). A VM can run an MS-DOS–based application in either the virtual 8086 mode or protected mode of the microprocessor.

Although most MS-DOS–based applications run fine in a window or as a full-screen application, some may not. To ensure absolute backward compatibility for all MS-DOS–based applications, Windows 95 provides a separate operating mode called "single MS-DOS application mode." When in this mode, Windows 95 runs only one MS-DOS–based application at a time. No Windows-based applications run in that mode; in fact, none of the graphical user interface (GUI) components of the system are even loaded.

Windows 95 supports the complete set of MS-DOS system functions and interrupts and provides extensions that permit MS-DOS–based applications to take advantage of long filenames and other Windows 95 features, such as exclusive volume locking, virtual machine services, and program information file management.

Disk utilities and other applications that directly modify file system structures, such as directory entries, must request exclusive use of the volume before making modifications to the structures. Windows 95 provides a set of input and output control (IOCTL) functions to manage exclusive volume use. Exclusive use prevents applications from inadvertently changing the file system while a disk utility is trying modify it.

Virtual machine services enable Microsoft MS-DOS–based applications to take advantage of features provided by Windows 95 when the applications run in a window. MS-DOS–based applications can retrieve and, optionally, set the title of the window in which they run. Virtual machine services also allow MS-DOS–based applications to periodically check the state of an internal close flag and terminate if the flag is set. Windows 95 sets this flag when the user chooses the Close command from the system menu of the window in which the MS-DOS–based application runs. Close-aware applications enable the Close command, which gives the user an alternate way to exit the application and close the window.

Program information file management lets Microsoft Windows–based applications create, examine, and modify program information files (.PIF files). These files contain the detailed information needed by the operating system to prepare virtual machines for running Microsoft MS-DOS–based applications. Installation programs and other applications can open the files, retrieve and set information in the files, and display the information to the user for editing.

For more information, see the following articles in this guide: Article 23, "MS-DOS Extensions," Article 24, "Long Filenames," Article 25, "Exclusive Volume Locking," Article 26, "Program Information File Management," and Article 27, "Virtual Machine Services."

Windows-Based Applications

Windows 95 supports 16-bit applications written for Windows version 3.*x* as well as 32-bit applications that use the Win32 or Microsoft® Win32s® API. For 16-bit applications, Windows 95 preserves the cooperative multitasking model used in Windows version 3.*x*; that is, all 16-bit applications share the same virtual address space, the same message queue, and the same thread of execution. By contrast, each 32-bit Windows-based application has its own address space, a private message queue, and one or more threads of execution. In addition, each 32-bit thread is preemptively multitasked.

All new applications should be 32-bit applications developed using the Win32 API. For information about porting a 16-bit application to Win32, see Article 4, "Version Differences."

Shell Features and Extensions

Windows 95 includes a number of component object module (COM) interfaces and functions that applications can use to enhance various aspects of the shell. This section describes the aspects of the shell that applications can enhance.

Shell Namespace

A namespace is a collection of symbols, such as file and directory names or database keys. The Windows 95 shell uses a single hierarchical namespace to organize all objects of interest to the user, including files, storage devices, printers, and network resources—in short, anything that can be viewed using Windows Explorer. The namespace is similar to the directory structure of a file system except that the namespace contains objects other than files and directories.

The Windows 95 shell provides a COM interface and several functions that allow an application to browse the namespace and retrieve information about the objects in the namespace. For more information about the shell's namespace, its COM interface, and related functions, see Article 11, "Shell's Namespace."

Shortcuts

A shortcut (also called a shell link) is a data object that contains information used to access another object located anywhere in the shell's namespace. A shortcut allows an application to access an object without having to know the current name and location of the object. Objects that can be accessed through shortcuts include files, folders, disk drives, printers, and network resources.

Windows 95 includes a COM interface that an application can use to implement shortcuts. For example, an application that manipulates documents might use shortcuts to provide the user with a list of the most recently opened documents. For more information about shortcuts, see Article 14, "Shell Links."

Shell Extensions

An application developer can extend the Windows 95 shell in a number of different ways. Extending the shell involves adding information to the system registry or writing an OLE COM in-process server (InProcServer32).

A context menu handler is a type of shell extension that modifies the contents of a context menu. The system displays a context menu when the user clicks or drags an object using mouse button 2. The context menu contains commands that apply specifically to the object that was clicked or dragged.

Most context menus have a Properties command that displays the property sheet for the selected item. A property sheet contains information about an object in a set of overlapping windows called pages. A property sheet handler is a shell extension that adds pages to a system-defined property sheet or replaces pages in a Control Panel application's property sheet.

The system uses icons to represent files in the shell's namespace. By default, the system displays the same icon for all files that have the same filename extension. An icon handler can override the default and set the icon for a particular file.

A copy hook handler is an shell extension that approves or disapproves the moving, copying, deleting, or renaming of a file object.

For more information about extending the shell, see Article 12, "Shell Extensions."

File Viewers and Parsers

The shell includes a Quick View command that allows the user to view the contents of a file without having to run the application that created it and without even requiring the presence of the application. When the user chooses Quick View from the File menu or from the context menu for a file, the system runs the file viewer associated with the selected file. The shell uses the filename extension to determine which viewer to run.

A file viewer provides the user interface for viewing a file. It is an OLE component object implemented in an in-process server DLL. You can provide file viewers for new file formats or replace an existing viewer with one that includes more functionality. For more information about file viewers, see Article 16, "File Viewers."

A file viewer works in conjunction with a file parser, which is a DLL that provides the low-level parsing needed to generate the "quick view" of a file of a given type. You can extend the file viewing capabilities of Windows 95 by supplying additional file parsers. Each file parser is responsible for a specific type or class of file and is associated with a display engine. For example, you can allow a quick view to be generated for a .DOC file by creating a file parser to support the file type and associating the file parser with the word processor display engine. For more information about file parsers, see Article 17, "File Parsers."

Control Panel Applications

A Control Panel application is a special purpose DLL that lets the user configure the Windows environment. Even though Windows provides a number of standard Control Panel applications, you can create additional applications to let the user examine and modify the settings and operation modes of specific hardware and software. For information about creating Control Panel applications, see the documentation included in the Win32 SDK.

Screen Savers

A screen saver is an application that the system automatically starts when the mouse and keyboard have been idle for a period of time. A screen saver avoids damage to the display caused by static images on the screen or conceals sensitive information left on the screen. The property sheet for the display allows the user to select from a list of screen savers, specify how much time should elapse before the screen saver is started, configure screen savers, and preview screen savers. For information about how to create a screen saver, see the documentation included in the Win32 SDK.

System Features

This section describes some of the main features of Windows 95 that you can use in your Windows-based applications.

Registry

The registry is a central storage location that contains current information about the computer hardware configuration, installed software applications, settings and preferences of the current user, and associations between types of files and the applications that access and manipulate their contents. Much of the information that was stored in initialization files in previous versions of the Windows operating system is now stored in the Windows 95 registry.

Mentions of the registry occur in several places in documentation for Windows and Win32. *The Windows Interface Guidelines for Software Design* has a chapter containing a general discussion of the registry. A chapter in the *Microsoft Windows 95 Resource Kit* explains how to integrate an application into Windows 95 by storing information in the registry. This guide also includes an article that addresses registry coding issues for a program that installs a software application. Finally, the documentation included in the Win32 SDK provides a detailed description of the functions and structures that provide an application with access to the registry.

Fonts

Fonts are used to draw text on video displays and other output devices. In Windows 95, a *font* is a collection of characters and symbols that share a common design. The three major elements of this design are typeface, style, and size. A typeface is a set of characters that share common characteristics, such as stroke width and the presence or absence of serifs. For example, Arial® and Courier are each typefaces. The font style refers to font characteristics, such as italic and bold. Font size refers to the point size of a font. Applications may use the Font common dialog box to display available fonts and allow users to select the typeface, style, and size.

Windows 95 provides functions and related structures that allow applications to enumerate the available fonts on the system and select a specific font.

In addition to enumerating and selecting fonts, Windows 95 provides a set of functions and related structures that allow developers to perform the following tasks:

- Use a stock font to draw text.
- Check the text capabilities of a device.
- Set the text alignment.
- Draw text from different fonts on the same line.
- Rotate lines of text.
- Retrieve character outlines of a TrueType font.
- Use portable TrueType metrics to achieve a WYSIWYG (what you see is what you get) effect.
- Use PANOSE™ numbers of a TrueType font.
- Create and install customized fonts.

For more information about fonts, see the documentation included in the Win32 SDK.

Printing

Windows 95 provides a complete set of functions that allow applications to print on a variety of devices: laser printers, vector plotters, raster printers, and fax machines. One of the chief features of these functions is their support of device independence. Instead of issuing device-specific commands to draw output on a particular printer or plotter, an application calls high-level functions from graphics device interface (GDI). The various printing components in Windows 95 interact with GDI to convert the high-level commands to raw device commands and spool the print job to the printer.

In addition to GDI, the following Windows 95 components are involved in printing.

Device driver   A Windows DLL that supports the Windows device driver interface (DDI). A device driver generates raw device commands when it processes calls to DDI functions made by GDI. The commands are processed by the printer when it prints the image.

Print spooler	The primary component of the printing interface. The print spooler is a Windows executable file that manages the printing process. Print management involves retrieving the location of the correct printer driver, loading the driver, converting high-level function calls to journal records, storing the journal records on disk as a print job, and so on.
Print processor	A Windows DLL that reads and converts journal records into DDI calls.
Port monitor	A Windows DLL that passes the raw device commands over the network, through a parallel port, or through a serial port to the device.

Windows 95 provides functions that allow applications to monitor many aspects of the printing process. Applications may enumerate and obtain information about these aspects:

- Monitors for a specified server.
- Print jobs for a specified printer.
- Ports that are available for printing on a specified server.
- Printer drivers installed on a specified printer server.
- Available printers, print servers, domains, or print providers.
- Print processors installed on the specified server.
- Data types that a specified print processor supports.

For more information about printing, see the documentation included in the Win32 SDK.

File System

The file allocation table (FAT) file system is the original file system of MS-DOS. Except for the introduction of 16-bit FAT in MS-DOS version 3.0, this file system has remained essentially unchanged since MS-DOS version 2.0. Windows 95, however, introduces the following major change: the enhancement of the FAT file system to support long filenames. A long filename is a name for a file or directory that exceeds the standard 8.3 filename format.

The protected-mode FAT file system is the default file system used by Windows 95 for mass storage devices, such as hard disk and floppy disk drives. Protected-mode FAT is compatible with the MS-DOS FAT file system, using file allocation tables and directory entries to store information about the contents of a disk drive. The protected-mode FAT file system also supports long filenames, storing these names as well as the date and time that the file was created and the date that the file was last accessed in the FAT file system structures.

Win32-based applications automatically have access to long filenames through the use of the Win32 file management functions as well as the common dialog boxes used to open and save files. Applications should support long filenames and use long filenames for displaying all document and data filenames in the shell, in title bars, in dialog boxes and controls, and with icons.

For more information about the file system, see Article 23, "MS-DOS Extensions" and Article 24, "Long Filenames."

Plug and Play

Plug and Play is the name of a new industry standard for personal computers that lets personal computers (PCs) and attached hardware work together automatically. The goal of the Plug and Play technology is to make it easier than ever before for users to change the hardware configuration of their computers.

The most obvious beneficiaries of Plug and Play are the users of mobile PCs, whose hardware configurations change whenever they use a PCMCIA (Personal Computer Memory Card International Association) card or docking station. Every PC user, though, will benefit from Plug and Play; anyone who has ever had trouble setting up a new modem, sound card, or compact disc read-only memory (CD-ROM) drive understands the need for this technology.

Most of the Plug and Play architecture is implemented in new hardware, updated device drivers, and Windows itself; for most Windows-based applications, little extra code is required to support Plug and Play. A Windows-based application should be enabled for Plug and Play if it uses hardware that could be reconfigured, added to a system, or removed from a system while the application is running. Any Windows-based application that can be run on a mobile PC or that depends on the state of the monitor or other external devices should check for changes to the system hardware and take appropriate action when changes occur.

The system uses the following messages to send information about configuration changes to Windows applications.

WM_DEVICECHANGE	Tells applications about device changes. It is the most important Plug and Play message. The *wParam* parameter of this message contains an event code that an application can use to react to the change. For example, the DBT_DEVICEQUERYREMOVE event code asks an application for permission to remove a device. An application can return TRUE to grant permission or FALSE to deny it.
WM_DISPLAYCHANGE	Alerts applications to changes in the resolution of the screen.
WM_POWERBROADCAST	Tells applications about changes in the system's power status, including pending standby requests.

For more information about these messages, see the documentation included in the Win32 SDK. For information about the Plug and Play system architecture and how to write Plug and Play device drivers, see the Windows 95 DDK. For information about the design of Plug and Play hardware, see the *Hardware Design Guide for Microsoft Windows 95*.

Win32 Application Programming Interface

The Microsoft Win32 API allows applications to exploit the power of 32 bits using the Windows family of operating systems. The Win32 functions, messages, and structures form a consistent and uniform API for all of Microsoft's 32-bit platforms: Windows 95, Microsoft® Windows NT™, and Windows version 3.1 with Win32s. Using the Win32 API, you can develop applications that run successfully on all platforms while still being able to take advantage of unique features and capabilities of any given platform.

With a few minor exceptions, Microsoft ensures consistent and uniform behavior of the Win32 API across all platforms. Differences in the implementation of the Win32 functions depend on the capabilities of the underlying features of the platform. The most notable difference is that some Win32 functions carry out their tasks only on the more powerful platforms. For example, security functions are only available on the Windows NT operating system. Most other differences are system limitations, such as restrictions on the range of values or the number of items a given function can manage. For more information about system limitations, see Article 3, "Win32 Limitations in Windows 95."

The Win32 API provides a wide and varied set of functions, messages, and structures that give your 32-bit applications access to the unique features and capabilities of the Windows operating system. The Win32 API can be grouped into these functional categories:

- Graphics Device Interface (GDI)
- Windows Management
- System Services
- Multimedia
- Remote Procedure Calls (RPC)

Graphics Device Interface

Graphics device interface (GDI) provides functions and related structures that an application can use to generate graphical output for displays, printers, and other devices. Using GDI functions, you can draw lines, curves, closed figures, paths, text, and bitmapped images. The color and style of the items you draw depends on the drawing objects — that is, pens, brushes, and fonts — that you create. You can use pens to draw lines and curves, brushes to fill the interiors of closed figures, and fonts to write text.

Applications direct output to a given device by creating a device context (DC) for the device. The device context is a GDI-managed structure containing information about the device, such as its operating modes and current selections. An application creates a DC by using device context functions. GDI returns a device context handle, which is used in subsequent calls to identify the device. For example, using the handle, an application can retrieve information about the capabilities of the device, such as its technology type (display, printer, or other device) and the dimensions and resolution of the display surface.

Applications can direct output to a physical device, such as a display or printer, or to a "logical" device, such as a memory device or metafile. Logical devices give applications the means to store output in a form that is easy to send subsequently to a physical device. Once an application records output in a metafile, it can play that metafile any number of times, sending the output to any number of physical devices.

Applications use attribute functions to set the operating modes and current selections for the device. The operating modes include the text and background colors, the mixing mode (also called the binary raster operation) that specifies how colors in a pen or brush combine with colors already on the display surface, and the mapping mode that specifies how GDI maps the coordinates used by the application to the coordinate system of the device. The current selections identify which drawing objects are used when drawing output.

Window Management

Window management gives applications the means to create and manage a user interface. Using the window management functions, you create and use windows to display output, prompt for user input, and carry out the other tasks necessary to support interaction with the user. Nearly all applications create at least one main window.

Applications define the general behavior and appearance of their windows by creating window classes and corresponding window procedures. The window class identifies default characteristics, such as whether the window processes double clicks of the mouse buttons or has a menu. The window procedure contains the code that defines the behavior of the window, carries out requested tasks, and processes user input.

Applications generate output for a window using the GDI functions. Because all windows share the display screen, applications do not receive access to the entire screen. Instead, the system manages all output so that it is aligned and clipped to fit within the corresponding window. Applications can draw in a window in response to a request from the system or while processing input messages. When the size or position of a window changes, the system typically sends a message to the application requesting that it paint any previously unexposed area of its window.

Applications receive mouse and keyboard input in the form of messages. The system translates mouse movement, mouse button clicks, and keystrokes into input messages and places these messages in the message queue for the application. The system automatically provides a queue for each application. The application uses message functions to extract messages from the queue and dispatch them to the appropriate window procedure for processing.

Applications can process the mouse and keyboard input directly or let the system translate this low-level input into command messages by using menus and keyboard accelerators. You use menus to present a list of commands to the user. The system manages all the actions required to let the user choose a command and then sends a message identifying the choice to the window procedure. Keyboard accelerators are application-defined combinations of keystrokes that the system translates into messages. Accelerators typically correspond to commands in a menu and generate the same messages.

Applications often respond to command messages by prompting the user for additional information with dialog boxes. A dialog box is a temporary window that displays information or requests input. A dialog box typically includes controls — small, single-purpose windows — that represent buttons and boxes through which the user makes choices or enters information. There are controls for entering text, scrolling text, selecting items from a list of items, and so on. Dialog boxes manage and process the input from these controls, making this information available to the application so that it can complete the requested command.

Window management functions provide other features related to windows. For example, the clipboard functions provide the means to copy and paste information within the same window, between windows in the same application, and between windows in different applications. Applications also use the clipboard functions to carry out dynamic data exchange (DDE). DDE operations let applications exchange information without requiring specific direction from the user.

System Services

System services are a set of functions that give applications access to the resources of the computer and the features of the underlying operating system, such as memory, file systems, and processes. An application uses system services functions to manage and monitor the resources that it needs to complete its work. For example, an application uses memory management functions to allocate and free memory and uses process management and synchronization functions to start and coordinate the operation of multiple applications or multiple threads of execution within a single application.

System services functions provide access to files, directories, and input and output (I/O) devices. The file I/O functions give applications access to files and directories on disks and other the storage devices on a given computer and on computers in a network. These functions support a variety of file systems, from the MS-DOS FAT file system to the CD-ROM file system (CDFS). The network functions create and manage connections to shared resources, such as directories and printers, on computers in the network. Communications functions read from and write to communications ports as well as control the operating modes of these ports.

System services functions provide methods for applications to share resources with other applications. For example, you can make useful procedures available to all applications by placing these procedures in DLLs. Applications access these procedures by using DLL functions to load the libraries and retrieve the addresses of the procedures. You can share useful data, such as bitmaps, icons, fonts, and strings, by adding this data as "resources" to the file for an application or DLL. Applications retrieve the data by using the resource functions to locate the resources and load them into memory.

System services functions provide access to information about the system and other applications. System information functions let applications determine specific characteristic about the computer, such as whether a mouse is present and what dimensions elements of the screen have. Registry and initialization functions let applications store application-specific information in system files so that new instances of the application or even other applications can retrieve and use the information.

System services also let applications share information with applications running on the same computer or on other computers in a network. Applications can copy information between processes by using the mailslot and pipe functions to carry out interprocess communication (IPC). For operating systems that provide security features, the security functions give applications access to secure data as well as protect data from intentional or unintentional access or damage.

System services functions provide features that applications can use to handle special conditions during execution, such as handling errors, logging events, and handling exceptions. There are features that applications can use to debug and improve performance. For example, debugging functions permit single-step control of the execution of other processes, and performance monitoring allows for detailing the path of execution through a process.

Multimedia

Multimedia functions give applications access to high-quality audio and video. Multimedia functions let you enhance and expand the capabilities of your application, giving users the ability to combine these forms of communication with more traditional forms of computer output. Using multimedia functions, applications can create documents and presentations that incorporate music, sound effects, and video clips as well as text and graphics. The multimedia functions provide services for audio, video, file I/O, media control, joysticks, and timers.

Applications use audio functions to play and record audio data using waveform, Musical Instrument Digital Interface (MIDI), and auxiliary audio formats. When playing audio, an application can mix sounds by routing selected audio to specified devices. To ensure efficient storage of audio data, the audio functions provide access to audio compressors and decompressors through the Audio Compression Manager (ACM).

Applications use video functions to capture video clips, compress the clips, and control their playback. An application captures video clips by using simple messages to access video and wave audio acquisition hardware, such as a video tape machine, and to stream selected video clips to disk. To store video data efficiently, an application can use the video compressors and decompressors provided by the Installable Compression Manager (ICM). Applications can play back video clips either on the computer screen or on other media devices by using the Media Control Interface (MCI) indirectly through the functions of the MCIWnd window class.

Applications use file I/O functions to store and retrieve the different types of multimedia data. An application can use unbuffered and buffered I/O with multimedia files, access and navigate Resource Interchange File Format (RIFF) files, and integrate custom I/O functions for multimedia data types. Of particular significance is the audio-video interleaved (AVI) file format, which provides for storing digital video clips consisting of both video and audio data. An AVI file is a RIFF file that has an extensible file architecture. This means that an application can customize AVI files to store and retrieve nonstandard data streams.

The Media Control Interface (MCI) provides a common set of high-level commands through which applications control media devices, such as animation devices, audio compact discs (CDs), digital-video devices, MIDI sequencers, video overlay devices, video disks, VISCA tape recorders (VCRs), and waveform (digital sound) devices. To communicate with a device, an application sends messages or command strings through MCI. The corresponding device handler interprets the message or string and executes the appropriate command at the device.

Applications use joystick functions to provide support for up to two joystick devices. An application can retrieve information about a joystick, calibrate the sensitivity of the device, and receive messages related to movement and button activity. Multimedia timer functions provide high-resolution timing for single or periodic events.

Remote Procedure Calls

Remote procedure calls (RPCs) give applications the means to carry out distributed computing, enabling them to tap the resources and computational power of computers on a network. Using RPC, you create distributed applications, each consisting of a client that presents information to the user and a server that stores, retrieves, and manipulates data and generally handles the bulk of the computing tasks for the client. Shared databases, remote file servers, and remote printer servers are examples of distributed applications.

A distributed application, running as a process in one address space, makes procedure calls that execute in an address space on another computer. Within the application, such calls appear to be standard local procedure calls, but these calls activate stub procedures that interact with the RPC run-time library to carry out the necessary steps to execute the call in the remote address space. RPC manages the network communications needed to support these calls, even the details such as network protocols. This means distributed applications need little or no network-specific code, making development of such applications relatively easy.

Microsoft RPC is just one part of a complete environment for distributed computing defined by the Open Software Foundation (OSF), a consortium of companies that was formed to define the components of a complete environment supporting distributed computing. Microsoft's implementation of RPC is compatible with the OSF standard with minor differences. Client or server applications written using Microsoft RPC version 1.0 will interoperate with any Distributed Computing Environment (DCE) RPC client or server whose run-time libraries implement the connection-based model and run over a supported protocol.

Extension Libraries

Extension libraries give applications services and capabilities beyond the basic services of the Win32 API. The extension libraries either expand on services already provided by the Win32 API or provide unique services that are commonly used by Win32 applications. There are the following extension libraries:

- Common Controls
- Common Dialog Boxes
- Data Decompression
- File Installation
- Dynamic Data Exchange (DDE) Management
- Network DDE

Common Controls and Dialog Boxes

The Windows 95 shell incorporates a number of control windows and dialog boxes that help give Windows 95 its distinctive look and feel. Because these controls and dialog boxes are supported by DLLs that are a part of Windows 95, they are available to all applications. Using the common controls and dialog boxes helps keep an application's user interface consistent with that of the shell and other applications. Because developing a control or dialog box can be a substantial undertaking, using the common controls and dialog boxes can also save you a significant amount of development time.

The common controls are a set of control windows that are supported by the common control library, COMCTL32.DLL. Like other control windows, a common control is a child window that an application uses in conjunction with another window to perform I/O tasks. The common control DLL includes a programming interface that applications use to create and manipulate the controls as well as to receive user input from them. For more information about common controls, see the documentation included in the Win32 SDK.

The common dialog boxes provide a ready-made user interface that you can use to retrieve various kinds of information from the user. They are supported by the common dialog box library, COMDLG32.DLL. The library includes dialog boxes for selecting and creating colors, finding and replacing strings, opening and saving files, and setting printer options. For more information about the common dialog boxes, see the documentation included in the Win32 SDK.

Data Decompression and File Installation

The data decompression and file installation libraries provide useful functions for applications that install files. The data decompression library provides functions that applications use to expand files that have been compressed using the Microsoft File Compression Utility (COMPRESS.EXE). The file installation library provides functions that make it easier for applications to analyze currently installed files and install new files properly.

DDEML and Network DDE

The DDE management and network DDE libraries simplify the process of exchanging data with other applications. The DDE management library (DDEML) provides functions that minimize the amount of code needed in an application to carry out dynamic data exchange and gives an application the means to exchange data without requiring user interaction. The network DDE library provides functions that an application can use to connect to DDE servers on other computers in the network. The functions minimize the amount of code that an application needs to access the network; they also ensure security across network connections.

Win32 Software Development Kit

The Win32 SDK includes the tools and resources you need to build 32-bit applications that use the Win32 API. The Win32 SDK contains the following components:

- Win32s components for building Win32-based applications that run on Windows version 3.*x* platforms.
- 32-bit header files and libraries for building Win32 applications that run with the Windows 95 and Windows NT operating systems.
- Retail and debug versions of the Windows 95 core system DLLs.
- Applications and utilities that aid in the development process.
- Sample source code that demonstrates how to implement the Win32 API.
- Documentation of the Win32 API and information describing how to use Win32 to develop Windows 95–based applications.
- Online text of the style guide for Windows-based applications, *The Windows Interface Guidelines for Software Design*.
- Articles from the Windows 95 Knowledge Base.

For a description of the features and contents of the Win32 SDK as well as instructions on how to install and use it, see the *Getting Started* booklet included in the Win32 SDK.

OLE

OLE is a set of API services that allows an application to create documents consisting of information from different applications. Each piece of information is represented as an object and can consist of text, bitmap images, vector graphics, and even voice annotation and video clips. Representing information as objects makes it easier for applications to exchange, incorporate, and process data from applications created by different vendors. Applications that take advantage of OLE can interact seamlessly, allowing the user to focus on creating and managing information rather than on remembering how to perform procedures.

OLE associates two major types of data with an object: presentation data and native data. An object's presentation data is information needed to render the object on a display device, while its native data is all the information needed for an application to edit the object.

An object can be linked to or embedded in a document. Linking is a process whereby only an object's presentation data and a reference (or pointer) to its native data are placed in a document. The actual native data associated with the object exists in another location, such as in a file on disk. Whenever an application updates the object, it appears updated within the document. To the user, a linked object acts as if it were wholly contained within the document. In contrast, embedding places an object's presentation data and its native data physically within a document. All information necessary to edit the object is contained in the document.

Embedding makes a document larger, but it allows the object to be transferred with the document to another computer and to be edited on a different computer. Linked objects cannot "travel" with documents outside the local file system of the computer, but they are more efficient than embedded objects because a single instance of the object's data can serve many different documents.

OLE not only gives applications the ability to add linked and embedded objects to documents but also includes the following powerful features that you incorporate into your Windows-based applications.

Visual editing	Lets the user directly activate an object in-place within a document without switching to a different window. This includes operations such as in-place editing, displaying, recording, and playing.
Nested objects	Lets the user directly manipulate an object nested within another other object and to establish links to nested objects.

Drag and drop	Lets the user drag an object from one application window to another or to drop an object inside another object.
Storage-independent links	Allows links between embedded objects that are not stored as files on disk, enabling embedded objects within the same or different documents to update one another's data, whether or not they are recognized by the file system.
Adaptable links	Enables links between objects to be maintained in certain move or copy operations.
OLE automation	Enables the creation of command sets that operate both within and across applications. For example, a user can activate a command from a word processing application that sorts a range of cells in a spreadsheet created by a different application.
Version management	Allows an object to contain information about the application and the version of the application that created it.
Object conversion	Allows an object type to be converted so that different applications can be used with the same object. For example, an object created with one brand of spreadsheet could be converted so that it could be interpreted by a different spreadsheet application for editing.

OLE is supported by Windows version 3.1, Windows NT, and Windows 95, allowing your application to work the same way on all Windows platforms. The OLE documentation included in the Win32 SDK contains a set of DLLs, sample source code, extensive online information, and tools to assist in adding OLE capabilities to Windows-based applications.

Telephony Application Programming Interface

Telephony application programming interface (TAPI) makes it possible to create applications that combine the capabilities of the personal computer with the telephone. TAPI was created in cooperation with telecommunications companies, personal computer manufacturers, and software vendors as the standard for integrating telephones with PCs running the Windows operating system.

By integrating the PC and the telephone networks, TAPI makes possible the following new classes of applications.

Screen-based telephony	Provides a visual interface for accessing existing phone features and makes new features possible that cannot be implemented due to the today's limited telephone user interface.
Communications management	Provides end-user programmability that enables intelligent filtering and forwarding of telephone communications.
Personal productivity	Automates telephone calls and integrates them into personal productivity software. Calls can be automatically dialed to save time, and call details can be logged.
Integrated messaging	Allows the user to access their different electronic communications media, such as electronic mail, voice mail, and faxes from a single point on the desktop or from a remote location.
Ubiquitous voice on the desktop	Digitizes audio from the telephone directly into the PC, or retrieves audio seamlessly from a voice server and plays it back over a phone's speaker.
Conferencing	Provides video conferences as well as less bandwidth intensive tasks, such as sharing documents or "virtual whiteboards," to create a richer communications medium and attain the benefits of proximity at a distance.
Wide area data networking	Provides cleaner integration with the global telephone network, which facilitates fax and data communications from the PC.
Vertical solutions	Integrates telephone communications with business information systems. For example, an incoming call can be routed to the first available agent by a computer-based queuing system, and the customer's record "popped" onto the agent's screen before they even pick up the phone with caller identification-like functionality.

TAPI provides a standard interface, allowing an application to take advantage of the many capabilities and services of the telephone. At the same time, TAPI isolates an application from the complexity and variability of the underlying telephone network, greatly simplifying the application development task. In addition, TAPI is independent of the method of connection between the PC and telephone. This gives maximum flexibility to integrate the PC with the telephone system.

TAPI is part of the Microsoft Windows Open Services Architecture (WOSA), which provides a single set of open-ended interfaces to enterprise computing services. WOSA services, such as TAPI, consist of two interfaces. Developers write to an applications programming interface (API). The other interface, referred to as the service provider interface (SPI), is used to establish the connection to the specific telephone network.

Applications can combine TAPI with other capabilities of Windows to provide a combination of services. For example, an application can use TAPI to establish a connection and then use the Windows audio functionality to record and play back voice information over the connection.

For more information about TAPI, see the documentation included in the Win32 SDK.

Messaging Application Programming Interface

Windows 95 includes the messaging application programming interface (MAPI). You can use MAPI to add messaging features to your Windows-based applications that make it easy for users to electronically share information, such as charts and reports.

The MAPI architecture is designed to make it easy to write powerful messaging-enabled applications that are independent of the underlying messaging system. To achieve this, MAPI provides two interfaces: the API, which provides messaging services to an application, and the service-provider interface (SPI), which provides the link to the messaging system. MAPI provides a layer of functionality between an application and the underlying messaging system, allowing them to be developed independently of one other.

MAPI services are high-level (compared to most networking functions) and allow you to implement sophisticated messaging features with a small amount of code. You deal only with functions for sending, receiving, and addressing messages; the underlying messaging system is completely transparent. MAPI also provides other functionality such as access to address books—that is, customized lists of message recipients.

MAPI supports existing standards such as the X.400 API Association's Common Messaging Calls (CMC). By using the CMC or Simple MAPI, you can easily add message capabilities to an existing application's user interface. For example, a word processing program can include a Send Message command that sends a document as a mail message to a recipient. MAPI also supports application macro languages, such as those used in Microsoft® Excel and Word. For example, a spreadsheet user can write a macro that automatically sends a monthly budget spreadsheet to a designated recipient when the file is updated with new sales figures.

You can also use CMC or Simple MAPI to create an application that is centered around messaging capabilities. One example is a scheduling application in which users can view the schedules of their coworkers and send meeting requests to the coworkers' calendars. Another example is a forms-routing application that sends an expense report to a series of recipients and records their approval or disapproval.

MAPI also supports workgroup applications that require full access to all of the back-end messaging services, including the message store, address book or directory, and transport functions. These applications include e-mail clients, workflow automation programs, and bulletin board services. For example, a workflow application might allow a user to inspect a message stored in a certain project folder to see if the appropriate workers have signed off on their tasks. This application could also include a sophisticated search and store feature that retrieves relevant files from a bulletin board system and stores them in the folders of certain recipients. Advanced workgroup applications take advantage of Extended MAPI.

For more information about MAPI, see the documentation included in the Win32 SDK.

Pen

Every computer running Windows 95 can display and manipulate data that was collected on a pen-enabled system. These capabilities are provided by a dynamic-link library, either PKPD.DLL or PKPD32.DLL. A Windows-based application can use pen data in the following ways:

- To display a signature for letters or faxes.
- To verify signatures collected on a pen-based mobile computer.
- To display graphics, maps, or handwritten notes that have been drawn on a pen-based system.

Displaying and manipulating *ink*, the common term for pen data, is only a subset of the pen services available to Windows-based applications. Pen-enabled applications use the entire set of Pen functions to add ink collection and recognition to their feature sets. Pen services for Microsoft Windows 95 requires the PENWIN.DLL or PENWIN32.DLL library for all of the functionality of pen data collection. The library is supplied by the pen tablet or computer manufacturer that bundles Microsoft pen services with their product. (Pen-enabled systems use the same pen display library that is available on every Windows 95 computer for pen data manipulation and display: PKPD.DLL or PKPD32.DLL.)

For more information about the pen capabilities of Windows 95, see Article 9, "Displaying and Using Pen Data." The *Programmer's Guide to Pen Services for Microsoft Windows 95*, which is included in the Win32 SDK, provides information about using the entire set of pen API to collect, recognize, manipulate, and display ink.

International Applications

Within six months of its final release, Windows 95 will be available in 30 different language versions. To support all of these languages, Microsoft has developed three separate code bases: one for single-byte character sets (SBCS), one for double-byte character sets (DBCS), and one for the languages of the Middle East.

The DBCS versions, which ship to the Far East, include the input method editor (IME) for complex writing systems, an end-user defined character (EUDC) editor, and all the code for passing DBCS (mixture of 8- or 16-bit) characters through the user interface. For more information about the input method editor, see Article 30, "Using Input Method Editors." For more information about creating applications that can handle DBCS characters, see Article 29, "Using Double-Byte Characters."

The versions for the Middle East support both left to right and right to left text placement as well as special ligature and text justification (*Kashida*) handling. For more information about developing applications for the Middle East, see Article 31, "Writing Applications for Middle-Eastern Languages."

To make localization easy, you should develop all language-dependent user-interface elements as Win32 resources. Using resources allows you to create versions of your application in any number of languages without having to recompile your application's components. For more information about resources, see the documentation included in the Win32 SDK.

For more information about internationalization issues, see Article 28, "International Guidelines," and read the *International Handbook for Software Design*, which is available in the Microsoft Developer Network Development Library.

A R T I C L E   2

Creating Great Applications

About Creating Great Applications

The Microsoft® Windows® 95 user interface is based on a datacentric design; that is, rather than focusing on applications, the user interface design emphasizes data and tasks that involve the manipulation of data. The interface has been designed to allow the user to browse for data and documents and to edit them directly without necessarily having to locate an appropriate editor or application first. This type of design frees the user to focus on information and tasks rather than on applications and how they interact.

This article briefly describes some of the features you should use and guidelines you should follow to ensure that your application is a "great" Windows 95–based application. A great Windows 95–based application is one that integrates seamlessly with the user interface in Windows 95 and conforms to the system's datacentric design principles. In addition to reading this article, you should follow the user interface guidelines presented in *The Windows Interface Guidelines for Software Design*.

File Information

Throughout the Windows 95 shell, files appear as icons. When you click on a file's icon using mouse button 2, the system displays a context menu containing commands that perform actions on the file. One of the commands, Properties, displays a special dialog box called a property sheet that contains information about the file. By viewing a file's property sheet, the user can find out information about a file without having to open it.

By default, a file's property sheet contains general information about the file, including its name, size, location, creation date, attributes, and so on. The following illustration shows the default property sheet for a typical file.

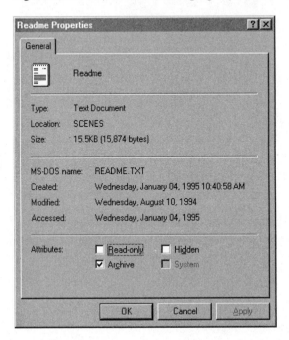

If your application creates files with additional properties that the user may be interested in, you should add more pages to the property sheets for the files. One way to add property sheet pages to an application using OLE structured storage is to store documents in compound files (also called docfiles) and use the Document Summary Information Property Set to store summary information and editing statistics for the documents. When the user activates the property sheet for the document, the shell automatically gathers the summary information and editing statistics from the document and adds them to the property sheet as two additional pages. The following illustration shows a property sheet with Summary and Statistics pages added based on data gathered from the document.

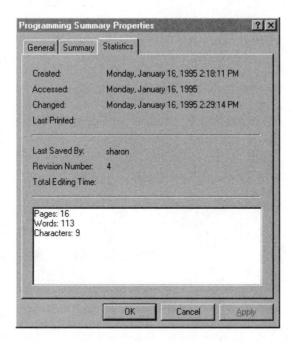

For more information about saving document information using the OLE Document Summary Information Property Set, see the OLE documentation included in the Microsoft® Win32® Software Development Kit (SDK).

Another way to add pages to file property sheets is to write a shell extension (OLE InProcServer32) that includes a property sheet handler. Whenever the user activates the property sheet for a file, the system checks the registry to see if any property sheet handlers are registered for the file type. If there are some registered, the system calls the handlers before displaying the property sheet. The handlers can add any number of pages to the property sheet before it is displayed. For more information about shell extensions and property sheet handlers, see Article 12, "Shell Extensions."

Long Filenames

Windows 95 allows users and applications to create and use long filenames for their files and directories. A long filename is a name for a file or directory that is longer than the standard 8.3 filename format. In the past, long filenames typically appeared on network servers that used file systems other than the Microsoft® MS-DOS® file allocation table (FAT) file system. In Windows 95, however, long filenames are available for use with network servers and with local disk drives supporting the protected-mode FAT file system.

An application should support long filenames and display them correctly. You can use the **SHGetFileInfo** function in your application to retrieve the long filename for a file as well as the file's icon, type name, attributes, and so on. If you include the File Open and Save As common dialog boxes in your application, you can use the OFN_LONGNAMES value to direct the dialog boxes to display and return long filenames. Before an application displays a long filename, it should hide the filename extension. For example, the application should display a filename like "My letter to Mom" instead of "My letter to Mom.Doc." An application can hide filename extensions on a file-specific basis by using the **SHGetFileInfo** function.

The following illustration shows a folder containing documents with long filenames.

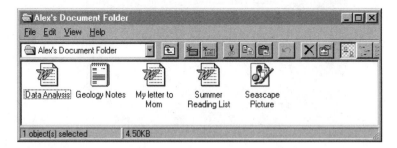

If an application is used to view or edit a document or data file, the title bar of the window that contains the file should display the long filename for the file. If the title bar also includes the application's name, it should appear to the right of the filename. Displaying the filename first places the emphasis on the document or data rather than on the application. For more information about long filenames, see Article 24, "Long Filenames."

You should also support Universal Naming Convention (UNC) path names for files in your application. Using UNC names enables users to browse documents on the network directly and to open an application's files on remote machines without needing to know the location of the file on the network or having to make an explicit network connection.

Context Menus

A context menu is a pop-up menu containing a set of commands that are specific to a particular object. Window 95 provides a context menu for all objects that appear in the shell, including files, folders, printers, and so on. A context menu appears when the user clicks an object using mouse button 2. Because context menus are displayed at the pointer's current location, they eliminate the need for the user to move the pointer to the menu bar or toolbar. They also help eliminate screen clutter.

You should provide context menus for all objects in an application and should display the context menu whenever the user clicks an object using mouse button 2. Each context menu should include a Properties command that displays a property sheet for the object.

In addition to displaying a context menu for objects, an application should also display a context menu when the user clicks the small icon in the title bar using mouse button 2. The commands in the context menu should operate on the object that is open in the window, not on the window itself. To see an example of a context menu associated with a title bar icon, click the title bar icon of a folder window in the shell using mouse button 2. For more information about context menus, see Article 12, "Shell Extensions."

Icons

If your application supports OLE, you should make sure that the icons for your embedded and linked objects are consistent with the shell. For example, when the user drags an icon from the shell into your container, the icon and its name should stay the same.

You should support interactions with embedded icons the same way that the shell does. For example, when the user selects the icon for an embedded object, you should dither the icon with the system highlight color rather than enclosing it in a rectangle that has resizing handles.

Shortcuts

A shortcut (also called a shell link) is a data object that contains information used to access another object in the system, such as a file, folder, disk drive, or printer. A shortcut has an icon associated with it; the user accesses the object associated with a shortcut by double-clicking the shortcut's icon. The associated object can be stored anywhere in the system.

Typically, the user creates shortcuts to gain quick access to objects stored in subfolders on the same machine or to shared folders on other machines. For example, the user can create a shortcut to a Microsoft Word document located in a subfolder and can place the shortcut icon on the desktop. The user can later start Word and open the document simply by double-clicking the shortcut icon. If the document is later moved or renamed, the system takes steps to update the shortcut the next time the user selects it.

An application should support shortcuts. For example, a word processing application might allow the user to drag and drop a shortcut icon into a document file. An application should also correctly dereference shortcuts. For example, if the user specifies the filename of a shortcut when using an application's Open command on the File menu, the application should open the object associated with the shortcut, not the shortcut file itself. For more information about shortcuts, see Article 14, "Shell Links."

Clipboard Data Transfer Operations

Windows 95 supports two types of clipboard data transfer operations—those involving menu commands (such as Cut, Copy, and Paste) and those involving the direct manipulation of objects (drag and drop). An application should support both types extensively.

You should support the OLE style of drag and drop. If you support drag and drop, the user can easily move data among the desktop, folders, and other applications. You should support dragging with mouse button 2 and display a context menu at the end of the drag operation, as the shell does. At a minimum, the menu should include these commands: Move Here, Copy Here, Create Shortcut(s) Here, and Cancel. For more information about supporting the OLE style of drag and drop, see Article 7, "Dragging and Dropping."

You should make sure your application's menu-based data transfer model works well with the shell. You should test various scenarios, such as copying a shortcut or file in a shell folder to the clipboard and then pasting the shortcut or file into your application. Also, if your application supports shortcuts to its documents, you should offer a link to your OLE data object when the user drags an object out of a document.

Common Controls and Dialog Boxes

The Windows 95 shell incorporates a number of control windows and dialog boxes that help give Windows 95 its distinctive look and feel. Because these controls and dialog boxes are supported by DLLs that are a part of Windows 95, they are available to all applications. You should use the common controls and dialog boxes—rather than developing similar controls and dialog boxes of your own—because they help keep your application's user interface consistent with that of the shell and other applications. Because developing a control or dialog box can be a substantial undertaking, using the common controls and dialog boxes can also save you a significant amount of development time.

Common Controls

The common controls are a set of control windows that are supported by the common control library, which is a DLL called COMCTRL32.DLL. Like other control windows, a common control is a child window that an application uses in conjunction with another window to perform input and output (I/O) tasks. The common control DLL includes a programming interface that you use to create and manipulate the controls and dialog boxes and to receive user input from them. This section describes some of the controls provided by the common control DLL.

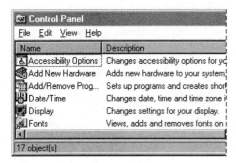

Header Control. A header control provides headings for columns of text or numbers. It can be divided into many parts, and each part can have its own heading text. The user can adjust the width of the columns by dragging the dividers that separate the parts.

Property Sheet. A property sheet displays the properties of an object, such as a document file or a cell in a spreadsheet. Related properties can be grouped together and placed on separate, overlapping pages within the property sheet. Each page has a tab that the user can select to bring the page to the foreground.

An application can create a special type of property sheet called a wizard control. The control displays a sequence of pages that guide the user through the steps of an operation, such as setting up a device or creating a birthday card.

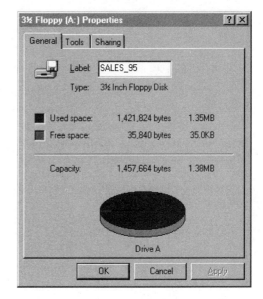

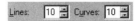

Up-Down Control. An up-down control consists of a pair of arrow buttons that the user can click to increment or decrement a value, such as a scroll position or a number displayed in an accompanying edit control.

Tree View Control. A tree view control displays a hierarchical list of items, such as the headings in a document, the entries in an index, or the files and directories on a disk. By clicking an item, the user can expand or collapse the associated list of subordinate items. The user can select items, edit item labels, and drag items from one location to another.

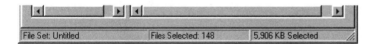

Status Window. A status window displays information that may be useful to the user. It is typically positioned along the bottom of a window and can be divided into parts to display different types of information simultaneously.

Toolbar. A toolbar contains buttons that carry out commands when the user selects them. Typically, the buttons correspond to menu items, providing a quicker, more direct way for the user to access an application's commands.

Progress Bar. A progress bar indicates the progress of a lengthy operation. It consists of a rectangle that is gradually filled with color, from left to right, as the operation progresses.

List View Control. A list view control displays a collection of related items, each consisting of an icon and a descriptive label. The items can be arranged and displayed in different ways to suit the user's preferences. The user can select items, edit item labels, and drag items from one location to another.

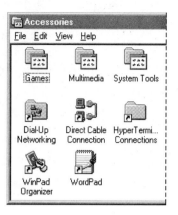

Trackbar. A trackbar allows the user to select a value from a range of consecutive values. To select a value, the user drags the trackbar's slider to the desired position.

Common Dialog Boxes

Windows 95 provides several common dialog boxes that your application can use to obtain various kinds of information from the user. There are the following types of common dialog boxes.

Dialog box	Description
Color	Enables the user to select and create colors.
Find	Enables the user to specify a search string.
Open	Enables the user to specify the location and filename of a file to be opened.
Page Setup	Enables the user to set the attributes of a printed page, including the paper type, the paper source, the page orientation, and the width of the page margins.
Print	Enables the user to configure a printer for a particular print job. The user can set print job parameters, such as the print quality, print range, and number of copies.
Replace	Enables the user to specify strings for use in a search and replace operation.
Save As	Enables the user to specify the location and name of a file to be saved.

For more information about the common dialog boxes, see the documentation included in the Win32 SDK. Note that the Print Setup dialog box provided in previous versions of Windows is now obsolete; new applications should use the Page Setup dialog box.

The Open and Save As common dialog boxes accessed from the File menu are especially useful because they support many features of the Windows 95 shell, including shell links, long filenames, and direct browsing of the network. If you cannot use the Open and Save As dialog boxes, you should incorporate the following features into your open and save dialog boxes to ensure that they are consistent with the shell, the Windows accessories, and other applications:

- Support the same namespace hierarchy as the shell; that is, Desktop should be at the root of the hierarchy, followed by all folders and objects on the desktop, including My Computer, My Network, and so on. For more information about the shell namespace, see Article 11, "Shell's Namespace."

- Support shortcuts (also known as shell links). Note that opening a shortcut should open the target of the shortcut rather than the shortcut file itself. For more information about shortcuts, see Article 14, "Shell Links."

- Display filenames with the corresponding icons and filename extensions removed, as the shell does.

- Allow the user to browse the network hierarchy directly.

- Make sure that all of your dialog boxes (not just your open and save dialog boxes) use only nonbold fonts. In addition, you should use the DS_3DLOOK style to give your dialog boxes the three-dimensional look used throughout the system.

Other Development Considerations

In addition to supporting common controls and dialog boxes, an application should include other new shell features, such as context menus, property sheets (with extensions), the details view, and so on. For more information about context menus and property sheets, see Article 12, "Shell Extensions."

If your application supports 256 colors, you should use the Windows halftone palette, as the shell does. It helps system performance because the system does not need to load a new palette every time the execution focus switches between the shell and your application. For more information about palettes, see the documentation included in the Win32 SDK.

Windows 95 Help

The Windows Help application has been improved for Windows 95. It includes many new features that you can use to provide help information that is task- or object-specific as well as readily accessible and unobtrusive. You should consider including the following features in your application's help file:

- Provide context-sensitive help for your dialog boxes and documents. The user can access context-sensitive help by clicking mouse button 2 (if there is no context menu available) or pressing the F1 key to display help information for a specific object or element in the application. The following illustration shows context-sensitive help for a control in a dialog box.

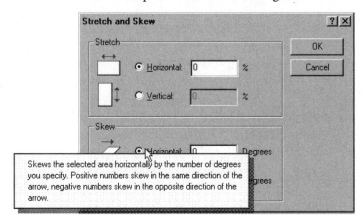

- Use secondary windows for procedural help. A secondary window does not have menus, and it remains open until it is explicitly closed.

- Embed shortcut buttons in your help text. A shortcut button allows the user to start an application from within a help file.

- Use sizable topic windows to make help text easier to read.

- Consider using the built-in support for training cards.

For more information about the Windows 95 Help application, see the documentation included in the Win32 SDK and the documentation included with the Microsoft Windows Help Compiler.

Multiple Instances

You should not let the user open multiple views of the same document. Multiple views confuse the user and conflict with the datacentric design of Windows 95.

When the user attempts to open a document file associated with an application, typically by double-clicking the document file's icon, the application should determine if the document file is already open. If it is, the application should check whether the current user has attempted to open the file. The application should do more than just compare user names because the user may be logged onto more than one computer. If the current user already has the document file open, the application should immediately restore the window containing the open document file.

If the current user has not attempted to open the document file (meaning that someone else on the network has), the application should prompt the user with the following message.

```
This document has already been opened by <name>. Would you like to
make a copy?
```

If the user does not want to make a copy, the application should exit; otherwise, it should make a copy.

You should also handle the case where the user double-clicks an application's icon when the application is already running. If the application's default action is to open a blank document when the user double-clicks the icon, the application should present the user with a list of currently opened documents. Opening a new document, however, should be the default action.

Pen Input

An application should support pen input so that it is easy to use on pen-based platforms, such as notebook computers and desktop tablets. The following list briefly describes what you need to do to support pen input:

- Use functions from the Windows pen application programming interface (API) to activate the pen in your application. If you activate the pen, the user can enter text using handwriting recognition and edit documents using gestures.

- Incorporate ink-edit controls into your application. Ink-edit controls allow the user to enter scribbled notes, drawings, and signatures.

- Add other natural pen-oriented features and gestures to your application.

For more information about supporting pen input, see Article 9, "Displaying and Using Pen Data."

Application Installation Guidelines

You should follow the Windows 95 guidelines for installing your application so that it works well when running with Windows 95. Some of the important installation guidelines follow:

- Create a subdirectory in the Applications directory at the root of the hard disk and store your application's executable file and any sample files there. If the Applications directory does not exist at the root of the hard disk, your installation program should create it. If you have any other executable or data files, such as .DLL and .HLP files that are specific to your application, your program should create another subdirectory named Application Extensions in the Applications directory. It should copy the remaining files (except shared files) to this new subdirectory.

- Copy all system-wide shared files (files shared by applications from many different vendors) to the \Applications\Shared Components directory. If this directory does not exist, your installation program should create it. If a given file already exists in this directory, your program should overwrite it with your file *only if* your file is a more recent version.

- Copy all shared files (files shared by applications from the same vendor) to a vendor-specific directory in the \Applications\Shared Components directory. If the vendor-specific directory does not exist, your installation program should create it.

- Place a single icon (shortcut) for your main application either directly in the Programs folder of the Start menu or in a subfolder of the Programs folder. If your installation program adds a shortcut, the user can easily start your application from the Start menu. However, your program should not overload the Start menu. To prevent overloading that menu, you may want your installation program to prompt the user to choose which shortcuts to add.

- Register your application-specific icons and commands as described in "Registry" later in this article.

- Support the Add/Remove Programs application in Control Panel so that the shell automatically runs your installation and uninstall programs. Note that on some types of hardware, the shell automatically runs your installation program as soon as the user inserts the floppy disk or compact disc (CD).

For more information about installing your application to run with Windows 95, see Article 10, "Installing Applications."

Registry

Integrating your application into the Windows 95 shell requires that you make full and correct use of the system registry. Your installation program should add the following items to the registry:

- Register your application under the **HKEY_LOCAL_MACHINE\ SOFTWARE** key. Your installation program should include keys for your company name, product name, and version number.

- Store user-specific initialization data under the **HKEY_CURRENT_USER\ SOFTWARE** key. Your installation program should not store initialization data in the WIN.INI file.

- Add application-specific paths to the registry so that Windows sets the PATH environment appropriately when starting your application. Your installation program should set the path in the **HKEY_LOCAL_MACHINE** root under the **\SOFTWARE\Microsoft\Windows\CurrentVersion\AppPaths** key and create a new key having the same name as your application's executable file. Under this new key, your program should create the Path value name and assign it a path using the same format as that expected by the PATH environment variable.

- Register an icon for each type of data file created by your application. When the system displays one of your data files in the shell, the registered icon for that file's type appears along with the file's name. If your installation program does not register icons for data files, the system will generate icons for them, but they may not be as distinctive as you would like them to be.

- Register data-specific commands for your data files; these commands appear in the context menus for your data files. For example, if your application creates sound files, your installation program might register a Play command that enables the user to play a sound by choosing Play from the context menu.

- Register a "Print To command" for your data files. Including a printto canonical verb in the registry enables the user to print your data files by performing a drag and drop operation to a specific printer object. Note, however, that the printto canonical verb does not add a command to the context menu of your data files.

For a description of additional items you should add as well as instructions about how to add the items described in the preceding list, see Article 10, "Installing Applications."

Windows 95 Logo Requirements

This section describes the technical requirements that software programs and hardware devices must meet to qualify for the Windows 95 Logo. These requirements are periodically updated. For information about updates, contact Microsoft.

General Requirements for Applications

The requirements for the Windows 95 Logo apply to the following four main types of programs:

- File-based applications—that is, applications that provide Open, Save, and Close File menu options.

- Applications that are not file-based and applications that run exclusively in full screen mode. An application that runs exclusively in full screen mode is one that cannot run in a window or be minimized.

- Utilities (for example, virus scanners and disk management programs).

- Development tools (for example, compilers and linkers).

To qualify for the Windows 95 Logo, an application must meet the appropriate requirements in the following list. The first five requirements apply to all types of applications.

1. An application must use the Win32 application programming interface (API) and must be compiled using a 32-bit compiler that generates an executable file of the Portable Executable (PE) format. If your application is not represented in the PE format (for example, it uses interpreted code), the "run-time engine" must be a Win32 executable file in the PE format. For example, if you develop an application in Microsoft® Access, your application is an .MDB file, not an .EXE, but ACCESS.EXE would need to be a Win32 PE format executable file.

2. An application must support the Windows 95 shell and user interface. At a minimum, an application must meet the following requirements:

   - Register both 16- by 16-pixel and 32- by 32-pixel icons for each file type and the application.

   - Follow the user interface guidelines described in *The Windows Interface Guidelines for Software Design*. An application should also use the system-defined dialog boxes and controls.

   - Use the system metrics for setting the size of elements within the application.

   - Use the system-defined colors.

   - Use mouse button 2 for context menus (and *not* for any other purpose).

   - Follow the Windows 95 application installation guidelines to make the application properly visible in the shell. At a minimum, this means that you should use the registry, you should not add information to the WIN.INI or SYSTEM.INI file, and you should provide complete uninstall capabilities with your application. The installation process must also be automated. For more information about installation guidelines, see Article 10, "Installing Applications."

   For detailed guidelines about supporting the shell and user interface, see *The Windows Interface Guidelines for Software Design*.

3. An application must be tested on the latest version of Microsoft® Windows NT™. If the application uses features that are available only in Windows 95, the features must degrade gracefully in Windows NT. Conversely, if it uses features available only in Windows NT, the features must degrade gracefully in Windows 95. The application must run successfully with both Windows 95 and Windows NT, unless architectural differences between the two operating system prevent it.

4. An application must support long filenames and use them to display all document and data filenames in the shell, in title bars, in dialog boxes and controls, and with icons. An application should also hide the extensions of filenames that are displayed within the application itself.

5. An application should process Plug and Play events. For example, it should be aware of slow links and should react to system messages that occur when a new device is attached or removed.

The next three requirements apply to file-based applications that do not run in full screen mode. Some games and children's software run exclusively in full screen mode and *need not follow* these three requirements:

6. An application must support Universal Naming Conventions (UNC) names for paths.

7. An application must support OLE containers or objects, or both. It must also support the OLE style of drag and drop. An application should also support OLE automation and compound files (with document summary information included).

8. An application must support simple mail enabling using the Messaging Application Programming Interface (MAPI) or the Common Messaging Call (CMC) API; that is, it must include Send Mail functionality.

The following items are modified requirements for utilities, such as disk optimizers and anti-virus software:

9. Same as number 1, except for components that must use exclusive volume locking functions, soft interrupts, or components that must talk directly to 16-bit drivers. The user interface and other components of these applications must be 32 bits and use the Windows 95 thunking mechanism to access the 16-bit components.

10. Same as number 2.

11. Same as number 3, except for products like disk utilities implementing platform-specific functionality that does not make sense in Windows NT version 3.5.

12. Same as number 4.

13. Numbers 5 through 8 are recommended, but not required. However, number 6 *is* required if your product accesses network resources.

The following items are modified requirements for compilers and other development tools:

14. In addition to the requirements that follow, if Windows is one of the target platforms of a compiler or development tool, the compiler or tool must be capable of generating applications that can meet all of the Windows 95 Logo requirements.

15. Same as number 1.

16. Same as number 2, except that when icons are registered for each file type and the application, common source filename extensions, such as .C, .CPP, .H, and .HPP, are excluded.

17. Same as number 3.

18. Same as number 4.

19. Same as number 5.

20. Same as number 6.

21. Compilers and development tools must support OLE in the following ways:

- Support the OLE style of drag and drop (recommended within the tool's design environment).

- Support OLE automation (recommended, but not required).

- Provide an easy way to create applications with OLE container or object support, or provide this functionality by default.

22. Same as number 8 (recommended, but not required).

Personal Computer Systems

For a personal computer (PC) system to qualify for the Windows 95 Logo, it must meet a minimum set of requirements as outlined below and pass the System Compatibility Test (SCT) for Windows 95. The SCT tests are included in the Microsoft Windows 95 Device Driver Kit (DDK), along with instructions for OEM participation. System testing is OEM-administered, and results are sent to Microsoft Compatibility Labs (MCL).

A PC system must meet the following requirements:

1. 80386 or compatible processor. (However, 33-megahertz 80486 or better is recommended.)

2. 4 megabytes (MB) random-access memory (RAM). (However, 8 MB is recommended.)

3. Plug and Play basic input/output system (BIOS) version 1.0a or later that reads back all resources. (A BIOS that soft-sets all resources is recommended.)

4. Molded-in or permanently printed icon labels on the computer case for built-in ports. Ideally, icons on the cable connectors should match the icons on the computer case.

5. Optional read-only memory (ROM) chips on expansion cards must use the Plug and Play header format documented in the Plug and Play BIOS specification.

6. A Video Graphics Array (VGA) display adapter that uses a packed-pixel frame buffer and provides a resolution of at least 640 by 480 pixels and 8 bits per pixel (bpp) for desktop systems and a 64-shade gray scale for mobile systems. (However, VGA 1024 by 768 pixels and 8 bpp is recommended for desktop systems, and 64 colors is recommended for mobile systems.)

7. One parallel port that supports IEEE-P1284-I mode protocols for compatibility mode and nibble mode. The system must be capable of receiving the parallel device's identifier in nibble mode. (However, ECP P1284-I is recommended.)

8. One integrated or separate serial port, with 1-16550A required for mobile systems. Also recommended are 1-16550A for desktop systems, an additional PS/2® style port, pen devices with a barrel button, and serial infrared devices meeting the Infrared Data Association (IrDA) specification.

9. Advanced Power Management (APM) version 1.1 is required for mobile systems. (However, it is recommended also for desktop systems.)

If the system ships with expansion cards or peripheral devices integrated onto the motherboard, it is recommended that the cards or devices meet the Windows 95 Logo specifications defined in this article and use 32-bit Windows 95–based device drivers.

For more information about qualifying a PC for the Windows 95 Logo, see the *Hardware Design Guide for Windows 95*.

Hardware Peripheral Devices

For a peripheral device to qualify for the Windows 95 Logo, it must meet the requirements described in the *Hardware Design Guide for Windows 95* and pass the compatibility tests conducted by MCL. For information about prequalifying test tools and MCL device and driver submission details, see the Windows 95 DDK. The Windows 95 DDK also contains detailed information about designing Windows 95–based device drivers.

To carry the Windows 95 Logo, a device driver must support the following Plug and Play capabilities in Windows 95:

1. Retrieves configuration information from Configuration Manager.

2. Is dynamically loadable.

3. Is dynamically reconfigurable.

4. Reacts to system messages that occur when a device is attached or removed.

An ideal Windows 95–based Plug and Play driver requires minimal user inter-action to be properly selected. In addition, the settings for the device may need to change based on which user is logged in, whether the machine is docked or not, or both.

Display Adapters

Display adapters must meet the following requirements:

1. Support the VGA graphics standard.

2. Support at least a 640- by 480-pixel, 8 bpp display driver. Desktop systems must be able to display at least 256 colors, and mobile systems must support an 8 bpp driver and map colors into at least a 64 gray scale display so that changes to higher-resolution external monitors can be made without restarting Windows 95.

3. Use a packed-pixel frame buffer with at least 8 bpp.

4. Use a VGA BIOS that, if it exists separately, has its base address fixed at C000h. (However, an alternate address is recommended.)

5. Use a standard VGA with a page frame and I/O address resource that can be static—that is, not relocatable.

6. Support the Video Electronics Standards Association (VESA) ergonomic timings.

7. Be capable of being disabled if a conflicting VGA expansion card is added to the system.

8. Provide at least one alternate configuration in case of conflict during initial program load (IPL) boot (non-VGA display resources only). The VGA BIOS must be able to use alternate configuration register addresses.

9. Have the display adapter circuitry come up active when power is turned on or the system is reset. This requirement applies only to an Industry Standard Architecture (ISA) Plug and Play display adapter expansion cards used as a system boot device.

Audio Adapters

Audio adapters must meet the following requirements:

1. Be able to produce 22 kilohertz (kHz), 8-bit, monaural, output-only sound (minimum performance).

2. Support either Sound Blaster™ or the Microsoft Windows Sound System to use built-in drivers for Windows 95.

3. Use a one-eighth inch miniature phone jack wired for stereo as the output connector.

4. Map the base input and output (I/O) address to configurations compatible with either Sound Blaster or the Microsoft Sound System.

5. Support at least all interrupt request (IRQ) signals used either by Sound Blaster or the Microsoft Windows Sound System.

6. Support the selection of at least three available Direct Memory Access (DMA) channels, either 8 bit or 16 bit, if DMA is supported.

7. Support disabling in case of resource conflicts with other devices.

Storage Devices

This section lists the requirements for storage devices, including floppy disk controllers, ATA (IDE) adapters, ATA (IDE) peripherals, small computer system interface (SCSI) host adapters, and SCSI devices.

Floppy Disk Controllers

Floppy disk controllers must meet the following requirements:

1. Use at least three static I/O addresses: 3F2h, 3F4h, and 3F5h.

2. Support IRQ6.

3. Support at least DMA 2, if DMA is used. The controller should be capable of selecting at least two other available DMA channels, either 8 bit or 16 bit.

4. Be capable of being independently disabled.

ATA (IDE) Adapters

ATA (IDE) adapters must meet the following requirements:

1. Use the first device attached to the adapter as the boot device.

2. Use the standard I/O addresses: 1F0h through 1F7h and 3F6h.

3. Support at least IRQ14.

4. Be capable of being disabled if an ATA (IDE) expansion card is added to the system. In addition, if a single adapter card contains a floppy disk drive controller, the adapter must be able to independently disable the floppy drive controller if a conflict occurs.

ATA (IDE) Peripherals

ATA (IDE) peripherals must meet the following requirements:

1. Support the ATA Packet Interface (ATAPI) protocol for CD-ROMs defined in SFF-8020 version 1.2.

2. Comply with the requirements specified in the ATA 2 specification.

3. Set the signature after an ATA Read or ATA Identify Command is received.

4. Implement the SEEK command and set the DSC bit when the ATAPI seek is complete, but not change the drive select bit.

5. Return the CANNOT READ MEDIUM - INCOMPATIBLE FORMAT additional sense code qualifier when a READ is received on an audio track.

6. Support CD-DA.

7. Support the READ_CD command sector types mode 2 form 1, mode 2 form 2, mode 1 form 1, and mode 1 form 2.

8. Support the Test_Unit_Ready command.

SCSI Host Adapters

SCSI host adapters must meet the following requirements:

1. Meet the standards described in the current version of the Plug and Play SCSI specification.

2. Support the SCSI Configured Auto-Magically (SCAM) Level 1 protocol for automatic SCSI identifier assignment.

3. Use the 50-pin, high-density shielded device connector defined in the SCSI-2 standard (external SCSI peripheral subsystems only).

4. Select at least three available DMA channels, either 8 bit or 16 bit, if DMA is supported.

5. Support disabling in case of resource conflicts with other devices.

6. Support automatic switchable termination for Plug and Play operation of internal, external, or mixed SCSI configurations.

SCSI Devices

SCSI devices must meet the following requirements:

1. Meet the standards described in the current version of the Plug and Play SCSI specification.

2. Support the SCSI Configured Auto-Magically (SCAM) Level 1 protocol for automatic SCSI identifier assignment.

3. Use the 50-pin, high-density shielded device connector defined in the SCSI-2 standard (external SCSI peripheral subsystems only).

4. Use the drivers and receivers that meet the specifications defined in the single-ended alternative of the SPI.

5. Use cables that conform to the cable requirements defined in clause 6 of the SPI specification.

6. Ensure that external SCSI peripherals contain two connectors for the SCSI cable: a SCSI in connector and a SCSI out connector. The last peripheral in the chain uses a terminator on the SCSI out connector.

7. Support the attachment of a permanent terminator to the end of the cable for internal SCSI peripherals.

8. Ensure that internal SCSI peripherals do not terminate the SCSI bus.

9. Ensure that terminations conform to the terminator requirements in the SPI specification over the terminator power (TERMPWR) voltage range of 4.0 to 5.25 VDC.

10. Power terminators from the TERMPWR line on the SCSI bus.

11. Provide overcurrent protection for the TERMPWR line or lines.

12. Ensure that only terminators draw power from TERMPWR.

13. Implement the SCSI Bus Parity signal defined in the SCSI-2 specifications.

Parallel Port Devices

Parallel port devices (printers) must meet the following requirements:

1. Meet the standards described in the current version of the Plug and Play Parallel Port Device specification.
2. Comply with IEEE P1284-I.
3. Support the compatibility and nibble mode protocols to read the device identifier from the peripheral.

External Communications Devices

An external communications device must be able to identify itself using the identification method described in the Plug and Play External COM Device Specification.

Modems

Modems must meet the following requirements:

1. Support at least 9600 bits per second (bps) V.32 with V42/V42bis protocol for data modems.
2. Support the TIA-602 (Hayes®-compatible) AT command set, with extensions for flow control, V42/V42bis.
3. Support fax capabilities of at least 9600 bps V.29 with class 1 (TIA-578A).
4. Support Plug and Play device identification, using the appropriate Plug and Play specification (for example, ISA bus, COM port, PCMCIA slot, or LPT port).
5. Support the 16550A compatible universal asynchronous receiver-transmitter (UART) interface.

Network Adapters

Network adapters must meet the following requirements:

1. Support the network driver interface specification (NDIS) 3.1 network device driver, which allows dynamic starting and stopping of the network card.
2. Provide a means of automatically enabling the adapter as a boot device or enabling the adapter as a nonbootable device, if the network adapter is designed with Remote Initial Program Load (RIPL) capability.
3. Do not hook Interrupt 18 and Interrupt 19 on ISA bus systems. This is a requirement for an ISA Plug and Play card.
4. Support at least seven IRQ signals and enable/disable.
5. Select at least three available DMA channels, either 8 bit or 16 bit, if DMA is supported.
6. Support disabling in case of resource conflicts with other devices.

A R T I C L E   3

Win32 Limitations in Windows 95

About Windows 95 System Limitations

Microsoft® Windows® 95 implements some Microsoft® Win32® functions and messages differently than Microsoft® Windows NT™. If you intend to run 32-bit applications on both platforms, you need to understand these differences to minimize development and debugging time.

General Limitations

Some Win32 functions and messages, such as for security and event logging, are not supported by Windows 95. Windows 95 provides stub routines for these unsupported functions so that applications designed for other operating systems that fully support the Win32 application programming interface (API) can run with Windows 95 without errors.

By design, Win32 functions that take string parameters can handle either Unicode™ (wide character) or ANSI strings. However, Windows 95 does not implement the Unicode (or wide character) version of most Win32 functions. With few exceptions, these functions are implemented as stubs that simply return an error value. However, Windows 95 does provide Unicode implementations of the following functions.

ExtTextOut	**MessageBox**
GetCharWidth	**MessageBoxEx**
GetTextExtentExPoint	**TextOut**
GetTextExtentPoint	

In addition, Windows 95 implements the **MultiByteToWideChar** and **WideCharToMultiByte** functions for converting strings to and from Unicode.

Although all Boolean functions in the documentation for the Microsoft Win32 Software Development Kit (SDK) are described as returning 1 for TRUE and zero for FALSE, these return values are not necessarily true for Win32 functions in Windows 95. Instead, these functions are guaranteed to return a *nonzero* value for TRUE and zero for FALSE.

Window Management (User)

Windows 95 implements some window management features in 16 bits. The use of 16 bits imposes some restrictions on parameters in functions and messages and places limits on internal storage. For example, the standard edit control is limited to somewhat less than 64 kilobytes (K) of text. In some cases, Windows 95 provides new features that can be used to avoid these restrictions and limitations, such as the rich edit control in which the amount of text is limited only by available memory.

The *wParam* parameter for the **SendMessageCallback**, **SendMessageTimeout**, and **SendNotifyMessage** functions is limited to a 16-bit value.

In Windows 95, the *wParam* parameter in list box messages, such as LB_INSERTSTRING or LB_SETITEMDATA, is limited to a 16-bit value. One effect of this limit is that list boxes cannot contain more than 32,767 items. Although the number of items is restricted, the total size, in bytes, of the items in a list box is limited only by available memory. In contrast, a 64K data limit is imposed by Windows version 3.1.

Windows 95 permits up to 16,364 window handles and 16,364 menu handles. Although these limits are less than in Windows NT, they are significantly greater than the limits imposed by Windows version 3.1.

In Windows 95, the **ActivateKeyboardLayout**, **GetKeyboardLayoutName**, and **UnloadKeyboardLayout** functions do not support extended error code values; that is, you cannot retrieve errors for these functions by using the **GetLastError** function.

In Windows 95, only one desktop is available while the system runs. Although the thread desktop functions, **GetThreadDesktop** and **SetThreadDesktop**, are available under Windows 95, they do not do anything.

Any private application message must be defined above WM_USER + 0x100. A value above this will ensure that there is no collision between private messages and dialog box control messages.

Windows 95 automatically applies the standard three-dimensional shading and color scheme to dialog boxes created by applications marked as version 4.0 or later. Applications that are marked for earlier versions can still get the three-dimensional appearance by applying the DS_3DLOOK style to dialog boxes. If this style is used, the system automatically applies the three-dimensional look without requiring the application to check the operating system version. This is useful, for example, in applications developed for Windows NT version 3.5. The DS_3DLOOK style is ignored in Windows NT version 3.1.

The IDC_SIZE and IDC_ICON values used with the **LoadCursor** function are obsolete and should not be used in a Windows 95–based application or in a Win32-based application that is marked as version 4.0.

In Windows 95, the MB_ICONQUESTION style used with the **MessageBox**, **MessageBoxEx**, and **MessageBoxIndirect** functions is obsolete. Win32-based applications should use the MB_ICONEXCLAMATION style instead. Similarly, applications should use the MB_ICONINFORMATION style instead of the MB_ICONASTERISK style and the MB_ICONSTOP style instead of the MB_ICONHAND style.

Graphics Device Interface (GDI)

Windows 95 uses a 16-bit world coordinate system and restricts x- and y-coordinates for text and graphics to the range ±32K. Windows NT uses a 32-bit world coordinate system and allows coordinates in the range ±2 gigabytes (GB). If you pass full 32-bit coordinates to text and graphics functions in Windows 95, the system truncates the upper 16 bits of the coordinates before carrying out the requested operation.

Because Windows 95 uses a 16-bit coordinate system, the sum of the coordinates of the bounding rectangle specified by the **Arc**, **Chord**, **Pie**, **Ellipse**, and **RoundRect** functions cannot exceed 32K. In addition, the sum of the *nLeftRect* and *nRightRect* parameters or the *nTopRect* and *nBottomRect* parameters cannot exceed 32K.

In Windows 95, regions are allocated from the 32-bit heap and can, therefore, be as large as available memory. (In Windows version 3.1, regions were limited to 64K.) All other logical objects, however, share the 64K local heap. In addition, the number of region handles cannot exceed 16K.

To ensure that adequate space is always available for logical objects, applications should always delete objects when no longer needed. The following functions create objects that are placed in the local heap and have corresponding functions used to delete the objects.

Object	Create with	Delete with
Bitmap	**CreateBitmap,** **CreateBitmapIndirect,** **CreateCompatibleBitmap,** **CreateDIBitmap,** **CreateDIBSection,** **CreateDiscardableBitmap**	**DeleteObject**
Brush	**CreateBrushIndirect,** **CreateDIBPatternBrush,** **CreateDIBPatternBrushPt,** **CreateHatchBrush,** **CreatePatternBrush,** **CreateSolidBrush**	**DeleteObject**
Color space	**CreateColorSpace**	**DeleteColorSpace**
Device context (DC)	**CreateDC,** **GetDC**	**DeleteDC,** **ReleaseDC**
Enhanced metafile	**CloseEnhMetaFile,** **CopyEnhMetaFile,** **GetEnhMetaFile,** **SetEnhMetaFileBits**	**DeleteEnhMetaFile**
Enhanced metafile DC	**CreateEnhMetaFile**	**CloseEnhMetaFile**
Extended pen	**ExtCreatePen**	**DeleteObject**
Font	**CreateFont,** **CreateFontIndirect**	**DeleteObject**
Memory DC	**CreateCompatibleDC**	**DeleteDC**
Metafile	**CloseMetaFile,** **CopyMetaFile,** **GetMetaFile,** **SetMetaFileBitsEx**	**DeleteMetaFile**
Metafile DC	**CreateMetafile**	**CloseMetaFile**
Palette	**CreatePalette**	**DeleteObject**
Pen	**CreatePen,** **CreatePenIndirect**	**DeleteObject**
Region	**CombineRgn,** **CreateEllipticRgn,** **CreateEllipticRgnIndirect,** **CreatePolygonRgn,** **CreatePolyPolygonRgn,** **CreateRectRgn,** **CreateRectRgnIndirect,** **CreateRoundRectRgn,** **ExtCreateRegion,** **PathToRegion**	**DeleteObject**

Physical objects have always existed in global memory and are, therefore, not limited.

Windows 95 does not support world transformations that involve either shearing or rotations. The **ExtCreateRegion** function fails if the transformation matrix is anything other than a scaling or translation of the region.

In Windows 95, pens and brushes have several limitations. The **ExtCreatePen** function supports solid colors only (the PS_SOLID style), and the styles PS_ALTERNATE and PS_USERSTYLE are not supported. Geometric pens (the PS_GEOMETRIC style) are limited to the BS_SOLID brush style specified in the **LOGBRUSH** structure passed to **ExtCreatePen.** In addition, the following pen styles are supported in paths only.

PS_ENDCAP_FLAT	PS_JOIN_BEVEL
PS_ENDCAP_ROUND	PS_JOIN_MITER
PS_ENDCAP_SQUARE	PS_JOIN_ROUND

Windows 95 does not support the dashed or dotted pen styles, such as PS_DASH or PS_DOT, in wide lines. The BS_DIBPATTERN brush style is limited to an 8- by 8-pixel brush.

Windows 95 does not support brushes from bitmaps or device independent bitmaps (DIBs) that are larger than 8 by 8 pixels. Although bitmaps larger than 8 by 8 pixels can be passed to the **CreatePatternBrush** or **CreateDIBPatternBrush** function, only a portion of the bitmap is used to create the brush.

Windows 95 does not provide automatic tracking of the brush origin. An application is responsible for using the **UnrealizeObject**, **SetBrushOrgEx**, and **SelectObject** functions each time it paints using a pattern brush.

Windows 95 does not support the CBM_CREATEDIB value for the **CreateDIBitmap** function. The **CreateDIBSection** function should be used instead to create a DIB. **CreateDIBSection** is also available in Windows NT version 3.5.

If the **biCompression** member of the **BITMAPINFOHEADER** structure is the BI_BITFIELDS value, the **bmiColors** member of the **BITMAPINFO** structure contains three doubleword color masks that specify the red, green, and blue components, respectively, of each pixel. Windows 95 only supports these color masks for 16 and 32 bits per pixel (bpp).

16bpp	The blue mask is 0x001F, the green mask is 0x03E0, and the red mask is 0x7C00.
16bpp	The blue mask is 0x001F, the green mask is 0x07E0, and the red mask is 0xF800.
32bpp	The blue mask is 0x000000FF, the green mask is 0x0000FF00, and the red mask is 0x00FF0000.

If the *lpvBits* parameter is NULL, the **GetDIBits** function fills in the dimensions and format of the bitmap in the **BITMAPINFO** structure pointed to by the *lpbi* parameter. In this case, if the function is successful, the return value in Windows 95 is the total number of scan lines in the bitmap. In Windows NT versions 3.1 and 3.5, however, the return value is 1 (TRUE), indicating success.

Deletion of drawing objects is slightly different in Windows 95 than in Windows NT. In Windows NT, if a drawing object (pen or brush) is deleted while it is still selected into a DC, the **DeleteObject** function fails. In Windows 95, the function succeeds, but the result is a nonfunctioning object. This nonfunctioning object is automatically destroyed when the DC is deleted.

When a path is constructed in Windows 95, only the following functions are recorded: **ExtTextOut**, **LineTo**, **MoveToEx**, **PolyBezier**, **PolyBezierTo**, **Polygon**, **Polyline**, **PolylineTo**, **PolyPolygon**, **PolyPolyline**, and **TextOut**.

In Windows 95, the **GetGraphicsMode** and **SetGraphicsMode** functions only support the GM_COMPATIBLE value. The GM_ADVANCED value is not supported.

In Windows 95, the **DeviceCapabilities** function returns −1 when called with the DC_FILEDEPENDENCIES value because that capability is not supported. In Windows 95, **DeviceCapabilities** supports the following additional capabilities.

DC_DATATYPE_PRODUCED	Retrieves an array of strings containing the data types that the printer driver supports. A return value of −1 indicates that the printer driver only understands device-specific commands (in other words, "RAW" data) that are native to the printer. A return value of 2 or more indicates the number of strings in the array.
DC_EMF_COMPLIANT	Returns a flag that indicates if the specified printer driver is capable of accepting an enhanced metafile (EMF) spooled by the system (that is, the printer driver is EMF-compliant). The function returns 1 if the printer driver is EMF-compliant and −1 if the printer driver is not.

Although Windows 95 imposes no restrictions on the **PlayEnhMetaFile** and **PlayEnhMetaFileRecord** functions, the files and records that these functions execute are subject to the limitations described in this section. For example, the functions ignore records that attempt to draw outside of the 16-bit coordinate space or that apply shearing or rotation to world transformations.

In Windows 95, the maximum length of the description string for an enhanced metafile is 16K. This limit applies to the **GetEnhMetaFileDescription**, **GetEnhMetaFileHeader**, and **GetEnhMetaFile** functions.

In Windows 95, the **dmDeviceName** member of the **DEVMODE** structure specifies the "friendly" name of the printer, which may be set to any user-defined value. Windows 95, however, does not support the the following members; they are included for compatibility with Windows NT.

dmBitsPerPel	**dmFormName**
dmDisplayFlags	**dmPelsHeight**
dmDisplayFrequency	**dmPelsWidth**

Windows 95 does not support print monitor dynamic-link libraries (DLLs) that have been developed for Windows NT. To add a monitor using the **AddMonitor** function, you must specify a monitor DLL that has been explicitly created for Windows 95. The following printing and print spooling functions are not available in Windows 95.

AddForm	**FindFirstPrinterChangeNotification**
AddPrinterConnection	**FindNextPrinterChangeNotification**
ConnectToPrinterDlg	**GetForm**
DeleteForm	**ResetPrinter**
DeletePrinterConnection	**SetForm**
EnumForms	**WaitForPrinterChange**
FindClosePrinterChangeNotification	

In Windows 95, the **SetPrinter** function ignores the **pShareName** member of the **PRINTER_INFO_2** structure. Windows 95 does not support the **PRINTER_INFO_3** and **PRINTER_INFO_4** structures used with the **SetPrinter**, **GetPrinter**, and **EnumPrinters** functions. The **PRINTER_INFO_5** structure, which is available in Windows 95, is not supported in Windows NT versions 3.1 and 3.5.

The PRINTER_ENUM_CONNECTIONS value used with the **EnumPrinters** function is not supported in Windows 95. The **DOC_INFO_2** structure used with the **StartDocPrinter** function and the **PORT_INFO_2** structure used with the **EnumPorts** function are not supported in Windows NT versions 3.1 and 3.5.

Windows 95 supports the DRAWPATTERNRECT printer escape.

Win32-based applications that send output to PostScript™ printers should use the **GetDeviceCaps** function to check for the PC_PATHS value to determine whether to use path functions or printer escapes to draw paths. Applications should use paths functions whenever possible. The following example shows how to check for this capability.

```
// Determine whether to use path functions on the device.
// hDC is the output device.

OSVERSIONINFO osvi;

osvi.dwOSVersionInfoSize = sizeof(osvi);
GetVersionEx(&osvi);

if ((osvi.dwPlatformId == VER_PLATFORM_WIN32_NT) ||
    ((osvi.dwPlatformId == VER_PLATFORM_WIN32_WINDOWS) &&
      (GetDeviceCaps(hDC, POLYCAPS) & PC_PATHS)))
    bUsePaths = TRUE;
else
    bUsePaths = FALSE;
```

In Windows 95, printer drivers typically set this capability to zero. This means that Win32-based applications sending output to Postscript printers need to use the **ExtEscape** function and the printer-specific escapes to draw paths at the printer. (The **Escape** function cannot be used for this.)

In Windows NT, the string specified in the *lpszDeviceName* parameter of the **EnumDisplaySettings** function must be of the form "\\ .\Display*X*", where *X* can be 1, 2, or 3. In Windows 95, *lpszDeviceName* must be NULL.

System Services (Kernel)

The extended error codes returned by the **GetLastError** function are not guaranteed to be the same in Windows 95 and Windows NT. This difference applies to extended error codes generated by calls to GDI, window management, and system services functions.

Windows 95 does not support asynchronous file input and output (I/O), except on serial devices. Therefore, the **ReadFile** and **WriteFile** functions will fail if you pass in an overlapped region on anything other than a serial device. The **GetOverlappedResult** function works only on serial devices or on files opened by using the **DeviceIoControl** function.

In Windows 95, the **ReadFileEx** and **WriteFileEx** functions will fail if you pass in the handle of a serial device (for example, COM2). **ReadFile** and **WriteFile**, however, accept the handle of a serial device.

In Windows NT, the **FileTimeToDosDateTime** and **DosDateTimeToFileTime** functions allow dates up to 12/31/2107. In Windows 95, these functions allow dates up to 12/31/2099.

The precision of the time for a file on a file allocation table (FAT) file system volume is 2 seconds. If Windows 95 is connected through a network to a different file system, the time precision is limited only by the remote device.

In Windows NT, the **DeleteFile** function fails if you attempt to delete a file that is open for normal I/O or is opened as a memory mapped file. In Windows 95, **DeleteFile** deletes such files. Because deleting open files may cause loss of data and application failure, you must take every precaution to close files before attempting to delete them by using **DeleteFile**.

In Windows 95, fixed memory blocks cannot be reallocated to be movable. The GMEM_MODIFY and GMEM_MOVEABLE combination of values has no effect when a memory block is reallocated by using the **GlobalReAlloc** function. Similarly, the LMEM_MODIFY and LMEM_MOVEABLE combination has no effect when a memory block is reallocated by using the **LocalReAlloc** function.

In Windows 95, committing memory for a page that is already committed is an expensive operation that has no ultimate effect (it is expensive because additional storage is allocated and subsequently freed for each committed page). When committing memory by using the **VirtualAlloc** function, an application should specify only the pages that actually need to be committed.

Although applications can request that memory allocation be at a specific virtual address, applications must not depend on any given address range always being available on every operating system. Applications can query the address space by using the **GetSystemInfo** function.

In Windows 95, memory allocated by Win32-based applications falls in the address range 4 megabytes (MB)–2GB for private memory and 2GB–3GB for shared memory (shared mapped files). The PAGE_WRITECOPY and PAGE_GUARD access protection values are not supported. Instead of using the PAGE_GUARD value and handling the EXCEPTION_GUARD_PAGE exception, applications can use the PAGE_NOACCESS value and handle the EXCEPTION_ACCESS_VIOLATION exception.

The SEC_IMAGE and SEC_NOCACHE values for the *fdwProtect* parameter of the **CreateFileMapping** function are not supported in Windows 95. In addition, the *dwMaximumSizeHigh* parameter of **CreateFileMapping** is ignored in Windows 95, so applications should specify zero for the parameter.

In Windows 95, shared memory mapped files that are created by using the **MapViewOfFileEx** function appear in the same address space across all 32-bit processes in the system. If you pass in a specific base offset in the *lpvBase* parameter of **MapViewOfFileEx** and the function succeeds, you are guaranteed that the same memory region is available in every process. This is not true in Windows NT because **MapViewOfFileEx** fails for any process that already has the given memory region in use.

Coherence guarantees that the data accessible in a file view is an identical copy of the file's contents on disk. In Windows 95, file views derived from a single file-mapping object are coherent only if the file is accessed through one of the views. A view of a file is not guaranteed to be coherent if the file is accessed by normal file I/O functions, such as **ReadFile** or **WriteFile**, or by views created from a different file-mapping object.

If you close a file handle that was used to create a file mapping object, both Windows NT and Windows 95 hold the file open until you unmap the last view of the file by using the **UnmapViewOfFile** function. However, Windows NT holds the file open with no sharing restrictions, whereas Windows 95 holds it open using the sharing restrictions of the original file handle. To ensure exclusive access to a file in Windows NT, the file handle must remain open for the life of the file-mapping object. Because Windows 95 retains the sharing restrictions, both the file handle and the handle to the file-mapping object may be closed after calling **MapViewOfFile** and exclusive access to the file is ensured.

In Windows 95, if the FILE_MAP_COPY value is specified for the *fdwAccess* parameter of **MapViewOfFile** (or **MapViewOfFileEx**), the *hMapObject* parameter must have been created with the PAGE_WRITECOPY value. Also, the *dwOffsetHigh* parameter of **MapViewOfFile** (or **MapViewOfFileEx**) is ignored, so applications should specify zero for the parameter.

Windows 95 implements copy-on-write file mappings slightly differently than Windows NT. In Windows 95, a call to **MapViewOfFile** with FILE_MAP_COPY returns an error unless PAGE_WRITECOPY was used with the **CreateFileMapping** function. In both Windows NT and Windows 95, creating the map with PAGE_WRITECOPY and the view with FILE_MAP_COPY produces a view to the file that makes the pages swappable and prevents modifications from going to the original data file. In Windows 95, PAGE_WRITECOPY must be passed to **CreateFileMapping**, but this is optional in Windows NT.

If you share mapping between multiple processes by using the **DuplicateHandle** or **OpenFileMapping** function and one process writes to a view, the modifications will not be propagated to the other process in Windows NT. However, the modifications will be propagated in Windows 95. The original file, though, will not change on either platform.

In Windows 95, the **CreateFile** function does not support the standard "\\ .\C:" and "\\ .\PhysicalDrive0" formats used to gain access to the logical or physical drives. To gain access, applications must specify a virtual device (VxD) name instead and use the **DeviceIoControl** function to send requests through the VxD to the logical and physical drives. For more information, see Article 20, "Device I/O Control."

In Windows 95, the **DuplicateHandle** function cannot duplicate handles of registry keys as it can in Windows NT. The function returns an error if an application attempts to duplicate the handle of a registry key. In addition, when a file handle is duplicated, the duplicated handle will not be granted more access than the original.

The **LoadLibrary** function does not support loading 16-bit DLLs into a Win32 process.

Thread locales, which are retrieved and set by using the **GetThreadLocale** and **SetThreadLocale** functions, are static and can only be changed at system boot time.

In Windows 95, the **FlushInstructionCache** function always returns TRUE. Windows 95 supports single processor machines only.

In Windows 95, a call to the **FreeResource** function must be included for every call to the **LoadResource** function. The call to **FreeResource** allows the system to discard a resource that an application no longer needs. Windows NT automatically frees resources, so a call to **FreeResource** is not required.

The SYNCHRONIZE standard access rights flag is not supported in Windows 95. The following functions are affected.

DuplicateHandle	**OpenSemaphore**
MsgWaitForMultipleObjects	**WaitForMultipleObjects**
OpenEvent	**WaitForMultipleObjectsEx**
OpenMutex	**WaitForSingleObject**
OpenProcess	**WaitForSingleObjectEx**

The Windows 95 registry does not allow key names containing control characters. In addition, if the *lpszSubKey* parameter is an empty string, the **RegDeleteKey** function deletes the key identified by the *hKey* parameter.

In Windows 95, the **RegCreateKeyEx** function creates a non-volatile key even if the REG_OPTION_VOLATILE value is specified.

Multimedia

The **sndAlias** macro is not supported in Windows 95. In addition, the SND_ALIAS and SND_ALIAS_ID values for the **PlaySound** function are not supported in Windows 95.

The Windows 95 multimedia functions are not designed to be used by two or more threads in the same process. Although most multimedia functions will work if they are called by multiple threads, some are likely to fail. Functions that are particularly likely to fail include **PlaySound**, any of the functions that prepare or unprepare headers, and any of the open and close functions. **PlaySound** can never be used simultaneously by multiple threads in the same process. The functions that prepare or unprepare headers and the open and close functions can be used simultaneously by multiple threads in the same process, but only if they do not pass the same structure.

A R T I C L E   4

Version Differences

About Version Differences

The Microsoft® Windows® 95 operating system supports Windows-based applications that have a subsystem version number of either 3.*x* or 4.0. An application's subsystem version number is set by the linker. This article describes the differences in the way Windows 95 treats applications based on their subsystem version numbers. It is intended to help you identify areas in an application written for Windows version 3.*x* that you must revise to take advantage of the new features provided by Windows 95.

General Window Management Differences

When a version 4.0 application uses the **SetWindowLong** function (with GWL_STYLE) to change a window's style, Windows 95 sends the window a WM_STYLECHANGING message before changing the style. The message's *lParam* parameter is the address of a **STYLESTRUCT** structure. The **styleOld** and **styleNew** members of the structure specify the old and new styles. By processing WM_STYLECHANGING, an application can inspect the styles and perhaps change them.

Windows 95 sends the WM_STYLECHANGED message after changing the style. Again, the *lParam* parameter is the address of a **STYLESTRUCT** structure that specifies the new styles. The application can use WM_STYLECHANGED to update any style-dependent information stored in the application's internal data structures.

Windows 95, however, does not send the WM_STYLECHANGING and WM_STYLECHANGED messages to a version 3.*x* application.

A version 4.0 application cannot use the **SetWindowLong** function to set the WS_EX_TOPMOST style for a window or to remove the style from a window. The application must use the **SetWindowPos** function to set or remove the WS_EX_TOPMOST style.

Windows 95 automatically adds and removes the WS_EX_WINDOWEDGE style for windows in both version 3.*x* and 4.0 applications. In a version 3.*x* application, Windows 95 adds the WS_EX_WINDOWEDGE style to a window if the window would have a dialog border or a sizable border in version 3.1. Windows 95 removes the WS_EX_WINDOWEDGE style if the window's style changes so that it would no longer have a dialog border or sizable border in version 3.1. Windows 95 uses similar criteria for adding and removing the WS_EX_WINDOWEDGE style for a Windows version 4.0 application, except that any window that has a title bar receives the WS_EX_WINDOWEDGE style, regardless of the window's other border styles.

When the user drags the icon of a minimized window created by a version 3.*x* application, Windows 95 sends the window a WM_QUERYDRAGICON message to retrieve the cursor to use while dragging. Windows 95 also sends WM_QUERYDRAGICON to retrieve the icon to display in the task-switch window that appears when the user presses the ALT+TAB key combination. Windows 95 does not send WM_QUERYDRAGICON to a window created by a version 4.0 application. Instead, the application is expected either to use the WM_SETICON and WM_GETICON messages or to set the big and small icons when registering the window class.

When a window in a version 4.0 application loses the mouse capture as a result of a call to the **SetCapture** function, the window receives the message WM_CAPTURECHANGED, but Windows 95 sends the message asynchronously. In other words, the window receives the message, but possibly not right away. Some of the ways in which a window can lose the mouse capture include:

- The user activated a different application by clicking one of its windows.
- The **DefWindowProc** function changed the capture in response to a WM_CANCELMODE message.
- Another window using the same message queue called the **SetCapture** function. (All 16-bit applications share the same queue, but each 32-bit thread has its own queue.)

If a child window in a version 3.*x* application has WS_EX_NOPARENTNOTIFY as a window style, Windows 95 disregards the style when the user clicks the child window. That is, Windows 95 sends the WM_PARENTNOTIFY message to all windows in the parent chain regardless of whether the child window has the style. If a child window in a version 4.0 application has the style, Windows 95 does not send WM_PARENTNOTIFY messages when the user clicks the child window.

In a version 3.x application, it is possible for the horizontal coordinate on the left side of a window's client area to be greater than that on the right side. This happens because version 3.x sometimes incorrectly handles an empty client rectangle that contains a vertical scroll bar. (Fixing the problem would cause some applications to generate general protection faults.) In a version 4.0 application, it is not possible for the horizontal coordinate of the left side of a client area to be greater than that of the right side.

Dialog Boxes

A dialog box created by a version 4.0 application automatically receives the DS_3DLOOK style. This style gives three-dimensional borders to child controls in the dialog box and draws the entire dialog box using the three-dimensional color scheme. The DS_3DLOOK style is available to a dialog box created by a version 3.x application, but you must explicitly add the style to the dialog box template. The application that creates the dialog box determines the version number of the dialog box.

Windows 95 performs a strict validation check on the DS_ styles specified in a dialog box template. If the template contains any styles that Windows 95 does not recognize and a version 4.0 application is creating the dialog box, the creation fails. If a version 3.x application is creating the dialog box, the system debugger generates a warning, but Windows 95 creates the dialog box anyway.

Buttons

The parent window of a button (except push buttons) in a version 3.x application receives a WM_CTLCOLORBTN message when the button is about to be drawn. In a version 4.0 application, however, the parent window of a button receives the WM_CTLCOLORSTATIC message, which retrieves a color appropriate for drawing text on the background of the dialog box. Windows 95 sends WM_CTLCOLORSTATIC to retrieve the background and text colors for the text area of check boxes, radio buttons, and group buttons. An application should process WM_CTLCOLORSTATIC in order to correctly set the colors of any dialog box item that contains text and appears directly on the dialog area.

Windows 95 perform default handling of the WM_CTLCOLORBTN message differently depending on an application's version. For a version 3.x application, the default handling for button colors is to use the COLOR_WINDOW value for the background color and the COLOR_WINDOWTEXT value for the foreground color. For a version 4.0 application, Windows 95 uses the COLOR_3DFACE value for the background and the COLOR_BTNTEXT value for the foreground.

In a version 3.*x* application, a push button's outer top left corner is nonwhite because the button is typically drawn on a white background. If the border was white, the background would appear to bleed into the button. In a version 4.0 application, a push button's outer top left corner is white in color (COLOR_3DHILIGHT) because the button is typically drawn on a nonwhite background (COLOR_3DFACE).

Edit Controls

In a version 3.*x* application, an edit control that is the descendant of an inactive window takes the input focus when the user clicks the control; an edit control in a version 4.0 application does not. Not taking the input focus prevents the situation where the user can enter text into what appears to be an inactive window.

An edit control in a version 3.*x* application retrieves its text and background colors by sending the WM_CTLCOLOREDIT message to its parent window. In a version 4.0 application, an edit control sends the WM_CTLCOLOREDIT or WM_CTLCOLORSTATIC message. If the edit control is disabled or read-only, it sends WM_CTLCOLORSTATIC; otherwise, it sends WM_CTLCOLOREDIT. In addition, a disabled multiline edit control in a version 4.0 application uses the COLOR_GRAYTEXT value as its text color.

A multiline edit control in a version 4.0 application has a proportional scroll box (thumb), but a multiline edit control in a version 3.*x* application does not.

In a version 3.*x* application, the *wParam* parameter of the EM_REPLACESEL message is not used. In a version 4.0 application, the *wParam* parameter is a flag that specifies whether the replacement operation can be undone.

List Boxes

In a version 4.0 application, a list box that is part of a combo box uses the WM_CAPTURECHANGED notification message to hide its drop-down list if it is open. For more information, see "Combo Boxes" later in this article.

The DDL_EXCLUSIVE flag of the **DlgDirList** function does not have the expected result in a version 3.*x* application. Specifically, the flag does not exclude read-write files from the list. In a version 4.0 application, the DDL_EXCLUSIVE flag excludes read-write files.

If a list box in a version 3.*x* application has either the WS_HSCROLL or WS_VSCROLL style, the list box receives both horizontal and vertical scroll bars. Although one of the scroll bars is typically hidden, Windows 95 displays the hidden scroll bar if its scrolling range becomes greater than zero. In a version 4.0 application, a list box does not receive a horizontal scroll bar, unless it has the WS_HSCROLL style. Likewise, it does not receive a vertical scroll bar unless it has the WS_VSCROLL style.

When creating a list box in a version 3.*x* application, Windows 95 always increases the size of the list box by adding the border width to each side. This is done because Windows 95 assumes that the dimensions specified by the application or the dialog template are for the client area of the list box. Unfortunately, increasing the size in this way makes aligning a list box rather difficult. Windows 95 does not increase the size when creating a list box in a version 4.0 application; Windows 95 assumes that the specified size includes the borders.

Combo Boxes

A combo box in a version 4.0 application passes the control color messages (WM_CTLCOLOR*) from its child components (edit control and list box) to the parent window of the combo box. In a version 3.*x* application, a combo box passes those messages to the **DefWindowProc** function.

A combo box in a version 4.0 application uses the WM_CAPTURECHANGED message to hide its drop-down list box if it is open. Windows 95 sends the message when another window takes the mouse capture, which typically happens when the user clicks another window. In a version 3.*x* application, a combo box does not use WM_CAPTURECHANGED to hide the drop-down list.

A combo box in a version 3.*x* application uses the WM_CTLCOLORLISTBOX message to retrieve the text and background colors. In a version 4.0 application, a combo box uses the WM_CTLCOLOREDIT or WM_CTLCOLORSTATIC message instead. The combo box uses WM_CTLCOLORSTATIC if it is disabled or contains a read-only selection field (in an edit control); otherwise, it uses WM_CTLCOLOREDIT.

In a version 3.*x* application, the background of the static text area in read-only combo boxes is filled with the system highlight color (COLOR_HILIGHT). In a version 4.0 application, Windows 95 fills the background of the static text area only for a combo box that is not owner drawn.

In a version 4.0 application, Windows 95 adds the ODS_COMBOBOXEDIT value to the **itemState** member of the **DRAWITEMSTRUCT** structure when Windows 95 sends the WM_DRAWITEM message to the parent window of an owner-drawn combo box to draw an item in the selection field. The ODS_COMBOBOXEDIT value tells the parent window that the drawing takes place in the selection field of the combo box rather than in the list box.

Menus

A 16-bit version 3.*x* application that creates or loads a menu is considered to be the owner of the menu. However, when the application exits, the menu is "orphaned" until no 16-bit version components for Windows version 3.*x* remain. For 16-bit version 4.0 applications and all 32-bit applications, the application that creates the menu is the owner, and the menu is destroyed as soon as the application exits. Unlike graphics device interface (GDI) objects, there is no way to change the ownership of a menu.

In a version 3.*x* application, the Close command cannot be deleted from the System menu of an multiple document interface (MDI) child window. In a version 4.0 application, the Close command can be deleted.

Windows 95 increases the width of hierarchical, owner-drawn menu items in a version 3.*x* application. Some applications rely on this increased width and use it to include icons that simulate toolbars. In a version 4.0 application, Windows 95 does not automatically increase the width of hierarchical, owner-drawn menu items.

The *wParam* parameter of the WM_MENUSELECT message is interpreted differently depending on the subsystem version number of the application and whether the application is written for 16 or 32 bits:

- In a 16-bit version 3.*x* application, the *wParam* parameter is the handle of the pop-up menu if the selected item activates a pop-up menu.
- In a 16-bit version 4.0 application, *wParam* is the identifier of the menu item, regardless of whether the item activates a pop-up menu.
- In a 32-bit application (both subsystem versions), the low-order word of *wParam* is the identifier of the menu item or, if the item activates a pop-up menu, the index of the pop-up menu. This high-order word contains the menu flags.

System Bitmaps and Colors

In 16-bit version 3.*x* applications, purpose windows, such as dialog boxes, message boxes, and system-defined control windows, receive WM_CTLCOLOR messages when they are about to be drawn. The high-order word of the *lParam* parameter indicates the type of special purpose window about to be drawn (CTLCOLOR_BTN, CTLCOLOR_EDIT, and so on). By default, a special purpose window passes the WM_CTLCOLOR message to the parent or owner window (for both subsystem versions), allowing the parent or owner to set the foreground and background colors of the special purpose window. The same is true for 32-bit applications, except that the special purpose window receives one or more of the following messages instead of WM_CTLCOLOR.

WM_CTLCOLORBTN	WM_CTLCOLORMSGBOX
WM_CTLCOLORDLG	WM_CTLCOLORSCROLLBAR
WM_CTLCOLOREDIT	WM_CTLCOLORSTATIC
WM_CTLCOLORLISTBOX	

In 32-bit applications, the message itself indicates the type of special purpose window about to be drawn. The *lParam* parameter contains the window's 32-bit handle.

Display drivers for Windows version 3.*x* provide the bitmaps, icons, and cursors used by previous versions of Windows. Because Windows 95 renders and scales the system bitmaps, icons, and cursors itself, its display drivers do not (and should not) contain any OBM_, OIC_, or OCR_ resources.

For a version 3.*x* application, the default handling of the window messages WM_CTLCOLORSTATIC and WM_CTLCOLORDLG is to use the COLOR_WINDOW value for the background and the COLOR_WINDOWTEXT value for the foreground. For a version 4.0 application, Windows 95 uses the COLOR_3DFACE value for the background and the COLOR_WINDOWTEXT value for the foreground.

When an application calls the **GetClientRect** function to retrieve the client rectangle of a minimized window created by a version 3.*x* application, Windows 95 retrieves the old dimensions for a minimized window (0, 0, 36, 36). For a minimized window in a version 3.1 or 4.0 application, Windows 95 retrieves 0, 0, **GetSystemMetrics**(SM_CXMINIMIZED), **GetSystemMetrics** (SM_CYMINIMIZED). These metrics change if the user changes the title bar height or minimized window width by using Control Panel. In other words, the **GetClientRect** function returns the dimensions of the entire minimized window, preventing an application from causing a general protection (GP) fault because of an unexpectedly empty client rectangle.

System Metrics

When a version 3.*x* application calls the **GetSystemMetrics** function to retrieve the SM_CYVSCROLL or SM_CYHSCROLL metric value, the function returns a value that is one pixel more than the actual height of the corresponding type of standard scroll bar. Windows 95 adds a pixel because applications written for previous versions of windows routinely subtract one pixel from the return value. Subtracting one pixel accounts for the way a standard scroll bar in a version 3.*x* application overlaps the border of the window in which it resides. A version 4.0 application receives the actual height of the scroll bar.

When a version 3.*x* application retrieves the SM_CXDLGFRAME and SM_CYDLGFRAME system metric values, **GetSystemMetrics** returns a value that is one pixel less that the actual frame width or height. A version 4.0 application receives the actual width or height.

GetSystemMetrics returns one pixel more than the actual height of a title bar when a version 3.*x* application requests the SM_CYCAPTION system metric value. A version 4.0 application receives the actual height of the title bar.

GetSystemMetrics returns one pixel less than the actual height of a menu bar when a version 3.*x* application requests the SM_CYMENU system metric value. A version 4.0 application receives the actual height of the menu bar.

When a version 3.*x* application calls **GetSystemMetrics** to retrieve the SM_CYFULLSCREEN value (height of a maximized window's client area), the function returns a value that is one pixel less than the actual height. This is because **GetSystemMetrics** returns one pixel more than the actual title bar height when an application retrieves the SM_CYCAPTION value. (The sum of the height of a maximized window's client area and the height of a title bar must equal the height of the working area of the screen.) A version 4.0 application receives the actual height of the maximized window's client area when it requests the SM_CYFULLSCREEN value.

Parameter Validation

If a 32-bit version 3.*x* application specifies invalid class styles when calling the **RegisterClass** function, Windows 95 strips out the invalid bits and generates warnings in the system debugger, but allows **RegisterClass** to succeed anyway. If a 32-bit version 4.0 application passes invalid class styles to **RegisterClass**, the function fails.

In a version 3.*x* application, Windows 95 does not validate the **length** member of the **WINDOWPLACEMENT** structure that is passed to the window placement functions, **GetWindowPlacement** and **SetWindowPlacement**. The **length** member, however, is validated for a version 4.0 application; Windows 95 fails these functions if the value of **length** is incorrect.

Windows 95 does not validate the **cbSize** member of the **STARTUPINFO** structure specified in the **CreateProcess** and **GetStartupInfo** functions for applications written for Windows version 3.*x*. The **cbSize** member is validated, however, for version 4.0 applications.

In the debugging version of Windows 95, the system fills the specified buffer with zeros up to the length specified by the *cbSize* parameter when a version 4.0 application calls the **LoadString** function. The buffer is not filled with zeros for a version 3.*x* application.

P A R T   2

Developing Applications for Windows 95

A R T I C L E   5

Using Common Controls and Dialog Boxes

About Using Common Controls and Dialog Boxes

The Microsoft® Windows® 95 shell looks quite a bit different from the shell used currently by Windows version 3.1*x* and Microsoft® Windows NT™. This new shell includes Windows 95 Explorer, which integrates the functionality of File Manager and Program Manager in Windows 3.1*x*. Windows 95 Explorer uses many of the new Windows 95 common controls and follows the guidelines specified in *The Windows Interface Guidelines for Software Design*.

Because Windows 95 Explorer follows the interface guidelines so closely and uses many of the new Windows 95 controls, developers may want to use it as a model for their new Windows 95–based applications. This article explains how a developer can create an Explorer-like application that displays real-estate listings for houses.

This article is based on the article "Creating a Windows 95 Explorer-like Application" and the CHICOAPP sample application, both by Nancy Cluts, available in the Microsoft Developer Network Development Library.

Appearance of Windows 95 Explorer

Windows 95 Explorer includes some new interface objects, such as a toolbar, a status bar, a tree view control, and a list view control. These controls work together to provide a usable and intuitive interface for the objects contained in the system. For more information about these new controls, see the documentation included in the Microsoft® Win32® Software Development Kit (SDK) and the six part series of articles entitled "Win32 Common Controls" in the Microsoft Developer Network Development Library (under Technical Articles), written by Nancy Cluts.

The new controls are provided in a dynamic-link library (DLL), which is called COMCTL32.DLL. The COMCTL32.DLL file is included in Windows 95 and will also be supported in Microsoft® Win32s® (running with Windows version 3.1*x*) and in Windows NT. The new controls are 32 bit only; they will not be supported in 16-bit Windows environments.

The following illustration shows the Windows 95 Explorer.

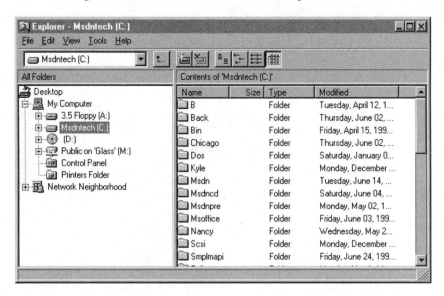

Designing the Sample Application

The sample application displays a real estate listing with the following functionality:

- A toolbar at the top of the screen with tooltip controls for easy access to commands.
- A status window at the bottom of the screen displaying the currently selected city and the number of houses listed for that city.
- A tree view control displaying the cities that have houses for sale.
- A list view control displaying the houses for sale.
- A pop-up context menu that can be displayed by mouse clicking.
- Property sheets for viewing and changing house properties.
- Long filename support for saving and opening house listing files.

The following illustration shows the finished application. It displays the main screen with an open listing for the city of Seattle.

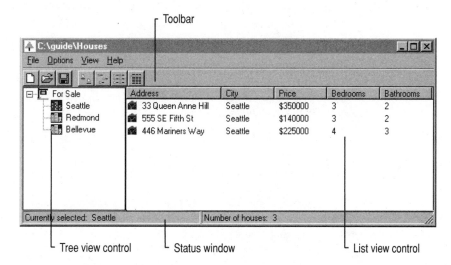

The application-defined structures used to hold the data for the sample application follow. For more information about how these structures are used, see the section "Parsing and Storing the Data" later in this article.

```
typedef struct tagCITYINFO
{
    char szCity[MAX_CITY];   // city name
    int NumHouses;           // number of houses listed in city
    HTREEITEM hItem;         // handle of tree view item
} CITYINFO;

typedef struct tagHOUSEINFO
{
    char szAddress[MAX_ADDRESS];  // address
    char szCity[MAX_CITY];        // city
    int iPrice;                   // price
    int iBeds;                    // number of bedrooms
    int iBaths;                   // number of bathrooms
    int iImage;                   // bitmap index for house
    char szAgent[MAX_CITY];       // listing agent
    char szNumber[MAX_CITY];      // listing agent's phone number
} HOUSEINFO;
```

The following constants and global variables are used in the sample application.

```
// Global variables
#define NUM_BUTTONS 8
#define TEMP_LEN 10

// Structure containing information about the for sale listing.
LISTINFO g_Listing;

// Arrays to hold house and city information.
HOUSEINFO rgHouses[MAX_HOUSES];
CITYINFO  rgCities[MAX_CITIES];

// File input and output (I/O) global variables.
OPENFILENAME OpenFileName;
TCHAR         szDirName[MAX_PATH]   = TEXT("");
TCHAR         szFile[MAX_PATH]      = TEXT("\0");
TCHAR         szFileTitle[MAX_PATH];

// Filter specification for the OPENFILENAME structure.
TCHAR szFilter[] = TEXT("Text Files (*.TXT)\0*.TXT\0All Files
(*.*)\0*.*\0");

char *lpBufPtr;
```

Creating the Common Control Windows

Because the windows used in the sample application are part of the Windows 95 common control library, you must call **InitCommonControls** to ensure that COMCTL32.DLL is loaded before calling any functions that use the new common controls. The status window has two parts: the left part, which displays the currently selected city, and the right part, which displays the number of houses listed for that city. The following example demonstrates how the status bar is implemented and calls helper functions to create the toolbar and the list view and tree view windows.

```
BOOL CreateAppWindows( HWND hwndParent )
{
    RECT rcl;
    int lpSBParts[2];
    static TCHAR szBuf[MAX_PATH];

    // Make sure that the common control library is loaded.
    InitCommonControls();

    // Get the size and position of the parent window.
    GetClientRect(hwndParent, &rcl);
```

```
// First, create the status window.
g_Listing.hWndStatus = CreateStatusWindow(
WS_CHILD | WS_BORDER | WS_VISIBLE,  // window styles
TEXT(""),                           // default window text
hwndParent,                         // parent window
ID_STATUS);                         // identifier

if (g_Listing.hWndStatus == NULL)
    MessageBox (NULL, TEXT("Status Bar not created!"), NULL,
              MB_OK );

// Make the multiple parts for the status window.
lpSBParts[0] = (rcl.right - rcl.left) / 2;
lpSBParts[1] = -1;
SendMessage(g_Listing.hWndStatus, SB_SETPARTS, (WPARAM)2,
(LPARAM)&lpSBParts);

// Set the text for the status window.
ChangeSBText(g_Listing.hInst, g_Listing.hWndStatus, -1);

// Next, create the toolbar.
g_Listing.hWndToolBar = CreateTheToolbar(hwndParent);

if (g_Listing.hWndToolBar == NULL )
    MessageBox (NULL, "Toolbar Bar not created!", NULL, MB_OK);

// Create the list view window.
g_Listing.hWndListView = LV_CreateListView(hwndParent,
g_Listing.hInst, g_Listing.NumHouses, &rgHouses[0]);

if (g_Listing.hWndListView == NULL)
{
    MessageBox (NULL, "Listview not created!", NULL, MB_OK );
    return FALSE;
}

// Create the tree view window, and initialize its
// image list.
g_Listing.hWndTreeView = TV_CreateTreeView(hwndParent,
g_Listing.hInst, g_Listing.NumCities, rgCities);

if (g_Listing.hWndTreeView == NULL)
{
    MessageBox(NULL, TEXT("Tree View not created!"), NULL, MB_OK);
    return FALSE;
}

return TRUE;
}
```

```
VOID ChangeSBText(HINSTANCE hInst, HWND hwnd, int iNumSelected)
{
    static TCHAR szBuf1[MAX_LEN];
    static TCHAR szBuf2[MAX_LEN];
    static TCHAR szSelected[MAX_LEN];
    TCHAR szText[MAX_ITEMLEN];
    int NumHouses;

    if (szBuf1[0] == '\0')
        LoadString (hInst, IDS_SELECTED, szBuf1, sizeof(szBuf1));

    if (szBuf2[0] == '\0')
        LoadString (hInst, IDS_NUMHOUSES, szBuf2, sizeof(szBuf2));

    if (iNumSelected == -1)
    {
        lstrcpy( szSelected, TEXT("None"));
        NumHouses = 0;
    }
    else
    {
        lstrcpy( szSelected, rgCities[iNumSelected].szCity);
        NumHouses = rgCities[iNumSelected].NumHouses;
    }

    wsprintf(szText, TEXT("%s %s"), szBuf1, szSelected);
    SendMessage(hwnd, SB_SETTEXT, 0, (LPARAM)szText);

    wsprintf(szText, TEXT("%s %d"), szBuf2, NumHouses);
    SendMessage(hwnd, SB_SETTEXT, 1, (LPARAM)szText);
}
```

To make a toolbar, create a bitmap for each button and then create a larger bitmap by stringing together each of the small bitmaps into one long bitmap. The standard toolbar bitmaps are built into COMCTL32.DLL. You can add these images to your toolbar by using the TB_ADDBITMAP message. In the following example, three of the standard file bitmaps (new, open, and save) and four of the view bitmaps (large icon, small icon, list view, and details view) are included in the toolbar. The TBBUTTON structure is filled in with the predefined bitmap indices for the desired bitmaps.

```
// Toolbar buttons.
TBBUTTON tbButtons[] = {
    { STD_FILENEW, IDM_NEW, TBSTATE_ENABLED, TBSTYLE_BUTTON, 0, 0L, 0},
    { STD_FILEOPEN, IDM_OPEN, TBSTATE_ENABLED, TBSTYLE_BUTTON, 0,
      0L, 0},
    { STD_FILESAVE, IDM_SAVE, TBSTATE_ENABLED, TBSTYLE_BUTTON, 0,
      0L, 0},
    { 0, 0, TBSTATE_ENABLED, TBSTYLE_SEP, 0, 0L, 0},
```

```
        { VIEW_LARGEICONS, IDM_LARGEICON, TBSTATE_ENABLED, TBSTYLE_BUTTON,
          0, 0L, 0},
        { VIEW_SMALLICONS, IDM_SMALLICON, TBSTATE_ENABLED, TBSTYLE_BUTTON,
          0, 0L, 0},
        { VIEW_LIST, IDM_LISTVIEW, TBSTATE_ENABLED, TBSTYLE_BUTTON, 0, 0L,
          0},
        { VIEW_DETAILS, IDM_REPORTVIEW, TBSTATE_ENABLED, TBSTYLE_BUTTON,
          0, 0L, 0},
};
```

In the code that creates the toolbar, the application calls the **CreateToolbarEx**
function, specifying HINST_COMMCTRL as the handle of the instance,
IDB_STD_SMALL_COLOR as the bitmap identifier, and a pointer to the
TBBUTTON structure. Note that the number of buttons specified is 4
because the last 4 buttons (the view buttons) come from a different bitmap.

```
HWND CreateTheToolbar(HWND hWndParent)
{
    HWND hWndToolbar;
    TBADDBITMAP tb;
    int index, stdidx;

    hWndToolbar = CreateToolbarEx(hWndParent,
        WS_CHILD | WS_BORDER | WS_VISIBLE |
        TBSTYLE_TOOLTIPS, ID_TOOLBAR, 11, (HINSTANCE)HINST_COMMCTRL,
        IDB_STD_SMALL_COLOR, (LPCTBBUTTON)&tbButtons,
        4, 0, 0, 100, 30, sizeof(TBBUTTON));

    // Add the system-defined view bitmaps.
    tb.hInst = HINST_COMMCTRL;
    tb.nID = IDB_VIEW_SMALL_COLOR;
    stdidx = SendMessage(hWndToolbar, TB_ADDBITMAP, 12, (LPARAM)&tb);

    // Update the indices to the bitmaps.
    for (index = 4; index < NUM_BUTTONS; index++)
        tbButtons[index].iBitmap += stdidx;

    // Add the view buttons.
    SendMessage(hWndToolbar, TB_ADDBUTTONS, 4, (LONG) &tbButtons[4]);

    return (hWndToolbar);
}
```

The next step is to create the list view and tree view windows. In the following
example, the tree view control is one-fourth the width of the window's client
area, and its height takes into account the vertical size of the toolbar and status bar.
The example demonstrates how to create the tree view window. For this example,
the values that determine the size of the controls are hard-coded. Applications
should obtain these values by calling the **GetSystemMetrics** function.

```
HWND TV_CreateTreeView (HWND hWndParent, HINSTANCE hInst,
                        int NumCities, CITYINFO *pCity)
{
    HWND hwndTree;        // handle to tree view window
    RECT rcl;             // rectangle for setting size of window
    HBITMAP hBmp;         // handle to bitmap
    HIMAGELIST hIml;      // handle to image list

    // Get the size and position of the parent window.
    GetClientRect(hWndParent, &rcl);

    // Create the tree view window, make it 1/4 the width of the
    // parent window, and take the status bar and toolbar into
    // account.
    hwndTree = CreateWindow (
        WC_TREEVIEW,                // window class
        "",                         // no default text
        WS_VISIBLE | WS_CHILD | WS_BORDER | TVS_HASLINES |
            TVS_HASBUTTONS | TVS_LINESATROOT,
        0, 27,                      // x,y
        (rcl.right - rcl.left)/4,   // cx
        rcl.bottom - rcl.top - 45,  // cy
        hWndParent,                 // parent
        (HMENU) ID_TREEVIEW,        // identifier
        hInst,                      // instance
        NULL );
    if (hWndTree == NULL)
        return NULL;

    // First, create the image list that is needed.
    hIml = ImageList_Create(BITMAP_WIDTH, BITMAP_HEIGHT,FALSE,
    2, 10);

    // Load the bitmaps, and add them to the image lists.
    hBmp = LoadBitmap(hInst, MAKEINTRESOURCE(FORSALE_BMP));
    idxForSale = ImageList_Add(hIml, hBmp, NULL);
    hBmp = LoadBitmap(hInst, MAKEINTRESOURCE(CITY_BMP));
    idxCity = ImageList_Add(hIml, hBmp, NULL);
    hBmp = LoadBitmap(hInst, MAKEINTRESOURCE(SELCITY_BMP));
    idxSelect = ImageList_Add(hIml, hBmp, NULL);

    // Make sure that all of the bitmaps are added.
    if (ImageList_GetImageCount(hIml) != 3)
        return FALSE;
```

```
    // Associate the image list with the tree view control.
    TreeView_SetImageList(hwndTree, hIml, idxForSale);

    // Initialize the tree view by adding "Houses For Sale."
    TV_InitTreeView(hInst, hwndTree);

    return (hwndTree);
}

VOID TV_InitTreeView(HINSTANCE hInst, HWND hwndTree)
{
    TCHAR szText[MAX_CITY];

    // Add the root item "Houses for Sale."
    LoadString(hInst, IDS_FORSALE, szText, MAX_LEN);
    hTPrev = (HTREEITEM)TVI_ROOT;
    iImage = idxForSale;
    hParent = (HTREEITEM)NULL;
    iSelect = idxForSale;
    hTRoot = TV_AddOneItem(szText, hwndTree, -1 );

    // Reset the previous item and image.
    hParent = hTRoot;
    hTPrev = (HTREEITEM)TVI_FIRST;
    iImage = idxCity;
    iSelect = idxSelect;
}
```

In the following example, you create the list view window, make it three-fourths the width of the parent window's client area, place it on the right side, and account vertically for the toolbar and status bar.

```
HWND LV_CreateListView (HWND hWndParent, HINSTANCE hInst,
                        int NumHouses, HOUSEINFO *pHouse)
{
    HWND hWndList;          // handle to list view window
    RECT rcl;              // rectangle for setting size of window
    HICON hIcon;           // handle to icon
    int index;             // index used in FOR loops
    HIMAGELIST hSmall, hLarge; // handles to image lists
    LV_COLUMN lvC;         // list view column structure
    char szText[64];       // place to store some text
    int iWidth;            // column width

    // Get the size and position of the parent window.
    GetClientRect(hWndParent, &rcl);
```

```
// Create the list view window, make it 3/4 the size of the
// parent window, and take the status bar and toolbar into
// account.
iWidth = (rcl.right - rcl.left) - ((rcl.right - rcl.left)/4);
hWndList = CreateWindowEx( 0L,
    WC_LISTVIEW,                                // list view class
    "",                                         // no default text
    WS_VISIBLE | WS_CHILD | WS_BORDER | LVS_REPORT,  // styles
    (rcl.right - rcl.left)/4, 27,               // x, y
    iWidth, rcl.bottom - rcl.top - 42,          // cx, cy
    hWndParent,                                 // parent
    (HMENU) ID_LISTVIEW,                        // identifier
    hInst,                                      // instance
    NULL );

if (hWndList == NULL )
  return NULL;

// First, initialize the image lists that are needed.
// Create an image list for the small and large icons.
// FALSE specifies large icons, and TRUE specifies small icons.
hSmall = ImageList_Create( 16, 16, TRUE, 1, 0 );
hLarge = ImageList_Create( 32, 32, FALSE, 1, 0 );

// Load the icons, and add them to the image lists.
hIcon = LoadIcon ( hInst, MAKEINTRESOURCE(HOUSE_ICON));
if ((ImageList_AddIcon(hSmall, hIcon) == -1) ||
    (ImageList_AddIcon(hLarge, hIcon) == -1))
    return NULL;

// Associate the image list with the list view control.
ListView_SetImageList(hWndList, hSmall, LVSIL_SMALL);
ListView_SetImageList(hWndList, hLarge, LVSIL_NORMAL);

// Initialize the LV_COLUMN structure.
// The mask specifies that the .fmt, .cx, width,
// and .isubitem members of the structure are valid.
lvC.mask = LVCF_FMT | LVCF_WIDTH | LVCF_TEXT | LVCF_SUBITEM;
lvC.fmt = LVCFMT_LEFT;   // left-align the column
lvC.cx = iWidth / NUM_COLUMNS + 1; // width of column,
                                   // in pixels

lvC.pszText = szText;
```

```
    // Add the columns.
    for (index = 0; index < NUM_COLUMNS; index++)
    {
        lvC.iSubItem = index;
        LoadString( hInst,
        IDS_ADDRESS + index,
        szText,
        sizeof(szText));
        if (ListView_InsertColumn(hWndList, index, &lvC) == -1)
        return NULL;
    }

    return (hWndList);

}
```

Sizing Issues

After creating the windows, you will need to resize the application's main window. To resize all of the windows at the same time, use the **DeferWindowPos** function. **DeferWindowPos** updates a structure that contains multiple window positions. You use this function as you would use the window enumeration functions; that is, you begin, defer, and end. The following example illustrates how to resize all of the windows.

```
BOOL ResizeWindows(HWND hwnd)
{
    RECT rcl;
    HDWP hdwp;

    // Get the client area of the parent window.
    GetClientRect(hwnd, &rcl);

    // Defer four windows.
    hdwp = BeginDeferWindowPos(4);
    if (hdwp == NULL)
        return FALSE;

    // First, reset the status bar size.
    DeferWindowPos(hdwp, g_Listing.hWndStatus, NULL, 0, 0,
        rcl.right - rcl.left, 20, SWP_NOZORDER | SWP_NOMOVE);

    // Next, reset the toolbar size.
    DeferWindowPos(hdwp, g_Listing.hWndToolBar, NULL, 0, 0,
        rcl.right - rcl.left, 20, SWP_NOZORDER | SWP_NOMOVE);
```

```
        // Next, reset the tree view size.
        DeferWindowPos(hdwp, g_Listing.hWndTreeView, NULL, 0, 0,
            (rcl.right - rcl.left ) / 4, rcl.bottom - rcl.top - 45,
            SWP_NOZORDER | SWP_NOMOVE);

        // Last, reset the list view size.
        DeferWindowPos(hdwp, g_Listing.hWndListView, NULL,
            (rcl.right - rcl.left ) / 4, 25,
            (rcl.right - rcl.left) - ((rcl.right - rcl.left)/4),
            rcl.bottom - rcl.top - 42,
            SWP_NOZORDER );

        return (EndDeferWindowPos(hdwp));
}
```

Parsing and Storing the Data

Once the windows are created and resized, you need a method for reading in and storing the house listing data. The easiest way to store the house listing data is to save it to an ASCII file. The file should contain the following information:

- Number of cities
- City name (one name per line)
- Number of houses
- Information about each house (one house per line with each item of information separated by commas)

The ASCII file has the following form.

```
3
Bellevue
Redmond
Seattle
9
 100 Main Street,Redmond,175000,3,2,Joan Smith,555-1212
 523 Pine Lake Road,Redmond,125000,4,2,Ed Jones,555-1111
 1212 112th Place SE,Redmond,200000,4,3,Mary Wilson,555-2222
 22 Lake Washington Blvd,Bellevue,2500000,4,4,Joan Smith,555-1212
 33542 116th Ave. NE,Bellevue,180000,3,2,Ed Jones,555-1111
 64134 Nicholas Lane,Bellevue,250000,4,3,Mary Wilson,555-2222
 33 Queen Anne Hill,Seattle,350000,3,2,Joan Smith,555-1212
 555 SE Fifth St,Seattle,140000,3,2,Ed Jones,555-1111
 446 Mariners Way,Seattle,225000,4,3,Mary Wilson,555-2222
```

To parse the file, use the **sscanf** function and then convert some of the strings to integers, copy data to the structure, and update the file pointer. The structures used contain information about the houses, the cities, and the current state of the application. You should fill out a CITYINFO structure for each city listed and a HOUSEINFO structure for each house listed. When saving the information to a file, you reverse the procedure.

Using the Common Dialog Boxes

To support long filenames, use the new common dialog boxes to open and save the house listing information. If you have existing code written for the Windows version 3.1 common dialog boxes, you will be able to recompile some of it, and the application will display the new dialog boxes. You will need to hide the filename extension (.TXT, in this case) before setting the caption text for the main window. As shown in the following illustration, the new File Open common dialog box has no problem with long filenames, such as "Listing for the Puget Sound" or "Another saved listing."

The following example demonstrates how to use the common dialog boxes to open and save a file. It also shows how to read and parse the file to initialize the structures.

```
BOOL OpenNewFile( HWND hWnd )
{
    HANDLE hFile;
    DWORD dwBytesRead;
    DWORD dwFileSize;

    lstrcpy( szFile, TEXT(""));
    lstrcpy( szFileTitle, TEXT(""));
```

```
OpenFileName.lStructSize        = sizeof(OPENFILENAME);
OpenFileName.hwndOwner          = hWnd;
OpenFileName.hInstance          = (HANDLE) g_Listing.hInst;
OpenFileName.lpstrFilter        = szFilter;
OpenFileName.lpstrCustomFilter  = (LPTSTR) NULL;
OpenFileName.nMaxCustFilter     = 0L;
OpenFileName.nFilterIndex       = 1L;
OpenFileName.lpstrFile          = szFile;
OpenFileName.nMaxFile           = sizeof(szFile);
OpenFileName.lpstrFileTitle     = szFileTitle;
OpenFileName.nMaxFileTitle      = sizeof(szFileTitle);
OpenFileName.lpstrInitialDir    = NULL;
OpenFileName.lpstrTitle         = TEXT("Open a File");
OpenFileName.nFileOffset        = 0;
OpenFileName.nFileExtension     = 0;
OpenFileName.lpstrDefExt        = TEXT("*.txt");
OpenFileName.lCustData          = 0;
OpenFileName.Flags              = OFN_SHOWHELP | OFN_PATHMUSTEXIST
                                  | OFN_FILEMUSTEXIST
                                  | OFN_HIDEREADONLY;

if (GetOpenFileName(&OpenFileName))
{
if ((hFile = CreateFile((LPCTSTR)OpenFileName.lpstrFile,
    GENERIC_READ,
    FILE_SHARE_READ,
    NULL,
    OPEN_EXISTING,
    FILE_ATTRIBUTE_NORMAL,
    (HANDLE)NULL)) == (HANDLE)-1)
{
    MessageBox( hWnd, TEXT("File open failed."), NULL, MB_OK );
    return FALSE;
}

// Get the size of the file.
dwFileSize = GetFileSize(hFile, NULL);
if (dwFileSize == 0xFFFFFFFF)
{
    MessageBox( NULL, TEXT("GetFileSize failed!"), NULL, MB_OK);
    return FALSE;
}
```

```
        // Allocate a buffer for the file to be read into.
        lpBufPtr = (TCHAR *)GlobalAlloc( GMEM_FIXED, dwFileSize );
        if (lpBufPtr == NULL)
        {
            MessageBox( NULL, TEXT("GlobalAlloc failed!"), NULL, MB_OK);
            CloseHandle( hFile );
            return FALSE;
        }

        // Read its contents into a buffer.
        ReadFile(hFile,(LPVOID)lpBufPtr, dwFileSize, &dwBytesRead, NULL);

        if (dwBytesRead == 0)
        {
            MessageBox( hWnd, TEXT("Zero bytes read."), NULL, MB_OK );
            CloseHandle(hFile);
            GlobalFree(lpBufPtr);
            return FALSE;
        }

        // Close the file.
        CloseHandle(hFile);

        // Parse the file buffer.
        return (ParseFile());
        }
        else
        {
        ProcessCDError(CommDlgExtendedError(), hWnd );
        return FALSE;
        }
}

BOOL ParseFile ( VOID )
{
    int count, result, index;
    TCHAR szTemp[MAX_PATH], szBeds[TEMP_LEN], szBaths[TEMP_LEN];
    TCHAR * lpSave;
    HTREEITEM hPrev;

    // Initialize the tree view and list view windows.
    InitTreeAndList();

    lpSave = lpBufPtr;

    // Read in the first line to get the number of cities.
    sscanf( lpBufPtr, TEXT("%s\n"), szTemp);
    g_Listing.NumCities = atoi(szTemp);
```

```
            // Move the buffer pointer.
            while (*lpBufPtr != 0x0A)
               lpBufPtr++;
            lpBufPtr++;

            if (g_Listing.NumCities == 0 || g_Listing.NumCities > MAX_CITIES)
            {
                MessageBox(NULL, TEXT("Number of cities must be between 1 and
16"), NULL, MB_OK);
                GlobalFree(lpBufPtr);
                return FALSE;
            }

            // Read a city for each line.
            for (count= 0; count < g_Listing.NumCities; count++)
            {
                sscanf( lpBufPtr, TEXT("%s\n"), rgCities[count].szCity);

                // Move the buffer pointer.
                while (*lpBufPtr != 0x0A)
                    lpBufPtr++;
                lpBufPtr++;

                // Add the city to the tree view control.
                hPrev = TV_AddOneItem( rgCities[count].szCity,
                g_Listing.hWndTreeView, count);
            }

            // Get the number of houses.
            sscanf( lpBufPtr, TEXT("%s\n"), szTemp);
            g_Listing.NumHouses = atoi(szTemp);

            // Move the buffer pointer.
            while (*lpBufPtr != 0x0A)
            lpBufPtr++;
            lpBufPtr++;

            if (g_Listing.NumHouses == 0 || g_Listing.NumHouses > MAX_HOUSES)
            {
            MessageBox(NULL, TEXT("Number of houses must be between 1 and 256"),
NULL, MB_OK);
                GlobalFree(lpBufPtr);
                return FALSE;
            }
```

```
    // Read the house information for each line.
    for (count= 0; count < g_Listing.NumHouses; count++)
    {
        result = sscanf(lpBufPtr,
        TEXT("%[^','],%[^','],%[^','],%[^','],%[^','],%[^','],%s"),
        rgHouses[count].szAddress,rgHouses[count].szCity,
        szTemp, szBeds, szBaths, rgHouses[count].szAgent,
        rgHouses[count].szNumber);

        rgHouses[count].iPrice = atoi(szTemp);
        rgHouses[count].iBeds = atoi(szBeds);
        rgHouses[count].iBaths = atoi(szBaths);

        // Move the buffer pointer.
        while (*lpBufPtr != 0x0A)
            lpBufPtr++;
        lpBufPtr++;

    // Increment the house count for the city.
    for (index=0;index < g_Listing.NumCities; index++)
    {
        if (lstrcmp(rgHouses[count].szCity, rgCities[index].szCity) ==
         0)
        {
            rgCities[index].NumHouses++;
            break;
        }
    }
    }
    // Free up the buffer.
    GlobalFree(lpBufPtr);

    // Then add the cities and houses to the list view and
    // tree view controls.

    return TRUE;
}

VOID UpdateListView( HWND hwndLV, int iSelected )
{
    int count, index;

    LV_RemoveAllItems(hwndLV);
```

```
                    for (index = 0, count = 0; count < g_Listing.NumHouses; count++)
                    {
                        if (lstrcmp(rgHouses[count].szCity,
                            rgCities[iSelected].szCity) == 0)
                        {
                            // Add the house to the list view control.
                            if (!LV_AddItem(hwndLV, index, &rgHouses[count]))
                                MessageBox(NULL, TEXT("LV_AddItem failed!"), NULL,
                                MB_OK);
                            index++;
                        }
                    }
                }


BOOL SaveToFile( HWND hWnd )
{
    HANDLE hFile;
    DWORD dwOpen;
    DWORD dwBytesWritten;
    TCHAR buf[MAX_PATH];
    DWORD dwFileSize;

    dwFileSize = GetDataBufferAndSize();
    if (dwFileSize == 0)
    {
        MessageBox(NULL,TEXT( "GetDataBufferAndSize failed!"), NULL,
                    MB_OK);
        return FALSE;
    }


    dwOpen = CREATE_ALWAYS;

    // Open the file.
    if ((hFile = CreateFile((LPCTSTR)OpenFileName.lpstrFile,
            GENERIC_WRITE,
            FILE_SHARE_WRITE,
            NULL,
            dwOpen,
            FILE_ATTRIBUTE_NORMAL,
            (HANDLE)NULL)) == (HANDLE)-1)
    {
        sprintf( buf, TEXT("Could not create file %s"),
            OpenFileName.lpstrFile );
        MessageBox( hWnd, buf, NULL, MB_OK );
        return FALSE;
    }
```

```
                    // Write its contents into a file.
                    if (WriteFile( hFile, (LPCVOID)lpBufPtr, dwFileSize,
                        &dwBytesWritten, NULL) == FALSE)
                    {
                        MessageBox( hWnd, TEXT("Error writing file."), NULL, MB_OK );
                        return FALSE;
                    }

                    // Close the file.
                    CloseHandle(hFile);

                    // Free up the file buffer.
                    GlobalFree(lpBufPtr);

                    return TRUE;
                }
                VOID InitTreeAndList( VOID )
                {
                    g_Listing.NumCities = 0;
                    g_Listing.NumHouses = 0;
                    g_Listing.iSelected = -1;
                    g_Listing.iSelHouse = -1;
                    TreeView_DeleteAllItems(g_Listing.hWndTreeView);
                    ListView_DeleteAllItems(g_Listing.hwndListView);
                    TV_InitTreeView(g_Listing.hInst, g_Listing.hWndTreeView);

                }
```

Handling Notification Messages

Notification messages are used extensively to manipulate the behavior and appearance of controls. Because status windows, toolbars, list view controls, and tree view controls all expect notification messages, you must ensure that each control gets the notifications it needs. In the main window procedure for the application, trap the WM_NOTIFY message and either handle the notification messages directly or pass them to handler functions.

```
case WM_NOTIFY:
    lpToolTipText = (LPTOOLTIPTEXT)lParam;
    if (lpToolTipText->hdr.code == TTN_NEEDTEXT)
    {
        LoadString(g_Listing.hInst,
                    lpToolTipText->hdr.idFrom,  // string ID == cmd ID
                    szBuf,
                    sizeof(szBuf));
        lpToolTipText->lpszText = szBuf;
    }
```

```
if (TV_NotifyHandler(hWnd, message, wParam, lParam, &g_Listing))
{
    // Update the list view control to show houses
    // in the selected city.
    UpdateListView(g_Listing.hWndListView, g_Listing.iSelected);

    // Update the status text.
    ChangeSBText(g_Listing.hInst, g_Listing.hWndStatus,
                 g_Listing.iSelected );
}
LV_NotifyHandler(hWnd, message, wParam, lParam, g_Listing.hInst);
break;
```

For the toolbar, the sample application only traps the TTN_NEEDTEXT
notification message, which is sent whenever the system needs to display a tooltip
control associated with a toolbar button. In response to this notification message,
the application must load the appropriate text string into the **lpszText** member of
the **LPTOOLTIPTEXT** structure.

The tree view window's notification handler, however, only handles the
TVN_SELCHANGED notification message, which is sent to the tree view window
whenever the selection changes.

```
LRESULT TV_NotifyHandler(HWND hWnd, UINT uMsg, WPARAM wParam, LPARAM
                         lParam, LISTINFO *pList)
{
    static NM_TREEVIEW *pNm;

    pNm = (NM_TREEVIEW *)lParam;
    if (pNm->hdr.idFrom != ID_TREEVIEW)
        return 0L;

    switch(pNm->hdr.code)
    {
        case TVN_SELCHANGED:
            pList->iSelected = (int)(pNm->itemNew.lParam);
            return 1;
            break;
        default:
            break;
    }
return 0L;
```

In response, the application needs to update the list view control and status bar to reflect the house listings for the newly selected city.

```
VOID UpdateListView( HWND hwndLV, int iSelected )
{
    int count, index;

    // Remove the previous items.
    LV_RemoveAllItems(hwndLV);

    // Loop through the house listings.
    for (index = 0, count = 0; count < g_Listing.NumHouses; count++)
    {
        // Check whether the house is listed for the new city.
         if (strcmp(rgHouses[count].szCity,
             rgCities[iSelected].szCity) == 0)
        {
            // If it is, add the house to the list view control.
            if (!LV_AddItem(hwndLV, index, &rgHouses[count]))
                MessageBox(NULL, "LV_AddItem failed!", NULL, MB_OK);
            index++;
        }
    }
}
```

Handling notification messages for the list view window is a bit more complicated. The application implements the list view control using a callback function that receives the text for each item, so the notification handler needs to trap the LVN_GETDISPINFO notification message and fill in the **pszText** member of the **LV_ITEM** structure with the appropriate text, depending on the column.

The application also processes the LVN_COLUMNCLICK notification message in the list view notification handler. This notification message is sent whenever the user clicks a column heading in the list view control. In response, the application must sort the items in the list view control based on the criteria presented in the selected column. For example, if the user clicks the Bedrooms column, the application sorts the list in ascending order by the number of bedrooms for the item (that is, the house). The application uses a simple callback function that is called by using the **ListView_SortItems** macro. The callback function sorts the data using simple math (returning the greater of two values) for the columns that have integer sort criteria and using the **strcmp** function for the columns that have string sort criteria.

```
LRESULT LV_NotifyHandler(HWND hWnd, UINT uMsg, WPARAM wParam,
                         LPARAM lParam, HINSTANCE hInst)
{
    LV_DISPINFO *pLvdi = (LV_DISPINFO *)lParam;
    NM_LISTVIEW *pNm = (NM_LISTVIEW *)lParam;
    HOUSEINFO *pHouse = (HOUSEINFO *)(pLvdi->item.lParam);
    static TCHAR szText[TEMP_LEN];

    if (pNm->hdr.idFrom != ID_LISTVIEW)
        return 0L;

    switch(pLvdi->hdr.code)
    {
        case LVN_GETDISPINFO:
            switch (pLvdi->item.iSubItem)
            {
                case 0:     // address
                    pLvdi->item.pszText = pHouse->szAddress;
                    break;

                case 1:     // city
                    pLvdi->item.pszText = pHouse->szCity;
                    break;

                case 2:     // price
                    sprintf(szText, "$%u", pHouse->iPrice);
                    pLvdi->item.pszText = szText;
                    break;

                case 3:     // number of bedrooms
                    sprintf(szText, "%u", pHouse->iBeds);
                    pLvdi->item.pszText = szText;
                    break;

                case 4:     // number of bathrooms
                    sprintf(szText, "%u", pHouse->iBaths);
                    pLvdi->item.pszText = szText;
                    break;

                default:
                    break;
            }
            break;

        case LVN_COLUMNCLICK:
            // The user clicked on one of the column headings,
            // so sort by this column.
            ListView_SortItems(pNm->hdr.hwndFrom,ListViewCompareProc,
                        (LPARAM)(pNm->iSubItem));
            break;
```

```
            default:
                break;
        }
        return 0L;
}


int CALLBACK ListViewCompareProc(LPARAM lParam1, LPARAM lParam2,
                                 LPARAM lParamSort)
{
    HOUSEINFO *pHouse1 = (HOUSEINFO *)lParam1;
    HOUSEINFO *pHouse2 = (HOUSEINFO *)lParam2;
    int iResult;

    if (pHouse1 && pHouse2)
    {
        switch( lParamSort)
        {
            case 0:     // sort by address
                iResult = lstrcmpi(pHouse1->szAddress,
                    pHouse2->szAddress);
                break;

            case 1:     // sort by city
                iResult = lstrcmpi(pHouse1->szCity, pHouse2->szCity);
                break;

            case 2:     // sort by price
                iResult = pHouse1->iPrice - pHouse2->iPrice;
                break;

            case 3:     // sort by number of bedrooms
                iResult = pHouse1->iBeds - pHouse2->iBeds;
                break;

            case 4:     // sort by number of bathrooms
                iResult = pHouse1->iBaths - pHouse2->iBaths;
                break;

            default:
                iResult = 0;
                break;


        }

    }
    return(iResult);
}
```

Adding Pop-up Context Menus

At this point, the application is functional, but you still need to add the pop-up menu that is displayed when the user clicks mouse button 2. There are two ways to do this. The easiest method is to trap the WM_CONTEXTMENU message and check the *wParam* parameter to see if the click occurred in the list view window. WM_CONTEXTMENU is sent whenever the user clicks mouse button 2. Another method is to handle the NM_RCLICK notification message and call the **ListView_HitTest** macro to determine which item, if any, the user has clicked. NM_RCLICK is sent whenever the user clicks mouse button 2 in the list view window.

To display a context menu for an item, you load the menu and call the **TrackPopupMenu** function. When the user chooses an item from the menu, the appropriate command is generated and sent to the window procedure in the form of a WM_COMMAND message.

```
case WM_CONTEXTMENU:
    // Mouse button 2 has been clicked.
    if ((HWND)wParam == g_Listing.hWndListView)
    {
        //.Get the menu for the pop-up menu from the resource file.
        hMenu = LoadMenu(g_Listing.hInst, "HousePopupMenu");
        if (!hMenu)
            break;

        // Get the first submenu in it for TrackPopupMenu.
        hMenuTrackPopup = GetSubMenu(hMenu, 0);

        // Draw the "floating" pop-up menu, and track it.
        TrackPopupMenu(hMenuTrackPopup,
                    TPM_LEFTALIGN | TPM_RIGHTBUTTON,
                    LOWORD(lParam), HIWORD(lParam),
                    0, g_Listing.hWndListView, NULL);

        // Destroy the menu.
        DestroyMenu(hMenu);
    }
    break;
```

Incorporating Property Sheets

Property sheets (also known as tabbed dialog boxes) allow users to view and change the properties of an item. In the sample application, the item is a house listing. Each property sheet contains one or more overlapping windows (called *pages*) that contain a logical grouping of properties. The user switches between pages by clicking tabs that label each property page. The sample contains two property sheets: one allowing the user to view and change the properties for a particular house listing (for example, address and city) and the other displaying information about the listing agent (for example, name and phone number). The following illustration shows the House Listing property sheet page. (An illustration of the Listing Agent property sheet page is found later in this section.)

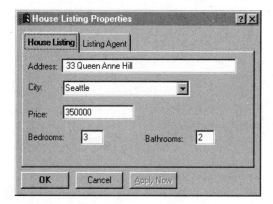

Processing a property sheet page is similar to processing a dialog box with one major difference. When you process a property sheet page, you handle notification messages instead of the commands generated for the OK and Cancel buttons. You should process the property sheet pages in the following manner:

- Save the original values for the item in response to the WM_INITDIALOG message.

- Reset the values of the item in response to the PSN_KILLACTIVE and PSN_APPLY notification messages.

- Reset the values of the item in response to a PSN_RESET notification message.

- Set the edit fields in the page for the item in response to the PSN_SETACTIVE notification message.

To initialize the property sheet pages, you need to determine which house is currently selected and save that information for future reference. The first property sheet page displayed is the House Listing page. Responding to the WM_INITDIALOG message gives you the first chance to determine the currently selected house. The following example determines the index of the selected house within the global array of houses.

```
static char szAddSave[MAX_ADDRESS];
BOOL bErr;
int index, count;
LV_ITEM lvItem;
    .
    .
    .
  case WM_INITDIALOG:
    // Fill in the list box with the cities.
    for (index = 0; index < g_Listing.NumCities; index++)
        SendDlgItemMessage(hDlg, IDE_CITY, CB_INSERTSTRING,
                           (WPARAM)(-1),
                           (LPARAM)(rgCities[index].szCity));

    // Get the index to the selected list view item.
    index = ListView_GetNextItem(g_Listing.hWndListView,
                            -1, MAKELPARAM(LVNI_SELECTED, 0));

    // Get the house address.
    lvItem.iItem = index;
    lvItem.iSubItem = 0;
    lvItem.mask = LVIF_TEXT;
    lvItem.cchTextMax = sizeof(szAddSave);
    lvItem.pszText = szAddSave;
    ListView_GetItem(g_Listing.hWndListView,&lvItem);

    // Find the house in the list.
    for (count=0; count < g_Listing.NumHouses; count++)
    {
        if (strcmp(lvItem.pszText, rgHouses[count].szAddress) == 0)
            break;
    }
    g_Listing.iSelHouse = count;
    .
    .
    .
```

The Listing Agent property sheet page allows the user to view and change the name and phone number of the listing agent associated with the selected house. The code used to handle this page is quite similar to that used for the House Listing page, except that the szAgent and szNumber members of the array of HOUSEINFO structures are modified instead of the other house-specific fields.

The following illustration shows the Listing Agent property sheet page.

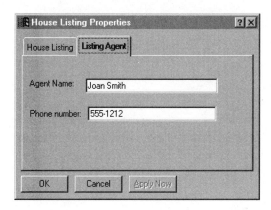

ARTICLE 6

Using the Registry

About Using the Registry

The registry is a central storage location that contains current information about the computer hardware configuration, installed software applications, settings and preferences of the current user, and associations between types of files and the applications that access and manipulate their contents. Much of the information that was stored in initialization files in early versions of the Microsoft® Windows® operating system is now stored in the registry in Windows 95.

Mentions of the registry occur in several places in the documentation for Windows 95 and in the Microsoft® Win32® Software Development Kit (SDK). The documentation included in the Win32 SDK provides a detailed description of the functions and structures that provide an application with access to the registry. *The Windows Interface Guidelines for Software Design* has a chapter containing a general discussion of the registry. The *Microsoft Windows 95 Resource Kit* devotes a chapter to integrating an application into the Windows 95 operating system by storing information in the registry. If you are unfamiliar with the registry or the arrangement of information within it, you should read about the registry before beginning this article. This article assumes you are already familiar with the registry and focuses on using the registry functions to navigate and load the registry as part of installing an application.

After briefly introducing registry terminology, this article identifies procedures involved in working with the registry when installing a software product. Other issues, such as the general registry structure and Windows 95 style recommendations, are mentioned in support of the registry coding described here.

This article describes how to record the following types of information in the registry:

- Application state information
- Application path information
- Filename extensions
- New data files
- Icons
- Icon commands
- Uninstall information

This article frequently refers to a fictitious company called Buzz Productions, whose fictitious product is named BeeSounds. The product is comprised of an executable file named BUZZER.EXE, a dynamic-link library (DLL) named BUZZEXT.DLL, and a help file named BUZZER.HLP. Data files used by the product are identified by the .BZZ filename extension.

Introducing the Registry

The registry is a hierarchical database. The database is made up of keys that are linked together to form hierarchies or tree structures. The keys are the fundamental entities in the database. The registry has six keys, also called root keys, that serve as entrypoints to the database for any application. Links provide a mechanism to traverse the database from a root key to other keys. The link between two keys also serves to establish the relationship of a subkey. A subkey is further from the root of the hierarchy than the other key in the link.

Each key has a name and a default value. A key can also have other named values associated with it. A value can be named or unnamed and has its own storage area for a data value. The data value can store binary, numerical, string, or other types of data.

The registry contains information that is critical to the correct operation of the computer. Before accessing and modifying the contents of the registry, you should make a back up copy of the registry. You can do this using the RegEdit utility.

Note   The registries for Windows 95 and Microsoft® Windows NT™ differ in how they handle class information associated with a key. The Windows 95 registry treats all classes alike. If you pass in a valid *lpszClass* buffer pointer to **RegQueryInfoKey** but do not pass in a valid *lpcchClass* pointer (that is, if you pass in NULL), Windows 95 lets the function call proceed.

The Window NT registry, however, distinguishes the different classes. In Windows NT, if you pass in a valid *lpszClass* buffer pointer to **RegQueryInfoKey** but do not pass in a valid *lpcchClass* pointer (that is, if you pass in NULL), the system returns the ERROR_INVALID_PARAMETER error value.

Registering Application State Information

Application state information identifies information about a specific release of a software product, such as the product name, version number, user preferences, and component location. The registry provides two entry level hierarchies for storing this information. Application state information for the current version of a software product that is user-specific is stored in the registry in the following portion of the **HKEY_CURRENT_USER** hierarchy.

```
HKEY_CURRENT_USER
    Software
        BuzzProductions
            BeeSounds
                Version2.00
```

Application state information for the current version of a software product that is specific to an installation (and relevant to all users) is stored in the following portion of the **HKEY_LOCAL_MACHINE** hierarchy.

```
HKEY_LOCAL_MACHINE
    SOFTWARE
        BuzzProductions
            BeeSounds
                Version2.00
```

You can add additional keys and values under your application's **Version** key in each hierarchy. Key names are canonical; they cannot be changed, so you can use them to group the information types being stored. Key values can easily be changed and are ideal for storing information that changes, such as user preferences.

If the amount of installation-specific and user version information exceeds a few thousand bytes, you might still want to create an initialization (.INI) file.

Registering Application Path Information

Application path information identifies where the application file (.EXE file), application extension files (.DLL files), and other support files for an application are stored in the Windows 95 file system. By following the conventions recommended in *The Windows Interface Guidelines for Software Design*, the files for the BeeSounds sample product would be installed in the following directories.

Filename	Directory
BUZZER.EXE	\Program Files\BeeSounds
BUZZEXT.DLL	\Program Files\BeeSounds\System
BUZZER.HLP	\Program Files\BeeSounds\System
*.BZZ (data files)	\Program Files\BeeSounds\System

The registry stores directory information that locates the installed application files and their associated application extension files in one or more keys of the **HKEY_LOCAL_MACHINE** hierarchy. For the BUZZER.EXE file, the key is inserted in the following hierarchy.

```
HKEY_LOCAL_MACHINE
     SOFTWARE
         Microsoft
             Windows
                 CurrentVersion
                     App Paths
                         BUZZER.EXE
```

Each installed application file should have a key under the **App Paths** key named after the application file.

The **BUZZER.EXE** key has two values. The Default value specifies the path to the application file. The optional Path value specifies the paths to other application files.

Note If an application shares application extension files, the installation program should create a **SharedDLLs** key under the **CurrentVersion** key. Under the **SharedDLLs** key, the installation program should create a key and a data value for each shared file. The key name for each shared file must specify the path and filename of the shared file. The data value associated with the key for a shared file tracks the number of applications that share the application extension file.

You can expand the capabilities of an application by adding keys under the **CurrentVersion** key in both the **HKEY_CURRENT_USER** and the **HKEY_LOCAL_MACHINE** hierarchies.

For example, you can automatically start your application whenever Windows 95 starts up by adding the **Run** key beneath the **CurrentVersion** key and by including a data value for the **Run** key that specifies the command line to start the application.

You can automatically restart an application that was interrupted by a system shutdown when Windows 95 starts up by adding the **RunOnce** key beneath the **CurrentVersion** key and by including a data value for the **RunOnce** key that specifies the command line to restart the application. The command line must specify the path to the application file, appropriate data files, and any options needed to restore the application.

Registering Filename Extensions

You can distinguish new file types by registering the filename extensions in the registry. Every file type that you install in the registry requires at least two registry keys. One of the mandatory keys specifies the filename extension. The other mandatory key specifies the application identifier and defines a long (40 character) description of the application identifier or class name that end users will see. Additional keys can specify a class identifier and a short (15 character) description of the application identifier or class name.

The registry stores filename extensions in the **HKEY_CLASSES_ROOT** hierarchy. The keys needed to register the filename extension used by the BeeSounds data files follow. Note that the CLSID class identifier is not a literal value; it is a unique identifier that can be obtained by running the UUIDGEN.EXE utility included in the Win32 SDK.

```
HKEY_CLASSES_ROOT
    .BZZ = BeeSounds
    BeeSounds·
        CLSID
    CLSID
        {CLSID identifier}
            AuxUserType
                2
```

Registering Data Files for Creation

If you would like users to be able to create new data files for an application directly from the desktop or folder without running the application, you should register the filename extension for creation.

The registry stores information that is used for data file creation in the **HKEY_CLASSES_ROOT** hierarchy. The keys needed to register data files used by the BeeSounds data files follow. The **ShellNew** key has a value associated with it. The value used is the default value, and it contains the string "NullFile".

```
HKEY_CLASSES_ROOT
    .BZZ
        ShellNew
```

Registering Icons

Windows 95 determines the icon to display for each file from information stored in the registry. If you would like the user to distinguish data files used by your application from other generic (unidentified) files stored on the file system, you can install icons to associate with a specific file type and register the icon and file association in the registry.

The registry stores icon information in the **HKEY_CLASSES_ROOT** hierarchy. The keys needed to register an icon for data files used by the BeeSounds data files follow. The **DefaultIcon** key has a value associated with it. The value used is the default value, and it contains a string identifying the path and file that contains the icon, and either an positive index value or a negative resource identifier that specifies the icon resource within the file. The value can be "%", indicating an instance-specific icon (for more infomation about instance-specific icons, see Article 12, "Shell Extensions").

The following example shows a sample **DefaultIcon** key and its associated value:

```
HKEY_CLASSES_ROOT
    BeeSounds
        DefaultIcon = "C:\BEE\buzzer.exe, 1"
```

The file containing the icon can be an application file, an application extension file, or a resource file containing one or more resources. If the first resource in a file is the icon you want to associate with a file, you can omit the comma and index value from the data of the default value.

Registering Icon Commands

Clicking with mouse button 2 on an icon displays a menu of commands that can be executed with the icon. Support for many of these commands is provided by the container (folder or desktop) containing the icon. However, containers do not provide support for the primary commands (Open, Edit, Play, and Print) that can be executed with an icon, nor do they provide support for custom commands. For each primary command or custom command that you want to provide to the user, you must register information for the command. For example, the BeeSounds product supports the Play primary command and the custom command "Play in Reverse."

The registry stores information for icon command support in the hierarchy of **HKEY_CLASSES_ROOT**. The keys needed to register data files used by the BeeSounds data files follow. The **Shell** key has a value associated with it. The value's name is default, and it has contains the string "Play, Play_In_Reverse".

```
HKEY_CLASSES_ROOT
    BeeSounds
        Shell
            Play
                command = "C:\WINDOWS\buzzer.exe /play %1"
            Play_In_Reverse
                command = C:\WINDOWS\buzzer.exe /reverse %1"
```

The **Play** key has a value associated with it. The value used is the default value, and it contains the text that is displayed in the menu. This value must be localized (for example, "&Play"). If key name matches the menu text, you do not need to specify a value for the key. The command key under the **Play** key specifies as its value the command line that implements the Play command.

The **Play_In_Reverse** key uses the default value that contains the "Play In Reverse" text that appears in the menu. The command key found under the **Play_In_Reverse** key specifies as its value the command line that implements the "Play in Reverse" command.

When displaying the menu for an icon, the system lists the order of the commands as they appear under the **Shell** key. You can override that sequence by specifying a preferred sequence as a comma-delineated key list in the default value of the **Shell** key. The first command listed in the menu becomes the default command for an icon.

Registering Uninstall Information

Windows 95 includes a property sheet for Control Panel for installing and removing applications. Users might need to remove an application to recover disk space or to move the application to another location. To facilitate this, you should provide an uninstall program with your software application that removes the files and their settings and records information about the application in the registry.

The registry stores uninstall information in the **HKEY_LOCAL_MACHINE** hierarchy. The keys needed to register uninstall information for the BUZZER.EXE application follow.

```
HKEY_LOCAL_MACHINE
    SOFTWARE
        Microsoft
            Windows
                CurrentVersion
                    Uninstall
                        BUZZER.EXE
```

The **BUZZER.EXE** key has two named values that are required for each application key in the Uninstall hierarchy. The DisplayName value specifies a text string that the Add/Remove Programs property sheet of Control Panel displays to the user. The UninstallString value specifies the command line that runs the uninstall program, and it must specify the path, application file, and needed command-line arguments. For the BeeSounds product, this value is "c:\Program Files\BeeSounds\NOBUZZ.EXE /q."

The following example registers the uninstall information for the BeeSounds product.

```
case  IDM_REGUNINSTALL:            //register uninstall information

// 1. Navigate to the CurrentVersion key.
// 2. Create CurrentVersion\Uninstall\BUZZER.EXE key(s).
// 3. Create DisplayName and UninstallString values for BUZZER.EXE key.
// 4. Close the keys.

    // Prepare to navigate to the CurrentVersion key.
    hKey = HKEY_LOCAL_MACHINE;
    lstrcpy(lpszChildKey,
        (LPCSTR)"SOFTWARE\\Microsoft\\Windows\\CurrentVersion");
    dwReserved = 0;
    hChildKey = NULL;
    lpszKeyValue = szKeyValue;

    if (ERROR_SUCCESS == RegOpenKeyEx(hKey, lpszChildKey, dwReserved,
        KEY_READ|KEY_WRITE, &hChildKey))
    {
        MessageBox(hwnd, lpszChildKey, "Register Uninstall",MB_OK);
    }
    else {
        MessageBox(hwnd,"Key is not immediate child of other key",
            "Register App Path",MB_OK);
        break;
    }

    // Prepare to create Uninstall\BUZZER.EXE key(s).
    hKey = hChildKey;
    // Identify the filename extension.
    lstrcpy(lpszChildKey,(LPCSTR)"Uninstall\\BUZZER.EXE");
    lstrcpy(lpszClassType,"");       // class identifier for new key

    dwReserved = 0;
    hChildKey = NULL;
    fdwOptions = REG_OPTION_NON_VOLATILE;

    dwDisposition = 0L;      // clear returning parameter for create
    lpdwDisposition = &dwDisposition;

    dwDisposition2 = 0L;     // clear return parameter for nested create
    lpdwDisposition2 = &dwDisposition2;
```

```
if (ERROR_SUCCESS == RegCreateKeyEx(hKey, lpszChildKey, dwReserved,
        lpszClassType, fdwOptions,
        KEY_ALL_ACCESS, NULL, &hChildKey, lpdwDisposition))
{
    switch (dwDisposition){

    case REG_CREATED_NEW_KEY:
        // Create the DisplayName and UninstallString values.
        MessageBox(hwnd,"Create BUZZER.EXE a Success",
            "Creating key",MB_OK);

        lstrcpy (lpszKeyValueName, (LPCSTR)"DisplayName");
        lstrcpy (lpszKeyValue,
            (LPCSTR)"BeeSounds Removal Application");
        RegSetValueEx(hChildKey, lpszKeyValueName, dwReserved,
            REG_SZ, lpszKeyValue, sizeof(*szKeyValue));

        lstrcpy (lpszKeyValueName, (LPCSTR)"UninstallString");
        lstrcpy (lpszKeyValue,
            (LPCSTR)"C:\\Program Files\\BeeSounds\\NOBUZZ.EXE /q");
        RegSetValueEx(hChildKey, lpszKeyValueName, dwReserved,
            REG_SZ, lpszKeyValue, sizeof(*szKeyValue));

        RegCloseKey(hChildKey);
        RegCloseKey(hKey);
        break;

    case REG_OPENED_EXISTING_KEY:
    // This case should not apply, assuming it is a new installation
    // or the CurrentVersion hierarchy was copied and then deleted.
    // Therefore, delete the existing key and create a new one.

        MessageBox(hwnd,"Create BUZZER.EXE failed",
            "Creating key",MB_OK);

        RegDeleteKey(hKey, hChildKey);
        RegCreateKeyEx(hKey, lpszChildKey, dwReserved,
            lpszClassType, fdwOptions,
            KEY_ALL_ACCESS, NULL, &hChildKey, lpdwDisposition2);
```

```
            if (dwDisposition2 == REG_CREATED_NEW_KEY)
            {
            // The second try worked. Now add values.
            lstrcpy (lpszKeyValueName, (LPCSTR)"DisplayName");
            lstrcpy (lpszKeyValue,
                (LPCSTR)"BeeSounds Removal Application");
            RegSetValueEx(hChildKey, lpszKeyValueName, dwReserved,
                REG_SZ, lpszKeyValue, sizeof(*szKeyValue));

            lstrcpy (lpszKeyValueName, (LPCSTR)"UninstallString");
            lstrcpy (lpszKeyValue,
                (LPCSTR)"C:\\Program Files\\BeeSounds\\NOBUZZ.EXE /q");
            RegSetValueEx(hChildKey, lpszKeyValueName, dwReserved,
                REG_SZ, lpszKeyValue, sizeof(*szKeyValue));

            RegCloseKey(hChildKey);
            RegCloseKey(hKey);
            }
            break;

        default:          // other status returned?
            MessageBox(hwnd,"Function successful,
                but status unexpected", "Creating key",MB_OK);
        }
    }
    else {
        MessageBox(hwnd,"Error--Couldn't create key",
            "Creating key",MB_OK);
    }

    // The second attempt did not create a new key.
    if (dwDisposition2 != REG_CREATED_NEW_KEY)
    {  // Place the error correction code here.
    }

    break;
```

If an application is being removed, the usage count for each shared and system-wide shared application extension file needs to be decremented. If the usage count for a file reaches zero, the user should be given the option of deleting the file.

A R T I C L E   7

Dragging and Dropping

About Dragging and Dropping

This article is based in part on "Drag and Drop Target Practice: Implementing OLE 2.0 Support in Your Applications," (*Microsoft Developers Network News*, January 1994), by Sara Williams.

A Microsoft® Windows® 95–based application should fully support the source and target drag and drop capabilities provided by OLE. One of the most attractive features of drag and drop in OLE is that the code that handles the actual data transfer—your implementation of the **IDataObject** interface—is reusable. You will be able to use the same code to implement cut and paste. OLE separates what the user does to cause the data transfer from how the applications actually transfer the data. This allows you to use the same "back-end" **IDataObject** interface for any number of ways that the user may want to transfer data.

This article explains the general concepts that you need to know to support OLE drag and drop capabilities in your applications and lists the basic steps for implementing drag and drop support.

General OLE Concepts

One of the most attractive aspects of OLE is that it is completely modular. It is designed so that each component can exist, for the most part, on its own. For example, you can add drag and drop support to your application without bothering with in-place activation, automation, or compound storage.

Even if your application only uses a small part of OLE, the Component Object Model (COM) enables other applications to know what your application's OLE capabilities are. COM is the fundamental, underlying model that OLE is based upon; all OLE objects are also component objects.

COM stipulates that any component object must control its own life span and be able to tell other objects about its capabilities in a strictly defined manner. To control its life span, a component object maintains a reference count. Capabilities are grouped into logical sets called interfaces; each interface is a set of member functions necessary to support a certain capability. The "strictly defined manner" that component objects must use is itself an interface, which is called **IUnknown**. Because all OLE interfaces are derived from **IUnknown**, they are component objects. **IUnknown** has three member functions: **QueryInterface**, **AddRef**, and **Release**.

An object uses **QueryInterface** to tell other objects about its capabilities. If the object implements the requested interface, it returns a pointer to the interface. If it does not implement it, it returns the E_NOTIMPL error value stating that the object does not support the requested interface. **AddRef** and **Release** are used to control the object's life span. An object's **AddRef** member function is called when another object holds a pointer to the object, and the **Release** member function is called when the pointer is no longer needed. If a call to **Release** causes the object's reference count to go to zero, the object can safely unload itself.

COM provides a couple of immediate benefits:

- An object can determine in advance if another object supports a certain feature. If the other object does not support the feature, the calling object can react accordingly.

- Objects do not remain in memory longer (or shorter) than necessary, and they do not rely on the user to launch or close them.

OLE's new data transfer mechanism is a crucial element of drag and drop support. Data transfer in OLE allows objects to be very specific about the data that they transfer. Instead of simply being able to transfer a plain old bitmap, an object can now transfer a bitmap of the object's contents rendered for a printer device and stored in a stream to be released by OLE.

To accomplish this, OLE uses the **IDataObject** interface and the **FORMATETC** and **STGMEDIUM** structures. Applications implement **IDataObject** to accomplish all data transfer in OLE; it includes member functions that set and retrieve an object's data, enumerate the available data formats, and receive data change notifications. **FORMATETC** and **STGMEDIUM** provide the specific details about the data that is being transferred—that is, the target device, aspect, storage medium, and release method.

Every drag and drop operation involves two objects: a source and a target. The source object contains the data to be dragged, and the target object accepts the dragged data.

Adding Drop Source Capabilities

To enable your application to become the source of a drag and drop operation, follow these steps:

1. Initialize the OLE libraries. Any application that uses the OLE libraries must check the version of the libraries and call the **OleInitialize** function during its initialization.

   You should use the **GetBuildVersion** function to make sure that the system's OLE libraries are at least as recent as the ones for which the application was written.

   Before you call any other OLE functions, you must call **OleInitialize** to initialize the OLE libraries. Because each call to **OleInitialize** must have a matching call to the **OleUninitialize** function, you should maintain an *fOleInitialized* flag so that you will know whether to call **OleUninitialize** when your application exits.

2. Implement the **IDropSource** interface. Not including the member functions that it inherits from **IUnknown**, **IDropSource** has only two member functions: **QueryContinueDrag** and **GiveFeedback**. OLE calls **QueryContinueDrag** intermittently during the drag operation. Its parameters include the state of the keyboard, which the drop source uses to control the drag operation. The drop source returns the S_OK value to continue dragging, the DRAGDROP_CANCEL value to cancel dragging, or the DRAGDROP_DROP value to drop the object.

3. OLE calls **GiveFeedback** to tell the drop source to update the cursor and ask the source window for visual feedback about what would happen if the user dropped at the current point. It sounds like a lot of work to update the cursor, but OLE will use its default cursors if the value DRAGDROP_S_USEDEFAULTCURSORS is returned.

4. Implement the **IDataObject** interface, which is used by OLE applications to tansfer data. In a drag and drop operation, the drop source gives OLE a pointer to its **IDataObject** implementation. OLE saves the pointer and passes it to the drop target when the cursor first enters the target window and when the drop occurs. Fortunately, you only need to implement the following (non-**IUnknown**) **IDataObject** member functions for drag and drop support: **GetData**, **GetDataHere**, **QueryGetData**, and **EnumFormatEtc**.

5. Call the **DoDragDrop** function to begin the drag operation. After you have detected that the user wants to drag something, you should call **DoDragDrop**. OLE uses the **IDataObject** and **IDropSource** pointers that are passed in, along with its list of registered drop targets, to control the drag operation. When the drag operation is complete, **DoDragDrop** returns either the DRAGDROP_S_DROP or DRAGDROP_S_CANCEL value. In addition, OLE returns a **DWORD** in the address pointed to by *pdwEffect* that tells how the drop should affect the source data—that is, whether the operation was a move, copy, link, or scroll. You should look at the *pdwEffect* value and modify the source data as necessary.

6. Call **OleUninitialize**. Before an OLE application exits, it must call **OleUninitialize** to release the OLE libraries. You should check your *fOleInitialized* flag before calling **OleUninitialize** and should only call **OleUninitialize** if **OleInitialize** returned successfully.

Adding Drop Target Capabilities

To enable your application to become a drop target, follow these steps:

1. Initialize the OLE libraries. You should check the build version and call the **OleInitialize** function exactly as you would for a drop source.

2. Call the **RegisterDragDrop** function. OLE keeps a list of the windows that are drop targets. Every window that accepts dropped objects must register itself and its **IDropTarget** interface pointer. Then when the user drags the object over a drop target window, OLE has the **IDropTarget** interface pointer handy.

3. Implement the **IDropTarget** interface. OLE uses the **IDropTarget** interface pointer that you registered with **RegisterDragDrop** to keep you informed of the state of a drop operation.

   When the cursor first enters a registered drop target window, OLE calls the **IDropTarget::DragEnter** member function. In this member function, you should ensure that your application can create the dragged object if it is dropped. Your application may also display visual feedback showing where the dropped object will appear, if appropriate.

   When the cursor moves around inside a drop target window, OLE calls the **IDropTarget::DragOver** member function, just as Windows 95 sends WM_MOUSEMOVE messages. Here you should update any visual feedback that your application displays to reflect the current cursor position. When the cursor leaves a drop target window, OLE calls the **IDropTarget::DragLeave** member function. In your **DragLeave** member function, you should remove any feedback you displayed during **DragOver** or **DragEnter**.

OLE calls your **IDropTarget::Drop** member function when the user drops the object. To be precise, a drop occurs when the drop source returns the DRAGDROP_DROP value from the **IDropSource::QueryContinueDrag** member function. In your **Drop** member function, you should create an appropriate object from **IDataObject** that is passed as a parameter. The following example shows how to implement **IDropTarget::Drop**.

```
STDMETHODIMP CDropTarget::Drop (LPDATAOBJECT pDataObj,
    DWORD grfKeyState, POINTL pointl, LPDWORD pdwEffect)
{
    FORMATETC fmtetc;
    SCODE sc = S_OK;

    UndrawDragFeedback(); // removes any visual feedback

    // QueryDrop returns TRUE if the application can accept
    // a drop based on the current key state, requested action,
    // and cursor position.
    if (pDataObj && QueryDrop(grfKeyState,pointl,FALSE,pdwEffect)) {
        m_pDoc->m_lpSite = CSimpleSite::Create(m_pDoc);
        m_pDoc->m_lpSite->m_dwDrawAspect = DVASPECT_CONTENT;

        // Initialize the FORMATETC structure.
        fmtetc.cfFormat = NULL;
        fmtetc.ptd = NULL;
        fmtetc.lindex = -1;
        fmtetc.dwAspect = DVASPECT_CONTENT; // draws object's content
        fmtetc.tymed = TYMED_NULL;
        HRESULT hrErr = OleCreateFromData
            (pDataObj,IID_IOleObject,OLERENDER_DRAW,
            &fmtetc, &m_pDoc->m_lpSite->m_OleClientSite,
            m_pDoc->m_lpSite->m_lpObjStorage,
            (LPVOID FAR *)&m_pDoc->m_lpSite->m_lpOleObject);
        if (hrErr == NOERROR)
            // The object was created successfully.
        else
            // The object creation failed.
            sc = GetScode(hrErr);
    }
    return ResultFromScode(sc);
}
```

4. Call the **RevokeDragDrop** function. Before a drop target window is destroyed, it must call **RevokeDragDrop** to allow OLE to remove the window from its list of drop targets.

5. Uninitialize the OLE libraries. Like a drop source, your application needs to uninitialize the OLE libraries before terminating.

Other Drag and Drop Considerations

You can use OLE drag and drop to add drag and drop support within your own application. There is nothing to stop your application from being both a drop source and a drop target or from accepting dropped objects from itself.

This article does not discuss reference counting, although it is a crucial part of implementing a stable OLE application.

Scrap Files

Windows 95 allows the user to transfer objects within a data file to the desktop or a folder. The result of the transfer operation is a file icon called a scrap. An OLE application automatically supports the creation of scrap files if its **IDataObject** interface supports enough data formats so that the drop target can create either an embedding or a shortcut object. You do not need to add any other functionality to your application to allow the user to create a scrap file. However, there are two optional features you may wish to add to your application: round-trip support and caching additional data formats in a scrap file. Round-trip support means that an object can be dragged out of a document and into a new container and then dragged from the new container back into the original document.

Round-Trip Support

When the user transfers a scrap into your application, it should integrate the scrap as if it were being transferred from its original source. For example, if a selected range of cells from a spreadsheet is transferred to the desktop, they become a scrap. If the user transfers the resulting scrap into a word processing document, the cells should be incorporated as if they were transferred directly from the spreadsheet. Similarly, if the user transfers the scrap back into the spreadsheet, the cells should be integrated as if they were originally transferred within that spreadsheet.

Your application must include code that integrates a scrap into a document; otherwise, the embedding object of the scrap is copied into the document rather than the data associated with the scrap. To retrieve the data for the scrap, your application must examine the class identifier, CLSID, of the scrap object by retrieving the CF_OBJECTEDESCRIPTOR file format data. If the application recognizes the CLSID, the application should transfer the native data into the document rather than calling the **OleCreateFromData** function.

Caching Additional Data Formats

When an **IDataObject** is dropped onto a file system folder, such as the desktop, the shell receives the CLSID of the object and looks for the list of clipboard formats to be cached in the scrap file. The list is located in the following registry location.

```
HKEY_CLASSES_ROOT\CLSID\{clsid}\DataFormats\PriorityCacheFormats
```

The clipboard formats should be added to the registry as the names of named values (the value should be empty). The additional formats give the user more choices when copying the scrap file and opening the Paste Special dialog box from another application. You should choose only useful formats to keep the scrap file from becoming too large. For example, Windows 95 WordPad scrap-caches the RTF format, and Windows 95 Paint scrap-caches the CF_BITMAP format.

```
HKEY_CLASSES_ROOT\CLSID\{D3E34B21-9D75-101A-8C3D-
00AA001A1652}\DataFormats\PriorityCacheFormats,"#8",,""

HKEY_CLASSES_ROOT\CLSID\{73FDDC80-AEA9-101A-98A7-
00AA00374959}\DataFormats\PriorityCacheFormats,"Rich Text Format",,""
```

Delayed Rendering

You can specify the list of clipboard formats to be delay-rendered under the **HKEY_CLASSESROOT\CLSID\{*clsid*}\DataFormats\ PriorityCacheFormats** key. The **IDataObject** of a scrap object with this CLSID will offer these formats in addition to the native data and cached data. When the drop target requests one of these formats, the shell runs the application and renders the format from the active object. However, you should avoid using this mechanism because it does not work if the server is not available or if the application is a non-OLE application.

Clipboard Formats for Shell Data Transfers

Windows 95 allows the user to transfer data objects between applications and the shell. The user can transfer data objects, such as printers, files, shortcuts, and folders, either by dragging and dropping them or by using the Cut, Copy, and Paste menu commands. Both transfer methods involve the clipboard.

Windows 95 defines several clipboard formats that you must support to transfer objects between your application and the shell. The Windows header files do not include predefined clipboard format identifiers for these clipboard formats. Instead, they provide a set of clipboard format names and corresponding values. To obtain an identifier for a clipboard format, you simply pass the format's value to the **RegisterClipboardFormat** function. The following table lists the values and corresponding clipboard format names.

Value	Format name
CFSTR_SHELLIDLIST	"Shell IDList Array"
CFSTR_SHELLIDLISTOFFSET	"Shell Object Offsets"
CFSTR_NETRESOURCES	"Net Resource"
CFSTR_FILEDESCRIPTOR	"FileGroupDescriptor"
CFSTR_FILECONTENTS	"FileContents"
CFSTR_FILENAME	"FileName"
CFSTR_PRINTERGROUP	"PrinterFriendlyName"
CFSTR_FILENAMEMAP	"FileNameMap"

The following sections describe the clipboard formats used to transfer data between applications and the shell.

"FileName" Format

The global memory object contains a single null-terminated and fully qualified filename. This format is supported for compatibility with applications written for Windows version 3.1. New applications should support the CF_HDROP clipboard format instead of the "FileName" format.

"FileNameMap" Format

The "FileNameMap" format is used with the CF_HDROP clipboard format to rename a list of files that are copied to a new location during a copy and paste operation or a drag and drop operation. Data in the "FileNameMap" format consist of a double-null terminated list of filenames that correspond to the filenames in the CF_HDROP data. When the files listed in the CF_HDROP data are copied to the new location, the files receive the new names specified in the "FileNameMap" data. For example, if the CF_HDROP data contains two files with the names c:\temp.000 and c:\temp.001, the "FileNameMap" data contains the following list of filenames.

```
"new.txt\0another.txt\0\0"
```

If the files are copied to c:\target, they receive the following names.

```
c:\target\new.txt(was c:\temp.000)
c:\target\another.txt(was c:\temp.001)
```

The system stores files in the recycle bin using a coding system for the filenames (dcxxxx.ext). When the user drags or copies files from the recycle bin, the system uses the filenames specified in the "FileNameMap" format to rename the files.

CF_HDROP Format

The global memory object contains a **DROPFILES** structure. If the object was copied to the clipboard as part of a drag and drop operation, the **pt** member of **DROPFILES** includes the coordinates of the point where the drop occurred. The **pFiles** member is the offset to a double–null-terminated list of filenames. An application can retrieve information from the data object by passing the object's handle to the **DragQueryInfo**, **DragQueryFile**, **DragQueryDropFileInfo**, and **DragQueryPoint** functions.

"PrinterFriendlyName" Format

This format is similar to the CF_HDROP format, except that the **pFiles** member of the **DROPFILES** structure is the address of a double–null-terminated list of printer "friendly" names.

"FileContents" Format

The data object contains the contents of one or more files in a format that can be written to a file. When a group of files is being transferred, the target of the drag and drop operation can use the **lindex** member of the **FORMATETC** structure to indicate which file to retrieve. The names and attributes of each file are contained in the "FileGroupDescriptor" data.

"FileGroupDescriptor" Format

The data object contains the filenames and attributes of a group of files being transferred during an OLE style drag and drop operation. The data object consists of a **FILEGROUPDESCRIPTOR** structure and any number of **FILEDESCRIPTOR** structures (one for each file in the group).

"Shell Object Offsets" Format

The global memory object contains an array of **POINT** structures. The first structure specifies the screen coordinates of a group of shell objects, and the remaining structures specify the relative offsets of each item in the group. All coordinates are in pixels.

"Net Resource" Format

The global memory object contains a list of network resources. The memory object consists of a **NRESARRAY** structure and any number of **NETRESOURCE** structures (one for each network resource in the list). Note that the string parameters (**LPSTR** types) in the **NETRESOURCE** structure contain offsets instead of addresses.

"Shell IDList Array" Format

The global memory object contains an array of item identifier lists. The memory object consists of a **CIDA** structure that contains offsets to any number of item identifier lists (**ITEMIDLIST** structures). The first structure in the array corresponds to a folder, and subsequent structures correspond to file objects within the folder.

Additional Information

For more information about how to support drag and drop in your applications, you can read the following documentation:

- OLE documentation included in the Microsoft® Win32® Software Development Kit (SDK).

  Information covered includes drag and drop operations as well as the **IDataObject** function and the **FORMATETC** and **STGMEDIUM** structures. The SimpDnD and Outline samples demonstrate drag and drop implementation.

- *Inside OLE 2* by Craig Brockschmidt, published by Microsoft® Press.

  This book provides a thorough description of data transfer and drag and drop operations.

Reference

The following structures define the clipboard formats used to transfer data between applications and the shell.

DROPFILES

```
typedef struct _DROPFILES {
    DWORD pFiles; // offset of file list
    POINT pt;      // drop point (coordinates depend on fNC)
    BOOL fNC;      // see below
    BOOL fWide;    // TRUE if file contains wide characters,
                   // FALSE otherwise
} DROPFILES, FAR * LPDROPFILES;
```

Defines the CF_HDROP and CF_PRINTERS clipboard formats. In the case of CF_HDROP, the data that follows is a double–null-terminated list of filenames. For CF_PRINTERS, the data that follows are the printer friendly names.

fNC

Nonclient area flag. If this member is TRUE, **pt** specifies the screen coordinates of a point in a window's nonclient area. If it is FALSE, **pt** specifies the client coordinates of a point in the client area.

FD_FLAGS

```
typedef enum {
    FD_CLSID = 0x0001,
    FD_SIZEPOINT = 0x0002,
    FD_ATTRIBUTES = 0x0004,
    FD_CREATETIME = 0x0008,
    FD_ACCESSTIME = 0x0010,
    FD_WRITESTIME = 0x0020,
    FD_FILESIZE = 0x0040,
    FD_LINKUI = 0x8000,
} FD_FLAGS;
```

Specifies an enumerate type that defines the flags used with the **dwFlags** member of the **FILEDESCRIPTOR** structure.

FILEDESCRIPTOR

```
typedef struct _FILEDESCRIPTOR { // fod
    DWORD    dwFlags;            // see below
    CLSID    clsid;              // file class identifier
    SIZEL    sizel;              // width and height of file icon
    POINTL   pointl;             // screen coordinates of file object
    DWORD    dwFileAttributes;   // file attribute flags (FILE_ATTRIBUTE_)
    FILETIME ftCreationTime;     // time of file creation
    FILETIME ftLastAccessTime;   // time of last access to file
    FILETIME ftLastWriteTime;    // time of last write operation
    DWORD    nFileSizeHigh;      // high-order word of file size, in bytes
    DWORD    nFileSizeLow;       // low-order word of file size, in bytes
    CHAR     cFileName[ MAX_PATH ]; // name of file (null-terminated)
} FILEDESCRIPTOR, *LPFILEDESCRIPTOR;
```

Describes the properties of a file that is being copied by means of the clipboard during an OLE drag and drop operation.

dwFlags

Array of flags that indicate which of the other structure members contain valid data. This member can be a combination of these values:

FD_ACCESSTIME	The **ftLastAccessTime** member is valid.
FD_ATTRIBUTES	The **dwFileAttributes** member is valid.
FD_CLSID	The **clsid** member is valid.
FD_CREATETIME	The **ftCreationTime** member is valid.
FD_FILESIZE	The **nFileSizeHigh** and **nFileSizeLow** members are valid.
FD_LINKUI	Treat the operation as "Link."
FD_SIZEPOINT	The **sizel** and **pointl** members are valid.
FD_WRITESTIME	The **ftLastWriteTime** member is valid.

FILEGROUPDESCRIPTOR

```
typedef struct _FILEGROUPDESCRIPTOR { // fgd
    UINT cItems;             // number of elements in fgd
    FILEDESCRIPTOR fgd[1]; // array of file descriptor structures
} FILEGROUPDESCRIPTOR, * LPFILEGROUPDESCRIPTOR;
```

Defines the CF_FILEGROUPDESCRIPTOR clipboard format.

NRESARRAY

```
typedef struct _NRESARRAY { // anr
    UINT       cItems; // number of elements in nr
    NETRESOURCE nr[1];  // see below
} NRESARRAY, * LPNRESARRAY;
```

Defines the CF_NETRESOURCE clipboard format.

nr

Array of **NETRESOURCE** structures that contain information about network resources. The string members (**LPSTR** types) in the structure contain offsets instead of addresses.

ARTICLE 8

Creating Multimedia Applications

About Multimedia Applications

Microsoft® Windows® version 3.0 was the first Windows-based system support for multimedia. This system shipped in the summer of 1991. The multimedia support enabled the Windows operating system to speak, play music, synthesize sounds, show high-quality color images, and access time-dependent data using compact disc read-only memory (CD-ROM). Until that time, Windows had been silent except for system beeps. Later in 1991, the introduction of the Media Control Interface (MCI) allowed Windows to control video and audio recorders, laser disk players, and virtually any other audio or video device.

To enable multimedia, personal computers (PCs) running Windows needed to be equipped with high-performance hardware as well as new drivers for audio, video, and storage. In response to that need, computer manufacturers began introducing PCs specifically designed for Windows multimedia in consultation with Microsoft and with guidance from the Multimedia PC Marketing Council, which was formed to set performance specifications for video, audio, and CD-ROM subsystems. Companies also introduced multimedia upgrade kits for the large, installed base of silent PCs.

As a result of these improvements, Windows has become the leading multimedia PC platform, and hardware and developer support has skyrocketed. Every major PC manufacturer makes multimedia-ready models, and there are more than a dozen multimedia upgrade kits available for Windows.

Future Directions in Multimedia

Multimedia is experiencing a technological explosion. Advances in video and audio compression algorithms provide new uses for PC multimedia. Traditional publishing and entertainment industries are converging with multimedia as well. To participate fully in this evolution, companies need to identify the significant trends, new products, and business opportunities likely to influence the future of multimedia.

Perhaps the most important trend is the rapid adoption of Microsoft Windows on multimedia-ready computers for the home. Both market share and sales rates of home computers are growing, driven largely by falling hardware prices. Continued growth of Windows-based multimedia in the home depends on three factors: ease of use, high-quality video performance, and the availability of great titles.

Microsoft's Plug and Play specification for multimedia components, from audio to video capture adapters, provides the ease of use essential to the continued acceptance of multimedia hardware in the home. For the user, this means hardware that automatically configures itself upon installation, eliminating the need to adjust dip switches or configure drivers.

Video playback has increased in Windows by up to 50 percent, and improved standards for high-performance video rendering are being developed.

In addition to displaying enhanced video, Windows-based computers will be used more frequently for high-quality video capture and editing. Several manufacturers are already demonstrating MPEG-quality video running with Windows, and Microsoft is working with hardware and software developers to specify a true MPEG implementation for Windows. As a result of this work, inexpensive MPEG decoding hardware is becoming available for Windows.

Future work will center on specifying requirements for video and bus performance; implementing MPEG, MPEG 2, and motion JPEG hardware-assisted compression; and using the capabilities of Windows 95 and Microsoft® Windows NT™.

Introduction to Writing Multimedia Applications

The remainder of this article covers three main issues related to creating Windows multimedia applications:

- Working with or without multimedia hardware.
- Coping with unavailable resources.
- Yielding resources to other applications.

This article is only an overview of some of the global issues. For discussions of specific categories of multimedia applications and the Windows API that supports each class, see the multimedia documentation included in the Microsoft® Win32® Software Development Kit (SDK).

Classes of Applications

Multimedia applications fall into two general classes: applications that are completely dependent on multimedia support in Windows and applications that take advantage of the support if multimedia hardware is available. Applications in the latter class are called "multimedia aware," because they recognize the multimedia hardware but are not fully dependent on it.

Multimedia-Dependent Applications

Some applications make sense only in a multimedia environment. For example, a speak and spell tutor requires support for playing sounds. The application will not run on a computer that has no multimedia support. Developers should strive to create applications that either fail gracefully or have reduced functionality if a feature they require is unavailable.

Multimedia-Aware Applications

An application that is multimedia aware uses multimedia hardware if it is available. If a user, for example, starts a multimedia-aware application on a computer that does not have a sound card, the application simply disables the audio portion of its interface and continues to run.

Selected Multimedia Components

Applications can be sensitive to the presence of multimedia support or to individual components. For example, an application that displays text and uses animations, waveform, the Musical Instrument Digital Interface (MIDI), and compact disc (CD) audio sounds in various places might at first seem impossible without multimedia support. However, if the application were an encyclopedia that displayed mostly text, occasionally augmented by multimedia inserts, it could provide most of its functionality on a computer with no special multimedia hardware. It would only need the standard Windows window management and graphics device interface (GDI) libraries to display its text.

Video Performance Guidelines

This section discusses issues related to maximizing video performance in multimedia applications.

Window Size and Position

To achieve the best video playback rate (that is, the most frames per second), the playback window must be horizontally aligned on a four-pixel boundary. Without this alignment, playback may be slower by up to 50 percent.

The system typically aligns the playback window automatically. However, if an application plays an audio-video interleaved (AVI) file into a window that is not near the upper left corner of a pop-up window, the automatic alignment does not occur. (In this case, the playback window could move off the screen or could move back and forth repeatedly.) Because automatic alignment is not guaranteed, every programmer must ensure that the upper left corner of a playing AVI file is either on a pixel whose number is evenly divisible by four in the horizontal direction or in the upper left corner of a pop-up window that the system can safely align for the application.

Stretching video playback can slow performance significantly. Performance suffers whenever an AVI file is played back at any size other than its actual dimensions. It is impaired even if the playback size is smaller than the AVI frame size.

Video Compression

To improve image and audio quality, you should avoid compressing an AVI file more than once. You should combine uncompressed pieces of video in your editing system before compressing the final product. Using this method not only promotes image and audio quality, it is faster as well, because editing is always faster with uncompressed video.

To achieve better video compression, you should follow these guidelines:

- Capture the video on high-end equipment.
- Keep noise out of the signal to prevent even worse noise in the compressed video.
- Use a low-pass filter to decrease noise.

You can use the **AVISaveOptions** or **ICCompressorChoose** function to display a dialog box that lists compression options. One of these options is "quality." A higher quality setting equates to a larger frame. If you set a target data rate, the highest quality setting uses the entire data rate. However, a lower quality setting results in an even smaller data rate than you requested. Typically, you should set the target data rate in the dialog box and set the quality to maximum.

Interleave Options

Although interleave options are unimportant for editing, they are important for video at run time. At run time, the interleave should be 1:1.

Data and Frame Rates

The data rate your application uses depends on the speed of the CD-ROM player on your target platforms. For single-speed players, 150 kilobytes (K) per second is a reasonable rate.

Most video cards will support 15 fps at sizes up to 320 by 240 pixels. In fact, most video cards will support good full-screen playback at 15 fps if the AVI file is that size or less. If the video is larger than 320 by 240 pixels, however, the performance of full-screen playback is very poor.

Most developers test their applications on a variety of hardware platforms to gauge the data and frame rates.

Key Frames

Most applications use the default setting for key frames. Using fewer key frames can produce a slightly better image quality. However, if the target system cannot keep up with the data rate during playback, an application will stall for a longer time than it would otherwise and performance will suffer. A higher setting for key frames will cause fewer frames to be skipped when playback cannot keep up with the data rate.

Palette Flashing

It is important to avoid palette flashing when an application plays different AVI files and shows different bitmaps. The PALMAP sample application found in the Samples subdirectory of the Win32 SDK shows how to generate an optimal palette from a variety of pictures. Applications should create such a palette using all the AVI files and images to be displayed and should realize this palette when processing the WM_QUERYNEWPALETTE and WM_PALETTECHANGED messages. To cause a video to play mapped to the chosen palette and to avoid palette flashing, MCI applications can send the **MCI_REALIZE** command with the MCI_DGV_REALIZE_BKGD value (or the **realize** command with the "background" flag). Similarly, applications can use the **DrawDibDraw** function with the DDF_BACKGROUNDPAL value when drawing bitmaps.

General Programming Guidelines

This section discusses issues related to developing multimedia applications.

Calling Functions From Within Callback Functions

Win32 applications can call virtually any API element from within a callback function. For Windows 16-bit applications, however, the list of functions that you can safely call is still very small. The list includes the following functions:

- **midiOutLongMsg**
- **midiOutShortMsg**
- **OutputDebugStr**
- **PostMessage**
- **timeGetSystemTime**
- **timeGetTime**
- **timeKillEvent**
- **timeSetEvent**

Applications that require cross-platform portability must take this restriction into account.

Multiple-Thread Limitations

The Windows 95 multimedia functions are not designed to be used by two or more threads in the same process. Although most multimedia functions will work if they are called by multiple threads, some are likely to fail. Functions that are particularly likely to fail include **PlaySound**, any of the functions that prepare or unprepare headers, and any of the open and close functions. The **PlaySound** function can never be used simultaneously by multiple threads in the same process. The functions that prepare or unprepare headers and the open and close functions can be used simultaneously by multiple threads in the same process, but only if they do not pass the same structure.

Resource Availability

Ideally, an application uses a device or feature only when it is needed and closes it when it is no longer required. If a resource is not available, the application should either continue without it (for example, disable the button that plays sound) or ask the user to release the device or feature from another application.

Unfortunately, loading on demand can result in significant timing delays, especially if a dynamic-link library (DLL) has to be loaded and initialized. A good compromise is to open the device before it is required and release it when another application requires it or when the application terminates. An application will know whether the device is available well before it needs to use it, so it can avoid the delays associated with loading code. To load on demand well, an application must process any WM_ACTIVATEAPP messages it receives. If an application receives WM_ACTIVATEAPP with a *wParam* value of zero, it should close any devices that it has open when it is no longer active. A subsequent WM_ACTIVATEAPP message with a nonzero *wParam* value indicates that the application should attempt to reopen any devices it needs because it is active once again.

An application can determine the availability of the multimedia features it uses and selectively disable the parts that are not going to work. The application has the option of notifying the user of the reduced functionality.

An application that tolerates limited functionality must check the error return code after each attempt to open a device so that it can avoid failing when the system configuration changes. You can inform the user either directly (through a dialog box) or indirectly (by disabling a button) that a feature has been lost.

Yielding Resources to Other Applications

Applications that hold devices open for long periods should process the WM_ACTIVATEAPP messages sent to them so that other applications can also use multimedia capabilities. For example, during a game that allows the user to speak a part by recording his or her own voice, the user might decide to bring up Sound Recorder to alter a sound file recorded previously. If the game does not yield control of the waveform-audio output device, Sound Recorder will not work as expected.

As a rule, applications should not play animations or sounds while they are inactive. An exception to this general rule is an application that plays audio CDs, because the user may want to continue playing a CD while running another application. If an application needs to use a CD drive that is unavailable because another application has it open, the application must tell the user about the conflict.

An application should also give the user the option of turning off certain multimedia features, particularly sounds. (This is often done using a menu.) The user may want a background application to play MIDI files or may want to hear an audio CD while using an application. Also, the user may get tired of hearing the same sounds from an application repeatedly.

Hardware Compatibility

The existence of multimedia DLLs on a system does not guarantee that appropriate device drivers are available. For example, the system may be installed on a computer with no sound card, or it may have no multimedia features at all. The existence of multimedia API elements does not mean that all of the multimedia personal computer (MPC) standard features are available either.

In addition, the presence of a CD-ROM device does not mean that it meets MPC specifications. Documentation for an application should inform the user that application performance may suffer if the user does not have MPC- or MPC2-compatible hardware. An application should either fail gracefully (with a message at startup) or tolerate the unavailability of multimedia support at run time.

You should also consider the role of your installation program in this process. If your installation program cannot find multimedia support and consequently disables your application's features, you should provide some way to enable these features if the user later adds multimedia support (for example, a sound card). You could require the user to rerun the installation program, or, preferably, you could put a detection mechanism into the startup code for the application (checking, for example, the registry for the existence of the device). The application does not need to know which sound driver to add; it must simply recognize that the multimedia API elements are now supported. This is easy to detect at run time.

The ability to load and unload drivers on demand adds another layer of compli-
cation to an application's use of multimedia. Because the number of available
device drivers during the run time of an application may vary, it is not sufficient
to simply enumerate them at application startup. To use every available driver while
running, an application should check for the WM_DEVICECHANGE message to
discover whether a device is changing.

A R T I C L E   9

Displaying and Using Pen Data

About Displaying and Using Pen

A subset of the pen services for Microsoft® Windows® 95 is available on every Windows 95 system through the pen display dynamic-link library (DLL) called *PKPD.DLL* or *PKPD32.DLL*. Functions in this library allow any Windows 95–based application to display and manipulate pen data (also called "ink") that was originally collected on a pen-enabled system. A few practical applications for these services might include:

- Using Windows-based applications to display a signature for letters or faxes.
- Verifying signatures collected on a pen-based mobile computer.
- Animating the display of ink for presentations or games.
- Merging, compressing, and storing ink collected on pen-based systems, which might later be recognized as text on a pen-based system.
- Displaying graphics, maps, or handwritten notes that have been drawn on a pen-based system.

The *Programmer's Guide to Pen Services for Microsoft Windows 95*, which is included in the Microsoft® Win32® Software Development Kit (SDK), provides information about using the entire set of pen functions to collect, recognize, manipulate, and display ink. The set of functions supported in the Windows 95 pen display library is limited to manipulating and displaying ink. Chapter 4, "The Inking Process," in that guide describes the functions available for displaying pen data, most of which are also available in the pen display library.

This article concentrates on the functions most likely to be used in the pen data display library on a standard Windows 95 system. It also presents a sample application that allows you to display pen data using various methods. The following topics are presented in both overview and sample code descriptions:

- Retrieving pen data from a file and saving pen data to a file.
- Scaling pen data.
- Compressing, decompressing, and trimming pen data.
- Animating the display of pen data.
- Retrieving information about pen data.

The final section of this article provides guidelines for writing Windows 95–based applications so that they will run successfully on pen-enabled systems. Although the pen services automatically supply user interface tools to the user so that your application can be used without a keyboard, you should be aware of the issues described in this article to ensure that your application works well in a pen-enabled environment.

Overview of Pen Services

Pen services for Microsoft Windows 95 provide all of the software requirements for operating a pen-based system. This includes data collection from a tablet- or screen-based pen device, display of ink, routing of data to one or more DLLs for character recognition, and the ability to persist data. It also includes Windows conrols for pen input, which are used to recognize ink as text or create ink drawings, and tools, such as the on-screen keyboard. The first five chapters in the *Programmer's Guide to Pen Services for Microsoft Windows 95* provide a comprehensive overview of these topics. You should read these chapters in addition to this article if you need more information about pen services.

This section compares the pen display library functions in Windows 95 to the total set of pen services.

Data Collection and Recognition

Pen data can be collected on a pen-enabled system by using either high-level or low-level calls to pen functions. High-level programming provides defaults for most steps and makes pen data collection and recognition straightforward. Low-level programming adds a few more function calls to the process; however, data collection and recognition are essentially the same using both programming methods. The high-level method is described here because of its simplicity. For more information about this method, see Chapter 2, "Starting Out with System Defaults," in *Programmer's Guide to Pen Services for Microsoft Windows 95*.

At the highest level, a pen-aware application makes a call to the **DoDefaultInput** pen function, passing it a window handle. After this, the window and its child windows start receiving messages generated by the pen services. The first message allows the application to enable or disable itself or its child windows as pen targets. By default, all child windows are set as targets, capable of accepting pen input. Another set of messages sets up each target window's inking information, such as pen color, width, clipping range, and so on. After more "overhead" messages of this sort, the application is required to create an object in memory to collect the data. This object can be a recognition context object (**HRC**) or a pen data object (**HPENDATA**). The latter is relevant to this article , because it is the type of data that can be read and displayed using the pen display library functions.

As pen data arrives to each target window, the window is notified by a message, and the collected pen data is placed into the created object (**HRC** or **HPENDATA**) by default. Finally, when ink input ends, each target window receives a data-ending message. If an **HPENDATA** object was created, the application has the opportunity to duplicate or save the data. If an **HRC** object was created, the default behavior is to send the data to a recognizer. A recognizer is a DLL that is loaded to translate pen strokes into characters. When the recognizer has finished, the window receives a results message, and the default behavior of the pen services is to send the recognizer's "best guess" to the target window as a string of **WM_CHAR** messages.

Display of Data

Pen services for Microsoft Windows 95 require the PENWIN.DLL or PENWIN32.DLL library for all of the functionality of pen data collection. The library is supplied by the pen tablet or computer manufacturer that bundles the services with their product.

Pen-enabled systems, however, use the same pen display library that is available on every Windows 95 system for pen data manipulation and display: PKPD.DLL or PKPD32.DLL. The remainder of this article provides information about these services. Because of the overlap of use by both pen-enabled and penless systems, you will find a few functions in the pen display library that are included primarily for pen-enabled systems. These are noted and usually discussed after the functions that are more relevant to displaying ink on standard Windows 95 systems.

Functions in the Pen Display Library

Before turning to the sample application, it might be helpful to provide some information about the pen display library functions used by the application and to describe the categories of functions in the pen display library. It is also highly recommended that you read Chapter 4, "The Inking Process," of the *Programmer's Guide to Pen Services for Microsoft Windows 95* for a more information about these functions and consult the reference documentation in that guide for any individual function descriptions.

The functions in the pen display library can be organized into groups according to the following activities:

- Creating pen data objects.
- Scaling pen data.
- Displaying pen data.
- Examining pen data.
- Editing or copying pen data.
- Compressing pen data.
- Using inkset objects.

Each of these groups and the functions that comprise them are discussed in this section. Functions in Pen Windows version 1.0 that have been superseded by the Pen Windows version 2.0 are not generally discussed in this section.

Before the pen display library functions are presented, it is important to describe exactly what constitutes pen data. Pen data is a collection of strokes composed of coordinate points. When ink is drawn, all of the points collected while the pen is down on the tablet comprise a "pen down stroke." (The time durations collected while the pen is not on the tablet are called a "pen up stroke.") After pen data is collected, it is stored in a pen data (or **HPENDATA**) object. This pen data object is accessed through a window handle, similar to the way that handles are used to access other Windows objects, such as device contexts.

Internally, a pen data object is composed of a main header followed by a sequence of strokes. The main header provides information, such as the number of strokes and points, the bounding rectangle, the ink color and width, and so on.

Each stroke contains a set of data points, which indicate the positions of the pen during the stroke, and a stroke header, which indicates the number of points in the stroke and when the stroke occurred.

Each point is initially stored in pen tablet coordinates with a resolution of 0.001 inch and an origin in the upper left corner of the tablet. The resolution can be scaled later to a different display resolution if needed.

Additional information provided by the original equipment manufacturer (OEM) for the pen tablet may also be contained in the stroke. If OEM data exists, it follows the point data in the stroke.

The following illustration shows the format of a pen data (**HPENDATA**) object.

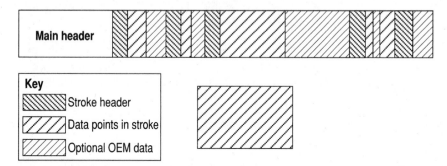

Key	
Stroke header	
Data points in stroke	
Optional OEM data	

Creating Pen Data Objects

Three functions are associated with the creation of pen data objects:

- **CreatePenDataEx**
- **DuplicatePenData**
- **DestroyPenData**

Although **CreatePenDataEx** has many parameters, most are only useful when creating a pen data object used to accept pen input. Applications using the Windows 95 display libraries on systems without a pen should normally set the *uScale* parameter to the PDTS_STANDARDSCALE value and pass zero or NULL to the other parameters.

DuplicatePenData makes a copy in memory of the pen data object and returns a handle to it.

Any memory allocated for pen data objects created by using **CreatePenDataEx** or **DuplicatePenData** can and must eventually be freed by using **DestroyPenData**.

Scaling Pen Data

Three functions are associated with the scaling of pen data points:

- **MetricScalePenData**
- **OffsetPenData**
- **ResizePenData**

MetricScalePenData scales the pen data to display resolutions corresponding to the Windows mapping modes. For example, passing the PDTS_HIENGLISH value to **MetricScalePenData** is equivalent to MM_HIENGLISH resolution, passing the PDTS_HIMETRIC value is equivalent to MM_HIMETRIC resolution, passing the PDTS_LOMETRIC value is equivalent to MM_LOMETRIC resolution, and so on. The original tablet coordinates are the same as the Windows mapping mode called MM_HIENGLISH (0.001 inch).

OffsetPenData can be used to offset the bounding rectangle within the pen data coordinates. For example, you can pass negative values to this function to move the rectangle containing the points to the left or top edge.

ResizePenData is useful for arbitrarily scaling points to fall within a given rectangle. You might want to use this function on pen data to scale it to a predetermined window size.

Note that rescaling pen data to a lower resolution causes information to be lost. If you need to maintain the highest resolution possible for your pen data, you may want to use the **DrawPenDataEx** function to scale your data to a window because that method leaves the original data alone and only scales the points as they are displayed.

Displaying Pen Data

Four functions are associated with displaying pen data:

- **DrawPenDataEx**
- **DrawPenData** (not available in PKPD32.DLL)
- **RedisplayPenData**
- **CreatePenDataRegion**

Of these functions, **DrawPenDataEx** is the most useful for systems that are not pen-enabled. **DrawPenDataEx** is very versatile and handles all of the details of drawing pen data to the device context that it is passed. It has the ability to draw all strokes, a selected range of strokes, or a selected range of points. It also has the ability to animate the drawing of ink, playing back the strokes in their original succession and duration, by reading the timing information stored with each stroke. Part of the animation process involves automatic calls made by **DrawPenDataEx** to a callback function that you specify. Along with the address of a callback function, an **ANIMATEINFO** structure is also passed to this function to provide more information about the animation. The sample application and accompanying text describes this process in greater detail.

The other functions listed here are used less often on standard Windows 95 systems. **DrawPenData** is a 16-bit display function that has been superseded by **DrawPenDataEx**. **RedisplayPenData** is primarily designed for displaying ink immediately after a user has drawn it (such as in an ink control) so that pen data objects can be merged.

CreatePenDataRegion is also primarily used on pen-enabled systems that use "gestures" to communicate system-level commands to the operating system, such as cutting or pasting operations. Gestures are pen movements (such as "circle-P") that require immediate ink display anywhere on the screen.

Examining Pen Data

Nine functions are used to examine the contents of a pen data object:

- **GetPenDataAttributes**
- **GetStrokeAttributes** and **SetStrokeAttributes**
- **GetStrokeTableAttributes** and **SetStrokeTableAttributes**
- **BeginEnumStrokes**, **GetPenDataStroke**, and **EndEnumStrokes**
- **HitTestPenData**

GetPenDataAttributes is used to retrieve information from the pen data object's main header, such as the bounding rectangle, the total number of points and strokes, the time that the pen data was created, and the device sampling rate. This function is used in the sample application to retrieve the bounding rectangle of ink before it is scaled. It is also used to determine the scaling and compression of the pen data object.

Most of the other functions in this group provide access to individual or group stroke attributes either indirectly through a function call or by providing direct access to the pen data object in memory.

GetStrokeAttributes and **SetStrokeAttributes** retrieve and modify, respectively, the attributes of individual strokes, including the pen state (up or down), the ink color and width, and the time that the stroke was recorded.

GetStrokeTableAttributes and **SetStrokeTableAttributes** retrieve and modify, respectively, attributes that are shared by a group of strokes. For example, if all strokes use a red pen color and a width of 1, that attribute can be modified for all strokes by using only one call to **SetStrokeTableAttributes**.

BeginEnumStrokes returns a far pointer to the **HPENDATA** object within the global heap, **GetPenDataStroke** retrieves pointers to point data within the **HPENDATA** object, and **EndEnumStrokes** unlocks the pen data memory block and invalidates any pointers retrieved.

HitTestPenData determines if a given point lies on or near a point in the pen data object.

Editing or Copying Pen Data

Functions in this group can be organized into three subgroups. The first subgroup of functions adds strokes to or extracts strokes from a pen data object.

ExtractPenDataStrokes	Copies and, optionally, deletes strokes from a pen data object.
InsertPenDataStroke	Inserts a stroke into an existing pen data object.
RemovePenDataStrokes	Deletes a contiguous set of strokes from a pen data object in memory.

The second subgroup of functions adds points to or extracts points from an existing stroke.

ExtractPenDataPoints	Copies points from a specified stroke in a pen data object to a buffer, optionally removing the points.
GetPointsFromPenData	Copies points from a stroke in a pen data object to a buffer (superseded by **ExtractPenDataPoints**).
InsertPenDataPoints	Inserts points into an existing stroke in a pen data object.
AddPointsPenData	Appends a set of points to a stroke in a pen data object (used mainly by pen-enabled systems).

The third subgroup performs operations on the entire pen data object.

InsertPenData	Merges two separate pen data objects into a single object.
PenDataToBuffer	Writes the data in an existing **HPENDATA** object to a serial buffer. The function is used to transfer pen data to a file or the clipboard.
PenDataFromBuffer	Creates and loads an **HPENDATA** object with the data from the serial buffer created by **PenDataToBuffer**. The function is used to transfer pen data from a file or the clipboard.

Compressing Pen Data

Data compression plays an important role in pen-based computing. The high sampling rates of a pen device, combined with large amounts of input, result in large blocks of pen data. The pen display library offers two methods of compression, each with advantages and disadvantages depending on the intended use of the pen data. These two functions are associated with data compression:

- **CompressPenData**
- **TrimPenData**

CompressPenData is generally used to compress pen data before saving it to disk or passing it to the clipboard. It is also used to decompress the data before it is used again. Compressed data must be decompressed to be used by most functions in the pen display library. Compression provides from 60 to 70 percent reduction in pen data size with no loss of data when the data is decompressed (this is called *lossless* compression).

TrimPenData, in contrast, irreversibly removes data from the pen data object. Much of the information stored in a pen data object can be removed if the data is only to be used for display purposes. Some of the data that you might want to trim from a pen data object includes colinear and duplicate points, empty strokes, timing and "up stroke" information, OEM hardware information, and so on.

Using Inkset Objects

An *inkset object* consists of time intervals for either individual strokes or a collection of strokes. In turn, the interval of each stroke consists of the times at which the stroke begins and ends. In this way, a pen-based application can refer to a stroke not only by the points it contains but also by the time interval in which the stroke occurs.

Timing information principally serves recognizers. It provides them with an additional characteristic of the raw data that may offer clues for interpretation.

Timing information, though, has other uses as well. For example, it enables an application to accurately verify a signature by comparing not only the coordinates but also the duration of each stroke against a copy of the original signature. This type of verification is an effective safeguard against forgery because of the difficulty of simultaneously duplicating both the pattern and duration of the original signature.

Because inkset objects are more complicated than can be easily described in this article and because they are not used in the sample application, see the *Programmer's Guide to Pen Services for Microsoft Windows 95*, which is included in the Win32 SDK, for more information about their use.

AN_PKPD Sample Application

The sample application discussed in this article is called AN_PKPD. It is based on another animation sample called ANIMATE (provided for pen application developers in the SAMPLES\WIN16\PEN directory of the Win32 SDK), which collects, displays, saves, and loads pen data. The ANIMATE sample requires a pen tablet and the installation of the pen services for Microsoft Windows 95. The AN_PKPD sample, on the other hand, requires only Windows 95, the pen data, and either PKPD.DLL or PKPD32.DLL, both of which are supplied with Windows 95.

Sample pen data files, generated from the ANIMATE sample, are provided with the source code for AN_PKPD so that the sample application has some data to work with. These pen data files contain nothing more than pen data objects that are saved directly to disk without compression or any other alteration. You can, however, save these files in compressed format after displaying them. It is suggested that you do not overwrite the original files if you decide to save them as compressed files.

Reading, Writing, and Compressing Pen Data

The application-defined LoadSave function loads and saves pen data information. The original pen data supplied with the sample files was generated using the ANIMATE sample and is not compressed or trimmed. In the AN_PKPD sample, you have the option of saving any of the files that you load and display. If you do save a file, it is saved in a compressed state. If it has been displayed as "clipped" data (drawn to the original scale, not scaled to a window), it is also in reduced resolution rather than tablet resolution and is trimmed of excess pen data. It is suggested that you do not overwrite the original files if you save them as compressed files.

This section describes the LoadSave function, which calls two internal functions, ReadPenData and WritePenData. The full source for all three functions is at the end of this section.

After retrieving a filename by using the FGetFileName local function, the **CreatePenDataEx** function is called to create an **HPENDATA** object that is accessed by the *vhpndt* variable.

```
vhpndt = CreatePenDataEx((LPPENINFO)NULL, PDTS_STANDARDSCALE, 0, 0);
```

CreatePenDataEx specifies the data scaling as the PDTS_STANDARDSCALE value, which is equivalent to PDTS_HIENGLISH (.001 inch per logical unit). This keeps the scaling of the pen data at the highest possible resolution initially—that is, at the same resolution as the pen tablet. All pen tablets are scaled at .001 inches per logical unit.

After opening the file and getting a file handle (*hfile*), the *fOpen* variable is checked to determine whether the function was called for reading or writing pen data. If it was called for reading a file, the **DestroyPenData** function is called on the pen data object to remove any existing ink from a previously displayed file. Then the pen data is read into the pen data object by calling the ReadPenData local function. ReadPenData uses the Windows **lread** function internally to read the data into the buffer and the pen display library's **PenDataFromBuffer** function to place that data in the pen data object created by **CreatePenDataEx**.

Next, the **GetPenDataAttributes** function is called to determine whether or not the pen data was compressed when it was saved. If the data was compressed, the **CompressPenData** function is called to decompress it. Pen display library functions do not work on compressed data.

The following example shows this process in the LoadSave function.

```
if (fOpen)
{
    if (vhpndt)  DestroyPenData(vhpndt);
    vhpndt = ReadPenData(hfile);
    // Determine whether the pen data is compressed.
    vnPDTS = GetPenDataAttributes(vhpndt, NULL, GPA_PDTS);
    // If it is compressed, decompress it.
    if ((vnPDTS & PDTS_COMPRESSED) == PDTS_COMPRESSED)
        CompressPenData(vhpndt, CMPD_DECOMPRESS, 0);

Redraw();
}
```

The final step of loading a file is to call the Redraw local macro, which basically invalidates the window. Redraw can be expanded in the following manner.

```
PostMessage(vhwndOut, WM_USER, 0, 0);
```

In the window procedure for *vhwndOut*, the WM_USER message is handled as follows.

```
    .
    .
    .


    case WM_USER:  // for Redraw macro
        InvalidateRect(hwnd, NULL, TRUE);
        if (IsWindow(vhdlg))
            EnableWindow(GetDlgItem(vhdlg, IDD_PBCLEAR), vhpndt != NULL);
        SetFocus(vhwndOut);      // catch Esc
        break;

    .
    .
    .
```

When data is saved by using the LoadSave function, it is automatically compressed by using the **CompressPenData** function. Then the internal WritePenData function is called; it uses the pen display library **PenDataToBuffer** function and the Windows **_lwrite** function to write the data to a buffer and then to the file. Finally, the pen data in memory is decompressed to its original state so that it can be displayed again.

Compression of pen data is not mandatory, but it is often very useful because it can achieve as much as 70% reduction in size on the disk. To compare compressed and noncompressed pen file sizes, try loading one of the sample pen data files and then save it with a different name. The difference is quite apparent. Here is an example showing WritePenData that compresses, saves, and decompresses the data.

```
if (fOpen)
{

     .
     .
     .

// Load the pen data here.

     .
     .
     .

}
else{
    // Compress the pen data before saving it.
    CompressPenData(vhpndt, CMPD_COMPRESS, 0);
    WritePenData(hfile, vhpndt);
    // Decompress the pen data for further displaying.
    CompressPenData(vhpndt, CMPD_DECOMPRESS, 0);
 }
```

Following are the complete listings for the application-defined LoadSave, ReadPenData, and WritePenData functions.

```
VOID NEAR PASCAL
LoadSave(
   BOOL fOpen)
   {
   HCURSOR hCursor = SetCursor(LoadCursor(NULL, IDC_WAIT));
   HFILE hfile;
   static char const szOpenTitle[] = "Open File";
   static char const szSaveTitle[] = "Save File";
```

```
if (!*vszFile)
    lstrcpy((LPSTR)vszFile, vszSaveFileDef);
if (FGetFileName(vhwndAN, fOpen, vszFile))
    {
    OFSTRUCT of;
    if (!vhpndt)
      // Create a pen data object to read pen data into.
      vhpndt = CreatePenDataEx((LPPENINFO)NULL, PDTS_STANDARDSCALE, 0, 0);

    if ((hfile = OpenFile((LPSTR)vszFile, &of,
      fOpen? OF_READ: OF_CREATE)) != HFILE_ERROR)
      {
      if (fOpen)
       {
          if (vhpndt)  DestroyPenData(vhpndt);
          vhpndt = ReadPenData(hfile);
          // Determine whether the pen data is compressed.
          vnPDTS = GetPenDataAttributes(vhpndt, NULL, GPA_PDTS);
          // If it is compressed, decompress it.
          if ((vnPDTS & PDTS_COMPRESSED) == PDTS_COMPRESSED)
             CompressPenData(vhpndt, CMPD_DECOMPRESS, 0);

          Redraw();
       }
       else{
          // Compress the pen data before saving it.
          CompressPenData(vhpndt, CMPD_COMPRESS, 0);
          WritePenData(hfile, vhpndt);
          // Decompress the pen data for further displaying.
          CompressPenData(vhpndt, CMPD_DECOMPRESS, 0);
       }
       _lclose(hfile);
       }
    else ErrBox("error opening file", szOpenTitle);
    }
else if (fOpen)
    InfoBox("did not get file", szOpenTitle);
else
    InfoBox("did not save file", szOpenTitle);
SetCursor(hCursor);
```

```
//  ReadPenData - reads pen data from a file. The file format at this
//  point is a UINT value representing the size of the pen data,
//  followed by that many bytes of pen data.
//
//  Before calling this function, the caller should have already
//  opened the file specified by hfile and ensured that the
//  file pointer is offset to the beginning of the pen data.
//  When the function returns, the file pointer will be offset
//  to the end of the pen data in the file.
HPENDATA NEAR PASCAL ReadPenData(    // return handle to pen data
   HFILE hfile)    // handle of open file
   {
   HPENDATA hpndt = NULL;
   LONG     cb, cbRead, cbHpndt;
   BYTE     lpbBuf[cbBufMax];     // buffer
   DWORD    dwState = 0L;         // required init
   BOOL     fError = FALSE;

   if (!hfile
      || (cb = _lread(hfile, &cbHpndt, sizeof(LONG))) == HFILE_ERROR
      || cb != sizeof(LONG))
         return NULL;

   while (cbHpndt > 0)
      {
      if ((cbRead = _lread(hfile, lpbBuf, (UINT)min(cbHpndt, cbBufMax)))
         == HFILE_ERROR
         || PenDataFromBuffer(&hpndt, 0, lpbBuf, cbBufMax, &dwState) < 0)
         {
         if (hpndt)
            DestroyPenData(hpndt);
         return NULL;
         }
      cbHpndt -= cbRead;
      }

   return hpndt;
   }
```

```
//  WritePenData - writes pen data into a file, preceded by a UINT
//  consisting of the size of the pen data, in bytes.
//
//  Before calling this function, the caller should have
//  already opened the file specified by hfile and ensured that
//  the file pointer is correctly placed.  When the function
//  returns, the file pointer will be offset to the end of the
//  pen data in the file. The function fails if the pen data is
//  larger than 64K.
BOOL NEAR PASCAL WritePenData(   // returns true if successful
   HFILE hfile,           // handle to open file
   HPENDATA hpndt)        // pen data to write
   {
   BYTE lpbBuf[cbBufMax];
   DWORD dwState = 0L;  // required initialization
   LONG cb;
   LONG cbSize;

   if (!hfile || !hpndt)
      return FALSE;

   if (GetPenDataAttributes(hpndt, (LPVOID)&cbSize, GPA_SIZE) < 0)
      return FALSE;

   if (_lwrite(hfile, (LPCSTR)&cbSize, sizeof(LONG)) == HFILE_ERROR)
      return FALSE;

   while ((cb = PenDataToBuffer(hpndt, lpbBuf, cbBufMax, &dwState)) > 0L)
      if (_lwrite(hfile, lpbBuf, (UINT)cb) == HFILE_ERROR)
         return FALSE;

   return cb >= 0;
   }
```

Scaling and Trimming Pen Data

It may or may not be necessary to scale pen data for your application. If your application only requires that the pen data be drawn to the scale of the client window, pen services take care of the scaling of the drawing (not the pen data) during the **DrawPenDataEx** function. All you need do is pass in the rectangle of the client window as a parameter along with a handle to a device context for the window.

If you want to keep the aspect ratios the same as when the ink was drawn on the tablet, you will need to scale the pen data to fit your display. You can do this on a point by point basis with each pen data point, or you can use the built-in scaling capabilities of the pen services.

The example in this section, taken from the ANOutWndProc window procedure's WM_PAINT case, demonstrates how you might go about setting the proper scale for the pen data and trimming unneeded data from the pen data object. In the AN_PKPD sample, the ANDLG dialog box structure contains an fRenderScale member that determines whether to scale the output to the client window or "clip" the drawing, based on the selection in the Drawing Options dialog box. Clipping means that the pen data is displayed in its original aspect ratios and is not confined to the client window area.

When the Scale option is chosen in the Rendering section of the Drawing Options dialog box, vandlg.fRenderScale is set true and the Windows **GetClientRect** function is called to retrieve the rectangle into which the drawing will be scaled.

```
if (vandlg.fRenderScale)              // scale to window
    GetClientRect(hwnd, &r);
```

When Clip is chosen in the Rendering section of the Drawing Options dialog box, vandlg.fRenderScale is set to FALSE and the pen data is to drawn to its original scale. In this case, you will probably want to fit the entire pen data on the display, although some of it may fall outside the client window, thereby being clipped.

In the sample application, this is done by calling the **MetricScalePenData** function and scaling the pen data to its lowest possible resolution. The lowest display resolution for pen data corresponds to the MM_TEXT mapping mode in Windows, which is set by using the Windows **SetMapMode** function. Following this, unneeded data is trimmed from the pen data by calling the **TrimPenData** function.

```
else
if (vfScaled == FALSE)
 {
    // Display in same aspect ratio as the original ink, and
    // clip the pen data if it is outside the window.

    // Scale the pen data to display the coordinates and trim the
    // excess data.
    if(MetricScalePenData(vhpndt, PDTS_DISPLAY))
        TrimPenData(vhpndt, TPD_COLLINEAR |     // duplicate strokes
                            TPD_EMPTYSTROKES | // strokes w/o points
                            TPD_USER |         // header info
                            TPD_PENINFO |      // OEM data
                            TPD_OEMDATA ,      // OEM data
                            0);
```

```
// Use the following function if there is no animation or
// up strokes.
//TrimPenData(vhpndt, TPD_EVERYTHING, 0);

// Set the mapping mode to the same as PDTS_DISPLAY.
SetMapMode(hdc, MM_TEXT);
```

Although the **TrimPenData** function can be called with the TPD_EVERYTHING value only, doing this removes timing data necessary for correct animation as well as up strokes, which you might want to examine using this sample application.

The **GetPenDataAttributes** function is called next to retrieve the new bounding rectangle of the pen data. This rectangle is used to determine if the data fits on the screen and also used to calculate an aspect ratio if the data does not fit or needs to be further resized. The screen width and height are then retrieved to determine if the new scaling will fit on the screen.

```
// Get the bounding rectangle of the pen data in PDTS_DISPLAY
// mapping mode.
GetPenDataAttributes(vhpndt, &r, GPA_RECTBOUND);
nMapWidth = r.right - r.left;
nMapHeight = r.bottom - r.top;

// Get the screen resolution.
nDisplayWidth=GetDeviceCaps(hdc, HORZRES);
nDisplayHeight=GetDeviceCaps(hdc, VERTRES);
```

If the scaling mode is still too large, the data can be resized to fit the screen by using the **ResizePenData** function. Note that the use of **ResizePenData** is only recommended for one-time resizing. Resolution is lost when data is repeatedly resized.

In the example used to resize the data, an aspect ratio is determined from the bounding rectangle of the pen data and the rectangle is reduced for margins to 80% of the screen size. This new rectangle is then passed to **ResizePenData**, which does the work of modifying the coordinates of each of the points in the pen data object.

```
// If the pen data is still too big, resize it to fit on the screen.
if (r.right > nDisplayWidth || r.bottom > nDisplayHeight)
{

    // Resize the rectangle, maintaining the aspect ratio.
    if(nMapWidth > nMapHeight)
        AspectRatio = (float)nDisplayWidth/(float)nMapWidth;
    else
        AspectRatio = (float)nDisplayHeight/(float)nMapHeight;
```

```
                    // Reduce slightly for margins on the screen.
                    AspectRatio *= (float) 0.8;

                    // Set the right and bottom of the rectangle to a new size.
                    r.right = (int) (AspectRatio * (float)r.right);
                    r.bottom = (int) (AspectRatio * (float)r.bottom);

                    // Resize the pen data to a new rectangle.
                    ResizePenData(vhpndt, &r);
        }
```

Remember that when data is reduced in scale by using **MetricScalePenData** or **ResizePenData**, data is lost. Rescaling it to a higher resolution will not regain the lost data. If you save the data at this point, you should not overwrite the original file.

There are, of course, other methods than those shown here to display ink in the correct aspect ratio. For example, you could use **GetPenDataAttributes** to retrieve the rectangle of ink and then size a window to the same aspect ratio and let the **DrawPenDataEx** function scale the drawing into that window.

The following example demonstrates the effect of setting the Rendering option in the Drawing Options dialog box to either Scale or Clip.

```
LRESULT CALLBACK            // return LRESULT
ANOutWndProc(               // drawing window procedure
    HWND hwnd,              // == vhwndOut
    UINT message,
    WPARAM wParam,
    LPARAM lParam)
    {
    LRESULT lRet = 1L;
    static char const szBoxTitle[] = "DrawPenDataEx";
    int nDisplayWidth, nDisplayHeight, nMapWidth, nMapHeight;

    switch (message)
        {
      case WM_USER:  // for Redraw macro

        .
        .
        .


      case WM_CHAR:

        .
        .
        .
```

```
case WM_PAINT:

     .
     .
     .

         if (vandlg.fRenderScale)               // scale to window
            GetClientRect(hwnd, &r);
         else
          if (vfScaled == FALSE)
            {
               // Display in the same aspect ratio as the original ink, and
               // clip the pen data if it is outside the window.

               // Scale the pen data to display the coordinates and trim the
               // excess data.
               if(MetricScalePenData(vhpndt, PDTS_DISPLAY))
                  TrimPenData(vhpndt, TPD_COLLINEAR |        // duplicate strokes
                                      TPD_EMPTYSTROKES |     // strokes w/o points
                                      TPD_USER |             // header info
                                      TPD_PENINFO |          // OEM data
                                      TPD_OEMDATA ,          // OEM data
                                      0);

               // Use the following function if there is no animation or
               // up strokes.
               //TrimPenData(vhpndt, TPD_EVERYTHING, 0);

               // Set the mapping mode to the same as PDTS_DISPLAY.
               SetMapMode(hdc, MM_TEXT);

               // Get the bounding rectangle of the pen data in the PDTS_DISPLAY
               // mapping mode.
               GetPenDataAttributes(vhpndt, &r, GPA_RECTBOUND);
               nMapWidth = r.right - r.left;
               nMapHeight = r.bottom - r.top;

               // Get the screen resolution.
               nDisplayWidth=GetDeviceCaps(hdc, HORZRES);
               nDisplayHeight=GetDeviceCaps(hdc, VERTRES);

               // If the pen data is still too big, resize it to fit on the screen.
               if (r.right > nDisplayWidth || r.bottom > nDisplayHeight)
               {
                  // Resize the rectangle, maintaining the aspect ratio.
                  if(nMapWidth > nMapHeight)
                    AspectRatio = (float)nDisplayWidth/(float)nMapWidth;
                  else
                    AspectRatio = (float)nDisplayHeight/(float)nMapHeight;
```

```
                    // Reduce slightly for margins on the screen.
                    AspectRatio *= (float) 0.8;

                    // Set the right and bottom of the rectangle to a new size.
                    r.right = (int) (AspectRatio * (float)r.right);
                    r.bottom = (int) (AspectRatio * (float)r.bottom);

                    // Resize the pen data to the new rectangle.
                    ResizePenData(vhpndt, &r);
}
// Do scaling only once.
vfScaled = TRUE;
```

Displaying the Pen Data

The AN_PKPD.RC resource file sets a menu with two drawing procedure options: AnimatePenData and DrawPenDataEx. The **DrawPenDataEx** function is used for both procedures.

For nonanimated drawing (IDM_DRAWPARTIAL selection), the local macro DrawPenDataPartial is used.

```
#define DrawPenDataPartial(hdc, lprect, hpndt, s0, s1, p0, p1)\
  DrawPenDataEx(hdc, lprect, hpndt, s0, s1, p0, p1, NULL, NULL, 0)
```

Starting and ending strokes and starting and ending points, which can be set in the Drawing Options dialog box, are sent to the **DrawPenDataEx** function. The following example shows the result of selecting **DrawPenDataEx** from the DrawProc menu before loading pen data.

```
case DPDPART:  // partial drawing
  default:
    DrawPenDataPartial(hdc, // DC
      &r,                   // rectangle for scaling and clipping
      vhpndt,               // pen data
      vandlg.uStrk0,        // first stroke to draw
      vandlg.uStrk1,        // last stroke to draw
      vandlg.uPt0,          // first point in first stroke to draw
      vandlg.uPt1);         // last point in last stroke to draw
    break;
  }
```

The second way that **DrawPenDataEx** is used in the sample application is for animation. Animation is a process by which **DrawPenDataEx** draws the pen data using timing information stored when the ink was originally drawn by the user and timing information passed to the function when it is called. Animation requires a callback function and an **ANIMATEINFO** structure.

To animate pen data, the *lpai* parameter of **DrawPenDataEx** must be the address of an **ANIMATEINFO** structure. The AN_PKPD sample application fills in this structure with the following information.

```
ANIMATEINFO ai =
{
    sizeof(ANIMATEINFO),                      // structure size
    vandlg.uSpeedPct,                         // speed as a percent
    MakeMs(vandlg.uCBPeriodCode),             // callback period in ms.
    vandlg.fSkipUp? AI_SKIPUPSTROKES: 0,      // options
    0L,                                       // lParam
    0L                                        // reserved
};
```

The second member of this structure (set here to vandlg.uSpeedPct) sets an animation speed relative to the original speed at which it was drawn. A setting of 100% produces the original speed. The third member sets the callback period. If this is set to None in the dialog box, the callback function is never called and you lose access to the dialog box until animation has finished.

The fourth member of this structure allows you to set options—in this case, the option of skipping "up strokes," which comprise the timing information recorded when the pen is not on the tablet.

To enable animation, you must also supply the address of a callback function to **DrawPenDataEx**. The AN_PKPD sample application uses a callback function called AnimateProc, which is defined as follows.

```
AnimateProc(                    // animation callback procedure
    HPENDATA hpndt,             // pen data
    UINT wStroke,               // current stroke
    UINT cPnts,                 // number of points yet to draw
    UINT FAR *lpuSpeedPct,      // address of speed percent
    LPARAM lParam)              // application value
```

The animation callback function is typically used to allow for user activity to occur during animation. For example, the user may want to change the speed of the animation. For this reason, a pointer to the **uSpeedPct** member of the **ANIMATEINFO** structure is passed to the animation callback function so that it can be set by the function. The AnimateProc callback function in the application also displays the number of callbacks calls made in the window title of the application, if the user has selected Callback Display from the View menu.

The following example shows the code involved in the three methods of displaying data in the AN_PKPD sample application. Note that some sections of code, indicated by ellipses, have been removed in order to show only code sections relevant to displaying data. For the complete listing, see the sample application.

AN_PKPD.RC

```
.
.
.


    POPUP "&DrawProc"
    BEGIN
        MENUITEM "&AnimatePenData",          IDM_DRAWEX, CHECKED
        MENUITEM "DrawPenDataE&x",            IDM_DRAWPARTIAL
    END
```

AN_PKPD.C

```
.
.
.


// Defines


.
.
.


#define DPDEX             (IDM_DRAWEX - IDM_DRAWEX)
#define DPDPART           (IDM_DRAWPARTIAL - IDM_DRAWEX)


.
.
.


// Type definitions
typedef struct tagANDLG // dialog box initialization [default values in brackets]
    {
    UINT uStrk0;         // first stroke to render [0]
    UINT uPt0;           // point offset in first stroke [0]
    UINT uStrk1;         // last stroke to render [-1]
    UINT uPt1;           // point offset in last stroke [-1]
    BOOL fSkipUp;        // FALSE to animate upstrokes, TRUE to skip them
    BOOL fAutoRepeat;    // FALSE to end after one rendering, TRUE to repeat to tap
    UINT uCBPeriodCode;  // callback period code [CALLBACKNEVER]
    UINT uSpeedPct;      // speed of animation [100%]
    BOOL fRenderScale;   // TRUE to scale pen data to output window, FALSE to clip
    }
```

```
    ANDLG, FAR *LPANDLG;

  .
  .
  .


// Macros

  .
  .
  .


// Draw only part of the pen data.
#define DrawPenDataPartial(hdc, lprect, hpndt, s0, s1, p0, p1)\
    DrawPenDataEx(hdc, lprect, hpndt, s0, s1, p0, p1, NULL, NULL, 0)

  .
  .
  .


//----------------------------------------------------------------------------
LRESULT CALLBACK        // returns LRESULT
ANOutWndProc(           // drawing window procedure
    HWND hwnd,          // == vhwndOut
    UINT message,
    WPARAM wParam,
    LPARAM lParam)
    {

    .
    .
    .


    switch (message)
        {
      case WM_USER:  // for Redraw macro

    .
    .
    .


      case WM_CHAR:

    .
    .
    .
```

```
case WM_PAINT:

    .
    .
    .

  if (vhpndt)
     {
     PAINTSTRUCT ps;
     HDC hdc = BeginPaint(hwnd, &ps);

     vfDrawing = TRUE;        // set semaphore

     if (hdc)
        {
        RECT r;
        int iRet;
        int nWidthDPD = 1;
        COLORREF crDPD = RGB(0, 255, 255);  // cyan default for DrawPenData pen
        ANIMATEINFO ai =
           {
           sizeof(ANIMATEINFO),                  // structure size
           vandlg.uSpeedPct,                     // speed as a percent
           MakeMs(vandlg.uCBPeriodCode),         // callback Period in ms.
           vandlg.fSkipUp? AI_SKIPUPSTROKES: 0,  // options
           0L,                                   // lParam
           0L                                    // reserved
           };

           .
           .
           .

        // Scaling done here. For more information, see "Scaling
        // and Trimming Pen Data."

           .
           .
           .

        switch (nDrawProc)
           {
        case DPDEX:                    // animation
           vcCB = 0;                   // animation callback counter
           vfReqCxl = FALSE;           // reset
           ShowCancel(vandlg.uCBPeriodCode != CALLBACKNEVER);
```

```
        iRet = DrawPenDataEx(
            hdc,                    // handle to DC
            &r,                     // rectangle for scaling and clipping
            vhpndt,                 // pen data
            vandlg.uStrk0,          // first stroke
            vandlg.uStrk1,          // last stroke
            vandlg.uPt0,            // first point in first stroke
            vandlg.uPt1,            // last point in last stroke
            vlpfnAnimateProc,       // AnimateProc callback function
            &ai,
            0);

        if (iRet < 0 && iRet >= -10)
            {

            .
            .
            .


            // Error handling code goes here.


            .
            .
            .


        vfReqCxl = FALSE;
        break;

    case DPDPART:  // partial drawing
    default:
        DrawPenDataPartial(hdc, // DC
            &r,                  // rectangle for scaling and clipping
            vhpndt,              // pen data
            vandlg.uStrk0,       // first stroke to draw
            vandlg.uStrk1,       // last stroke to draw
            vandlg.uPt0,         // first point in first stroke to draw
            vandlg.uPt1);        // last point in last stroke to draw
        break;
        }

ClearAppQueue();  // handle message backlog, if any

if (vandlg.fAutoRepeat)
    Redraw();
}
```

```
        EndPaint(hwnd, &ps);
        vfDrawing = FALSE;
        }

    .
    .
    .


//-------------------------------------------------------------------------
BOOL CALLBACK                 // return LRESULT; NB _export to ensure correct ds
AnimateProc(                  // animation callback procedure
    HPENDATA hpndt,           // pen data
    UINT wStroke,             // current stroke
    UINT cPnts,               // number of points yet to draw
    UINT FAR *lpuSpeedPct,    // address of speed percent
    LPARAM lParam)            // application value
    {
    BOOL fRet = !vfReqCxl;    // set in dialog box and File menu
    hpndt, wStroke, cPnts, lParam;   // unused

    if (fRet)
        {
        char sz[cbSzTMax];

        if (!vcCB)
            ShowCancel(TRUE);

        ClearAppQueue();      // handle message backlog in app. queue

        *lpuSpeedPct = vandlg.uSpeedPct;   // get latest speed setting

        wsprintf((LPSTR)sz, (LPSTR)"CB=%u", ++vcCB);
          if (vfCB)
            SetWindowText(vhwndAN, (LPSTR)sz);

        // vfReqCxl may have gotten set in ANOutWndProc's WM_PAINT if the
        // user, for example, changed the window size during a callback.
        fRet = !vfReqCxl;
        }

    return fRet;
    }
```

Enabling Your Applications For Pen-Based Systems

Windows 95 implements pen services that all developers of Windows 95–based applications need to be aware of, regardless of whether their applications make use of the functions found in the Pen Windows version 2.0. Windows 95 can run on mobile platforms, and physical keyboards may not be available for these devices. In addition, applications for Far-Eastern markets may need to function without keyboard input. To ensure that your Windows 95–based applications work appropriately on systems that do not use a keyboard, use the guidelines listed in this section.

For personal computer systems that have a pen installed, Windows 95 provides the pen user with a base level of functionality that includes handwriting edit controls and lens buttons. For Windows 95–based applications to work well when the pen is the only input device, application developers need to implement the functionality described below and to design the interface to work well with a pen.

Handwriting Edit Controls

When the version stamp on your application identifies it as a Windows 95–based application, all edit controls will be replaced by handwriting edit (hedit) controls. To ensure that your application uses hedit controls appropriately, follow the guidelines in this section.

To support hedit controls, mark your application as a Windows 95–based application.

You should also keep these points in mind when designing your application to use hedit controls:

- The behavior of the hedit control may not be exactly identical to that of a standard edit control.

- A hedit control may not cause the display of a dialog box to change; it may display the lens tool or confirmation dialog boxes.

- If the focus leaves the dialog box, it may not indicate that the user is finished with the field. Pen-related derivative dialog boxes can be disabled on a case-by-case basis at WM_CTLINIT message and HN_BEGINDIALOG or HN_ENDDIALOG notification message time.

Lens Buttons

Single-line hedit controls can include a lens button that the user chooses to open a writing window over the control if space permits and if the control is scrollable. This pop-up window acts like a dialog box for entering text. When the window is dismissed, it sends the text to the hedit control. To ensure that your application uses lens buttons appropriately, follow the guidelines in this section.

To support lens buttons, include these elements in your application:

- Give multiline edit controls access to the lens tool for multiline edit controls.
- Leave plenty of room in your hedit controls for the lens button. You should create all single-line hedit controls with the WS_AUTOHSCROLL style even if you think they are wide enough. (Lens buttons will not appear in hedit controls that do not include this style.)

You should also keep these points in mind when designing your application to use lens buttons:

- Editing may not only occur within the hedit control.
- A hedit control may never cause a dialog box to appear.
- The focus may not have gone away when the hedit control loses focus; the focus may be in the lens control (which is a child of the hedit control).

A R T I C L E   1 0

Installing Applications

About Installing Applications

This article describes a standard set of guidelines for installing applications to run with the Microsoft® Windows® 95 operating system. The purpose of these guidelines is to enable all application developers to support the same general method of installation for applications. The prime benefit is for users, many of whom have said they prefer a consistent installation method so that they do not need to learn a different method with each new software purchase. These guidelines also benefit the application developer by helping to standardize the organization and management of application files, thereby making initial installations, updates, and application removals easier.

Installation Program

The installation program plays the primary role in carrying out application installation. The program retrieves information from the user and the computer and installs the files and information needed to run the application successfully. Every installation program carries out these basic steps:

1. Determines the user's hardware and software configuration and available disk space.

2. Copies application executable and data files to the appropriate directories on the hard disk.

3. Sets up the execution environment for the application by modifying existing files and adding entries to the registry.

An installation program (or a companion program) should also be prepared to update or remove an already installed application.

You are responsible for designing and implementing the installation program for your application. Windows does not provide a default installation program, but it does provide an Add/Remove Programs application in Control Panel that helps guide the user through starting the installation, update, or removal process. When the user chooses to install an application, Add/Remove Programs automatically checks the floppy and compact disc read-only memory (CD-ROM) drives for installation programs, searching for filenames such as SETUP.EXE and INSTALL.EXE. If a file is found and the user agrees to finish the installation, Add/Remove Programs starts the program and exits. After that, the started program is responsible for guiding the user through the rest of the installation process.

Designing the Installation Program

Your installation program should be a "good" Windows-based application, employing the standard Windows graphical user interface, presenting users with options and status. It is recommended that you use the InstallShield SE Toolkit included in the Microsoft® Win32® Software Development Kit (SDK) to develop your installation programs. You should also read relevant sections of *The Windows Interface Guidelines for Software Design* for information about designing an application that is consistent with the look and feel of the Windows shell. It will also give you information about easy-to-implement features that will add value to your application and make use of new usability functionality in the shell.

Your installation program should always offer setup options. The following options are recommended.

Typical setup	Installs the application with all of the most common settings and copies the most commonly used files. This should be the default setup option.
Compact setup	Copies the fewest number of files needed to operate your application. This option is useful for laptops and computers on which disk space is at a premium.
Custom setup	Allows the user to determine the details of the installation, such as the directories to receive the files and the application features to enable. This option, which is typically used by the power user, should also include an option to set up components left out during a typical or compact setup.
Silent setup	Runs setup without user interaction. This should just be a command line option so that your installation program can be run within a batch script.

Your installation program should always supply defaults. In particular, it should supply a common response to every option so that all the user has to do is press the ENTER key.

Your installation program should never ask the user to install a disk more than once and should make the computer beep when it is time for the user to insert a new disk.

Your installation program should always include a progress indicator to show users how far along they are in the setup procedure.

Your installation program should always give the user a chance to cancel the setup process before it is finished. Your program should keep a log of files that have been copied and settings that have been made so that it can clean up a canceled installation. If the installation is canceled, your program should remove any registry entries it may have made, remove any shortcuts it may have added to the desktop, and delete any files it may have copied onto the user's hard disk.

Determining the Configuration

Your installation program should determine the hardware and software configuration of the user's computer before copying files and setting the environment. It is important for the installation program to verify that everything needed to successfully run the application is available. For example, if your application depends on specific hardware or software, your installation program should make sure the hardware or software is present. If it is not, the program should notify the user immediately and recommend a course of action.

Your installation program should always tell the user how much disk space is needed. For custom setup, the installation program should adjust the "space needed" figure as the user selects and deselects options. Your installation program should verify that enough disk space is present for the options that the user selects. If there is not enough free space, the program should notify the user but give the user the option to override the warning.

Your installation program should always determine whether any of the files to be installed are already on the hard disk. This is especially important for shared files, such as commonly used dynamic-link libraries (DLLs). If the files already exist, your installation program should check the version number to ensure that it is not replacing a file with an older version. In other words, the installation program should always make sure the most recent version of a file is installed on the user's disk.

Copying Files

Your installation program should copy all necessary executable and data files to the appropriate directories. It should never copy files to the Windows or System directories. Instead, it should create a directory in the Program Files directory and copy its files there. If the Program Files directory does not exist on the root of the hard disk, your installation program should create it.

It is recommended that your installation program use a long filename for the directory, such as the application name or another descriptive and unique name. Your program should copy the main executable file for your application and any other executable or data files that the user may want to open directly to the newly created directory. For example, if your application's name is "My Wizzy Application.Exe", your installation program should create the \Program Files\My Wizzy Application directory, and copy My Wizzy Application.Exe to that directory.

If you have any other executable or data files, such as .DLL and .HLP files that are specific to your application, your installation program should create a subdirectory, named System, in your application's directory. It should copy the remaining files (except shared files) to this new directory. For example, if your application has a DLL named MWASUP.DLL, your installation program should create the \Program Files\My Wizzy Application\System directory and copy the DLL there.

If any of your executable or data files are shared, your installation program needs to copy the files to yet another directory, depending on how widely the file is to be shared. A file is *system-wide shared* if many applications from different vendors use it. For example, the VBRUN300.DLL file is a system-wide shared file, because it is used by any application built with Visual Basic. A file is a *shared file* if it is shared by a set of applications from the same vendor. A common example of this would be an office suite that might use the same drawing program for its word processor as it does for its spreadsheet.

Your installation program should copy all system-wide shared files to the Windows SYSTEM directory. If a given file already exists in this directory, the program should overwrite it with your application file *only if* your file is a more recent version. The **GetFileTime**, **GetFileVersionInfo**, and **GetFileInformationByHandle** functions can be used to determine which file is more recent. After copying a DLL file, your installation program should increment the usage counter for the DLL in the registry. For more information about the usage counter, see "Adding Entries to the Registry" later in this article.

Your installation program should copy all shared files to a System directory in the \Program Files\Common Files directory. If the directory does not exist, the installation program should create it. Again, it is recommended that your program use a descriptive and unique name. For example, if there is a shared file named My Wizzy Speller.Exe, your program should create a directory named \Program Files\Common Files\System and copy the file there. The location of the Program Files and Common Files directories is registered (using the macro **REGSTR_PATH_SETUP**) in the **HKEY_LOCAL_MACHINE** root under the **SOFTWARE\Microsoft\Windows\CurrentVersion** key. The value names are ProgramFilesDir and CommonFilesDir.

When your installation program installs applications on computers running Microsoft® Win32s® with Windows version 3.*x*, it needs to be aware that the system does not support long filenames. Your installation program will need to use the short 8.3 filename equivalent for Program Files and Common Files, which is Progra~1 and Common~1, respectively.

Using a WININIT.INI File to Replace DLLs in Windows 95

Installation programs often need to replace old .DLL files with new versions. However, Windows 95 does not allow a .DLL file to be replaced if the DLL is currently loaded into memory. To solve this problem, your installation program must copy the new .DLL files to the user's machine, giving each new .DLL file a temporary name that is different from that of the corresponding old .DLL file. Your installation program must also copy a file called WININIT.INI to the user's machine. The WININIT.INI file is processed by the WININIT.EXE program when the system is restarted, before any DLLs are loaded. The WININIT.INI file specifies the destination path and filename for each new DLL.

The WININIT.INI file contains a [rename] section that specifies the source and destination path and filenames for the new DLLs. The entries in the [rename] section have the following syntax.

```
DestinationFileName=SourceFileName
```

The following syntax is used to delete a file.

```
NUL=SourceFileName
```

The following example shows a [rename] section from a WININIT.INI file.

```
[rename]
C:\WINDOWS\Fonts\arial.ttf=C:\WINDOWS\Fonts\arial.win
C:\WINDOWS\SYSTEM\advapi32.dll=C:\WINDOWS\SYSTEM\advapi32.tmp
```

When the system is restarted, it searches for a WININIT.INI file and, if it finds one, runs WININIT.EXE on the file. After processing the file, WININIT.EXE renames it to WININIT.BAK.

The DestinationFileName and SourceFileName must both be short (8.3) names instead of long filenames because WININIT.EXE is a non-Windows application and runs before the protected mode disk system is loaded. Because long filenames are only visible when the protected mode disk system is loaded, WININIT.EXE will not see them, and therefore, will not process them.

WININIT.INI is not supported in Microsoft® Windows NT™. To replace DLLs already loaded in memory, use the **MoveFileEx** function.

Setting Up the Environment

Your installation program needs to set up the proper environment for your application. The environment consists of application-specific entries in the initialization files, the registry, and the Start button.

Setting Initialization Files

Windows does not require the AUTOEXEC.BAT and CONFIG.SYS files. Because these files may not be present on the hard disk, you should make sure that your application does not require entries in those files.

Windows does not require you to modify the PATH environment variable. Instead, Windows looks for your .EXE and .DLL files in the application-specific path specified in the registry. Your installation program is responsible for setting the application-specific path when it installs the application.

Windows does not require an application to load device drivers at boot time. This means that your application does not need to specify drivers in the CONFIG.SYS file. Instead, your application can dynamically load the drivers when it starts by using the virtual device loader functions of Windows or the **CreateFile** and **DeviceIoControl** functions of Win32.

Your installation program should *not* make entries in the WIN.INI file. It should use the registry instead. If you have information that you do not want to put in the registry, your installation program should create a private initialization file and place it in the same directory that contains your application's executable files.

Adding Entries to the Registry

Your installation program should add information about your application to the registry. In particular, it should always add the following entries.

HKEY_LOCAL_MACHINE\SOFTWARE*CompanyName\ProductName\Version*
Stores information pertaining to this particular copy of the application.

HKEY_CURRENT_USER\SOFTWARE
Stores user-specific preferences. This is information that application vendors used to store in the WIN.INI file. For example Microsoft Word might store the fact that a user wants the automatic save feature turned off here.

Your installation program should always add application-specific paths to the registry for your application. If your installation program registers a path, Windows sets the PATH environment to be the registered path when it starts your application. Your program sets the path in the **HKEY_LOCAL_MACHINE** root under the application paths key **\SOFTWARE\Microsoft\Windows\CurrentVersion\AppPaths** (using the **REGSTR_PATH_APPPATHS** macro). Your installation program must create a new key having the same name as your application's executable file. Under this new key, it creates the Path value name and assigns it a path using the same format as expected by the PATH environment variable.

The following example shows application-specific paths for both Windows® Excel, Excel.Exe, and My Wizzy Application.Exe.

```
HKEY_LOCAL_MACHINE
  SOFTWARE\Microsoft\Windows\CurrentVersion\AppPaths
    Excel.Exe
      Default=D:\Program Files\MS Office\Excel\Excel.Exe
      Path= D:\Program Files\MS Office\Excel\Excel.Exe;D:\Program
         Files\Common Files\MS Office;

    My Wizzy App.Exe
        Default=d:\Program Files\My Wizzy Application\My Wizzy
           Application.Exe
        Path= D:\Program Files\My Wizzy Application;D:\Program Files\My
           Wizzy Application\Application Extensions;
```

In the preceding example, the Default value specifies the full path to the corresponding executable file. This value is typically used by Windows in the Start Run command. If the user types the name of your application but Windows fails to find it in the current path, Windows uses this value to locate and start your application.

Your installation program should keep track of shared DLLs. When installing an application that uses shared DLLs, it should increment the usage counter for the DLL in the registry. When removing an application, it should decrement the usage counter. If the result is zero, the user should be given the option of deleting the DLL. The user should be warned that other applications may actually need the DLL and will not work if it is missing. The following example shows the general format for usage counters in the registry.

```
\HKEY_LOCAL_MACHINE\SOFTWARE\Microsoft\Windows\CurrentVersion\SharedDLLs
   C:\Program Files\Common Files\System\vbrun300.DLL=3
```

Supporting Context Menu Operations

Your installation program can provide support for context menu operations, such as Open, Print, and Print To, by setting appropriate registry entries. The context menu appears when the user clicks mouse button 2 on a document associated with your application.

Enabling Print in the registry gives the shell instructions about what to execute when the user chooses Print from the context menu. Usually an application will display a dialog box that says " Printing page n of N on LPTX."

Enabling Print To in the registry specifies the default action for "drag print." Print To displays the same dialog box as Print when you drag it to a specific printer. The Print To option is not displayed on the context menu, so it does not bring up anything (that is, it cannot be chosen).

The following example shows how to set commands for the context menu for files having the .WRI filename extension.

```
HKEY_CLASSES_ROOT\.wri = wrifile
HKEY_CLASSES_ROOT\wrifile = Write Document
HKEY_CLASSES_ROOT\wrifile\DefaultIcon =
    C:\Progra~1\Access~1\WORDPAD.EXE,2
HKEY_CLASSES_ROOT\wrifile\shell\open\command = WORDPAD.EXE %1
HKEY_CLASSES_ROOT\wrifile\shell\print\command =
    C:\Progra~1\Access~1\WORDPAD.EXE /p "%1"
HKEY_CLASSES_ROOT\wrifile\shell\printto\command =
    C:\Progra~1\Access~1\WORDPAD.EXE /pt "%1" "%2" "%3" "%4"
```

In the preceding commands, the %1 parameter is the filename, %2 is the printer name, %3 is the driver name, and %4 is the port name. In Windows 95, you can ignore the %3 and %4 parameters (the printer name is unique in Windows 95).

Adding the Application to the Start Button

Your installation program can still create a "Program Group" in the Programs folder by using dynamic data exchange (DDE) as used in Windows version 3.1, but this is no longer the preferred method. Instead, your installation program should add an icon for your primary application to the Start menu. The program can, optionally, prompt the user to choose which program icons to place in the menu. However, icons should not be added for every application in your package, and an extensive hierarchy of programs and folders should not be created on the Start menu.

To add an icon to the Start menu, your installation program should create a link to your application's executable file and place the link in the directory named \WINDOWS\STARTMEN\PROGRAMS. (Note that the Windows directory should actually be the path returned by the **GetWindowsDirectory** function.) An installation program can create a link by using the **IShellLink** interface.

Using Filename Extensions

In Windows 95, filename extensions should always describe a file type. Your installation program should not rename old or backup files by giving them filename extensions like .001, .BAK, or .XX1. If the file type does not change, the program should give the file a new name. For example, it can use long filenames to change the old version of a filename, such as SAMPLE.DLL being changed to Copyof SAMPLE.DLL.

The following table lists filename extensions currently used in Windows. You should not use these filename extensions, unless your file fits the given type description.

Extension	Type description
386	Windows virtual device driver
3GR	Screen grabber for Microsoft® MS-DOS®–based applications
ACM	Audio Compression Manager driver
ADF	Administration configuration files
ANI	Animated mouse cursor
AVI	Video clip
AWD	Fax viewer document
AWP	Fax key viewer
AWS	Fax signature viewer
BAK	Backed-up file
BAT	MS-DOS batch file
BFC	Briefcase
BIN	Binary data file
BMP	Picture (Windows bitmap)
CAB	Windows setup file
CAL	Windows Calendar file
CDA	CD audio track

Extension	Type description
CFG	Configuration file
CNT	Help contents
COM	MS-DOS–based program
CPD	Fax cover page
CPE	Fax cover page
CPI	International code page
CPL	Control Panel application
CRD	Windows Cardfile document
CSV	Command-separated data file
CUR	Cursor (pointer)
DAT	System data file
DCX	Fax viewer document
DLL	Application extension (dynamic-link library)
DOC	WordPad document
DOS	MS-DOS–based file (also extension for NDIS2 net card and protocol drivers)
DRV	Device driver
EXE	Application
FND	Saved search results
FON	Font file
FOT	Shortcut to font
GR3	Windows version 3.0 screen grabber
GRP	Program group file
HLP	Help file
HT	HyperTerminal file
ICM	Image color matching (ICM) profile
ICO	Icon
IDF	MIDI instrument definition
INF	Setup information
INI	Configuration settings
KBD	Keyboard layout
LGO	Windows logo driver
LIB	Static-link library
LNK	Shortcut
LOG	Log file

Extension	Type description
MCI	MCI command set
MDB	File viewer extension
MID	MIDI sequence
MIF	MIDI instrument file
MMF	Microsoft Mail message file
MMM	Animation
MPD	Mini-port driver
MSG	Microsoft Exchange mail document
MSN	The Microsoft Network home base
MSP	Windows Paintbrush picture
NLS	Natural language services driver
PAB	Microsoft Exchange personal address book
PCX	Picture (PCX format)
PDR	Port driver
PF	ICM profile
PIF	Shortcut to MS-DOS–based application
PPD	PostScript® printer description file
PRT	Printer formatted file (result of Print to File option)
PST	Microsoft Exchange personal information store
PWL	Password list
QIC	Backup set for Microsoft Backup
REC	Windows Recorder file
REG	Application registration file
RLE	Picture (RLE format)
RMI	MIDI sequence
RTF	Document (rich text format)
SCR	Screen saver
SET	File set for Microsoft Backup
SHB	Shortcut into a document
SHS	Scrap
SPD	PostScript printer description file
SWP	Virtual memory storage
SYS	System file

Extension	Type description
TIF	Picture (TIFF format)
TMP	Temporary file
TRN	Translation file
TSP	Windows telephony service provider
TTF	TrueType font
TXT	Text document
VBX	Visual Basic control file
VER	Version description file
VXD	Virtual device driver
WAV	Sound wave
WPC	WordPad file converter
WRI	Windows Write document
XAB	Microsoft Mail address book

You should also investigate filename extensions commonly used by popular applications so that you can avoid creating a new extension that might conflict with them, unless you intend to replace or supersede the functionality of those applications.

Register Document Types

Your installation program should register every file type used that is not provided by Windows 95:

- For the files of interest to the user, such as document types, the installation program should register both an icon and a description. It should provide good OLE/shell verbs and also add a "ShellNew" entry so your document type shows up in the "New" menu. This menu is available when the user clicks mouse button 2 on any container or chooses the File menu in a folder window.

- For files that the user would have a good reason to double-click, the installation program should provide the file with a good icon and description and also a registered "open" action so that the user can double-click it.

- For files that are less interesting to the user, such as .INI or configuration files, the installation program should provide the file with a good icon and description. The best way to do this is to consistently use predefined filename extensions, such as .INI, .SYS, and .TXT.

- For files of little interest to the user, the installation program should minimally register a file type so that there is a decent description in "Details" view (and possibly an icon). If the program does not register the type, the file is identified by whatever the filename extension may be. Registering the type ensures that the file is identified by the description and related icon.

Network Issues

Most corporate customers would like to run their applications from a network server. To support running from a server, you need to provide your installation application in both a server and client package. The server package consists of executable files, DLLs, data files, and any files that must be shared across the network. The client package consists of the portions of the application that are user-specific, including registry settings, details about the user's configuration, and information about how to locate the server package.

Generally, you should have two installation programs or modes for installing the packages: an administrative installation program that an administrator runs for preparing the server and a client installation program that runs on each client machine and sets up the connection to the server. The client installation program should also have a batch or silent installation option so that an administrator can deploy your application with automatic software distribution tools. Ideally, the client installation functions are built into the application so that it configures itself when it starts (perhaps by reading options set by the administrative installation program).

Corporate customers typically run Windows from a shared copy on a server. The following directories are stored on the server; your application and client installation program may or may not have write access to these directories.

```
\Windows
    \Command
    \Inf
    \Fonts
    \Help
    \Hyperterm
    \Pif
    \System
        \Color
        \Iosubsys
        \Viewers
        \VMM32
```

You should use the **GetSystemDirectory** function to find the System subdirectory. To find the Windows directory, look in the following registry location.

```
HKEY_LOCAL_MACHINE\Software\Microsoft\Windows\CurrentVersion\Setup
    SharedDir=
```

Your application should store files that cannot be shared (machine-specific files) in a "machine" directory with write access. The machine directory contains files and settings that are specific to a particular machine. If one user changes settings, anyone else who uses that computer gets those settings. If the machine has user profiles turned on, Windows copies the user-specific settings into and out of the machine directory when the user logs on and off. That way, if a user changes a machine setting (that is, a hardware setting), every user is affected, but if the user changes a user-specific setting, the change affects only that user.

The machine directory should not contain any executable files. You can find the machine directory by calling the **GetWindowsDirectory** function. The following files and directories are stored in the machine directory.

WIN.COM	\Spool
WININIT.EXE	\Desktop
*.INI	\Startmen
*.GRP	\Nethood

Your application and installation program should fully support Universal Naming Convention (UNC) paths. If an application is being installed on a network path, the installation program should store a UNC path in any shortcuts it makes for the Start menu. Your installation program can use the Windows network functions (**WinNet***) to determine if a path is a network path.

You should consider what configuration settings an administrator might want to set for a user and what restrictions an administrator might want to place on a user (for example, not letting a user access a configuration menu). You should put these settings and restrictions in a System Policy template (.ADM) file.

For more information about network issues relating to Windows 95, see the *Microsoft Windows 95 Resource Kit*.

CD-ROM Considerations

Autorun is a feature that is supported on CD-ROM drives. When the user loads a compact disc (CD) into the drive, Windows 95 automatically runs a file on the CD. The file to run must be specified in an AUTORUN.INF file located in the CD's root directory. The following example shows a typical entry in an AUTORUN.INF file.

```
[AutoRun]
OPEN=myprog.exe
```

The autorun feature can be disabled by the device manager or by an entry in the SYSTEM.INI file. Your application must not rely on the autorun feature being available. Also, the autorun feature should not be used to automatically install your application on a user's hard disk without the user being asked first.

If you provide your application on a CD, your installation program should give the user the choice of running the application from the CD or installing it on the hard disk. You should keep the following points in mind when using the autorun feature:

- Even if the user chooses to run your application from the CD, your program will need to copy some files to the hard disk (for example, writable files and files containing the user's preferences).

- If you include a shortcut on the desktop, your application should display a message when the user selects the shortcut and the CD is not loaded.

Installing Fonts

By carrying out these steps, you can write a single font installation routine that works for both Microsoft® Windows NT™ and Windows 95:

1. Determine whether the platform is Windows 95 or Windows NT. This distinction is important because Windows 95 allows a shared network installation where most system files, including fonts, are stored on a centrally managed server. To determine the platform, look in the following registry location for a "SharedDir" value.

```
HKeyLocalMachine\Software\Microsoft\Windows\CurrentVersion\Setup
```

The data value of "SharedDir" is the UNC name of the server and sharepoint of the shared directory. In most cases, a shared directory is marked as read-only by the system administrator, so your installation program should also check to see if it can write to this location. If it cannot, it should let the user install the fonts in a different location, or stop the setup process.

2. Check whether the TrueType® font being installed is already present on the system by using the **EnumFontsEx** function. If that font is present, the program should check to see if its version is newer by matching the installed font name with the filename on the disk. The font name is stored in the following registry location for both Windows 95 and Windows NT.

```
HKeyLocalMachine\Software\Microsoft\Windows\CurrentVersion\Fonts
```

The subkeys in this registry location contain the full name of the font file as the value key, followed by the filename of the .TTF file as the key data. If the filename in the registry is just a filename with no path information, the font is installed in the \WINDOWS\FONTS directory for Windows 95 or the \WINDOWS\SYSTEM directory for Windows NT. Because TrueType font files do not carry a version resource, your program will need to retrieve the version string from the 'name' table in the .TTF file.

- Before copying the .TTF file to the appropriate directory, the installation program should check to see if the filename already exists in that directory. If it does, the program should rename your .TTF file to some other name, perhaps by appending a number to the end of the basename.

- After copying the .TTF file to the user's disk, the installation program should inform the system that it wants the font to be available. The program should pass it the .TTF filename directly by using the **AddFontResource** function. Windows 95 and Windows NT do not require the creation of .FOT files.

- To make the font installation permanent, the installation program should add the font name and filename to the registry by writing both of the values to the following registry location.

```
HKeyLocalMachine\Software\Microsoft\Windows\CurrentVersion\Fonts
```

Removing an Application

Your installation program can direct the Add/Remove Programs application in Control Panel to list your application as an application that can be "automatically removed" by adding the following entries to the registry.

HKEY_LOCAL_MACHINE
\Software\Microsoft\Windows\CurrentVersion\Uninstallapplication-name
   DisplayName=product-name
   UninstallString=full-path-to-program command-line-parameters

Add/Remove Programs displays the product name specified by the **DisplayName** value in its list of applications that can be removed. Windows uses the value specified by the **UninstallString** value to start the uninstall program to carry out the removal of the application. This string needs to completely specify the command-line parameters needed to execute the uninstall program and remove the application. A full path is required. If both the DisplayName and UninstallString values are not complete, Add/Remove Programs will not list the application.

Windows needs to know when the removal of the application is done, so it requires the **UninstallString** value to specify the uninstall program that actually carries out the removal. A batch file or other program that starts the removal program should not be specified.

Your installation program should use casual names, including spaces, for the *application-name* and **DisplayName** value. Casual names help keep the tree comprehensible for users who browse the registry. The registry locations are defined as constants for C programmers in the REGSTR.H header file. Descriptions of the macros follow.

REGSTR_PATH_UNINSTALL	Path to uninstall branch
REGSTR_VAL_UNINSTALLER_DISPLAYNAME	DisplayName
REGSTR_VAL_UNINSTALLER_COMMANDLINE	UninstallString

The uninstall program must display a user interface that informs the user that the removal process is taking place. It is recommended that you use the sample uninstall program in the InstallShield SE Toolkit as the starting point for your own uninstall program. The sample illustrates the appropriate user interface and application removal tasks.

Your uninstall program should provide a silent option that allows the user to run it remotely. The uninstall program should also display clear and helpful messages for any errors it encounters during the removal of the application. Windows will only detect and report a failure to start the uninstall program.

Because computers running Microsoft® Win32s® and Windows NT do not provide Add/Remove Programs in Control Panel, your installation program needs to include an Icon in the Applications program group so that the user can launch the uninstall program.

To summarize, an uninstall program should complete the following steps:

- Remove all information used by the application from the registry. If decrementing a DLL's usage count results in a usage count of zero, the uninstall program should display a message offering to delete the DLL or save it in case it may be needed later.
- Remove any shortcuts to the application from the desktop.
- Remove all program files related to the application. The uninstall program should not remove files that the user created with the application unless the user agrees to delete them. If the user's files are stored in the application's directory tree, the uninstall program should ask the user if the files should be moved to a new directory.
- Remove empty directories left by the application.

Quick Checklist for Planning an Installation Program

You should keep the following points in mind when you plan an installation program for your application:

- Store private initialization (.INI) files in the application directory if the application is running locally or in the directory returned by the **GetWindowsDirectory** function if the application is shared.
- Do not copy files to the Windows or System directories. If you include fonts with your application, you should put the fonts in the Fonts folder.
- Tell the user how much space the installation will take and use a progress indicator.
- Make sure to create all directories in the user selected path.
- Do not assume that floppies are on Drive A.
- Always supply defaults.
- Name your installation program SETUP.EXE.

PART 3

Extending the Windows 95 Shell

ARTICLE 11

Shell's Namespace

About the Shell's Namespace

A *namespace* is a collection of symbols, such as database keys or file and directory names. The Microsoft® Windows® 95 shell uses a single hierarchical namespace to organize all objects of interest to the user: files, storage devices, printers, network resources, and anything else that can be viewed using Windows 95 Explorer. The root of this unified namespace is the Windows 95 desktop.

In many ways, the shell's namespace is analogous to a file system's directory structure. However, the namespace contains more types of objects than just files and directories. Familiar file system concepts, such as *filename* and *path*, have been replaced by more general and powerful associations. This article discusses some of these associations, outlines the organization of the shell's namespace, and describes the functions and interfaces associated with the namespace.

Folders and File Objects

A *folder* is a collection of items in the shell's namespace. A folder is analogous to a file system directory, and many folders are, in fact, directories. However, there are also other types of folders, such as remote computers, storage devices, the desktop folder, the Control Panel, the Printers folder, and the Fonts folder. A folder may contain other folders as well as items called *file objects*. A file object may be an actual file, or it can be a Control Panel application, a printer, or another type of object. Each type of folder can only contain certain kinds of file objects; for example, you cannot move a Control Panel application into a file system directory.

Because there are many kinds of folders and file objects, each folder is a OLE component object model (COM) object that "knows" how to enumerate its contents and carry out other actions. More precisely, each folder implements the **IShellFolder** interface. Retrieving the **IShellFolder** object for a shell folder is referred to as *binding* to the folder. An application that binds to a folder must eventually free the **IShellFolder** interface object by calling its **Release** member function.

You can bind to the desktop folder (retrieve the folder's **IShellFolder** interface) by using the **SHGetDesktopFolder** member function. You can enumerate subfolders by using the **IShellFolder::EnumObjects** member function. You can bind to a subfolder of any given folder by using the **IShellFolder::BindToObject** member function. Using these three functions, an application can navigate throughout the shell's entire namespace.

Item Identifiers and Pointers to Item Identifier Lists

Objects in the shell's namespace are assigned item identifiers and item identifier lists. An *item identifier* uniquely identifies an item within its parent folder. An *item identifier list* uniquely identifies an item within the shell's namespace by tracing a path to the item from the desktop. A pointer to an item identifier list, which is sometimes called a PIDL (pronounced *piddle*), is used with many functions.

Item identifiers and PIDLs are much like the filenames and paths used in a file system. However, they share this important difference: item identifiers and PIDLs are binary data structures that never appear to the user. Item names called *display names* that can be shown to the user are described later.

An item identifier is defined by the variable-length **SHITEMID** structure. The first two bytes of this structure specify its size, and the format of the remaining bytes depends on the parent folder, or more precisely on the software that implements the parent folder's **IShellFolder** interface. Except for the first two bytes, item identifiers are not strictly defined, and applications should make no assumptions about their format. To determine whether two item identifiers are equal, an application can use the **IShellFolder::CompareIDs** member function.

The **ITEMIDLIST** structure defines an element in an item identifier list (the only member of this structure is an **SHITEMID** structure). An item identifier list consists of one or more consecutive **ITEMIDLIST** structures packed on byte boundaries, followed by a 16-bit zero value. An application can walk a list of item identifiers by examining the size specified in each **SHITEMID** structure and stopping when it finds a size of zero.

Item identifier lists are almost always allocated using the shell's allocator (an **IMalloc** interface that you can retrieve by using the **SHGetMalloc** function). For example, some shell functions create an item identifier list and return a PIDL to it. In such cases, it is usually the application's responsibility to free the PIDL using the shell's allocator. Note that the **SHGetMalloc** function retrieves the task allocator for OLE applications.

Folder Locations

Certain folders have special meanings for the shell. An application can use shell functions to retrieve the locations of these special folders and to enable the user to browse for specific folders.

Some special folders are *virtual folders*—so called because they are not actual directories on any storage device, local or remote. Virtual folders like the desktop folder, the My Computer folder, and the Network Neighborhood folder make a unified namespace possible by serving as containers for any number of storage devices and network resources. Other virtual folders contain file objects, such as printers, that are not part of the file system.

File system directories that the shell uses for specific purposes are also considered special folders. Examples include the Programs folder (which contains the user's program groups) and the desktop directory (which is used to physically store files that have been copied to the desktop folder). The locations of special file system folders are stored in the registry under the **HKEY_CURRENT_USER/Software/ Microsoft/Windows/CurrentVersion/Explorer/Shell Folders** key.

You can use the **SHGetSpecialFolderLocation** function to retrieve the location of a special folder, which can be virtual or part of the file system. The function returns a PIDL, which the application must eventually free using the shell's allocator. If the folder is part of the file system, you can convert the PIDL to a file system path by using the **SHGetPathFromIDList** function. For a list of special folders, see the description of the **SHGetSpecialFolderLocation** function.

To display a dialog box that enables the user to browse for a folder, you can use the **SHBrowseForFolder** function. An application might use this function to prompt the user for a directory or remote computer. This function can also be used to browse for network printers, even though printers are not considered folders. An application can specify the root folder to browse from. For example, to prompt the user for a program group, you might call **SHBrowseForFolder** specifying the PIDL for the Programs folder as the root.

Item Enumeration

An application that uses the **IShellFolder** interface for a folder can determine the folder's contents by using the **EnumObjects** member function. This member function creates an *item enumeration object,* which is a set of item identifiers that can be retrieved by using the **IEnumIDList** interface.

One or more item identifiers can be retrieved from the enumeration object by using the **IEnumIDList::Next** member function. Calling this function repeatedly allows an application to retrieve all of the item identifiers one or more at a time. Using other member functions, you can skip items in the sequence, return to the beginning of the sequence, or "clone" the enumeration object to save its state.

When you are finished using the enumeration object, you must free it by calling the **IEnumIDList::Release** member function.

Display Names and Filenames

Because item identifiers are binary data structures, each item in a shell folder also has a *display name,* which is a string that can be shown to the user. You can use member functions in the **IShellFolder** interface to retrieve an item's display name, to find an item with the specified display name, or to change an item's display name.

The **IShellFolder::GetDisplayNameOf** member function can be used to retrieve a display name. The actual string returned depends on the type of display name specified. Values identifying the different types of display names are defined by the **SHGNO** enumerated type and have the SHGDN prefix. The type of display name that an application requests might depend on whether an item is shown by itself or within its parent folder. (A shared directory might be labeled Public on 'bill' in the former case and simply Public in the latter case.)

A special type of display name is one that can be converted back to an item identifier by using the **IShellFolder::ParseDisplayName** member function. You might use this type of display name as a parameter to the **ShellExecute** function or as a command-line argument for an application. For items within the file system, the display name for parsing is the same as the file system path. You can also convert a PIDL to a file system path by using the **SHGetPathFromIDList** function.

The **IShellFolder::SetNameOf** member function can be used to change the display name of a file object or subfolder. Changing an item's display name also changes its item identifier, so the function returns a PIDL containing the new item identifier. For file objects or folders within the file system, changing the display name renames the file or directory.

Object Attributes and Interfaces

Every file object and folder has attributes that determine, among other things, what actions can be carried out on it. An application can determine the attributes of any file object or folder and can retrieve interfaces for items in a shell folder.

To determine the attributes of a file object or folder, an application can use the **IShellFolder::GetAttributesOf** member function. Attributes include capabilities (such as whether a file object can be deleted or can be a drop target), display attributes (such as whether a folder is shared), contents flags (such as whether a folder has subfolders), as well as other attributes (such as whether an object is a folder, whether it is part of the file system, and so on). For a list of attributes, see the description of the **IShellFolder::GetAttributesOf** member function.

An application can retrieve interfaces that can be used to carry out actions on a file object or folder by using the **IShellFolder::GetUIObjectOf** member function. For example, the application can display the property sheets for a file object by retrieving the object's **IContextMenu** interface and activating the Properties command.

Using the Shell's Namespace

This section contains examples that demonstrate the functions and interfaces associated with the shell's namespace.

Using PIDLs and Display Names

This section presents an example illustrating how to retrieve the location of a special folder, walk an item identifier list, and use the **IShellFolder** interface to retrieve display names. The example is a Microsoft® Win32®-based console application that prints the display names of the folders a user would have to open to get to the Programs folder. To display them, the application would carry out these steps:

1. Retrieve the PIDL (obtain a pointer to an item identifier list) for the Programs folder by using the **SHGetSpecialFolderLocation** function.

2. Bind to the desktop folder (retrieve the folder's **IShellFolder** interface) by using the **SHGetDesktopFolder** function.

3. Walk the item identifier list and process elements as follows: print the subfolder's display name, bind to the subfolder, and release the parent folder's **IShellFolder** interface.

Before carrying out any of the preceding steps, the application uses the **SHGetMalloc** function to retrieve a pointer to the shell's **IMalloc** interface, which it saves in the following global variable.

```
// Global pointer to the shell's IMalloc interface.
LPMALLOC g_pMalloc;
```

The following example shows the application's **main** function. This function carries out all of the steps described previously, although it calls the application-defined GetNextItemID and CopyItemID functions to walk the item identifier list and the application-defined PrintStrRet function to print the display names. These application-defined functions are described later in this section.

```
// main - the application's entrypoint function
int __cdecl main()
{
    LPITEMIDLIST pidlPrograms;
    LPSHELLFOLDER pFolder;

    // Get the shell's allocator.
    if (!SUCCEEDED(SHGetMalloc(&g_pMalloc)))
        return 1;

    // Get the PIDL for the Programs folder.
    if (SUCCEEDED(SHGetSpecialFolderLocation(NULL,
            CSIDL_PROGRAMS, &pidlPrograms))) {

        // Start with the desktop folder.
        if (SUCCEEDED(SHGetDesktopFolder(&pFolder))) {
            LPITEMIDLIST pidl;

            // Process each item identifier in the list.
            for (pidl = pidlPrograms; pidl != NULL;
                    pidl = GetNextItemID(pidl)) {
                STRRET sName;
                LPSHELLFOLDER pSubFolder;
                LPITEMIDLIST pidlCopy;

                // Copy the item identifier to a list by itself.
                if ((pidlCopy = CopyItemID(pidl)) == NULL)
                    break;

                // Display the name of the subfolder.
                if (SUCCEEDED(pFolder->lpVtbl->GetDisplayNameOf(
                        pFolder, pidlCopy, SHGDN_INFOLDER,
                        &sName)))
                    PrintStrRet(pidlCopy, &sName);

                // Bind to the subfolder.
                if (!SUCCEEDED(pFolder->lpVtbl->BindToObject(
                        pFolder, pidlCopy, NULL,
                        &IID_IShellFolder, &pSubFolder))) {
                    g_pMalloc->lpVtbl->Free(g_pMalloc, pidlCopy);
                    break;
                }
```

```
                   // Free the copy of the item identifier.
                   g_pMalloc->lpVtbl->Free(g_pMalloc, pidlCopy);

                   // Release the parent folder and point to the
                   // subfolder.
                   pFolder->lpVtbl->Release(pFolder);
                   pFolder = pSubFolder;
              }

              // Release the last folder that was bound to.
              if (pFolder != NULL)
                   pFolder->lpVtbl->Release(pFolder);
         }

         // Free the PIDL for the Programs folder.
         g_pMalloc->lpVtbl->Free(g_pMalloc, pidlPrograms);
    }

    // Release the shell's allocator.
    g_pMalloc->lpVtbl->Release(g_pMalloc);
    return 0;
}
```

Following is the GetNextItemID function. Given a pointer to an element in an item identifier list, the function returns a pointer to the next element (or NULL if there are no more elements). The **main** function calls this function to walk the item identifier list for the Programs folder.

```
// GetNextItemID - points to the next element in an item identifier
//      list.
// Returns a PIDL if successful or NULL if at the end of the list.
// pdil - previous element
LPITEMIDLIST GetNextItemID(LPITEMIDLIST pidl)
{
    // Get the size of the specified item identifier.
    int cb = pidl->mkid.cb;

    // If the size is zero, it is the end of the list.
    if (cb == 0)
        return NULL;

    // Add cb to pidl (casting to increment by bytes).
    pidl = (LPITEMIDLIST) (((LPBYTE) pidl) + cb);

    // Return NULL if it is null-terminating or a pidl otherwise.
    return (pidl->mkid.cb == 0) ? NULL : pidl;
}
```

Following is the CopyItemID function. Given a pointer to an element in an item identifier list, the function allocates a new list containing only the specified element followed by a terminating zero. The **main** function uses this function to create single-element PIDLs, which it passes to **IShellFolder** member functions.

```
// CopyItemID - creates an item identifier list containing the
//      first item identifier in the specified list.
// Returns a PIDL if successful or NULL if out of memory.
LPITEMIDLIST CopyItemID(LPITEMIDLIST pidl)
{
    // Get the size of the specified item identifier.
    int cb = pidl->mkid.cb;

    // Allocate a new item identifier list.
    LPITEMIDLIST pidlNew = (LPITEMIDLIST)
        g_pMalloc->lpVtbl->Alloc(g_pMalloc, cb + sizeof(USHORT));
    if (pidlNew == NULL)
        return NULL;

    // Copy the specified item identifier.
    CopyMemory(pidlNew, pidl, cb);

    // Append a terminating zero.
    *((USHORT *) (((LPBYTE) pidlNew) + cb)) = 0;

    return pidlNew;
}
```

The **IShellFolder::GetDisplayNameOf** member function returns a display name in a **STRRET** structure. The display name may be returned in one of three ways, which is specified by the **uType** member of the **STRRET** structure. The **main** function calls the following PrintStrRet function to print the display name.

```
// PrintStrRet - prints the contents of a STRRET structure.
// pidl - PIDL containing the display name if STRRET_OFFSET
// lpStr - address of the STRRET structure
void PrintStrRet(LPITEMIDLIST pidl, LPSTRRET lpStr)
{
    LPSTR lpsz;
    int cch;

    switch (lpStr->uType) {

        case STRRET_WSTR:
            cch = WideCharToMultiByte(CP_OEMCP, WC_DEFAULTCHAR,
                lpStr->pOleStr, -1, NULL, 0, NULL, NULL);
            lpsz = (LPSTR) g_pMalloc->lpVtbl->Alloc(g_pMalloc, cch);
```

```
            if (lpsz != NULL) {
                WideCharToMultiByte(CP_OEMCP, WC_DEFAULTCHAR,
                    lpStr->pOleStr, -1, lpsz, cch, NULL, NULL);
                printf("%s\n", lpsz);
                g_pMalloc->lpVtbl->Free(g_pMalloc, lpsz);
            }
            break;

        case STRRET_OFFSET:
            printf("%s\n", ((char *) pidl) + lpStr->uOffset);
            break;

        case STRRET_CSTR:
            printf("%s\n", lpStr->cStr);
            break;
    }
}
```

Browsing for Folders

The following example uses the **SHBrowseForFolder** function to prompt the user for a program group. The Programs directory is specified as the root.

```
// Main_OnBrowse - browses for a program folder.
// hwnd - handle of the application's main window
//
// Uses the global variable g_pMalloc, which is assumed to point
//      to the shell's IMalloc interface.
void Main_OnBrowse(HWND hwnd)
{
    BROWSEINFO bi;
    LPSTR lpBuffer;
    LPITEMIDLIST pidlPrograms;  // PIDL for Programs folder
    LPITEMIDLIST pidlBrowse;    // PIDL selected by user

    // Allocate a buffer to receive browse information.
    if ((lpBuffer = (LPSTR) g_pMalloc->lpVtbl->Alloc(
            g_pMalloc, MAX_PATH)) == NULL)
        return;

    // Get the PIDL for the Programs folder.
    if (!SUCCEEDED(SHGetSpecialFolderLocation(
            hwnd, CSIDL_PROGRAMS, &pidlPrograms))) {
        g_pMalloc->lpVtbl->Free(g_pMalloc, lpBuffer);
        return;
    }
```

```
        // Fill in the BROWSEINFO structure.
        bi.hwndOwner = hwnd;
        bi.pidlRoot = pidlPrograms;
        bi.pszDisplayName = lpBuffer;
        bi.lpszTitle = "Choose a Program Group";
        bi.ulFlags = 0;
        bi.lpfn = NULL;
        bi.lParam = 0;

        // Browse for a folder and return its PIDL.
        pidlBrowse = SHBrowseForFolder(&bi);
        if (pidlBrowse != NULL) {

            // Show the display name, title, and file system path.
            MessageBox(hwnd, lpBuffer, "Display name", MB_OK);
            if (SHGetPathFromIDList(pidlBrowse, lpBuffer))
                SetWindowText(hwnd, lpBuffer);

            // Free the PIDL returned by SHBrowseForFolder.
            g_pMalloc->lpVtbl->Free(g_pMalloc, pidlBrowse);
        }

        // Clean up.
        g_pMalloc->lpVtbl->Free(g_pMalloc, pidlPrograms);
        g_pMalloc->lpVtbl->Free(g_pMalloc, lpBuffer);
}
```

Reference

The following interfaces, member functions, structures, macros, and types are associated with the shell's namespace.

Interfaces and Member Functions

IShellFolder

Designates an interface implemented by the shell and used to determine the contents of a folder. The **IShellFolder** interface has the following member functions.

BindToObject	Retrieves the specified interface for the specified subfolder.
BindToStorage	Reserved; this function is not currently implemented.
CompareIDs	Compares two item identifier lists and returns the result.
CreateViewObject	Reserved for use by the shell; do not use.
EnumObjects	Enumerates the objects in the folder.
GetAttributesOf	Retrieves the attributes of the specified file object or subfolder.
GetDisplayNameOf	Retreives the display name of a file object or subfolder.
GetUIObjectOf	Creates an OLE interface that can be used to carry out operations on a file object or subfolder.
ParseDisplayName	Translates a display name into an item identifier list.
SetNameOf	Sets the display name of the specified file object or subfolder and changes its identifier accordingly.

Like all OLE interfaces, **IShellFolder** also includes the **QueryInterface**, **AddRef**, and **Release** member functions.

IShellFolder::ParseDisplayName

```
HRESULT IShellFolder::ParseDisplayName(
    LPSHELLFOLDER pIface, HWND hwndOwner, LPBC pbcReserved,
    LPWSTR lpwszDisplayName, ULONG *pchEaten,
    LPITEMIDLIST *ppidl, ULONG *pdwAttributes
    );
```

Translates a file object or folder's display name into an item identifier.

- Returns the NOERROR value if successful or an OLE-defined error value otherwise.

pIface
Address of the **IShellFolder** interface. In C++, this parameter is implicit.

hwndOwner
Handle of the owner window that the client should specify if it displays a dialog box or message box.

pbcReserved
Reserved; this parameter is always NULL.

lpwszDisplayName
Address of a null-terminated Unicode string specifying the display name. This parameter must be a display name for parsing—that is, a display name retrieved using the SHGDN_FORPARSING value.

pchEaten
> Address of an unsigned long value that receives the number of characters of the display name that were parsed.

ppidl
> Address that receives a pointer to the new item identifier list for the object. If an error occurs, a NULL pointer is returned in this address.

> The returned item identifier list specifies the relative path (from the parent folder) that corresponds to the specified display name. It contains only one **SHITEMID** structure followed by a terminating zero.

pdwAttributes
> Address that receives the attributes of the file object.

This member function is similar to the **IParseDisplayName::IParseDisplayName** member function defined by OLE.

IShellFolder::EnumObjects

```
HRESULT IShellFolder::EnumObjects(
    LPSHELLFOLDER pIface, HWND hwndOwner, DWORD grfFlags,
    LPENUMIDLIST *ppenumIDList
    );
```

Creates an item enumeration object (an **IEnumIDList** interface) that can be used to enumerate the contents of a folder.

- Returns the NOERROR value if successful or an OLE-defined error value otherwise.

pIface
> Address of the **IShellFolder** interface. In C++, this parameter is implicit.

hwndOwner
> Handle of the owner window that the client should specify if it displays a dialog box or message box.

grfFlags
> Flags determining which items to include in the enumeration. For a list of possible values, see the description of the **SHCONTF** type.

ppenumIDList
> Address that receives a pointer to the **IEnumIDList** interface created by this member function. If an error occurs, a NULL pointer is returned in this address.

The calling application must free the returned **IEnumIDList** object by calling its **Release** member function.

This member function is similar to the **IOleContainer::EnumObjects** member function defined by OLE.

IShellFolder::BindToObject

```
HRESULT IShellFolder::BindToObject(
    LPSHELLFOLDER pIface, LPCITEMIDLIST pidl, LPBC pbcReserved,
    REFIID riid, LPVOID *ppvOut
    );
```

Creates an **IShellFolder** object for a subfolder.

• Returns the NOERROR value if successful or an OLE-defined error value otherwise.

pIface
Address of the **IShellFolder** interface. In C++, this parameter is implicit.

pidl
Address of an **ITEMIDLIST** structure that identifies the subfolder relative to its parent folder.

pbcReserved
Reserved; applications should specify NULL for this parameter.

riid
Identifier of the interface to return. This parameter is almost always the IID_IShellFolder interface identifier.

ppvOut
Address that receives the interface pointer. If an error occurs, a NULL pointer is returned in this address.

IShellFolder::BindToStorage

This member function is reserved for future use and is not currently implemented.

IShellFolder::CompareIDs

```
HRESULT IShellFolder::CompareIDs(
    LPSHELLFOLDER pIface, LPARAM lParam,
    LPCITEMIDLIST pidl1, LPCITEMIDLIST pidl2
    );
```

Determines the relative ordering of two file objects or folders, given their item identifier lists.

- Returns a handle to a result code. If this member function is successful, the CODE field of the status code (SCODE) has the following meaning:

CODE field	Meaning
Less than zero	The first item should precede the second ($pidl1 < pidl2$).
Greater than zero	The first item should follow the second ($pidl1 > pidl2$).
Zero	The two items are the same ($pidl1 = pidl2$).

pIface
Address of the **IShellFolder** interface. In C++, this parameter is implicit.

lParam
Value specifying the type of comparison to perform. The calling application should always specify zero, indicating that the two items should be sorted by name.

pidl1 and *pidl2*
Addresses of two **ITEMIDLIST** structures that uniquely identify the items to be compared. Both item identifier lists are relative to the parent folder.

IShellFolder::CreateViewObject

This member function is reserved for use by the shell and should not be called by applications.

IShellFolder::GetAttributesOf

```
HRESULT IShellFolder::GetAttributesOf(
    LPSHELLFOLDER pIface, UINT cidl, LPCITEMIDLIST *apidl,
    ULONG *rgfInOut
    );
```

Retrieves the attributes of one or more file objects or subfolders.

- Returns the NOERROR value if successful or an OLE-defined error value otherwise.

pIface

   Address of the **IShellFolder** interface. In C++, this parameter is implicit.

cidl

   Number of file objects to get the attributes of.

apidl

   Address of an array of pointers to **ITEMIDLIST** structures, each of
   which uniquely identifies a file object relative to the parent folder. Each
   ITEMIDLIST structure must contain exactly one **SHITEMID** structure
   followed by a terminating zero.

rgfInOut

   Address of an array of values that specify file object attributes. The calling
   application should initialize each array element by specifying which file
   object attributes to retrieve.

This member function returns the actual attributes of each file object in the
corresponding array element; it may return all attributes or just the requested
attributes.

The following attribute flags may be returned by this member function. File object
attributes include capability flags, display attributes, contents flags, and miscellaneous attributes.

A file object's capability flags may include zero or more of these values:

SFGAO_CANCOPY	The specified file objects or folders can be copied (same value as the DROPEFFECT_COPY value).
SFGAO_CANDELETE	The specified file objects or folders can be deleted.
SFGAO_CANLINK	It is possible to create shortcuts for the specified file objects or folders (same value as the DROPEFFECT_LINK value).
SFGAO_CANMOVE	The specified file objects or folders can be moved (same value as the DROPEFFECT_MOVE value).
SFGAO_CANRENAME	The specified file objects or folders can be renamed.
SFGAO_CAPABILITYMASK	Mask for the capability flags.
SFGAO_DROPTARGET	The specified file objects or folders are drop targets.
SFGAO_HASPROPSHEET	The specified file objects or folders have property sheets.

A file object's display attributes may include zero or more of these values:

SFGAO_DISPLAYATTRMASK	Mask for the display attributes.
SFGAO_GHOSTED	The specified file objects or folders should be displayed using a ghosted icon.
SFGAO_LINK	The specified file objects are shortcuts.
SFGAO_READONLY	The specified file objects or folders are read-only.
SFGAO_SHARE	The specified folders are shared.

A file object's contents flags may include zero or more of these values:

SFGAO_CONTENTSMASK	Mask for the contents attributes.
SFGAO_HASSUBFOLDER	The specified folders have subfolders (and are, therefore, expandable in the left pane of Windows 95 Explorer).

A file object may have zero or more of the following miscellaneous attributes:

SFGAO_FILESYSANCESTOR	The specified folders contain one or more file system folders.
SFGAO_FILESYSTEM	The specified folders or file objects are part of the file system (that is, they are files, directories, or root directories).
SFGAO_FOLDER	The specified items are folders.
SFGAO_REMOVABLE	The specified file objects or folders are on removable media.
SFGAO_VALIDATE	Validate cached information.

IShellFolder::GetUIObjectOf

```
HRESULT IShellFolder::GetUIObjectOf(
    LPSHELLFOLDER pIface, HWND hwndOwner, UINT cidl,
    LPCITEMIDLIST *apidl, REFIID riid, UINT *prgfReserved,
    LPVOID *ppvOut
    );
```

Returns an interface that can be used to carry out actions on the specified file objects or folders—typically, to create context menus or carry out drag and drop operations.

- Returns the NOERROR value if successful or an OLE-defined error value otherwise.

pIface
Address of the **IShellFolder** interface. In C++, this parameter is implicit.

hwndOwner
Handle of the owner window that the client should specify if it displays a dialog box or message box.

cidl
Number of file objects or subfolders specified by *apidl*.

apidl
Address of an array of pointers to **ITEMIDLIST** structures, each of which uniquely identifies a file object or subfolder relative to the parent folder. Each item identifier list must contain exactly one **SHITEMID** structure followed by a terminating zero.

riid
Identifier of the interface to return. This parameter can be a pointer to the IID_IExtractIcon, IID_IContextMenu, IID_IDataObject, or IID_IDropTarget interface identifier.

prgfReserved
Reserved for future versions of Windows; must be NULL.

ppvOut
Address that receives the interface pointer. If an error occurs, a NULL pointer is returned in this address.

IShellFolder::GetDisplayNameOf

```
HRESULT IShellFolder::GetDisplayNameOf(
    LPSHELLFOLDER pIface, LPCITEMIDLIST pidl, DWORD uFlags,
    LPSTRRET lpName
    );
```

Retrieves the display name for the specified file object or subfolder.

- Returns the NOERROR value if successful or an OLE-defined error value otherwise.

pIface
: Address of the **IShellFolder** interface. In C++, this parameter is implicit.

pidl
: Address of an **ITEMIDLIST** structure that uniquely identifies the file object or subfolder relative to the parent folder.

uFlags
: Flag indicating the type of display name to return. For a list of possible values, see the description of the **SHGNO** enumerated type.

lpName
: Address of a **STRRET** structure in which to return the display name. The string returned in this structure depends on the type of display name requested.

IShellFolder::SetNameOf

```
HRESULT IShellFolder::SetNameOf(
    LPSHELLFOLDER pIface, HWND hwndOwner, LPCITEMIDLIST pidl,
    LPCOLESTR lpszName, DWORD uFlags, LPITEMIDLIST *ppidlOut
    );
```

Changes the name of a file object or subfolder, changing its item identifier in the process.

- Returns the NOERROR value if successful or an OLE-defined error value otherwise.

pIface
: Address of the **IShellFolder** interface. In C++, this parameter is implicit.

hwndOwner
: Handle of the owner window that the client should specify if it displays a dialog box or message box.

pidl
: Address of an **ITEMIDLIST** structure that uniquely identifies the file object or subfolder relative to the parent folder.

lpszName
: Address of a null-terminated string that specifies the new display name.

uFlags
: Flag indicating the type of name specified by *lpszName*. For a list of possible values, see the description of the **SHCONTF** enumerated type.

ppidlOut

Address in which the member function returns a pointer to the new **ITEMIDLIST** structure. This parameter can be NULL, and the member function does not return the new structure for the object in that case.

If this parameter is not NULL, this member function frees the specified **ITEMIDLIST** structure and allocates a new one using the task allocator. The calling application is responsible for freeing the new **ITEMIDLIST** structure. If an error occurs, the member function returns NULL in this address.

IEnumIDList

Designates an interface used to enumerate item identifiers. The **IShellFolder::EnumObjects** member function creates an **IEnumIDList** interface. The **IEnumIDList** interface has the following member functions.

Clone	Creates a new item enumeration object having the same contents and state as the given one.
Next	Retrieves one or more item identifiers and advances the current position.
Reset	Returns to the beginning of the enumeration sequence.
Skip	Skips over one or more items in the enumeration sequence.

Like all OLE interfaces, **IEnumIDList** also includes the **QueryInterface**, **AddRef**, and **Release** methods.

IEnumIDList::Clone

```
HRESULT Clone(IEnumIDList FAR * pEnumIDList,
    IEnumIDList **ppenum);
```

Creates a new item enumeration object with the same contents and state as the current one.

- Returns the NOERROR value if successful or an OLE-defined error value otherwise.

pEnumIDList

Address of the **IEnumIDList** interface. In C++, this parameter is implicit.

ppenum

Address that receives a pointer to the new enumeration object. The calling application must eventually free the new object by calling its **Release** member function.

This member function makes it possible to record a particular point in the enumeration sequence and then return to that point at a later time.

IEnumIDList::Next

```
HRESULT Next(IEnumIDList FAR * pEnumIDList,
    ULONG celt, LPITEMIDLIST *rgelt, ULONG *pceltFetched);
```

Retrieves the specified number of item identifiers in the enumeration sequence and advances the current position.

- Returns the NOERROR value if successful, the S_FALSE value if there are no more items in the enumeration sequence, or an OLE-defined error value if an error occurs.

pEnumIDList
Address of the **IEnumIDList** interface. In C++, this parameter is implicit.

celt
Specifies the number of elements in the array pointed to by the *rgelt* parameter.

rgelt
Address of an array in which to return the item identifiers. The calling application must free the item identifiers by using the task allocator (retrieved by using the **SHGetMalloc** function).

pceltFetched
Address of a value that receives a count of the item identifiers actually returned in *rgelt*. The count can be smaller than the value specified in the *celt* parameter. This parameter can be NULL if, and only if, *celt* is one.

If this member function returns any value other than NOERROR, no entries in the *rgelt* array are valid on exit. They are all in an indeterminate state.

IEnumIDList::Reset

```
HRESULT Reset(IEnumIDList FAR * pEnumIDList,);
```

Returns to the beginning of the enumeration sequence.

- Returns the NOERROR value if successful or an OLE-defined error value otherwise.

pEnumIDList
Address of the **IEnumIDList** interface. In C++, this parameter is implicit.

IEnumIDList::Skip

```
HRESULT Skip(IEnumIDList FAR * pEnumIDList,
    ULONG celt);
```

Skips over the specified number of elements in the enumeration sequence.

- Returns the NOERROR value if successful or an OLE-defined error value otherwise.

pEnumIDList
Address of the **IEnumIDList** interface. In C++, this parameter is implicit.

celt
Number of item identifiers to skip.

Functions

The following functions are used with the shell's namespace.

BrowseCallbackProc

```
int BrowseCallbackProc(HWND hwnd, UINT uMsg, LPARAM lParam,
    LPARAM lpData);
```

Specifies an application-defined callback function that is used with the **SHBrowseForFolder** function. A browse dialog box calls this function to notify it about events. The **BFFCALLBACK** type defines a pointer to this callback function.

- Returns zero.

hwnd
Handle of the browse dialog box. The callback function can send the following messages to the window:

BFFM_ENABLEOK	Enables the OK button if *wParam* is nonzero or disables it if *wParam* is zero.
BFFM_SETSELECTION	Selects the specified folder. *lParam* is the PIDL of the folder to select if *wParam* is FALSE, or it is the path of the folder otherwise.
BFFM_SETSTATUSTEXT	Sets the status text to the null-terminated string specified by *lParam*.

uMsg

Value identifying the event. This parameter can be one of these values:

BFFM_INITIALIZED	The browse dialog box has finished initializing. *lpData* is NULL.
BFFM_SELCHANGED	The selection has changed. *lpData* is a pointer to the item identifier list for the newly selected folder.

lParam

Message-specific value. For more information, see the description of *uMsg*.

lpData

Application-defined value that was specified in the **lParam** member of the **BROWSEINFO** structure.

SHAddToRecentDocs

```
void SHAddToRecentDocs(UINT uFlags, LPCVOID pv);
```

Adds a document to the shell's list of recently used documents or clears all documents from the list. The user accesses the list through the Start menu of the Windows taskbar.

- No return value.

uFlags

Flag that indicates the meaning of *pv*. This parameter can be one of these values:

SHARD_PATH	*pv* is the address of a path string.
SHARD_PIDL	*pv* is the address of an item identifier list.

pv

Address of a buffer that contains the path and filename of the document, or the address of an **ITEMIDLIST** structure that contains an item identifier list uniquely identifying the document. If this parameter is NULL, the function clears all documents from the list.

SHBrowseForFolder

```
LPITEMIDLIST SHBrowseForFolder(LPBROWSEINFO lpbi);
```

Displays a browse dialog box that enables the user to select a shell folder.

- Returns a pointer to an item identifier list that specifies the location of the selected folder relative to the root of the namespace. If the user chooses the Cancel button in the dialog box, the return value is NULL.

lpbi

Address of a **BROWSEINFO** structure that contains information used to display the dialog box.

The calling application is responsible for freeing the returned item identifier list using the shell's task allocator.

SHChangeNotify

```
void SHChangeNotify(LONG wEventId, UINT uFlags,
    LPCVOID dwItem1, LPCVOID dwItem2);
```

Notifies the system of an event that an application has performed. An application should use this function if it performs an action that may affect the shell.

- No return value.

wEventId

Array of flags that specifies the events. This parameter can be a combination of these values:

SHCNE_ASSOCCHANGED	Changed a file type association.
SHCNE_ATTRIBUTES	Changed a file's attributes.
SHCNE_CREATE	Created a file.
SHCNE_DELETE	Deleted a file.
SHCNE_DRIVEADD	Added a network drive.
SHCNE_DRIVEADDGUI	Added a network drive by way of a graphic user interface (GUI).
SHCNE_DRIVEREMOVED	Removed a network drive.
SHCNE_INTERRUPT	Performed the event as a result of a system interrupt.
SHCNE_MEDIAINSERTED	Added removable media, such as a compact-disc read-only memory (CD-ROM) drive.
SHCNE_MEDIAREMOVED	Removed a removable medium, such as a CD-ROM drive.
SHCNE_MKDIR	Created a new directory.
SHCNE_NETSHARE	Shared a resource on the network.
SHCNE_NETUNSHARE	Stopped sharing a resource.
SHCNE_RENAMEFOLDER	Renamed a folder.
SHCNE_RENAMEITEM	Renamed an item in a folder.
SHCNE_RMDIR	Removed a directory.

SHCNE_SERVERDISCONNECT	Disconnected a network server.
SHCNE_UPDATEDIR	Updated the contents of a directory.
SHCNE_UPDATEIMAGE	Changed an image in the system global image list.
SHCNE_UPDATEITEM	Changed the properties of a printer or file.

uFlags

Flag that indicates the meaning of *dwItem1* and *dwItem2*. This parameter can be one of these values:

SHCNF_DWORD	The *dwItem1* and *dwItem2* parameters are double-word values.
SHCNF_FLUSH	Flushes the system event buffer. The function does not return until the system is finished processing the given event.
SHCNF_FLUSHNOWAIT	Flushes the system event buffer. The function returns immediately regardless of whether the system is finished processing the given event.
SHCNF_IDLIST	*dwItem1* and *dwItem2* are the addresses of item identifier lists.
SHCNF_PATH	*dwItem1* and *dwItem2* are paths.
SHCNF_PRINTER	*dwItem1* and *dwItem2* are printer "friendly" names.

dwItem1

First event-dependent value.

dwItem2

Second event-dependent value.

SHFileOperation

```
int SHFileOperation(LPSHFILEOPSTRUCT lpFileOp);
```

Performs a copy, move, rename, or delete operation on a file system object.

- Returns zero if successful or nonzero if an error occurs.

lpFileOp

Address of an **SHFILEOPSTRUCT** structure containing information that the function needs to carry out the operation.

SHFreeNameMappings

```
void SHFreeNameMappings(HANDLE hNameMappings);
```

Frees a filename mapping object that was retrieved by the **SHFileOperation** function.

- No return value.

hNameMappings
Handle of the filename mapping object to free.

SHGetDesktopFolder

```
HRESULT SHGetDesktopFolder(LPSHELLFOLDER *ppshf);
```

Retrieves the **IShellFolder** interface for the desktop folder, which is the root of the shell's namespace.

- Returns the NOERROR value if successful or an OLE-defined error result otherwise.

ppshf
Address that receives an **IShellFolder** interface pointer for the desktop folder. The calling application is responsible for eventually freeing the interface by calling its **Release** member function.

SHGetFileInfo

```
DWORD SHGetFileInfo(LPCSTR pszPath,
    DWORD dwFileAttributes, SHFILEINFO FAR *psfi, UINT cbFileInfo,
    UINT uFlags);
```

Retrieves information about an object in the file system, such as a file, a folder, a directory, or a drive root.

- Returns a value whose meaning depends on the *uFlags* parameter. If *uFlags* specifies the SHGFI_EXETYPE value, the return value indicates the type of the executable file. For more information, see the comments below.

  If *uFlags* includes the SHGFI_ICON or SHGFI_SYSICONINDEX value, the return value is the handle of the system image list that contains the large icon images. If the SHGFI_SMALLICON value is also included, the return value is the handle of the image list that contains the small icon images.

  If *uFlags* does not include the SHGFI_EXETYPE, SHGFI_ICON, SHGFI_SYSICONINDEX, or SHGFI_SMALLICON values, the return value is nonzero if successful or zero otherwise.

pszPath

> Address of a buffer that contains the path and filename. Both absolute and relative paths are valid. If *uFlags* includes the SHGFI_PIDL value, *pszPath* must be the address of an **ITEMIDLIST** structure that contains the list of item identifiers uniquely identifying the file within the shell's namespace.

dwFileAttributes

> Array of file attribute flags (FILE_ATTRIBUTE_ values). If *uFlags* does not include the SHGFI_USEFILEATTRIBUTES value, this parameter is ignored.

psfi and *cbFileInfo*

> Address and size, in bytes, of the **SHFILEINFO** structure that receives the file information.

uFlags

> Flag that specifies the file information to retrieve. This parameter can be a combination of these values:

SHGFI_ATTRIBUTES	Retrieves the file attribute flags. The flags are copied to the **dwAttributes** member of the structure specified by *psfi*.
SHGFI_DISPLAYNAME	Retrieves the display name for the file. The name is copied to the **szDisplayName** member of the structure specified by *psfi*.
SHGFI_EXETYPE	Returns the type of the executable file if *pszPath* identifies an executable file. For more information, see the comments below.
SHGFI_ICON	Retrieves the handle of the icon that represents the file and the index of the icon within the system image list. The handle is copied to the **hIcon** member of the structure specified by *psfi*, and the index is copied to the **iIcon** member. The return value is the handle of the system image list.
SHGFI_ICONLOCATION	Retrieves the name of the file that contains the icon representing the file. The name is copied to the **szDisplayName** member of the structure specified by *psfi*.
SHGFI_LARGEICON	Modifies SHGFI_ICON, causing the function to retrieve the file's large icon.
SHGFI_LINKOVERLAY	Modifies SHGFI_ICON, causing the function to add the link overlay to the file's icon.

SHGFI_OPENICON	Modifies SHGFI_ICON, causing the function to retrieve the file's open icon. A container object displays an open icon to indicate that the container is open.
SHGFI_PIDL	Indicates that *pszPath* is the address of an **ITEMIDLIST** structure rather than a path name.
SHGFI_SELECTED	Modifies SHGFI_ICON, causing the function to blend the file's icon with the system highlight color.
SHGFI_SHELLICONSIZE	Modifies SHGFI_ICON, causing the function to retrieve a shell-sized icon. If this value is not specified, the function sizes the icon according to the system metric values.
SHGFI_SMALLICON	Modifies SHGFI_ICON, causing the function to retrieve the file's small icon.
SHGFI_SYSICONINDEX	Retrieves the index of the icon within the system image list. The index is copied to the **iIcon** member of the structure specified by *psfi*. The return value is the handle of the system image list.
SHGFI_TYPENAME	Retrieves the string that describes the file's type. The string is copied to the **szTypeName** member of the structure specified by *psfi*.
SHGFI_USEFILEATTRIBUTES	Indicates that the function should use *dwFileAttributes*. This flag must be set when retrieving an icon for a file that does not exist.

To retrieve the executable file type, *uFlags* must specify only SHGFI_EXETYPE. The return value specifies the type of the executable file:

0	Nonexecutable file or an error condition
LOWORD = NE or PE HIWORD = 3.0, 3.5, or 4.0	Windows-based application
LOWORD = MZ HIWORD = 0	Microsoft® MS-DOS® .EXE, .COM, or .BAT file
LOWORD = PE HIWORD = 0	Win32-based console application

SHGetInstanceExplorer

```
HRESULT SHGetInstanceExplorer(IUnknown **ppunk);
```

Retrieves the address of Windows 95 Explorer's **IUnknown** interface.

- Returns the NOERROR value if successful or the E_FAIL value otherwise.

ppunk
  Address of a value that receives the address of Windows 95 Explorer's **IUnknown** interface.

SHGetMalloc

```
HRESULT SHGetMalloc(LPMALLOC * ppMalloc);
```

Retrieves a pointer to the shell's **IMalloc** interface. A shell extension must use this interface to allocate memory that is later freed by the shell.

- Returns the NOERROR value if successful or E_FAIL otherwise.

ppMalloc
  Address of a value that receives the address of the shell's **IMalloc** interface.

SHGetPathFromIDList

```
BOOL SHGetPathFromIDList(LPCITEMIDLIST pidl,
    LPSTR pszPath);
```

Converts an item identifier list to a file system path.

- Returns TRUE if successful or FALSE if an error occurs—for example, if the location specified by *pidl* is not part of the file system.

pidl
  Address of an item identifier list that specifies a file or directory location relative to the root of the namespace (the desktop).

pszPath
  Address of a buffer that receives the file system path. The size of this buffer is assumed to be MAX_PATH bytes.

SHGetSpecialFolderLocation

```
HRESULT SHGetSpecialFolderLocation(HWND hwndOwner,
    int nFolder, LPITEMIDLIST * ppidl);
```

Retrieves the location of a special folder.

- Returns the NOERROR value if successful or an OLE-defined error result otherwise.

hwndOwner
   Handle of the owner window that the client should specify if it displays a dialog box or message box.

nFolder
   Value specifying the folder to retrieve the location for. This parameter can be one of these values:

CSIDL_BITBUCKET	Recycle bin—file system directory containing file objects in the user's recycle bin. The location of this directory is not in the registry; it is marked with the hidden and system attributes to prevent the user from moving or deleting it.
CSIDL_CONTROLS	Control Panel—virtual folder containing icons for Control Panel applications.
CSIDL_DESKTOP	Windows desktop—virtual folder at the root of the namespace.
CSIDL_DESKTOPDIRECTORY	File system directory used to physically store file objects on the desktop (not to be confused with the desktop folder itself).
CSIDL_DRIVES	My Computer—virtual folder containing everything on the local computer: storage devices, printers, and Control Panel. The folder may also contain mapped network drives.
CSIDL_FONTS	Virtual folder containing fonts.
CSIDL_NETHOOD	File system directory containing objects that appear in Network Neighborhood.
CSIDL_NETWORK	Network Neighborhood—virtual folder representing the top level of the network hierarchy.

CSIDL_PERSONAL	File system directory that serves as a common repository for documents.
CSIDL_PRINTERS	Printers folder—virtual folder containing installed printers.
CSIDL_PROGRAMS	File system directory that contains the user's program groups (which are also file system directories).
CSIDL_RECENT	File system directory that contains the user's most recently used documents.
CSIDL_SENDTO	File system directory that contains Send To menu items.
CSIDL_STARTMENU	File system directory containing Start menu items.
CSIDL_STARTUP	File system directory that corresponds to the user's Startup program group.
CSIDL_TEMPLATES	File system directory that serves as a common repository for document templates.

ppidl
Address that receives a pointer to an item identifier list specifying the folder's location relative to the root of the namespace (the desktop).

SHLoadInProc

```
HRESULT SHLoadInProc(REFCLSID rclsid);
```

Creates an instance of the specified object class from within the context of the shell's process.

- Returns the NOERROR value if successful or an OLE-defined error result otherwise.

rclsid
Class identifier (CLSID) of the object class to be created.

Structures, Macros, and Types

The following structures, macros, and types are used with the shell's namespace.

BROWSEINFO

```
typedef struct _browseinfo {
    HWND hwndOwner;              // see below
    LPCITEMIDLIST pidlRoot;     // see below
    LPSTR pszDisplayName;       // see below
    LPCSTR lpszTitle;           // see below
    UINT ulFlags;               // see below
    BFFCALLBACK lpfn;           // see below
    LPARAM lParam;              // see below
    int iImage;                 // see below
} BROWSEINFO, *PBROWSEINFO, *LPBROWSEINFO;
```

Contains parameters for the the **SHBrowseForFolder** function and receives information about the folder selected by the user.

hwndOwner

Handle of the owner window for the dialog box.

pidlRoot

Address of an item identifier list (an **ITEMIDLIST** structure) specifying the location of the "root" folder to browse from. Only the specified folder and its subfolders appear in the dialog box. This member can be NULL, and the namespace root (the desktop folder) is used in that case.

pszDisplayName

Address of a buffer that receives the display name of the folder selected by the user. The size of this buffer is assumed to be MAX_PATH bytes.

lpszTitle

Address of a null-terminated string that is displayed above the tree view control in the dialog box. This string can be used to specify instructions to the user.

ulFlags

Value specifying the types of folders to be listed in the dialog box as well as other options. This member can include zero or more of these values:

BIF_BROWSEFORCOMPUTER	Only returns computers. If the user selects anything other than a computer, the OK button is grayed.
BIF_BROWSEFORPRINTER	Only returns printers. If the user selects anything other than a printer, the OK button is grayed.
BIF_DONTGOBELOWDOMAIN	Does not include network folders below the domain level in the tree view control.
BIF_RETURNFSANCESTORS	Only returns file system ancestors. If the user selects anything other than a file system ancestor, the OK button is grayed.
BIF_RETURNONLYFSDIRS	Only returns file system directories. If the user selects folders that are not part of the file system, the OK button is grayed.
BIF_STATUSTEXT	Includes a status area in the dialog box. The callback function can set the status text by sending messages to the dialog box.

lpfn

Address an application-defined function that the dialog box calls when events occur. For more information, see the description of the **BrowseCallbackProc** function. This member can be NULL.

lParam

Application-defined value that the dialog box passes to the callback function, if one is specified.

iImage

Variable that receives the image associated with the selected folder. The image is specified as an index to the system image list.

CIDA

```
typedef struct _IDA {
    UINT cidl;        // number of array elements
    UINT aoffset[1];  // see below
} CIDA, * LPIDA;
```

Corresponds to the CF_IDLIST clipboard format.

aoffset
> Array of offsets relative to the beginning of the **CIDA** structure. The first element is the offset of the **ITEMIDLIST** structure for a folder (absolute from the root). Subsequent elements are offsets of **ITEMIDLIST** structures for file objects (relative from the parent folder).

SHCONTF

```
typedef enum tagSHCONTF {
    SHCONTF_FOLDERS = 32,          // for shell browser
    SHCONTF_NONFOLDERS = 64,       // for default view
    SHCONTF_INCLUDEHIDDEN = 128,   // for hidden or system objects
} SHCONTF;
```

Specifies an enumerated type that defines flags used with the **IShellFolder::EnumObjects** member function.

SHFILEINFO

```
typedef struct _SHFILEINFO { // shfi
    HICON hIcon;                         // see below
    int   iIcon;                         // see below
    DWORD dwAttributes;                  // see below
    char  szDisplayName[MAX_PATH];       // see below
    char  szTypeName[80];                // see below
} SHFILEINFO;
```

Contains information about a file object.

hIcon
> Handle of the icon that represents the file.

iIcon
> Index of the icon image within the system image list.

dwAttributes
> Array of flags that indicates the attributes of the file object. For information about the flags, see the description of the **IShellFolder::GetAttributesOf** member function.

szDisplayName
> String that contains the name of the file as it appears in the Windows shell, or the path and filename of the file that contains the icon representing the file.

szTypeName
> String that describes the type of the file.

This structure is used with the **SHGetFileInfo** function.

SHFILEOPSTRUCT

```
typedef struct _SHFILEOPSTRUCT { // shfos
    HWND          hwnd;                        // see below
    UINT          wFunc;                       // see below
    LPCSTR        pFrom;                       // see below
    LPCSTR        pTo;                         // see below
    FILEOP_FLAGS  fFlags;                      // see below
    BOOL          fAnyOperationsAborted;       // see below
    LPVOID        hNameMappings;               // see below
    LPCSTR        lpszProgressTitle;           // see below
} SHFILEOPSTRUCT, FAR *LPSHFILEOPSTRUCT;
```

Contains information that the **SHFileOperation** function uses to perform file operations.

hwnd

Handle of the dialog box used to display information about the status of the operation. If **fFlags** includes the FOF_CREATEPROGRESSDLG value, this parameter is the handle of the parent window for the progress dialog box created by the system.

wFunc

Operation to perform. This member can be one of these values:

FO_COPY	Copies the files specified by **pFrom** to the location specified by **pTo**.
FO_DELETE	Deletes the files specified by **pFrom** (**pTo** is ignored).
FO_MOVE	Moves the files specified by **pFrom** to the location specified by **pTo**.
FO_RENAME	Renames the files specified by **pFrom**.

pFrom

Address of a string that contains the names of the source files.

pTo

Address of a string that specifies the destination for the moved, copied, or renamed file.

fFlags

Flags that control the file operation. This member can be a combination of these values:

FOF_ALLOWUNDO	Preserves undo information, if possible.
FOF_CONFIRMMOUSE	Not implemented.
FOF_FILESONLY	Performs the operation only on files if a wildcard filename (*.*) is specified.
FOF_MULTIDESTFILES	Indicates that the **pTo** member specifies multiple destination files (one for each source file) rather than one directory where all source files are to be deposited.
FOF_NOCONFIRMATION	Responds with "yes to all" for any dialog box that is displayed.
FOF_NOCONFIRMMKDIR	Does not confirm the creation of a new directory if the operation requires one to be created.
FOF_RENAMEONCOLLISION	Gives the file being operated on a new name (such as "Copy #1 of...") in a move, copy, or rename operation if a file of the target name already exists.
FOF_SILENT	Does not display a progress dialog box.
FOF_SIMPLEPROGRESS	Displays a progress dialog box, but does not show the filenames.
FOF_WANTMAPPINGHANDLE	Fills in the **hNameMappings** member. The handle must be freed by using the **SHFreeNameMappings** function.

fAnyOperationsAborted

Value that receives TRUE if the user aborted any file operations before they were completed or FALSE otherwise.

hNameMappings

Handle of a filename mapping object that contains an array of **SHNAMEMAPPING** structures. Each structure contains the old and new paths for each file that was moved, copied, or renamed. This member is used only if **fFlags** includes FOF_WANTMAPPINGHANDLE.

lpszProgressTitle

Address of a string to use as the title for a progress dialog box. This member is used only if **fFlags** includes FOF_SIMPLEPROGRESS.

If **pFrom** or **pTo** are unqualified names, the current directories are taken from the global current drive and directory settings as managed by the **GetCurrentDirectory** and **SetCurrentDirectory** functions.

The **SHGetNameMappingPtr** macro retrieves a pointer to the filename mapping object returned in the **hNameMappings** member of this structure. The **SHGetNameMappingCount** macro retrieves the number of **SHNAMEMAPPING** structures in the object.

SHNAMEMAPPING

```
typedef struct _SHNAMEMAPPING { // shnm
    LPSTR pszOldPath; // address of old path
    LPSTR pszNewPath; // address of new path
    int   cchOldPath; // number of characters in old path
    int   cchNewPath; // number of characters in new path
} SHNAMEMAPPING, FAR *LPSHNAMEMAPPING;
```

Contains the old and new paths for each file that was moved, copied, or renamed by the **SHFileOperation** function.

STRRET

```
typedef struct _STRRET { // str
    UINT uType; // see below
    union
    {
        LPWSTR pOleStr;       // address of OLE string to free
        UINT   uOffset;       // offset into item identifier list
        char   cStr[MAX_PATH]; // buffer to receive display name
    } DUMMYUNIONNAME;
} STRRET, *LPSTRRET;
```

Contains strings returned from **IShellFolder** member functions, such as **GetDisplayNameOf**.

uType

Value that specifies the desired format of the string. This member can be one of these values:

STRRET_CSTR	The string is returned in **cStr**.
STRRET_OFFSET	The string is located at **uOffset** bytes from the beginning of the item identifier list.
STRRET_WSTR	The string is at the address pointed to by **pOleStr**.

The system may or may not provide the display name in the desired format. When **IShellFolder::GetDisplayNameOf** returns, **uType** indicates the format.

SHGetNameMappingCount

```
int SHGetNameMappingCount(HANDLE hNameMappings)
```

Retrieves the number of **SHNAMEMAPPING** structures in a filename mapping object.

- Returns the number of **SHNAMEMAPPING** structures.

hNameMappings
Handle of a filename mapping object retrieved by the **SHFileOperation** function.

The **SHGetNameMappingCount** macro is defined as follows.

```
#define SHGetNameMappingCount(_hnm) \
    DSA_GetItemCount(_hnm)
```

SHGetNameMappingPtr

```
lpshnm = SHGetNameMappingPtr(HANDLE hNameMappings, int iItem)
```

Retrieves the address of a **SHNAMEMAPPING** structure contained in a file mapping object.

- Returns the address of the **SHNAMEMAPPING** structure specified by *iItem*.

hNameMappings
Handle of a filename mapping object retrieved by the **SHFileOperation** function.

iItem
Index of the **SHNAMEMAPPING** structure to be retrieved.

The **SHGetNameMappingPtr** macro is defined as follows.

```
#define SHGetNameMappingPtr(_hnm, _iItem) \
    (LPSHNAMEMAPPING)DSA_GetItemPtr(_hnm, _iItem)
```

SHGNO

```
typedef enum tagSHGDN {
    SHGDN_NORMAL = 0,             // see below
    SHGDN_INFOLDER = 1,           // see below
    SHGDN_FORPARSING = 0x8000,    // see below
} SHGNO;
```

Specifies an enumerated type that defines flags used with the **IShellFolder::GetDisplayNameOf** and **IShellFolder::SetNameOf** member functions.

SHGDN_NORMAL
> Default display name that is suitable for a file object displayed by itself, as shown in the following examples.

File system path	Corresponding display name
C:\WINDOWS\FILE.TXT	File
\\COMPUTER\SHARE	Share on computer
C:\ (where drive C has the volume name My Drive)	My Drive (C)

SHGDN_INFOLDER
> Display name that is suitable for a file object displayed within its respective folder, as shown in the following examples.

File system path	Corresponding display name
C:\WINDOWS\FILE.TXT	File
\\COMP\SHARE	User
C:\ (where drive C has the volume name My Drive)	My Drive (C)

SHGDN_FORPARSING
> Display name that can be passed to the **ParseDisplayName** member function of the parent folder's **IShellFolder** object.

File system path	Corresponding display name
C:\WINDOWS\FILE.TXT	C:\WINDOWS\FILE.TXT
\\COMP\SHARE	\\COMP\SHARE
C:\ (where drive C has the volume name My Drive)	C:\

A R T I C L E   1 2

Shell Extensions

About Shell Extensions

In Microsoft® Windows® 95, applications can extend the shell in a number of ways. A *shell extension* enhances the shell by providing additional means of manipulating file objects, by simplifying the task of browsing through the file system and networks, or by giving the user easier access to tools that manipulate objects in the file system. For example, a shell extension can assign an icon to each file or add commands to the context menu and File menu for a file.

Windows 95 supports two groups of shell extensions. The first group are registered for each type of file:

- Context menu handlers. They add items to the context menu for a particular file object. (The context menu is displayed when the user clicks a file object with mouse button 2.)

- Icon handlers. They typically add instance-specific icons for file objects. They can also be used to add icons for all files belonging to the same class.

- Data handlers. They provide a type-specific **IDataObject** interface to be passed to the OLE **DoDragDrop** function.

- Drop handlers. They provide type-specific drop behavior to files that can accept drag and drop objects.

- Property sheet handlers. They add pages to the property sheet dialog box that the shell displays for a file object. The pages are specific to a class of files or a particular file object.

The second group of shell extensions are associated with file operations such as move, copy, rename, and so on:

- Copy hook handlers. They are called when a folder object is about to be copied, moved, deleted, or renamed. They can either allow or prevent the operation.

- Drag and drop handlers. They are context menu handlers that the system calls when the user drops an object after dragging it to a new position.

The design of a shell extension is based on the OLE Component Object Model (COM). The shell accesses an object through interfaces. An application implements the interfaces in a shell extension dynamic-link library (DLL), which is essentially an OLE in-process server DLL.

This article explains how to create shell extensions and describes how the shell interacts with them.

Shell Extension Terms

You should be familiar with the following shell extension terms before proceeding.

file object
A file object is an item within the shell. The most familiar file objects are files and directories. However, a file object may not actually be a part of the file system; it may only appear that way. For example, printers, Control Panel applications, and network shares, servers, and workgroups are also considered to be file objects.

file class
Each file object is a member of a file class. The file class refers to the code that "owns" the manipulation of files belonging to the class. For example, text files and Microsoft Word documents are examples of file classes. Each file class has specific shell extensions associated with it. When the shell is about to take an action involving a file object, it uses the file class to determine the shell extensions to load.

handler
A handler is the code that implements a particular shell extension.

Registry Entries for Extending the Shell

An application that creates and maintains files, such as a spreadsheet, word processor, or graphics application, typically adds two keys to the system registry: a file association key and an application identifier key. The file association key maps a filename extension to an application identifier. For example, a word processing application might register the following key under **HKEY_CLASSES_ROOT**.

```
HKEY_CLASSES_ROOT
    .doc=AWordProcessor
```

The value name (.doc) specifies the filename extension, and the value (AWordProcessor) denotes the key name that contains the information about the application handling the filename extension.

The application identifier key is the second registry entry made by an application handling files.

```
HKEY_CLASSES_ROOT
    AWordProcessor=A Word Processor
```

The value (A Word Processor) is a string describing the application that recognizes files having the given filename extension. (In this case, it is the .DOC filename extension.)

Extending the shell requires that you add other entries below the file association and application identifier keys. The system checks these entries to determine the commands to add to various shell menus, when to load an extension DLL, where to find the DLL, and so on.

There are several registry keys that allow you to extend the shell without having to write any code at all. These keys let you set the default icon for a class of files or add commands to the File menu and its New submenu in Windows 95 Explorer.

Setting Default Icons for File Classes

The system uses icons to represent file objects in the shell. Typically, all files of the same class have the same icon. By adding the **DefaultIcon** key to the file association key for a particular file class, you can specify the icon that the system displays for all files of the class. The value of the **DefaultIcon** key specifies the executable file (or DLL) that contains the icon and the index of the icon within the file.

```
HKEY_CLASSES_ROOT
    .doc=AWordProcessor
        DefaultIcon=C:\MYDIR\MYAPP.EXE,1
```

If the registry does not contain a **DefaultIcon** key for a particular file class, the system uses the default icon for the class. One of the advantages of using a class icon is that it requires no programming; the shell handles displaying the icon for the class.

By writing an icon handler, you give each instance of a file a different icon. For more information about icon handlers, see "Icon Handlers" later in this article.

Modifying the Context Menu for a File Class

When the user clicks a file object using mouse button 2, the system displays a context menu for the object. The context menu contains a set of menu items that allow the user to perform various operations on the file object, such as opening or printing it. A context menu contains two types of items: dynamic items and static items. Dynamic items are added to a context menu by a context menu handler (described later in this article).

Static menu items are listed in the system registry and are automatically added to a context menu by the system. Because static items are listed in the system registry based on their class, the context menus for all file objects belonging to a particular class receive the same set of static items.

You specify static menu items for a file class by adding a **shell** key below the application identifier key of the file class and then adding verb and command value entries below the shell key. Following is the registry format for static items.

```
HKEY_CLASSES_ROOT
    <applicationID> = <"description">
        shell
            <verb> = <"menu-item text">
                command = <"command string">
```

Each verb value entry specifies a menu-item text string for the system to add to the context menu. The command value entry specifies the action that the system takes when the user chooses the menu item. Typically, the *command string* value specifies the path and filename of an application and includes command-line options that direct the application to perform an action on the corresponding file object. For example, the following registry keys add an Open command and a Print command to the context menu for all files with the .WRI filename extension.

```
HKEY_CLASSES_ROOT
  wrifile = Write Document
      shell
        open
          command = C:\Progra~1\Access~1\WORDPAD.EXE %1
            print
          command = C:\Progra~1\Access~1\WORDPAD.EXE /p "%1"
            printto
          command =
            C:\Progra~1\Access~1\WORDPAD.EXE /pt "%1" "%2" "%3" "%4"
```

In the preceding commands, the %1 parameter is the filename, %2 is the printer name, %3 is the driver name, and %4 is the port name. In Windows 95, you can ignore the %3 and %4 parameters (the printer name is unique in Windows 95).

The system defines a set of verbs called *canonical verbs* that introduce an element of language-independence to context menus. When you include a canonical verb in the registry, the system automatically generates a localized menu item string for the verb before adding it to the context menu. The canonical verbs include the open, print, explore, find, openas, and properties verbs. The printto verb is also canonical, but it is a special case because it is never actually displayed. Instead, it allows the user to print a file by dragging it to a printer object. Canonical verbs are also used with context menu handlers.

If the open canonical verb is included in the registry entries for a file class, the system adds an Open menu item to the corresponding context menu and makes it the default item. If the open verb is not included, the menu item corresponding to the verb listed in the registry is the default item. A context menu handler can change the default item. For more information about context menu handlers, see "Context Menu Handlers" later in this article.

Modifying the New Submenu

The File menu in a file system folder contains a New submenu that, by default, includes the Shortcut and Folder commands. These commands allow the user to create new shortcuts and folders within the current folder. The New submenu can also include other nondefault commands that let the user create new files of various types within the current folder, such as sound files, text files, and bitmap files. For example, the New submenu might include a Sound command that creates a .WAV file in the current folder.

If your application creates a type of file that the user may want to create from within a file system folder, you should consider adding a command for it to the New submenu. For example, suppose you have created a graphics application that creates files with the .XYZ filename extension. You could add a command, such as XYZ Picture, that creates a new .XYZ file or launches your application and opens a new .XYZ file for editing.

You add a command to the New submenu by including a **ShellNew** key below the file association key for your filetype. When the system needs to create the New submenu, it searches through the file association entries for instances of the **ShellNew** key. When it finds an instance of **ShellNew**, the system retrieves the string associated with the application identifier key (xyzfile) and adds the string to the New submenu as a new command. Note that an Open command must be registered below the application identifier key; otherwise, the system does not add the Open command to the New submenu.

The following example shows the registry entries needed to add the XYZ Picture command to the New submenu.

```
HKEY_CLASSES_ROOT
    .xyz="xyzfile"
        ShellNew
            NullFile=""
    .
    .
    .
    xyzfile="XYZ Picture"
        shell
            open
                command="C:\XYZ\XYZAPP.EXE %1
```

The data names for the **ShellNew** key specify the method to use to create a new file of the type designated by the filename extension. There are four possible data names and values for the **ShellNew** key.

Data name	Value	Description
NullFile	""	Creates an empty (null) file. If this data name is specified, Data and FileName are ignored.
Data	*binary-value*	Creates a file that contains the data specified by *binary-value*. This data name is ignored if either NullFile or FileName is specified.
FileName	*path-name*	Creates a copy of the file specified by *path-name*. This data name is ignored if NullFile is specified.
Command	*path-name*	Executes the command specified by *path-name* when the file is created. For example, the command might start a wizard.

Registering Shell Extensions

A shell extension must be registered in the Windows registry. The class identifier of each handler must be registered under the **HKEY_CLASSES_ROOT\CLSID** key. The **CLSID** key contains a list of class identifier key values, such as {00030000-0000-0000-C000-000000000046}. Each class identifier key is a globally unique identifier (GUID) generated by the UUIDGEN tool. Within each class identifier key, the handler adds an **InProcServer32** key that gives the location of the handler's DLL. It is best to give the complete path for the handler; using the complete path keeps the handler independent of the current path and speeds up the load time for the DLL.

The information that the shell uses to associate a shell extension handler with a file type is stored under the **shellex** key. The shell also uses several other special keys under **HKEY_CLASSES_ROOT** to look for shell extensions: *****, **Folder**, **Drives**, **Printers**, and keys for network providers. Descriptions of the keys follow:

- You can use the * key to register handlers that the shell calls whenever it creates a context menu or property sheet for a file object in the following manner.

```
HKEY_CLASSES_ROOT
  * = *
    shellex
      ContextMenuHandlers
          {00000000-1111-2222-3333-00000000000001}
      PropertySheetHandlers
          {00000000-1111-2222-3333-00000000000002}
```

The shell uses instances of the ExtraMenu and SummaryInfo handlers to add to the context menus and property sheets for every file object.

- You can use **Folder** key to register a shell extension for directories in the file system. You can register context menu handlers, copy hook handlers, and property sheet handlers in the same way you register these handlers for the * key. An additional handler, the drag and drop handler, applies only to the **Folder** and **Printers** keys. An example showing the **Folder** key follows.

```
Folder = Folder
  shellex
    DragDropHandlers
        {00000000-1111-2222-3333-00000000000004}
    CopyHookHandlers
        {00000000-1111-2222-3333-00000000000005}
```

- You can use the **Drives** key for the same registrations as the **Folder** key, but the **Drives** key is called only for root paths (for example, C:\).

- The **Printers** key allows the same registrations as the **Folder** key, but it uses additional handlers for printer events, deletion or removal of printers (through the copy hook handler), and printer properties (with property sheet handlers and context menu handlers).

To avoid conflicts with other classes, you must use real GUIDs, not the sample strings shown in the previous examples.

Debugging Tips

The shell automatically unloads a DLL when the DLL's usage count is zero, but only after the DLL has not been used for a period of time. The inactive period may be unacceptably long at times, especially when a shell extension DLL is being debugged. You can shorten the inactive period by adding the following information to the registry.

```
HKLM
    Software
        Microsoft
            Windows
                CurrentVersion
                    Explorer
                        AlwaysUnloadDll
```

AlwaysUnloadDll shortens the inactive period so that DLLs are unloaded quickly.

While debugging your extension, you may want to shut down the Windows 95 shell without closing the currently running applications. To do so, follow these steps:

1. From the Start menu on the Windows taskbar, choose Shut Down.

2. While holding down the CTRL+ALT+SHIFT key combination, click the No button in the Shut Down Windows dialog box.

How the Shell Accesses Shell Extension Handlers

The shell uses two interfaces to initialize instances (objects created by **IClassFactory::CreateInstance**) of shell extensions: **IShellExtInit** and **IPersistFile**. The shell uses the **IShellExtInit** interface to initialize instances of context menu handlers, drag and drop handlers, and property sheet handlers. The shell uses **IPersistFile** to initialize instances of icon handlers, data handlers, and drop handlers. This interface is defined by OLE.

The **IShellExtInit** interface adds an additional member function, **Initialize**, to the standard **IUnknown** interface. A handler's **Initialize** function should keep a copy of the parameters that the shell passes to the function for later use. An example showing how to initialize instances follows.

```
STDMETHODIMP CShellExt::Initialize(LPCITEMIDLIST pIDFolder,
    LPDATAOBJECT pDataObj, HKEY hRegKey)
{
    // Initialize can be called more than once.
    if (m_pDataObj)
        m_pDataObj->Release();

    // Save the object pointer.
    if (pDataObj) {
        m_pDataObj = pDataObj;
        pDataObj->AddRef();
    }

    // Duplicate the registry handle.
    if (hRegKey)
        RegOpenKeyEx(hRegKey, NULL, 0L, MAXIMUM_ALLOWED,
            &this->hRegKey);

    return NOERROR;
}
```

A shell extension handler must implement three functions: an entrypoint function (often called DllMain or LibMain), **DllCanUnloadNow**, and **DllGetClassObject**.

DllCanUnloadNow and **DllGetClassObject** are essentially the same as they would be for any OLE in-process server DLL. The use of **DllCanUnloadNow** is shown in the following example.

```
STDAPI DllCanUnloadNow(void)
{
    // g_cRefThisDll must be placed in the instance-specifc
    // data section.
    return ResultFromScode((g_cRefThisDll==0) ? S_OK : S_FALSE);
}
```

DllGetClassObject needs to expose the class factory for the object in the DLL. For more information about exposing the class factory, see the OLE documentation included in the Microsoft® Win32® Software Development Kit (SDK). The following example shows how to expose the class factory.

```
// DllGetClassObject - a DLL entrypoint function used by
// most in-process server DLLs.

STDAPI DllGetClassObject(REFCLSID rclsid, REFIID riid, LPVOID *ppvOut)
{
    *ppvOut = NULL; // assume failure

    if (IsEqualIID(rclsid, CLSID_ShellExtension)) {
        return CShellExtSample_Create(riid, ppvOut);
    } else {
        return CLASS_E_CLASSNOTAVAILABLE;
    }
}
```

Context Menu Handlers

A *context menu handler* is a shell extension that adds menu items to any of the shell's context menus. There are two types of context menu handlers. Each type has a different purpose, but the same implementation. *Context menu extensions* are used when the user clicks a file object by using mouse button 2, and *drag and drop handlers* are used when the user drags a file object using mouse button 2. This section describes the types of context menu handlers, how they are used, how they are added to the registry, and the interfaces that they must implement.

Context Menu Extensions

When the user clicks mouse button 2 on an item within the shell's namespace (that is, file, directory, server, work group, and so on), it creates the default context menu for the type of item and then loads context menu extensions that are registered for the type (and its base type) so that they can add extra menu items. The context menu extensions are registered at the following location.

```
HKCR\{ProgID}\shellex\ContextMenuHandlers
```

IContextMenu Interface

An application implements a context menu handler interface, **IContextMenu**, to add menu items to the context menu for a file object. The shell displays the object's context menu when the user clicks the object with mouse button 2. The menu items can be either class-specific (that is, applicable to all files of a particular type) or instance-specific (that is, applicable to an individual file).

When the user clicks a file object by using mouse button 2, the system passes the address of the object's context menu to the context menu handler, which should use the handle only to add items to the menu. The handler should not delete or modify existing menu items, because other handlers may add items either before or after it does. In addition, the shell adds items to the menu after all context menu handlers have been called.

Context menu handlers are entered in the registry under the **shellex** key within an application's information area. The **ContextMenuHandlers** key lists the names of subkeys that contain the CLSID of each context menu handler. An example showing the **ContextMenuHandlers** key follows.

```
ContextMenuHandlers
    {00000000-1111-2222-3333-00000000000001}
```

You can register multiple context menu handlers for a file type.

In addition to the standard **IUnknown** member functions, the context menu handler interface uses the **QueryContextMenu**, **InvokeCommand**, and **GetCommandString** member functions.

When the user selects one of the menu items added by a context menu handler, the shell calls the handler's **IContextMenu::InvokeCommand** member function to let the handler process the command. If multiple context menu handlers are registered for a file type, the value of the **ContextMenuHandlers** key determines the order of the commands.

When the system is about to display a context menu (or the File menu on the menu bar) for a file object, the system calls the context menu handler's **QueryContextMenu** member function. The context menu handler inserts menu items by position (MF_POSITION) directly into the context menu by calling the **InsertMenu** function. The following example shows that menu items must be string items (MF_STRING).

```
STDMETHODIMP CShellExt::QueryContextMenu(HMENU hMenu,
    UINT indexMenu, UINT idCmdFirst, UINT idCmdLast, UINT uFlags)
{
    UINT idCmd = idCmdFirst;
    char szMenuText[64];
    char szMenuText2[64];
    char szMenuText3[64];
    char szMenuText4[64];
    BOOL bAppendItems=TRUE;

    if ((uFlags & 0x000F) == CMF_NORMAL) {
        lstrcpy(szMenuText, "&New .GAK menu 1, Normal File");
        lstrcpy(szMenuText2, "&New .GAK menu 2, Normal File");
        lstrcpy(szMenuText3, "&New .GAK menu 3, Normal File");
        lstrcpy(szMenuText4, "&New .GAK menu 4, Normal File");
```

```
    } else if (uFlags & CMF_VERBSONLY) {
        lstrcpy(szMenuText, "&New .GAK menu 1, Shortcut File");
        lstrcpy(szMenuText2, "N&ew .GAK menu 2, Shortcut File");
        lstrcpy(szMenuText3, "&New .GAK menu 3, Shortcut File");
        lstrcpy(szMenuText4, "&New .GAK menu 4, Shortcut File");
    } else if (uFlags & CMF_EXPLORE) {
        lstrcpy(szMenuText, "&New .GAK menu 1,
            Normal File right click in Explorer");
        lstrcpy(szMenuText2, "N&ew .GAK menu 2,
            Normal File right click in Explorer");
        lstrcpy(szMenuText3, "&New .GAK menu 3,
            Normal File right click in Explorer");
        lstrcpy(szMenuText4, "&New .GAK menu 4,
            Normal File right click in Explorer");
    } else if (uFlags & CMF_DEFAULTONLY) {
        bAppendItems = FALSE;
    } else {
        char szTemp[32];
        bAppendItems = FALSE;
    }

    if (bAppendItems) {
        InsertMenu(hMenu, indexMenu++, MF_SEPARATOR | MF_BYPOSITION,
            0, NULL);
        InsertMenu(hMenu, indexMenu++, MF_STRING | MF_BYPOSITION,
            idCmd++, szMenuText);
        InsertMenu(hMenu, indexMenu++, MF_SEPARATOR | MF_BYPOSITION,
            0, NULL);
        InsertMenu(hMenu, indexMenu++, MF_STRING | MF_BYPOSITION,
            idCmd++, szMenuText2);
        InsertMenu(hMenu, indexMenu++, MF_SEPARATOR | MF_BYPOSITION,
            0, NULL);
        InsertMenu(hMenu, indexMenu++, MF_STRING | MF_BYPOSITION,
            idCmd++, szMenuText3);
        InsertMenu(hMenu, indexMenu++, MF_STRING | MF_BYPOSITION,
            idCmd++, szMenuText4);

        // Must return the number of menu items added.
        return ResultFromShort(idCmd-idCmdFirst);
    }
    return NOERROR;
}
```

The system calls the **InvokeCommand** member function when the user selects a menu item that the context menu handler added to the context menu. The **InvokeCommand** function in the following example handles the commands associated with the menu items added by the previous example.

```
STDMETHODIMP CShellExt::InvokeCommand(LPCMINVOKECOMMANDINFO lpcmi)
{
    HRESULT hr = E_INVALIDARG;

    // If the high-order word of lpcmi->lpVerb is not NULL, this
    // function was called by an application and lpVerb is a command
    // that should be activated. Otherwise, the shell has called this
    // function, and the low-order word of lpcmi->lpVerb is the
    // identifier of the menu item that the user selected.
    if (!HIWORD(lpcmi->lpVerb)) {
        UINT idCmd = LOWORD(lpcmi->lpVerb);

        switch (idCmd) {
            case 0:
                hr = DoGAKMenu1(lpcmi->hwnd, lpcmi->lpDirectory,
                    lpcmi->lpVerb, lpcmi->lpParameters, lpcmi->nShow);
                break;

            case 1:
                hr = DoGAKMenu2(lpcmi->hwnd, lpcmi->lpDirectory,
                    lpcmi->lpVerb, lpcmi->lpParameters, lpcmi->nShow);
                break;

            case 2:
                hr = DoGAKMenu3(lpcmi->hwnd, lpcmi->lpDirectory,
                    lpcmi->lpVerb, lpcmi->lpParameters, lpcmi->nShow);
                break;

            case 3:
                hr = DoGAKMenu4(lpcmi->hwnd, lpcmi->lpDirectory,
                    lpcmi->lpVerb, lpcmi->lpParameters, lpcmi->nShow);
                break;
        }
    }
    return hr;
}
```

Windows calls the **GetCommandString** member function to get a language-independent command string or the help text for a context menu item.

Drag and Drop Handlers

Drag and drop handlers implement the **IContextMenu** interface. In fact, a drag and drop handler is simply a context menu handler affecting the menu that the shell displays when a user drags and drops a file object with mouse button 2. Because this menu is called the drag and drop menu, shell extensions that add items to this menu are called drag and drop handlers. Drag and drop handlers work the same way as context menu handlers.

Note that drag and drop handlers are registered under the key of folder types (typically the Directory key). To change the behavior of the dragged object (**IDataObject**), you need to implement a data handler.

Icon Handlers

An application can customize the icons that the shell displays for the application's file types. The icon interface also allows an application to specify icons for folders and subfolders within the application's file structure.

An application can specify icons for its file types in two ways. The simplest way is to specify a class icon to be used for all files of a particular file type by adding a **DefaultIcon** key to the registry under the program information. For information about specifying a class icon, see "Setting Default Icons for File Classes" earlier in this article.

An application can use the %1 value with the **DefaultIcon** key. This value denotes that each file instance of this type can have a different icon. The application must supply an icon handler for the file type and add an **IconHandler** key to the **shellex** key for the application. An application can have only one entry for the **IconHandler** key, and the value of its key denotes the CLSID of the icon handler.

```
shellex
    IconHandler
        {00000000-1111-2222-3333-00000000000003}
DefaultIcon = %1
```

To have customized icons, an application must provide an icon handler that implements the **IExtractIcon** interface. The system follows these steps when it is about to display an icon for a file type that has instance-specific icons:

1. Retrieves the class identifier of the handler.
2. Creates a handler object by calling the **CoCreateInstance** function with the CLSID.
3. Initializes the instance by calling the **IPersistFile::Load** member function.
4. Uses the **QueryInterface** member function to get to the **IExtractIcon** interface.
5. Calls the **IExtractIcon::GetIconLocation** and **IExtractIcon::Extract** member functions.

The **IExtractIcon** interface has the **Extract** and **GetIconLocation** member functions in addition to the usual **IUnknown** member functions.

The system calls the **GetIconLocation** member function to get the location and index of an icon to display. Typically, the icon location is an executable or DLL filename, but it can be any file.

The system calls the **Extract** member function when it needs to display an icon for a file that does not reside in an executable or DLL file. Applications usually have the file icons in their executable or DLL files, so icon handlers can simply implement this member function as a return-only function that returns the E_FAIL error value. You need to implement the **Extract** member function only if the icon image is stored in a file in an application-defined format. When the icon for a file is in a separate .ICO file (or any other type of file), the icon handler must extract the icon for the shell and return it in this member function.

Property Sheet Handlers

Another way the shell can be extended is by custom property sheets. When the user selects the properties for a file, the shell displays a standard property sheet. If the registered file type has a property sheet handler, the shell allows the user to access additional sheets that the handler provides. Property sheet handlers implement the **IShellPropSheetExt** interface.

Property sheet handlers are entered in the registry under the **shellex** key within an application's information area. The **PropertySheetHandlers** key lists the names of subkeys that contain the class identifier of each context menu handler, as shown in the following example.

```
PropertySheetHandlers
    {00000000-1111-2222-3333-00000000000002}
```

You can register multiple property sheet handlers for a file type. In this case, the order of the subkey names in the **PropertySheetHandlers** key determines the order of the additional property sheets. You can use a maximum of 24 (the value of MAXPROPPAGES) pages in a property sheet.

Adding Property Sheet Pages

The property sheet handler uses the **AddPages** member function in addition to the usual **IUnknown** member functions. The system calls the **AddPages** member function when it is about to display a property sheet. The system calls each property sheet handler registered to the file type to allow the handlers to add pages to the property sheets. The following example shows how to implement the **AddPages** member function.

```
STDMETHODIMP CSamplePageExt::AddPages(LPFNADDPROPSHEETPAGE lpfnAddPage,
    LPARAM lParam)
{
    PROPSHEETPAGE psp;
    HPROPSHEETPAGE hpage;

    psp.dwSize      = sizeof(psp);   // no extra data
    psp.dwFlags     = PSP_USEREFPARENT | PSP_USERELEASEFUNC;
    psp.hInstance   = (HINSTANCE)g_hmodThisDll;
    psp.pszTemplate = MAKEINTRESOURCE(DLG_FSPAGE);
    psp.pfnDlgProc  = FSPage_DlgProc;
    psp.pcRefParent = &g_cRefThisDll;
    psp.pfnRelease  = FSPage_ReleasePage;
    psp.lParam      = (LPARAM)hdrop;

    hpage = CreatePropertySheetPage(&psp);
    if (hpage) {
        if (!lpfnAddPage(hpage, lParam))
            DestroyPropertySheetPage(hpage);
    }
    return NOERROR;
}
```

Replacing Control Panel Pages

The **ReplacePage** member function is called only by Control Panel applications. It allows you to replace the property sheet of a standard Control Panel application with a custom page. For example, if a mouse manufacturer adds extra buttons to its mouse, the manufacturer can replace the standard Mouse Control Panel's "Buttons" property sheet page. The **ReplacePage** member function is not called by the shell because the shell does not have any property sheet pages that can be replaced by a shell extension. Currently, only Control Panel applications call this member function, but other property sheet suppliers could use this member function to allow their property sheet pages to be replaced.

Each property sheet handler that allows a property sheet page to be replaced must specify the registry location where other handlers that replace pages register themselves. For standard Control Panel applications, this location is defined by the **REGSTR_PATH_CONTROLSFOLDER** macro in the REGSTR.H file. The macro defines the key under the **HKEY_LOCAL_MACHINE** key in which all Control Panel property sheet page replacement handlers must register. For example, a property sheet handler that needs to replace a property sheet page for the Mouse Control Panel would register a property sheet extension handler in the following registry location.

```
HKEY_LOCAL_MACHINE
  REGSTR_PATH_CONTROLSFOLDER
    Mouse
      shellex
        PropertySheetHandlers = NewMousePage
          NewMousePage = {00000000-1111-2222-3333-00000000000002}
```

In addition, a property sheet handler that allows replaceable pages must define identifiers for each page that can be replaced.

Standard Control Panel applications define this location in the REGSTR.H and CPLEXT.H header files. In REGSTR.H, the controls folder macro **REGSTR_PATH_CONTROLSFOLDER** defines the key under the **HKEY_LOCAL_MACHINE** key in which all Control Panel property sheet page replacement handlers must register. CPLEXT.H defines the subkey for each Control Panel application that contains a replacable property sheet page: **\Mouse** for a Mouse Control Panel application and **\Keyboard** for a Keyboard Control Panel application.

Standard Control Panel applications define these identifiers in CPLEXT.H. For example, CPLPAGE_MOUSE_BUTTONS defines the identifier for the Mouse Control Panel's Buttons page, and CPLPAGE_KEYBOARD_SPEED defines the identifier for the Keyboard Control Panel's Speed page.

Copy Hook Handlers

A *copy hook handler* is a shell extension that the shell calls before copying, moving, deleting, or renaming a folder object. The copy hook handler does not perform the task itself, but the handler provides approval for the task. When the shell receives approval from the copy hook handler, it performs the actual file system operation (that is, copies, moves, deletes, or renames). Copy hook handlers are not informed about the success of the operation, so they cannot monitor actions that occur to folder objects.

The shell initializes the copy hook handler interface directly—that is, without using an **IShellExtInit** or **IPersistFile** interface first. A folder object can have multiple copy hook handlers. The copy hook handler interface has one member function, **CopyCallBack**, in addition to the standard **IUnknown** member functions.

The shell calls the **CopyCallBack** member function before it copies, moves, deletes, or renames a folder object. The function returns an integer value that indicates whether the shell should perform the operation. The shell will call each copy hook handler registered for a folder object until either all the handlers have been called or any handler returns the IDCANCEL value. The handler can also return the IDYES value to specify that the operation should be carried out or the IDNO value to specify that the operation should not be performed.

Data Handlers

When a file is dragged from the shell (or copied to the clipboard from the shell), the shell creates a default **IDataObject** interface that supports standard clipboard formats (CF_HDROP, "Shell IDList Array", and so on). An application can add more clipboard formats by providing a data handler for the file type. A data handler must support both the **IPersistFile** and **IDataObject** interfaces. The shell initializes a data handler by calling the **IPersistFile::Load** member function. When a data handler is provided, the default **IDataObject** interface delegates some member function calls to the data handler so that the additional clipboard data formats become available to the drop target.

You register a data handler by adding a **DataHandler** key and class identifier for the handler under the **shellex** key for the file type as shown in the following example.

```
shellex
    DataHandler = {00000000-1111-2222-3333-00000000000003}
```

Drop Handlers

By default, a file is not a drop target. By providing a drop handler for the file types created by your application, you can make the files into drop targets. A drop handler must support both the **IPersistFile** and **IDropTarget** interfaces. The shell initializes a drop handler by calling the **IPersistFile::Load** member function. When the user drags an object over one of your application's files or drops an object onto one of its files, the system calls the appropriate member functions of the **IDropTarget** interface.

You register a drop handler by adding a **DropHandler** key and class identifier for the handler under the **shellex** key for the file type as shown in the followng example.

```
shellex
    DropHandler = {00000000-1111-2222-3333-00000000000003}
```

Reference

The following interfaces, member functions, and structures are associated with shell extensions.

Interfaces and Member Functions

IContextMenu

Designates an interface that enables the shell to retrieve extensions to context menus. The **IContextMenu** interface has the following member functions.

GetCommandString	Retrieves the language-independent name of a menu command or the help text for a menu command.
InvokeCommand	Carries out a menu command, either in response to user input or otherwise.
QueryContextMenu	Adds commands to a context menu.

Like all OLE interfaces, **IContextMenu** also includes the **QueryInterface**, **AddRef**, and **Release** member functions.

IContextMenu::GetCommandString

```
HRESULT IContextMenu::GetCommandString(
    LPCONTEXTMENU pIface, UINT idCmd, UINT uFlags,
    UINT *pwReserved, LPSTR pszName, UINT cchMax);
```

Retrieves the language-independent command string or the help text for a context menu item.

- Returns the NOERROR value if successful or an OLE-defined error code otherwise.

pIface
Address of the **IContextMenu** interface. In C++, this parameter is implicit.

idCmd
Menu item identifier offset.

uFlags
　　Flag specifying the information to retrieve. This parameter can be one of these values:

GCS_HELPTEXT	Returns the help text for the menu item.
GCS_VALIDATE	Validates that the menu item exists.
GCS_VERB	Returns the language-independent command name for the menu item.

pwReserved
　　Reserved. Applications must specify NULL when calling this member function, and handles must ignore this parameter when called.

pszName and *cchMax*
　　Address and size of the buffer that receives the null-terminated string.

The language-independent command name is a name that can be passed to the **IContextMenu::InvokeCommand** member function to activate a command by an application. The help text is a description that Windows 95 Explorer displays in its status bar; it should be reasonably short (under 40 characters).

IContextMenu::InvokeCommand

```
HRESULT IContextMenu::InvokeCommand(
    LPCONTEXTMENU pIface, LPCMINVOKECOMMANDINFO lpici);
```

Carries out the command associated with a context menu item.

- Returns the NOERROR value if successful or an OLE-defined error code otherwise.

pIface
　　Address of the **IContextMenu** interface. In C++, this parameter is implicit.

lpici
　　Address of a **CMINVOKECOMMANDINFO** structure containing information about the command.

The shell calls this member function when the user chooses a command that the handler added to a context menu. This member function may also be called by an application without any corresponding user action.

IContextMenu::QueryContextMenu

```
HRESULT IContextMenu::QueryContextMenu(
    LPCONTEXTMENU pIface, HMENU hmenu, UINT indexMenu,
    UINT idCmdFirst, UINT idCmdLast, UINT uFlags
    );
```

Adds menu items to the specified menu. The menu items should be inserted at a given position in the menu, and their menu item identifiers must be in a given range.

- Returns an **HRESULT** structure in which, if successful, the **code** member contains the menu identifier offset of the last menu item added.

pIface
   Address of the **IContextMenu** interface. In C++, this parameter is implicit.

hmenu
   Handle of the menu. The handler should specify this handle when calling the **InsertMenu** or **InsertMenuItem** function.

indexMenu
   Zero-based position at which to insert the first menu item.

idCmdFirst and *idCmdLast*
   Minimum and maximum values that the handler can specify for menu item identifiers. The actual identifier of each menu item should be *idCmdFirst* plus a menu identifier offset in the range zero through (*idCmdLast–idCmdFirst*).

uFlags
   Flag specifying zero or more of these values:

CMF_DEFAULTONLY	The user is activating the default action, typically by double-clicking. A context menu extension or drag and drop handler should not add any menu items if this value is specified. A namespace extension should add only the default item, if any.
CMF_EXPLORE	Context menu handlers should ignore this value. This value is specified if the context menu is for an object in the left pane of Windows 95 Explorer.
CMF_NORMAL	Indicates normal operation. A context menu extension, namespace extension, or drag and drop handler can add any menu items.
CMF_VERBSONLY	Context menu handlers should ignore this value. This value is specified if the context menu is for a shortcut object.

The remaining bits of the low-order word are reserved by the system. The high-order word may be used for context-specific communications.

An extension must not modify other menu items or insert menu items at a location other than that specified by *indexMenu*. Such an extension will not work in a future version of the Windows operating system.

ICopyHook

Designates an interface that allows a copy hook handler to prevent a folder or printer object from being copied, moved, deleted, or renamed. The shell calls a copy hook handler whenever file system directories are about to be copied, moved, deleted, or renamed and whenever the status of a printer is about to change.

The shell creates the copy hook handler interface directly—that is, without using the **IShellExtInit** or **IPersistFile** interface first. A folder object can have multiple copy hook handlers.

A copy hook handler interface has one member function, **CopyCallBack**, in addition to the standard **QueryInterface**, **AddRef**, and **Release** member functions.

ICopyHook::CopyCallback

```
UINT CopyCallback(ICopyHook FAR * pCopyHook,
    HWND hwnd, UINT wFunc, UINT wFlags, LPCSTR pszSrcFile,
    DWORD dwSrcAttribs, LPCSTR pszDestFile, DWORD dwDestAttribs);
```

Either allows the shell to carry out a copy, move, delete, or rename operation on a folder object, or prevents the shell from carrying out the operation. The shell calls each copy hook handler registered for a folder object until either all the handlers have been called or any handler returns the IDCANCEL value.

- Returns an integer value that indicates whether the shell should perform the operation. It can be one of the following values:

    IDCANCEL   Prevents the current operation and cancels any pending operations.

    IDNO   Prevents the operation on this folder, but continues with any other operations (for example, a batch copy operation).

    IDYES   Allows the operation.

pCopyHook
Address of the **ICopyHook** interface. In C++, this parameter is implicit.

hwnd
Handle of the window that the copy hook handler should use as the parent window for any user interface elements the handler may need to display. If the FOF_SILENT value is specified, the member function should ignore this parameter.

wFunc

Operation to perform. This parameter can be one of these values:

FO_COPY	Copies the file specified by *pszSrcFile* to the location specified by *pszDestFile*.
FO_DELETE	Deletes the file specified by *pszSrcFile*.
FO_MOVE	Moves the file specified by *pszSrcFile* to the location specified by *pszDestFile*.
FO_RENAME	Renames the file specified by *pszSrcFile*.
PO_DELETE	Deletes the printer specified by *pszSrcFile*.
PO_PORTCHANGE	Changes the printer port. *pszSrcFile* and *pszDestFile* contain double-null terminated lists of strings. Each list contains the printer name followed by the port name. The port name in *pszSrcFile* is the current printer port, and the port name in *pszDestFile* is the new printer port.
PO_RENAME	Renames the printer specified by *pszSrcFile*.
PO_REN_PORT	Combination of PO_RENAME and PO_PORTCHANGE.

wFlags

Flags that control the operation. This parameter can be a combination of these values:

FOF_ALLOWUNDO	Preserves undo information, if possible.
FOF_CONFIRMMOUSE	Not implemented.
FOF_FILESONLY	Not implemented. The shell calls a copy hook handler only for folder objects, not files.
FOF_MULTIDESTFILES	Indicates that the **SHFileOperation** function specifies multiple destination files (one for each source file) rather than one directory where all the source files are to be deposited. A copy hook handler typically ignores this value.
FOF_NOCONFIRMATION	Responds with "yes to all" for any dialog box that is displayed.
FOF_NOCONFIRMMKDIR	Does not confirm the creation of any needed directories if the operation requires a new directory to be created.
FOF_RENAMEONCOLLISION	Gives the file being operated on a new name (such as, "Copy #1 of ...") in a copy, move, or rename operation if a file of the target name already exists.
FOF_SILENT	Displays no progress dialog box.
FOF_SIMPLEPROGRESS	Displays a progress dialog box, but the dialog box does not show the names of the files.

pszSrcFile
    Address of a string that contains the name of the source file.

dwSrcAttribs
    Attributes of the source file. This parameter can be a combination of any of the file attribute (FILE_ATTRIBUTE_) flags defined in the Windows header files.

pszDestFile
    Address of a string that contains the name of the destination file.

dwDestAttribs
    Attributes of the source file. This parameter can be a combination of any of the file attribute (FILE_ATTRIBUTE_) flags defined in the Windows header files.

IExtractIcon

Designates an interface that enables the shell to retrieve icons for file objects. The **IExtractIcon** interface has the following member functions.

GetIconLocation	Retrieves the icon location for a file object.
Extract	Extracts an icon from the specified location.

Like all OLE interfaces, **IExtractIcon** also includes the **QueryInterface**, **AddRef**, and **Release** member functions.

IExtractIcon::GetIconLocation

```
HRESULT IExtractIcon::GetIconLocation(
    LPEXTRACTICON pIface, UINT uFlags, LPSTR szIconFile,
    UINT cchMax, int *piIndex, UINT *pwFlags
    );
```

Retrieves the location and index of an icon.

- Returns the NOERROR value if the function returned a valid location or the S_FALSE value if the shell should use a default icon.

pIface
    Address of the **IExtractIcon** interface. In C++, this parameter is implicit.

uFlags
    Flags. This parameter can be zero or these values:

GIL_FORSHELL	The icon is to be displayed in a shell folder.
GIL_OPENICON	The icon is for a folder that is open.

szIconFile and *cchMax*

Address and size of the buffer that receives the icon location. The icon location is a null-terminated string that typically specifies the name of an icon file.

piIndex

Address of an integer that receives the icon index.

pwFlags

Address of an unsigned integer that receives zero or more of these values:

GIL_DONTCACHE	The shell should use the **Extract** member function rather than look up the icon in its internal cache.
GIL_NOTFILENAME	The location is not a filename. Instead, it is an extension-specific string that identifies the icon. The caller must use the **Extract** member function to retrieve the icon image no matter what flags are returned.
GIL_PERCLASS	All file objects of this class have the same icon.
GIL_PERINSTANCE	Each file object of this class has its own icon.
GIL_SIMULATEDOC	The shell should create a document icon using the specified icon.

IExtractIcon::Extract

```
HRESULT IExtractIcon::Extract(
    LPEXTRACTICON pIface, LPCSTR pszFile, UINT nIconIndex,
    HICON *phiconLarge, HICON *phiconSmall, UINT nIconSize
    );
```

Extracts an icon image from the specified location.

- Returns the NOERROR value if the function extracted the icon or the S_FALSE value if the calling application should extract the icon by calling the **ExtractIcon** function.

pIface

Address of the **IExtractIcon** interface. In C++, this parameter is implicit.

pszFile

Address of a null-terminated string specifying the icon location. This parameter must be a string returned by the **GetIconLocation** member function.

nIconIndex

Icon index.

phiconLarge and *phiconSmall*

Addresses of variables that receive the handles of the large and small icons, respectively.

nIconSize
> Value specifying the size, in pixels, of the large icon required. The size specified can be the width or height. The width of an icon always equals its height.

The icon location and index are the same values as returned by the **IExtractIcon::GetIconLocation** member function. If this function returns S_FALSE, these values must specify an icon filename and index. If this function does not return S_FALSE, the calling application should make no assumptions about the meanings of the *pszFile* and *nIconIndex* parameters.

IShellPropSheetExt

Designates an interface that allows a property sheet handler to add or replace pages in the property sheet for a file object. The **IShellPropSheetExt** interface has the following member functions.

AddPages   Adds one or more pages to a property sheet for a file object.

ReplacePage   Replaces a page in a property sheet for a Control Panel object.

Like all OLE interfaces, **IShellPropSheetExt** also includes the **QueryInterface**, **AddRef**, and **Release** member functions.

IShellPropSheetExt::AddPages

```
HRESULT AddPages(IShellPropSheetExt FAR * pProp,
    LPFNADDPROPSHEETPAGE lpfnAddPage, LPARAM lParam);
```

Adds one or more pages to a property sheet that the shell displays for a file object. When it is about to display the property sheet, the shell calls the **AddPages** member function of each property sheet handler registered to the file type.

- Returns the NOERROR value if successful or an OLE-defined error value otherwise.

pProp
> Address of the **IShellPropSheetExt** interface. In C++, this parameter is implicit.

lpfnAddPage

Address of a callback function that the property sheet handler calls to add a page to the property sheet. The function takes a property sheet handle returned by the **CreatePropertySheetPage** function and the *lParam* parameter passed to the **AddPages** member function. For more information about the callback function, see the description of the **AddPropSheetPageProc** function in the documentation included with the Win32 Software Development Kit (SDK).

lParam

Parameter to pass to the function pointed to by *lpfnAddPage*.

For each page it needs to add to a property sheet, a property sheet handler fills a **PROPSHEETPAGE** structure, calls **CreatePropertySheetPage**, and then calls the function pointed to by *lpfnAddPage*.

IShellPropSheetExt::ReplacePage

```
HRESULT ReplacePage(IShellPropSheetExt FAR * pProp,
    UINT uPageID, LPFNADDPROPSHEETPAGE lpfnReplacePage, LPARAM lParam);
```

Replaces a page in a property sheet for a Control Panel object.

- Returns the NOERROR value if successful or an OLE-defined error value otherwise.

pProp

Address of the **IShellPropSheetExt** interface. In C++, this parameter is implicit.

uPageID

Identifier of the page to replace. The values for this parameter for Control Panels can be found in CPLEXT.H.

lpfnReplacePage

Address of a function that the property sheet handler calls to replace a page to the property sheet. The function takes a property sheet handle returned by the **CreatePropertySheetPage** function and the *lParam* parameter passed to the **ReplacePage** member function.

lParam

Parameter to pass to the function pointed to by *lpfnReplacePage*.

To replace a page, a property sheet handler fills a **PROPSHEETPAGE** structure, calls **CreatePropertySheetPage**, and then calls the function pointed to by *lpfnReplacePage*.

IShellExtInit

Designates an interface used to initialize a property sheet extension, context menu extension, or drag and drop handler. The **IShellExtInit** interface has the following member functions.

Initialize   Initializes the shell extension.

Like all OLE interfaces, **IShellExtInit** also includes the **QueryInterface**, **AddRef**, and **Release** member functions.

IShellExtInit::Initialize

```
HRESULT IShellExtInit::Initialize(
    LPSHELLEXTINIT pIface, LPCITEMIDLIST pidlFolder,
    LPDATAOBJECT lpdobj, HKEY hkeyProgID
    );
```

Initializes a property sheet extension, context menu extension, or drag and drop handler.

- Returns the NOERROR value if successful or an OLE-defined error value otherwise.

pIface
    Address of the **IShellExtInit** interface. In C++, this parameter is implicit.

pidlFolder
    Address of an **ITEMIDLIST** structure (item identifier list) that uniquely identifies a folder. This parameter is NULL for property sheet extensions and context menu extensions. For nondefault drag and drop menu extensions, this parameter must specify the target folder.

lpdobj
    Address of an **IDataObject** interface object that can be used to retrieve the objects being acted upon.

hkeyProgID
    Registry key for the file object or folder type.

This is the first member function that the shell calls (besides **AddRef**, **Release**, and **QueryInterface**) after it creates an instance of a property sheet extension, context menu extension, or drag and drop handler.

The meanings of some parameters depend on the extension type. For drag and drop handlers, the item identifier list specifies the destination folder (the drop target), the **IDataObject** interface identifies the items being dropped, and the registry key specifies the file class of the destination folder (typically, it is "Directory").

For property sheet extensions and context menu extensions, the item identifier list specifies the folder that contains the selected file objects, the **IDataObject** interface identifies the selected file objects, and the registry key specifies the file class of the file object that has the focus.

Structures

The following structures are used with shell extensions.

CMINVOKECOMMANDINFO

```
typedef struct _CMInvokeCommandInfo {
    DWORD cbSize;          // sizeof(CMINVOKECOMMANDINFO)
    DWORD fMask;           // see below
    HWND hwnd;             // see below
    LPCSTR lpVerb;         // see below
    LPCSTR lpParameters;   // see below
    LPCSTR lpDirectory;    // see below
    int nShow;             // see below
    DWORD dwHotKey;        // see below
    HANDLE hIcon;          // see below
} CMINVOKECOMMANDINFO, *LPCMINVOKECOMMANDINFO;
```

Contains information about a context menu command.

fMask

Value specifying zero or more of these flags:

CMIC_MASK_HOTKEY	Specifies that **dwHotKey** is valid.
CMIC_MASK_ICON	Specifies that **hIcon** is valid.
CMIC_MASK_FLAG_NO_UI	Prevents the system from displaying user inter-face elements (for example, error messages) while carrying out a command.

hwnd

Handle of the window that owned the context menu, such as the desktop, Windows 95 Explorer, or the tray. An extension might specify this handle as the owner window of any message boxes or dialog boxes that it displays.

lpVerb

32-bit value containing zero in the high-order word and the menu-identifier offset of the command to carry out in the low-order word. The shell specifies this value (using the **MAKEINTRESOURCE** macro) when the user chooses a menu command.

If the high-order word is not zero, this member is the address of a null-terminated string specifying the language-independent name of the command to carry out. This member is typically a string when a command is being activated by an application. The system provides predefined constant values for the following command strings:

Value	String
CMDSTR_NEWFOLDER	"NewFolder"
CMDSTR_VIEWDETAIL	"ViewDetails"
CMDSTR_VIEWLIST	"ViewList"

lpParameters

Optional parameters. This member is always NULL for menu items inserted by a shell extension.

lpDirectory

Optional working directory name. This member is always NULL for menu items inserted by a shell extension.

nShow

Flag to pass to the **ShowWindow** function if the command displays a window or starts an application.

dwHotKey

Optional hot key to assign any application activated by the command. If **fMask** does not specify CMIC_MASK_HOTKEY, this member is ignored. A shell extension should ignore this member.

hIcon

Icon to use for any application activated by the command. If **fMask** does not specify CMIC_MASK_ICON, this member is ignored. A shell extension should ignore this member.

The address of this structure is passed to the **IContextMenu::InvokeCommand** member function.

ITEMIDLIST

```
typedef struct _ITEMIDLIST { // idl
    SHITEMID mkid;  // list of item identifers
} ITEMIDLIST, * LPITEMIDLIST;
typedef const ITEMIDLIST * LPCITEMIDLIST;
```

Contains a list of item identifiers. For more information, see Article 11, "Shell's Namespace."

SHITEMID

```
typedef struct _SHITEMID {        // mkid
    USHORT cb;        // size of identifier, including cb itself
    BYTE   abID[1]; // variable-length item identifier
} SHITEMID, * LPSHITEMID;
typedef const SHITEMID  * LPCSHITEMID;
```

Defines an item identifier.

ARTICLE 13

Application Desktop Toolbars

About Application Desktop Toolbars

An *application desktop toolbar* (also called an appbar) is a window that is similar to the Microsoft® Windows® 95 taskbar. It is anchored to an edge of the screen, and it typically contains buttons that give the user quick access to other applications and windows. The system prevents other applications from using the desktop area occupied by an appbar. Any number of appbars can exist on the desktop at any given time.

Windows provides an application programming interface (API) that lets you take advantage of appbar services provided by the system. The services help ensure that application-defined appbars operate smoothly with one another and with the taskbar. The system maintains information about each appbar and sends the appbars messages to notify them about events that can effect their size, position, and appearance.

Sending Messages

An application uses a special set of messages, called appbar messages, to add or remove an appbar, set an appbar's size and position, and retrieve information about the size, position, and state of the taskbar. To send an appbar message, an application must use the **SHAppBarMessage** function. The function's parameters include a message identifier, such as ABM_NEW, and the address of an **APPBARDATA** structure. The structure members contain information that the system needs to process the given message.

For any appbar message, the system uses some members of the **APPBARDATA** structure and ignores the others. However, because the system always uses the **cbSize** and **hWnd** members, an application must fill these members for every appbar message. The **cbSize** member specifies the size of the structure, and the **hWnd** member is the handle of the appbar's window.

Some appbar messages request information from the system. When processing these messages, the system copies the requested information into the **APPBARDATA** structure.

Registration

The system keeps an internal list of appbars and maintains information about each bar in the list. The system uses the information to manage appbars, perform services for them, and send them notification messages.

An application must register an appbar (that is, add it to the internal list) before it can receive appbar services from the system. To register an appbar, an application sends the ABM_NEW message. The accompanying **APPBARDATA** structure includes the handle of the appbar's window and an application-defined message identifier. The system uses the message identifier to send notification messages to the window procedure of the appbar window. For more information about appbar notification messages, see "Notification Messages" later in this article.

An application unregisters an appbar by sending the ABM_REMOVE message. Unregistering an appbar removes it from the system's internal list of appbars. The system no longer sends notification messages to the appbar nor prevents other applications from using the screen area occupied by the appbar. An application should always send ABM_REMOVE before destroying an appbar.

Size and Position

An application should set an appbar's size and position so that it does not interfere with any other appbars or the taskbar. Every appbar must be anchored to a particular edge of the screen, and multiple appbars can be anchored to an edge. However, if an appbar is anchored to the same edge as the taskbar, the system ensures that the taskbar is always on the outermost edge.

To set the size and position of an appbar, an application first proposes a screen edge and bounding rectangle for the appbar by sending the ABM_QUERYPOS message. The system determines whether any part of the screen area within the proposed rectangle is occupied by the taskbar or another appbar, adjusts the rectangle (if necessary), and returns the adjusted rectangle to the application.

Next, the application sends the ABM_SETPOS message to set the new bounding rectangle for the appbar. Again, the system may adjust the rectangle before returning it to the application. For this reason, the application should use the adjusted rectangle returned by ABM_SETPOS to set the final size and position. The application can use the **MoveWindow** function to move the appbar into position.

By using a two-step process to set the size and position, the system allows the application to provide intermediate feedback to the user during the move operation. For example, if the user drags an appbar, the application might display a shaded rectangle indicating the new position before the appbar actually moves.

An application should set the size and position of its appbar after registering it and whenever the appbar receives the ABN_POSCHANGED notification message. An appbar receives this notification message whenever a change occurs in the taskbar's size, position, or visibility state and whenever another appbar on the same side of the screen is resized, added, or removed.

An appbar should send the ABM_ACTIVATE message whenever it receives the WM_ACTIVATE message. Similarly, whenever an appbar receives a WM_WINDOWPOSCHANGED message, it should send a corresponding ABM_WINDOWPOSCHANGED message. Sending these messages ensures that the system properly sets the Z order of any autohide appbars on the same edge.

Autohide Application Desktop Toolbars

An autohide appbar is one that is normally hidden, but becomes visible when the user moves the mouse cursor to the screen edge that the appbar is associated with. The appbar hides itself again when the user moves the mouse cursor out of the bar's bounding rectangle.

Although the system allows a number of different appbars at any given time, it allows only one autohide appbar at a time for each screen edge on a first come, first served basis. The system automatically maintains the Z order of an autohide appbar (within its Z order group only).

An application uses the ABM_SETAUTOHIDEBAR message to register or unregister an autohide appbar. The message specifies the edge for the appbar and a flag that specifies whether the appbar is to be registered or unregistered. The message fails if an autohide appbar is being registered, but one is already associated with the specified edge. An application can retrieve the handle of the autohide appbar associated with an edge by sending the ABM_GETAUTOHIDEBAR message.

An autohide appbar does not need to register as a normal appbar; that is, it does not need to be registered by sending the ABM_NEW message. An appbar that is not registered by ABM_NEW overlaps any appbars anchored on the same edge of the screen.

Notification Messages

The system sends messages to notify an appbar about events that can effect its position and appearance. The messages are sent in the context of an application-defined message. The application specifies the identifier of the message when it sends the ABM_NEW message to register the appbar. The notification code is in the *wParam* parameter of the application-defined message.

An appbar receives the ABN_POSCHANGED notification message when the taskbar's size, position, or visibility state changes, when another appbar is added to the same edge of the screen, or when another appbar on the same edge of the screen is resized or removed. An appbar should respond to this notification message by sending ABM_QUERYPOS and ABM_SETPOS messages. If an appbar's position has changed, it should call the **MoveWindow** function to move itself to the new position.

The system sends the ABN_STATECHANGE notification message whenever the taskbar's autohide or always-on-top state has changed—that is, when the user checks or unchecks the "Always on top" or "Auto hide" check box on the taskbar's property sheet. An appbar can use this notification message to set its state to conform to that of the taskbar, if desired.

When a full-screen application is started or when the last full-screen application is closed, an appbar receives the ABN_FULLSCREENAPP notification message. The *lParam* parameter indicates whether the full-screen application is opening or closing. If it is opening, the appbar must drop to the bottom of the Z order. The appbar should restore its Z order position when the last full-screen application has closed.

An appbar receives the ABN_WINDOWARRANGE notification message when the user selects the Cascade, Tile Horizontally, or Tile Vertically command from the task bar's context menu. The system sends the message two times, before rearranging the windows (*lParam* is TRUE) and after arranging the windows (*lParam* is FALSE).

An appbar can use ABN_WINDOWARRANGE messages to exclude itself from the cascade or tile operation. To exclude itself, the appbar should hide itself when *lParam* is TRUE and show itself when *lParam* is FALSE. If an appbar hides itself in response to this message, it does not need to send the ABM_QUERYPOS and ABM_SETPOS messages in response to the cascade or tile operation.

Using Application Desktop Toolbars

This section includes examples that demonstrate how to perform the following tasks:

- Register an application desktop toolbar (appbar).
- Set its size and position.
- Process the notification messages that the system sends to a registered appbar.

Registering an Application Desktop Toolbar

An application must register an appbar by sending the ABM_NEW message. Registering an appbar adds it to the system's internal list and provides the system with a message identifier to use to send notification messages to the appbar. Before exiting, an application must unregister the appbar by sending the ABM_REMOVE message. Unregistering removes the appbar from the system's internal list and prevents the bar from receiving appbar notification messages.

The function in the following example either registers or unregisters an appbar, depending on the value of a Boolean flag parameter.

```
// RegisterAccessBar - registers or unregisters an appbar.
// Returns TRUE if successful or FALSE otherwise.
// hwndAccessBar - handle of the appbar
// fRegister - register and unregister flag
//
// Global variables
//      g_uSide - screen edge (defaults to ABE_TOP)
//      g_fAppRegistered - flag indicating whether the bar is registered
BOOL RegisterAccessBar(HWND hwndAccessBar, BOOL fRegister)
{
    APPBARDATA abd;

    // Specify the structure size and handle of the appbar.
    abd.cbSize = sizeof(APPBARDATA);
    abd.hWnd = hwndAccessBar;

    if (fRegister) {

        // Provide an identifier for notification messages.
        abd.uCallbackMessage = APPBAR_CALLBACK;
```

```
                    // Register the appbar.
                    if (!SHAppBarMessage(ABM_NEW, &abd))
                        return FALSE;
                    g_uSide = ABE_TOP;         // default edge
                    g_fAppRegistered = TRUE;
                } else {

                    // Unregister the appbar.
                    SHAppBarMessage(ABM_REMOVE, &abd);
                    g_fAppRegistered = FALSE;
                }
                return TRUE;
            }
```

Setting the Size and Position

An application should set an appbar's size and position after registering the appbar,
after the user user moves or sizes the appbar, and whenever the appbar receives the
ABN_POSCHANGED notification message. Before setting the size and position of
the appbar, the application queries the system for an approved bounding rectangle
by sending the ABM_QUERYPOS message. The system returns a bounding rectangle that does not interfere with the taskbar or any other appbar. The system
adjusts the rectangle purely by rectangle subtraction; it makes no effort to preserve
the rectangle's initial size. For this reason, the appbar should readjust the rectangle,
as necessary, after sending ABM_QUERYPOS.

Next, the application passes the bounding rectangle back to the system by using
the ABM_SETPOS message. Then it calls the **MoveWindow** function to move the
appbar into position.

The following example shows how to set an appbar's size and position.

```
// AppBarQuerySetPos - sets the size and position of an appbar.
// uEdge - screen edge to which the appbar is to be anchored
// lprc - current bounding rectangle of the appbar
// pabd - address of APPBARDATA structure with the hWnd and
//     cbSize members filled
void PASCAL AppBarQuerySetPos(UINT uEdge, LPRECT lprc, PAPPBARDATA pabd)
{
    int iHeight = 0;
    int iWidth = 0;

    pabd->rc = *lprc;
    pabd->uEdge = uEdge;
```

```
    // Copy the screen coordinates of the appbar's bounding
    // rectangle into the APPBARDATA structure.
    if ((uEdge == ABE_LEFT) ||
            (uEdge == ABE_RIGHT)) {
        iWidth = pabd->rc.right - pabd->rc.left;
        pabd->rc.top = 0;
        pabd->rc.bottom = GetSystemMetrics(SM_CYSCREEN);
    } else {
        iHeight = pabd->rc.bottom - pabd->rc.top;
        pabd->rc.left = 0;
        pabd->rc.right = GetSystemMetrics(SM_CXSCREEN);
    }

    // Query the system for an approved size and position.
    SHAppBarMessage(ABM_QUERYPOS, pabd);

    // Adjust the rectangle, depending on the edge to which the
    // appbar is anchored.
    switch (uEdge) {
        case ABE_LEFT:
            pabd->rc.right = pabd->rc.left + iWidth;
            break;

        case ABE_RIGHT:
            pabd->rc.left = pabd->rc.right - iWidth;
            break;

        case ABE_TOP:
            pabd->rc.bottom = pabd->rc.top + iHeight;
            break;

        case ABE_BOTTOM:
            pabd->rc.top = pabd->rc.bottom - iHeight;
            break;
    }

    // Pass the final bounding rectangle to the system.
    SHAppBarMessage(ABM_SETPOS, pabd);

    // Move and size the appbar so that it conforms to the
    // bounding rectangle passed to the system.
    MoveWindow(pabd->hWnd, pabd->rc.left, pabd->rc.top,
        pabd->rc.right - pabd->rc.left,
        pabd->rc.bottom - pabd->rc.top, TRUE);
}
```

Processing Notification Messages

An appbar receives a notification message when the state of the task bar changes, when a full screen application starts (or the last one closes), or when an event occurs that can affect the appbar's size and position. The following example shows how to process the various notification messages.

```
// AppBarCallback - processes notification messages sent by the system.
// hwndAccessBar - handle of the appbar
// uNotifyMsg - identifier of the notification message
// lParam - message parameter
void AppBarCallback(HWND hwndAccessBar, UINT uNotifyMsg,
    LPARAM lParam)
{
    APPBARDATA abd;
    UINT uState;

    abd.cbSize = sizeof(abd);
    abd.hWnd = hwndAccessBar;

    switch (uNotifyMsg) {
        case ABN_STATECHANGE:

            // Check to see if the taskbar's always-on-top state has
            // changed and, if it has, change the appbar's state
            // accordingly.
            uState = SHAppBarMessage(ABM_GETSTATE, &abd);
            SetWindowPos(hwndAccessBar,
                (ABS_ALWAYSONTOP & uState) ? HWND_TOPMOST : HWND_BOTTOM,
                0, 0, 0, 0, SWP_NOMOVE | SWP_NOSIZE | SWP_NOACTIVATE);
            break;

        case ABN_FULLSCREENAPP:

            // A full screen application has started, or the last full
            // screen application has closed. Set the appbar's
            // Z order appropriately.
            if (lParam) {
                SetWindowPos(hwndAccessBar,
                    (ABS_ALWAYSONTOP & uState) ?
                                                HWND_TOPMOST : HWND_BOTTOM,
                    0, 0, 0, 0,
                    SWP_NOMOVE | SWP_NOSIZE | SWP_NOACTIVATE);
            } else {
                uState = SHAppBarMessage(ABM_GETSTATE, &abd);
                if (uState & ABS_ALWAYSONTOP)
                    SetWindowPos(hwndAccessBar, HWND_TOPMOST,
                        0, 0, 0, 0,
                        SWP_NOMOVE | SWP_NOSIZE | SWP_NOACTIVATE);
            }
```

```
                case ABN_POSCHANGED:

                    // The taskbar or another appbar has changed its
                    // size or position.
                    AppBarPosChanged(&abd);
                    break;
            }
    }
```

The following function adjusts an appbar's bounding rectangle and then calls the application-defined AppBarQuerySetPos function (included in the previous section) to set the bar's size and position accordingly.

```
// AppBarPosChanged - adjusts the appbar's size and position.
// pabd - address of an APPBARDATA structure that contains information
//      used to adjust the size and position
void PASCAL AppBarPosChanged(PAPPBARDATA pabd)
{
    RECT rc;
    RECT rcWindow;
    int iHeight;
    int iWidth;

    rc.top = 0;
    rc.left = 0;
    rc.right = GetSystemMetrics(SM_CXSCREEN);
    rc.bottom = GetSystemMetrics(SM_CYSCREEN);

    GetWindowRect(pabd->hWnd, &rcWindow);
    iHeight = rcWindow.bottom - rcWindow.top;
    iWidth = rcWindow.right - rcWindow.left;

    switch (g_uSide) {
        case ABE_TOP:
            rc.bottom = rc.top + iHeight;
            break;

        case ABE_BOTTOM:
            rc.top = rc.bottom - iHeight;
            break;

        case ABE_LEFT:
            rc.right = rc.left + iWidth;
            break;
```

```
          case ABE_RIGHT:
              rc.left = rc.right - iWidth;
              break;
          }
          AppBarQuerySetPos(g_uSide, &rc, pabd);
      }
```

Reference

The following function, structure, messages, and notification messages are associated with appbars.

Function and Structure

The following function and structure are used with appbars.

SHAppBarMessage

```
WINSHELLAPI UINT APIENTRY SHAppBarMessage(DWORD dwMessage,
    PAPPBARDATA pabd);
```

Sends an appbar message to the system.

- Returns a message-dependent value. For more information, see the documentation for the individual appbar messages.

dwMessage
Identifier of the appbar message to send. This parameter can be one of these values:

ABM_ACTIVATE	Notifies the system that an appbar has been activated.
ABM_GETAUTOHIDEBAR	Retrieves the handle of the autohide appbar associated with a particular edge of the screen.
ABM_GETSTATE	Retrieves the autohide and always-on-top states of the Windows taskbar.
ABM_GETTASKBARPOS	Retrieves the bounding rectangle of the Windows taskbar.
ABM_NEW	Registers a new appbar and specifies the message identifier that the system should use to send notification messages to the appbar.

ABM_QUERYPOS	Requests a size and screen position for an appbar.
ABM_REMOVE	Unregisters an appbar, removing the bar from the system's internal list.
ABM_SETAUTOHIDEBAR	Registers or unregisters an autohide appbar for an edge of the screen.
ABM_SETPOS	Sets the size and screen position of an appbar.
ABM_WINDOWPOSCHANGED	Notifies the system when an appbar's position has changed.

pabd

Address of an **APPBARDATA** structure. The content of the structure depends on the value of *dwMessage*.

APPBARDATA

```
typedef struct _AppBarData { // abd
    DWORD  cbSize;            // sizeof(APPBARDATA)
    HWND   hWnd;             // handle of appbar
    UINT   uCallbackMessage; // see below
    UINT   uEdge;           // see below
    RECT   rc;              // see below
    LPARAM lParam;          // see below
} APPBARDATA, *PAPPBARDATA;
```

Contains information that the system uses to process appbar messages.

uCallbackMessage

Application-defined message identifier. The application uses the specified identifier for notification messages that it sends to the the appbar identified by the **hWnd** member. This member is used when sending the ABM_NEW message.

uEdge

Flag that specifies an edge of the screen. This member can be one of these values:

ABE_BOTTOM	Bottom edge
ABE_LEFT	Left edge
ABE_RIGHT	Right edge
ABE_TOP	Top edge

This member is used when sending the ABM_GETAUTOHIDEBAR, ABM_QUERYPOS, ABM_SETAUTOHIDEBAR, and ABM_SETPOS messages.

rc

 RECT structure that contains the bounding rectangle, in screen coordinates, of an appbar or the Windows taskbar. This member is used when sending the ABM_GETTASKBARPOS, ABM_QUERYPOS, and ABM_SETPOS messages.

lParam

 Message-dependent value. This member is used with the message ABM_SETAUTOHIDEBAR.

This structure is used with the **SHAppBarMessage** function.

Messages

An application sends appbar messages to register an appbar with the system; to set an appbar's size, position, and state; to retrieve information about the Windows taskbar; and so on. To send an appbar message, an application uses the **SHAppBarMessage** function. There are the following appbar messages.

ABM_ACTIVATE

```
SHAppBarMessage(ABM_ACTIVATE, pabd);
```

Notifies the system that an appbar has been activated. An appbar should call this message in response to the WM_ACTIVATE message.

- Always returns TRUE.

pabd

 Address of an **APPBARDATA** structure that identifies the appbar to activate. You must specify the **cbSize** and **hWnd** members when sending this message; all other members are ignored.

This message is ignored if the **hWnd** member of the structure pointed to by *pabd* identifies an autohide appbar. The system automatically sets the Z order for an autohide appbar.

ABM_GETAUTOHIDEBAR

```
hwndAutoHide = (HWND) SHAppBarMessage(ABM_GETAUTOHIDEBAR, pabd);
```

Retrieves the handle of the autohide appbar associated with an edge of the screen.

- Returns the handle of the autohide appbar. The return value is NULL if an error occurs or if no autohide appbar is associated with the given edge.

pabd
> Address of an **APPBARDATA** structure that specifies the screen edge. You must specify the **cbSize**, **hWnd**, and **uEdge** members when sending this message; all other members are ignored.

ABM_GETSTATE

```
fuState = (UINT) SHAppBarMessage(ABM_GETSTATE, pabd);
```

Retrieves the autohide and always-on-top states of the Windows taskbar.

- Returns zero if the taskbar is not in the autohide or always-on-top state. Otherwise, the return value is one or both of these values:

  ABS_ALWAYSONTOP   The taskbar is in the always-on-top state.

  ABS_AUTOHIDE   The taskbar is in the autohide state.

pabd
> Address of an **APPBARDATA** structure. You must specify the **cbSize** and **hWnd** members when sending this message; all other members are ignored.

ABM_GETTASKBARPOS

```
fResult = (BOOL) SHAppBarMessage(ABM_GETTASKBARPOS, pabd);
```

Retrieves the bounding rectangle of the Windows taskbar.

- Returns TRUE if successful or FALSE otherwise.

pabd
> Address of an **APPBARDATA** structure whose **rc** member receives the bounding rectangle, in screen coordinates, of the taskbar. You must specify the **cbSize** and **hWnd** members when sending this message; all other members are ignored.

ABM_NEW

```
fRegistered = (BOOL) SHAppBarMessage(ABM_NEW, pabd);
```

Registers a new appbar and specifies the message identifier that the system should use to send notification messages to the appbar. An appbar should send this message before sending any other appbar messages.

- Returns TRUE if successful or FALSE if an error occurs or the appbar is already registered.

pabd
> Address of an **APPBARDATA** structure that contains the new appbar's window handle and message identifier. You must specify the **cbSize**, **hWnd**, and **uCallbackMessage** members when sending this message; all other members are ignored.

ABM_QUERYPOS

```
SHAppBarMessage(ABM_QUERYPOS, pabd);
```

Requests a size and screen position for an appbar. The message proposes a screen edge and a bounding rectangle for the appbar. The system adjusts the bounding rectangle so that the appbar does not interfere with the Windows taskbar or any other appbars. An appbar should send this message before sending the ABM_SETPOS message.

- Always returns TRUE.

pabd
> Address of an **APPBARDATA** structure. The **uEdge** member specifies a screen edge, and the **rc** member contains the proposed bounding rectangle. When the **SHAppBarMessage** function returns, **rc** contains the approved bounding rectangle. You must specify the **cbSize**, **hWnd**, **uEdge**, and **rc** members when sending this message; all other members are ignored.

ABM_REMOVE

```
SHAppBarMessage(ABM_REMOVE, pabd);
```

Unregisters an appbar, removing it from the system's internal list. The system no longer sends notification messages to the appbar nor prevents other applications from using the screen area occupied by the appbar.

- Always returns TRUE.

pabd
> Address of an **APPBARDATA** structure that contains the handle of the appbar to unregister. You must specify the **cbSize** and **hWnd** members when sending this message; all other members are ignored.

This message causes the system to send the ABN_POSCHANGED notification message to all appbars.

ABM_SETAUTOHIDEBAR

```
fSussess = (BOOL) SHAppBarMessage(ABM_SETAUTOHIDEBAR, pabd);
```

Registers or unregisters an autohide appbar for an edge of the screen. The system allows only one autohide appbar for each edge on a first come, first served basis.

- Returns TRUE if successful or FALSE if an error occurs or an autohide appbar is already registered for the given edge.

pabd
> Address of an **APPBARDATA** structure. The **uEdge** member specifies the screen edge. The **lParam** parameter is set to TRUE to register the appbar or FALSE to unregister it. You must specify the **cbSize**, **hWnd**, **uEdge**, and **lParam** members when sending this message; all other members are ignored.

ABM_SETPOS

```
SHAppBarMessage(ABM_SETPOS, pabd);
```

Sets the size and screen position for an appbar. The message specifies a screen edge and a bounding rectangle for the appbar. The system may adjust the bounding rectangle so that the appbar does not interfere with the Windows taskbar or any other appbars.

- Always returns TRUE.

pabd

Address of an **APPBARDATA** structure. The **uEdge** member specifies a screen edge, and the **rc** member contains the bounding rectangle. When the **SHAppBarMessage** function returns, **rc** contains the approved bounding rectangle. You must specify the **cbSize**, **hWnd**, **uEdge**, and **rc** members when sending this message; all other members are ignored.

This message causes the system to send the ABN_POSCHANGED notification message to all appbars.

ABM_WINDOWPOSCHANGED

```
SHAppBarMessage(ABM_WINDOWPOSCHANGED, pabd);
```

Notifies the system when an appbar's position has changed. An appbar should call this message in response to the WM_WINDOWPOSCHANGED message.

- Always returns TRUE.

pabd

Address of an **APPBARDATA** structure that identifies the appbar to activate. You must specify the **cbSize** and **hWnd** members when sending this message; all other members are ignored.

This message is ignored if the **hWnd** member of the structure pointed to by *pabd* identifies an autohide appbar.

Notification Messages

The system sends notification messages to an appbar to notify it about events. The message identifier for the notification messages is an application-defined value that is set when the application sends the ABM_NEW message. The system sends the following notification messages to an appbar.

ABN_FULLSCREENAPP

```
ABN_FULLSCREENAPP
fOpen = (BOOL) lParam;
```

Notifies an appbar when a full-screen application is opening or closing. When a full-screen application is opening, an appbar must drop to the bottom of the Z order. When it is closing, the appbar should restore its Z order position. This notification message is sent in the form of an application-defined message that is set by the ABM_NEW message.

- No return value.

fOpen
    Flag specifying whether a full-screen application is opening or closing. This parameter is TRUE if it is opening or FALSE if it is closing.

ABN_POSCHANGED

Notifies an appbar when an event has occurred that may effect the appbar's size and position. Events include changes in the taskbar's size, position, and visibility state as well as the addition, removal, or resizing of another appbar on the same side of the screen.

- No return value.

An appbar should respond to this notification message by sending the messages ABM_QUERYPOS and ABM_SETPOS. If its position has changed, the appbar should call the **MoveWindow** function to move itself to the new position.

ABN_STATECHANGE

```
ABN_STATECHANGE
```

Notifies an appbar that the taskbar's autohide or always-on-top state has changed; that is, the user has checked or unchecked the "Always on top" or "Auto hide" check box on the taskbar's property sheet. An appbar can use this notification message to set its state to conform to that of the taskbar, if desired.

- No return value.

ABN_WINDOWARRANGE

```
ABN_WINDOWARRANGE
fBeginning = (BOOL) lParam;
```

Notifies an appbar that the user has selected the Cascade, Tile Horizontally, or Tile Vertically command from the taskbar's context menu.

- No return value.

fBeginning
> Flag specifying whether the cascade or tile operation is beginning. This parameter is TRUE if the operation is beginning and the windows have not yet been moved. It is FALSE if the operation has completed.

The system sends this notification message twice—first with *lParam* set to TRUE and then with *lParam* set to FALSE. The first notification is sent before the windows are cascaded or tiled, and the second is sent after the cascade or tile operation has occurred.

ARTICLE 14

Shell Links

About Shell Links

A *shell link* is a data object that contains information used to access another object in the shell's namespace—that is, any object visible through Microsoft® Windows® 95 Explorer. The objects that can be accessed through shell links include files, folders, disk drives, and printers. A shell link allows the user or an application to access an object from anywhere in the namespace; the user or application does not need to know the current name and location of the object.

The user creates a shell link by choosing the Create Shortcut command from an object's context menu. The system automatically creates an icon for the shell link by combining the object's icon with a small arrow (known as the system-defined link overlay icon) that appears in the lower left corner of the icon. A shell link that has an icon is called a *shortcut*; however, the terms shell link and shortcut are often used interchangeably. Typically, the user creates shortcuts to gain quick access to objects stored in subfolders or in shared folders on other machines. For example, a user can create a shortcut to a Microsoft Word document located in a subfolder and place the shortcut icon on the desktop. Later the user can start Word and open the document simply by double-clicking the shortcut icon. If the document is later moved or renamed, the system takes steps to update the shortcut the next time the user selects it.

Applications can also create and use shell links and shortcuts. For example, a word processing application might create a shell link to implement a list of the most recently used documents. An application creates a shell link by using the **IShellLink** interface to create a shell link object and uses the **IPersistFile** or **IPersistStream** interface to store the object in a file or stream. This article describes the **IShellLink** interface and explains how to use the interface to create and resolve shell links from within a Windows-based application.

Because the design of shell links is based on the OLE Component Object Model (COM), you should be familiar with the basic concepts of COM and OLE programming before reading this article. For more information, see the OLE documentation included in the Microsoft Windows Software Development Kit (SDK).

Link Resolution

If a user creates a shortcut to an object and the name or location of the object is subsequently changed, the system automatically takes steps to update, or *resolve*, the shortcut the next time the user selects it. However, if an application creates a shell link and stores it in a stream, the system does not automatically attempt to resolve the link. The application must resolve the link by calling the **IShellLink::Resolve** member function.

When a shell link is created, the system saves information about the link. When resolving a link (either automatically or if **IShellLink::Resolve** is called), the system first retrieves the path associated with the shell link by using a pointer to the shell link's identifier list. (For more information about the identifier list, see "Item Identifiers and Identifier Lists" later in this article.) The system searches for the associated object in that path and, if it finds the object, resolves the link. If the system cannot find the object, it looks in the same directory for an object that has the same file creation time and attributes, but a different name. This type of search resolves a link to an object that has been renamed.

If the system still cannot find the object, it searches the subdirectories of the current directory, looking recursively though the directory tree for a match with either the same name or creation time. If the system does not find a match after that, it displays a dialog box prompting the user for a location. An application can suppress the dialog box by specifying the SLR_NO_UI value in a call to **IShellLink::Resolve**.

Initialization of the Component Object Library

Before an application can create and resolve shortcuts, it must initialize the component object library by calling the **CoInitialize** function. Each call to **CoInitialize** requires a corresponding call to the **CoUninitialize** function, which an application should call when it terminates. The call to **CoUninitialize** ensures that the application does not terminate until it has received all of its pending messages.

Location-Independent Names

The system provides location-independent names for shell links to objects stored in shared folders. If the object is stored locally, the system provides the local path and filename for the object. If the object is stored remotely, the system provides the Universal Naming Convention (UNC) network resource name for the object. Because the system provides location-independent names, a shell link can serve as a universal name for a file that can be transferred to other machines.

Link Files

When the user creates a shortcut to an object by choosing the Create Shortcut command from the object's context menu, Windows stores the information it needs to access the object in a link file—that is, a binary file that has the .LNK filename extension. A link file contains the following information:

- The location (path) of the object referenced by the shortcut (called the "corresponding object" in this article).
- The working directory of the corresponding object.
- The list of arguments that the system passes to the corresponding object when the **IContextMenu::InvokeCommand** member function is activated for the shortcut.
- The show (SW_) command used to set the initial show state of the corresponding object.
- The location (path and index) of the shortcut's icon.
- The shortcut's description string.
- The hot key for the shortcut.

When a link file is deleted, the corresponding object is not affected.

If you create a shortcut to another shortcut, the system simply copies the link file rather than creating a new link file. This is important to remember if you are assuming that the shortcuts will remain independent of each other.

An application can register a filename extension as a "shortcut" file type. If a file has a filename extension that has been registered as a shortcut file type, the system automatically adds the system-defined link overlay icon (a small arrow) to the file's icon. To register a filename extension as a shortcut file type, you must add the "IsShortcut" value to the registry description of the filename extension. Note that the shell must be restarted for the overlay icon to take effect.

```
HKEY_CLASSES_ROOT
 .xyz    (Default) = "XYZApp"
 .
 .
 .
 XYZApp  IsShortcut = ""
```

Location in the Namespace

A shortcut can exist on the desktop or anywhere in the shell's namespace. Similarly, the object that is associated with the shortcut can also exist anywhere in the shell's namespace. An application can use the **IShellLink::SetPath** member function to set the path and filename for the associated object, and the **IShellLink::GetPath** member function to retrieve the current path and filename for the object.

Working Directory

The working directory is the directory where the corresponding object of a shortcut loads or stores files when the user does not identify a specific directory. A link file contains the name of the working directory for the corresponding object. An application can set the name of the working directory for the corresponding object by using the **IShellLink::SetWorkingDirectory** member function and can retrieve the name of the current working directory for the corresponding object by using the **IShellLink::GetWorkingDirectory** member function.

Command-Line Arguments

A link file contains command-line arguments that the shell passes to the corresponding object when the user selects the link. An application can set the command-line arguments for a shortcut by using the **IShellLink::SetArguments** member function. It is useful to set command-line arguments when the corresponding application, such as a linker or compiler, takes special flags as arguments. An application can retrieve the command-line arguments from a shortcut by using the **IShellLink::GetArguments** member function.

Show Command

When the user double-clicks a shortcut, the system starts the application associated with the corresponding object and sets the initial show state of the application based on the show command specified by the shortcut. The show command can be any of the SW_ values included in the description of the **ShowWindow** function. An application can set the show command for a shortcut by using the **IShellLink::SetShowCmd** member function and can retrieve the current show command by using the **IShellLink::GetShowCmd** member function.

Shortcut Icon and Description

Like other shell objects, a shortcut has an icon. The user accesses the object associated with a shortcut by double-clicking the shortcut's icon. When the system creates an icon for a shortcut, it uses the bitmap of the corresponding object and adds the system-defined link overlay icon (a small arrow) to the lower left corner. An application can set the location (path and index) of a shortcut's icon by using the **IShellLink::SetIconLocation** member function. An application can retrieve the current location (path and index) of a shortcut's icon by using the **IShellLink::GetIconLocation** member function.

A shortcut also has a description, which is a brief string that appears below the shell link icon. By default, the description consists of the words "Shortcut to" followed by the filename of the object. The user can edit the description string by selecting it and entering a new string. An application can set the description string by using the **IShellLink::SetDescription** member function and can retrieve the current description string by using the **IShellLink::GetDescription** member function.

Hot Key

A shortcut object can have a hot key associated with it. A hot key allows the user to use the shortcut by pressing a particular combination of keys. An application can set the hot key for a shortcut by using the **IShellLink::SetHotkey** member function and can retrieve the current hot key for a shortcut by using the **IShellLink::GetHotkey** member function.

Item Identifiers and Identifier Lists

The shell uses object identifiers within the shell namespace. All of the objects that are visible in the shell (files, directories, servers, workgroups, and so on) have an identifier that is unique among the objects within the parent folder. These identifiers are called item identifiers, and they have the **SHITEMID** data type as defined in the SHLOBJ.H header file. An item identifier is a variable-length byte stream that contains information for identifying an object within a folder. Only the creator of an item identifier knows the content and format of the identifier. The only part of an item identifier that the shell uses is the first two bytes, which specify the size of the identifier.

Each parent folder has its own item identifier that identifies it within its own parent folder. Thus, any shell object can be uniquely identified by a list of item identifiers. A parent folder keeps a list of identifiers for the items in the folder. The list has the **ITEMIDLIST** data type. Item identifier lists are allocated by the shell and may be passed across shell interfaces, such as **IShellFolder**. It is important to remember that each identifier in an item identifier list is only meaningful within the context of the parent folder.

An application can use the **IShellLink::SetIDList** member function to set a shortcut's item identifier list. This function is useful when setting a shortcut to an object that is not a file, such as a printer or disk drive. An application can retrieve a shortcut's item identifier list by using the **IShellLink::GetIDList** member function.

Using Shell Links

This section contains examples that demonstrate how to create and resolve shortcuts from within a Windows-based application.

Creating a Shortcut to a File

The CreateLink function in the following example creates a shortcut. The parameters include a pointer to the name of the file to link to, a pointer to the name of the shortcut that you are creating, and a pointer to the description of the link. The description consists of the string, "Shortcut to *filename*," where *filename* is the name of the file to link to.

Because CreateLink calls the **CoCreateInstance** function, it is assumed that the **CoInitialize** function has already been called. CreateLink uses the **IPersistFile** interface to save the shortcut and the **IShellLink** interface to store the filename and description.

```
// CreateLink - uses the shell's IShellLink and IPersistFile interfaces
//   to create and store a shortcut to the specified object.
// Returns the result of calling the member functions of the interfaces.
// lpszPathObj - address of a buffer containing the path of the object
// lpszPathLink - address of a buffer containing the path where the
//   shell link is to be stored
// lpszDesc - address of a buffer containing the description of the
//   shell link

HRESULT CreateLink(LPCSTR lpszPathObj,
    LPSTR lpszPathLink, LPSTR lpszDesc)
{
    HRESULT hres;
    IShellLink* psl;

    // Get a pointer to the IShellLink interface.
    hres = CoCreateInstance(&CLSID_ShellLink, NULL,
        CLSCTX_INPROC_SERVER, &IID_IShellLink, &psl);
    if (SUCCEEDED(hres)) {
        IPersistFile* ppf;
```

```
        // Set the path to the shortcut target, and add the
        // description.
        psl->lpVtbl->SetPath(psl, lpszPathObj);
        psl->lpVtbl->SetDescription(psl, lpszDesc);

        // Query IShellLink for the IPersistFile interface for saving the
        // shortcut in persistent storage.
        hres = psl->lpVtbl->QueryInterface(psl, &IID_IPersistFile,
            &ppf);

        if (SUCCEEDED(hres)) {
            WORD wsz[MAX_PATH];

            // Ensure that the string is ANSI.
            MultiByteToWideChar(CP_ACP, 0, lpszPathLink, -1,
                wsz, MAX_PATH);

            // Save the link by calling IPersistFile::Save.
            hres = ppf->lpVtbl->Save(ppf, wsz, TRUE);
            ppf->lpVtbl->Release(ppf);
        }
        psl->lpVtbl->Release(psl);
    }
    return hres;
}
```

Resolving A Shortcut

An application may need to access and manipulate a shortcut that was created previously. This operation is referred to as "resolving" the shortcut.

The application-defined ResolveIt function in the following example resolves a shortcut. Its parameters include a window handle, a pointer to the path of the shortcut, and the address of a buffer that receives the new path to the object. The window handle identifies the parent window for any message boxes that the shell may need to display. For example, the shell can display a message box if the link is on unshared media, if network problems occur, if the user needs to insert a floppy disk, and so on.

The ResolveIt function calls the **CoCreateInstance** function and assumes that the **CoInitialize** function has already been called. Note that ResolveIt needs to use the **IPersistFile** interface to store the link information. **IPersistFile** is implemented by the **IShellLink** object. The link information must be loaded before the path information is retrieved, which happens later in the example. Failing to load the link information causes the calls to the **IShellLink::GetPath** and **IShellLink::GetDescription** member functions to fail.

```
HRESULT ResolveIt(HWND hwnd, LPCSTR lpszLinkFile, LPSTR lpszPath)
{
    HRESULT hres;
    IShellLink* psl;
    char szGotPath[MAX_PATH];
    char szDescription[MAX_PATH];
    WIN32_FIND_DATA wfd;

    *lpszPath = 0; // assume failure

    // Get a pointer to the IShellLink interface.
    hres = CoCreateInstance(&CLSID_ShellLink, NULL,
            CLSCTX_INPROC_SERVER, &IID_IShellLink, &psl);
    if (SUCCEEDED(hres)) {
        IPersistFile* ppf;

        // Get a pointer to the IPersistFile interface.
        hres = psl->lpVtbl->QueryInterface(psl, &IID_IPersistFile,
            &ppf);
        if (SUCCEEDED(hres)) {
            WORD wsz[MAX_PATH];

            // Ensure that the string is Unicode.
            MultiByteToWideChar(CP_ACP, 0, lpszLinkFile, -1, wsz,
                MAX_PATH);

            // Load the shortcut.
            hres = ppf->lpVtbl->Load(ppf, wsz, STGM_READ);
            if (SUCCEEDED(hres)) {

                // Resolve the link.
                hres = psl->lpVtbl->Resolve(psl, hwnd, SLR_ANY_MATCH);
                if (SUCCEEDED(hres)) {

                    // Get the path to the link target.
                    hres = psl->lpVtbl->GetPath(psl, szGotPath,
                        MAX_PATH, (WIN32_FIND_DATA *)&wfd,
                        SLGP_SHORTPATH );
                    if (!SUCCEEDED(hres)
                        HandleErr(hres); // application-defined function
```

```
                            // Get the description of the target.
                            hres = psl->lpVtbl->GetDescription(psl,
                                szDescription, MAX_PATH);
                            if (!SUCCEEDED(hres))
                                HandleErr(hres);
                            lstrcpy(lpszPath, szGotPath);
                    }
                }
            // Release the pointer to the IPersistFile interface.
            ppf->lpVtbl->Release(ppf);
            }
        // Release the pointer to the IShellLink interface.
        psl->lpVtbl->Release(psl);
        }
        return hres;
}
```

Creating a Link to a Nonfile Object

Creating a shortcut to a nonfile object, such as a printer, is similar to creating a shortcut to a file. The main difference is that, rather than setting the path to the file, you must set the identifier list to the printer. To set the identifier list, you must call the **IShellLink::SetIDList** member function, specifying the address of an identifier list.

Each object within the shell's namespace has an item identifier, a variable-length byte stream containing information that identifies the object within its folder. The shell often concatenates item identifiers into null-terminated lists consisting of any number of item identifiers.

In general, if you need to set a shortcut to an item that does not have a filename, such as a printer, you will already have a pointer to the object's **IShellFolder** interface. The **IShellFolder** interface is used to create namespace extensions.

Once you have the class identifier for the **IShellFolder** interface, you can call the **CoCreateInstance** function to get the address of the interface. Then you can call the interface to enumerate the objects in the folder and retrieve the address of the item identifier for the object that you are searching for. Finally, you can use the address in a call to the **IShellLink::SetIDList** member function to create a shortcut to the object.

Reference

The following interface is used with shell links.

Interfaces and Member Functions

IShellLink

Designates an interface that allows an application to create and resolve shell links.
The **IShellLink** interface has the following member functions.

GetArguments	Retrieves the command-line arguments associated with a shell link object.
GetDescription	Retrieves the description string for a shell link object.
GetHotkey	Retrieves the hot key for a shell link object.
GetIconLocation	Retrieves the location (path and index) of the icon for a shell link object.
GetIDList	Retrieves the list of item identifiers for a shell link object.
GetPath	Retrieves the path and filename of a shell link object.
GetShowCmd	Retrieves the show (SW_) command for a shell link object.
GetWorkingDirectory	Retrieves the name of the working directory for a shell link object.
Resolve	Resolves a shell link by searching for the shell link object and updating the shell link path and its list of identifiers, if necessary.
SetArguments	Sets the command-line arguments associated with a shell link object.
SetDescription	Sets the description string for a shell link object.
SetHotkey	Sets the hot key for a shell link object.
SetIconLocation	Sets the location (path and index) of the icon for a shell link object.
SetIDList	Sets the list of item identifiers for a shell link object.
SetPath	Sets the path and filename of a shell link object.
SetRelativePath	Sets the relative path for a shell link object.
SetShowCmd	Sets the show (SW_) command for a shell link object.
SetWorkingDirectory	Sets the name of the working directory for a shell link object.

Like all OLE interfaces, **IShellLink** also includes the **QueryInterface**, **AddRef**,
and **Release** member functions.

IShellLink::GetArguments

```
HRESULT GetArguments(ISHELLLINK FAR * pShlLnk,
    LPSTR pszArgs, int cchMaxPath);
```

Retrieves the command-line arguments associated with a shell link object.

- Returns the NOERROR value if successful or an OLE-defined error value otherwise.

pShlLnk
    Address of the **IShellLink** interface. In C++, this parameter is implicit.

pszArgs
    Address of a buffer that receives the command-line arguments.

cchMaxPath
    Maximum number of characters to copy to the buffer pointed to by *pszArgs*.

IShellLink::GetDescription

```
RESULT GetDescription(ISHELLLINK FAR * pShlLnk,
    LPSTR pszName, int cchMaxName);
```

Retrieves the description string for a shell link object.

- Returns the NOERROR value if successful or an OLE-defined error value otherwise.

pShlLnk
    Address of the **IShellLink** interface. In C++, this parameter is implicit.

pszName
    Address of a buffer that receives the description string.

cchMaxName
    Maximum number of characters to copy to the buffer pointed to by *pszName*.

IShellLink::GetHotkey

```
HRESULT GetHotkey(ISHELLLINK FAR * pShlLnk,
    WORD *pwHotkey);
```

Retrieves the hot key for a shell link object.

- Returns the NOERROR value if successful or an OLE-defined error value otherwise.

pShlLnk
> Address of the **IShellLink** interface. In C++, this parameter is implicit.

pwHotkey
> Address of the hot key. The virtual-key code is in the low-order byte, and the modifier flags are in the high-order byte. The modifier flags can be a combination of these values:

HOTKEYF_ALT	ALT key
HOTKEYF_CONTROL	CTRL key
HOTKEYF_EXT	Extended key
HOTKEYF_SHIFT	SHIFT key

IShellLink::GetIconLocation

```
HRESULT GetIconLocation(ISHELLLINK FAR * pShlLnk,
    LPSTR pszIconPath, int cchIconPath, int *piIcon);
```

Retrieves the location (path and index) of the icon for a shell link object.

- Returns the NOERROR value if successful or an OLE-defined error value otherwise.

pShlLnk
> Address of the **IShellLink** interface. In C++, this parameter is implicit.

pszIconPath
> Address of a buffer that receives the path of the file containing the icon.

cchIconPath
> Maximum number of characters to copy to the buffer pointed to by *pszIconPath*.

piIcon
> Address of a value that receives the index of the icon.

IShellLink::GetIDList

```
HRESULT GetIDList(ISHELLLINK FAR * pShlLnk,
    LPITEMIDLIST * ppidl);
```

Retrieves the list of item identifiers for a shell link object.

- Returns the NOERROR value if successful or an OLE-defined error value otherwise.

pShlLnk

Address of the **IShellLink** interface. In C++, this parameter is implicit.

ppidl

Address of a pointer to a list of item identifiers.

IShellLink::GetPath

```
HRESULT GetPath(IShellLink FAR * pShlLnk,
    LPSTR pszFile, int cchMaxPath, WIN32_FIND_DATA *pfd, DWORD fFlags);
```

Retrieves the path and filename of a shell link object.

- Returns the NOERROR value if successful or an OLE-defined error value otherwise.

pShlLnk

Address of the **IShellLink** interface. In C++, this parameter is implicit.

pszFile

Address of a buffer that receives the path and filename of the shell link object.

cchMaxPath

Maximum number of bytes to copy to the buffer pointed to by *pszFile*.

pfd

Address of a **WIN32_FIND_DATA** structure that contains information about the shell link object.

fFlags

Flags that specify the type of path information to retrieve. This parameter can be a combination of these values:

SLGP_SHORTPATH	Retrieves the standard short (8.3) filename.
SLGP_UNCPRIORITY	Retrieves the Universal Naming Convention (UNC) path for the file.

IShellLink::GetShowCmd

```
HRESULT GetShowCmd(ISHELLLINK FAR * pShlLnk,
    int *piShowCmd);
```

Retrieves the show command for a shell link object.

- Returns the NOERROR value if successful or an OLE-defined error value otherwise.

pShlLnk

Address of the **IShellLink** interface. In C++, this parameter is implicit.

piShowCmd

Address of the show command. For a list of show commands, see the description of the **ShowWindow** function.

IShellLink::GetWorkingDirectory

```
HRESULT GetWorkingDirectory(ISHELLLINK FAR * pShlLnk,
    LPSTR pszDir, int cchMaxPath);
```

Retrieves the name of the working directory for a shell link object.

- Returns the NOERROR value if successful or an OLE-defined error value otherwise.

pShlLnk

Address of the **IShellLink** interface. In C++, this parameter is implicit.

pszDir

Address of a buffer that receives the name of the working directory.

cchMaxPath

Maximum number of characters to copy to the buffer pointed to by *pszDir*.
The name of the working directory is truncated if it is longer than the maximum specified by this parameter.

IShellLink::Resolve

```
HRESULT Resolve(ISHELLLINK FAR * pShlLnk, HWND hwnd,
    DWORD fFlags);
```

Resolves a shell link. The system searches for the shell link object and, if necessary, updates the shell link path and its list of identifiers.

- Returns the NOERROR value if successful or an OLE-defined error value otherwise.

pShlLnk

Address of the **IShellLink** interface. In C++, this parameter is implicit.

hwnd

Handle of a window that the shell uses as the parent window for a dialog box. The shell displays the dialog box if it needs to prompt the user for more information while resolving a shell link.

fFlags

Action flags. This parameter can be a combination of these values:

SLR_ANY_MATCH	Resolves the link, displaying a dialog box if the system needs information from the user.
SLR_NO_UI	Prevents the shell from displaying a dialog box if it cannot resolve the shell link. When this value is specified, the high-order word of this parameter specifies a time-out duration, in milliseconds. The function returns if the link cannot be resolved within the time-out duration. If the high-order word is set to zero, the time-out duration defaults to 3000 milliseconds (3 seconds).
SLR_UPDATE	Directs the shell to update the path to the link and the list of identifiers if the link object has been changed. If this value is used, it is not necessary to call the **IPersistFile::IsDirty** member function to determine whether the link object has changed.

When this member function is called, the system retrieves the path associated with the current link object and searches for the object in that path. If the system finds the object, it resolves the link. If the system cannot find the object, it looks in the same directory for an object with the same file creation time and attributes, but with a different name. This type of search resolves a link to an object that has been renamed.

If the system still cannot find the link object, it searches the subdirectories of the current directory. It does a recursive search of the directory tree looking for a match with either the same name or creation time. If it does not find a match after that, the shell displays a dialog box prompting the user for a location. An application can suppress the dialog box by specifying the SLR_NO_UI value in a call to this member function.

IShellLink::SetArguments

```
HRESULT SetArguments(ISHELLLINK FAR * pShlLnk,
    LPCSTR pszArgs);
```

Sets the command-line arguments for a shell link object.

- Returns the NOERROR value if successful or an OLE-defined error value otherwise.

pShlLnk
> Address of the **IShellLink** interface. In C++, this parameter is implicit.

pszArgs
> Address of a buffer that contains the new command-line arguments.

This member function is useful when creating a link to an application that takes special flags as arguments, such as a compiler.

IShellLink::SetDescription

```
HRESULT SetDescription(ISHELLLINK FAR * pShlLnk,
    LPCSTR pszName);
```

Sets the description for a shell link object. The description can be any application-defined string.

- Returns the NOERROR value if successful or an OLE-defined error value otherwise.

pShlLnk
> Address of the **IShellLink** interface. In C++, this parameter is implicit.

pszName
> Address of a buffer containing the new description string.

IShellLink::SetHotkey

```
HRESULT SetHotkey(ISHELLLINK FAR * pShlLnk,
    WORD wHotkey);
```

Sets a hot key for a shell link object.

- Returns the NOERROR value if successful or an OLE-defined error value otherwise.

pShlLnk
> Address of the **IShellLink** interface. In C++, this parameter is implicit.

wHotkey
> Hot key. The virtual-key code is in the low-order byte, and the modifier flags are in the high-order byte. The modifier flags can be a combination of the values specified in the description of the **IShellLink::GetHotkey** member function.

Setting a hot key allows the user to activate the object by pressing a particular combination of keys.

IShellLink::SetIconLocation

```
HRESULT SetIconLocation(ISHELLLINK FAR * pShlLnk,
    LPCSTR pszIconPath, int iIcon);
```

Sets the location (path and index) of the icon for a shell link object.

- Returns the NOERROR value if successful or an OLE-defined error value otherwise.

pShlLnk
Address of the **IShellLink** interface. In C++, this parameter is implicit.

pszIconPath
Address of a buffer that contains the path of the file containing the icon.

iIcon
Index of the icon.

IShellLink::SetIDList

```
HRESULT SetIDList(ISHELLLINK FAR * pShlLnk,
    LPCITEMIDLIST pidl);
```

Sets the list of item identifiers for a shell link object.

- Returns the NOERROR value if successful or an OLE-defined error value otherwise.

pShlLnk
Address of the **IShellLink** interface. In C++, this parameter is implicit.

pidl
Address of a list of item identifiers.

This member function is useful when an application needs to set a shell link to an object that is not a file, such as a Control Panel application, a printer, or another computer.

IShellLink::SetPath

```
HRESULT SetPath(ISHELLLINK FAR * pShlLnk,
    LPCSTR pszFile);
```

Sets the path and filename of a shell link object.

- Returns the NOERROR value if successful or an OLE-defined error value otherwise.

pShlLnk
> Address of the **IShellLink** interface. In C++, this parameter is implicit.

pszFile
> Address of a buffer that contains the new path.

IShellLink::SetRelativePath

```
HRESULT SetRelativePath(ISHELLLINK FAR * pShlLnk,
    LPCSTR pszPathRel, DWORD dwReserved);
```

Sets the relative path to the shell link object.

- Returns the NOERROR value if successful or an OLE-defined error value otherwise.

pShlLnk
> Address of the **IShellLink** interface. In C++, this parameter is implicit.

pszPathRel
> Address of a buffer that contains the new relative path.

dwReserved
> Reserved; must be zero.

This function sets the relative path for a shortcut that is saved in a stream using the **IPersistStream** interface, or to override the default relative path tracking for a shortcut. When a shortcut is saved in a file, the system keeps track of the relative path between the file in which the shortcut is saved and the target of the shortcut (if there is one). If the link is broken, the system uses **SetRelativePath** to attempt to restore the link. For a shortcut is saved in a stream instead of a file, **SetRelativePath** allows an application to set the link between the shortcut and its target.

IShellLink::SetShowCmd

```
HRESULT SetShowCmd(ISHELLLINK FAR * pShlLnk,
    int iShowCmd);
```

Sets the show command for a shell link object. The show command sets the initial show state of the window.

- Returns the NOERROR value if successful or an OLE-defined error value otherwise.

pShlLnk
Address of the **IShellLink** interface. In C++, this parameter is implicit.

iShowCmd
Show command. For a list of the show commands, see the description of the **ShowWindow** function.

IShellLink::SetWorkingDirectory

```
HRESULT SetWorkingDirectory(ISHELLLINK FAR * pShlLnk,
    LPCSTR pszDir);
```

Sets the name of the working directory for a shell link object.

- Returns the NOERROR value if successful or an OLE-defined error value otherwise.

pShlLnk
Address of the **IShellLink** interface. In C++, this parameter is implicit.

pszDir
Address of a buffer that contains the name of the new working directory.

The working directory must be set only if the object requires it to be set. For example, if an application creates a shell link to a Microsoft Word document that uses a template residing in a different directory, the application would use this method to set the working directory.

ARTICLE 15

Taskbar Notification Area

About the Taskbar Notification Area

The Microsoft® Windows® 95 taskbar includes a notification area where an
application can put an icon to indicate the status of an operation or to notify the
user about an event. For example, an application might put a printer icon in the
taskbar to show that a print job is under way. The notification area is at the right
end of the taskbar (if the taskbar has a horizontal orientation) or at the bottom
(if the taskbar has a vertical orientation).

An icon in the taskbar can have a tooltip control associated with it. In addition, the
system can send notification messages to the application whenever a mouse event
occurs in the bounding rectangle of the icon.

Sending Messages

An application sends messages to add, modify, or delete taskbar icons. To send
a message, an application must use the **Shell_NotifyIcon** function. The function
parameters include the identifier of the message to send, such as NIM_ADD, and
the address of an **NOTIFYICONDATA** structure. The structure members contain
information that the system needs to process the given message.

To add an icon to the taskbar's notification area, send the NIM_ADD message.
The **NOTIFYICONDATA** structure that accompanies the message specifies the
handle of the icon, the identifier of the icon, and, if desired, the tooltip text for the
icon. If the taskbar has the Show Clock option selected, the system places the new
icon to the immediate left of the clock. Otherwise, the icon appears on the right side
or at the bottom of the toolbar. Any existing icons are shifted to the left to make
room for the new icon.

An application can delete an icon from the taskbar notification area by sending the
NIM_DELETE message. It can send the NIM_MODIFY message to modify the
information that the system maintains for a taskbar icon, including its icon handle,
tooltip text, and callback message identifier.

Receiving Callback Messages

Each taskbar icon can have an application-defined callback message associated with it. If an icon has a callback message, the system will send the message to the application whenever a mouse event occurs within the icon. In this way, the system can notify an application whenever the user clicks or double-clicks the icon, or moves the mouse cursor into the icon's bounding rectangle.

An application defines an icon's callback message when it adds the icon to the taskbar. The **uCallbackMessage** member of the **NOTIFYICONDATA** structure included with the NIM_ADD message specifies the identifier of the callback message. When a mouse event occurs, the system sends the callback message to the window identified by the **hWnd** member. The message's *lParam* parameter is the identifier of the mouse message that the system generated as a result of the mouse event. For example, when the mouse cursor moves into a taskbar icon, the *lParam* parameter of the resulting callback message contains the WM_MOUSEMOVE identifier. The *wParam* parameter contains the identifier of the taskbar icon in which the mouse event occurred.

Using the Taskbar Notification Area

This section includes examples that demonstrate how to add icons to the taskbar notification area and how to process callback messages for taskbar icons.

Adding and Deleting Icons

You add an icon to the taskbar notification area by filling a **NOTIFYICONDATA** structure and then sending the structure by means of the NIM_ADD message. The structure members must specify the handle of the window that is adding the icon and the icon identifier and icon handle. You can also specify tooltip text for the icon, and, if you need to receive mouse messages for the icon, the identifier of the callback message that the system should use to send the message to your window.

The function in the following example demonstrates how to add an icon to the taskbar.

```
// MyTaskBarAddIcon - adds an icon to the taskbar notification area.
// Returns TRUE if successful or FALSE otherwise.
// hwnd - handle of the window to receive callback messages
// uID - identifier of the icon
// hicon - handle of the icon to add
// lpszTip - tooltip text
```

```
BOOL MyTaskBarAddIcon(HWND hwnd, UINT uID, HICON hicon, LPSTR lpszTip)
{
    BOOL res;
    NOTIFYICONDATA tnid;

    tnid.cbSize = sizeof(NOTIFYICONDATA);
    tnid.hWnd = hwnd;
    tnid.uID = uID;
    tnid.uFlags = NIF_MESSAGE | NIF_ICON | NIF_TIP;
    tnid.uCallbackMessage = MYWM_NOTIFYICON;
    tnid.hIcon = hicon;
    if (lpszTip)
        lstrcpyn(tnid.szTip, lpszTip, sizeof(tnid.szTip));
    else
        tnid.szTip[0] = '\0';

    res = Shell_NotifyIcon(NIM_ADD, &tnid);

    if (hicon)
        DestroyIcon(hicon);

    return res;
}
```

To delete an icon from the taskbar notification area, you must fill a
NOTIFYICONDATA structure and send it to the system in the context of an
NIM_DELETE message. When deleting a taskbar icon, you need to specify only
the **cbSize**, **hWnd**, and **uID** members, as the following example shows.

```
// MyTaskBarDeleteIcon - deletes an icon from the taskbar
//      notification area.
// Returns TRUE if successful or FALSE otherwise.
// hwnd - handle of the window that added the icon
// uID - identifier of the icon to delete
BOOL MyTaskBarDeleteIcon(HWND hwnd, UINT uID)
{
    BOOL res;
    NOTIFYICONDATA tnid;

    tnid.cbSize = sizeof(NOTIFYICONDATA);
    tnid.hWnd = hwnd;
    tnid.uID = uID;

    res = Shell_NotifyIcon(NIM_DELETE, &tnid);
    return res;
}
```

Receiving Mouse Events

If you specify a callback message for a taskbar icon, the system sends the message to your application whenever a mouse event occurs in the icon's bounding rectangle. The *wParam* parameter specifies the identifier of the taskbar icon, and the *lParam* parameter specifies the mouse message that the system generated as a result of the mouse event.

The function in the following example is from an application that adds a battery icon and a printer icon to the taskbar. The application calls the function when it receives a callback message. The function determines if the user has clicked one of the icons and, if a click has occurred, calls an application-defined function to display status information.

```
// On_MYWM_NOTIFYICON - processes callback messages for taskbar icons.
// wParam - first message parameter of the callback message
// lParam - second message parameter of the callback message
void On_MYWM_NOTIFYICON(WPARAM wParam, LPARAM lParam)
{
    UINT uID;
    UINT uMouseMsg;

    uID = (UINT) wParam;
    uMouseMsg = (UINT) lParam;

    if (uMouseMsg == WM_LBUTTONDOWN) {
        switch (uID) {
            case IDI_MYBATTERYICON:

                // The user clicked the battery icon. Display the
                // battery status.
                ShowBatteryStatus();
                break;

            case IDI_MYPRINTERICON:

                // The user clicked the printer icon. Display the
                // status of the print job.
                ShowJobStatus();
                break;

            default:
                break;
        }
    }
    return;
}
```

Reference

The following function, structure, and messages are associated with the taskbar notification area.

Function and Structure

The following function and structure are used with the taskbar notification area.

Shell_NotifyIcon

```
WINSHELLAPI BOOL WINAPI Shell_NotifyIcon(DWORD dwMessage,
    PNOTIFYICONDATA pnid);
```

Sends a message to the system to add, modify, or delete a taskbar icon.

- Returns TRUE if successful or FALSE otherwise.

dwMessage
Identifier of the message to send. This parameter can be one of these values:

NIM_ADD	Adds an icon to the taskbar notification area.
NIM_DELETE	Deletes an icon from the taskbar notification area.
NIM_MODIFY	Modifies an icon in the taskbar notification area.

pnid
Address of an **NOTIFYICONDATA** structure. The content of the structure depends on the value of *dwMessage*.

NOTIFYICONDATA

```
typedef struct _NOTIFYICONDATA { // nid
    DWORD cbSize;             // sizeof(NOTIFYICONDATA)
    HWND hWnd;                // see below
    UINT uID;                 // see below
    UINT uFlags;              // see below
    UINT uCallbackMessage;    // see below
    HICON hIcon;              // see below
    char szTip[64];           // see below
} NOTIFYICONDATA, *PNOTIFYICONDATA;
```

Contains information that the system needs to process taskbar notification area messages.

hWnd

Handle of the window that receives notification messages associated with an icon in the taskbar notification area.

uID

Application-defined identifier of the taskbar icon.

uFlags

Array of flags that indicate which of the other structure members contain valid data. This member can be a combination of these values:

NIF_ICON	The **hIcon** member is valid.
NIF_MESSAGE	The **uCallbackMessage** member is valid.
NIF_TIP	The **szTip** member is valid.

uCallbackMessage

Application-defined message identifier. The system uses the specified identifier for notification messages that it sends to the window identified by **hWnd** whenever a mouse event occurs in the bounding rectangle of the icon.

hIcon

Handle of the taskbar icon to add, modify, or delete.

szTip

Tooltip text to display for the taskbar icon.

Messages

An application sends messages to add, modify, or delete taskbar icons. To send a message, an application uses the **Shell_NotifyIcon** function. The following messages are associated with taskbar icons.

NIM_ADD

```
fAdded = Shell_NotifyIcon(NIM_ADD, pnid);
```

Adds an icon to the taskbar notification area.

- Returns TRUE if successful or FALSE otherwise.

pnid

Address of an **NOTIFYICONDATA** structure that contains information about the icon to add.

NIM_DELETE

```
fDeleted = Shell_NotifyIcon(NIM_DELETE, pnid);
```

Deletes an icon from the taskbar notification area.

- Returns TRUE if successful or FALSE otherwise.

pnid
> Address of an **NOTIFYICONDATA** structure that contains information about the taskbar icon to delete.

NIM_MODIFY

```
fModified = Shell_NotifyIcon(NIM_MODIFY, pnid);
```

Changes the icon, tooltip text, or notification message identifier for an icon in the taskbar notification area.

- Returns TRUE if successful or FALSE otherwise.

pnid
> Address of an **NOTIFYICONDATA** structure that contains the information used to change the icon, tooltip text, or notification message identifier for the taskbar icon.

P A R T   4

Using Windows 95 Features

ARTICLE 16

File Viewers

About File Viewers

The Microsoft® Windows® 95 shell allows the user to browse the information in the file system and on the network. The Quick View feature of the shell allows the user to quickly view the contents of a file without having to run the full application that created it and without even the presence of the application. To view the file contents, the user selects a file and chooses the Quick View command from the context menu of the selection (or from the File menu). The following illustration shows the context menu.

In response to the user choosing the Quick View command, the shell activates a file-specific viewer for the selected file. The shell uses the extension of the file to determine which viewer to activate. A file viewer associates itself with file classes and filename extensions in the system registry.

A file viewer is an OLE component object (not a compound document object) implemented inside a 32-bit in-process server dynamic-link library (DLL), which is associated, in turn, with the file viewer's class identifier. A file viewer provides the user interface for viewing a file. Menu items, a toolbar, and a status bar are standard parts of the file viewer interface. A file viewer can optionally add other functionality for further shell integration.

A file viewer object, which is separate from the class factory object in the in-process server, uses the standard OLE **IPersistFile** interface as well as the **IFileViewer** interface described later in this article. The shell does not interact directly with file viewer objects. Instead, the shell starts an instance of a small program called Quick View (QUIKVIEW.EXE) for each file to be viewed. Each instance of Quick View defines a process for a file viewer, giving the viewer its own message queue. Although Quick View is a Windows executable file, it is not a complete Windows-based application. It associates a path with a file viewer, creates an instance of the file viewer object, and instructs the file viewer to load and display the file.

Because a file viewer is an OLE component object, additional interfaces and functionality can be added in future versions of Windows to support new features. For example, a file viewer can act as an OLE container application and can perform in-place activation of embedded objects inside the file being viewed. A file viewer can let the user make a selection in a document and copy the selection to the clipboard or use the selection in a drag and drop operation. However, such functionality is entirely up to the developer of the file viewer. This article describes the basic functionality that a file viewer must provide and discusses user interface guidelines that all developers of file viewers should follow.

Adding or Replacing File Viewers

The File Viewer interfaces allow you to add file viewers to Windows 95. For example, you may need to add a file viewer that supports a new file format or provides additional functionality. To understand how to add a file viewer to Windows 95, it is important first to understand how the default file viewers work.

The shell calls the Quick View program to display a file. Quick View manages the file viewing process and presents error messages for error conditions returned by the display engines—a collection of DLLs that draws the viewer window and displays the file. Windows 95 includes display engines for word processing documents, spreadsheets, databases, vector graphics, and raster graphics. File parser DLLs are associated with a particular display engine and are specific to a type or class of files. For example, spreadsheet and database files are associated with the spreadsheet or database display engine. These DLLs are typically between 25K and 75K in size and do all the low-level parsing of the files to be viewed.

There are two methods to add file viewing functionality to Windows 95. First, a particular file parser DLL may be added to the system. The advantage of this method is that file parsers are relatively straightforward to write and debug. The disadvantage is that the limitations built into the default display engines (such as no printing and no cut, copy, and paste operations) remain even when a new file parsing DLL is used. For more information about the interface between the file parsers and the display engines, see Article 17, "File Parsers."

The second method of including file viewing functionality in Windows 95 is to add one or more DLLs that work directly with Quick View. The interaction between QUIKVIEW.EXE and the display engines is the subject of this article. An example of one of these file viewing systems for ASCII files is found in the Samples subdirectory of the Microsoft® Win32® Software Development Kit (SDK). The main advantage of this method is that the code you write can support whatever file viewing functionality you wish to provide. This may be particularly important if your file format does not display well with one of the four default display engines. For example, an accounting package might have this problem. The main disadvantage of this method is that writing for the Quick View interface requires more development and testing effort.

The remainder of this article discusses the interaction between QUIKVIEW.EXE and the display engines. The discussion is split into three sections. The first section describes the entries in the registry necessary to support associations between a pathname and a file viewer. The second section describes how the shell starts Quick View and outlines the steps Quick View performs to locate an appropriate file viewer and activate it. The last section describes the structure and implementation of a file viewer OLE component, including the recommended user interface features.

The file viewing technology used by the Quick View feature in Windows 95 was developed jointly by Microsoft Corporation and Systems Compatibility Corporation.

File Viewer Registration

During installation, a file viewer should ensure that entries exist in the registry that accurately associate a file with the class identifier of the file viewer's in-process server DLL. The file viewer's installation program may merge the contents of a registration (.REG) file into the registry. A file viewer can register itself for more than one file type if it can handle multiple file formats. If a file type has more than one registered file viewer, the shell activates the most recently registered viewer for the file type when the user chooses the Quick View command.

Determining File Types

The Quick View program attempts a simple association using the filename extension. If there is no filename extension or if there are no file viewers registered for the filename extension, Quick View calls each registered file viewer to see if any of them recognize the file. If more than one file viewer is registered for the same filename extension, Quick View calls each file viewer starting with the last one in the list. If Quick View cannot find a file viewer that can read the file, the Quick View operation fails and Quick View displays the following message.

```
There are no viewers registered for this type of file. Would you like to
try the default viewer?
```

The default viewer displays a hexadecimal dump using the word processing engine.

For more information, see "Quick View Program" later in this article.

Structure of Registry Entries

The following registry structure is required for Quick View to associate a class identifier or filename extension with the class identifier of a file viewer.

```
HKEY_CLASSES_ROOT
    \QuickView
        \<extension> = <human-readable document type>
            \{<CLSID>} = <human-readable viewer name>
            \{<CLSID>} = <human-readable viewer name>
            \{<CLSID>} = <human-readable viewer name>

        ...[More extension entries for additional file types]
            ...

    \CLSID
        \{<CLSID>} = <human-readable viewer name>
            \InprocServer32 = <full path to file viewer DLL>
                            = ThreadingModel = "Apartment"

        ...[More class IDs for file viewers and other object servers]
```

A description of the registry entries follows.

Entry	Description
HKEY_CLASSES_ROOT	Root of the registry.
QuickView	Top-level key under which associations are stored.
CLSID	16-byte OLE class identifier spelled out in hexadecimal digits in the form of 12345678-1234-1234-1234-1234567890AB with the hyphens included. All class identifiers are surrounded by curly braces when stored in the registry.
human-readable document type	String describing the file type associated with the class identifier or filename extension that can be displayed to the user. A file viewer can change the type when it is installed so that the name always reflects the preferred viewer. For example, this string might be "Windows Write Document."
human-readable viewer name	String that describes the vendor of the file viewer, as it might be displayed in an About box, such as "Company ABC Write Document Viewer."
<extension>	Three-character filename extension with the period, as is consistent with the standard 8.3 filename format—for example, .WRI.

CLSID and **InprocServer32** are standard OLE (32-bit) subkey names. The "ThreadingModel = Apartment" entry is required for file viewers. The apartment threading model, which is new for OLE in Windows 95 and Microsoft® Windows NT™ version 3.51, allows the **OleInitialize** and **CoInitialize** functions to be called from multiple threads.

The **QuickView** key can have any number of filename extension subkeys, each representing a registered file type. Each filename extension subkey can have one or more class identifier subkeys, each representing a registered file viewer object. The most recently registered file viewer appears first in the list of class identifier subkeys, and it is the first one found when Quick View enumerates the registered file viewers.

Note The file viewer class identifier should always differ from the file type class identifier because the application that created the file may already be using the class identifier to identify the application as a compound document server.

Each class identifier stored under the filename extension subkeys must correspond to an entry of the same class identifier stored under the top-level key called **CLSID**. This is the standard location for storing information for OLE object servers. For file viewers, there must be an **InprocServer32** subkey under the file viewer's class identifier key. The value of the **InprocServer32** subkey is the full path to the file viewer DLL. You should store the full path and not depend on the DLL being in the path of the Windows 95 environment. **InprocServer32** is a standard OLE subkey where the path to a component object server is stored. Using this subkey allows the Quick View program to use standard OLE member functions to access and create objects from file viewer servers.

Registering a File Viewer

This section shows how to register a hypothetical file viewer for "AcmeWord Document" files with the .AWD filename extension. The file viewer is implemented in an in-process server DLL called ACMEWRDV.DLL. The DLL has this class identifier: 00021116-0000-0000-C000-000000000046. The program that installs the file viewer creates the following registry entries.

```
HKEY_CLASSES_ROOT
    \QuickView
        \.AWD = AcmeWord Document
            \{00021117-0000-0000-C000-000000000046} = AcmeWord Document
                                                               Viewer
    \CLSID
        \{00021117-0000-0000-C000-000000000046} = AcmeWord Document
                                                           Viewer
            \InprocServer32 = c:\acmeword\acmewrdv.dll
                            = ThreadingModel = "Apartment"
```

The .REG file, which is an ASCII text file, contains these entries. (Note that wrapped lines are indented on the second line.)

```
HKEY_CLASSES_ROOT\QuickView\.AWD = AcmeWord Document
HKEY_CLASSES_ROOT\QuickView\.AWD \{00021117-0000-0000-C000-
    000000000046} = AcmeWord Document Viewer
HKEY_CLASSES_ROOT\CLSID\{00021117-0000-0000-C000-000000000046} =
    AcmeWord Document Viewer
HKEY_CLASSES_ROOT\CLSID\{00021117-0000-0000-C000-000000000046}
    \InprocServer32 = c:\acmeword\acmewrdv.dll
                    = ThreadingModel = "Apartment"
```

The Quick View program uses these registry entries to associate a path with the class identifier of a file viewer's in-process server DLL.

Quick View Program

The Quick View program (QUIKVIEW.EXE) acts on behalf of the shell to locate and activate a file viewer for a given path. There is a one to one correspondence between each running instance of Quick View and each file being displayed in a file viewer. Each instance of Quick View defines a process for a file viewer, giving the file viewer its own message queue. Quick View turns over execution of the process to the file viewer until the file viewer shuts down.

Quick View Execution and Error Conditions

The lifetime of each instance of the Quick View program consists of the following steps:

1. When the user chooses the Quick View or Print command, the shell starts an instance of QUIKVIEW.EXE for each selected file (by using the Win32 **CreateProcess** or **WinExec** function). The shell may specify a show command, and Quick View passes the command to the file viewer. The command-line argument that the shell passes to Quick View has the following options.

Option	Meaning
-f:*pathname*	Path of the file to view or print. Universal Naming Convention (UNC) filenames are allowed. If this option is not specified, Quick View terminates without displaying any messages.
-v	File to be opened for viewing in the file viewer. If this option is specified, Quick View ignores all of the options described below. This is the default option in the absence of both **-v** and **-p**.
-d	Quick View and the file viewer to suppress all user interface (UI) elements if **-p** is also specified. Quick View suppresses any error messages, and the file viewer should not display any dialog boxes for printing. Quick View ignores this option in the absence of **-p**.
-p	File to be opened for printing. If **-v** is also present, Quick View ignores this option.
-&:*pathname*	Printer driver to use to print the file. Quick View ignores this option in the absence of **-p**. If **-p** is present but **-&** is not, Quick View instructs the file viewer to use the default printer driver.

2. Quick View starts and checks for a path on the command line. If there is no path, the user has attempted to start Quick View by itself and the program immediately terminates without displaying any messages.

3. Quick View parses the filename extension from the path given in the **-f** option. If no filename extension is given, Quick View proceeds to stage E1 (error condition 1). Otherwise, Quick View uses the following procedure to find a file viewer class identifier associated with the given filename extension.

   a. Quick View attempts to open the **HKEY_CLASS_ROOT\QuickView** *extension* key, where *extension* is parsed from the path.

      i.   If the filename extension maps to a type such as the following one, **HKEY_CLASS_ROOT***extension* = *typename*, and there is a registry entry with the form **HKEY_CLASS_ROOT***typename***\QuickView = ***, Quick View looks for file viewer class identifiers under the key **HKEY_CLASS_ROOT\QuickView***. If a key with the **HKEY_CLASS_ROOT*\QuickView = *** form exists, the system attempts to use all the viewers listed under the "*" section.

      ii. Otherwise, Quick View begins enumerating the file viewer class identi-fiers under the **HKEY_CLASS_ROOT\QuickView***extension* key. If the enumeration fails (that is, there is nothing in the registry to enumerate), Quick View closes the key and proceeds to stage E2. Otherwise, Quick View reads the first file viewer class identifier in the enumeration and proceeds to step 4.

   b. If an error occurs in step 4, the enumeration continues until all file viewer class identifiers have been tried. If no file viewer is activated, Quick View closes the key from (a) and proceeds to stage E2.

4. Given a class identifier of a file viewer DLL, Quick View attempts to create an instance of a file viewer object of the given class by using the following procedure.

   a. Quick View calls a function to create an instance of a file viewer object, specifying parameters that include the class identifier and IID_IPersistFile interface identifier. This instructs OLE to load the DLL listed under the class identifier's **InprocServer32** subkey, obtain an instance of the object from the DLL, and return an **IPersistFile** interface pointer to the object. If the instance cannot be created because of lack of memory, Quick View proceeds to stage E4. If it fails for some other reason, Quick View proceeds to stage E3. (Note that, because DLL objects are involved, a call to the **QueryInterface** member function will not fail with the REGDB_IID_NOTREG error value, which typically signals a corrupted registry. That error is generated only when LRPC proxies and stubs are involved.)

b. Given the **IPersistFile** interface pointer *pIPersistFile*, Quick View calls the **Load** member function of the **IPersistFile** interface, specifying the path of the file and the STGM_READ and STGM_SHARE_DENY_NONE values, which instruct the object to open the file for read access. If **Load** fails, Quick View calls the **Release** member function of *pIPersistFile* and proceeds to stage E4 if the error is due to a lack of memory. Otherwise, Quick View proceeds to stage E3.

c. Quick View obtains the file viewer object's **IFileViewer** interface by specifying the IID_IFileViewer interface identifier in a call to the **QueryInterface** member function of *pIPersistFile*. Quick View calls the **Release** member function of *pIPersistFile*, regardless of the outcome. If this call fails due to lack of memory, Quick View proceeds to stage E4. Otherwise, Quick View proceeds to stage E3.

d1. If the **-v** option was present or both the **-v** and **-p** options were absent, Quick View calls the **ShowInitialize** member function of *pIFileViewer*, which instructs the file viewer to load the file and perform any preshowing initialization that is prone to failure (including the creation of windows, the loading of resources, and so on). This is the file viewer's one chance to fail. If it fails, Quick View proceeds to stage E4 if the error is due to lack of memory or to stage E3 otherwise. If **ShowInitialize** succeeds, Quick View calls the **Show** member function of *pIFileViewer*, specifying the show command that was passed to Quick View's **WinMain** function. **Show** does not return until the user closes the file viewer, and it always returns NOERROR in that case. If **Show** is called before **ShowInitialize**, it returns E_UNEXPECTED.

d2. If the **-p** option was present (and the **-v** option was absent), Quick View calls the **PrintTo** member function of *pIFileViewer* specifying the path of the printer driver provided in the **-&** option (or NULL if **-&** was absent) and a value indicating if the **-d** option was present on the command line (UI suppression flag). **PrintTo** does not return until printing is complete or an error occurs. If an error occurs, the file viewer is responsible for notifying the user if the UI suppression flag is FALSE.

e. When **Show** or **PrintTo** returns (whichever was called in steps d1 or d2), Quick View calls the **Release** member function of *pIFileViewer*, regardless of the return value. If the file viewer successfully executed the **IFileViewer::ShowInitialize** member function, the **Release** member function will not fail. **Release** fails only if it is called before **ShowInitialize**. If **PrintTo** fails but the **-d** option was not specified on the command line, Quick View assumes that the file viewer displayed a message to indicate printing failed, and Quick View fails without displaying a message in that case. In any case, Quick View proceeds to step 5.

5. Quick View releases any interface pointers that it may have had and calls **OleUninitialize** (which calls **CoFreeUnusedLibraries** internally). Quick View then terminates normally.

Quick View may encounter these four error conditions (stages E1 through E4) during the lifetime of an instance.

E1. If Quick View fails to associate the path with a file viewer class identifier (using a filename extension), it displays this message.

```
There are no viewers for this type of file. Would you like to
try the default viewers.
```

If the user clicks No, Quick View terminates. If the user clicks Yes, Quick View displays the Searching dialog box, enumerates all registered file viewers (regardless of file type or filename extension), and attempts to have each one load and display the file. Quick View tries each file viewer of a given class identifier once. If no file viewer successfully displays the file, Quick View removes the Searching dialog box and displays this message.

```
Error opening or reading file.
```

When the user closes the dialog box, Quick View terminates.

E2. If Quick View successfully determines the file type but fails to enumerate any file viewers associated with the filename extension, it displays the Searching dialog box and attempts to have each registered viewer display the file, trying each file viewer class identifier once. If that fails, the Quick View removes the Searching dialog box and displays this message.

```
There are no viewers capable of viewing <human-readable document
type> files.
```

When the user closes the dialog box, Quick View terminates.

E3. If Quick View successfully locates an initial file viewer but fails to view the file for any reason other than an out of memory condition, Quick View displays the Searching dialog box and continues enumerating viewers under the class identifier or filename extension key currently in use (steps 3d or 4c). If Quick View tries all viewers registered for the type unsuccessfully, processing continues as in stage E2 by trying all registered viewers regardless of registered type.

E4. If an out of memory condition occurs for one file viewer, it is likely that other viewers will not succeed either. In that case, Quick View displays a dialog box (using MB_ICONEXCLAMATION) with this message.

```
There is not enough memory to view or print <filename>. Quit one
or more files or programs, and then try again.
```

A file viewer can return a number of error values to Quick View. When Quick View receives an error value, it displays an error message. Quick View recognizes the following error values.

FV_E_BADFILE	((HRESULT)0x8534E102L)
FV_E_EMPTYFILE	((HRESULT)0x8534E108L)
FV_E_FILEOPENFAILED	((HRESULT)0x8534E105L)
FV_E_INVALIDID	((HRESULT)0x8534E106L)
FV_E_MISSINGFILES	((HRESULT)0x8534E104L)
FV_E_NOFILTER	((HRESULT)0x8534E100L)
FV_E_NONSUPPORTEDTYPE	((HRESULT)0x8534E101L)
FV_E_NOVIEWER	((HRESULT)0x8534E10AL)
FV_E_OUTOFMEMORY	((HRESULT)0x8534E107L)
FV_E_PROTECTEDFILE	((HRESULT)0x8534E109L)
FV_E_UNEXPECTED	((HRESULT)0x8534E103L)

Pinned Windows

The shell can request Quick View to display a new file in the same window as that used by the previous file viewer; that is, Quick View can "pin" a viewer window. Quick View communicates the shell's request by sending a WM_DROPFILES message to the file viewer. The message contains an internal drop files structure whose members include the path of the new file to be displayed. A file viewer uses the same code to handle both the "pinned" state and drag and drop operations in which the file viewer displays a file that the user has dragged and dropped on the file viewer's window.

Quick View implements the **IFileViewerSite** interface, which allows a file viewer to retrieve the handle of the current pinned window, if there is any, or set a new pinned window. When Quick View calls a file viewer's **IFileViewer::ShowInitialize** member function, the file viewer receives the address of Quick View's **IFileViewerSite** interface. If the file viewer saves the address of the interface, it should call the **IFileViewerSite::AddRef** member function to increment the reference count.

Only one pinned window can exist at a time. A file viewer uses the **IFileViewerSite::SetPinnedWindow** member function to set a new pinned window and the **IFileViewerSite::GetPinnedWindow** member function to retrieve the handle of the current pinned window.

When Quick View calls the file viewer's **IFileViewer::Show** member function, the file viewer receives the address of a **FVSHOWINFO** structure that includes a optional **RECT** structure. A valid **RECT** structure is a hint from the shell that the file viewer window should be pinned; the file viewer should set the size and position of its window based on the information in the structure.

If the file viewer window receives a WM_DROPFILES message, it should fill in the **strNewFile** member of the **FVSHOWINFO** structure with the path of the new file to be displayed, fill the **rect** member with the size and position of the viewer window, and set the appropriate values in the **dwFlags** member. The file viewer should also fill the **punkrel** member with the address of an interface that the new file viewer should call to release the previous file viewer. Doing this allows the previous file viewer to perform cleanup operations. The new file viewer may be the same as the current file viewer if the current one supports the new file. If the old file viewer is the same as the new one, the release does not do anything because the reference count is greater than zero.

If a file viewer returns a file but Quick View cannot find a viewer for the new file, it calls the **IFileViewer::Show** member function for the old file viewer with the FVSIF_NEWFAILED value. The file viewer can either terminate or continue showing the previous file.

Searching Dialog Box

When Quick View must enumerate more than one file viewer from the registry, it displays a dialog box containing a message that reads, as follows.

```
Searching for a viewer to display or print the <human-readable
document type> in <filename>. Press Cancel to stop the search.
```

If the document type is not known, the following message appears.

```
Searching for a viewer to display or print <filename>.
Press Cancel to stop the search.
```

Quick View animates the magnifying glass icon in the dialog box to indicate that Quick View is searching the hard disk. Pressing the Cancel button stops any search in progress and closes Quick View without performing any further actions or providing any user interface.

File Viewer Structure and Implementation

A file viewer is an OLE component object in an in-process server DLL where the object implements the **IPersistFile** and **IFileViewer** interfaces. The in-process server exports the **DllGetClassObject** and **DllCanUnloadNow** functions, implements a class factory object with the **IClassFactory** interface, and implements the file viewer object with the interfaces required. The following illustration shows the structure of a file viewer.

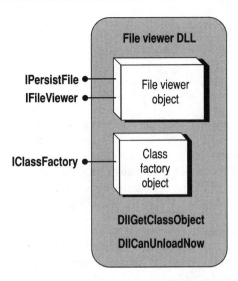

There are a number of reasons why a file viewer is best implemented in a DLL with the given interfaces. In general, a DLL is faster to load and usually comes in a small package. In the future, these same DLLs will provide other nonuser interface features, such as content indexing, and a component object DLL will be the most efficient and fastest way to access those features. In some cases, a file viewer object may need to display pop-up windows and process messages through its own message loop as in Windows 95. The DLL structure still allows this when used in conjunction with a stub process like Quick View, which gives the file viewer DLL the right to execute a message loop.

The **IPersistFile** interface in the file viewer object is intended to be a general mechanism through which the object is given a path for a file. From then on, the component that loaded the object can ask it to do any number of things with the file. Through Quick View, the Windows 95 shell asks the object to show the file by using the **IFileViewer::ShowInitialize** and **IFileViewer::Show** member functions or asks the object to print the file to a specific printer by using the **IFileViewer::PrintTo** member function. In the future, the shell may ask the object to perform content indexing, which would happen through an interface other than **IFileViewer**. For this reason, the file loading member functions of **IPersistFile** are separate from the operations that perform on the file, which is why **IFileViewer** was not just extended with its own **Load** member function. This latter option is a little more efficient (because it avoids **IPersistFile** entrypoint functions that are not implemented), but the design given here is easier to extend.

IFileViewer Interface

The shell uses the **IFileViewer** interface to tell a file viewer object when to show its user interface for the file being viewed or to print the file. In addition to the usual **IUnknown** members, the interface includes the **ShowInitialize**, **Show**, and **PrintTo** member functions.

Before calling the **Show** member function, the shell calls **ShowInitialize** to instruct the file viewer to perform any creations, allocations, or loading. **ShowInitialize** may fail, whereas **Show** may not because Quick View needs to know, before anything becomes visible and before transferring control to the file viewer, whether the file viewer can show the file. If the file viewer can show the file, Quick View hides its Searching dialog box before the file viewer window appears.

The **ShowInitialize** member function should return the same FV_ error codes listed in "Structure of Registry Entries" earlier in this article. Although the sample file viewer included in the Win32 SDK uses a more generic form of error codes, new file viewer DLLs should use the FV_ form.

The **Show** member function is similar to the Windows **ShowWindow** function in that it receives a Show command indicating how the file viewer should initially display its window. The meaning of the Show command is exactly the same as for **ShowWindow**. In general, Quick View passes the Show command from its **WinMain** function directly to **IFileViewer::Show**, which passes the command to **ShowWindow**. Since Quick View obtains this parameter from the shell, this design enables the shell to open a file viewer in the minimized, normal, or maximized state and even allows the shell to hide a file viewer (with the SW_HIDE value). There is no extra overhead in providing this flexibility. Note that the Windows 95 shell always starts Quick View with the SW_SHOWNORMAL value.

The only case when **Show** may fail is if **ShowInitialize** has not been called. In that case, it returns the E_UNEXPECTED status code (SCODE). Otherwise, **Show** must return the NOERROR error code.

The **PrintTo** member function is like **Show** in that it does not return until it finishes printing or an error occurs. If an error occurs, the file viewer object is responsible for informing the user of the problem. When calling **PrintTo**, the shell specifies the name of the printer driver that the file viewer should use to print the file. The shell also specifies a flag that indicates whether the file viewer should display any UI elements, including error message, during the print operation. If the flag is FALSE, the file viewer may show Print dialog boxes, Printer Setup dialog boxes, error messages, and so on.

The interface identifier of **IFileViewer** is defined in the Windows header files as the IID_IFileViewer interface identifier.

File Viewer Creation

You can create a file viewer that interacts appropriately with Quick View by following these steps:

1. Define the file viewer object to use the **IPersistFile** and **IFileViewer** interfaces. The object must also implement a separate **IUnknown** interface that does not delegate calls in aggregation situations. In general, a file viewer object creates or attaches to a window that displays a file's contents.

2. Implement the **Load** and **GetCurFile** member functions (as well as the **IUnknown** member functions) of the **IPersistFile** interface. The **IsDirty** member function can simply return **ResultFromScode**(S_FALSE) because a file viewer does not modify the file, and the **Save** and **SaveCompleted** member functions should simply return **ResultFromScode**(E_NOTIMPL). **Load** stores the filename, but delays opening the file until the later call to the **IFileViewer::ShowInitialize** member function. **GetCurFile** returns **ResultFromScode**(E_UNEXPECTED) if **Load** has not yet been called. Otherwise, it copies the pathname and returns the NOERROR error code.

3. Implement the **IFileViewer::ShowInitialize** and **IFileViewer::Show** member functions (as well as the **IUnknown** member functions of **IFileViewer**). **ShowInitialize** must perform all operations that are prone to failure such that if **ShowInitialize** succeeds, **Show** will never fail. The implementation of these two member functions is like an implementation of an application's **WinMain** function, where **ShowInitialize** registers window classes (using the instance handle that the DLL receives in its **DllEntryPoint** function, not the instance of Quick View), creates the necessary windows to meet the UI guidelines, and loads the file as read-only with the path given in **IPersistFile::Load**. Then **Show** displays the contents of that file in the viewport window, shows the top-level file viewer window, and enters a message loop. To enhance the appearance of the UI, the file should be loaded and completely displayed in the viewport window before the windows are made visible.

   Show does not return until the user has closed the window; that is, Quick View waits for **Show** to return before terminating. Quick View delegates the responsibility of the message loop to the **Show** member function, so **ShowInitialize** and **Show** look and behave exactly like a **WinMain** function in any application (the code is just stored in a DLL).

   Note that the path in the **IPersistFile::Load** member function may be a uniform naming convention (UNC) path. Functions such as Win32 **OpenFile** and OLE **StgOpenStorage** automatically handle UNC paths. If you open a file any other way, you must be sure to handle UNC paths properly.

4. Define the class factory object with the **IClassFactory** interface and implement the interface completely to create a file viewer object. The class factory must support aggregation and server locking, as required by the **IClassFactory** interface.

5. Implement the **DllGetClassObject** function to create an instance of the class factory mentioned in step 4 and return a pointer to one of its interfaces, as required for any component object DLL.

6. Implement the **DllCanUnloadNow** function to return the appropriate code, depending on the number of file viewer objects in service and the number of lock counts implemented by using the **IClassFactory::LockServer** member function, as required for any component object DLL.

7. Include the Print To feature by using the **IFileViewer::PrintTo** member function. This step is optional. If this feature is not implemented, the member function must return **ResultFromScode**(E_NOTIMPL).

8. Finish the DLL implementation by using the **DllEntryPoint** function, as required for any Win32 DLL.

In general, only the implementations of **IPersistFile::Load** and the **IFileViewer** member functions are specific to a file viewer. The other steps that deal with creating an OLE component object are standard OLE mechanisms. For more information about these mechanisms, including objects and interfaces, see the OLE documentation included in the Win32 SDK as well as Chapters 3 and 4 of *Inside OLE 2* from Microsoft® Press.

File Viewer User Interface Guidelines

This section describes the minimal user interface recommended for a file viewer. These guidelines are provided to promote a consistent user interface in all file viewers. You should follow these guidelines as closely as possible and include viewer-specific features within the context of these guidelines.

Window Appearance

A file viewer's main window should have Minimize, Maximize, and Close buttons and these top-level menu items: File, View, and Help (the contents of these menus is described later). A file viewer should also include a toolbar and a status window. The appearance and contents of the viewport window, which occupies all space not used by the toolbar and status window, is left to the developer. However, the viewport window typically has proportional scroll bars if the file contents are not entirely visible in the viewport.

The following illustration shows the typical initial state of a file viewer window. The initial state can be minimized or maximized if the file viewer is given a different show command through the **IFileViewer::Show** member function.

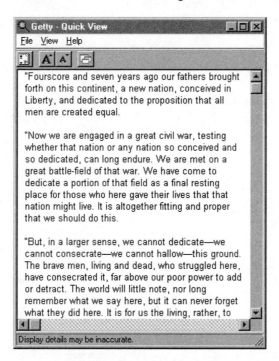

A file viewer can include other top-level menu items for file-specific features. For example, a file viewer should include an Edit menu with a single &Copy item to allow the user to make a selection in the viewport window and copy it to the clipboard. However, such extensions are not part of the basic user interface for a file viewer.

You should also use the new window flags in Windows 95 to create a three-dimensional window appearance and use scroll bars with proportional scroll boxes.

File Menu Items

The standard file viewer File menu has the following four items (as well as separators), two of which are optional. A file viewer can add other items to the menu, but in most cases there is no need for other items.

Menu item string	Result of selecting the menu item
"&Open File for Editing"	Locates and starts the application that can open and edit the file. After successfully starting the application, the file viewer should hide its window immediately, shut down, and eventually return from **IFileViewer::Show**, after which the Quick View process terminates. If the file viewer fails to start the application, it should display the following message.
	`There is no application available that can open this file.`
Separator	Not applicable.
"Page Set&up" (optional)	Activates the standard Page Setup dialog box (or an application-specific dialog box if desired), the results of which affect the display of the file in the viewport window. The effects of the Page Setup command last only for the duration of the file viewer and do not affect the contents of the disk file. This menu item should appear if the file viewer supports printing and only if the Print menu item appears as well.
"&Print\tCtrl+P" (optional)	Activates the standard Print/Printer Setup property sheet. Any changes made to the printer setup that would affect the display of the file in the viewport window last only for the duration of the file viewer and do not affect the contents of the disk file. This menu item should appear only if the file viewer supports printing a file without starting the full application.
Separator	Not applicable.
"E&xit"	Hides the window, closes the file, destroys all the windows, performs other necessary cleanup, and returns with the NOERROR error code from **IFileViewer::Show**. The window should be hidden before cleanup happens to avoid marring its appearance, when the system destroys the toolbar and other controls.

View Menu Items

The View menu of a standard file viewer has the following items.

Menu item string	Result of selecting the menu item
"&Toolbar"	Toggles the visibility of the toolbar. This item is checked when the toolbar is visible and unchecked when it is hidden.
"&Status Bar"	Toggles the visibility of the status window. This item is checked when the status line is visible and unchecked when it is hidden.
"&Page View"	Toggles between a full-sized view and a single-page view.
"Replace &Window"	Toggles between reusing the current window to view a file and creating a new window to view a file.
Separator	Not applicable.
"&Landscape"	Toggles between landscape and portrait view when in page view.
"&Rotate"	Rotates a raster graphic image 90 degrees every time the image is selected.
Separator	Not applicable.
"&Font"	Displays a dialog box that allows the user to select a font and point size for viewing word processing documents and spreadsheets.

Help Menu Items

The standard file viewer Help menu has the following items.

Menu item string	Result of selecting the menu item
"&Help Topics"	Activates WINHELP.EXE with the file viewer's help file.
"&About *fileviewer name*"	Displays an About dialog box for the file viewer. The About dialog box identifies the vendor of the file viewer.

A file viewer can also add other help items and context-sensitive help.

Toolbar Buttons

A file viewer must include a toolbar with a single button tied to the Open File for Editing menu item on the File menu described previously. The image in this button is a 16- by 15-pixel bitmap derived from the icon of the application that would be started if the user opened the file from the shell (using the shell's association route). The image is obtained by calling the **SHGetFileInfo** function with the path of the file. If this function fails, a file viewer can include a button that contains its own image and attempt to start the parent application, or the file viewer can remove the button and disable the Open File for Editing menu item on the File menu. This single button must be the leftmost item on the toolbar and must be separated from any other buttons that are specific to the file viewer.

The following illustration show the Open File for Editing menu item.

⌐ Open File for Editing

Other buttons should correspond roughly to the functions present in the file viewer menus. A file viewer that supports a Font menu item should have Increase Font Size and Decrease Font Size buttons. Other file viewer classes may need to include printing and rotation buttons on the toolbar.

A standard toolbar button is the Replace Window button. The default behavior for file viewers is for a new file viewer instance to be created whenever the user chooses the Quick View menu item. When the Replace Window button is toggled to the on position, however, a new instance is not created; instead, the contents of the relevant file viewer window are replaced by a view of the new file.

All buttons should have a corresponding tooltip control that displays some context information when the mouse cursor is positioned on the button. The standard Windows 95 toolbar control provides built-in support for tooltip controls such that you only have to provide the text string. The following illustration shows a tooltip control for a toolbar button.

The recommended tooltip strings for various toolbar buttons follow.

Toolbar button	Tooltip string
Open File for Editing	"Open File for Editing"
Font Increase	"Increase Font Size"
Font Decrease	"Decrease Font Size"
Small View	"Toggle view size"
Landscape	"Toggle portrait/landscape"
Rotate [Again]	"Rotate image 90 degrees"
Replace Window	"Replace Window"

Status Window Messages

A file viewer should display status window messages for the system menu and all top-level and pop-up menu items. The messages for the system menu and other menu items used by the default Windows 95 file viewers follow.

[Menu] item	Message
[System]	"Commands for manipulating this and other windows."
[System] Restore	"Restores this window to normal size." "Expands this window to full screen size."
[System] Move	"Move this window to another screen location."
[System] Size	"Resizes this window."
[System] Minimize	"Collapses this window to an icon."
[System] Maximize	"Expands this window to full screen size."
[System] Close	"Closes this window."
[System] Switch To...	"Switch to another task."
[File]	"Contains commands for opening the file and quitting Quick View."
[File] Open File for Editing	"Opens the file for editing."
[File] Page Setup	"Changes the page setup for printing."
[File] Print...	"Prints the file contents."
[File] Exit	"Quits Quick View."
[View]	"Contains commands for customizing this window."
[View] Toolbar	"Shows or hides the toolbar."
[View] Status Bar	"Shows or hides the status bar."
[View] Page View	"Switches between document and page views."
[View] Replace Window	"Displays new files in current Quick View window."
[View] Landscape	"Switches between portrait and landscape."
[View] Rotate (Again)	"Rotates the image by 90 degrees."
[View] Font	"Changes the display font."
[Help]	"Contains commands for displaying Help and information about Quick View."
[Help] Help Topics	"Displays the Help Contents and Index."
[Help] About	"Displays program information, version number and copyright."

The following standard messages for other conditions not related to menu items are implemented in the Windows 95 default file viewers:

- In the inactive state, when the user is doing nothing else, the status line should read as follows.

```
Display details may be inaccurate.
```

This line should be the first visible message when the file viewer appears.

- When the mouse cursor is positioned over the viewport window, the status window should read as follows.

```
To edit, click Open File for Editing on the File menu.
```

Note that the document type is specific for the file viewer in use, as shown in the following illustration.

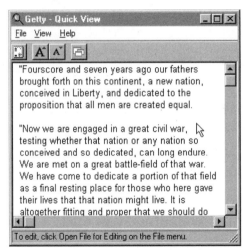

- The status window should reflect longer versions of tooltip messages when tooltip controls are displayed. For example, a longer version of the "Increase Font Size" tooltip is "Increase the font size of the display" shown at the same time in the status window.

Viewport Window Contents and Context Menu

The viewport window is where you provide most file-specific UI elements. The viewport occupies all space in the client area of the main window not used for the toolbar and status bar. It displays the file contents in whatever mode is applicable, and it is sensitive to the user-selected printer and page setup as well as other View menu commands.

If the contents of the file are too large to be completely displayed within the viewport, the file viewer should provide scroll bars (with proportional scroll boxes) to shift the image. If the contents of the file are smaller than the viewport window, no scroll bars should appear. In addition, the file contents should not be initially scaled to fill the viewport window unless the user selects scaling through the View menu commands.

The only other requirement for the viewport window is that it should provide a context menu for the file. The context menu should appear when the user clicks the viewport with the mouse button 2. The context menu should include the following items.

Menu item string	Equivalent found on other menu
"&Open File for Editing"	Open File for Editing command on the File menu
Separator	Not applicable
"Page Se&tup" (optional)	Page Setup command on the File menu
"&Print" (optional)	Print command on the File menu (note, no accelerator)
Separator	Not applicable

A file viewer may add more items as necessary. The Toolbar and Status bar menu items commands on the View menu should not appear in the context menu.

Drag and Drop Functionality

The default file viewers in Windows 95 allow the user to drag a file from the desktop or Explorer and drop the file on a file viewer's window. A file viewer should show the small document icon that includes the "+" sign when the mouse is over the file viewer's window before the drop takes place. The Replace Window command in the View menu controls whether another file viewer window is displayed or the same window is reused.

Sophisticated File Viewers

This article only describes the minimal file viewer UI. There are, of course, many other possibilities besides just rudimentary printing and viewing capabilities. One useful feature is the ability to copy data from a document either to the clipboard or in a drag and drop operation. In such cases, the file viewer needs to provide the ability to select data in the file, a Copy command (on an Edit menu as well as in a context menu), and the ability to pick up the selection and drag it elsewhere. However, the file viewer should not be a drop target and should not support the Cut and Paste commands on the Edit menu (or other variants) because those operations modify the file.

If the parent application creating the files that are handled in a specific file viewer is an OLE compound document container, the file viewer itself must be sensitive to viewing a compound document. That means that the file viewer itself will support some minimal container features and will, of course, use OLE to load and display compound document objects in the file itself. If the file viewer also supports in-place activation, it can activate inside-out objects in-place to allow the user to select and copy data from embeddings. While there are no standards for such functionality in Windows 95, there will be in future versions of Windows.

Reference

A file viewer in-process server DLL must implement the **IFileViewer** and **IPersistFile** interfaces. This section describes the **IFileViewer** interface and its member functions. For information about the **IPersistFile** interface and its member functions, see the OLE documentation included in the Win32 SDK.

Interfaces and Member Functions

IFileViewer

Designates an interface that allows a registered file viewer to be notified when it must show or print a file. The Windows 95 shell calls this interface when the user selects the Quick View command from a file's context menu and the file is a type that the file viewer recognizes. The **IFileViewer** interface has the following member functions:

PrintTo	Prints a file.
Show	Displays a file.
ShowInitialize	Prepares to display a file.

Like all OLE interfaces, **IFileViewer** also includes the **QueryInterface**, **AddRef**, and **Release** member functions.

IFileViewer::PrintTo

```
HRESULT PrintTo(IFileViewer FAR * pFileViewer,
    LPSTR pszDriver, BOOL fSuppressUI);
```

Prints a file.

- Returns the NOERROR value if successful or an OLE-defined error value otherwise.

pFileViewer

Address of the **IFileViewer** interface. In C++, this parameter is implicit.

pszDriver

Address of a buffer that contains the name of the printer device driver that should print the file. If this parameter is NULL, the file viewer determines which device driver to use.

fSuppressUI

User interface suppression flag. If this parameter TRUE, the file viewer should not display any UI whatsoever, including error messages, during the print operation. If this parameter FALSE, the file viewer can show dialog boxes, as needed.

The shell specifies the name of the file to print by calling the file viewer's **IPersistFile::Load** member function.

IFileViewer::Show

```
HRESULT Show(IFileViewer FAR * pFileViewer,
    LPFVSHOWINFO pvsi);
```

Displays a file.

- Returns the NOERROR value if successful or the E_UNEXPECTED value if the **IFileViewer::ShowInitialize** member function was not called before **IFileViewer::Show**.

pFileViewer

Address of the **IFileViewer** interface. In C++, this parameter is implicit.

pvsi

Address of an **FVSHOWINFO** structure containing information that the file viewer uses to display the file. A file viewer can return information to the shell by modifying the members of the structure.

The shell specifies the name of the file to display by calling the file viewer's **IPersistFile::Load** member function.

IFileViewer::Show can fail only if **IFileViewer::ShowInitialize** was not called first, and the return value must be E_UNEXPECTED in that case. Otherwise, **IFileViewer::Show** must return NOERROR.

IFileViewer::ShowInitialize

```
HRESULT ShowInitialize(IFileViewer FAR * pFileViewer,
    LPFILEVIEWERSITE lpfsi);
```

Allows a file viewer to determine whether it can display a file and, if it can, to perform initialization operations before showing the file.

- Returns the NOERROR value if successful or an OLE-defined error value otherwise.

pFileViewer
Address of the **IFileViewer** interface. In C++, this parameter is implicit.

lpfsi
Address of a **IFileViewerSite** interface. A file viewer uses this interface to retrieve the handle of the current pinned window or to specify a new pinned window.

The shell calls this member function before the **IFileViewer::Show** member function. The shell specifies the name of the file to display by calling the file viewer's **IPersistFile::Load** member function.

IFileViewer::ShowInitialize must perform all operations that are prone to failure so that if it succeeds, **IFileViewer::Show** will not fail.

IFileViewerSite

Designates an interface that allows a file viewer to retrieve the handle of the current pinned window or to set a new pinned window. The pinned window is the window in which the current file viewer is displaying a file. When the user selects a new file to view, the shell directs the file viewer to display the new file in the pinned window rather than to create a new window.

The **IFileViewerSite** interface has the following member functions.

GetPinnedWindow	Retrieves the handle of the current pinned window.
SetPinnedWindow	Sets a new pinned window.

Like all OLE interfaces, **IFileViewerSite** also includes the **QueryInterface**, **AddRef**, and **Release** member functions.

IFileViewerSite::GetPinnedWindow

```
HRESULT GetPinnedWindow(IFileViewerSite FAR * pFileVS,
    HWND *phwnd);
```

Retrieves the handle of the current pinned window, if it exists.

- Returns the NOERROR value if successful or an OLE-defined error value otherwise.

pFileVS

Address of the **IFileViewer** interface. In C++, this parameter is implicit.

phwnd

Address of a window handle of the current pinned window or NULL if no pinned window exists.

IFileViewerSite::SetPinnedWindow

```
HRESULT SetPinnedWindow(IFileViewerSite FAR * pFileVS,
    HWND hwnd);
```

Sets a new pinned window.

- Returns the NOERROR value if successful or an OLE-defined error value otherwise.

pFileVs

Address of the **IFileViewer** interface. In C++, this parameter is implicit.

hwnd

Handle of the new pinned window or NULL if there is to be no pinned window.

When the user selects a new file to view, the shell directs the file viewer to display the new file in the pinned window instead of creating a new window.

Structure

The following structure is used with file viewers.

FVSHOWINFO

```
typedef struct {
    DWORD     cbSize;     // size of structure, in bytes
    HWND      hwndOwner;  // see below
    int       iShow;      // see below
    DWORD     dwFlags;    // see below
    RECT      rect;       // see below
    LPUNKNOWN punkrel;    // see below
    OLECHAR   strNewFile[MAX_PATH];  // see below
} FVSHOWINFO, *LPFVSHOWINFO;
```

Contains information that the **IFileViewer::Show** member function uses to display a file.

hwndOwner

Handle of the owner window. When a file viewer creates a window to display a file, it should specify this handle as the owner of the window.

iShow

Show command. For a list of show commands, see the description of the **ShowWindow** function.

dwFlags

Show information flags. This member can be a combination of these values:

FVSIF_CANVIEWIT	The file viewer can display the file.
FVSIF_NEWFAILED	The file viewer specified a new file to display, but no viewer could display the file. The file viewer should either terminate or continue to display the previous file.
FVSIF_NEWFILE	A drag and drop operation has dropped a file on the file viewer window. The file viewer passes the name of the file to the shell by copying the name to **strNewFile**. The shell attempts to load a file viewer that can display the new file.
FVSIF_PINNED	A pinned window exists. A file viewer should either use the pinned window to display the file or set a new pinned window and display the file in it.
FVSIF_RECT	**rect** contains valid data.

rect

Address of a **RECT** structure that specifies the size and position of the file viewer's window. This member is valid only if **dwFlags** includes the FVSIF_RECT value.

punkrel

Address of an interface whose **Release** member function is called by a new file viewer to release the previous file viewer. This member is used when a drag and drop operation drops a file on the file viewer's window.

strNewFile

Address of a string that specifies the name of a new file to display. A file viewer sets this member when a drag and drop operation drops a file on the file viewer's window.

The shell uses this structure to pass information to a file viewer, and a file viewer uses it to return information to the shell.

ARTICLE 17

File Parsers

About File Parsers

A file parser is a dynamic-link library (DLL) that provides the low-level parsing needed to generate a "quick view" for a file of a given type. File parsers work in conjunction with the file viewing components of the Microsoft® Windows® 95 operating system. These components are the shell, the Quick View program (QUIKVIEW.EXE), display engines, and file parsers. The shell responds to user requests to generate a quick view for a file by calling the Quick View program. The program manages the process, directing one of the display engines to draw the Quick View window and fill it with a view of the file. The display engine uses a file parser to determine the contents of the file and to draw those contents correctly.

You can extend the file viewing capabilities of Windows 95 by supplying additional file parsers. Each file parser is responsible for a specific type or class of file and is associated with one of the display engines. For example, you can allow a quick view to be generated for a .DOC file by creating a file parser to support that file type and associating the file parser with the word processor display engine.

This article describes the file parser interface and explains how to write file parsers for word processing documents, spreadsheets, databases, bitmapped graphics, and vector graphics. The functions, macros, and structures described here can be found with the file parser sample code in the Samples subdirecory of the Microsoft® Win32® Software Development Kit (SDK). For information about extending the file viewing capabilities in other ways, see Article 16, "File Viewers."

The file viewing technology used in the Quick View feature of the Microsoft Windows 95 operating system has been jointly developed by Microsoft Corporation and Systems Compatibility Corporation.

Adding or Removing File Parsers

For performance reasons, the file viewer builds a cache of the file parsers in the system the first time the Quick View feature is used. This cache is stored in the registry. If a file parser is added or removed, this cache must be rebuilt. To make the system rebuild the cache, set verify data not equal to zero under the following key.

```
\\HKEY_LOCAL_MACHINE\SOFTWARE\SCC\Viewer Technology\MS1
```

File Parser Functions

Every file parser must implement the following functions.

VwStreamCloseFunc   **VwStreamSectionFunc**

VwStreamOpenFunc   **VwStreamSeekFunc**

VwStreamReadFunc   **VwStreamTellFunc**

VwStreamReadRecordFunc

The display engine calls these functions to display a file of the type supported by the file parser.

The display engine starts the file viewing process by calling **VwStreamOpenFunc**, sending the name of a file to the file parser. The first responsibility of any parser is to verify that the given file has the proper format and can be processed. If the file is viewable, the file parser returns a value to the display engine acknowledging the request.

Once the parser completes verification of the file, the display engine calls **VwStreamSectionFunc**, directing the file parser to identify the type and name of the first section of the file to be processed. A *section* is a portion of the file in which all the data is of one type; it forms a logical breaking point for the processing of the file. The standard section types are word processing, spreadsheet, database, bitmapped graphics, and vector graphics. A file can consist of a single section, multiple sections of the same type, or a combination of sections of different types. The actions that the display engine takes to display the file depend on the type of section currently being processed. The file parser must call the **SOPutSectionType** and **SOPutSectionName** functions to output the section type and to set the section name.

Before the file parser returns from **VwStreamSectionFunc**, it may need to provide the display engine with additional information. If the portion to be processed is a word processing section, the file parser must set entries for the font table by using the **SOPutFontTableEntry** function. If it is a spreadsheet section, the file parser must set the column width by calling the **SOPutColumnInfo** function. If it is a database section, the file parser must set the field format by calling the **SOPutFieldInfo** function. The file parser can also set the date base used by spreadsheets and databases to calculate dates by using the **SOSetDateBase** function. In addition, the file parser can set header entries by calling the **SOPutHdrEntry** function.

After the section type and general information is set, the display engine requests data for the section by calling **VwStreamReadFunc**. The file parser fulfills this request by calling the stream output functions. These functions pass the data to the display engine in a form that is easiest for the engine to display, copy to the clipboard, or write to disk.

The stream output functions used by the file parser depend on the section type. For word processing sections, the file parser uses the **SOPutParaSpacing**, **SOPutCharAttr**, and **SOPutChar** functions to set the spacing for paragraphs, set the style attributes for characters, and output characters. For spreadsheet sections, the parser uses the **SOPutDataCell** and **SOPutTextCell** functions to output the content (data or text) of cells. For database sections, it uses the **SOPutField** and **SOPutVarField** functions to output the data of fields. The parser uses the **SOPutBitmapHeader** and **SOPutScanLineData** functions for bitmapped graphics sections and the **SOVectorAttr** and **SOVectorObject** functions for vector graphics sections.

To set a break for a paragraph, cell, or field, the file parser calls the **SOPutBreak** function with an appropriate value, either SO_PARABREAK, SO_CELLBREAK, or SO_RECORDBREAK. The return value from **SOPutBreak** tells the file parser how to proceed. If it is the SO_STOP value, the file parser stops all processing and returns from **VwStreamReadFunc**.

The file parser continues to output data until it reaches the end of the section. The parser must end a section by calling **SOPutBreak** with the SO_SECTIONBREAK value. If this is the last section in the file, the file parser indicates that the end of the file has been reached by using the SO_EOFBREAK value instead.

If there are subsequent sections left in the file, the display engine calls the **VwStreamSectionFunc** function again to request the type and name of the next section, and processing continues just as it did for the first section.

After the last section, the display engine calls **VmStreamCloseFunc** to indicate that processing is complete and that no further requests for data will be made. The file parser must close the file and any related files it has opened and clean up resources, such as freeing memory.

If an error occurs while a file is parsed, the file parser should call the **SOBailOut** function to notify the display engine of the error condition. The parser must immediately return from **VwStreamReadFunc** after calling the **SOBailOut** function.

Restartable Parsing

You must design the file parser so that parsing can be efficiently restarted at discrete locations within the file. The goal is to give the display engine the best performance without it having to store a completely converted copy of a file.

To facilitate restartable parsing, the display engine incorporates a module, which is called the *chunker*, that essentially caches data from the parser. The chunker does not cache all the data, only the data that the display engine has most recently requested. However, it does cache state data for restartable locations in the file. This means that as long as the parser maintains its own internal data in a way that can be efficiently restarted, the display engine and the parser can work cooperatively to locate and restart processing at the cached locations.

The file parser is responsible for determining the best locations for restarting parsing. It does this by calling the **SOPutBreak** function. The chunker assumes that each break is a restartable location in the file. Before calling **SOPutBreak**, however, the file parser must save up-to-date data about the location so that it can quickly retrieve and begin processing the data at the location if requested to do so.

The display engine uses the **VwStreamSeekFunc** and **VwStreamTellFunc** functions to direct the file parser to a restartable location.

Word Processing Sections

Word processing sections contain text organized as paragraphs, tables, and subdocuments. Of these, paragraphs and tables can have attributes, such as indentation, tab stops, and spacing. The text in word processing sections consists of characters having attributes, such as typeface, height, and weight. Word processing sections can also include embedded objects, allowing bitmapped art and other graphics to be included with the text.

A file parser processes the text associated with a word processing section when the display engine calls the **VwStreamReadFunc** function. The file parser must set all attributes before calling the **SOPutChar** function or other text output functions. The file parser must never automatically set an attribute as a default. If the state of a current attribute is not known, the file parser must not set it.

Paragraph Attributes

The file parser sets the attributes of a paragraph before outputting characters for the paragraph. The attributes are the alignment, indent, spacing, tab stops, and margins.

The file parser sets the alignment to be left, right, centered, or justified by using the **SOPutParaAlign** function and sets the left, right, and first line indents by using the **SOPutParaIndents** function. The file parser sets the spacing before and after the paragraph and between lines of the paragraph by using the **SOPutParaSpacing** function. The file parser sets tab stops by using the **SOPutTabStop** function, calling the function once for each tab stop. To mark the start and end of a tab stop definition, the file parser calls the **SOStartTabStops** and **SOEndTabStops** functions. The file parser sets page margins for the paragraph by using the **SOPutParaMargins** function.

Tables

The file parser can add tables to text output by using the **SOBeginTable** and **SOEndTable** functions to mark the start and end of the table definition and can format the rows and cells in tables by using the **SOPutTableRowFormat** and **SOPutTableCellInfo** functions. The file parser uses the character and paragraph functions to output the text for each cell and set the attributes.

The file parser marks the end of each cell and each row by using the **SOPutBreak** function with the SO_TABLECELLBREAK and SO_TABLEROWBREAK values. A file parser must insert a cell break after each cell and a row break at the end of each row. If a file parser inserts a row break before inserting as many cells as were defined for the row, the remaining cells are assumed to be empty. Empty cells may be inserted in the middle of a row by inserting consecutive cell breaks.

Row and cell formats must be defined before the last cell of a row. After defining the row properties by using the **SOPutTableRowFormat** function, the parser must call the **SOPutTableCellInfo** function for each cell in the row. After a row is defined, the row properties are assumed to apply to subsequent rows until new row properties are specified. A filter may, thus, define an entire table by specifying the row and cell properties once and then using the appropriate row and cell breaks.

You can add borders to cells by setting the **pLeftBorder**, **pRightBorder**, **pTopBorder**, and **pBottomBorder** members of the **SOTABLECELLINFO** structure to appropriate values when setting the cell format.

You can add tabs to cells by using the special character, the SO_CHCELLTAB value. This character is defined for cells that are merged with their neighbors and acts as a tab that moves the current text position to the location of the next boundary that would have existed if the cells had not been merged.

Subdocuments

The file parser adds subdocuments—that is, headers, footers, footnotes, and comments—to the document by using the **SOPutBreak** function. The file parser must call **SOPutBreak** with the SO_SUBDOCBEGINBREAK value to start a subdocument and with the SO_SUBDOCENDBREAK value to end it.

After ending a subdocument, the file parser must restore character and paragraph attributes to their state before the subdocument was started. The file parser can use the **SUUserPushData** and **SUUserPopData** functions to save and restore nested subdocument information. A parser can nest subdocuments without limit. The following example shows when to save and restore this information.

```
This is a <Bold On> test

    // At this point, the filter should save its internal
    // information to reflect the fact that bold is on.
    SOPutBreak(SO_SUBDOCBEGINBREAK);
    SoPutSubdocInfo(...);
<Subdoc Begin> This is a <Bold Off>subdocument<Subdoc End>

    // At this point, the filter should restore its internal
    // information to reflect the fact that bold is on.
    SOPutBreak(SO_SUBDOCENDBREAK);

document <Bold Off>of mine.
```

File parsers are not expected to correctly exit a subdocument when run from a regular paragraph break (with the SO_PARABREAK value) inside the subdocument. The display engine lets the file parser run to the subdocument's end break (that is, the SO_SUBDOCENDBREAK value) and returns the SO_STOP value to it.

Characters and Character Attributes

The file parser outputs characters by using the **SOPutChar** function. It can specify extra properties for a character, such as grouped or hidden, when outputting by using the **SOPutCharX** function. The file parser outputs special characters, such as tabs, hard line breaks, hard page breaks, and hyphens by using the **SOPutSpecialCharX** function.

Before outputting characters, the file parser sets character attributes by using the **SOPutCharAttr**, **SOPutCharFontById**, **SOPutCharFontByName**, and **SOPutCharHeight** functions. These functions set the style, font, height, and width of the character. The **SOPutCharAttr** function lets the file parser set style attributes, such as italic, underline, and strikeout. The **SOPutCharFontById** and **SOPutCharFontByName** functions can specify any font that the parser added to the font table during processing of the **VwStreamSectionFunc** function. The **SOPutCharHeight** function sets the character height, in half points.

Embedded Objects

The file parser can embed graphics objects in the text of a paragraph section by using the **SOPutEmbeddedObject** function. The function inserts the embedded graphics object at the current location.

Spreadsheet Sections

The file parser outputs content (data or text) for cells in a spreadsheet by using the **SOPutDataCell** and **SOPutTextCell** functions. Before outputting cell data, the file parser must get the range of columns to be output by using the **SOGetInfo** function with the SOINFO_COLUMNRANGE value. When **SOGetInfo** returns, the low-order word of its *pInfo* parameter identifies the first column of data to generate output for, and the high-order word identifies the last column. The file parser should only call **SOPutDataCell** or **SOPutTextCell** for cells within the range indicated by a call to **SOGet**. When there is no more data within a range of columns, the file parser must call the **SOPutBreak** function with either the SO_EOFBREAK or SO_SECTIONBREAK value, whichever applies. This must be done for each range of columns in the document.

For example, if the first column is 10 and the last column is 19, the filter reads the file from its current position, but it only calls **SOPutDataCell** or **SOPutTextCell** for cells that belong in columns 10 through column 19, inclusively. (The column numbers are zero based.) The parser skips over cells that belong in columns outside of this range. The filter must produce cells for *all* columns in the range, filling in with empty cells, if necessary. As before, the filter continues until **SOPutBreak** returns the SO_STOP value.

In general, the file parser should carry out the following steps:

1. Determine the desired range of columns.
2. Determine the next cell available from the input file.
3. If the cell is not in the given range of columns, jump to step 2.
4. If the cell is not empty, call **SOPutDataCell** or **SOPutTextCell** with the current data. Otherwise, call **SOPutDataCell** for a cell of the SO_CELLEMPTY type.
5. Update local variables, such as row and column numbers.
6. Call **SOPutBreak** with the SO_CELLBREAK value.
7. If **SOPutBreak** returns the SO_STOP value, return from the **VwStreamReadFunc** function.
8. If at the beginning of the next section, call **SOPutBreak** with the SO_SECTIONBREAK value and return.
9. If at the end of the file, call **SOPutBreak** with the SO_EOFBREAK value and return.
10. Repeat steps 2 through 10.

When the chunker saves local data for various seek positions in a document, it does so within **SOPutBreak**, when the break is of the SO_CELLBREAK type. Thus, when a file parser has its local data restored for a random seek position, the data will reflect the state of the file parser during its call to **SOPutBreak** for the last cell of the previous chunk in the current range of cells. Any tracking done by the parser, such as the current row number, should be updated before **SOPutBreak** is called for each cell.

Every horizontal range of columns, specified by *dwExtraData* in each call to your **VwStreamReadFunc** function, must eventually be terminated by a call to **SOPutBreak** with SO_EOFBREAK or SO_SECTIONBREAK value, whichever is applicable. The type of break depends on the input file. A file parser must not put a section break at the end of the file, and an end-of-file (EOF) break, of course, cannot occur anywhere but at the actual end of the file.

For example, if the input document contains a single spreadsheet that is 30 columns wide, the display engine can call the parser with three different ranges of columns: 0 to 11, 12 to 23, and 24 to 29. The file parser calls **SOPutBreak** with an EOF break three times, once for each time it reaches the end of the file while processing a given range.

When calling **SOPutBreak** with a section break, the file parser must be sure that the seek position is at the beginning of the next section—that is, the file position where the file parser needs to be when **VwStreamSectionFunc** is next called. Any one of the calls to **SOPutBreak** for a section break may be the one that sets the seek position for the top of the next section.

Database Sections

The file parser outputs data and text for a database by using the **SOPutField**, **SOPutMoreVarField**, and **SOPutVarField** functions. The parser uses the **SOPutField** function for fields of a fixed size. The other functions are used for variable length fields. The parser sets field information by using the **SOPutFieldInfo** function while processing the **VmStreamSectionFunc** function.

Bitmapped Sections

The file parser starts a bitmapped section by calling the **SOPutSectionType** function with the SO_BITMAP value when processing the **VmStreamSectionFunc** function. The file parser must also set the bitmap header information for the section by using the **SOPutBitmapHeader** function before returning from **VmStreamSectionFunc**. The information in the bitmap header allows the chunker to allocate storage for other bitmap information, such as the palette. This means that the file parser must call **SOPutBitmapHeader** before any other bitmapped section functions.

Palettes

The file parser must generate a palette for those sections that have the color palette value, SO_COLORPALETTE, set in the **wImageFlags** member of the **SOBITMAPHEADER** structure. The parser uses the **SOStartPalette**, **SOPutPaletteEntry**, and **SOEndPalette** functions to define the color palette for a bitmapped section. Only one palette may be defined for a bitmapped section.

All **SOCOLORREF** members set during the stream read can use RGB (red, green, blue) values, palette index values, or palette-relative RGB values. All settings of these values must be done through the **SOPALETTEINDEX**, **SORGB**, or **SOPALETTERGB** macro. For more information about these types of color values, see the description of the **COLORREF** value.

Tiles and Scan Lines

A bitmap image in a bitmapped section consists of tiles and scan lines. A *tile* is a rectangular portion of an image, containing at least one scan line. An image is one or more tiles wide and one or more tiles long. A *tile column* is the horizontal positioning of a tile; the tiles that have their x-coordinate equal to zero belong to tile column zero, with tile column numbers incrementing in the direction of the increasing x-coordinates.

The file parser specifies its tile length in terms of scan lines. Once the length is specified, the display engine always requests bitmap data as whole tiles; that is, it tells the parser to stop only on integral multiples of the tile length. For formats that contain multiple tiles, file parsers should set the tile length to the minimum number of scan lines required for a single tile. Formats that are not stored in tiles should have the tile width set equal to the image width and the tile length set to one scan line.

The following values are expected to be valid when tiles are created.

```
TILESACROSS = (ImageWidth+TileWidth-1)/TileWidth
TILESDOWN = (ImageLength+TileLength-1)/TileLength
TILESPERIMAGE=TILESACROSS*TILESDOWN
```

To output bitmap data, the file parser outputs a scan line at a time, in sequential order, by using the **SOPutScanLineData** function. All of the scan line must belong to the same tile column. After each scan line, the file parser calls the **SOPutBreak** function with the SO_SCANLINEBREAK value. As is normally the case, the return value from **SOPutBreak** indicates whether the file parser should return from the **VwStreamReadFunc** function.

Building Scan Lines

The file parser builds the scan line data as a continuous stream of bits that define each pixel. Each pixel is packed into an array of bytes in such a way that if the data were written out in hexadecimal or binary numbers, the pixels could be read in order from left to right. That is, for a 4-bit-per-pixel format, the first pixel is stored in the high-order bits of the first byte (bit 7, bit 6, bit 5, and bit 4), and the second pixel is stored in low-order bits of that byte (bit 3, bit 2, bit 1, and bit 0). Thus, if the first eight pixels of a 4-bit-per-pixel scan line have the hex values of 0, 2, C, 9, A, 4, 3, and F, the first four bytes of scan line data would be 02, C9, A4, and 3F.

If the parser provides a palette for the image, the data for each pixel is interpreted as an index into the palette. If no palette exists for the image, the bits for each pixel specify either a true color (24-bit only) or a gray scale value. For 24-bit color, each 3 bytes of a scan line represent the intensities of red, green, and blue of a single pixel. When the scan line has been completely specified, the parser must call the **SOPutBreak** function with the SO_SCANLINEBREAK value, except for the last line of the bitmap. The last line of the bitmap must end with a break of the SO_SECTIONBREAK or SO_EOFBREAK type, whichever applies.

The following example illustrates the use of the bitmapped functions in the simplest possible case: a parser with scan line data stored one tile wide and with the same format that parsers are required to provide it, so the data requires no additional processing after being read in. This example also does not check for EOF or read errors.

```
WORD   wBytesRead;
WORD   wBufSize = Proc.ScanLineBufSize;

do
{
...

xread( hFile, Proc.ScanLineBuf, wBufSize, &wBytesRead );

SOPutScanLineData( Proc.ScanLineBuf, hProc );

...

} while( SOPutBreak( SO_SCANLINEBREAK, 0, hProc ) == SO_CONTINUE );
```

Vector Graphics Sections

The file parser starts a vector graphics section by calling the **SOPutSectionType** function with the vector value, SO_VECTOR, while processing the **VmStreamSectionFunc** function. The file parser must also set the vector header by using the **SOPutVectorHeader** function before returning from **VmStreamSectionFunc**. The information in the **SOVECTORHEADER** structure defines the size and attributes of the rectangle in which vector graphics are drawn.

The vector graphics functions are similar to the primitive GDI functions, but they include extensions that are based on the file formats being supported. All vector graphics objects are described in two-dimensional space on a logical coordinate system. The direction and resolution of the x- and y-axis is defined in the **SOVECTORHEADER** structure.

The file parser uses two functions to transfer data. The **SOVectorAttr** function sets attributes related to drawing vector graphics objects, and the **SOVectorObject** function defines a vector graphics object to be drawn. The parser specifies an identifier, a data size, and the address of data when it calls a function. The identifier specifies the action to take and the size and data-defined details of the action. Each action has a corresponding structure in which the data must be given. For example, to define a logical font, the parser must set the members of the **SOLOGFONT** structure and pass the structure to **SOVectorAttr**.

Although vector graphics functions are similar to the graphics device interface (GDI) functions, they are not exactly the same. For example, this means the members of the **SOLOGFONT** and **LOGFONT** structures are not necessarily the same.

After drawing every object, the file parser should call the **SOPutBreak** function with the SO_VECTOROBJECTBREAK value.

Writing a File Parser

File parsers should be contained in a set of source and include files as follows, where *XXX* represents a mnemonic for the data format. For specific examples, see the sample ASCII filter files identified in the following table.

Generic filename	Contents	Sample ASCII filter file
VS_*XXX*.C	Code	VS_ASC.C
VSD_*XXX*.C	Data	VSD_ASC.C
VS_*XXX*.H	Type definitions	VS_ASC.H
VSP_*XXX*.H	Portability information	VSP_ASC.H

The portability information file makes porting of filters between 16- and 32-bit versions of Windows and multiple Microsoft® Windows NT™ platforms easier. To allow file parsers to be used for content indexing, a set of include files is provided that will allow conditional compilations to yield executable DLLs for all of these needs from the same set of source files.

Your VSP_*XXX*.H file should look something like the following. (For further information, see the corresponding ASCII filter file.)

- The structure type and name of the static data.

```
#define VwStreamStaticType   ???
#define VwStreamStaticName   ???
```

The parser must not change the contents of the structure, because it is shared among all instances of the parser.

- The structure type and name of the dynamic data.

```
#define VwStreamDynamicType   ???
#define VwStreamDynamicName   ???
```

VwStreamDynamicName is for consistency and has no real use, because all dynamic data is accessed through the pseudonym **Proc**. Each instance of the parser has a separate copy of dynamic data.

- The structure type and name of the save data.

```
#define VwStreamSaveType   ???
#define VwStreamSaveName   ???
```

VwStreamSaveName should reference an element that is in the **VwStreamDynamicType** structure. The data in this structure is saved after every call to **VwStreamSectionFunc** and **VwStreamReadFunc** and restored before every call to **VwStreamReadFunc**.

- The structure type and name of the section data.

```
#define VwStreamSectionType   ???
#define VwStreamSectionName   ???
```

If neither of these is defined, the file parser is assumed to be *single section only*. **VwStreamSectionName** should reference an element that is in the **VwStreamDynamicType** structure. The data in this structure is saved after each call to **VwStreamSectionFunc** and is guaranteed to contain the current section's data on entry to **VwStreamReadFunc**.

The example below shows the relationship of the various save areas to the dynamic data structure.

```
typedef struct {
 ...
} VwStreamSaveType;
typedef struct {
 ...
} VwStreamSectionType;
typedef struct {
 ...
    VwStreamSectionType VwStreamSectionName; // multisection only
    VwStreamSaveType VwStreamSaveName;
} VwStreamDynamicType;
```

- The stream identifier name and count.

```
#define VwStreamIdName    ???
#define VwStreamIdCount   ???
```

VwStreamIdName is the name of the FILTER_DESC array in VSD_*XXX*.C, and **VwStreamIdCount** is the number of elements in this array. Like the static data, this data should never be changed by a parser.

- The name of the include file. All the structure types used by the parser should be defined in this file.

```
#define VwInclude              "vs_xxx.h"
#define VwStreamUserSaveType   ???
#define VwStreamGenSeekName    ???
#define VwStreamOpenFunc       xxx_stream_open
#define VwStreamSeekFunc       xxx_stream_seek
#define VwStreamTellFunc       xxx_stream_tell
#define VwStreamReadFunc       xxx_stream_read
#define VwStreamReadRecordFunc xxx_stream_readrecord
#define VwStreamSectionFunc    xxx_stream_section
#define VwStreamCloseFunc      xxx_stream_close
#define VwGetInfoFunc          xxx_getinfo
#define VwGetRtnsFunc          xxx_getrtns
#define VwGetDataFunc          xxx_getdata
#define VwSetDataFunc          xxx_setdata
#define VwAllocProcFunc        xxx_alloc_proc
#define VwFreeProcFunc         xxx_free_proc
#define VwLocalUpFunc          xxx_local_up
#define VwLocalDownFunc        xxx_local_down
#define VwGetSectionDataFunc   xxx_getsectiondata
#define VwSetSectionDataFunc   xxx_setsectiondata
```

- The top of the VS_*XXX*.C file should look like this.

```
#include "VSP_XXX.H"
#include "VSCTOP.H"
#include "VS_XXX.PRO"
```

Reference

The following functions, helper functions, and structures are associated with file parsers.

Functions

The following functions are used with file parsers.

VwStreamCloseFunc

```
VOID VwStreamCloseFunc(SOFILE hFile, HPROC reserved);
```

Closes the file. The file parser must carry out any necessary cleanup, such as closing any other open files related to the given file.

- No return value.

hFile
> Handle of the file for execute input and output (XIO) routines.

reserved
> Reserved; do not use.

VwStreamOpenFunc

```
INT VwStreamOpenFunc(SOFILE hFile, INT wFileId,
    U_BYTE VWPTR * pFileName, SOFILTERINFO VWPTR * pFilterInfo,
    HPROC reserved);
```

Checks the validity of the specified file and returns information about the file parser.

- Returns the VWERR_OK value if successful or one of the following error values otherwise:

VWERR_BADFILE	Corrupt or unreadable file
VWERR_EMPTYFILE	Empty file
VWERR_PROTECTEDFILE	Password-protected or encrypted file
VWERR_SUPFILEOPENFAILS	Supplementary file failed to open

hFile
> Handle of the file for execute input and output (XIO) routines.

wFileId
> Identifier for the file.

pFileName
> Address of the null-terminated string specifying the base name of the file. This string does not include path information.

pFilterInfo
> Address of the **SOFILTERINFO** structure that receives information about the file parser.

reserved
> Reserved; do not use.

VwStreamReadFunc

```
INT VwStreamReadFunc(SOFILE hFile, HPROC reserved);
```

Outputs characters, cells, or fields, depending on the current section type and file contents.

- Returns zero if successful or −1 if the end of the file is reached.

hFile
Handle of the file for execute input and output (XIO) routines.

reserved
Reserved; do not use.

VwStreamReadRecordFunc

```
VOID VwStreamReadRecordFunc(SOFILE hFile, DWORD dwData, HPROC reserved);
```

Outputs a single record by calling various stream output functions.

- No return value.

hFile
Handle of the file for execute input and output (XIO) routines.

dwData
Data to be saved for the record.

reserved
Reserved; do not use.

This function should output a single record and then call the **SOPutBreak** function with the SO_RECORDBREAK value before returning. The SO_EOFBREAK and SO_SECTIONBREAK conditions do not need to be trapped by this function.

VwStreamSectionFunc

```
INT VwStreamSectionFunc(SOFILE hFile, HPROC reserved);
```

Sets the parameters for a section.

- Always returns zero.

hFile
Handle of the file for execute input and output (XIO) routines.

reserved
Reserved; do not use.

At a minimum, this function should call the **SOPutSectionType** and **SOPutSectionName** functions to set the section type and name. The function should also set the cell width if the section is a spreadsheet or the field format if the section is a database.

The display engine calls the function after calling the **VwStreamOpenFunc** function but before calling the **VwStreamReadFunc** function. It is also called after any **VwStreamReadFunc** that ends with a call to the **SOPutBreak** function with the SO_SECTIONBREAK value.

VwStreamSeekFunc

```
INT VwStreamSeekFunc(SOFILE hFile, HPROC reserved);
```

Same definition as the line filters Seek function

- Returns zero if successful or −1 if the function fails.

hFile
    Handle of the file for execute input and output (XIO) routines.
reserved
    Reserved; do not use.

VwStreamTellFunc

```
INT VwStreamTellFunc(SOFILE hFile, HPROC reserved);
```

Same definition as the line filters Tell function.

- Returns zero if successful or −1 if the function fails.

hFile
    Handle of the file for execute input and output (XIO) routines.
reserved
    Reserved; do not use.

Helper Functions

SOBailOut

```
VOID SOBailOut(WORD wError, HPROC reserved);
```

Allows the file parser to return an error condition.

- No return value.

wError
   Error flag. This parameter can be one of these values:

SOERROR_BADFILE	Invalid file format
SOERROR_EOF	Unexpected end of file (EOF)
SOERROR_GENERAL	Unspecified error

reserved
   Reserved; do not use.

The parser should return from the **VwReadStreamFunc** function as soon as possible after this function is called.

SOBeginTable

```
VOID SOBeginTable(HPROC reserved);
```

Starts a table definition, indicating that the text in subsequent output calls is part of a table.

- No return value.

reserved
   Reserved; do not use.

This function must be called between paragraphs and before row and cell formats are specified.

SOEndColumnInfo

```
VOID SOEndColumnInfo(HPROC reserved);
```

Ends the definition of column information.

- No return value.

reserved
   Reserved; do not use.

The file parser must call this function immediately after setting the column information. This function can only be called from the **VwStreamSection** function.

SOEndFieldInfo

```
VOID SOEndFieldInfo(HPROC reserved);
```

Ends the definition of field information.

- No return value.

reserved
   Reserved; do not use.

The file parser must have previously called the **SOStartFieldInfo** function.

The file parser calls this function immediately after setting the field information. This function can only be called from the **VwStreamSection** function.

SOEndFontTable

```
VOID SOEndFontTable(HPROC reserved);
```

Ends the definition of a font table.

- No return value.

reserved
   Reserved; do not use.

The file parser must call this function immediately after setting font entries. This function can only be called from the **VwStreamSection** function.

SOEndPalette

```
VOID SOEndPalette( HPROC reserved );
```

Ends the definition of a color palette.

- No return value.

reserved
   Reserved; do not use.

The file parser calls this function immediately after specifying the last palette entry.

SOEndTable

```
VOID SOEndTable(HPROC reserved);
```

Ends a table definition, indicating that the text in subsequent output calls is no longer part of a table.

- No return value.

reserved
   Reserved; do not use.

The function must be called after a row break.

SOEndTabStops

```
VOID SOEndTabStops(HPROC reserved);
```

Ends the definition of tabs stops for a paragraph.

- No return value.

reserved
   Reserved; do not use.

To set tab stops, use the **SOPutTabStop** function.

The file parser calls this function immediately after setting the last tab stop for the paragraph.

SOGetInfo

```
VOID SOGetInfo(WORD wInfo, void VWPTR * pInfo, HPROC reserved);
```

Retrieves information about a spreadsheet.

- No return value.

wInfo
  Information type. If this parameter is the SOINFO_COLUMNRANGE value, the function retrieves the range of columns for a spreadsheet to read.

pInfo
  Address of a 32-bit variable that receives the first column number in the low-order word and the second column number in the high-order word.

reserved
  Reserved; do not use.

SOGetScanLineBuffer

```
WORD SOGetScanLineBuffer(VOID VWPTR * ppScanLineData, HPROC reserved );
```

Retrieves the address of the buffer for storing the current scan line.

- Returns the size, in bytes, of the scan line data buffer. The size is the maximum number of bytes that may be accessed using the returned address and is guaranteed to be sufficient to hold a scan line as wide as the entire tile.

ppScanLineData
  Address of the variable that receives the address of the scan line data buffer.

reserved
  Reserved; do not use.

This function is called from the **VwStreamReadFunc** function for each scan line produced.

This function sets the variable pointed to by *ppScanLineData* to the address where the scan line data should be built.

SOPutBitmapHeader

```
VOID SOPutBitmapHeader(PSOBITMAPHEADER pBitmapHeader, HPROC reserved);
```

Outputs information about a bitmap.

- No return value.

pBitmapHeader
> Address of the **SOBITMAPHEADER** structure that contains the bitmap header information.

reserved
> Reserved; do not use.

SOPutBreak

```
WORD SOPutBreak(WORD wType, DWORD dwInfo, HPROC reserved);
```

Sets a paragraph, cell, record, page, section, or other type of break.

- Returns the SO_STOP value to direct the file parser to stop processing and return or the SO_CONTINUE value to direct the file parser to continue processing.

wType
> Type of break. This parameter can one of these values:

SO_CELLBREAK	Regular cell break
SO_EOFBREAK	End of file (EOF) break, which implies a section break
SO_PARABREAK	Regular paragraph break
SO_RECORDBREAK	Regular record break
SO_SECTIONBREAK	Section break
SO_SUBDOCBEGINBREAK	Subdocument's begin break
SO_SUBDOCENDBREAK	Subdocument's end break

dwInfo
> Data to save for each record. This data is for database section breaks. For all other section types, this parameter should be zero.

reserved
> Reserved; do not use.

dwInfo is saved after every **SOPutBreak** function and, like the regular save information, should represent the next record, not the one just read.

In spreadsheet sections, the last cell in a section must have an associated SO_CELLBREAK break before either the SO_SECTIONBREAK or SO_EOFBREAK break.

In database sections, the last record in a section must have an associated SO_RECORDBREAK break before either the SO_SECTIONBREAK or SO_EOFBREAK break.

In word processing sections, the last paragraph does not need an SO_PARABREAK break before either the SO_SECTIONBREAK or SO_EOFBREAK break.

SOPutChar

```
VOID SOPutChar(WORD wCh, HPROC reserved);
```

Outputs a character, applying the current font, height, and attributes.

■ No return value.

wCh
   Character value. This parameter must be within the range specified by the current character set.

reserved
   Reserved; do not use.

The character is assumed to belong to the character set selected by the open function and is countable and visible.

SOPutCharAttr

```
VOID SOPutCharAttr(WORD wAttr, WORD wState, HPROC reserved);
```

Sets the style attributes for characters in text.

■ No return value.

wAttr
> Style attribute type. This parameter can be one of these values:

SO_BOLD	Bold
SO_CAPS	All capital letters
SO_DOTUNDERLINE	Dotted underline
SO_DUNDERLINE	Double underline
SO_ITALIC	Italic
SO_OUTLINE	Outlined rather than solid
SO_SHADOW	Shadow slightly beneath and behind
SO_SMALLCAPS	Small capital letters
SO_STRIKEOUT	Strikeout
SO_SUBSCRIPT	Subscript
SO_SUPERSCRIPT	Superscript
SO_UNDERLINE	Single underline
SO_WORDUNDERLINE	Underline

wState
> Style attribute state. This parameter can be the SO_ON or SO_OFF value.

reserved
> Reserved; do not use.

SOPutCharFontById

```
VOID SOPutCharFontById(DWORD dwFontId, HPROC reserved);
```

Sets the font for characters in text.

- No return value.

dwFontId
> Font identifier, relative to the previously given font table.

reserved
> Reserved; do not use.

SOPutCharFontByName

```
VOID SOPutCharFontByName(WORD wFontType, char VWPTR * pFontName, HPROC
reserved);
```

Sets the font for characters in text.

- No return value.

wFontType
Font family. This parameter can be one of these values:

SO_FAMILYDECORATIVE	Fancy display font
SO_FAMILYMODERN	Fixed width
SO_FAMILYROMAN	Variable width with serifs
SO_FAMILYSCRIPT	Handwriting
SO_FAMILYSWISS	Variable width without serifs
SO_FAMILYSYMBOL	Symbol font
SO_FAMILYUNKNOWN	Not known

pFontName
Address of a null-terminated string specifying the name of the font.

reserved
Reserved; do not use.

SOPutCharHeight

```
VOID SOPutCharHeight(WORD wHeight, HPROC reserved);
```

Sets the height, in half points, of a character in text.

▪ No return value.

wHeight
Height, in half points, of the character.

reserved
Reserved; do not use.

SOPutCharX

```
VOID SOPutCharX(WORD wCh, WORD wType, HPROC reserved);
```

Outputs a character, applying the specified character type.

▪ No return value.

wCh
Character value. This parameter must be within the range specified by the current character set.

wType
Type flag. This parameter can be one or more of these values:

SO_COUNT	The character is countable and may be deleted. Characters *without* this value are for display purposes and do not enter into character count calculations for write back.
SO_HIDDEN	The character is not visible on the display.
SO_LIMITEDIT	Consecutive characters of this type will be deleted as a group. No write back command will begin on one of these characters, but it may encompass a group of these characters.

reserved
Reserved; do not use.

The character is assumed to belong to the character set selected by the open function.

SOPutColumnInfo

```
VOID SOPutColumnInfo(PSOCOLUMN pColumn, HPROC reserved);
```

Sets column information.

▪ No return value.

pColumn
Address of the **SOCOLUMN** structure containing the column information.

reserved
Reserved; do not use.

The file parser must call the **SOStartColumnInfo** function before calling this function.

This function can only be called from the **VwStreamSection** function.

SOPutDataCell

```
VOID SOPutDataCell(PSODATACELL pCell, HPROC reserved);
```

Outputs data for a cell.

▪ No return value.

pCell
>   Address of a **SODATACELL** structure.

reserved
>   Reserved; do not use.

SOPutEmbeddedObject

```
VOID SOPutEmbeddedObject(PSOEMBEDDEDOBJECT pObject, HPROC reserved);
```

Sets an embedded graphics object.

- No return value.

pObject
>   Address of the **SOEMBEDDEDOBJECT** structure that contains information
>   about the object to be embedded.

reserved
>   Reserved; do not use.

The file parser must set the **SOEMBEDDEDOBJECT** structure with the
appropriate values.

SOPutField

```
VOID SOPutField(void VWPTR * pData, HPROC reserved);
```

Outputs data for a field.

- No return value.

pData
>   Address of the data for the field.

reserved
>   Reserved; do not use.

This function is used for all **wStorage** types except the SO_FIELDTEXTVAR
value.

SOPutFieldInfo

```
VOID SOPutFieldInfo(PSOFIELD pField, HPROC reserved);
```

Sets field information.

- No return value.

pField
> Address of the **SOFIELD** structure containing the field information.

reserved
> Reserved; do not use.

The file parser must call the **SOStartFieldInfo** function before calling this function.

This function can only be called from the **VwStreamSection** function.

SOPutFontTableEntry

```
VOID SOPutFontTableEntry(DWORD dwFontId, WORD wFontType,
    char VWPTR * pFontName, HPROC reserved);
```

Sets a font table entry.

- No return value.

dwFontId
> Font identifier. This parameter can be any number, but it must be unique within the font table.

wFontType
> Font family. This parameter can be one of these values:

SO_FAMILYDECORATIVE	Fancy display font
SO_FAMILYMODERN	Fixed width
SO_FAMILYROMAN	Variable width with serifs
SO_FAMILYSCRIPT	Handwriting
SO_FAMILYSWISS	Variable width without serifs
SO_FAMILYSYMBOL	Symbol font
SO_FAMILYUNKNOWN	Not known

pFontName
> Address of a null-terminated string specifying the name of the font.

reserved
> Reserved; do not use.

The file parser must call the **SOStartFontTable** function before calling this function. **SOPutFontTableEntry** must be called once for each font to be added to the table. Font identifiers must be unique, but they can be given in any order.

This function can only be called from the **VwStreamSection** function.

SOPutHdrEntry

```
VOID SOPutHdrEntry(char VWPTR *pLabel, char VWPTR * pData, WORD wId,
    HPROC reserved);
```

Sets strings for the header information.

- No return value.

pLabel
Label that the display engine should use when presenting this value.

pData
Value to display.

wId
Identifier for this item that the display engine and filter agree upon.

reserved
Reserved; do not use.

This function can only be called from the **VwStreamSection** function.

SOPutMoreText

```
VOID SOPutMoreText(WORD wCount, char VWPTR * pText, WORD bMore,
    HPROC reserved);
```

Outputs the text for a cell and indicates whether there is more text to be output for the cell.

- No return value.

wCount
Number of characters pointed to by *pText*. The number must not exceed 128 bytes.

pText
Address of the string of text characters to output.

bMore
More data flag. This parameter can be the SO_YES value to indicate more text to be output or the SO_NO value to indicate none.

reserved
Reserved; do not use.

This function is used to output a sequence of text initially started by using the **SOPutText** function.

If there is more text to output, the file parser must use a subsequent call or calls to the **SOPutMoreText** function to output the text. The 128 byte limit is for the convenience of the function processing **SOPutMoreText**.

SOPutMoreVarField

```
VOID SOPutMoreVarField(VOID VWPTR * pData, WORD wCount, WORD bMore,
    HPROC reserved);
```

Outputs data for a variable field and indicates whether there is more data to be output for the field.

- No return value.

pData
  Address of the data for the field.

wCount
  Number of bytes pointed to by *pData*. The number must not exceed 128 bytes.

bMore
  More data flag. This parameter can be the SO_YES value to indicate more data to be output or the SO_NO value to indicate none.

reserved
  Reserved; do not use.

This function can be called any number of times.

If there is more data to output, the file parser must use a subsequent call or calls to **SOPutMoreVarField** to output the data. The 128 byte limit is for the convenience of the function processing **SOPutMoreVarField**.

This function is used to output a sequence of data initially started by using the **SOPutVarField** function.

SOPutPaletteEntry

```
VOID SOPutPaletteEntry(unsigned char Red, unsigned char Green,
    unsigned char Blue, HPROC reserved);
```

Sets the colors for a palette entry.

- No return value.

Red
> Relative red intensity in the range 0 to 255.

Green
> Relative green intensity in the range 0 to 255.

Blue
> Relative blue intensity in the range 0 to 255.

reserved
> Reserved; do not use.

The file parser must call the **SOStartPalette** function before calling this function.

The order of calls to this function determines the order of entries in the color table for an image. The first palette entry is color 0, the color displayed for pixels with a value of 0; the second palette entry is color 1; and so on.

SOPutParaAlign

```
VOID SOPutParaAlign(WORD wType,HPROC reserved);
```

Sets the alignment for a paragraph.

- No return value.

wType
> Type of alignment. This parameter can be the SO_ALIGNLEFT, SO_ALIGNRIGHT, SO_ALIGNCENTER, or SO_ALIGNJUSTIFY value.

reserved
> Reserved; do not use.

SOPutParaIndents

```
VOID SOPutParaIndents(LONG dwLeft, LONG dwRight, LONG dwFirst,
    HPROC reserved);
```

Sets indents for a paragraph. Indents are relative to the corresponding left or right margin.

- No return value.

dwLeft
> Width, in twips, of the left indent. The indent is measured from the left page margin.

dwRight
    Width, in twips, of the right indent. The indent is measured from the right page margin.

dwFirst
    Width, in twips, of the left indent for the first line in the paragraph. The indent is measured from the left page margin.

reserved
    Reserved; do not use.

SOPutParaMargins

```
VOID SOPutParaMargins(LONG dwLeft, LONG dwRight, HPROC reserved);
```

Sets paragraph margins. The margins are relative to the left or right edge of the page.

- No return value.

dwLeft
    Width, in twips, of the left margin.

dwRight
    Width, in twips, of the right margin.

reserved
    Reserved; do not use.

SOPutParaSpacing

```
VOID SOPutParaSpacing(WORD wLineHeightType, DWORD dwLineHeight,
    DWORD dwSpaceBefore, DWORD dwSpaceAfter, HPROC reserved);
```

Sets the spacing for a paragraph.

- No return value.

wLineHeightType
    Type of line height. This parameter can be one of these values:

SO_HEIGHTATLEAST	Sets the line height to the height given by *dwLineHeight* or sets it to fit the tallest character in the line, whichever height is greater.
SO_HEIGHTAUTO	Sets the line height automatically to fit the tallest character in the line.
SO_HEIGHTEXACTLY	Sets the line height to the height given by *dwLineHeight*.

dwLineHeight
>   Baseline to baseline height, in twips.

dwSpaceBefore
>   Space before the paragraph, in twips.

dwSpaceAfter
>   Space after the paragraph, in twips.

reserved
>   Reserved; do not use.

SOPutScanLineData

```
VOID SOPutScanLineData(U_BYTE VWPTR * pScanLineData, HPROC reserved);
```

Sets the bit values in a single scan line of a bitmap.

- No return value.

pScanLineData
>   Address of the bitmap data for the current scan line.

reserved
>   Reserved; do not use.

The bitmap format must have been previously defined by using the **SOPutBitmapHeader** function.

SOPutSectionName

```
VOID SOPutSectionName(char VWPTR * pName, HPROC reserved);
```

Sets the name of a section.

- No return value.

pName
>   Address of a null-terminated string specifying the name of the section.

reserved
>   Reserved; do not use.

SOPutSectionType

```
VOID SOPutSectionType(WORD wType, HPROC reserved);
```

Outputs a section type.

- No return value.

wType

Section type. This parameter can be one of these values:

SO_BITMAP	Sets the section type to be a bitmap. When generating output for the section, the file parser should use only general and bitmap stream output functions.
SO_CELLS	Sets the section type to be a spreadsheet consisting of cells. When generating output for the section, the file parser should use only the general and spreadsheet stream output functions.
SO_FIELDS	Sets the section type to be a database consisting of fields. When generating output for the section, the file parser should use only the general and database stream output functions.
SO_PARAGRAPHS	Sets the section type to be a word processing document consisting of paragraphs. When generating output for the section, the file parser should use only general and word processing stream output functions.
SO_VECTOR	Sets the section type to be a vector graphics section consisting of graphics objects. When generating output for the section, the file parser should use only the general and vector graphics stream output functions.

reserved

Reserved; do not use.

SOPutSpecialCharX

```
VOID SOPutSpecialCharX(WORD wCh, WORD wType, HPROC reserved);
```

Outputs a special character, applying the specified character type.

- No return value.

wCh

Character value. This parameter can be one of these values:

SO_CHDATE	Automatic current date
SO_CHHHYPHEN	Nonbreaking hyphen
SO_CHHLINE	Hard line break
SO_CHHPAGE	Hard page break
SO_CHHSPACE	Nonbreaking space

SO_CHPAGENUMBER	Automatic page number
SO_CHSHYPHEN	Hyphen
SO_CHTAB	Tab
SO_CHTIME	Automatic current time
SO_CHUNKNOWN	Default character

wType

Type flag. This parameter can be one or more of these values:

SO_COUNT	The character is countable and may be deleted. Characters *without* this value are for display purposes and do not enter into character count calculations for write back.
SO_HIDDEN	The character is not visible on the display.
SO_LIMITEDIT	Consecutive characters of this type will be deleted as a group. No write back command will begin on one of these characters, but it may encompass a group of these characters.

reserved

Reserved; do not use.

SOPutSubdocInfo

```
VOID SOPutSubdocInfo(WORD wType, WORD wSubType, HPROC reserved);
```

Outputs subdocument data.

- No return value.

wType

Type of data. This parameter can be one of these values:

SO_COMMENT	The data is a comment.
SO_FOOTER	The data applies to the document footer.
SO_FOOTNOTE	The data applies to a footnote.
SO_HEADER	The data applies to the document header.

wSubType
Subtype of data. This parameter can be one of these values:

SO_BOTH	The data is for a header or footer on both left and right pages. This value is used with SO_HEADER or SO_FOOTER.
SO_LEFT	The data is for a header or footer on even pages only. This value is used with SO_HEADER or SO_FOOTER.
SO_RIGHT	The data is for a header or footer on odd pages only. This value is used with SO_HEADER or SO_FOOTER.
0 through 65535	The data is a footnote number. This value is used with SO_FOOTNOTE only.

If *wType* is SO_COMMENT, no subtype is needed.

reserved
Reserved; do not use.

SOPutTableCellInfo

```
VOID SOPutTableCellInfo(PSOTABLECELLINFO pCellInfo, HPROC reserved);
```

Sets cell information.

- No return value.

pCellInfo
Address of a **SOTABLECELLINFO** structure containing information about the cell.

reserved
Reserved; do not use.

SOPutTableRowFormat

```
VOID SOPutTableRowFormat(WORD wLeftEdge, WORD wRowHeight,
    WORD wRowHeightType, WORD wCellMargin, WORD wRowAlignment,
    WORD wNumCells, HPROC reserved );
```

Sets the format of a row in a table.

- No return value.

wLeftEdge
Position, in twips, of the left edge of the table, relative to the left margin.

wRowHeight
Row height, in twips.

wRowHeightType
Type of height for the row. This parameter can be one of these values:

SO_HEIGHTATLEAST	Sets the row height at least as high as that given by *wRowHeight*.
SO_HEIGHTAUTO	Sets the row height automatically to fit text in the row.
SO_HEIGHTEXACTLY	Sets the row height exactly as given by *wRowHeight*.

wCellMargin
White space on either side of text in a cell within the specified cell width. It is equal to half the total white space between adjacent cells.

wRowAlignment
Alignment of row within margins. This parameter can be the SO_ALIGNLEFT, SO_ALIGNRIGHT, or SO_ALIGNCENTER value.

wNumCells
Number of cells in the row.

reserved
Reserved; do not use.

SOPutTabStop

```
VOID SOPutTabStop(PSOTAB pTabs, HPROC reserved);
```

Sets a tab stop for the paragraph.

▪ No return value.

pTabs
Address of the **SOTAB** structure containing the tab stop information.

reserved
Reserved; do not use.

The file parser must call the **SOStartTabStops** function before calling this function and can set multiple tab stops for a paragraph by calling it multiple times. The file parser must not call any other output function while setting tab stops and must call the **SOEndTabStops** function after setting the last tab stop.

SOPutTextCell

```
VOID SOPutTextCell(PSOTEXTCELL pCell, WORD wCount, char VWPTR * pText,
    WORD bMore, HPROC reserved);
```

Outputs the text for a cell and indicates whether there is more text to be output for the cell.

- No return value.

pCell
Address of a **SOTEXTCELL** structure.

wCount
Number of characters pointed to by *pText*. The number must not exceed 128 bytes.

pText
Address of the string of text characters to be output.

bMore
More data flag. This parameter can be the SO_YES value to indicate more text to be output or the SO_NO value to indicate none.

reserved
Reserved; do not use.

If there is more text to be output, the file parser must use a subsequent call or calls to the **SOPutMoreText** function to output the text.

SOPutVarField

```
VOID SOPutVarField(void VWPTR * pData, WORD wCount, WORD bMore,
    HPROC reserved);
```

Outputs data for a variable field and indicates whether there is more data to be output for the field.

- No return value.

pData
Address of the data for the variable field.

wCount
Number of bytes pointed to by *pData*. The number must not exceed 128 bytes.

bMore

> More data flag. This parameter can be the SO_YES value to indicate more data to be output or the SO_NO value to indicate none.

reserved

> Reserved; do not use.

If there is more data to be output, the file parser must use a subsequent call or calls to the **SOPutMoreVarField** function to output the data.

SOPutVectorHeader

```
VOID SOPutVectorHeader(PSOVECTORHEADER pVectorHeader, HPROC reserved);
```

Outputs the vector header, specifying the display resolution, x- and y-axis orientation, background color, and color value type (RGB or palette).

- No return value.

pVectorHeader

> Address of a **SOVECTORHEADER** structure.

reserved

> Reserved; do not use.

SOSetDateBase

```
VOID SOSetDateBase(DWORD dwBase, WORD wFlags, HPROC reserved);
```

Sets the base date. All subsequent dates are calculated as the sum of the base date and the given date value.

- No return value.

dwBase

> Base number of Julian days to be automatically added to dates. All dates are entered in Julian day format in the following manner:

Jan. 1, 4713 B.C.	Julian Day 1
Jan. 1, 1 A.D.	Julian Day 1721424
Jan. 1, 1900	Julian Day 2415021
Jan. 1, 1904	Julian Day 2416481

> Formats supporting dates before 1582 are not supported.

wFlags
> Action flag. This parameter can be the SO_LOTUSHELL value to correct for the Lotus® 1-2-3® 1990 leap year bug.

reserved
> Reserved; do not use.

This function can only be called from the **VwStreamSection** function.

SOStartColumnInfo

```
VOID SOStartColumnInfo(HPROC reserved);
```

Starts the definition of column information.

- No return value.

reserved
> Reserved; do not use.

The file parser must call this function immediately before setting the information. This function can only be called from the **VwStreamSection** function.

SOStartFieldInfo

```
VOID SOStartFieldInfo(HPROC reserved);
```

Starts the definition of field information.

- No return value.

reserved
> Reserved; do not use.

The file parser calls this function immediately before setting field information. This function can only be called from the **VwStreamSection** function.

SOStartFontTable

```
VOID SOStartFontTable(HPROC reserved);
```

Starts the definition of a font table.

- No return value.

reserved
    Reserved; do not use.

The file parser must call this function immediately before setting font entries. This function can only be called from the **VwStreamSection** function.

SOStartPalette

```
VOID SOStartPalette(HPROC reserved);
```

Starts the definition of a color palette.

- No return value.

reserved
    Reserved; do not use.

The file parser calls this function immediately before defining palette entries.

SOStartTabStops

```
VOID SOStartTabStops(HPROC reserved);
```

Starts the definition of tab stops for a paragraph.

- No return value.

reserved
    Reserved; do not use.

To set tab stops, use the **SOPutTabStop** function.

The file parser calls this function immediately before setting the first tab stop for the paragraph.

SOVectorAttr

```
VOID SOVectorAttr(INT nItemId, DWORD wDataSize, VOID VWPTR *pData,
    HPROC reserved);
```

Sets attributes related to drawing vector graphics objects.

- No return value.

nItemId
> Action identifier. This parameter, which specifies the action to carry out and determines the appropriate values for *wDataSize* and *pData*, can be one of the vector attribute values in "Constants" later in this article.

wDataSize
> Size, in bytes, of data pointed to by *pData*.

pData
> Address of a buffer containing the information used to carry out the requested action. The meaning and format of the buffer depends on the value of *nItemId*.

reserved
> Reserved; do not use.

SOVectorObject

```
VOID SOVectorObject(INT nItemId, DWORD dwDataSize, VOID VWPTR *pData,
    HPROC reserved );
```

Draws or defines the given vector graphics object.

- No return value.

nItemId
> Action flag. This parameter, which specifies the action to carry out and determines the appropriate values for *wDataSize* and *pData*, can be one of the vector object values in "Constants" later in this article.

wDataSize
> Size, in bytes, of the data pointed to by *pData*.

pData
> Address of a buffer containing the information used to carry out the requested action. The meaning and format of the buffer depends on the value of *nItemId*.

reserved
> Reserved; do not use.

SUUserPopData

```
VOID SUUserPopData(VOID VWPTR * pData, HPROC reserved);
```

Pops user data. The data must have been pushed previously by using the **SUUserPushData** function.

- No return value.

pData
    Address of the **VwStreamUserSaveType** structure receiving the data.

reserved
    Reserved; do not use.

SUUserPushData

```
VOID SUUserPushData(VOID VWPTR * pData, HPROC reserved);
```

Pushes user data.

- No return value.

pData
    Address of a **VwStreamUserSaveType** structure containing the data to be saved.

reserved
    Reserved; do not use.

The data can be retrieved by using the **SUUserPopData** function.

SUUserRetrieveData

```
VOID SUUserRetrieveData(WORD wIndex, VOID VWPTR * pData, HPROC reserved);
```

Retrieves user data.

- No return value.

wIndex
    Index value specifying the data to retrieve. This value must have been previously returned by the **SUUserSaveData** function.

pData
    Address of the **VwStreamUserSaveType** structure receiving the data.

reserved
    Reserved; do not use.

The data must have been previously saved by using the **SUUserSaveData** function.

This function should not be used. The **SUUserPopData** function should be used instead.

SUUserSaveData

```
WORD SUUserSaveData(VOID VWPTR * pData, HPROC reserved);
```

Saves user data.

- Returns the index used to retrieve the data. Indexes are guaranteed to be zero-based and sequential.

pData
Address of a **VwStreamUserSaveType** structure containing the data to be saved.

reserved
Reserved; do not use.

This function should not be used. The **SUUserPushData** function should be used instead.

Macros

The following macros are used with file parsers.

SOANGLETENTHS

```
SOANGLETENTHS(AngleInTenthsOfADegree)
```

Sets the angle in tenths of a degree.

SOPALETTEINDEX

```
SOPALETTEINDEX(Index)
```

Creates a palette-index color value. *Index* must specify a valid palette entry index. When this color value is used, the system uses the color from the given palette entry.

SOPALETTERGB

```
SOPALETTERGB(Red, Green, Blue)
```

Creates a palette-relative RGB color value. *Red*, *Green*, and *Blue* specify the red, green, and blue color intensities and must be in the range 0 to 255. When this color value is specified, the system uses the palette entry that has the color that most closely matches this value.

SORGB

```
SORGB(Red, Green, Blue)
```

Creates an RGB color value. *Red*, *Green*, and *Blue* specify the red, green, and blue color intensities and must be in the range 0 to 255.

SOSETRATIO

```
SOSETRATIO(Numerator, Denominator)
```

Sets the ratio. *Numerator* and *Denominator* specify the ratio factors and must be values in the range 0 to 65,535.

Structures

The following structures are used with file parsers.

SOARCINFO

```
typedef struct SOARCINFOtag {
    SORECT Rect;       // see below
    SOANGLE StartAngle; // see below
    SOANGLE EndAngle;   // see below
} SOARCINFO, VWPTR *PSOARCINFO;
```

Contains information defining the arc to be drawn.

Rect
　　Rectangle that bounds the ellipse containing the arc.

StartAngle
　　Angle specifying the starting point of the arc. The angle is defined in tenths of a degree, counterclockwise from the positive x-axis. To set this member, use the **SOANGLETENTHS** macro.

EndAngle
　　Angle specifying the ending point of the arc. The angle is defined in tenths of a degree, counterclockwise from the positive x-axis. To set this member, use the **SOANGLETENTHS** macro.

SOBITMAPHEADER

```
typedef struct SOBITMAPHEADERtag {
    WORD wStructSize;    // see below
    WORD wImageFlags;    // see below
    WORD wImageWidth;    // see below
    WORD wImageLength;   // see below
    WORD wTileWidth;     // see below
    WORD wTileLength;    // see below
    WORD wBitsPerPixel;  // see below
    WORD wNPlanes;       // see below
    WORD wHDpi;          // see below
    WORD wVDpi;          // see below
} SOBITMAPHEADER, VWPTR *PSOBITMAPHEADER;
```

Contains information about the bitmap to be output.

wStructSize

Size, in bytes, of the structure.

wImageFlags

Image flags. This member can be a combination of one (and only one) color format value and other attribute values.

The color format can be one of these values:

SO_BGRCOLOR	Pixel values are RGB color values (24-bit only); bytes are stored consecutively in the order B,G,R.
SO_BLACKANDWHITE	Pixels are black or white (1 bit per pixel only).
SO_COLORPALETTE	Pixel values are indexes into the color palette for the bitmap.
SO_GRAYSCALE	Pixel values are gray scale values.
SO_RGBCOLOR	Pixel values are RGB color values (24-bit only); bytes are stored consecutively in the order R,G,B.

Other attributes can be a combination of these values:

SO_BOTTOMTOTOP	The image is provided in scan lines from the bottom up. The default is top to bottom.
SO_WHITEZERO	For gray scale images and black and white images only, a pixel with a value of zero is a white pixel, and increasing pixel values become darker. By default, a value of zero is defined as a black pixel with increasing values becoming lighter.

wImageWidth

Horizontal width, in pixels, of the image.

wImageLength

Vertical length, in pixels, of the image.

wTileWidth

Horizontal width, in pixels, of the tile.

wTileLength

Vertical length, in pixels, of the tile.

wBitsPerPixel

Number of consecutive bits that define the pixel color. The number is currently limited to 1, 4, 8, or 24.

wNPlanes

Color planes. This member must be 1.

wHDpi

Horizontal resolution, in pixels per inch, of the display on which the image originated. If the resolution is not known, this member can be zero.

wVDpi

Vertical resolution, in pixels per inch, of the display on which the image originated. If the resolution is not known, this member can be zero.

SOBORDER

```
typedef struct SOBORDERtag {
    WORD wWidth;        // see below
    SOCOLORREF rgbColor; // see below
    WORD wFlags;        // see below
} SOBORDER, VWPTR * PSOBORDER;
```

Contains information about the border around a cell in table.

wWidth

Width, in twips, of the border.

rgbColor

Color of the border. This member can be a RGB color value. To set this member, use the **SORGB** macro.

wFlags

Type of border and the edges to which it applies. This member can be a combination of the SO_BORDERNONE, SO_BORDERDOUBLE, SO_BORDERHAIRLINE, SO_BORDERTHICK, SO_BORDERSHADOW, and SO_BORDERDOTTED values.

SOCOLUMN

```
typedef struct SOCOLUMNtag {
    WORD wStructSize; // see below
    LONG dwWidth;     // see below
    char szName[40];  // see below
} SOCOLUMN, VWPTR * PSOCOLUMN;
```

Contains information about the columns in a spreadsheet.

wStructSize
Size, in bytes, of the structure.

dwWidth
Width, in characters, of the column.

szName
Null-terminated string specifying the name of the column.

SOCPARCANGLE

```
typedef struct SOCPARCANGLEtag {
    SOPOINT Center;      // center point
    SOANGLE SweepAngle;  // sweep angle
} SOCPARCANGLE, VWPTR *PSOCPARCANGLE;
```

Contains information defining an arc for use in vector graphics output.

SOCPPIEANGLE

```
typedef struct SOCPPIEANGLEtag {
    INT nRadius;         // radius
    SOANGLE StartAngle;  // starting angle
    SOANGLE SweepAngle;  // sweep angle
} SOCPPIEANGLE, VWPTR *PSOCPPIEANGLE;
```

Contains information defining a pie shape for use in vector graphics output.

SOCPTEXTATPOINT

```
typedef struct SOCPTEXTATPOINTtag {
    WORD wFormat;     // format of text
    INT nTextLength;  // text length
} SOCPTEXTATPOINT, VWPTR *PSOCPTEXTATPOINT;
```

Contains information defining the format and length of text for use in vector graphics output.

SODATACELL

```
typedef struct SODATACELLtag {
    WORD wStructSize;    //see below
    WORD wStorage;       //see below
    WORD wDisplay;       //see below
    DWORD dwSubDisplay;  //see below
    WORD wPrecision;     //see below
    WORD wAlignment;     //see below
    WORD wAttribute;     //see below
    union {
        SOINT32S Int32S; //see below
        SOINT32U Int32U; //see below
        BYTE IEEE4[4];   //see below
        BYTE IEEE8[8];   //see below
        BYTE IEEE10[10]; //see below
        BYTE BCD8[8];    //see below
    } uStorage;
} SODATACELL, VWPTR * PSODATACELL;
```

Contains information about the data to be placed in a cell of a spreadsheet.

wStructSize

Size, in bytes, of the structure.

wStorage

Storage type. This member can be one of these values:

SO_CELLBCD8I	Packed BCD excess-63.
SO_CELLEMPTY	The cell is empty.
SO_CELLERROR	The cell has an error condition.
SO_CELLIEEE4I	IEEE 4-byte in Intel® (PC) ordering.
SO_CELLIEEE8I	IEEE 8-byte in Intel (PC) ordering.
SO_CELLIEEE10I	IEEE 10-byte in Intel (PC) ordering.
SO_CELLINT32S	32-bit signed integer.
SO_CELLINT32U	32-bit unsigned integer.

wDisplay

Display type. This member can be one of these values:

SO_CELLBOOL	Boolean (0 = FALSE and 1 = TRUE).
SO_CELLDATE	Julian Days since the base date. **wStorage** may be either an IEEE or integer value.
SO_CELLDATETIME	Julian Days since the base date. **wStorage** may be either an IEEE or integer value.
SO_CELLDECIMAL	Decimal notation.
SO_CELLDOLLARS	Dollar sign.
SO_CELLEXPONENT	Exponential notation.
SO_CELLNUMBER	General number format.
SO_CELLPERCENT	Percent (not constrained to 0–100).
SO_CELLTIME	Decimal part of a day if **wStorage** is an IEEE value or seconds since 00:00 if **wStorage** is an integer value.

dwSubDisplay

Display subtype. The values depend on **wDisplay** value.

For SO_CELLNUMBER and SO_CELLDOLLARS, this member can be a combination of one negative-number format, thousands separator, and cell multiplier.

Negative Number Format

SO_CELLNEG_MINUS	Negative numbers have a minus sign.
SO_CELLNEG_MINUSRED	Negative numbers have a minus sign and are red.
SO_CELLNEG_PAREN	Negative numbers have parentheses.
SO_CELLNEG_PARENRED	Negative numbers have parentheses and are red.

Thousands Separator

SO_CELL1000SEP_COMMA	Commas as 1,000s separator.
SO_CELL1000SEP_NONE	No 1,000s separator.

Cell Multiplier

SO_CELLMULT_1	Used for all file parsers.
SO_CELLMULT_01	Used only for Microsoft® Excel viewer.
SO_CELLMULT_05	Used only for Lotus viewer.
SO_CELLMULT_005	Used only for Lotus viewer.
SO_CELLMULT_0005	Used only for Lotus viewer.
SO_CELLMULT_00005	Used only for Lotus viewer.
SO_CELLMULT_500	Used only for Lotus viewer.
SO_CELLMULT_5000	Used only for Lotus viewer.
SO_CELLMULT_0625	Used only for Lotus viewer.
SO_CELLMULT_015625	Used only for Lotus viewer.

For SO_CELLDATETIME, SO_CELLDATE, and SO_CELLTIME, this member can be a combination of one date separator, day format, month format, year format, day of week format, and time format.

Date Separator

SO_CELLDATESEP_MINUS

SO_CELLDATESEP_NONE

SO_CELLDATESEP_PERIOD

SO_CELLDATESEP_SPACE

Day Format

SO_CELLDAY_NONE

SO_CELLDAY_NUMBER

Month Format

SO_CELLMONTH_ABBREV

SO_CELLMONTH_FULL

SO_CELLMONTH_NONE

SO_CELLMONTH_NUMBER

Year Format

SO_CELLYEAR_ABBREV

SO_CELLYEAR_FULL

SO_CELLYEAR_NONE

Day of Week Format

SO_CELLDAYOFWEEK_ABBREV

SO_CELLDAYOFWEEK_FULL

SO_CELLDAYOFWEEK_NONE

Time Format

SO_CELLTIME_HHMM24

SO_CELLTIME_HHMMAM

SO_CELLTIME_HHMMHMS   For example, 14h45m

SO_CELLTIME_HHMMSS24

SO_CELLTIME_HHMMSSAM

SO_CELLTIME_HHMMSSHMS   For example, 14h45m34s

SO_CELLTIME_NONE

wPrecision

Precision or positioning value, depending on the **wDisplay** value.

For SO_CELLNUMBER and SO_CELLDOLLARS, this member specifies the number of places to the right of the decimal point.

For SO_CELLDATETIME, SO_CELLDATE, and SO_CELLTIME, this member specifies the position in the date time string of each element. It must be a combination of one value for each of the day of week position, month position, day position, year position, and time position.

Day of Week Position

SO_CELLDAYOFWEEK_1

SO_CELLDAYOFWEEK_2

SO_CELLDAYOFWEEK_3

SO_CELLDAYOFWEEK_4

SO_CELLDAYOFWEEK_5

Month Position

SO_CELLMONTH_1

SO_CELLMONTH_2

SO_CELLMONTH_3

SO_CELLMONTH_4

SO_CELLMONTH_5

Day Position

SO_CELLDAY_1

SO_CELLDAY_2

SO_CELLDAY_3

SO_CELLDAY_4

SO_CELLDAY_5

Year Position

SO_CELLYEAR_1

SO_CELLYEAR_2

SO_CELLYEAR_3

SO_CELLYEAR_4

SO_CELLYEAR_5

Time Position

SO_CELLTIME_1

SO_CELLTIME_2

SO_CELLTIME_3

SO_CELLTIME_4

SO_CELLTIME_5

wAlignment

Alignment of data in the cell. This member can be the SO_CELLLEFT, SO_CELLRIGHT, or SO_CELLCENTER value.

wAttribute

Attribute of data in the cell. This member can be a combination of the SO_CELLBOLD, SO_CELLITALIC, SO_CELLUNDERLINE, and SO_CELLSTRIKEOUT values.

Int32S

Signed 32-bit integer.

Int32U

Unsigned 32-bit integer.

IEEE4

Four-byte array representing an IEEE 4-byte floating-point number.

IEEE8

Eight-byte array representing an IEEE 8-byte floating-point number.

IEEE10

Ten-byte array representing an IEEE 10-byte floating-point number.

BCD8

Eight-byte array representing an excess-63 floating-point packed BCD.

SOEMBEDDEDGRAPHIC

```
typedef struct SOEMBEDDEDGRAPHICtag {
    SOPOINT Size;        // see below
    SORECT Crop;         // see below
    SOPOINT ScaledSize;  // see below
    WORD wBorder;        // see below
    DWORD dwFlags;       // see below
} SOEMBEDDEDGRAPHIC;
```

Contains information about the size and positioning of an embedded graphics object.

Size

Initial size of the image before scaling and cropping.

Crop

Cropping amount on the top, bottom, left, and right edges.

ScaledSize

Final size of the image after scaling and cropping.

wBorder

Border thickness, in twips. If this member is zero, there is no border.

dwFlags

Flags. This member can be a combination of these values:

SO_CENTERIMAGE	The image is centered in its final rectangle.
SO_MAINTAINASPECT	The image aspect ratio is preserved.

SOEMBEDDEDOBJECT

```
typedef struct SOEMBEDDEDOBJECTtag {
    WORD wStructSize;   // see below
    WORD wObjectType;   // see below
    char szFile[144];   // see below
    WORD wFIType;       // see below
    DWORD dwFileOffset; // see below
    SOEMBEDINFO Info;   // see below
} SOEMBEDDEDOBJECT, VWPTR * PSOEMBEDDEDOBJECT;
```

Contains information about an embedded object.

wStructSize

Size, in bytes, of the structure.

wObjectType

Type of object type. This member can be the SOEMBED_GRAPHIC or SO_UNKNOWN value.

szFile

Null-terminated string specifying the path and filename of the file that contains the object. If the object is in the current file, this member is NULL.

wFIType

File identifier for object's file. If the object type is the SO_UNKNOWN value, this member is zero.

dwFileOffset

Offset, in bytes, to the embedded object from the start of the given file.

Info

Union containing object-specific information.

SOEMBEDINFO

```
typedef union SOEMBEDINFOtag {
    SOEMBEDDEDGRAPHIC Graphic; // embedded graphics structure
} SOEMBEDINFO;
```

Contains information specific to embedded graphics objects.

SOFIELD

```
typedef struct SOFIELDtag {
    WORD wStructSize;
    LONG dwWidth;
    char szName[40];
    WORD wStorage;
    WORD wDisplay;
    DWORD dwSubDisplay;
    WORD wPrecision;
    WORD wAlignment;
} SOFIELD, VWPTR * PSOFIELD;
```

Contains information about a field in a database.

wStructSize
> Size, in bytes, of the structure.

dwWidth
> Width, in characters, of the column.

szName
> Null-terminated string specifying the name of the field.

wStorage
> Storage type. This member can be one of these values:

SO_CELLBCD8I	Packed BCD excess-63.
SO_CELLEMPTY	The cell is empty.
SO_CELLERROR	The cell has an error condition.
SO_CELLIEEE4I	IEEE 4-byte in Intel (PC) ordering.
SO_CELLIEEE8I	IEEE 8-byte in Intel (PC) ordering.
SO_CELLIEEE10I	IEEE 10-byte in Intel (PC) ordering.
SO_CELLINT32S	32-bit signed integer.
SO_CELLINT32U	32-bit unsigned integer.
SO_FIELDTEXTFIX	The field contains a string of fixed length.
SO_FIELDTEXTVAR	The field contains a string of unknown length.

wDisplay
> Display type. For more information, see the **wDisplay** member in the **SODATACELL** structure.

dwSubDisplay
> Display subtype. For more information, see the **dwSubDisplay** member in the **SODATACELL** structure.

wPrecision

> Precision or positioning value. For more information, see the **wPrecision** member in the **SODATACELL** structure.

> If **wStorage** is the SO_FIELDTEXTFIX value, this member specifies the number of characters in the string.

wAlignment

> Alignment of data in the cell. This member can be the SO_CELLLEFT, SO_CELLRIGHT, or SO_CELLCENTER value.

SOFILTERINFO

```
typedef struct SOFILTERINFOtag {
    INT wFilterCharSet;      // see below
    U_BYTE szFilterName[32]; // see below
} SOFILTERINFO;
```

Contains information identifying the file parser.

wFilterCharSet

> Character set used for text by the file parser. This member must be the SO_WINDOWS value.

szFilterName

> Null-terminated string specifying the name of the file parser. The name should identify either the format of the files being parsed or the product that created the files.

SOGROUPINFO

```
typedef struct SOGROUPINFOtag {
    WORD wStructSize;     // see below
    SORECT BoundingRect;  // see below
    INT nTransforms;      // see below
} SOGROUPINFO, VWPTR *PSOGROUPINFO;
```

Contains information about a group for use with vector graphics output.

wStructSize

> Size, in bytes, of the structure.

BoundingRect

> Rectangle that bounds all points displayed in the group. This rectangle does not cause clipping to occur. If clipping is needed, a clipping path must be selected.

nTransforms

> Number of transformation structures following this structure.

SOLOGBRUSH

```
typedef struct SOLOGBRUSHtag {
    WORD lbStyle;        // see below
    SOCOLORREF lbColor;  // see below
    INT lbHatch;         // see below
} SOLOGBRUSH, VWPTR *PSOLOGBRUSH;
```

Contains information defining a logical brush for use with vector graphics output.

lbStyle

Brush style. This member can be the SOBS_HATCHED, SOBS_HOLLOW, or SOBS_SOLID value.

lbColor

Color of the brush. This member can be an RGB or palette-relative value. To set this member, use the **SORGB** or **SOPALETTE** macro.

lbHatch

Hatch style. This member can be the SOHS_BDIAGONAL, SOHS_CROSS, SOHS_DIAGCROSS, SOHS_FDIAGONAL, SOHS_HORIZONTAL, or SOHS_VERTICAL value. This member is used only if **lbStyle** is the SO_HATCHED value.

For a complete definition of the members, see the **LOGBRUSH** structure.

SOLOGFONT

```
typedef struct SOLOGFONTtag {
    INT lfHeight;                       // font height
    INT lfWidth;                        // font width
    INT lfEscapement;                   // angle of text line
    INT lfOrientation;                  // angle of character baseline
    INT lfWeight;                       // font weight
    BYTE lfItalic;                      // italics
    BYTE lfUnderline;                   // underline
    BYTE lfStrikeOut;                   // strikeout
    BYTE lfCharSet;                     // character set
    BYTE lfOutputPrecision;             // output precision
    BYTE lfClipPrecision;               // clipping precision
    BYTE lfQuality;                     // output quality
    BYTE lfPitchAndFamily;              // pitch and family of font
    BYTE lfFaceName[SOLF_FACESIZE];     // typeface name of font
} SOLOGFONT, VWPTR *PSOLOGFONT;
```

Contains information that defines a logical font for use with vector graphics output. The **lfHeight** and **lfWidth** members must be in the same logical units as all of the other drawing commands. For a description of the members, see the **LOGFONT** structure.

SOLOGPEN

```
typedef struct SOLOGPENtag {
    INT loPenStyle;      // see below
    SOPOINT loWidth;     // see below
    SOCOLORREF loColor;  // see below
} SOLOGPEN, VWPTR *PSOLOGPEN;
```

Contains information that defines a logical pen for use with vector graphics output. For a complete definition of the members, see the **LOGPEN** structure.

loPenStyle
Pen Style. This member can be the SOPS_SOLID, SOPS_DASH, SOPS_DOT, SOPS_DASHDOT, SOPS_DASHDOTDOT, SOPS_NULL, or SOPS_INSIDEFRAME value.

loWidth
Width, in logical units, of the pen. The **x** member in the **POINT** structure is used, and the **y** member is ignored.

loColor
Color of the brush. This member can be an RGB or palette-relative value. To set this member, use the **SORGB** or **SOPALETTE** macro.

SOPARAINDENTS

```
typedef struct SOPARAINDENTStag {
    INT FirstLineIndent; // see below
    INT LeftIndent;      // see below
    INT RightIndent;     // see below
} SOPARAINDENTS, VWPTR *PSOPARAINDENTS;
```

Contains information about paragraph indents for use with vector graphics output.

FirstLineIndent
Distance, from the left edge of the frame, to indent the first line of each paragraph.

LeftIndent
Distance, from the left edge of the frame, to indent all lines but the the first line of each paragraph.

RightIndent
Distance, from the right edge of the frame, to indent all lines of each paragraph.

SOPATHINFO

```
typedef struct SOPATHINFOtag {
    WORD wStructSize;    // see below
    SORECT BoundingRect; // see below
    INT nTransforms;     // see below
} SOPATHINFO, VWPTR *PSOPATHINFO;
```

Contains information about a path for use with vector graphics output.

wStructSize
Size, in bytes, of the structure.

BoundingRect
Rectangle that bounds all points displayed in the path. This rectangle does not cause clipping to occur. If clipping is needed, a clipping path must be selected.

nTransforms
Number of transformation structures following this structure.

SOPOINT

```
typedef struct SOPOINTtag {
    INT x; // x-coordinate
    INT y; // y-coordinate
} SOPOINT, VWPTR *PSOPOINT;
```

Contains coordinates for a point.

SOPOLYINFO

```
typedef struct SOPOLYINFOtag {
    WORD wFormat; // see below
    INT nPoints;  // see below
} SOPOLYINFO, VWPTR *PSOPOLYINFO;
```

Contains information about the type and number of vertices of a polyline, polygon, spline, or Bézier curve.

wFormat
Format type. This member can be one of these values:

SOPT_BEZIERCLOSE	SOPT_POLYGON
SOPT_BEZIEROPEN	SOPT_POLYLINE
SOPT_CPPOLYGON	SOPT_SPLINECLOSE
SOPT_CPPOLYLINE	SOPT_SPLINEOPEN

nPoints
Number of vertices in the object.

SORECT

```
typedef struct SORECTtag {
    INT left;    // x-coordinate of upper left corner
    INT top;     // y-coordinate of upper left corner
    INT right;   // x-coordinate of lower right corner
    INT bottom;  // y-coordinate of lower right corner
} SORECT, VWPTR *PSORECT;
```

Contains the dimensions of a rectangle.

SOTAB

```
typedef struct SOTABtag {
    WORD wType;     // see below
    WORD wChar;     // see below
    WORD wLeader;   // see below
    LONG dwOffset;  // see below
} SOTAB, VWPTR * PSOTAB;
```

Contains information about tab stops.

wType
Type of tab stop. This member can be the SO_TABLEFT, SO_TABRIGHT, SO_TABCENTER, or SO_TABCHAR value.

wChar
Alignment character if **wType** is SO_TABCHAR. Tabs are aligned on this character.

wLeader
Repeating leader character for the tab. If this member is zero, there is no leader.

dwOffset
Offset of the tab from the left page margin.

SOTABLECELLINFO

```
typedef struct SOTABLECELLINFOtag {
    WORD wWidth;                // see below
    WORD wMerge;                // see below
    WORD wShading;              // see below
    PSOBORDER pLeftBorder;      // see below
    PSOBORDER pRightBorder;     // see below
    PSOBORDER pTopBorder;       // see below
    PSOBORDER pBottomBorder;    // see below
} SOTABLECELLINFO, VWPTR *PSOTABLECELLINFO;
```

Contains information about cells in a table.

wWidth

Width, in twips, of the cell.

wMerge

Merge flag specifying whether the cell is merged with any neighboring cells. This member can be a combination of these values: SO_MERGELEFT, SO_MERGERIGHT, SO_MERGEABOVE, and SO_MERGEBELOW.

wShading

Intensity value for background shading in the range of 0 to 255. If this member is zero, there is no background shading.

pLeftBorder

Left border.

pRightBorder

Right border.

pTopBorder

Top border.

pBottomBorder

Bottom border.

SOTEXTATARCANGLE

```
typedef struct SOTEXTATARCANGLEtag {
    SOARCINFO ArcInfo; // see below
    WORD wFormat;      // see below
    INT nTextLength;   // see below
} SOTEXTATARCANGLE, VWPTR *PSOTEXTATARCANGLE;
```

Contains information about text for use with vector graphics output.

ArcInfo

Arc information defining the arc relative to which the text is located. Only the starting angle is used to locate the point; the ending angle is ignored.

wFormat

Alignment format, indicating the relationship between the given point and the base line or bounding rectangle of the text. This member can be a combination of these values:

SOTA_BASELINE	Aligns the point and base line of the font.
SOTA_BOTTOM	Aligns the point and bottom of the bounding rectangle.
SOTA_CENTER	Aligns the point and horizontal center of the bounding rectangle.
SOTA_LEFT	Aligns the point and left side of the bounding rectangle.
SOTA_RIGHT	Aligns the point and right side of the bounding rectangle.
SOTA_TOP	Aligns the point and top of the bounding rectangle.

nTextLength

Length of text string that follows the structure.

SOTEXTATPOINT

```
typedef struct SOTEXTATPOINTtag {
    SOPOINT Point;    // see below
    WORD wFormat;     // see below
    INT nTextLength;  // see below
} SOTEXTATPOINT, VWPTR *PSOTEXTATPOINT;
```

Contains information about text at a point.

Point

Point that locates the text.

wFormat

Alignment format, indicating the relationship between the point and the base line or bounding rectangle of the text. This member can be a combination of these values:

SOTA_BASELINE	Aligns the point and base line of the font.
SOTA_BOTTOM	Aligns the point and bottom of the bounding rectangle.
SOTA_CENTER	Aligns the point and horizontal center of the bounding rectangle.
SOTA_LEFT	Aligns the point and left side of the bounding rectangle.
SOTA_RIGHT	Aligns the point and right side of the bounding rectangle.
SOTA_TOP	Aligns the point and top of the bounding rectangle.

nTextLength

Length of the text string that follows the structure.

SOTEXTCELL

```
typedef struct SOTEXTCELLtag {
    WORD wStructSize; // see below
    WORD wAlignment;  // see below
    WORD wAttribute;  // see below
} SOTEXTCELL, VWPTR * PSOTEXTCELL;
```

Contains information about the alignment and attributes of text in a spreadsheet cell.

wStructSize
    Size, in bytes, of the structure.

wAlignment
    Alignment. This member can be the SO_CELLLEFT, SO_CELLRIGHT, SO_CELLCENTER, or SO_CELLFILL value.

wAttribute
    Attributes. This member can be a combination of the SO_CELLBOLD, SO_CELLITALIC, SO_CELLUNDERLINE, and SO_CELLSTRIKEOUT values.

SOTEXTINRECT

```
typedef struct SOTEXTINRECTtag {
    SORECT Rect;       // see below
    WORD wFormat;      // see below
    INT nTextLength;   // see below
} SOTEXTINRECT, VWPTR *PSOTEXTINRECT;
```

Contains information about text for use with vector graphics output.

Rect
    Rectangle in which text is formatted.

wFormat
    Format of the string. This member can be a combination of these values:

SODT_BOTTOM	SODT_NOPREFIX
SODT_CALCRECT	SODT_RIGHT
SODT_CENTER	SODT_SINGLELINE
SODT_EXPANDTABS	SODT_TABSTOP
SODT_EXTERNALLEADING	SODT_TOP
SODT_LEFT	SODT_VCENTER
SODT_NOCLIP	SODT_WORDBREAK

nTextLength

Length of the text string that follows the structure.

SOTRANSFORM

```
typedef struct SOTRANSFORMtag {
    WORD wTransformFlags;  // see below
    SOPOINT Origin;        // see below
    INT xOffset;           // see below
    INT yOffset;           // see below
    SORATIO xScale;        // see below
    SORATIO yScale;        // see below
    SORATIO xSkew;         // see below
    SORATIO ySkew;         // see below
    SOANGLE RotationAngle; // see below
} SOTRANSFORM, VWPTR *PSOTRANSFORM;
```

Contains information about a transformation for use with vector graphics output.

wTransformFlags

Type of transformation. This member can be a combination of these values:

SOTF_NOTRANSFORM	SOTF_XSKEW
SOTF_ROTATE	SOTF_YOFFSET
SOTF_XOFFSET	SOTF_YSCALE
SOTF_XSCALE	SOTF_YSKEW

TSOTF_ROTATE may be combined only with SOTF_XOFFSET and SOTF_YOFFSET. In addition, no other values may be combined with SOTF_NOTRANSFORM.

Origin

Point of origin for all transformations, except for SOTF_XOFFSET and SOTF_YOFFSET.

xOffset and **yOffset**

Offset values to use for the SOTF_XOFFSET and OTF_YOFFSET transformations. The **x** and **y** members of this value are added to the x- and y-coordinates of all points in the transformed object.

xScale

Ratio to use for SOTF_XSCALE transformations. This ratio is used to scale the image on the x-axis from the given origin. To set this member, use the **SOSETRATIO** macro.

yScale

Ratio to use for SOTF_YSCALE transformations. This ratio is used to scale the image on the y-axis from the given origin. To set this member, use the **SOSETRATIO** macro.

xSkew

Ratio to use for SOTF_XSKEW transformations. This ratio used to skew the image horizontally from the given origin. To set this member, use the **SOSETRATIO** macro.

ySkew

Ratio to use for SOTF_YSKEW transformations. This ratio used to skew the image vertically from the given origin. To set this member, use the **SOSETRATIO** macro.

RotationAngle

Angle, in tenths of a degree, to use for SOTF_ROTATE transformations. All points are rotated this many degrees about the given origin. This value must be set by using the **SOANGLETENTHS** macro. A **SOANGLE** variable should not be set directly. Additional macros will be made available as needed.

The transformation equation follows.

```
x' = Origin.x + (xScale * (x-Origin.x)) + (xSkew*(y-Origin.y)) + xOffset
y' = Origin.y + (yScale * (y-Origin.y)) + (ySkew*(x-Origin.x)) + yOffset
```

SOVECTORHEADER

```
typedef struct SOVECTORHEADERtag {
    WORD wStructSize;      // see below
    SORECT BoundingRect; // see below
    WORD wHDPI;            // see below
    WORD wVDPI;            // see below
    WORD wImageFlags;      // see below
    SOCOLOR BkgColor;      // see below
} SOVECTORHEADER, VWPTR *PSOVECTORHEADER;
```

Contains information defining the size and attributes of the rectangle in which vector graphics are drawn.

wStructSize

Size, in bytes, of the structure.

BoundingRect

Rectangle that bounds all drawing commands.

wHDpI

Dots per inch resolution along the x-axis.

wVDpI

Dots per inch resolution along the y-axis.

wImageFlags
Image flags. This member can be a combination of these values:

SO_VECTORCOLORPALETTE	Uses a color palette. Color values must be palette entry indexes or palette-relative RGB values.
SO_VECTORRGBCOLOR	Uses RGB color values.
SO_XISLEFT	Has positive x-coordinates left of the y-axis.
SO_YISUP	Has positive y-coordinates up from the x-axis.

BkgColor
Color of the background in the bounding rectangle. This value must be set by using one of the three color macros: **SOPALETTEINDEX**, **SORGB**, or **SOPALETTERGB**. However, **SORGB** should not be used if a palette is defined.

Constants

The following vector object values and vector attribute values are used with the vector graphics functions.

Vector Object Values

SO_ARC
Draws an arc. *dwDataSize* must be 4 * **sizeof(SOPOINT)**, and *pData* must be the address of four **SOPOINT** structures.

SO_ARCCLOCKWISE
Draws an arc in the clockwise direction. *dwDataSize* must be 4 * **sizeof(SOPOINT)**, and *pData* must be the address of four **SOPOINT** structures.

SO_ARCANGLE
Draws an arc by defining the angles of the two points on the ellipse that locate the start and end of the arc. *dwDataSize* must be **sizeof(SOARCINFO)**, and *pData* must be the address of a **SOARCINFO** structure that defines the arc.

SO_ARCANGLECLOCKWISE
Draws an arc in the clockwise direction by defining the angles of the two points on the ellipse that locate the start and end of the arc. *dwDataSize* must be **sizeof(SOARCINFO)**, and *pData* must be the address of a **SOARCINFO** structure.

SO_CHORD
Draws a chord. *dwDataSize* must be 4 * **sizeof(SOPOINT)**, and *pData* must be the address of four **SOPOINT** structures.

SO_CHORDANGLE

Draws a chord by defining the angles of the two points on the ellipse that locate the start and end of the chord. *dwDataSize* must be **sizeof(SOARCINFO)**, and *pData* must be the address of a **SOARCINFO** structure that defines the chord in terms of the arc located on the chord.

SO_TEXTINRECT

Draws text in a rectangle. *dwDataSize* must be **sizeof(SOTEXTINRECT)** added to the length of the text string, and *pData* must be the address of a **SOTEXTINRECT** structure followed by the text string.

SO_ELLIPSE

Draws an ellipse. *dwDataSize* must be 2 * **sizeof(SOPOINT)**, and *pData* must be the address of two **SOPOINT** structures.

SO_FLOODFILL

Fills the area with the given color. *dwDataSize* must be **sizeof(SOPOINT)** added to **sizeof(SOCOLORREF)**, and *pData* must be the address of a variable containing the coordinates of the point to start at followed by the RGB color value to use to fill the area.

SO_LINE

Draws a line from point 1 to point 2 using the current pen. *dwDataSize* must be 2 * **sizeof(SOPOINT)**, and *pData* must be the address of two **SOPOINT** structures.

SO_PIE

Draws a pie shape. *dwDataSize* must be 4 * **sizeof(SOPOINT)**, and *pData* must be the address of four **SOPOINT** structures.

SO_PIEANGLE

Draws a pie by defining the angles of the two points on the ellipse that locate the start and end of the pie. *dwDataSize* must be **sizeof(SOARCINFO)**, and *pData* must be the address of a **SOARCINFO** structure that defines the pie in terms of the arc located on the pie.

SO_STARTPOLY

Starts drawing of a polygon. *dwDataSize* must be **sizeof(SOPOLYINFO)**, and *pData* must be the address of a **SOPOLYINFO** structure.

SO_POINTS

Specifies vertices of a polygon. *dwDataSize* must be N * **sizeof(SOPOINT)**, and *pData* must be the address of consecutively stored **SOPOINT** structures. At most, **SOMAXPOINTS** can be passed in a single SO_POINTS object. Multiple SO_POINTS objects can be generated to define all of the points associated with a polygon object. The number of points defined in SO_STARTPOLY must be defined using SO_POINTS before the object is closed with SO_ENDPOLY.

SO_ENDPOLY

Ends drawing of a polygon. *dwDataSize* must be zero, and *pData* must be NULL.

SO_RECTANGLE

Draws a rectangle. *dwDataSize* must be 2 * **sizeof(SOPOINT)**, and *pData* must be the address of two **SOPOINT** structures.

SO_ROUNDRECT

Draws a rectangle with rounded corners. *dwDataSize* must be 3 * **sizeof(SOPOINT)**, and *pData* must be address of the three **SOPOINT** structures.

SO_SETPIXEL

Sets the color of a pixel. *dwDataSize* must be **sizeof(SOPOINT)** added to **sizeof(SOCOLORREF)**, and *pData* must be the address of a variable containing the pixel point followed by the RGB color value to set.

SO_TEXTATPOINT

Draws text at the given point. *dwDataSize* must be **sizeof(SOTEXTATPOINT)** added to the length of the text string, and *pData* must be the address of a **SOTEXTATPOINT** structure followed by the text string.

SO_TEXTATARCANGLE

Draws text at the given location. *dwDataSize* must be **sizeof(SOTEXTATARCANGLE)** added to the length of the text string, and *pData* must be the address of a **SOTEXTATARCANGLE** structure followed by the text string.

SO_BEGINPATH

Starts the definition of a path. *dwDataSize* must be **sizeof(SOPATHINFO)** added to **GroupInfo.nTransforms * sizeof(SOTRANSFORM)**, and *pData* must be the address of a **SOPATHINFO** structure followed by the number of **SOTRANSFORM** structures defined in the **nTransforms** member of the **SOPATHINFO** structure. The transformations will occur to all objects in the path in the order supplied. For more information about these transformations, see the SO_OBJECTTRANSFORM vector atttribute value.

This item is used to begin the definition of a path. Paths are a collection of points connected by lines that form opened or closed objects. Multiple subpaths may be created using SO_CLOSESUBPATH while defining a path. Note that the current object and group transformations will also apply during creation of a path. This allows maximum flexibility with transforming paths. Any object can be rendered to create the path. However, due to current limitations, text objects will not be added to the path. Multiple levels of paths are also allowed.

SO_ENDPATH

Ends the definition of a path. *dwDataSize* must be zero, and *pData* must be NULL.

SO_CLOSESUBPATH

Closes the current subpath. *dwDataSize* must be zero, and *pData* must be NULL.

SO_DRAWPATH

Strokes, fills, or both strokes and fills the current path with the current pen and brush. Since the group, path, and object transformations were applied when the path was created, they are not applied again. *dwDataSize* must be **sizeof(WORD)**, and *pData* must be the address of a variable containing the SODP_STROKE or SODP_FILL value, or both.

SO_BEGINGROUP

Starts the definition of a group. *dwDataSize* must be **sizeof(SOGROUPINFO)** added to **GroupInfo.nTransforms * sizeof(SOTRANSFORM)**, and *pData* must be the address of a **SOGROUPINFO** structure followed by the number of **SOTRANSFORM** structures defined in the **nTransforms** member of the **SOGROUPINFO** structure. The transformations will occur to all objects in the group in the order supplied. For more information about these transformations, see the SO_OBJECTTRANSFORM vector attribute value.

SO_ENDGROUP

Ends the definition of a group. *dwDataSize* must be zero, and *pData* must be NULL.

SO_CPSET

Moves the current pen position to this point. *dwDataSize* must be **sizeof(SOPOINT)**, and *pData* must be the address of the variable containing the point.

SO_CPLINE

Draws a line from the current pen position. *dwDataSize* must be **sizeof(SOPOINT)**, and *pData* must be the address of a variable containing the point to draw to.

SO_CPRECTANGLE

Draws a rectangle starting at the current pen position. *dwDataSize* must be **sizeof(SOPOINT)**, and *pData* must be the address of a variable containing the point to be the opposite corner of the rectangle.

SO_CPELLIPSE

Draws an ellipse around the current point with an x- and y-radius described by the **SOPOINT** data. *dwDataSize* must be **sizeof(SOPOINT)**, and *pData* must be the address of a variable containing the x- and y-radius values.

SO_CPARCTRIPLE

Draws a circle arc from the current point through the first point and ending at the second point. *dwDataSize* must be 2 * (**sizeof(SOPOINT)**, and *pData* must be the address of two **SOPOINT** structures.

SO_CPARCANGLE

Draws an arc from the current point pivoting around the center point of the specified sweep angle. *dwDataSize* must be **sizeof(SOCPARCANGLE)**, and *pData* must be the address of a **SOCPARCANGLE** structure that gives the center point of the arc and the sweep angle.

SO_CPPIEANGLE
> Draws a pie with the current position as the center and with the given start and sweep angles. *dwDataSize* must be **sizeof(SOCPPIECANGLE)**, and *pData* must be the address of a **SOCPPIEANGLE** structure that gives the radius of the circle.

SO_BEGINSYMBOL
> Starts the definition of a symbol. A symbol is collection of vector commands that together make up a single symbol. Symbols are considered in the wrapping algorithm of frame text. *dwDataSize* must be **sizeof(SORECT)**, and *pData* must be the address of a **SORECT** structure that identifies the bounding rectangle of all commands used within the symbol.

SO_ENDSYMBOL
> Ends the definition of a symbol. *dwDataSize* must be zero, and *pData* must be NULL.

SO_BEGINTEXTFRAME
> Starts the definition of a text frame. A text frame is used in conjunction with SO_TEXTINPARA to wrap text within a frame. Text is wrapped according to the SO_PARAINDENTS vector attribute value. Symbols are included in the wrapping algorithm. *dwDataSize* must be **sizeof(SORECT)**, and *pData* must be the address of a **SORECT** structure that identifies the bounding rectangle of the text frame.

SO_ENDTEXTFRAME
> Ends the definition of a text frame. *dwDataSize* must be zero, and *pData* must be NULL.

SO_TEXTINPARA
> Draws the text string in the current font and text attributes at the current wrap location. The wrap location is moved by the text extent. Any words that would extend beyond the right indent of the frame are wrapped. This object is only valid within a text frame. *dwDataSize* must be **sizeof(INT)** added to the length of the text string, and *pData* must be the address of a integer variable containing the size of the text string that follows.

SO_PARAEND
> Ends a paragraph. *dwDataSize* must be zero, and *pData* must be NULL.

Vector Attribute Values

SO_SELECTFONT

Selects the given font. *dwDataSize* must be **sizeof(SOLOGFONT)**, and *pData* must be the address of a **SOLOGFONT** structure.

SO_SELECTPEN

Selects the given pen. *dwDataSize* must be **sizeof(SOLOGPEN)**, and *pData* must be the address of a **SOLOGPEN** structure.

SO_SELECTBRUSH

Selects the given brush. *dwDataSize* must be **sizeof(SOLOGBRUSH)**, and *pData* must be the address of a **SOLOGBRUSH** structure.

SO_POLYFILLMODE

Sets the polygon-filling mode. *dwDataSize* must be **sizeof(INT)**, and *pData* must be the address of a variable containing either the SOPF_ALTERNATE or SOPF_WINDING value.

SO_TEXTCHAREXTRA

Sets the text character extra value. *dwDataSize* must be **sizeof(INT)**, and *pData* must be the address of a variable containing a value. This attribute affects text objects.

SO_DRAWMODE

Sets the drawing mode used when drawing the pen and interiors. *dwDataSize* must be **sizeof(INT)**, and *pData* must be the address of a variable containing one of these values:

SOR2_BLACK	SOR2_NOT
SOR2_COPYPEN	SOR2_NOTCOPYPEN
SOR2_MASKNOTPEN	SOR2_NOTMASKPEN
SOR2_MASKPEN	SOR2_NOTMERGEPEN
SOR2_MASKPENNOT	SOR2_NOTXORPEN
SOR2_MERGENOTPEN	SOR2_WHITE
SOR2_MERGEPEN	SOR2_XORPEN
SOR2_NOP	

SO_TEXTCOLOR

Sets the foreground color. *dwDataSize* must be **sizeof(SOCOLORREF)**, and *pData* must be the address of a variable containing a RGB or palette-relative color value. To set this value, use the **SORGB** or **SOPALETTE** macro.

SO_BKMODE

Sets the background mode. *dwDataSize* must be **sizeof(INT)**, and *pData* must be the address of a variable containing either the SOBK_OPAQUE or SOBK_TRANSPARENT value.

SO_BKCOLOR

Sets the background color used for styled lines, hatched brushes, and text when the background mode is SOBK_OPAQUE. *dwDataSize* must be **sizeof(SOCOLORREF)**, and *pData* must be the address of a variable containing an RGB or palette-relative color value. To set this value, use the **SORGB** or **SOPALETTE** macro.

SO_OBJECTTRANSFORM

Sets object transformations. *dwDataSize* must be **sizeof (INT)** added to nCount * **sizeof(SOTRANSFORM)**, and *pData* must be one INT (*nCount*) followed by that number of **SOTRANSFORM** structures. The transformations will occur in the order supplied.

SO_CLIPMODE

Sets the clipping mode. *dwDataSize* must be **sizeof(WORD)**, and *pData* must be the address of a variable containing either the SO_DONOTCLIP or SO_CLIPTOPATH value.

SO_POINTRELATION

Sets the coordinate orientation. *dwDataSize* must be **sizeof(INT)**, and *pData* must be the address of a variable containing the SOPR_ABSOLUTE or SOPR_RELATIVE value.

SO_PARAINDENTS

Sets the paragraph indents within a text frame, defining the first, left, and right indents of paragraph text being built into the frame. These values are only valid when within a text frame. All values are in the current coordinate system. *dwDataSize* must be **sizeof(SOPARAINDENTS)**, and *pData* must be the address of a **SOPARAINDENTS** structure.

SO_PARAALIGN

Sets the alignment of paragraph text being built into a text frame. *dwDataSize* must be **sizeof(WORD)**, and *pData* must be the address of a 16-bit variable containing the SO_ALIGNLEFT, SO_ALIGNCENTER, SO_ALIGNRIGHT, or SO_ALIGNJUSTIFY value.

A R T I C L E   1 8

Briefcase Reconcilers

About Briefcase Reconcilers

A briefcase reconciler gives the Windows 95 Briefcase the means to reconcile different versions of a document. A briefcase reconciler combines different *input* versions of a document to produce a single, new *output* version of the document. You may need to create a briefcase reconciler to support your type of document. This article describes briefcase reconcilers and explains how to create them.

Reconciliation

A *document* is a collection of information that can be copied and changed. A document is said to have *versions* if the content of at least two copies of the document are different. Reconciliation produces a single version of a document from two or more initial versions. Typically, the final version is a combination of information from the initial versions with the most recent or most useful information preserved.

Reconciliation is initiated by the Briefcase when it determines that two or more copies of the same document are different. The Briefcase, which is called the *initiator* in this context, locates and starts the briefcase reconciler associated with the given document type. The reconciler compares the documents and determines which portions of the documents to retain. Some reconcilers may require user interaction to complete reconciliation. Others may complete reconciliation without user interaction. The reconciler can be contained within an application or be an extension implemented as a dynamic-link library (DLL).

Some briefcase reconcilers may create *residues*. A residue is a document, usually having the same file type as the initial document, that contains information *not* saved in the merged version. Residues are typically used to give authors a quick way to determine what information from their original document is not in the final merged version. If a reconciler supports residues, it creates one residue for each of the original versions of the document. Residues are not created unless the initiator requests them. The Briefcase does not currently request residues, but future initiators may.

Some briefcase reconcilers work in conjunction with the Briefcase to provide the user with a means to terminate reconciliation. This capability is useful for a user who may decide that the reconciliation should not proceed. A reconciler typically provides a *termination object* when the reconciliation requires user interaction and may be lengthy. In some environments, a reconciler may allow partial reconciliation, enabling a user to temporarily suspend a reconciliation and resume it later. The Briefcase does not currently support partial reconciliation, but future initiators may.

Creating a Briefcase Reconciler

You create a briefcase reconciler by implementing the reconciliation interfaces. At a minimum, a reconciler implements the **IReconcilableObject** interface and the **IPersistStorage** or **IPersistFile** interface. As the initiator, the Briefcase determines when reconciliation is needed and calls the **IReconcilableObject::Reconcile** member function to initiate reconciliation.

Although the **Reconcile** member function can provide a wide-ranging set of reconciliation capabilities, a briefcase reconciler carries out only minimal reconciliation in most cases. In particular, the Briefcase does not require the reconciler to support residue generation or to support the termination object. Also, the reconciler carries out a single top to bottom reconciliation and must not return the REC_E_NOTCOMPLETE value; that is, it should not attempt partial reconciliation.

The Briefcase provides the **IReconcileInitiator** interface. The briefcase reconciler can use the **IReconcileInitiator::SetAbortCallback** member function to set the termination object. The Briefcase does not use version identifiers and can, therefore, not provide previous versions of a document if a reconciler requests them using the corresponding member functions in **IReconcileInitiator**.

The Briefcase passes file monikers to **Reconcile** representing the versions of the document to be reconciled. The briefcase reconciler gains access to the versions by using either the **IMoniker::BindToObject** or **IMoniker::BindToStorage** member function. The latter is generally faster and is recommended. The reconciler must release any objects or storage to which it binds.

When the briefcase reconciler uses **BindToStorage**, it binds to storage that is either flat storage (a stream) or OLE-defined structured storage. If the reconciler expects flat storage, it should use **BindToStorage** to request the **IStream** interface. If the reconciler expects structured storage, it should request the **IStorage** interface. In both cases, it should request read-only direct (nontransacted) access to the storage; read-write access may not generally be available.

A minimal briefcase reconciler typically looks directly at the storage of the other versions and deals with embedded objects in a very primitive manner, such as merging two versions of the object by including both versions in the output version.

The initiator locates the appropriate briefcase reconciler by using a subset of the logic implemented by the **GetClassFile** function to determine the class of a given file and then looks in the registry for the reconciler class associated with the given file class. The Briefcase, like other shell components, determines the class of a file solely by the filename extension. A file's extension must have a registered class for the Briefcase to invoke a reconciler for the file. You must set a registry entry of the following form when installing your reconciler.

CLSID*clsid***\\Roles\\Reconciler***reconciler-classid*

The class must be quick loading, must be designated _MULTIPLEUSE, and, unless marshallers are provided for the reconciliation interface, must be an in-process server (contained in a DLL) rather than a local server (implemented in an .EXE file).

User Interaction

A briefcase reconciler should attempt to carry out reconciliation without user intervention. The more automated the reconciliation, the better the user's perception of the process.

In some cases, user intervention may be valuable. For example, a document system may require a user to review changes before accepting the merged version of a document or may require comments from the user explaining the changes that have been made. In these cases, the initiator, not the briefcase reconciler, is responsible for querying the user and carrying out the user's instructions.

In other cases, user intervention may be necessary. For example, when two versions have been edited in incompatible ways. In such cases, either the initiator or briefcase reconciler must query the user for instructions on how to resolve the conflict. In general, no initiator can rely on completing a reconciliation without expecting some user interaction. Reconcilers, on the other hand, have the option of interacting with the user to resolve conflicts or requiring the initiator to do so.

Embedded Objects

When reconciling a document, the briefcase reconciler itself may become an initiator if it discovers an embedded object of a type that it cannot reconcile. In this case, the reconciler needs to recursively reconcile each of the embedded objects and assume all the responsibilities of an initiator.

To carry out the recursion, the briefcase reconciler loads the object and queries for the appropriate interface. The handler for the object must support the interface. If any member function of the interface returns the OLE_E_NOTRUNNING value, the reconciler must run the object in order to carry out the operation. Because code for embedded objects is not always available, a reconciler must provide a solution for this condition. For example, the reconciler might include both old and new versions of the embedded object in the reconciled version. The reconciler must not attempt to reconcile across links.

The initiator stores the document versions being merged. In many cases, the initiator has access to the storage of each version and saves the result of reconciliation using similar storage. Sometimes, however, the initiator may have an in-memory object for which no persistent version is available. This situation can occur when a document containing open embedded objects must be reconciled before being saved. In such cases, the initiator saves the result of the reconciliation in the version found in memory.

The initiator uses the **IPersistStorage** interface to bind (load) the merged version. The initiator uses the **IPersistStorage::Load** member function if an initial version has already been created and uses the **IPersistStorage::InitNew** member function for the initial version. Once the merged version is loaded, the initiator uses **QueryInterface** to retrieve the address of the **IReconcilableObject** interface. This interface gives the initiator access to the storage of the existing residues and gives it a way to create storage for any new residues. Then the initiator directs the interface to carry out the reconciliation. The initiator actually queries for the **IPersistFile** interface before **IPersistStorage**. If the reconciler supports **IPersistFile**, the initiator manipulates the replica through the **IPersistFile** rather than **IPersistStorage** member functions. This permits reconciliation of files that are not stored as compound documents.

Once the reconciliation is complete, the initiator can save the merged version by using the **IPersistStorage** or **IPersistFile** interface. During reconciliation, the briefcase reconciler creates residues as needed and writes their persistent bits to storage. If the merged version is a stream, the **IStorage** interface passed to **IPersistStorage::Load** contains a stream named "Contents" with its storage state set to STATEBITS_FLAT. (You can set the state bits by using the **IStorage::Stat** member function.) After the merge is complete, the initiator saves the merged version by writing the data in an appropriate manner. It should ensure that STATEBITS_FLAT is set as appropriate for the storage.

Residues

The initiator indicates whether it wants residues by setting the *pstgNewResidues* parameter to a valid address when calling the **IReconcilableObject::Reconcile** member function. If the reconciler does not support the creation of residues, it must return immediately the REC_E_NORESIDUES value, unless the *dwFlags* parameter specifies the RECONCILEF_NORESIDUESOK value.

The briefcase reconciler returns residues to the initiator by creating new storage elements and copying them to the array pointed to by *pstgNewResidues*. For structured storage residues, the reconciler copies an **IStorage** interface, and for flat storage residues, it copies either an **IStream** or **IStorage** interface with the STATEBITS_FLAT flag set. The reconciler uses **IStorage** to create the necessary storage, using **IStorage::CreateStream** to create flat storage for a residue that is a stream and **IStorage::CreateStorage** to create structured storage.

The initiator prepares *pstgNewResidues* such that it contains no elements in the nonreserved part of the **IStorage** namespace. The briefcase reconciler places each residue in an element whose name corresponds to the order of its initial version. For example, the first residue is contained in "1," the second in "2," and so on. If the reconciled object itself produces a residue, that is found in the element named "0."

The briefcase reconciler commits each of the newly created elements individually, ensuring that the initiator has access to the information. The reconciler does not, however, commit *pstgNewResidues* itself. The initiator is responsible for committing this or otherwise disposing of it.

Reference

This section contains information about the reconciliation interfaces. When handling errors, a member function can return only those error values that are explicitly defined as possible return values. Furthermore, the member function must set all variables whose addresses are passed as parameters to NULL before returning from the error.

Interfaces and Member Functions

IReconcilableObject

The **IReconcilableObject** interface carries out the reconciliation of a document. This interface has the **GetProgressFeedbackMaxEstimate** and **Reconcile** member functions. The briefcase reconciler is responsible for implementing this interface.

IReconcilableObject::GetProgressFeedbackMaxEstimate

```
HRESULT IReconcilableObject::GetProgressFeedbackMaxEstimate(
    ULONG * pulProgressMax);
```

Retrieves an estimated measurement of the amount of work required to complete a reconciliation. This value corresponds to a similar value that is passed with the **IReconcileInitiator::SetProgressFeedback** member function during reconciliation. Reconcilers typically use this member function to estimate the work needed to reconcile an embedded document.

- Returns the S_OK value if successful. Otherwise, the member function returns one of the following error values:

OLE_E_NOTRUNNING   The object is an OLE embedded document that must be run before this operation can be carried out. The object state is unchanged as a result of the call.

E_UNEXPECTED   Unspecified error.

pulProgressMax
Address of the variable that receives the work estimate value.

The work estimate value, if available, is only approximate.

IReconcilableObject::Reconcile

```
HRESULT IReconcilableObject::Reconcile(
    IReconcileInitiator * pInitiator,
    DWORD dwFlags,
    HWND hwndOwner,
    HWND hwndProgressFeedback,
    ULONG ulcInput,
    IMoniker ** rgpmkOtherInput,
    LONG * plOutIndex,
    IStorage * pstgNewResidues,
    void * pvReserved);
```

Reconciles the state of an object with one or more other objects. The reconciliation updates the internal state of the object by merging the states of all objects to form a combined state.

- Returns one of the following success values if successful:

S_OK

> Reconciliation was completed successfully, and the changes must be propagated to the other objects.

S_FALSE

> No reconciliation actions were performed. The briefcase reconciler wishes to fall back to the initiator's bit copy implementation. This value may only be returned if RECONCILEF_ONLYYOUWERECHANGED is set in *dwFlags*.

REC_S_IDIDTHEUPDATES

> Reconciliation was completed successfully, and all the objects involved (the object implementing the **Reconcile** member function and all the other objects described by the passed-in monikers) have been updated appropriately. The initiator does not need, therefore, to do anything further to propagate the changes. The variable pointed to by *plOutIndex* should be set to −1L if **Reconcile** returns this value. The initiator will not save the source object's storage if **Reconcile** returns this value. This value may only be returned if RECONCILEF_YOUMAYDOTHEUPDATES was set in *dwFlags*.

REC_S_NOTCOMPLETE

> The briefcase reconciler completed some, but not all, of the reconciliation. It may need user interaction. The changes will not be propagated to other objects.

REC_S_NOTCOMPLETEBUTPROPAGATE

> The briefcase reconciler completed some, but not all, of the reconciliation. It may need user interaction. The changes will be propagated to the other objects.

Otherwise, the member function returns one of the following error values:

REC_E_NORESIDUES

> The briefcase reconciler does not support the generation of residues, so the request for residues is denied. The state of the object is unchanged.

REC_E_ABORTED

> The briefcase reconciler terminated reconciliation in response to a termination request from the initiator (for more information, see **IReconcileInitiator::SetAbortCallback**). The state of the object is unspecified.

REC_E_TOODIFFERENT

> Reconciliation cannot be carried out because the provided document versions are too dissimilar.

REC_E_INEEDTODOTHEUPDATES

> The object's **Reconcile** implementation was called with RECONCILEF_YOUMAYDOTHEUPDATES clear in *dwFlags*; the object's **Reconcile** implementation requires that value to be set in *dwFlags*.

OLE_E_NOTRUNNING

> The object is an OLE embedded object that must be run before this operation can be carried out. The state of the object is unchanged.

E_UNEXPECTED

> Unspecified error.

pInitiator

Address of the **IReconcileInitiator** interface for the initiator of the reconciliation process. This parameter must not be NULL.

dwFlags

Control flags for the reconciliation. This parameter may be zero or a combination of these values:

RECONCILEF_FEEDBACKWINDOWVALID

> *hwndProgressFeedback* is valid.

RECONCILEF_MAYBOTHERUSER

> The briefcase reconciler can prompt for user interaction if it is needed. Without this value, user interaction is not permitted. *hwndOwner* is valid.

RECONCILEF_NORESIDUESOK

> The briefcase reconciler can ignore requests for residues and carry out reconciliation. Reconcilers that do not support residues should check for this value whenever an initiator requests residues. Without this value, a reconciler that does not support residues must immediately return REC_E_NORESIDUES.

RECONCILEF_OMITSELFRESIDUE

>The briefcase reconciler can discard any residue associated with this object. Initiators typically use this value for reconciliations that loop from generation to generation.

RECONCILEF_ONLYYOUWERECHANGED

>The **Reconcile** member function is being called to propagate changes in the changed object to other unchanged objects. This value will only be set if the **HKEY_CLASSES_ROOT\CLSID***clsid_of_reconciler*\ **SingleChangeHook** key exists in the registry. If that key is not present in the registry, the initiator carries out reconciliation by making the other unchanged objects binary identical copies of the changed object. The *rgpmkOtherInput* monikers identify the other objects. This value will only be set in *dwFlags* if RECONCILEF_YOUMAYDOTHEUPDATES is also set. If the briefcase reconciler completes the updates itself successfully, REC_S_IDIDTHEUPDATES should be returned and the variable pointed to by *plOutIndex* should be set to −1L. Note that S_OK should not be returned on success if this value is set in *dwFlags*. The initiator will not save the source object's storage if **Reconcile** returns REC_S_IDIDTHEUPDATES. If the reconciler wishes to fall back to the initiator's bit copy implementation, it may return S_FALSE.

RECONCILEF_RESUMEDRECONCILIATION

>The briefcase reconciler should resume reconciliation, using the partial residues provided. Without this value, the reconciler should ignore any "considered but rejected" information in any of the input versions.

RECONCILEF_YOUMAYDOTHEUPDATES

>The briefcase reconciler may do the updates itself. Without this value, the reconciler may not do the updates itself. If reconciliation is completed successfully, the reconciler should return REC_S_IDIDTHEUPDATES if it did the updates itself or S_OK if it did not do the updates itself.

hwndOwner
Handle of the parent window to use for child windows that the briefcase reconciler creates. This parameter is valid only if the RECONCILEF_MAYBOTHERUSER value is specified in *dwFlags*.

hwndProgressFeedback
Handle of the progress feedback window displayed by the initiator. This parameter is valid only if RECONCILEF_FEEDBACKWINDOWVALID is specified in *dwFlags*. The briefcase reconciler may call the **SetWindowText** function using this window handle to display additional reconciliation status information to the user.

ulcInput
Number of versions or partial residues specified in *dwFlags*. This parameter must not be zero.

rgpmkOtherInput
> Address of an array that contains the addresses of the monikers to use to access the versions or partial residues to be reconciled.

plOutIndex
> Address of the variable that receives an index value indicating whether the result of the reconciliation is identical to one of the initial versions. The variable is set to −1L if the reconciliation result is a combination of two or more versions. Otherwise, it is a zero-based index, with 0 indicating this object, 1 indicating the first version, 2 indicating the second version, and so on.

pstgNewResidues
> Address of the **IStorage** interface used to store newly created residues. This parameter may be NULL to indicate that residues should not be saved.

pvReserved
> Reserved; must be NULL.

IReconcileInitiator

The **IReconcileInitiator** interface provides the briefcase reconciler with the means to notify the initiator of its progress, to set a termination object, and to request a given version of a document. This interface has the **SetArbortCallback** and **SetProgressFeedback** member functions. The initiator is responsible for implementing this interface.

IReconcileInitiator::SetAbortCallback

```
HRESULT IReconcileInitiator::SetAbortCallback(
    IUnknown * pUnkForAbort);
```

Sets the object through which the initiator can asynchronously terminate a reconciliation. A briefcase reconciler typically sets this object for reconciliations that are lengthy or involve user interaction.

- Returns the S_OK value if successful. Otherwise, the member function returns one of the following error values:

REC_E_NOCALLBACK	The initiator does not support termination of reconciliation operations and does not hold the specified object.
E_UNEXPECTED	Unspecified error.

pUnkForAbort
> Address of the **IUnknown** interface for the object. The initiator signals a request to terminate the reconciliation by using the **IUnknown::Release** member function to release the object. This parameter may be NULL to direct the initiator to remove the previously specified object.

The initiator can accept or reject the object. If the initiator accepts the object, the briefcase reconciler must later remove the object by subsequently calling this function with a NULL parameter when the reconciliation is complete. Because the reconciler removes the object after completing reconciliation, there may be times when the initiator releases the object after reconciliation is complete. In such cases, the reconciler ignores the request to terminate.

If the reconciliation is terminated, the **IReconcilableObject::Reconcile** member function must return either the REC_E_ABORTED or REC_E_NOTCOMPLETE value.

IReconcileInitiator::SetProgressFeedback

```
HRESULT IReconcileInitiator::SetProgressFeedback(
    ULONG ulProgress,
    ULONG ulProgressMax);
```

Indicates the amount of progress the briefcase reconciler has made toward completing the reconciliation. The amount is a fraction of 1 and is computed as the quotient of the *ulProgress* and *ulProgressMax*. Reconcilers should call this member function periodically during their reconciliation process.

- Returns the S_OK value if successful or the E_UNEXPECTED value if some unspecified error occurred.

ulProgress
Numerator of the progress fraction.

ulProgressMax
Denominator of the progress fraction.

The initiator typically uses this measure of progress to update a thermometer gauge or some other form of visual feedback for the user. The briefcase reconciler can change the value of *ulProgressMax* from call to call. This means successive calls to this member function do not necessarily indicate steady forward progress. Backward progress is legal, although not desirable. It is the responsibility of the initiator to determine whether backward progress should be revealed to the user.

INotifyReplica

The **INotifyReplica** interface provides the initiator with the means to notify an object that it may be subject to subsequent reconciliation. This interface has the **YouAreAReplica** member function. The briefcase reconciler is responsible for implementing this interface.

INotifyReplica::YouAreAReplica

```
HRESULT INotifyReplica::YouAreAReplica(
    ULONG ulcOtherReplicas,
    IMoniker ** rgpmkOtherReplicas);
```

Notifies on object that it may be subject to subsequent reconciliation through the **IReconilableObject::Reconcile** member function.

Briefcase calls **INotifyReplica** when objects are added to it.

- Returns the S_OK value if successful. Otherwise, the member function returns one of the following error values:

    E_UNEXPECTED   Unspecified error.

ulcOtherReplicas
    Number of other replicas of the object. This parameter must not be zero.

rgpmkOtherReplicas
    Address of an array that contains the addresses of the monikers to use to access the other replicas.

An object may be notified that it is a replica more than once. Briefcase reconcilers are not required to implement this interface. Initiators are not required to call this interface if it is implemented. However, an object's implementation of **IReconcilableObject::Reconcile** may reasonably fail if that object has not previously been notified through **INotifyReplica::YouAreAReplica** that it may be subject to reconciliation.

A R T I C L E   1 9

Passwords Control Panel

About the Passwords Control Panel

The Passwords Control Panel is a system-defined property sheet that allows the user to set security options and manage passwords for all password-protected services (also called password providers) in the system, including screen savers, electronic mail (email), and network logon. In addition, the Passwords Control Panel allows the user to set the Windows logon password and to keep passwords for other password-protected services identical to the Windows logon password. This means that the Windows logon password can work as a universal password for all password-protected services in the system.

The Passwords Control Panel includes a programming interface that allows an application to add property sheet pages. You should add a property sheet page to the Passwords Control Panel if your application provides security-related services that have properties the user can set.

If your application provides a password-protected service, the programming interface of the Passwords Control Panel allows you to add the name of your service to the control panel's list of password-protected services. If you add your service to the list, the user can change the password by using the Passwords Control Panel and keep the password identical to the Windows logon password.

This article describes the Passwords Control Panel and explains how to use its programming interface. The following illustration shows the Passwords Control Panel.

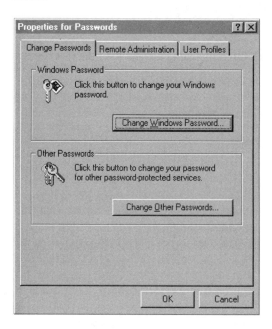

Adding a Property Sheet Page

You should add a property sheet page to the Passwords Control Panel if your application provides security-related functionality that goes beyond simply activating and changing passwords.

To add a property sheet page to the Passwords Control Panel, write a property sheet extension and register the extension with the Microsoft® Windows® 95 shell. A property sheet extension is a 32-bit dynamic-link library (DLL) that implements the **IShellPropSheetExt** interface. The Windows 95 shell calls a property sheet extension when the shell is about to display a property sheet. The extension provides code that creates a page, which the shell adds to the property sheet.

You register a property sheet extension by placing information into the system registry. The Windows 95 shell enumerates the property sheet extension DLLs first under the **\shellex\PropertySheetHandlers** registry key of the default class for system-wide property sheet pages and then under the **\shellex\PropertySheetHandlers** registry key of the object's class for class-specific property sheet pages.

For more information about creating and registering property sheet extensions, see Article 12, "Shell Extensions."

Managing Passwords

If your application provides a password-protected service, you should add your service to the Passwords Control Panel. When you add your service, the name of the service appears in the Select Password dialog box that appears when the user clicks the Change Other Passwords button. The user can change the password for the service by selecting the name and clicking the Change button and then filling in the resulting Change Password dialog box.

The name of your service also appears in the Change Windows Password dialog box with a check box next to it. By checking the check box, the user can choose to keep the password for the service identical to the Windows logon password. Likewise, the user can disassociate the service from the Windows logon password by unchecking the check box.

Including a Password User Interface

Any application that provides a password-protected service should make the password for the service accessible through the Passwords Control Panel. However, if the previous version of your application includes a user interface for setting a password, you may choose to retain that interface as well as making the password accessible through the Passwords Control Panel. If your application includes user interface elements for accomplishing tasks besides setting a password, you should make the change password functionality available both within the application's user interface and within the Passwords Control Panel. If you do not include the change password functionality in the user interface, you should make it available only through the Passwords Control Panel.

Your application should take into account that the user may have multiple keyboard languages installed. Such a user may inadvertently type a password in the wrong language and become confused when the password is rejected. Your application should check for multiple keyboard languages and alert the user when multiple languages are installed.

If your application includes a user interface for setting a password, you should use the Windows built-in change password dialog boxes to get password information from the user. For more information about the Windows change password dialog boxes, see "Change Password Dialog Boxes" later in this article.

Adding a Service to the Passwords Control Panel

If you add a service to the Passwords Control Panel, your installation program should add information about your service to the following location in the registry.

```
HKEY_LOCAL_MACHINE
    System
        CurrentControlSet
            Control
                PwdProvider
                    <Provider Name>
```

Provider Name is the name of your password-protected service. The name should be similar to the name of your executable file. The provider name is used when calling all password functions.

You must specify the following values for *Provider Name*.

Value name	Description
ChangePassword	Exported name of the **PPChangePassword** function.
Description	String that appears in the Select Password dialog box.
ProviderPath	Name of the executable module that provides the password-protected service.
GetPasswordStatus	Exported name of the **PPGetPasswordStatus** function.
Network Provider	Doubleword value that indicates whether the password-protected service provides network services. A network provider should set this value to 1. This value is optional.

In addition to adding information to the registry, you must provide a 32-bit DLL that exports the **PPChangePassword** function. Windows calls the function when the user wants to change the password associated with your password-protected service.

PPChangePassword is a Windows network function that uses a two-stage process to change a password. The function first determines whether it can change the password, and then it actually changes it. This two stage process is particularly important when the user is changing the Windows logon password because the logon password can have many other services associated with it, including network providers. For example, if a service that uses the Windows logon password is not running when the user changes the logon password, Windows shows a dialog box that explains the implications of changing the logon password. If the user goes ahead and changes the Windows logon password, the services with passwords that were not changed are displayed differently in the Change Windows Password and Select Password dialog boxes.

An application that is not a network provider can identify itself as load on demand. In this case, the application is loaded only when the user wants to change a password and is unloaded after the process is complete.

Adding a Service to the Windows Logon Password

When the user checks the check box associated with a password-protected service listed in the Change Windows Password dialog box, Windows calls the **PPChangePassword** function of the application that provides the service. The function attempts to change the password to the current Windows logon password, prompting the user for the old password first, if necessary. If the function fails, it should return an error value so that Windows can display the appropriate error message.

Removing a Service from the Windows Logon Password

When the user unchecks the check box associated with a password-protected service, Windows removes the service from the list of services associated with the Windows logon password. When the user clicks the Change Other Passwords button, Windows calls the application's **PPChangePassword** function. If the user does not change the password, Windows displays a dialog box asking the user whether to change the password for the service that was removed from the Windows logon password.

Changing the Windows Logon Password

The user changes the Windows logon password by clicking the Change Windows Password button, which causes Windows to display the Change Windows Password dialog box. In the dialog box, the user must enter the old and new Windows logon passwords, confirm the new logon password, and then click the OK button. Windows responds by calling the **PPChangePassword** function associated with each password-protected service that the user has added to the Windows logon password. Windows calls the function with the *dwAction* parameter set to the Passwd_Change_Pending value. If any **PPChangePassword** function returns an error value, Windows displays a dialog box that lists the services that cannot use the new Windows logon password. If the user continues to change the Windows logon password, Windows again calls the **PPChangePassword** function of each application that can change the password for its service. Windows sets the *dwAction* parameter to the Passwd_Change_Commit value this time.

Windows appends text to the name of each service whose password could not be changed, explaining that the service is no longer associated with the Windows logon password, even though it is checked. The user can then change the password.

Handling Error Conditions

If an application-defined error occurs while a password is being changed, the application should use the **MPRSetError** function to return an application-defined error value. If a standard error occurs, the application should return one of the following standard error values.

Error value	Meaning
ERROR_EXTENDED_ERROR	The application has a text error message to report.
WN_ACCESS_DENIED	There was a security violation.
WN_BAD_PASSWORD	An incorrect password was specified.
WN_BAD_POINTER	An invalid pointer was specified.
WN_BAD_VALUE	An invalid numeric value was specified.
WN_MORE_DATA	There is a warning that the buffer is too small.
WN_NOT_SUPPORTED	The function is not supported.
WN_SUCCESS	No error occurred; the function succeeded.
WN_WINDOWS_ERROR	A required Windows function failed.

Change Password Dialog Boxes

Windows includes built-in dialog boxes that you can use to get password information from the user. To display a built-in dialog box from within your application, implement the password functionality described previously, and then call the **PwdChangePassword** function. For example, when the user of an email application chooses the command to change the email password, the application can direct Windows to display a built-in change passwords dialog box.

Because Windows keeps track of which password-protected services are associated with the Windows logon password and which are not, Windows presents either the Change Other Passwords or Change Windows Password dialog box, whichever is appropriate.

For example, when the user of an email application chooses the command to change the email password, the application can direct Windows to display one of its built-in change passwords dialog boxes. Windows displays the appropriate dialog box, which depends on whether the user has associated the email password with the Windows logon password.

Using the Passwords Control Panel

The following example shows how to implement the **PPChangePassword** function.

```
#include <windows.h>
#include "mpr.h"

HANDLE hInstance;

#define USE_CRT_INIT 1

BOOL _stdcall _CRT_INIT(HINSTANCE hInstDLL, DWORD fdwReason,
    LPVOID lpReserved);
int FAR PASCAL LibMain(HINSTANCE hInst, WORD wDataSeg,
    WORD wcbHeapSize, LPSTR lpstrCmdLine);

SPIENTRY PPChangePassword(LPLOGONINFO lpAuthentInfo,
    LPLOGONINFO lpPreviousAuthentInfo, DWORD dwAction)
{
    switch (dwAction) {
        case PWDCHANGE_MASTERPWD_NOTIFY:

            // The Windows password has changed. A network provider can
            // add a new password to its store at this point.

            return WN_SUCCESS;

        case PWDCHANGE_PROVIDERPWD_PENDING:
            MessageBox((HWND) NULL,"Got PWDCHANGE_PROVIDERPWD_PENDING",
                "GenProv",MB_OK);

            // Do first-phase password change actions: query the server
            // to see if it is running, verify the old password, and so
            // on. Do not change the password in response to this
            // message. If there are no first-phase actions to do,
            // return WN_SUCCESS. Report errors (and error text, if
            // appropriate) by using NPSSetExtendedError
            // if there is a provider-specific extended error or
            // MPRSetError if the error can be expressed with a
            // WN_ error code. Return either ERROR_EXTENDED_ERROR or
            // the WN_ error code.

            return WN_SUCCESS;
```

```
        case PWDCHANGE_PROVIDERPWD_COMMIT:
            MessageBox(NULL,"Got PWDCHANGE_PROVIDERPWD_COMMIT",
                "GenProv",MB_OK);

            // Change the password. Report errors and display error
            // text, if appropriate, through NPSSetExtendedError
            // if there is a provider-specific extended error
            // or MPRSetError if the error can be expressed with a
            // WN_ error code. Return ERROR_EXTENDED_ERROR or the WN_
            // error code.

            return WN_SUCCESS;
    }

    return WN_SUCCESS;
}

BOOL _stdcall DllEntryPoint(HINSTANCE hInstDll, DWORD fdwReason,
    LPVOID lpReserved)
{

    static BOOL fInit = FALSE;

#if USE_CRT_INIT

    // Initialize the C run-time library before calling any of our code.
    if(fdwReason == DLL_PROCESS_ATTACH ||
            fdwReason == DLL_THREAD_ATTACH)
        if(!_CRT_INIT(hInstDll, fdwReason, lpReserved))
            return(FALSE);

#endif

    if(fdwReason == DLL_PROCESS_ATTACH) {
        hInstance = hInstDll;
    }
```

```
#if USE_CRT_INIT

    // Terminate the C run-time library after all of your code.
    if(fdwReason == DLL_PROCESS_DETACH ||
            fdwReason == DLL_THREAD_DETACH)
        if(!_CRT_INIT(hInstDll, fdwReason, lpReserved))
            return(FALSE);

#endif

    return TRUE;
}
```

Reference

The following functions are used with the Passwords Control Panel.

PPChangePassword

```
DWORD PPChangePassword(LPLOGONINFO lpAuthentInfo,
    LPLOGONINFO lpPreviousAuthentInfo, DWORD dwAction);
```

Informs a password provider that the user has successfully changed the password using the standard **PPChangePassword** dialog box. This notification message is useful if the password provider uses the Window logon password as the default password for network connections. Some password providers are not concerned with any feature of system logon except the password cache; these providers do not need to support this function.

- Returns the WN_SUCCESS value if successful or a WN_ error value otherwise.

lpAuthentInfo
    Address of a **LOGONINFO** structure that contains the name of the user who is currently logged on and the new password.

lpPreviousAuthentInfo
    Address of a **LOGONINFO** structure that contains the name of the user who is currently logged on and the old password.

dwAction

Action flag. This parameter can be one of these values:

PWDCHANGE_MASTERPWD_NOTIFY

> The logon password has changed. The password provider may need to perform an action, such as giving the new password to its redirector.

PWDCHANGE_PROVIDERPWD_CANCEL

> A password provider will receive this message if it has already received a first-phase notification (PWDCHANGE_PROVIDERPWD_ PENDING) and the password change action has been canceled (for example, in response to another password provider being unable to change its password).

PWDCHANGE_PROVIDERPWD_COMMIT

> This message is a commit-phase notification. The password provider should change the password in response to this message.

PWDCHANGE_PROVIDERPWD_PENDING

> The user wants to change a password that is maintained by the password provider. This message is a first-phase notification; the password provider should not change the password at this time. The password provider should do any precommit verification that is appropriate, such as checking that the old password is valid, if possible.

PPGetPasswordStatus

```
DWORD PPGetPasswordStatus(DWORD nIndex);
```

Queries a password provider about the status of its password. A password provider can report whether it is on or off (enabled or disabled) and whether it requires the user to type in the old password to change it. If a password provider does not support this function but does support **PPChangePassword**, it is assumed that the password is always enabled and that typing the old password is required.

- The return value depends on the *nIndex* parameter.

nIndex

Type of information to retrieve. This parameter can be one of these values:

PS_HASOLDPWD	Requests the "old password" status of the password. The return value is one of these values:
	PS_HASOLDPWD_ON PS_HASOLDPWD_OFF
PS_ONOFF	Requests the on or off status of the password. The return value is one of these values:
	PS_ONOFF_ON PS_ONOFF_OFF
PS_STORAGETYPE	Requests the storage type of the password. The return value is one of these values:
	PS_STORAGETYPE_LOCAL PS_STORAGETYPE_NETWORK

PwdChangePassword

```
DWORD PwdChangePassword(LPCTSTR lpProvider, HWND hwndOwner,
    DWORD dwFlags);
```

Changes the user's system logon password or a password provider's password. Master provider router (MPR) displays a dialog box for changing the password. If the user changes the logon password, MPR reencrypts the user's password cache with the new password. Password providers are notified through the **PPChangePassword** function.

- Returns the WN_SUCCESS value if successful or the WN_CANCEL value if the user cancels the operation.

lpProvider

Address of the name of the provider whose password is to be changed. If this parameter is NULL, the logon password is to be changed. Changing the logon password can also result in other password providers being notified to change their passwords, if the user has selected to synchronize a password provider's password with the Windows logon password.

hwndOwner

Handle of the owner window for the dialog box displayed by MPR.

dwFlags

Flag that causes MPR to display a dialog box that prompts only for the previous password. This parameter can be either zero or the CHANGEPWD_OLDPWDONLY value. The current logon password is given to the password provider as the new password. This flag is ignored if **PPChangePassword** is called to change the logon password—that is, if *lpProvider* is NULL. CHANGEPWD_OLDPWDONLY is intended for use by the system; an application should not use it.

PwdGetPasswordStatus

```
DWORD PwdGetPasswordStatus(LPCTSTR lpProvider, DWORD dwIndex,
    LPDWORD lpStatus);
```

Retrieves information about a password provider's password. The request is passed to the password provider through the **PPGetPasswordStatus** function.

- Returns the WN_SUCCESS value if successful or a WN_ error value otherwise.

lpProvider

Address of the name of the network provider that owns the password.

dwIndex

Type of information to retrieve. This parameter can be one of these values:

PS_HASOLDPWD	Indicates whether it is necessary to supply the previous password to change the current password. When the function returns, *lpStatus* includes one of these values: PS_HASOLDPWD_ON PS_HASOLDPWD_OFF
PS_ONOFF	Indicates whether the password is active. When the function returns, *lpStatus* includes one of these values: PS_ONOFF_ON PS_ONOFF_OFF
PS_SYNCMASTERPWD	Indicates whether the password should be kept the same as the Windows logon password. When the function returns, *lpStatus* includes one of these values: PS_SYNCMASTERPWD_ON PS_SYNCMASTERPWD_OFF
PS_STORAGETYPE	Indicates whether the password is stored locally or in a network location. When the function returns, *lpStatus* includes one of these values: PS_STORAGETYPE_LOCAL PS_STORAGETYPE_NETWORK

lpStatus

Address of a doubleword value that receives bit flag values. The meaning of the values depends on the *dwIndex* parameter.

PwdSetPasswordStatus

```
DWORD PwdSetPasswordStatus(LPCTSTR lpProvider, DWORD dwIndex,
    DWORD dwStatus);
```

Sets information about a password provider's password. Currently, this function can only determine whether the password is kept the same as the Windows logon password.

- Returns the WN_SUCCESS value if successful or a WN_ error value otherwise.

lpProvider

Address of the name of the network provider that owns the password.

dwIndex

Type of information to retrieve. Currently, only the PS_SYNCMASTERPWD value is supported.

dwStatus

Status flag. This parameter can be either the PS_SYNCMASTERPWD_ON or PS_SYNCMASTERPWD_OFF value.

ARTICLE 20

Device I/O Control

About Device I/O Control

Microsoft® Windows® 95 includes a device input and output control (IOCTL) interface that allows applications developed for the Microsoft® Win32® application programming interface (API) to communicate directly with virtual device drivers. Applications typically use this interface to carry out selected Microsoft® MS-DOS® system functions, to obtain information about a device, or to carry out input and output (I/O) operations that are not available through standard Win32 functions.

This article describes the device IOCTL interface, explains how to use the interface in applications, and describes how to implement the interface in virtual devices (VxDs). For information about the device IOCTL interface for other operating systems that support the Win32 API, see the documentation included in the Microsoft Win32 Software Development Kit (SDK).

Input and Output Control in Applications

You use the device IOCTL interface in an application to carry out "low-level" operations that are not supported by the Win32 API and that require direct communication with a VxD. Windows 95 implements the interface through the **DeviceIoControl** function, which sends commands and accompanying data directly to the given VxD. To use the interface, you open the VxD by using the **CreateFile** function, send commands to the VxD by using **DeviceIoControl**, and finally close the VxD by using the **CloseHandle** function.

Opening the VxD

You can open a static or dynamically loadable VxD by specifying the module name, filename, or registry entry identifying the VxD in a call to the **CreateFile** function. If the VxD exists and it supports the device IOCTL interface, **CreateFile** returns a device handle that you can use in subsequent calls to the **DeviceIoControl** function. Otherwise, the function fails and sets the last error value to ERROR_NOT_SUPPORTED or ERROR_FILE_NOT_FOUND. You can use the **GetLastError** function to retrieve the error value.

When you open a VxD, you must specify a name having the following form.

```
\\.\VxdName
```

VxDName can be the module name of the VxD, the name of the VxD file, or the name of a registry entry that specifies the filename.

CreateFile checks for a filename extension to determine whether *VxDName* specifies a file. If a filename extension (such as .VXD) is present, the function looks for the file in the standard search path. In the following example, **CreateFile** looks for the SAMPLE.VXD file in the standard search path.

```
HANDLE hDevice;

hDevice = CreateFile("\\\\.\\SAMPLE.VXD", 0, 0, NULL, 0,
    FILE_FLAG_DELETE_ON_CLOSE, NULL);
```

If *VxDName* has no filename extension, **CreateFile** checks the registry to see if the name is also a value name under the **KnownVxDs** key in **HKLM\System\ CurrentControlSet\Control\SessionManager**. If it is a value name, **CreateFile** uses the current value associated with the name as the full path of the VxD file. This method is useful for specifying VxDs that are not in the standard search path. In the following example, **CreateFile** searches the registry for the MYVXDPATH value.

```
hDevice = CreateFile("\\\\.\\MYVXDPATH", 0, 0, NULL, 0,
    FILE_FLAG_DELETE_ON_CLOSE, NULL);
```

If *VxDName* has no filename extension and is not in the registry, **CreateFile** assumes that the name is a VxD module name and searches the internally maintained device descriptor blocks for an already loaded VxD having the given name. In the following example, **CreateFile** opens the standard VxD named VWIN32.VXD.

```
hDevice = CreateFile("\\\\.\\VWIN32", 0, 0, NULL, 0,
    0, NULL);
```

In all cases, if **CreateFile** cannot find or load the VxD, it sets the last error value to ERROR_FILE_NOT_FOUND. If the function loads the VxD but the VxD does not support the device IOCTL interface, **CreateFile** sets the last error value to ERROR_NOT_SUPPORTED.

You can open the same VxD any number of times. **CreateFile** provides a unique handle each time you open a VxD, but it makes sure that no more than one copy of the VxD is loaded into memory. To ensure that the system removes the VxD from memory when you close the last instance of the VxD, use the FILE_FLAG_DELETE_ON_CLOSE value when opening dynamically loadable VxDs. Static VxDs cannot be removed from memory.

Although **CreateFile** has several parameters, only two parameters, *lpName* and *fdwAttrsAndFlags*, are useful when opening an VxD. The latter one, *fdwAttrsAndFlags*, can be zero, the FILE_FLAG_DELETE_ON_CLOSE value, or the FILE_FLAG_OVERLAPPED value. FILE_FLAG_OVERLAPPED is used for asynchronous operation and is described later in this article.

Sending Commands

You use **DeviceIoControl** to send commands to a VxD. You must specify the previously opened device handle, control code, and input and output parameters for the call. The device handle identifies the VxD, and the control code specifies an action for the VxD to perform. In the following example, the DIOC_GETVERSION control code directs the given VxD to return version information.

```
HANDLE hDevice
BYTE bOutput[4];
DWORD cb;

fResult = DeviceIoControl(
    hDevice,          // device handle
    DIOC_GETVERSION,  // control code
    NULL, 0,          // input parameters
    bOutput, 4, &cb,  // output parameters
    0);
```

The input and output parameters of **DeviceIoControl** include the addresses and sizes of any buffers needed to pass data into or out of the VxD. Whether you use these parameters depends on how the VxD processes the control code. You supply an input buffer if the VxD requires that you pass it data for processing, and you supply an output buffer if the VxD returns the results of processing. In the previous example, only the output parameters are supplied. These include the address of the output buffer; the size, in bytes, of the buffer; and the address of the variable to receive the count of bytes actually copied to the buffer by the VxD.

Although the Win32 header files define a set of standard control codes, Windows 95 does not support these standard codes. Instead, the meaning and value of control codes in Windows 95 are specific to each VxD. Different VxDs may support different control codes.

Some VxDs support the DIOC_GETVERSION control code, which directs the VxD to return version information in the output buffer. Although the version information can have any format that helps the application determine the version of the VxD, keeping the information to 4 bytes or less is recommended. The VxD returns the version information only if you supply a buffer and specify a nonzero size for the buffer.

If you opened the VxD using the FILE_FLAG_OVERLAPPED value, you must also provide an **OVERLAPPED** structure when calling **DeviceIoControl**. This structure contains information that the VxD uses to process the control code asynchronously.

Closing a VxD

When you have finished using a VxD, you can close the associated device handle by using the **CloseHandle** function, or you can let the operating system close the handle when the application terminates. The following example closes a VxD.

```
CloseHandle(hDevice);
```

Closing a VxD does not necessarily remove the VxD from memory. If you open a dynamically loadable VxD using the FILE_FLAG_DELETE_ON_CLOSE value, **CloseHandle** also removes the VxD if no other valid handles are present in the system. The system maintains a reference count for dynamically loadable VxDs, incrementing the count each time the VxD is opened and decrementing when the VxD is closed. **CloseHandle** checks this count and removes the VxD from memory when the count reaches zero. The system does not keep a reference count for static VxDs; it does not remove these VxDs when their corresponding handles are closed.

In rare cases, you may need to use the **DeleteFile** function to remove a dynamically loadable VxD from memory. For example, you use **DeleteFile** if another application has loaded the VxD and you just want to unload it. You also use **DeleteFile** if you have successfully loaded a VxD by using **CreateFile**, but the VxD does not support the device IOCTL interface. In such cases, **CreateFile** loads the VxD but provides no handle to close and remove the VxD. The following example removes the VxD named SAMPLE from memory.

```
DeleteFile("\\\\.\\SAMPLE");
```

In this example, SAMPLE is the module name of the VxD. (Do not specify the filename.) Be aware that the module name of a VxD is not necessarily the same as the VxD's filename without a filename extension. In general, avoid using **DeleteFile** to remove a VxD from memory.

Asynchronous Operations

You can direct a VxD to process a control code asynchronously. In an asynchronous operation, the **DeviceIoControl** function returns immediately, regardless of whether the VxD has finished processing the control code. Asynchronous operation allows an application to continue while the VxD processes the control code in the background. You request an asynchronous operation by specifying the address of an **OVERLAPPED** structure in the **DeviceIoControl** function. The **hDevice** member of **OVERLAPPED** specifies the handle of an event that the system sets to the signaled state when the VxD has completed the operation.

Asynchronous (overlapped) operations are useful for lengthy operations, such as formatting a disk. To perform an asynchronous operation, you must specify the FILE_FLAG_OVERLAPPED value when calling **CreateFile** to obtain a device handle. When calling **DeviceIoControl**, you must specify the address of an **OVERLAPPED** structure in the *lpOverlapped* parameter and the handle of a manual reset event in the **hEvent** member of the structure. The system ignores all other members.

If **DeviceIoControl** completes the operation before returning, it returns TRUE; otherwise, it returns FALSE. When the operation is finished, the system signals the manual reset event. You should call **GetOverlappedResult** when the thread that called **DeviceIoControl** needs to wait (that is, stop executing) until the operation has finished.

Using VWIN32 to Carry Out MS-DOS Functions

Windows 95 provides a VxD called VWIN32.VXD that supports a set of control codes that Win32 applications can use to carry out selected MS-DOS system functions. These system-defined control codes consist of the following values.

Control code (value)	Meaning
VWIN32_DIOC_DOS_INT13 (4)	Performs Interrupt 13h commands.
VWIN32_DIOC_DOS_INT25 (2)	Performs the Absolute Disk Read command (Interrupt 25h).
VWIN32_DIOC_DOS_INT26 (3)	Performs the Absolute Disk Write command (Interrupt 25h).
VWIN32_DIOC_DOS_IOCTL (1)	Performs the specified MS-DOS device I/O control function (Interrupt 21h Function 4400h through 4411h).

When a Windows 95–based application calls **DeviceIoControl** with the *dwIoControlCode* parameter set to one of the predefined control codes, the *lpvInBuffer* and *lpvOutBuffer* parameters must specify the addresses of **DIOC_REGISTERS** structures. The **DIOC_REGISTERS** structure specified by *lpvInBuffer* contains a set of register values that specify a command for the VxD to execute and any data that the VxD needs to execute the command. After completing the command, the VxD fills the **DIOC_REGISTERS** structure specified by *lpvOutBuffer* with the register values that resulted from executing the command. The meaning of the register values depends on the specified command.

Some interrupt functions require far pointers passed in segment:offset pairs where the segment is placed in a segment register. Because the 32-bit code does not have segments, the **DIOC_REGISTERS** structure contains no segment registers. To specify segment:offset pairs, place the full pointer into the structure member that corresponds to the register used to hold the offset portion of the real-mode pointer. For example, use **reg_EDX** for pointers that go into the DS:DX registers.

Many of the MS-DOS and BIOS functions require segment registers, but segment registers are not part of the **DIOC_REGISTERS** structure. To specify an address that includes a segment selector, use the structure member that corresponds to the offset of the real-mode segment:offset register pair to hold the entire address. For example, a pointer in the ES:DI registers would be put into the **reg_EDI** member.

When a Windows 95–based application uses the **DeviceIoControl** function to send commands to a VxD other than VWIN32.VXD, the meaning of the function's parameters are defined by the VxD. The system does not validate any parameter.

The system VxD, VWIN32.VXD, supports the IOCTL functions originally provided by MS-DOS Interrupt 21h. The following example shows how to call Get Media ID (Interrupt 21h Function 440Dh Minor Code 66h) from a Win32-based application.

```
#define VWIN32_DIOC_DOS_IOCTL 1

typedef struct _DIOC_REGISTERS {
    DWORD reg_EBX;
    DWORD reg_EDX;
    DWORD reg_ECX;
    DWORD reg_EAX;
    DWORD reg_EDI;
    DWORD reg_ESI;
    DWORD reg_Flags;
} DIOC_REGISTERS, *PDIOC_REGISTERS;
```

```
// Important: All MS_DOS data structures must be packed on a
// one-byte boundary.
#pragma pack(1)
typedef struct _MID {
    WORD  midInfoLevel;
    DWORD midSerialNum;
    BYTE  midVolLabel[11];
    BYTE  midFileSysType[8];
} MID, *PMID;
#pragma pack()

HANDLE hDevice;
DIOC_REGISTERS reg;
MID mid;
BOOL fResult;
DWORD cb;
int nDrive = 3;   // Drive C:

hDevice = CreateFile("\\\\.\\vwin32",
    0, 0, NULL, 0, FILE_FLAG_DELETE_ON_CLOSE, NULL);

reg.reg_EAX = 0x440D;       /* IOCTL for block devices          */
reg.reg_EBX = nDrive;       /* zero-based drive identifier       */
reg.reg_ECX = 0x0866;       /* Get Media ID command              */
reg.reg_EDX = (DWORD) &mid; /* receives media identifier info.   */
reg.reg_Flags = 0x0001;     /* assume error (carry flag is set)  */

fResult = DeviceIoControl(hDevice,
    VWIN32_DIOC_DOS_IOCTL,
    &reg, sizeof(reg),
    &reg, sizeof(reg),
    &cb, 0);

if (!fResult || (reg.reg_Flags & 0x0001))
    ; // error if carry flag is set

CloseHandle(hDevice);
```

Supporting Input-Output Control in VxDs

A VxD can support the device IOCTL interface by processing the message
W32_DEVICEIOCONTROL in the VxD's control procedure. You can take
advantage of the device IOCTL interface by providing a VxD that performs
privileged (ring 0) operations for your application.

Loading and Opening the VxD

When your application calls the **CreateFile** function, the system sends the W32_DEVICEIOCONTROL message to the control procedure of the specified VxD to determine if it supports the device IOCTL interface. The ESI register contains the address of a **DIOCParams** structure whose **dwIoControlCode** member specifies the DIOC_GETVERSION control code. A VxD that supports the device IOCTL interface must respond to the DIOC_GETVERSION control code by clearing the EAX register. (A VxD can also return version information in the buffer pointed to by the **lpvOutBuffer** member so long as the **cbOutBuffer** member is nonzero. If **cbOutBuffer** is zero, the calling application is not interested in version information, but the VxD must still return zero to indicate success.) If the VxD does not support the device IOCTL interface, it must place a nonzero value in EAX.

For dynamically loadable VxDs, the system sends a SYS_DYNAMIC_INIT control message to the VxD the first time that it is opened. If the VxD returns success, the system sends the W32_DEVICEIOCONTROL message with the DIOC_OPEN (identical in value to the DIOC_GETVERSION control code) control code. The VxD must return zero to inform the calling application that it supports W32_DEVICEIOCONTROL. The system sets the reference count for the VxD to 1. On every subsequent call to **CreateFile** for the VxD, the VxD receives the W32_DEVICEIOCONTROL message with the DIOC_OPEN control code and the reference count for the VxD is incremented.

The VxD receives a W32_DEVICEIOCONTROL message with the control code DIOC_CLOSEHANDLE if the application closes the device handle by calling the **CloseHandle** function, or if the operating system closes the handle when the application terminates (or **DeleteFile** if the VxD was not opened with the FILE_FLAG_DELETE_ON_CLOSE value). The VxD can use this notification to perform cleanup operations and release structures associated with the application. The reference count for the VxD is decremented before the message is sent. If the reference count has been decremented to zero, the VxD receives the SYS_DYNAMIC_EXIT message and is subsequently unloaded.

Processing Control Codes

When an application calls **DeviceIoControl**, the system calls the control procedure of the VxD identified by the given device handle. The EAX register contains the W32_DEVICEIOCONTROL message, and the ESI register contains the address of a **DIOCParams** structure. The structure contains all of the parameters that the application specified in the **DeviceIoControl** function as well as additional information. The VxD should examine the **dwIoControlCode** member of the **DIOCParams** structure to determine the action to perform. The **lpvInBuffer** member contains supporting data that the VxD needs to complete the action. After processing the control code, the VxD should copy any information that it needs to return to the application to the buffer specified by the **lpvOutBuffer** member.

If the VxD successfully processes the control code, it should clear the EAX register before returning. Otherwise, the VxD should set EAX to a nonzero value.

Asynchronous Operations

A VxD can determine whether an application has requested an asynchronous operation by checking the **lpoOverlapped** member of the **DIOCParams** structure. If **lpoOverlapped** specifies the address of an **OVERLAPPED** structure, the application has requested an asynchronous operation. In that case, the VxD should return -1 in the EAX register and then process the specified control code.

The operating system does not take any steps to make the application's memory available to the VxD at all times (in all contexts) for asynchronous operations. When implementing asynchronous operations, the VxD must use the appropriate virtual machine manager (VMM) services, such as **LinPageLock** with the PAGEMAPGLOBAL value, to make the application's memory pages available across contexts, including access to the **OVERLAPPED** structure.

When the VxD finishes processing the control code, it must notify the application by calling the **VWIN32_DIOCCompletionRoutine** service provided by VWIN32.VXD. The EBX register must contain the value of the **Internal** member of the **OVERLAPPED** structure. This member is reserved for operating system use only. In addition, if the VxD copies any data to the buffer specified by the **lpvOutBuffer** member of the **DIOCParams** structure, the VxD must specify the count of bytes copied to the buffer in the **InternalHigh** member of the **OVERLAPPED** structure. The remaining members of **OVERLAPPED**, **Offset** and **OffsetHigh**, can be used for developer-defined data.

Essentially, the **VWIN32_DIOCCompletionRoutine** service helps signal the event identified by the **hEvent** member of the **OVERLAPPED** structure. The application monitors the event to determine when the asynchronous operation is completed.

Reference

The following structures, system messages, and service are associated with the device IOCTL interface.

Structures

These structures are used to carry out device IOCTL functions.

DIOC_REGISTERS

```
typedef struct DIOCRegs {
    DWORD    reg_EBX;    // EBX register
    DWORD    reg_EDX;    // EDX register
    DWORD    reg_ECX;    // ECX register
    DWORD    reg_EAX;    // EAX register
    DWORD    reg_EDI;    // EDI register
    DWORD    reg_ESI;    // ESI register
    DWORD    reg_Flags;  // Flags register
} DIOC_REGISTERS;
```

Contains the register values for calling Interrupt 21h commands through the **DeviceIoControl** function. The meaning of the registers depends on the given command.

Some interrupt functions require far pointers passed in segment:offset pairs where the segment is placed in a segment register. Since the 32-bit code does not have segments, the **DIOC_REGISTERS** structure contains no segment registers. You should place the full pointer into the structure member that corresponds to the register used to hold the offset portion of the real-mode pointer. For example, use **reg_EDX** for pointers that go into the DS:DX registers.

DIOCParams

```
include vwin32.inc

DIOCParams STRUC
    Internal1           DD  ?  ; reserved
    VMHandle            DD  ?  ; handle of virtual machine
    Internal2           DD  ?  ; reserved
    dwIoControlCode     DD  ?  ; see below
    lpvInBuffer         DD  ?  ; see below
    cbInBuffer          DD  ?  ; see below
    lpvOutBuffer        DD  ?  ; see below
    cbOutBuffer         DD  ?  ; see below
    lpcbBytesReturned   DD  ?  ; see below
    lpoOverlapped       DD  ?  ; see below
    hDevice             DD  ?  ; handle of device
    tagProcess          DD  ?  ; see below
DIOCParams ENDS
```

Contains information that an application has passed to the virtual device driver (VxD) by calling the **DeviceIoControl** function.

dwIoControlCode

Control code to process. This member can be a developer-defined value or one of these system-defined values:

DIOC_CLOSEHANDLE — Notifies a VxD that an application has closed its device handle for the VxD. The VxD should perform cleanup operations and release any structures associated with the application.

DIOC_GETVERSION — Queries the VxD to determine if it supports the device IOCTL interface. If the VxD supports the interface, it must clear the EAX register. Otherwise, it must place a nonzero value in EAX. If **cbOutBuffer** is nonzero and the VxD supports the interface, the VxD should copy version information to the **lpvOutBuffer**.

lpvInBuffer
Address of a buffer that contains data needed to process the control code.

cbInBuffer
Size, in bytes, of the buffer pointed to by **lpvInBuffer**.

lpvOutBuffer
Address of a buffer that receives the results of processing the control code.

cbOutBuffer
Size, in bytes, of the buffer pointed to by **lpvOutBuffer**.

lpcbBytesReturned
Number of bytes copied to the buffer pointed to by **lpvOutBuffer**.

lpoOverlapped
Address of an **OVERLAPPED** structure that contains information used to complete the command asynchronously. If the command is to be completed synchronously, this member is NULL.

tagProcess
Information that the VxD can use to tag the current request along with **hDevice**. When the VxD receives a DIOC_CLOSEHANDLE control code for **hDevice** and **tagProcess**, it should perform appropriate cleanup operations.

System Message

The following system message is used to implement the device IOCTL interface of a VxD.

W32_DEVICEIOCONTROL

```
include VMM.INC

mov ebx, VMHandle          ; see below
mov eax, W32_DEVICEIOCONTROL
mov esi, OFFSET32 dioparams ; see below
VMMCall System_Control
```

Passes a control code and related information to a virtual device driver.

- Returns one of the following values in the EAX register:

0	The control code processed successfully.
−1	An asynchronous operation is in progress. A VxD must return this value only if the **lpoOverlapped** member of the **DIOCParams** structure is not NULL.
Error code	An error occurred. For a list of Win32 error codes, see the documentation included in the Win32 SDK.

VMHandle
> Handle of the virtual machine.

dioparams
> Address of a **DIOCParams** structure containing a control code and information that the VxD needs to process the control code.

This message is sent to a VxD when an application specifies the name of a VxD in the **CreateFile** function and when an application specifies the device handle of the VxD in a call to the **DeviceIoControl** or **CloseHandle** function. This message uses the ESI register.

Service

The following service is used with device IOCTL.

VWIN32_DIOCCompletionRoutine

```
mov ebx, Internal  ; see below
VxDCall VWIN32_DIOCCompletionRoutine
```

Notifies the system that an asynchronous operation in a virtual device driver is complete. The VxD calls this service after the asynchronous input and output (I/O) operation to signal the application.

- No return value.

Internal
> Event identifier. This parameter must be the same value initially passed to the VxD in the **Internal** member of the **OVERLAPPED** structure.

Before calling this service, the VxD must set the **InternalHigh** member of the **OVERLAPPED** structure to the number of bytes of return data.

A R T I C L E   2 1

System Policies

About System Policies

System administrators can use Microsoft® Windows® 95 system policies to control user and computer configurations from a single location on a network. System Policies propagate registry settings to a large number of computers without requiring the administrator to have detailed knowledge of the registry. There are many settings in the registry, and multiple registry settings must often be manipulated to achieve a particular result. The System Policies feature provides a layer of abstraction that makes it easier to control registry settings.

Instead of changing individual registry settings, a system administrator can specify policies. Each policy has some text that describes its effect. Some examples of policies follow:

- Disable file sharing.
- Display a custom logon banner.
- Remove the Run command from the Start menu.
- Use user-level security.

Registry Settings

Each policy is associated with one or more registry settings. When the administrator chooses to enforce a policy, the System Policies tool identifies registry changes that must be made and then makes the changes to the registries of the users and computers for which the policy applies. The administrator can specify policies for individual users, user groups, and individual computers. Default values can also be specified.

Policies have been implemented for most of the registry settings that an administrator might want to control and propagate. Although System Policies control only a subset of the registry, they are extensible. Application developers are encouraged to supply template files and implement policies for registry settings used by their products so that customers can plug the template files into a policy editor and control policies for the application.

Policy Editors and Downloaders

There are two administrative components involved in specifying policies: a policy editor and a policy downloader. A policy editor is an application that lets administrators specify registry settings for particular computers, users, and user groups, and a policy downloader is a small program installed on every client computer that merges the administrator's settings into the local registry.

The policy editor uses a template file, which is a text file describing registry settings and specifying how the settings should appear in the policy editor's user interface. The policy editor creates a policy file, which is a single file containing policy settings for a number of computers, users, and user groups. The policy file is a registry hive that is created and manipulated using Microsoft® Win32® functions. Windows 95 includes a policy editor, the System Policy Editor. Developers may create their own policy editors, but the editors must be able to read template files and be able to read and write policy files.

Windows 95 provides a policy downloader, which is built into Multiple Provider Router (MPR). Developers may also create their own policy downloaders. Policy downloaders may be installed so that MPR will call the installed component to do the downloading rather than doing so itself. Because the policy file format allows for extensions, developers may provide additional functionality.

Architecture

A computer's configuration is defined in terms of policies. The policies are ultimately stored in the local computer's registry. Every component that provides a policy is responsible for reading the registry at appropriate times and acting accordingly. For example, the policy that removes the Run command from the Start menu requires the shell code that displays the Start menu to check the appropriate registry setting to determine whether or not the shell is supposed to display the Run command. The policies are generic data items; the administrative tools and components have no information about them besides their names, their associated data, and where they reside in the registry. The only responsibilities of the administrative components are to allow the administrator to make policy settings and propagate those settings to the user's registry.

Policy Primitives

The following definitions are important for a complete understanding of policies:

- A policy is a permission or attribute for a particular item, action, or object. It is either enabled or disabled.
- A part is a subcomponent of a policy. A policy may have zero or more parts. Policy parts may have various data types, including Boolean values, numeric values, and string values. The values of the parts apply only if the policy is enabled.
- A category is a collection of similar policies.

Some policies do not need any parts. For instance, "Lock Desktop Links" could be a policy. For such a policy, it would be sufficient to say that it was either enabled or disabled. If it were enabled, the user could not modify his or her desktop links in any way. "Desktop Links" could be another policy, and it could have the Boolean parts "Create Links," "Delete Links," and "Modify Links." As another example, "Password Expiration" could be a policy, and "Number of days" (a numeric value) could be its part.

Policies and parts are analogous to a group of controls in a dialog box that are all enabled by a single check box. The check box, which corresponds to whether or not the policy is enabled, "turns on" the controls in the dialog box (the policy parts) and allows data to be entered into the controls. A policy with no parts (that is, no associated controls) is analogous to a single check box.

The following types of policies can be specified:

- A user-specific policy can be specified for each user or group. A default set of policies can be specified for users or groups who do not have sets of policies defined for them explicitly. Most policies are user-specific. User-specific policies are always merged into the **HKEY_CURRENT_USER** key of the registry.
- A machine-specific policy should not change according to user. A machine-specific policy applies to all users. It does not follow users when they move between different computers. Machine-specific policies are always merged into the **HKEY_LOCAL_MACHINE** key of the registry.

Policy Information

Any application or component can define a policy. The policy will appear in the administrator user interface, and information that the administrator sets about the policy will migrate to the local computer's registry. The application or component that defines a policy must check the registry appropriately to enforce its own policy.

Policy information is typically added to a local registry in the following sequence:

1. Categories, policies, and parts are described in a template (.ADM) file. The .ADM file format is described in "Template File Format" later in this article. An ADMIN.ADM file with all the policies that the system supports is shipped with Windows 95. Developers, however, may also provide their own template files.

2. The administrator runs the policy editor, which reads one or more policies and lists the available categories and policies. The administrator sets up the desired policies, and the policy editor uses registry functions to save the work to a policy (.POL) file. The format of policy files is described in "Policy File Format" later in this article.

3. After the user logs on (and user profiles are reconciled if they are enabled), the policy downloader is activated. It determines where to find the file on the network, opens the policy file, and merges the appropriate computer, user, and user group policies into the local registry.

Default User and Computer Names

There is a standard user name called DEFAULT USER and a standard computer name called DEFAULT COMPUTER. When the policy downloader updates machine- and user-specific policies, it first tries to find an entry in the policy file for the local computer name or user name. If the downloader does not find an entry, it looks for the DEFAULT USER or DEFAULT COMPUTER entry and uses those entries for the update. If there are no entries for a particular user or computer and default entries do not exist, no update takes place.

The DEFAULT USER and DEFAULT COMPUTER entries are powerful because administrators can set policies for a large number of users and computers and then manage the exceptions by creating specific user and computer entries in a .POL file.

Policy Downloading

Policy downloading can be set in one of the following three states:

- Off
- Automatic
- Manual

If policy downloading is off, no downloading takes place.

If policy downloading is set to automatic, MPR asks the primary network provider to provide a place to look on the network for the policy file. Microsoft® Windows NT™ and Novell® NetWare® providers both support this capability. (For example, for a Windows NT network, MPR looks in the primary domain controller's NETLOGON directory for a file named CONFIG.POL. For a NetWare version 3.*x* network, MPR looks on the preferred server's SYS\PUBLIC directory for a file named CONFIG.POL.) Any software vendor who provides a 32-bit network provider can support this capability by implementing the **NPGetPolicyPath** function. If policy downloading is set to automatic and the primary network provider does not support **NPGetPolicyPath**, no downloading takes place.

If policy downloading is set to manual, a specific path to the policy file must also be supplied. It can be either a Universal Naming Convention (UNC) path or a path beginning with a drive letter. (In the latter case, the drive letter must be appropriately mapped before downloading takes place.)

The default setting for policy downloading is automatic. No error messages are displayed if a policy file cannot be found in the location that the network provider suggests. This means that a site can install a number of Windows 95 clients and then deploy the policies at a later date. To deploy them, the administrator just needs to place the policy file(s) in the appropriate location(s) on the network, and the clients will immediately begin using them the next time they log on.

Policy Editor User Interface

This section describes the user interface of the System Policy Editor that ships with Windows 95. Other software vendors may, however, choose to use a different user interface.

The System Policy Editor requires an .ADM file describing the available policies to use. By default, it will use a file named ADMIN.ADM, but different template files may be specified using the Templates menu.

The main window of the System Policy Editor displays the users and computers that have entries in the policy file that is currently open. To create a new policy file, choose the New command on the File menu. A new policy file contains entries for the default user and default computer. To add entries for particular users or particular computers, use the Add User, Add Group, or Add Computer button. Note that policies for all of the entries shown in the main window are saved to one policy file. Typically, an administrator saves the policy file to the network location where the policy downloader looks by default.

The following illustration shows the main window of the System Policy Editor.

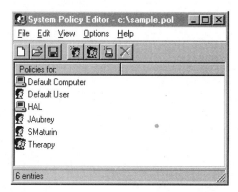

Double-clicking an entry, such as Default Computer, brings up a properties dialog box containing the policies for the entry. The Default Computer Properties dialog box shown in the following illustration has an upper section listing the policies and a lower section showing settings for a specific policy.

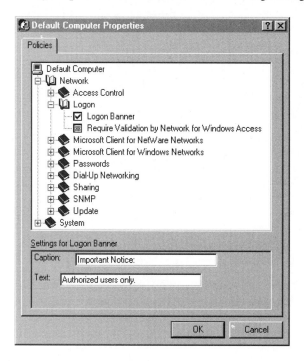

A check box in the properties dialog box has three states. If it is checked, the policy will be enforced; that is, the corresponding settings will be added to the registry when the policy is downloaded. If the check box is empty, the settings will be deleted from the registry when the policy is downloaded. If the check box is gray, the registry settings will not be changed when the policy is downloaded; that is, the user has the freedom to choose settings, assuming that the settings can be changed from the user interface.

For example, there is a user policy for desktop wallpaper. By checking that policy, the administrator specifies the particular wallpaper that the user will have. Even if the user uses the Display Control Panel application to change the wallpaper, the wallpaper specified by the administrator will appear the next time he or she logs on. If the administrator unchecks this policy, the wallpaper setting is deleted so that when the user logs on, there is no wallpaper. If the administrator makes the check box gray, nothing is enforced, and the user can choose the wallpaper.

As a second example, there is a user policy "Remove Run from Start menu" (under the **Shell/Restrictions** registry key). Checking this policy adds a registry setting that tells the shell not to include the Run command on the Start menu. By unchecking this policy, this registry key is deleted, and the shell displays the Run command. If the policy is left gray, the setting will not be changed. If the policy was already in force, it will stay that way, and the Run command will continue to be denied to the user. If the policy had not been applied already, the user would continue to see the Run command. Note that unlike the wallpaper example, the user cannot change this setting by using Control Panel or another user interface element.

The System Policy Editor can also operate directly on the local registry rather than on a policy file. This capability is useful for troubleshooting problems that may be policy-related, because it shows what policies are currently in place for a user on a particular computer. There is no policy file involved in this mode. To switch to the local registry view, use the Open Registry command on the File menu. Note that the check boxes will show only two states, checked and unchecked, because the registry settings for the policy are either present (the policy is on) or not present (the policy is off).

Template File Format

A template (.ADM) file describes a number of categories. Each category can contain zero or more policies, and each policy can contain zero or more parts. The following sections describe categories, policies, policy parts, and part types.

The ADMIN.ADM file that ships with Windows 95 identifies strings that are important for an internal localization tool by using two exclamation points (!!). Each of these strings is explicitly defined in the [strings] section of ADMIN.ADM. You do not need to use this mechanism when you create a template file.

Categories

A category is specified as follows.

CATEGORY *name* **TYPE** *category type*
  [**KEYNAME** *key name*]

  [... policy definition statements ...]

END CATEGORY

name
> Category name as it should appear in the System Policy Editor list box. It may
> optionally be enclosed by double quotation marks. (Names with spaces must be
> enclosed by double quotation marks.)

category type
> Type, which must be USER or MACHINE. It specifies whether the category is
> user-specific or machine-specific.

key name
> Optional registry key name to use for the category. If a key name is specified,
> it will be used by all child categories, policies, and parts, unless they specifically
> provide a key name of their own.

A policy definition statement may not appear more than once in a single category.

Policies

A policy is specified as follows.

POLICY *name*
  [**KEY** *key name*]
  [... part definition statements ...]
END POLICY

name
> Policy name as it should appear in the System Policy Editor list box. It may
> optionally be enclosed by double quotation marks. (Names with spaces must
> be enclosed by double quotation marks.)

key name
> Optional registry key name to use for the policy. If a key name is specified,
> it will be used by all child parts of the policy, unless they specifically provide
> a key name of their own.

Policy Parts

A policy part is specified as follows.

PART *name* **TYPE** *part type*
    type-dependent data
    [**KEYNAME** *key name*]
    VALUENAME *value name*
END PART

name
> Part name as it should appear in the System Policy Editor list box. It may optionally be enclosed by double quotation marks. (Names with spaces must be enclosed by double quotation marks.)

part type
> Policy part type. Part types are discussed individually in the following section.

type-dependent data
> Information about the part. Type-dependent data is discussed in the following section.

key name
> Optional key name to use. If no key name is specified, the previous key name in hierarchy is used.

value name
> Value name to use to set the data for this part.

Part Types

The following policy part types are defined:

CHECKBOX	Displays a check box. The value is set in the registry with the REG_DWORD type. The value will be nonzero if the check box is checked by the user and zero if it is unchecked.
COMBOBOX	Displays a combo box.
DROPDOWNLIST	Displays a combo box with a drop-down list style. The user may only choose from one of the entries supplied. The main advantage of a combo box with a drop-down list is that a number of extra registry edits may be specified, based on the user's selection.
EDITTEXT	Displays an edit field that accepts alphanumeric text. The text is set in the registry with the REG_SZ type.
LISTBOX	Displays a list box with "add" and "remove" buttons. This is the only part type that can be used to manage multiple values under one key.

NUMERIC

Displays an edit field with an optional spinner control (an up-down control) that accepts a numeric value. The value is set in the registry with the REG_DWORD type.

TEXT

Displays a line of static (label) text. There is no associated registry value with this part type.

Descriptions of these policy part types follow.

CHECKBOX Part Type

The CHECKBOX part type accepts the following options:

ACTIONLISTOFF

Specifies an optional action list to be used if the check box is turned off. For more information, see "Action Lists" later in this article.

ACTIONLISTON

Specifies an optional action list to be used if the check box is turned on. For more information, see "Action Lists" later in this article.

DEFCHECKED

Causes the check box to be initially checked.

VALUEOFF

Overrides the default "off" behavior of the check box if specified.

VALUEON

Overrides the default "on" behavior of the check box if specified.

The default behavior of a check box is to write the value 1 to the registry if it is checked and 0 if it is unchecked. VALUEON and VALUEOFF are used to override this behavior. For example, the following option writes "Fred" to the registry when the check box is checked.

```
VALUEON "Fred"
```

The following option writes the value 12 to the registry when the check box is unchecked.

```
VALUEOFF NUMERIC 12
```

COMBOBOX Part Type

The COMBOBOX part type accepts all the options that EDITTEXT does as well as the following option:

SUGGESTIONS   Begins a list of suggestions to be placed in the drop-down list. Suggestions are separated with spaces and can be enclosed by double quotation marks. The list ends with END SUGGESTIONS. Following is an example:

SUGGESTIONS
Alaska Alabama Mississippi "New York"
END SUGGESTIONS

DROPDOWNLIST Part Type

The DROPDOWNLIST part type accepts the following options:

ITEMLIST   Begins a list of the items in the drop-down list. The list must end with END ITEMLIST.

REQUIRED   Specifies that the policy editor will not allow a policy containing this part to be enabled unless a value has been entered for the part.

Each item in the ITEMLIST option must be specified as follows.

NAME *name* **VALUE** *value*
[**ACTIONLIST** *actionlist*]
...

name
    Text to be displayed in the drop-down list for this item.

value
    Value to be written as the part's value if this item is selected. Values are assumed to be strings, unless they are preceded by NUMERIC. The following example shows both string and numeric values.

```
VALUE "Some value"
VALUE NUMERIC 1
```

    If VALUE is followed by DELETE (for example, VALUE DELETE), the registry *valuename* and *value* pair will be deleted.

actionlist
    Optional action list to be used if this value is selected. For more information about action lists, see "Action Lists" later in this article.

EDITTEXT Part Type

The EDITTEXT part type accepts the following options:

DEFAULT *value*	Specifies the initial string to place in the edit field. If this option is not specified, the field is initially empty.
MAXLEN *value*	Specifies the maximum length of a string. The string in the edit field is limited to this length.
REQUIRED	Specifies that the policy editor will not allow a policy containing this part to be enabled, unless a value has been entered for this part.
OEMCONVERT	Sets the ES_OEMCONVERT style in the edit field so that typed text is mapped from ANSI to OEM and back.

LISTBOX Part Type

The VALUENAME option cannot be used with the LISTBOX part type, because there is no single value name associated with this type. By default, only one column appears in the list box, and for each entry a value is created whose name and value are the same. For instance, a "fred" entry in the list box would create a value named "fred" whose data was "fred".

The LISTBOX part type accepts the following options:

ADDITIVE	By default, the content of list boxes will "override" whatever values are set in the target registry. (That is, a control value is inserted in the policy file, which causes existing values to be deleted before the values set in the policy file are merged.) If this option is specified, existing values are not deleted, and the values set in the list box will be in addition to whatever values exist in the target registry.
EXPLICITVALUE	This option makes the user specify not only the value data, but the value name as well. The list box will show two columns for each item, one for the name and one for the data. This option cannot be used with the VALUEPREFIX option.
VALUEPREFIX *prefix*	The prefix specified is used in determining value names. If a prefix is specified, the prefix and an incremented integer will be used instead of the default value naming scheme described previously. For example, a prefix of "SomeName" will generate the value names "SomeName1", "SomeName2", and so on. The prefix can be empty (""), which will cause the value names to be "1", "2", and so on.

NUMERIC Part Type

The NUMERIC part type accepts the following options:

DEFAULT *value*	Specifies the initial numeric value for the edit field. If this option is not specified, the field is initially empty.
MAX *value*	Specifies the maximum value for the number. The default value is 9999.
MIN *value*	Specifies the minimum value for the number. The default value is 0.
REQUIRED	Specifies that the policy editor will not allow a policy containing this part to be enabled unless a value has been entered for this part.
SPIN *value*	Specifies increments to use for the spinner control. SPIN 0 removes the spinner control. SPIN 1 is the default.
TXTCONVERT	Writes values as REG_SZ strings ("1," "2," or "128") rather than as binary values.

TEXT Part Type

The TEXT part type accepts no type-specific data.

Action Lists

An action list is a set of arbitrary changes to the registry that are made in response to a control being in a certain state. For instance, if a check box is turned on, an application could install some virtual device drivers and record some other changes.

The syntax for an actionlist follows.

```
ACTIONLIST
  [KEYNAME key name]
  VALUENAME value name
  VALUE value
  [KEYNAME key name]
  VALUENAME value name
  VALUE value

  ....
END ACTIONLIST
```

The actionlist specifies a number of *key name*, *value name*, and *value* triplets. A key name is not required for every action, but if it is not listed, the key name from the previous action will be used. (This is useful for writing a number of values to one key.) Values are treated as strings unless they are preceded by NUMERIC, as in the following examples.

```
VALUE "Some value"
VALUE NUMERIC 1
```

If VALUE is followed by DELETE (for example, VALUE DELETE), the registry *valuename* and *value* pair will be deleted.

Comments

Comments can be added to a template (.ADM) file by preceding the line with two forward slashes (//) or a semicolon (;).

Conditional Expressions

Future policy editors may include new capabilities. If these new capabilities require revisions to the template file format, older versions of the System Policy Editor will not be able to read the new template files. You can use conditional expressions to ensure that any future template files you create will be compatible with older policy editors.

The System Policy Editor supports two conditional expressions. The first one allows you to include different parts of the template file, based on the version number. This expression has the following syntax.

#if VERSION *operator version_number*

.

.

.

[**#else**]

.

.

.

#endif

The *operator* can be one of the following symbols: >, >=, <, <=, ==, or !=. The *version_number* can be any integer; for Windows 95, the version number is 1.

The other conditional expression is **#ifdef**. This expression has the following syntax.

[#ifdef | #ifndef] *keyword*

.

.

.

[#else]

.

.

.

#endif

Keywords are implicitly understood by the policy editor. For example, a fictitious company named PolicyCorp might implement its own policy editor that could recognize the POLICYCORP keyword. This company could use the **#ifdef** and **#endif** conditional expressions to make sure its template files can be recognized by the Windows 95 System Policy Editor. (Because the Windows 95 System Policy Editor does not currently recognize any keywords, **#ifdef** always evaluates to FALSE and **#ifndef** always evaluates to TRUE.)

Policy File Format

A policy (.POL) file is a registry hive, which is created by using the Win32 **RegSaveKey** function.

The following top-level keys are defined:

- **Computers**
- **Groups**
- **GroupData**
- **Users**
- **Misc**

A policy downloader uses the following steps to download policies:

1. Locates the appropriate computer key, if any, under **Computers**. Beneath that key is an image of the registry settings to be merged. The policy downloader should walk through all the subkeys and values and merge those settings into the **HKEY_LOCAL_MACHINE** key, paying attention to the control codes that are defined in the following section.

2. Locates the appropriate groups key(s), if any, under **Groups**. Under the **Groups** keys is an image of the registry settings to be merged. These settings must be merged into the **HKEY_CURRENT_USER** key.

3. Locates the appropriate user key, if any, under **Users**. Under the **Users** key is an image of the registry settings to be merged. These settings must be merged into the **HKEY_CURRENT_USER** key.

Control Codes

Control codes are used to signify that special processing of a value or key name must take place. All control codes are prefixes to a value or key name and take the form of the code name (that is, **code.) directly followed by *value name* or *key name*.

The following control codes are defined for use with value names.

del.	Specifies that the value name following the control code should be deleted.
delvals.	Deletes all values under this key in the local registry before propagating values under this key from the policy file. When processing a particular key, a downloader must look for and process this value *first*. This control code is inserted by a list box control so that existing values are removed before the new values are added.
soft.	Specifies that it is a soft value. The downloader only propagates the value name following the control code if a value by that name does *not* exist in the local registry; that is, the downloader does not overwrite existing settings with soft values.

No control codes are currently defined for use with key names.

If a policy downloader encounters a control code that it does not understand, it must not process the key or value. If the control code is part of a value name, the policy downloader should skip that value in the hive file but continue to process other values under that key and its subkeys. If the control code is part of a key name, the downloader should ignore the key and not process any values under it or its subkeys. This behavior is important because it allows developers to create new control codes without breaking existing downloaders.

Developers may create new control codes in the same format as shown in the preceding table (that is, **code.). Developers who do so should notify Microsoft so that Microsoft can document the new codes.

Computers Key

Underneath the **Computers** key is a list of computers that have entries in the policy file. The steps to use in locating a **Computers** key follow:

1. Determine whether there is a key that is the same as the computer name. If there is such a key, merge the registry image beneath it into the **HKEY_LOCAL_MACHINE** key.
2. If the key is not there, determine whether there is a key called ".default". (This appears in the System Policy Editor user interface as Default Computer.) If a default key exists, merge the registry image beneath it.
3. If neither of the two steps work, do nothing.

Groups and GroupData Keys

Underneath the **Groups** key is a list of user groups who have entries in the policy file. Since a user may belong to many groups and those groups may have conflicting settings, it is important to specify an order in which groups are processed. This order is contained in the **GroupData\Priority** key, which has values in the form "1"="*group name*", "2"="*group name*", and so on. "1" is highest priority, and the priority diminishes as the number in the value name increases. The downloader reads the group priority values and then processes groups from lowest priority to highest; that is, the downloader begins with the highest numbered value and works to the value "1".

For each group in the priority list, the downloader determines if the user is a member of the group. If the user is in the group, the downloader should try to find a key with the group name under the **Groups** key. If such a key exists, the downloader merges the registry image under that key into the **HKEY_CURRENT_USER** key. It is not an error if a group is specified in the priority list but does not have an entry under the **Groups** key; it simply means that nothing happens. This process is repeated for each group in the priority list. (If a group has an entry under the **Groups** key but does not have an entry in the priority list, it is never processed.)

Users Key

Underneath the **Users** key is a list of computers that have entries in the policy file. The steps to use in locating a **Users** key follow:

1. Determine whether there is a key that is the same as the user name. If there is one, merge the registry image beneath it into the **HKEY_CURRENT_USER** key.

2. If the key is not there, determine whether there is a key called ".default". This appears in the System Policy Editor user interface as Default User. If a default key exists, merge the registry image beneath it.

3. If neither of the two steps work, do nothing.

Misc Key

The **Misc** key can be used by developers to store vendor-specific data. The naming convention for this key follows.

Misc*Vendor Name***\\Product Name***Version******data*

A software vendor may store any needed information in *data*. A key or value containing version information is highly recommended. As is recommended for the registry, *Version* should be "CurrentVersion" for the most current version of the product.

Installable Policy Downloaders

An installable policy downloader must be a Win32 dynamic-link library (DLL). It should export a named function that has the following form.

VOID FAR PASCAL ProcessPolicies(HWND *hwndOwner***,
LPSTR** *lpszPolicyFilePath***, LPSTR** *lpszUserName***,
LPSTR** *lpszComputerName***, DWORD** *dwFlags***);**

hwndOwner
Handle of the parent window.

lpszPolicyFilePath
Address of the full path and filename that MPR would have used to look for the policy file. The downloader may use this parameter, or ignore it and use a different path.

lpszUserName
  Address of the user name for the user who is logged on.

lpszComputerName
  Address of the local computer name.

dwFlags
  Flags. This parameter can be this value:

PP_DISPLAYERRORS	Displays error messages about errors encountered during downloading (including the file is not found, the network resource is not found, and so on). Otherwise, the function should fail silently if there is an error.

In addition to defining and exporting this function, an application must record it in the registry. The following entry should be added to the registry under the **HKEY_LOCAL_MACHINE\Network\Logon** key.

PolicyHandler = "*dll name, function name*"

In this example, *dll name* is the name of the DLL containing the function, and *function name* is the exported function name.

ARTICLE 22

Tool Help Functions

About Tool Help Functions

Tool help functions make it easier for developers to obtain information about currently executing Microsoft® Win32®-based applications. These functions are designed to streamline the creation of Win32-hosted tools, specifically Windows-based debugging applications.

The following topics are discussed in this article:

- Snapshots of the system
- Process walking
- Thread walking
- Module walking
- Heap lists and heap walking

Snapshots of the System

Snapshots are at the core of the tool help functions. A snapshot is a read-only copy of the current state of one or more of the following lists that reside in system memory: processes, threads, modules, and heaps.

Win32 processes that use tool help functions access these lists from snapshots instead of directly from the operating system. The lists in system memory change when processes are started and ended, threads are created and destroyed, executable modules are loaded and unloaded from system memory, and heaps are created and destroyed. The use of information from a snapshot prevents inconsistencies. Otherwise, changes to a list could possibly cause a thread to incorrectly traverse the list or cause an access violation (a GP fault). For example, if an application traverses the thread list while other threads are created or terminated, information that the application is using to traverse the thread list might become outdated and could cause an error for the application traversing the list.

You can take a snapshot of the system memory by using a function called **CreateToolhelp32Snapshot**. You can control the content of a snapshot by specifying one or more of the following values when calling this function: TH32CS_SNAPHEAPLIST, TH32CS_SNAPMODULE, TH32CS_SNAPPROCESS, and TH32CS_SNAPTHREAD.

The TH32CS_SNAPHEAPLIST and TH32CS_SNAPMODULE values are process specific. When these values are specified, the heap and module lists of the specified process are included in the snapshot. If no process identifier is specified, the current process is assumed. The TH32CS_SNAPTHREAD value always creates a system-wide snapshot even if a process identifier is passed to **CreateToolhelp32Snapshot**.

You can enumerate the heap or module state for all Win32 processes by specifying the TH32CS_SNAPALL value and the current process. Then, for each process in the snapshot that is not the current process, you can call **CreateToolhelp32Snapshot** again, specifying the process identifier and the TH32CS_SNAPHEAPLIST or TH32CS_SNAPMODULE value.

You can retrieve an extended error status code for **CreateToolhelp32Snapshot** by using the **GetLastError** function. For more information about **GetLastError**, see the documentation included in the Microsoft Win32 Software Development Kit (SDK).

When your process finishes using a snapshot, you should destroy it by using the **CloseHandle** function. Not destroying a snapshot causes the process to leak memory until the process exits, at which time the system reclaims the memory. For more information about **CloseHandle**, see the documentation included in the Win32 SDK.

Note The snapshot handle acts like a file handle and is subject to the same rules regarding which processes and threads it is valid in.

Process Walking

A snapshot that includes the Win32 process list contains information about each currently executing process. You can retrieve information for the first process in the list by using the **Process32First** function. After retrieving the first process in the list, you can traverse the process list for subsequent entries by using the **Process32Next** function. Both of these functions fill a **PROCESSENTRY32** structure with information about a process in the snapshot.

You can retrieve an extended error status code for **Process32First** and **Process32Next** by using the **GetLastError** function. For more information about **GetLastError**, see the documentation included in the Win32 SDK.

You can read the memory in a specific process into a buffer by using the **Toolhelp32ReadProcessMemory** function (or the **VirtualQueryEx** function).

Note   The contents of the **th32ProcessID** and **th32ParentProcessID** members of **PROCESSENTRY32** are Win32 process identifiers and can be used with other Win32 application programming interface (API) elements.

Thread Walking

A snapshot that includes the Win32 thread list contains information about each thread of each currently executing Win32 process. You can retrieve information for the first thread in the list by using the **Thread32First** function. After retrieving the first thread in the list, you can retrieve information for subsequent threads by using the **Thread32Next** function. Both of these functions fill a **THREADENTRY32** structure with information about individual threads in the snapshot.

You can enumerate the threads of a specific process by taking a snapshot that includes the threads and then by traversing the thread list, keeping information about the threads that have the same process identifier as the specified process.

You can retrieve an extended error status code for **Thread32First** and **Thread32Next** by using the **GetLastError** function. For more information about **GetLastError**, see the documentation included in the Win32 SDK.

Module Walking

A snapshot that includes the module list for a specified Win32 process contains information about each module, executable file, or dynamic-link library (DLL), used by the specified process. You can retrieve information for the first module in the list by using the **Module32First** function. Then after retrieving the first module in the list, you can retrieve information for subsequent modules in the list by using the **Module32Next** function. Both of these functions fill a **MODULEENTRY32** structure with information about the module.

You can retrieve an extended error status code for **Module32First** and **Module32Next** by using the **GetLastError** function. For more information about **GetLastError**, see the documentation included in the Win32 SDK.

Note   The module identifier, which is specified in the **th32ModuleID** member of **MODULEENTRY32**, has meaning only to the tool help functions. It is not a handle, nor is it usable by other Win32 API elements.

Heap Lists and Heap Walking

A snapshot that includes the heap list for a specified Win32 process contains identification information for each heap associated with the specified process and detailed information about each heap. You can retrieve an identifier for the first heap of the heap list by using the **Heap32ListFirst** function. After retrieving the first heap in the list, you can traverse the heap list for subsequent heaps associated with the process by using the **Heap32ListNext** function. Both of these functions fill a **HEAPLIST32** structure with the process identifier, the heap identifier, and flags describing the heap.

You can retrieve information about the first block of a heap by using the **Heap32First** function. After retrieving the first block of a heap, you can retrieve information about subsequent blocks of the same heap by using the **Heap32Next** function. **Heap32First** and **Heap32Next** fill a **HEAPENTRY32** structure with information for the appropriate block of a heap.

You can retrieve an extended error status code for **Heap32ListFirst**, **Heap32ListNext**, **Heap32First**, and **Heap32Next** by using the **GetLastError** function. For more information about **GetLastError**, see the documentation included in the Win32 SDK.

Note The heap identifier, which is specified in the **th32HeapID** member of the **HEAPENTRY32** structure, has meaning only to the tool help functions. It is not a handle, nor is it usable by other Win32 API elements.

Using the Tool Help Functions

This section contains examples demonstrating how to perform the following tasks:

- Access tool help functions.
- Take a snapshot and view the processes in the system address space.
- Traverse the threads listed in a snapshot.
- Traverse the modules listed for a specific process.

The following examples have been taken from the PVIEW95 application included in the Win32 SDK.

Note Each of the **HEAPENTRY32**, **HEAPLIST32**, **MODULEENTRY32**, **PROCESSENTRY32**, and **THREADENTRY32** structures that are used with the tool help functions has a **dwSize** member that must be initialized to the size of the structure before the structure is included in a call to a tool help function. The value of **dwSize** is used to indicate the version of the tool help functions used. If your application does not initialize **dwSize**, the tool help function will fail.

Accessing the Tool Help Functions

The tool help functions reside in the operating system kernel. The following example provides a platform-independent approach to accessing the tool help functions.

```
#include <tlhelp32.h> // needed for tool help declarations

// Type definitions for pointers to call tool help functions.
typedef BOOL (WINAPI *MODULEWALK)(HANDLE hSnapshot,
    LPMODULEENTRY32 lpme);
typedef BOOL (WINAPI *THREADWALK)(HANDLE hSnapshot,
    LPTHREADENTRY32 lpte);
typedef BOOL (WINAPI *PROCESSWALK)(HANDLE hSnapshot,
    LPPROCESSENTRY32 lppe);
typedef HANDLE (WINAPI *CREATESNAPSHOT)(DWORD dwFlags,
    DWORD th32ProcessID);

// File scope globals. These pointers are declared because of the need
// to dynamically link to the functions.  They are exported only by
// the Windows 95 kernel. Explicitly linking to them will make this
// application unloadable in Microsoft(R) Windows NT(TM) and will
// produce an ugly system dialog box.
static CREATESNAPSHOT pCreateToolhelp32Snapshot = NULL;
static MODULEWALK  pModule32First  = NULL;
static MODULEWALK  pModule32Next   = NULL;
static PROCESSWALK pProcess32First = NULL;
static PROCESSWALK pProcess32Next  = NULL;
static THREADWALK  pThread32First  = NULL;
static THREADWALK  pThread32Next   = NULL;

// Function that initializes tool help functions.
BOOL InitToolhelp32 (void)
{
    BOOL   bRet  = FALSE;
    HANDLE hKernel = NULL;
```

```
            // Obtain the module handle of the kernel to retrieve addresses of
            // the tool helper functions.
            hKernel = GetModuleHandle("KERNEL32.DLL");

            if (hKernel){
                pCreateToolhelp32Snapshot =
                    (CREATESNAPSHOT)GetProcAddress(hKernel,
                    "CreateToolhelp32Snapshot");

                pModule32First  = (MODULEWALK)GetProcAddress(hKernel,
                    "Module32First");
                pModule32Next   = (MODULEWALK)GetProcAddress(hKernel,
                    "Module32Next");

                pProcess32First = (PROCESSWALK)GetProcAddress(hKernel,
                    "Process32First");
                pProcess32Next  = (PROCESSWALK)GetProcAddress(hKernel,
                    "Process32Next");

                pThread32First  = (THREADWALK)GetProcAddress(hKernel,
                    "Thread32First");
                pThread32Next   = (THREADWALK)GetProcAddress(hKernel,
                    "Thread32Next");

                // All addresses must be non-NULL to be successful.
                // If one of these addresses is NULL, one of
                // the needed lists cannot be walked.
                bRet =  pModule32First && pModule32Next  && pProcess32First &&
                        pProcess32Next && pThread32First && pThread32Next &&
                        pCreateToolhelp32Snapshot;
            }
            else
                bRet = FALSE; // could not even get the module handle of kernel

            return bRet;
        }
```

Taking a Snapshot and Viewing Processes

The following function takes a snapshot of the currently executing processes in the system and walks through the list recorded in the snapshot.

```
BOOL GetProcessList (VOID)
{
    HANDLE          hSnapshot = NULL;
    BOOL            bRet      = FALSE;
    PROCESSENTRY32  pe32      = {0};
```

```
    // Take a snapshot of all processes currently in the system.
    hSnapshot = pCreateToolhelp32Snapshot(TH32CS_SNAPPROCESS, 0);
    if (hProcessSnap == (HANDLE)-1)
        return (FALSE);

    // Fill in the size of the structure before using it.
    pe32.dwSize = sizeof(PROCESSENTRY32);

    // Walk the snapshot of the processes, and for each process, get
    // information to display.
    if (pProcess32First(hProcessSnap, &pe32)) {
        BOOL          bGotModule = FALSE;
        MODULEENTRY32 me32       = {0};
        PINFO         pi         = {0};

        do {
            bGotModule = GetProcessModule(pe32.th32ProcessID,
                pe32.th32ModuleID, &me32, sizeof(MODULEENTRY32));
            if (bGotModule) {
                HANDLE hProcess;

                // Get the actual priority class.
                hProcess = OpenProcess (PROCESS_ALL_ACCESS,
                    FALSE, pe32.th32ProcessID);
                pi.dwPriorityClass = GetPriorityClass (hProcess);
                CloseHandle (hProcess);

                // Get the process's base priority value.
                pi.pcPriClassBase = pe32.pcPriClassBase;
                pi.pid            = pe32.th32ProcessID;
                pi.cntThreads     = pe32.cntThreads;
                lstrcpy(pi.szModName, me32.szModule);
                lstrcpy(pi.szFullPath, me32.szExePath);

                AddProcessItem(hListView, pi);
            }
        }
        while (pProcess32Next(hProcessSnap, &pe32));
        bRet = TRUE;
    }
    else
        bRet = FALSE;    // could not walk the list of processes

    // Do not forget to clean up the snapshot object.
    CloseHandle (hProcessSnap);
    return (bRet);
}
```

Traversing the Thread List

The following function takes a snapshot of the threads currently executing in the system and walks through the list recorded in the snapshot.

```
// Returns TRUE if the threads were successfully enumerated
//   and listed or FALSE if the threads could not be enumerated
//   or listed.
// hListView  - handle of the listview that lists thread information
// dwOwnerPID - identifier of the process whose threads are to
//   be listed
BOOL RefreshThreadList (HWND hListView, DWORD dwOwnerPID)
{
    HANDLE        hThreadSnap = NULL;
    BOOL          bRet        = FALSE;
    THREADENTRY32 te32        = {0};

    // Take a snapshot of all threads currently in the system.
    hThreadSnap = pCreateToolhelp32Snapshot(TH32CS_SNAPTHREAD, 0);
    if (hThreadSnap == (HANDLE)-1)
        return (FALSE);

    // Clear the current contents of the thread list view
    // (which are now old).
    ListView_DeleteAllItems(g_hwndThread);

    // Fill in the size of the structure before using it.
    te32.dwSize = sizeof(THREADENTRY32);

    // Walk the thread snapshot to find all the threads of the process.
    // If the thread belongs to the process, add its information
    // to the display list.
    if (pThread32First(hThreadSnap, &te32)) {
        do {
            if (te32.th32OwnerProcessID == dwOwnerPID) {
                TINFO ti;

                ti.tid        = te32.th32ThreadID;
                ti.pidOwner   = te32.th32OwnerProcessID;
                ti.tpDeltaPri = te32.tpDeltaPri;
                ti.tpBasePri  = te32.tpBasePri;

                AddThreadItem(hListView, ti);
            }
        }
        while (pThread32Next(hThreadSnap, &te32));
        bRet = TRUE;
    }
```

```
        else
            bRet = FALSE;              // could not walk the list of threads

        // Do not forget to clean up the snapshot object.
        CloseHandle (hThreadSnap);

        return (bRet);
}
```

Traversing the Module List

The following function takes a snapshot of the modules in the address space of a specified Win32 process and retrieves information for a specific module from the list recorded in the snapshot.

```
// Returns TRUE if there is information about the specified module
//    or FALSE if it could not enumerate the modules in the process
//    or the module is not found in the process.
// dwPID - identifier of the process that owns the module to
//    retrieve information about
// dwModuleID - tool help identifier of the module within the
//    process
// lpMe32 - structure to return data about the module
// cbMe32 - size of the buffer pointed to by lpMe32 (to ensure
//    the buffer is not overfilled)
BOOL GetProcessModule (DWORD dwPID, DWORD dwModuleID,
        LPMODULEENTRY32 lpMe32, DWORD cbMe32)
{
    BOOL            bRet        = FALSE;
    BOOL            bFound      = FALSE;
    HANDLE          hModuleSnap = NULL;
    MODULEENTRY32 me32          = {0};

    // Take a snapshot of all modules in the specified process.
    hModuleSnap = pCreateToolhelp32Snapshot(TH32CS_SNAPMODULE, dwPID);
    if (hModuleSnap == (HANDLE)-1)
        return (FALSE);

    // Fill the size of the structure before using it.
    me32.dwSize = sizeof(MODULEENTRY32);
```

```
    // Walk the module list of the process, and find the module of
    // interest. Then copy the information to the buffer pointed
    // to by lpMe32 so that it can be returned to the caller.
    if (pModule32First(hModuleSnap, &me32)) {
        do {
            if (me32.th32ModuleID == dwModuleID) {
                CopyMemory (lpMe32, &me32, cbMe32);
                bFound = TRUE;
            }
        }
        while (!bFound && pModule32Next(hModuleSnap, &me32));

        bRet = bFound;    // if this sets bRet to FALSE, dwModuleID
                          // no longer exists in specified process
    }
    else
        bRet = FALSE;               // could not walk module list

    // Do not forget to clean up the snapshot object.
    CloseHandle (hModuleSnap);

    return (bRet);
}
```

Reference

The following functions and structures are associated with the tool help services.

Functions

The following functions are used with tool help services.

CreateToolhelp32Snapshot

```
HANDLE WINAPI CreateToolhelp32Snapshot(DWORD dwFlags,
    DWORD th32ProcessID);
```

Takes a snapshot of the Win32 processes, heaps, modules, and threads used by the Win32 processes.

- Returns an open handle to the specified snapshot if successful or -1 otherwise.

dwFlags

Flags specifying portions of the system to include in the snapshot. These values are defined:

TH32CS_INHERIT	Indicates that the snapshot handle is to be inheritable.
TH32CS_SNAPALL	Equivalent to specifying the TH32CS_SNAPHEAPLIST, TH32CS_SNAPMODULE, TH32CS_SNAPPROCESS, and TH32CS_SNAPTHREAD values.
TH32CS_SNAPHEAPLIST	Includes the heap list of the specified Win32 process in the snapshot.
TH32CS_SNAPMODULE	Includes the module list of the specified Win32 process in the snapshot.
TH32CS_SNAPPROCESS	Includes the Win32 process list in the snapshot.
TH32CS_SNAPTHREAD	Includes the Win32 thread list in the snapshot.

th32ProcessID

Win32 process identifier. This parameter can be zero to indicate the current process. This parameter is used when the TH32CS_SNAPHEAPLIST or TH32CS_SNAPMODULE value is specified. Otherwise, it is ignored.

The snapshot taken by this function is examined by the other tool help functions to provide their results. Access to the snapshot is read only. The snapshot handle acts like a Win32 object handle and is subject to the same rules regarding which processes and threads it is valid in.

To retrieve an extended error status code generated by this function, use the **GetLastError** function.

To destroy the snapshot, use the **CloseHandle** function.

Heap32First

```
BOOL WINAPI Heap32First(LPHEAPENTRY32 lphe, DWORD th32ProcessID,
    DWORD th32HeapID);
```

Retrieves information about the first block of a heap that has been allocated by a Win32 process.

- Returns TRUE if information for the first heap block has been copied to the buffer or FALSE otherwise. The ERROR_NO_MORE_FILES error value is returned by the **GetLastError** function if the heap is invalid or empty.

lphe
> Address of a buffer containing a **HEAPENTRY32** structure.

th32ProcessID
> Identifier of the Win32 process context that owns the heap.

th32HeapID
> Identifier of the heap to enumerate.

The calling application must set the **dwSize** member of **HEAPENTRY32** to the size, in bytes, of the structure.

To access subsequent blocks of the same heap, use the **Heap32Next** function.

Heap32ListFirst

```
BOOL WINAPI Heap32ListFirst(HANDLE hSnapshot, LPHEAPLIST32 lphl);
```

Retrieves information about the first heap that has been allocated by a specified Win32 process.

- Returns TRUE if the first entry of the heap list has been copied to the buffer or FALSE otherwise. The ERROR_NO_MORE_FILES error value is returned by the **GetLastError** function when no heap list exists or the snapshot does not contain heap list information.

hSnapshot
> Handle of the snapshot returned from a previous call to the function **CreateToolhelp32Snapshot**.

lphl
> Address of a buffer containing a **HEAPLIST32** structure.

The calling application must set the **dwSize** member of **HEAPLIST32** to the size, in bytes, of the structure.

To retrieve information about other heaps in the heap list, use the **Heap32ListNext** function.

Heap32ListNext

```
BOOL WINAPI Heap32ListNext(HANDLE hSnapshot, LPHEAPLIST32 lphl);
```

Retrieves information about the next heap that has been allocated by a Win32 process.

- Returns TRUE if the next entry of the heap list has been copied to the buffer or FALSE otherwise. The ERROR_NO_MORE_FILES error value is returned by the **GetLastError** function when no more entries in the heap list exist.

hSnapshot
Handle of the snapshot returned from a previous call to the function **CreateToolhelp32Snapshot**.

lphl
Address of a buffer containing a **HEAPLIST32** structure.

The calling application must set the **dwSize** member of **HEAPLIST32** to the size, in bytes, of the structure.

To retrieve information about the first heap in a heap list, use the **Heap32ListFirst** function.

Heap32Next

```
BOOL WINAPI Heap32Next(LPHEAPENTRY32 lphe);
```

Retrieves information about the next block of a heap that has been allocated by a Win32 process.

- Returns TRUE if information about the next block in the heap has been copied to the buffer or FALSE otherwise. The ERROR_NO_MORE_FILES error value is returned by the **GetLastError** function when no more objects in the heap exist.

lphe
Address of a buffer containing a **HEAPENTRY32** structure.

The calling application must set the **dwSize** member of **HEAPENTRY32** to the size, in bytes, of the structure.

To retrieve information for the first block of a heap, use the **Heap32First** function.

Module32First

```
BOOL WINAPI Module32First(HANDLE hSnapshot, LPMODULEENTRY32 lpme);
```

Retrieves information about the first module associated with a Win32 process.

- Returns TRUE if the first entry of the module list has been copied to the buffer or FALSE otherwise. The ERROR_NO_MORE_FILES error value is returned by the **GetLastError** function if no modules exist or the snapshot does not contain module information.

hSnapshot
> Handle of the snapshot returned from a previous call to the function **CreateToolhelp32Snapshot**.

lpme
> Address of a buffer containing a **MODULEENTRY32** structure.

The calling application must set the **dwSize** member of **MODULEENTRY32** to the size, in bytes, of the structure.

To retrieve information about other modules associated with the specified process, use the **Module32Next** function.

Module32Next

```
BOOL WINAPI Module32Next(HANDLE hSnapshot, LPMODULEENTRY32 lpme);
```

Retrieves information about the next module associated with a Win32 process or thread.

- Returns TRUE if the next entry of the module list has been copied to the buffer or FALSE otherwise. The ERROR_NO_MORE_FILES error value is returned by the **GetLastError** function if no more modules exist.

hSnapshot
> Handle of the snapshot returned from a previous call to the function **CreateToolhelp32Snapshot.**

lpme
> Address of a buffer containing a **MODULEENTRY32** structure.

The calling application must set the **dwSize** member of **MODULEENTRY32** to the size, in bytes, of the structure.

To retrieve information about first module associated with a Win32 process, use the **Module32First** function.

Process32First

```
BOOL WINAPI Process32First(HANDLE hSnapshot, LPPROCESSENTRY32 lppe);
```

Retrieves information about the first Win32 process encountered in a system snapshot.

- Returns TRUE if the first entry of the process list has been copied to the buffer or FALSE otherwise. The ERROR_NO_MORE_FILES error value is returned by the **GetLastError** function if no processes exist or the snapshot does not contain process information.

hSnapshot
Handle of the snapshot returned from a previous call to the function **CreateToolhelp32Snapshot**.

lppe
Address of a **PROCESSENTRY32** structure.

The calling application must set the **dwSize** member of **PROCESSENTRY32** to the size, in bytes, of the structure.

To retrieve information about other processes recorded in the same snapshot, use the **Process32Next** function.

Process32Next

```
BOOL WINAPI Process32Next(HANDLE hSnapshot, LPPROCESSENTRY32 lppe);
```

Retrieves information about the next Win32 process recorded in a system snapshot.

- Returns TRUE if the next entry of the process list has been copied to the buffer or FALSE otherwise. The ERROR_NO_MORE_FILES error value is returned by the **GetLastError** function if no processes exist or the snapshot does not contain process information.

hSnapshot
Handle of the snapshot returned from a previous call to the function **CreateToolhelp32Snapshot**.

lppe
Address of a **PROCESSENTRY32** structure.

The calling application must set the **dwSize** member of **PROCESSENTRY32** to the size, in bytes, of the structure.

To retrieve information about the first process recorded in a snapshot, use the **Process32First** function.

Thread32First

```
BOOL WINAPI Thread32First(HANDLE hSnapshot, LPTHREADENTRY32 lpte);
```

Retrieves information about the first thread of any Win32 process encountered in a system snapshot.

- Returns TRUE if the first entry of the thread list has been copied to the buffer or FALSE otherwise. The ERROR_NO_MORE_FILES error value is returned by the **GetLastError** function if no threads exist or the snapshot does not contain thread information.

hSnapshot
> Handle of the snapshot returned from a previous call to the function **CreateToolhelp32Snapshot**.

lpte
> Address of a **THREADENTRY32** structure.

The calling application must set the **dwSize** member of **THREADENTRY32** to the size, in bytes, of the structure.

To retrieve information about other threads recorded in the same snapshot, use the **Thread32Next** function.

Thread32Next

```
BOOL WINAPI Thread32Next(HANDLE hSnapshot, LPTHREADENTRY32 lpte);
```

Retrieves information about the next thread of any Win32 process encountered in the system memory snapshot.

- Returns TRUE if the next entry of the thread list has been copied to the buffer or FALSE otherwise. The ERROR_NO_MORE_FILES error value is returned by the **GetLastError** function if no threads exist or the snapshot does not contain thread information.

hSnapshot
> Handle of the snapshot returned from a previous call to the function **CreateToolhelp32Snapshot**.

lpte
> Address of a **THREADENTRY32** structure.

The calling application must set the **dwSize** member of **THREADENTRY32** to the size, in bytes, of the structure.

To retrieve information about the first thread recorded in a snapshot, use the **Thread32First** function.

Toolhelp32ReadProcessMemory

```
BOOL WINAPI Toolhelp32ReadProcessMemory(DWORD th32ProcessID,
    LPCVOID lpBaseAddress, LPVOID lpBuffer, DWORD cbRead,
    LPDWORD lpNumberOfBytesRead);
```

Copies memory allocated to another process into an application-supplied buffer.

- Returns TRUE if successful.

th32ProcessID
   Identifier of the Win32 process whose memory is being copied. This parameter can be zero to copy the memory of the current process.

lpBaseAddress
   Base address in the specified process to read. Before transferring any data, the system verifies that all data in the base address and memory of the specified size is accessible for read access. If this is the case, the function proceeds. Otherwise, the function fails.

lpBuffer
   Address of the buffer that receives the contents of the address space of the specified process.

cbRead
   Number of bytes to read from the specified process.

lpNumberOfBytesRead
   Number of bytes copied to the specified buffer. If this parameter is NULL, it is ignored.

Structures

The following structures are used with tool help services.

HEAPENTRY32

```
typedef struct tagHEAPENTRY32
{
    DWORD  dwSize;            // size, in bytes, of structure
    HANDLE hHandle;           // handle of heap block
    DWORD  dwAddress;         // linear address of start of block
    DWORD  dwBlockSize;       // size, in bytes, of heap block
    DWORD  dwFlags;           // see below
    DWORD  dwLockCount;       // see below
    DWORD  dwResvd;           // reserved; do not use
    DWORD  th32ProcessID;     // see below
    DWORD  th32HeapID;        // see below
} HEAPENTRY32;
typedef HEAPENTRY32 *  PHEAPENTRY32;
typedef HEAPENTRY32 *  LPHEAPENTRY32;
```

Describes one entry (block) of a heap that is being examined.

dwFlags

Flags. These values are defined:

LF32_FIXED	The memory block has a fixed (unmovable) location.
LF32_FREE	The memory block is not used.
LF32_MOVEABLE	The memory block location can be moved.

dwLockCount

Lock count on the memory block. The lock count is incremented each time that the **GlobalLock** or **LocalLock** function is called on the block either by the application or the DLL that the heap belongs to.

th32ProcessID

Identifier of the Win32 process to examine. The contents of this member can be used by other Win32 functions and macros.

th32HeapID

Heap identifier in the owning process context. The contents of this member has meaning only to the tool help functions. It is not a handle, nor is it usable by other Win32 API elements.

HEAPLIST32

```
typedef struct tagHEAPLIST32 {
    DWORD dwSize;          // size, in bytes, of structure
    DWORD th32ProcessID;   // see below
    DWORD th32HeapID;      // see below
    DWORD dwFlags;         // see below
} HEAPLIST32;
typedef HEAPLIST32 *  PHEAPLIST32;
typedef HEAPLIST32 *  LPHEAPLIST32;
```

Describes an entry from a list that enumerates the heaps used by a specified process.

th32ProcessID
Identifier of the Win32 process to examine. The contents of this member can be used by other Win32 functions and macros.

th32HeapID
Heap identifier in the owning process context. The contents of this member has meaning only to the tool help functions. It is not a handle, nor is it usable by other Win32 API elements.

dwFlags
Flags. These values are defined:

HF32_DEFAULT	Process's default heap
HF32_SHARED	Shared heap

MODULEENTRY32

```
typedef struct tagMODULEENTRY32 {
    DWORD    dwSize;       // size, in bytes, of structure
    DWORD    th32ModuleID; // see below
    DWORD    th32ProcessID; // see below
    DWORD    GlblcntUsage; // see below
    DWORD    ProccntUsage; // see below
    BYTE   * modBaseAddr;  // see below
    DWORD    modBaseSize;  // see below
    HMODULE  hModule;      // see below
    char     szModule[MAX_MODULE_NAME32 + 1];
    char     szExePath[MAX_PATH];
} MODULEENTRY32;
typedef MODULEENTRY32 *  PMODULEENTRY32;
typedef MODULEENTRY32 *  LPMODULEENTRY32;
```

Describes an entry from a list that enumerates the modules used by a specified process.

th32ModuleID

Module identifier in the context of the owning process. The contents of this member has meaning only to the tool help functions. It is not a handle, nor is it usable by other Win32 API elements.

th32ProcessID

Identifier of the Win32 process being examined. The contents of this member can be used by other Win32 functions and macros.

GlblcntUsage

Global usage count on the module.

ProccntUsage

Module usage count in the context of the owning process.

modBaseAddr

Base address of the module in the context of the owning process.

modBaseSize

Size, in bytes, of the module.

hModule

Handle of the module in the context of the owning process.

szModule

String containing the module name.

szExePath

String containing the location (path) of the module.

Note **modBaseAddr** and **hModule** are valid *only* in the context of the process specified by **th32ProcessID**.

PROCESSENTRY32

```
typedef struct tagPROCESSENTRY32 {
    DWORD dwSize;                  // size, in bytes, of structure
    DWORD cntUsage;                // see below
    DWORD th32ProcessID;           // specified process
    DWORD th32DefaultHeapID;       // see below
    DWORD th32ModuleID;            // see below
    DWORD cntThreads;              // see below
    DWORD th32ParentProcessID;     // see below
    LONG  pcPriClassBase;          // see below
    DWORD dwFlags;                 // reserved; do not use
    char  szExeFile[MAX_PATH];     // see below
} PROCESSENTRY32;
typedef PROCESSENTRY32 *  PPROCESSENTRY32;
typedef PROCESSENTRY32 *  LPPROCESSENTRY32;
```

Describes an entry from a list that enumerates the processes residing in the system address space when a snapshot was taken.

cntUsage
> Number of references to the process. A process exists as long as its usage count is nonzero. As soon as its usage count becomes zero, a process terminates.

th32ProcessID
> Identifier of the Win32 process. The contents of this member can be used by other Win32 functions and macros.

th32DefaultHeapID
> Identifier of the default heap for the process. The contents of this member has meaning only to the tool help functions. It is not a handle, nor is it usable by other Win32 API elements.

th32ModuleID
> Module identifier of the process. The contents of this member has meaning only to the tool help functions. It is not a handle, nor is it usable by other Win32 API elements.

cntThreads
> Number of execution threads started by the process.

th32ParentProcessID
> Identifier of the Win32 process that created the process being examined. The contents of this member can be used by other Win32 functions and macros.

pcPriClassBase
> Base priority of any threads created by this process.

szExeFile
> Path and filename of the executable file for the process.

THREADENTRY32

```
typedef struct tagTHREADENTRY32{
    DWORD  dwSize;              // size, in bytes, of structure
    DWORD  cntUsage;           // see below
    DWORD  th32ThreadID;       // see below
    DWORD  th32OwnerProcessID; // see below
    LONG   tpBasePri;          // see below
    LONG   tpDeltaPri;         // see below
    DWORD  dwFlags;            // reserved; do not use
} THREADENTRY32;
typedef THREADENTRY32 *  PTHREADENTRY32;
typedef THREADENTRY32 *  LPTHREADENTRY32;
```

Describes an entry from a list that enumerates the threads executing in the system when a snapshot was taken.

cntUsage

Number of references to the thread. A thread exists as long as its usage count is nonzero. As soon as its usage count becomes zero, a thread terminates.

th32ThreadID

Identifier of the thread. The contents of this member has meaning only to the tool help functions. It is not usable by other Win32 API elements.

th32OwnerProcessID

Identifier of the process that created the thread. The contents of this member can be used by other Win32 functions and macros.

tpBasePri

Initial priority level assigned to a thread. These values are defined:

THREAD_PRIORITY_IDLE

Indicates a base priority level of 1 for IDLE_PRIORITY_CLASS, NORMAL_PRIORITY_CLASS, or HIGH_PRIORITY_CLASS processes, and a base priority level of 16 for REALTIME_PRIORITY_CLASS processes.

THREAD_PRIORITY_LOWEST

Indicates 2 points below normal priority for the priority class.

THREAD_PRIORITY_BELOW_NORMAL

Indicates 1 point below normal priority for the priority class.

THREAD_PRIORITY_NORMAL

Indicates normal priority for the priority class.

THREAD_PRIORITY_ABOVE_NORMAL

Indicates 1 point above normal priority for the priority class.

THREAD_PRIORITY_HIGHEST

Indicates 2 points above normal priority for the priority class.

THREAD_PRIORITY_TIME_CRITICAL

Indicates a base priority level of 15 for IDLE_PRIORITY_CLASS, NORMAL_PRIORITY_CLASS, or HIGH_PRIORITY_CLASS processes, and a base priority level of 31 for REALTIME_PRIORITY_CLASS processes.

tpDeltaPri

Change in the priority level of a thread. This value is a signed delta from the base priority level assigned to the thread.

For additional information about thread priority levels, see the documentation included in the Win32 SDK.

P A R T   5

Using Microsoft MS-DOS Extensions

A R T I C L E   2 3

MS-DOS Extensions

About MS-DOS Extensions

Microsoft® Windows 95® not only supports the complete set of Microsoft® MS-DOS® system functions and interrupts but also provides extensions that permit MS-DOS–based applications to take advantage of Windows 95 features, such as long filenames, exclusive volume locking, virtual machine services, message services, and program information file management. For more information about these topics, see the articles with those names in this guide. For more information about MS-DOS functions and interrupts, see the *Microsoft MS-DOS Programmer's Reference*. This article describes various MS-DOS extensions for Windows 95 and provides general information about the file system.

Windows 95 Version of MS-DOS

When running with Windows 95, MS-DOS–based applications can check the operating system version by using Get MS-DOS Version Number (Interrupt 21h, Function 30h). For Windows 95, this function returns 7 as the major version number and 0 as the minor version number.

If you need to know that the system is running MS-DOS version 7.0, you must use Interrupt 2Fh Function 4A33h. This function returns zero in the AX register for MS-DOS version 7.0 or higher and returns a nonzero value in AX for any other versions of the disk operating system. In addition to the AX register, this function uses the DS, SI, DX, and BX registers.

File System Support

Windows 95 supports the long filename file allocation table (FAT) when running Windows. Any physical file on this extended FAT file system will logically be associated with two names—namely, the *primary filename* (also referred to as the long filename) and its *alternate name or alias*. Windows 95 automatically generates the alias, and it is always in the standard 8.3 filename format. When a file is saved to disk, the system creates a directory entry for both the long filename and alias. Because the number of entries in the root directory is limited, it is best to store files in a directory below it to avoid filling up the root. For more information about the filename conventions and how the system generates the alias, see Article 24, "Long Filenames."

Filename Limitations Under Real Mode

If Windows 95 is started in single MS-DOS application mode (real mode), only the standard FAT file system (and not the long filename FAT file system) is supported. This means that long filenames that are created in a Windows environment will *not* be visible when the user exits to single MS-DOS application mode, although the names themselves are physically present on the media. Only the alias (the 8.3 filename) will be visible.

When down-level file systems (such as MS-DOS version 6.0, Windows version 3.1, Microsoft® Windows NT™ version 3.1, and OS/2® version 2.11) read a floppy disk that contains long filenames created using Windows 95, the long filename will not be visible; only the alias (the 8.3 filename) will be visible. However, Windows NT version 3.5 supports long filenames. Windows 95 will see the long filenames of files on a floppy disk that were created using Microsoft Windows NT version 3.5, and Windows NT version 3.5 will see the long filenames of files on a floppy disk that were created using Windows 95. Windows 95 will be able to see the long filenames on New Technology file system (NTFS), OS/2's high performance file system (HPFS), or Novell NetWare's file system if there are long filenames on the server.

Because down-level systems are not aware of long filenames, they will not preserve them. If you copy a file from a floppy disk to the hard disk on a down-level system, the long filename associated with the file is not copied over. If you edit a file on the floppy disk using the alias and then save a new copy back on the floppy disk using the down-level system, the long filename associated with the file will most likely be lost. If you take the floppy disk back to the Windows 95 system, only the alias will be associated with the file.

Preserving Filenames

Certain operations, such as copy, backup, and restore, using older versions of utilities that have not been updated to support long filenames will destroy the long filename. Running a utility called LFNBK that comes with Windows 95 before using older backup utilities will preserve the long filenames. Following are the steps for using LFNBK to backup and restore a disk:

1. Preserve the long filename and alias (the 8.3 filename) association by running **LFNBK /b** *drive-letter*, where *drive-letter* is the drive that you plan to back up.

2. Back up the drive (specified as *drive-letter* in the previous step) using an old backup program that is not be aware of long filenames.

3. Restore the backup files to a drive, when necessary at some later point, using an old restore program that is not be aware of long filenames.

4. Restore the long filenames on the drive, by running **LFNBK /r** *drive-letter*, where *drive-letter* is the drive where the files were restored to.

Searching Filenames

Searches of filenames apply to both the filename and its alias. The system presents a *single unified namespace* so that a single physical view of the file is preserved. However, if the result of a search shows only the long filename, it could be confusing to the user. For example, a set of files in a directory might include the following filenames and aliases.

Filename	Alias
LongFileName	LONGFI~1
File-1	FILE-1

A search of files in the directory using **DIR *1** would display the following information.

```
LONGFI~1    123    05-11-95    15:26    LongFileName
FILE-1      352    05-11-95    16:01    File-1
```

Note that the **DIR** command displays the alias first for compatibility with the older **DIR** format. However, a search utility that is aware of long filenames but displays only the filename, would also show both the *LongFileName* and *File-1* files. This could be confusing at first glance to the user because the *LongFileName* file does not have the number *1* as specified in the search criteria. The file was matched to the search pattern because its alias contains the number *1*.

The wildcard searches have been expanded in Windows 95. Using the old search criteria, the first * encountered caused all following characters to be ignored. However, in the preceding example, ***1** is a valid specification. More than one wildcard can be used in Windows 95 when specifying search criteria. For example, to search for all files that contain the word **mid** somewhere in the filename, ***mid*** can be specified as the search criteria.

Exclusive Volume Locking

Previously reserved fields in the file system directory entry are used for storing the last access date and the creation date and time. A file with a long filename, which is longer than 5 characters, will also cause the system to use previously reserved fields in the directory entry. In previous versions of MS-DOS and Windows, these reserved entries were zero. Older disk repair and checking utilities that have not been updated for Windows 95 might display errors about the disk because of the usage of these reserved entries. It is possible that an older disk repair utility could either destroy the long filename or the actual data in a file because it would mistakenly interpret the file as corrupted. For this reason, Windows 95 is designed to fail utilities that perform direct disk writes. This feature is called exclusive volume locking. A newer version of the utility that understands the newer on-disk file system structures will obtain an exclusive volume lock and proceed correctly.

Exclusive volume locking is also needed because the system is a multitasking system and disk utilities need exclusive access so that they can modify the file system without causing the file system to be inconsistent for the other executing applications. For more information, see Article 25, "Exclusive Volume Locking."

Storing Filenames

When an application stores filenames, it should follow these guidelines:

- Using an alias instead of a long filename can break the association with the file because certain operations, such as editing the file, can potentially change the alias. For example, if the server side of a network uses the alias instead of the long filename of a client file to store information related to the file, such as access permissions, it will be more susceptible to lose the association of permissions with the file. If the user edits the file on the client side, the alias may potentially change, and if it changes, the server side will lose the associated information.

- When an application caches the absolute path to a filename, the path itself can be a mixture of filenames and aliases. Because of this, applications that need to store a path should store a canonical form of the absolute path. Applications may use either Get Short Path Name (Interrupt 21h Function 7160h) or the Microsoft® Win32® **GetShortPathName** function to retrieve the canonical form of a path. Applications that need to determine if two files are the same can use the **nFileIndexHigh** and **nFileIndexLow** members of the **BY_HANDLE_FILE_INFORMATION** structure. Note, however, that **nFileIndexHigh** and **nFileIndexLow** might not be supported on real-mode file systems, such as Microsoft CD-ROM Extensions (MSCDEX), or real-mode networks.

- An installation program that needs to enter information into configuration files, such as CONFIG.SYS, should make sure it uses paths that only consist of 8.3 filename components, because the long filenames will not be visible at boot up time when startup files, such as CONFIG.SYS and AUTOEXEC.BAT, are processed. Again, the **GetShortPathName** function should be used for this purpose.

Filename Functions

With the exception of the **OpenFile** function, all of the functions in Windows version 3.*x* that require the application to pass in a filename (functions such as **LoadLibrary**, **WinExec**, **_lopen**, and **_lcreate**) have been updated to support long filenames. For compatibility reasons, functions that return filenames should return only aliases (8.3 filenames) to 16-bit Windows–based applications marked less than 4.0.

MS-DOS–based applications generally use the Interrupt 21h functions. Except for Extended Open/Create (Interrupt 21h Function 6Ch), the older Interrupt 21h functions have not changed in Windows 95. Extended Open/Create has been enhanced in Windows 95 to make use of the last access date for a file. To support long filenames, Windows 95 provides many new Interrupt 21h functions. Any MS-DOS–based application that will use long filenames must be updated to support the new functions. For information about the long filename Interrupt 21h functions, see Article 24, "Long Filenames."

Windows 95 supports the new Interrupt 21h long filename functions on as many file systems as possible. On file systems, such as MSCDEX, Flash, and real-mode network redirectors, that do not support long filenames, the system automatically translates the newer Interrupt 21h calls to the appropriate older Interrupt 21h calls, as long as the filename passed as a parameter is a valid alias (8.3 filename). Applications may use Get Volume Information (Interrupt 21h Function 71A0h) to retrieve information on the capabilities of the underlying file system.

Command Interpreter for Command

The **for** command in the command interpreter (COMMAND.COM) is modal. The default is **LFNFOR=OFF**, which causes the **for** command to use the old Interrupt 21h function calls. In that case, only aliases (8.3 filenames) can be used in the **for** command. If **LFNFOR=ON** is set, the **for** command uses the new Interrupt 21h functions, and long filenames can be used as part of the **for** command.

Long Command Lines

Although in previous versions of MS-DOS the limit for environment variables and batch file lines is 128 characters, it is 1024 characters in Windows 95. The limit for the keyboard buffer, however, is still 128 characters. Although 1024 and 128 are the standard limits, users may configure their systems to lower these limits.

In previous versions of MS-DOS, command-line arguments are located in the command tail of the program segment prefix (PSP). The command tail in the PSP is limited to 128 characters, including the leading byte that specifies the length of the command line and the trailing carriage return character. In Windows 95, if the command line is less than or equal to 126 characters, it is set in the command tail of the PSP. For command lines that are greater than 126 characters, an application should follow these steps:

1. Set the count byte in the command tail to 7Fh.

2. Fill in 7Eh bytes of the command tail followed by the carriage return character (0Dh).

3. Place the rest of the command line in the CMDLINE environment variable.

Reference

This section provides information about the following functions and structures.

Get Compressed File Size	Interrupt 21h Function 4302h
Lock/Unlock Removable Media	Interrupt 21h Function 440Dh Minor Code 48h
Eject Removable Media	Interrupt 21h Function 440Dh Minor Code 49h
Get Drive Map Info	Interrupt 21h Function 440Dh Minor Code 6Fh
Get First Cluster	Interrupt 21h Function 440Dh Minor Code 71h
Extended Open/Create	Interrupt 21h Function 6Ch
DRIVE_MAP_INFO	Get Drive Map Info returns information about the specified drive in this structure.
MID	This structure, which is used by Get Media ID (Interrupt 21h Function 440Dh Minor Code 66h) and Set Media ID (Interrupt 21h Function 440Dh Minor Code 46h), has been updated to support compact disc (CD) file systems. For information about using these functions, see the *Microsoft MS-DOS Programmer's Reference*.
PARAMBLOCK	This structure is needed by Lock/Unlock Removable Media.

Functions

The following functions are used with MS-DOS extensions.

Interrupt 21h Function 4302h Get Compressed File Size

```
mov ax, 4302h          ; Get Compressed File Size
mov dx, seg PathName   ; see below
mov ds, dx
mov dx, offset PathName
int 21h

jc error
```

Obtains the compressed size, in bytes, of a given file or directory.

- Clears the carry flag if successful. Otherwise, the function sets the carry flag and sets the AX register to an error value.

PathName
Address of a null-terminated string that specifies the file or directory to retrieve the file size for.

The function obtains the actual number of bytes of disk storage used to store the file. If the file is located on a volume that supports compression and the file is compressed, the value obtained is the compressed size of the specified file. If the file is not located on a volume that supports compression or if the file is not compressed, the value obtained is the file size, in bytes, rounded up to the nearest cluster boundary.

Interrupt 21h Function 440Dh Minor Code 48h Lock/Unlock Removable Media

```
mov ax, 440Dh          ; generic IOCTL
mov bx, DriveNum       ; see below
mov ch, 8              ; device category
mov cl, 48h            ; Lock or Unlock Removable Media
mov dx, seg ParamBlock ; see below
mov ds, dx
mov dx, offset ParamBlock
int 21h

jc  error
```

Locks or unlocks the volume in the given drive (preventing or permitting its removal) or returns the locked status of the given drive.

- Clears the carry flag and copies the number of pending locks on the given drive to the **NumLocks** member of the **PARAMBLOCK** structure if successful. Otherwise, the function sets the carry flag and sets the AX register to one of the following error values:

01h	The function is not supported.
B0h	The volume is not locked in the drive.
B2h	The volume is not removable.
B4h	The lock count has been exceeded.

DriveNum
> Drive to lock or unlock. This parameter can be 0 for default drive, 1 for A, 2 for B, and so on.

ParamBlock
> Address of a **PARAMBLOCK** structure that specifies the operation to carry out and receives a count of the number of locks on the drive.

Interrupt 21h Function 440Dh Minor Code 49h Eject Removable Media

```
mov ax, 440Dh      ; generic IOCTL
mov bx, DriveNum   ; see below
mov ch, 8          ; device category
mov cl, 49h        ; Eject Removable Media
int 21h

jc  error
```

Ejects the specified media.

- Clears the carry flag if successful. Otherwise, the function sets the carry flag and sets the AX register to one of the following error values:

01h	The function is not supported.
B1h	The volume is locked in the drive.
B2h	The volume is not removable.
B5h	The valid eject request has failed.

DriveNum
> Drive to eject. This parameter can be 0 for default drive, 1 for A, 2 for B, and so on.

If a given physical drive has more than one logical volume, all volumes must be unlocked by using Lock/Unlock Removable Media (Interrupt 21h Function 440Dh Minor Code 48h) before the drive will eject.

Interrupt 21h Function 440Dh Minor Code 6Fh Get Drive Map Info

```
mov ax, 440Dh               ; generic IOCTL
mov bx, DriveNum            ; see below
mov ch, 8                   ; device category
mov cl, 6Fh                 ; Get Drive Map Info
mov dx, seg DriveMapInfo    ; see below
mov ds, dx
mov dx, offset DriveMapInfo
int 21h

jc  error
```

Retrieves information about the specified drive.

DriveNum
Drive to obtain information about. This parameter can be 0 for the default drive, 1 for A, 2 for B, and so on.

DriveMapInfo
Address of the **DRIVE_MAP_INFO** structure that receives information about the specified drive.

Interrupt 21h Function 440Dh Minor Code 71h Get First Cluster

```
mov ax, 440Dh               ; generic IOCTL
mov bx, CharSet             ; see below
mov ch, 08h                 ; device category
mov cl, 71h                 ; Get First Cluster
mov dx, seg PathName        ; see below
mov ds, dx
mov dx, offset PathName
int 21h

jc error
```

Retrieves the first cluster of the specified file or directory.

- Clears the carry flag and sets DX:AX to the first cluster number if successful. Otherwise, the function sets the carry flag and returns either the ERROR_INVALID_FUNCTION or ERROR_ACCESS_DENIED value in AX.

CharSet
>   Character set of *PathName*. This parameter must be one of these values:

>   BCS_WANSI (0)   Windows ANSI character set

>   BCS_OEM (1)   Current OEM character set

>   BCS_UNICODE (2)   Unicode character set

PathName
>   Address of a null-terminated string containing the path of the file or directory
>   to retrieve the first cluster for.

The first cluster of a file is the first cluster of the FAT cluster chain describing
he data associated with the file. The first cluster of a directory is the first cluster of
the FAT cluster chain associated with the directory. It is the cluster that contains the
"." and ".." entries. The function finds any file or directory regardless of attribute
(system, hidden, or read-only). It does not find volume labels.

If your application is unable to accommodate a 32-bit cluster number, you must
check to see if the value returned in the DX register is greater than zero.

```
if(MAKELONG(regAX,regDX) > 0x0000FFF8)
    b32BitNum = TRUE;
else
    b32BitNum = FALSE;
```

It is the calling application's responsibility to check to see if the returned cluster
number is valid.

```
if((MAKELONG(regAX,regDX) < 2L) || (MAKELONG(regAX,regDX) > maxClus))
    bInvalidNum = TRUE;
else
    bInvalidNum = FALSE;
```

In the preceding example, the *maxClus* variable is the maximum legal cluster
number, as a **DWORD** type, computed from the drive parameters.

Interrupt 21h Function 6Ch Extended Open/Create

```
mov ah, 6Ch            ; Extended Open/Create
mov bx, ModeAndFlags   ; see below
mov cx, Attributes     ; see below
mov dx, Action         ; action to take
mov si, seg Filename   ; see below
mov ds, si
mov si, offset Filename
int 21h

jc error
mov [Handle], ax       ; file handle
mov [ActionTaken], cx  ; action taken to open file
```

Opens or creates a file having the given name and attributes.

- Clears the carry flag, copies the file handle to the AX register, and sets CX to one of the following values if successful:

ACTION_OPENED (0001h)

ACTION_CREATED_OPENED (0002h)

ACTION_REPLACED_OPENED (0003h)

Otherwise, this function sets the carry flag and sets the AX register to one of the following error values:

ERROR_INVALID_FUNCTION (0001h)

ERROR_FILE_NOT_FOUND (0002h)

ERROR_PATH_NOT_FOUND (0003h)

ERROR_TOO_MANY_OPEN_FILES (0004h)

ERROR_ACCESS_DENIED (0005h)

ModeAndFlags

Combination of access mode, sharing mode, and open flags. This parameter can be one value each from the access and sharing modes and any combination of open flags:

Access mode	Meaning
OPEN_ACCESS_READONLY (0000h)	
	Opens the file for reading only.
OPEN_ACCESS_WRITEONLY (0001h)	
	Opens the file for writing only.

Access mode	Meaning

OPEN_ACCESS_READWRITE (0002h)

Opens the file for reading and writing.

0003h

Reserved; do not use.

OPEN_ACCESS_RO_NOMODLASTACCESS (0004h)

Opens the file for reading only without modifying the file's last access date.

Sharing mode	Meaning

OPEN_SHARE_COMPATIBLE (0000h)

Opens the file with compatibility mode, allowing any process on a given computer to open the file any number of times.

OPEN_SHARE_DENYREADWRITE (0010h)

Opens the file and denies both read and write access to other processes.

OPEN_SHARE_DENYWRITE (0020h)

Opens the file and denies write access to other processes.

OPEN_SHARE_DENYREAD (0030h)

Opens the file and denies read access to other processes.

OPEN_SHARE_DENYNONE (0040h)

Opens the file without denying read or write access to other processes, but no process may open the file with compatibility mode.

Open flags	Meaning

OPEN_FLAGS_NOINHERIT (0080h)

If this flag is set, a child process created with Load and Execute Program (Interrupt 21h Function 4B00h) does not inherit the file handle. If the handle is needed by the child process, the parent process must pass the handle value to the child process. If this flag is not set, child processes inherit the file handle.

OPEN_FLAGS_NOCRITERR (2000h)

If a critical error occurs while MS-DOS is opening this file, Critical-Error Handler (Interrupt 24h) is not called. Instead, MS-DOS simply returns an error value to the program.

OPEN_FLAGS_COMMIT (4000h)

After each write operation, MS-DOS commits the file (flushes the contents of the cache buffer to disk).

Attributes

Attributes for files that are created or truncated. This parameter may be a combination of these values:

FILE_ATTRIBUTE_NORMAL (0000h)

>   The file can be read from or written to. This value is valid only if used alone.

FILE_ATTRIBUTE_READONLY (0001h)

>   The file can be read from, but not written to.

FILE_ATTRIBUTE_HIDDEN (0002h)

>   The file is hidden and does not appear in an ordinary directory listing.

FILE_ATTRIBUTE_SYSTEM (0004h)

>   The file is part of the operating system or is used exclusively by it.

FILE_ATTRIBUTE_VOLUME (0008h)

>   The name specified by *Filename* is used as the volume label for the current medium.

FILE_ATTRIBUTE_ARCHIVE (0020h)

>   The file is an archive file. Applications use this value to mark files for backup or removal.

Action

Action to take it the file exists or does not exist. This parameter can be a combination of these values:

FILE_CREATE (0010h)	Creates a new file if it does not already exist or fails if the file already exists.
FILE_OPEN (0001h)	Opens the file. The function fails if the file does not exist.
FILE_TRUNCATE (0002h)	Opens the file and truncates it to zero length (replaces the existing file). The function fails if the file does not exist.

The only valid combinations are FILE_CREATE combined with FILE_OPEN or FILE_CREATE combined with FILE_TRUNCATE.

Filename

Address of a null-terminated string specifying the name of the file to be opened or created. The name must be in the standard MS-DOS 8.3 filename format. The string must be a valid path for the volume associated with the given drive.

This function does not support long filenames. If the specified name is too long, this function truncates the name to the standard 8.3 format following the same naming scheme that the system uses when creating an alias for a long filename.

A file on a remote directory—that is, a directory on the network—cannot be opened, unless appropriate permissions for the directory exist.

Structures

The following structures are used with MS-DOS extensions.

DRIVE_MAP_INFO

```
DRIVE_MAP_INFO   struc
      dmiAllocationLength   db ?   ; see below
      dmiInfoLength         db ?   ; see below
      dmiFlags              db ?   ; see below
      dmiInt13Unit          db ?   ; see below
      dmiAssociatedDriveMap dd ?   ; see below
      dmiPartitionStartRBA  dq ?   ; see below
DRIVE_MAP_INFO   ends
```

Contains information about the drive specified in the call to Get Drive Map Info (Interrupt 2lh Function 440Dh Minor Code 6Fh).

dmiAllocationLength

Length of the buffer provided by the application calling Get Drive Map Info. This value should be the size of the **DRIVE_MAP_INFO** structure.

dmiInfoLength

Number of bytes that Get Drive Map Info used in the buffer provided by the calling application. Typically, this value is the size of the **DRIVE_MAP_INFO** structure.

dmiFlags

Flags describing the given drive. This member, which is filled by Get Drive Map Info, can be a combination of these values:

PROT_MODE_LOGICAL_DRIVE (01h)	A protected-mode driver is in use for this logical drive.
PROT_MODE_PHYSICAL_DRIVE (02h)	A protected-mode driver is in use for the physical drive corresponding to this logical drive.
PROT_MODE_ONLY_DRIVE(04h)	The drive is not available when running with MS-DOS.
PROT_MODE_EJECT (08h)	A protected-mode drive supports an electronic eject operation.
PROT_MODE_ASYNC_NOTIFY (10h)	The drive issues media arrival and removal notifications. This value is currently used for CD-ROM drives that are controlled by the protected-mode driver and that cause a broadcast message when media is removed or inserted without the application having to make a request to the drive. It can also be used by disk drivers.

dmiInt13Unit

Physical drive number of the given drive. This member, which is filled by Get Drive Map Info, can be one of these values:

00 - 7Fh	Floppy disk drive (00 for the first floppy drive, 01 for the second, and so on).
80 - FEh	Hard disk drive (80 for the first hard disk drive, 81 for the second, and so on).
FFh	The given drive does not map to a physical drive.

dmiAssociatedDriveMap

Logical drive numbers that are associated with the given physical drive. For example, a host drive C with child drive letters A and B would return with bits 0 and 1 set.

dmiPartitionStartRBA

Relative block address offset from the start of the physical volume to the start of the given partition.

Before an application makes a call to the Get Drive Map Info function, the **dmiAllocationLength** member must be set to the size of the **DRIVE_MAP_INFO** structure. All other members of the structure are filled in by Get Drive Map Info.

MID

```
MID struc
    midInfoLevel    dw 0            ; see below
    midSerialNum    dd ?            ; see below
    midVolLabel     db 11 dup (?)   ; see below
    midFileSysType  db 8 dup (?)    ; see below
MID ends
```

Contains information that uniquely identifies a disk or other storage medium.

midInfoLevel
Information level. This member must be zero.

midSerialNum
Serial number for the medium.

midVolLabel
Volume label for the medium. If the label has fewer than 11 characters, space characters (ASCII 20h) fill the remaining bytes in this member.

midFileSysType
Type of file system as an 8-byte ASCII string. This member can be one of these values:

FAT12	12-bit file allocation table (FAT)
FAT16	16-bit FAT
CDROM	High Sierra file system
CD001	ISO9660 file system
CDAUDIO	Audio disk

If the name has fewer than eight characters, space characters (ASCII 20h) fill the remaining bytes in this member.

PARAMBLOCK

```
PARAMBLOCK struc
    Operation db ?  ; see below
    NumLocks  db ?  ; see below
PARAMBLOCK ends
```

Contains information about locked drives.

Operation

Operation to carry out provided by the calling application of Lock/Unlock Removable Media (Interrupt 21h Function 440Dh Minor Code 48h). This member can be one of these values:

0	Locks the volume in the drive.
1	Unlocks the volume in the drive.
2	Returns the lock or unlock status.

All other values are reserved.

NumLocks

Number of locks pending on the given drive filled in by Lock/Unlock Removable Media.

ARTICLE 24

Long Filenames

About Long Filenames

Microsoft® Windows® 95 allows users and applications to create and use long names for their files and directories. A long filename is a name for a file or directory that exceeds the standard 8.3 filename format. In the past, long filenames typically appeared on network servers that used file systems other than the Microsoft® MS-DOS® file allocation table (FAT) file system. In Windows 95, however, long filenames are available for use with network servers and with local disk drives supporting the protected-mode FAT file system.

This article describes the long filename functions and explains how to create and use long filenames in applications written for MS-DOS and 16-bit Windows version 3.*x*. Microsoft® Win32®-based applications automatically have access to long filenames through the use of the corresponding Win32 file management functions.

Long Filenames and the Protected-Mode FAT File System

The protected-mode FAT file system is the default file system used by Windows 95 for mass storage devices, such as hard disk and floppy disk drives. Protected-mode FAT is compatible with the MS-DOS FAT file system, using file allocation tables and directory entries to store information about the contents of a disk drive. Protected-mode FAT also supports long filenames, storing these names as well as the date and time that the file was created and the date that the file was last accessed in the FAT file system structures.

The protected-mode FAT file system allows filenames of up to 256 characters, including the terminating null character. In this regard, it is similar to the Microsoft® Windows NT™ file system (NTFS), which allows filenames of up to 256 characters. Protected-mode FAT allows directory paths (excluding the filename) of up to 246 characters, including the drive letter, colon, and leading backslash. This limit of 246 allows for the addition of a filename in the standard 8.3 format with the terminating null character. The maximum number of characters in a full path, including the drive letter, colon, leading backslash, filename, and terminating null character, is 260.

When an application creates a file or directory that has a long filename, the system automatically generates a corresponding alias for that file or directory using the standard 8.3 format. The characters used in the alias are the same characters that are available for use in MS-DOS file and directory names. Valid characters for the alias are any combination of letters, digits, or characters with ASCII codes greater than 127, the space character (ASCII 20h), as well as any of the following special characters.

$ % ' - _ @ ~ ` ! ( ) { } ^ # &

The space character has been available to applications for filenames and directory names through the functions in current and earlier versions of MS-DOS. However, many applications do not recognize the space character as a valid character, and the system does not use the space character when it generates an alias for a long filename. MS-DOS does not distinguish between uppercase and lowercase letters in filenames and directory names, and this is also true for aliases.

The set of valid characters for long filenames includes all the characters that are valid for an alias as well as the following additional characters.

+ , ; = [ ]

Windows 95 preserves the case of the letters used in long filenames. However, the protected-mode FAT file system, which is not case sensitive, will not allow more than one file to have the same name except for case in the same directory. For example, files named *Long File Name* and *long file name* are not allowed to exist in the same directory. Although extended ASCII characters (characters with ASCII codes greater than 127) are also permitted in filenames, programs should avoid them, because the meanings of the extended characters may vary according to code page. On disk, the characters in the alias are stored using the OEM character set of the current code page, and the long filename is stored using Unicode format.

Although the protected-mode FAT file system is the default file system in Windows 95, it is not the only file system accessible to applications running with Windows 95. For example, applications that connect to network drives may encounter other file systems, such as NTFS. Before using long filenames for files and directories on a volume in a given drive, you must determine the maximum lengths of filenames and paths by using Get Volume Information (Interrupt 21h Function 71A0h). The function returns values that you can use to make sure your filenames and paths are within the limits of the file system.

In general, you should avoid using static buffers for filenames and paths. Instead, you should use the values returned by Get Volume Information to allocate buffers as you need them. If you must use static buffers, you should reserve 256 characters for filenames and 260 characters for paths. These are the maximum sizes currently recommended for Win32-based applications.

Filename Aliases

When an application creates a file or directory that has a long filename, the system automatically generates a corresponding short filename (alias) for that file or directory, using the standard 8.3 format. Aliases ensure that existing applications that do not handle long filenames can, nevertheless, access those files and directories.

If the long filename follows the standard 8.3 format, the alias has the same name except that all lowercase letters are converted to uppercase. For example, if the long filename is *Examples.Txt*, the corresponding alias will be *EXAMPLES.TXT*.

If the long filename does not follow the standard 8.3 format, the system automatically generates an alias, using the following scheme to ensure that the alias has a unique name. The system tries to create a name by using the first 6 characters of the long filename followed by a *numeric tail*. A numeric tail consists of the tilde (~) character followed by a number. The system starts with the number 1 in the numeric tail. If that filename already exists, it uses the number 2. It continues in this fashion until a unique name is found. If the long filename has a filename extension, the system will use the first three characters of the long filename's extension as the extension for the alias.

As the number of digits in the numeric tail grows, fewer characters in the long filename are used for the 8 characters in the alias. For example, the alias for *Long File Name.File* would be *LONGFI~10.FIL* if the names *LONGFI~1.FIL* through *LONGFI~9.FIL* already existed in the directory. Applications can override the default alias numbering scheme when creating a file by specifying the OPEN_FLAGS_ALIAS_HINT value and supplying a number to use in the call to Create or Open File (Interrupt 21h Function 716Ch).

A period is just another character in a long filename. Leading periods are allowed in a long filename, but trailing periods are stripped. A file can have multiple periods as part of its name. For example, *MyFile.081293.Document* is a valid filename, and its alias will be *MYFILE~1.DOC*. The first three characters after the last period in the filename are used as the filename extension for the alias, as long as the last period is not a leading period. A filename of *.login* is also valid, and its alias is *LOGIN~1*.

In a given directory, the long filename and its alias must uniquely identify a file. For example, if there is a file with the long filename *Long File Name* and the alias *LONGFI~1*, the system will not allow either *Long File Name* or *LONGFI~1* to be used as another file's long filename.

If a file with a long filename is copied or edited, the alias for the resulting file may be different from the original alias. For example, if the destination directory contains an alias that conflicts with the original alias, the system generates another unique alias. If a long filename *LongFileName* is associated with the *LONGFI~2* alias and is later copied to a different directory using the long filename, the alias in the destination directory might be *LONGFI~1* (unless a file with that name already existed in the destination directory). The system always generates new aliases during these operations and always chooses aliases that do not conflict with existing filenames. An application must never rely on an alias being the same for all copies and versions of a given file.

Applications can open, read, and write from a file using the alias without affecting the long filename. However, some operations on the alias, such as copy, move, backup, and restore, may result in the original long filename being destroyed. For example, older versions of utilities that do not support long filenames can destroy the long filename while performing those operations.

The system attempts to preserve a long filename, even when the file associated with it is edited by an application that is not aware of long filenames. Typically, these applications operate on a temporary copy of the file, and when the user elects to save the file, the application deletes the destination file or renames it to another name. The application then renames the temporary file to the destination name or creates a new file with new contents.

When an application makes a system call to delete or rename an alias, the system first gathers and saves a packet of information about the file and then performs the delete or rename operation. The information saved includes the long filename as well as the creation date and time, the last modification date and time, and the last access date of the original file. After the system performs the delete or rename operation, the system watches for a short period of time (the default is 15 seconds) to see if a call is made to create or rename a file with the same name. If the system detects a create or rename operation of a recently deleted alias, it applies the packet of information that it had saved to the new file, thus preserving the long filename.

Currently, Load and Execute Program (Interrupt 21h Function 4B00h) does not accept long filenames. If an application starts other applications, it must retrieve the filename alias for the given executable file and pass that alias to Load and Execute Program.

File and Directory Management

The standard MS-DOS file and directory management functions do not accept long filenames. You must, therefore, use the long filename functions to create and manage files and directories having long names. The long filename functions are similar to existing MS-DOS system functions. You copy function parameters to registers and issue an Interrupt 21h instruction to carry out the call. The function sets or clears the carry flag to indicate whether the operation was successful and may also return information in registers.

If a long filename function has a corresponding MS-DOS function, the number that identifies the long filename function is four digits long, beginning with the number 71 and ending in the same number as the corresponding MS-DOS function. For example, the long filename function Make Directory (Interrupt 21h Function 7139h) corresponds to MS-DOS Create Directory (Interrupt 21h Function 39h).

You can create or open a file having a long filename by using Create or Open File (Interrupt 21h Function 716Ch). This function takes the name and attributes of the file to create or open and returns a handle that you use to identify the file in subsequent calls to standard MS-DOS functions, such as Read File or Device (Interrupt 21h Function 3Fh) and Write File or Device (Interrupt 21h Function 40h).

You can set or retrieve the time and attributes for a file having a long filename by using Get or Set File Time (Interrupt 21h Function 57h) and Get or Set File Attributes (Interrupt 21h Function 7143h). You can move a file having a long filename by using Rename File (Interrupt 21h Function 7156h) or delete the file by using Delete File (Interrupt 21h Function 7141h).

You can create a directory having a long filename by using Make Directory (Interrupt 21h Function 7139h) or remove the directory by using Remove Directory (Interrupt 21h Function 713Ah).

You can set and retrieve the current directory by using Change Directory (Interrupt 21h Function 713Bh) and Get Current Directory (Interrupt 21h Function 7147h).

File Searches

You can search directories for selected files by using Find First File and Find Next File (Interrupt 21h Functions 714Eh and 714Fh). These functions search for and return information about files having long filenames and aliases (filenames in the standard 8.3 format). The functions return information in a **WIN32_FIND_DATA** structure, which contains both the filename and the corresponding alias, if any.

Unlike MS-DOS Find First File (Interrupt 21h Function 4Eh), the long filename version of Find First File allocates internal storage for the search operations and returns a handle that identifies the storage. This handle is used with Find Next File. To make sure the internal storage is freed, you must use Find Close (Interrupt 21h Function 71A1h) to end the search.

You pass the Delete File (Interrupt 21h Function 7141h) and Find First File functions a filename, which may contain wildcard characters, such as an asterisk (*) or question mark (?). Because Find First File, Find Next File, and Delete File examine long filenames and aliases during the search, some wildcard searches may yield unexpected results. For example, if the system has generated the alias *LONGFI~1* for the long filename *LongFileName*, a search for names that match the *1 pattern would always return the *LongFileName* file, even though that name does not end with a *1*. Searches are not case-sensitive. For example, a search for names that match the *mid* pattern will yield the same results as that for the *MID* pattern. In general, you should check both names returned in the **WIN32_FIND_DATA** structure to determine which of them matched the pattern.

Wildcard searches are more flexible in Windows 95 than in MS-DOS. In the preceding examples, *1 finds the filenames that end in a *1* and *mid* finds file-names that contain the characters *mid*. In MS-DOS and in Windows 95 searching on real-mode FAT directories, all characters after the first * are ignored.

Down-Level Systems

Long filenames, file last access date, and file creation date and time are not supported while the file system is in single MS-DOS application mode. They are not supported either in versions of MS-DOS that only use the real-mode FAT file system. These file systems and others that do not support long filenames are referred to as down-level systems. If you intend for an application to run with both Windows 95 and down-level systems, you should always check the system to determine whether it supports the long filename functions. The easiest way to check is to call Get Volume Information (Interrupt 21h Function 71A0h). This function returns an error if the system does not support the long filename functions.

Another way of handling down-level systems is to use a combination of calls to long filename and standard MS-DOS functions to carry out file management. In this case, you call the standard function only if the long filename function is not supported. To indicate an unsupported function, the system sets the AL register to zero but leaves the AH register and the carry flag unchanged. The following example shows how to combine long filename and standard functions to carry out a file or directory management operation.

```
stc                 ; set carry for error flag
                    ; set registers here for LFN function call
int 21h             ; call long filename function
jnc success         ; call succeeded, continue processing
cmp ax, 7100h       ; is call really not supported?
jne failure         ; supported, but error occurred
                    ; set registers here for MS-DOS function call
int 21h             ; call standard MS-DOS function
```

Application developers have to decide what to do when users save a file with a long filename to a down-level system. One approach is to imitate the behavior of the command interpreter (COMMAND.COM) and save the file using the alias without informing the user. A different approach is to have the application inform the user that the file system does not support long filenames and allow the user to save the file with a filename in the standard 8.3 format.

Last Access Date

The Windows 95 last access date is intended to reflect the last time a file was accessed for the purpose for which it was created. This date is intended to provide a means for applications, users, or both to determine which files have not been used recently. When an application saves a file, the system automatically resets the last access date. An application that cannot understand the contents of the files it is accessing should save the last access date and restore it after closing the file. For example, applications that back up a file, search files for strings, and scan for viruses should save and restore the last access date.

Applications should allow the system to set the last access date in the following cases:

- Running a program should set the last access date for the .EXE file.
- Loading a dynamic-link library (DLL) should set the last access date for the .DLL file.

- Editing or printing a document should set the last access date for the document file.

- In general, any use of a document by an application that creates or modifies that type of document should set the last access date (unless the document is being opened only to decide whether it is to be used in a find operation).

- Application use of peripheral files (.INI files and so on) should set the last access date.

Win32-based applications can preserve the last access date by using the **GetFileTime** and **SetFileTime** functions. Applications written for MS-DOS or Windows version 3.x can use Get Last Access Date and Time (Interrupt 21h Function 5704h) and Set Last Access Date and Time (Interrupt 21h Function 5705h), or they can open the file with Create or Open File (Interrupt 21h Function 716Ch) using the OPEN_ACCESS_RO_NOMODLASTACCESS (0004h) access mode.

Reference

The long filename functions described previously match the following Win32 file management functions.

Long filename function	Win32 function
Interrupt 21h Function 5704h Get Last Access Date and Time	**GetFileTime**
Interrupt 21h Function 5705h Set Last Access Date and Time	**SetFileTime**
Interrupt 21h Function 5706h Get Creation Date and Time	**GetFileTime**
Interrupt 21h Function 5707h Set Creation Date and Time	**SetFileTime**
Interrupt 21h Function 7139h Make Directory	**CreateDirectory**
Interrupt 21h Function 713Ah Remove Directory	**RemoveDirectory**
Interrupt 21h Function 713Bh Change Directory	**SetCurrentDirectory**
Interrupt 21h Function 7141h Delete File	**DeleteFile**
Interrupt 21h Function 7143h Get or Set File Attributes	**GetFileAttributes, SetFileAttributes**
Interrupt 21h Function 7147h Get Current Directory	**GetCurrentDirectory**

Long filename function	Win32 function
Interrupt 21h Function 714Eh Find First File	**FindFirstFile**
Interrupt 21h Function 714Fh Find Next File	**FindNextFile**
Interrupt 21h Function 7156h Rename File	**MoveFile**
Interrupt 21h Function 7160h Get Full Path Name	**GetFullPathName**
Interrupt 21h Function 7160h Get Short Path Name	**GetShortPathName**
Interrupt 21h Function 7160h Get Long Path Name	No Win32 function equivalent.
Interrupt 21h Function 716Ch Create or Open File	**CreateFile, OpenFile**
Interrupt 21h Function 71A0h Get Volume Information	**GetVolumeInformation**
Interrupt 21h Function 71A1h Find Close	**FindClose**
Interrupt 21h Function 71A6h Get File Info By Handle	**GetFileInformationByHandle**
Interrupt 21h Function 71A7h File Time To DOS Time	**FileTimeToDOSDateTime**
Interrupt 21h Function 71A7h DOS Time To File Time	**DOSDateTimeToFileTime**
Interrupt 21h Function 71A8h Generate Short Name	No Win32 function equivalent
Interrupt 21h Function 71A9h Server Create or Open File	No Win32 function equivalent
Interrupt 21h Function 71AAh Create Subst	No Win32 function equivalent
Interrupt 21h Function 71AAh Terminate Subst	No Win32 function equivalent
Interrupt 21h Function 71AAh Query Subst	No Win32 function equivalent

Note that Interrupt 21h Functions 71A2h through 71A5h exist, but they are for internal use by Windows 95 only.

Functions

The following functions are associated with long filenames.

Interrupt 21h Function 5704h Get Last Access Date and Time

```
mov ax, 5704h   ; Get Last Access Date and Time
mov bx, Handle  ; see below
int 21h

jc  error
mov [Date], dx  ; last access date
mov [Time], cx  ; currently not supported, always 0
```

Retrieves the last access date for the given file.

- Clears the carry flag and sets the CX register to zero and the DX register to these values if successful:

Bits	Contents
0–4	Day of the month (1–31)
5–8	Month (1 = January, 2 = February, and so on)
9–15	Year offset from 1980 (that is, add 1980 to get the actual year)

Otherwise, the function sets the carry flag and sets the AX register to an error value.

Handle
File handle.

Interrupt 21h Function 5705h Set Last Access Date and Time

```
mov ax, 5705h        ; Set Last Access Date and Time
mov bx, Handle       ; see below
mov cx, 0            ; time currently not supported, always 0
mov dx, AccessDate   ; see below
int 21h

jc  error
```

Sets the last access date for the given file.

- Clears the carry flag if successful. Otherwise, the function sets the carry flag and sets the AX register to an error value.

Handle
File handle.

AccessDate
New access date. The date is a packed 16-bit value with this form:

Bits	Contents
0–4	Day of the month (1–31)
5–8	Month (1 = January, 2 = February, and so on)
9–15	Year offset from 1980 (that is, add 1980 to get the actual year)

Interrupt 21h Function 5706h Get Creation Date and Time

```
mov ax, 5706h        ; Get Creation Date and Time
mov bx, Handle       ; see below
int 21h

jc  error
mov [Time], cx       ; creation time
mov [Date], dx       ; creation date
mov [MilliSeconds], si  ; number of 10 ms intervals in 2 seconds
```

Retrieves the creation date and time for the given file.

- Clears the carry flag and sets the CX, DX, and SI registers to these values if successful:

CX   Creation time. The time is a packed 16-bit value with the following form:

Bits	Contents
0–4	Second divided by 2
5–10	Minute (0–59)
11–15	Hour (0–23 on a 24-hour clock)

DX   Creation date. The date is a packed 16-bit value with the following form:

Bits	Contents
0–4	Day of the month (1–31)
5–8	Month (1 = January, 2 = February, and so on)
9–15	Year offset from 1980 (that is, add 1980 to get the actual year)

SI   Number of 10 millisecond intervals in 2 seconds to add to the MS-DOS time. The number can be a value in the range of 0 to 199.

Otherwise, the function sets the carry flag and sets the AX register to an error value.

Handle
File handle.

Interrupt 21h Function 5707h Set Creation Date and Time

```
mov ax, 5707h          ; Set Creation Date and Time
mov bx, Handle         ; see below
mov cx, Time           ; see below
mov dx, Date           ; see below
mov si, MilliSeconds   ; see below
int 21h

jc error
```

Sets the creation date and time for the given file.

- Clears the carry flag if successful. Otherwise, the function sets the carry flag and sets the AX register to an error value.

Handle
File handle.

Time
New creation time. The time is a packed 16-bit value with the following form:

Bits	Contents
0–4	Second divided by 2
5–10	Minute (0–59)
11–15	Hour (0–23 on a 24-hour clock)

Date
New creation date. The date is a packed 16-bit value with the following form:

Bits	Contents
0–4	Day of the month (1–31)
5–8	Month (1 = January, 2 = February, and so on)
9–15	Year offset from 1980 (that is, add 1980 to get the actual year)

MilliSeconds
Number of 10 millisecond intervals in 2 seconds to add to the MS-DOS time. The number can be a value in the range 0 to 199.

Interrupt 21h Function 7139h Make Directory

```
mov ax, 7139h     ; Make Directory
mov dx, seg Name  ; see below
mov ds, dx
mov dx, offset Name
int 21h


jc  error
```

Creates a new directory having the given name.

- Clears the carry flag if successful. Otherwise, the function sets the carry flag and sets the AX register to an error value.

Name
Address of a null-terminated string specifying the name of the directory to create. Long filenames are allowed.

Interrupt 21h Function 713Ah Remove Directory

```
mov ax, 713Ah      ; Remove Directory
mov dx, seg Name   ; see below
mov ds, dx
mov dx, offset Name
int 21h

jc  error
```

Removes the given directory. The directory must be empty.

- Clears the carry flag if successful. Otherwise, the function sets the carry flag and sets the AX register to an error value.

Name
    Address of a null-terminated string specifying the name of the directory to remove. Long filenames are allowed.

The root directory cannot be deleted.

Interrupt 21h Function 713Bh Change Directory

```
mov ax, 713Bh      ; Change Directory
mov dx, seg Path   ; see below
mov ds, dx
mov dx, offset Path
int 21h

jc  error
```

Changes the current directory to the directory specified by the given path.

- Clears the carry flag if successful. Otherwise, the function sets the carry flag and sets the AX register to an error value.

Path
    Address of a null-terminated string specifying the directory to change to. The path, which can include the drive letter, must be a valid path for the given volume. Long filenames are allowed.

The current or default directory is the directory that the system uses whenever an application supplies a filename that does not explicitly specify a directory. Similarly, the current or default drive is the drive the system uses whenever an application supplies a path that does not explicitly specify a drive. If a drive other than the default drive is specified as part of the new directory path, this function changes the current directory on that drive but does not change the default drive. Set Default Drive (Interrupt 21h Function 0Eh) can be used to change the default drive.

Interrupt 21h Function 7141h Delete File

```
mov ax, 7141h            ; Delete File
mov ch, MustMatchAttrs   ; see below
mov cl, SearchAttrs      ; see below
mov dx, seg Filename     ; see below
mov ds, dx
mov dx, offset Filename
mov si, WildcardAndAttrs ; see below
int 21h

jc error
```

Deletes the given file or files. If the specified filename contains a wildcard character, this function can delete multiple files that match the wildcard.

- Clears the carry flag if successful. Otherwise, the function sets the carry flag and sets the AX register to an error value.

MustMatchAttrs

Additional filter on the attributes specified in *SearchAttrs*. This parameter can be a combination of these values:

FILE_ATTRIBUTE_NORMAL (0000h)

> The file can be read from or written to. This value is valid only if used alone.

FILE_ATTRIBUTE_READONLY (0001h)

> The file can be read from, but not written to.

FILE_ATTRIBUTE_HIDDEN (0002h)

> The file is hidden and does not appear in an ordinary directory listing.

FILE_ATTRIBUTE_SYSTEM (0004h)

> The file is part of the operating system or is used exclusively by it.

FILE_ATTRIBUTE_VOLUME (0008h)

> The name specified by *Filename* is used as the volume label for the current medium.

FILE_ATTRIBUTE_DIRECTORY (0010h)

> The name specified by *Filename* is used as a directory, not a file.

FILE_ATTRIBUTE_ARCHIVE (0020h)

> The file is an archive file. Applications use this value to mark files for backup or removal.

SearchAttrs
> File attributes to search for. This parameter can be a combination of these
> values:
>
> FILE_ATTRIBUTE_NORMAL (0000h)
>
> FILE_ATTRIBUTE_READONLY (0001h)
>
> FILE_ATTRIBUTE_HIDDEN (0002h)
>
> FILE_ATTRIBUTE_SYSTEM (0004h)
>
> FILE_ATTRIBUTE_VOLUME (0008h)
>
> FILE_ATTRIBUTE_DIRECTORY (0010h)
>
> FILE_ATTRIBUTE_ARCHIVE (0020h)

Filename
> Address of a null-terminated string specifying the name of the file to delete.
> If *WildcardAndAttrs* is 1, the "*" and "?" wildcard characters are permitted
> in the filename. Long filenames are allowed.

WildcardAndAttrs
> Search criteria. This parameter must be one of these values:
>
> 0   Wildcard characters are not allowed in *Filename*. Any specified attributes
>   are ignored.
>
> 1   Wildcard characters are allowed in *Filename*. Files with specified attributes
>   are matched.

Wildcard searches are more flexible in Windows 95 than in MS-DOS. Both
long filenames and aliases are considered in searches. For example, *1 finds
Windows 95 filenames (both long filenames and aliases) that end in a *1*, and
mid finds filenames that contain the characters *mid*. In MS-DOS and in
Windows 95 searching on real-mode FAT directories, all characters after the
first * are ignored.

For more information about how *MustMatchAttrs* and *SearchAttrs* are used, see
the comments for Find First File (Interrupt 21h Function 714Eh).

Interrupt 21h Function 7143h Extended Get or Set File Attributes

```
mov ax, 7143h           ; Get or Set File Attributes
mov bl, Action          ; see below
mov cx, Attributes      ; see below
mov di, Date            ; see below
mov cx, Time            ; see below
mov si, MilliSeconds    ; see below
mov dx, seg Filename    ; see below
mov ds, dx
mov dx, offset Filename
int 21h


jc  error
; see below for return values
```

Retrieves or sets the file attributes, gets the compressed file size, or retrieves or sets the date and time for the given file.

- Clears the carry flag if successful.

  If *Action* is zero (retrieve attributes), the file attributes returned in the CX register may be a combination of the following values :

  FILE_ATTRIBUTE_NORMAL (0000h)

  FILE_ATTRIBUTE_READONLY (0001h)

  FILE_ATTRIBUTE_HIDDEN (0002h)

  FILE_ATTRIBUTE_SYSTEM (0004h)

  FILE_ATTRIBUTE_VOLUME (0008h)

  FILE_ATTRIBUTE_DIRECTORY (0010h)

  FILE_ATTRIBUTE_ARCHIVE (0020h)

If *Action* is 2 (get physical size of a compressed file), the size, in bytes, of the compressed file is returned in DX:AX. This value is the physical size of the compressed file—that is, the actual number of bytes that the compressed file occupies on disk.

If *Action* is 4 (get last write date/time) or 8 (get creation date/time), the CX register contains the time as a packed 16-bit value with the following form:

Bits	Contents
0–4	Second divided by 2
5–10	Minute (0–59)
11–15	Hour (0–23 on a 24-hour clock)

If *Action* is 4 (get last write date/time), 6 (get last access date), or 8 (get creation date/time), the DI register contains the date as a packed 16-bit value with the following form:

Bits	Contents
0–4	Day of the month (1–31)
5–8	Month (1 = January, 2 = February, and so on)
9–15	Year offset from 1980 (that is, add 1980 to get the actual year)

If *Action* is 8 (get creation date/time), the SI register contains the number of 10 millisecond intervals in 2 seconds to add to the MS-DOS time. The number can be a value in the range of 0 to 199.

If the function is not successful, it sets the carry flag and sets the AX register to an error value.

Action
Action to take. This parameter can be one of the following values:

0	Retrieve attributes.
1	Set specified attributes.
2	Get physical size of a compressed file.
3	Set last write date/time.
4	Get last write date/time.
5	Set last access date.
6	Get last access date.
7	Set creation date/time.
8	Get creation date/time.

Attributes

File attributes to set, which are used only if *Action* is 1. This parameter can be a combination of these values:

FILE_ATTRIBUTE_NORMAL (0000h)

> The file can be read from or written to. This value is valid only if used alone.

FILE_ATTRIBUTE_READONLY (0001h)

> The file can be read from, but not written to.

FILE_ATTRIBUTE_HIDDEN (0002h)

> The file is hidden and does not appear in an ordinary directory listing.

FILE_ATTRIBUTE_SYSTEM (0004h)

> The file is part of the operating system or is used exclusively by it.

FILE_ATTRIBUTE_ARCHIVE (0020h)

> The file is an archive file. Applications use this value to mark files for backup or removal.

Time

New time to set, which is used only if *Action* is 3 (set last write date/time) or 7 (set creation date/time) The time is a packed 16-bit value with the following form:

Bits	Contents
0–4	Second divided by 2
5–10	Minute (0–59)
11–15	Hour (0–23 on a 24-hour clock)

Date

New date to set, which is used only if *Action* is 3 (set last write date/time), 5 (set last access date), or 7 (set creation date/time). The date is a packed 16-bit value with the following form:

Bits	Contents
0–4	Day of the month (1–31)
5–8	Month (1 = January, 2 = February, and so on)
9–15	Year offset from 1980 (that is, add 1980 to get the actual year)

MilliSeconds

Number of 10 millisecond intervals in 2 seconds to add to the MS-DOS time. The number can be a value in the range 0 to 199. This value is only used if *Action* is 7 (set creation date/time).

Filename

Address of a null-terminated string specifying the name of the file to retrieve or set attributes for. Long filenames are allowed.

Interrupt 21h Function 7147h Get Current Directory

```
mov ax, 7147h         ; Get Current Directory
mov dl, Drive         ; see below
mov si, seg Buffer    ; see below
mov ds, si
mov si, offset Buffer
int 21h

jc  error
```

Copies the path of the current directory for the given drive to the buffer. The copied path does not include the drive letter or the leading backslash.

- Clears the carry flag and copies the path if successful. Otherwise, the function sets the carry flag and sets the AX register to an error value.

Drive

Drive number. This parameter can be 0 for current drive, 1 for A, 2 for B, and so on.

Buffer

Address of the buffer that receives the path. The buffer must be at least as big as the maximum allowed path for this volume that is returned by Get Volume Information (Interrupt 21h Function 71A0h).

Interrupt 21h Function 714Eh Find First File

```
mov ax, 714Eh              ; Find First File
mov ch, MustMatchAttrs     ; see below
mov cl, SearchAttrs        ; see below
mov dx, seg Filename       ; see below
mov ds, dx
mov dx, offset Filename
mov di, seg FindData       ; see below
mov es, di
mov di, offset FindData
mov si, DateTimeFormat     ; see below
int 21h

jc  error
mov [Handle], ax           ; search handle
mov [ConversionCode], cx   ; Unicode to OEM/ANSI conversion OK?
```

Searches a directory for the first file or directory whose name and attributes match the specified name and attributes.

- Clears the carry flag, copies information about the file to the specified buffer, returns the search handle in the AX register, and sets the CX register to a combination of the following values if successful:

0x0000   All characters in the primary and alternate name members in the structure specified by *FindData* were successfully converted from Unicode.

0x0001   The primary name returned in the structure specified by *FindData* contains underscore characters in place of characters that could not be converted from Unicode.

0x0002   The alternate name returned in the structure specified by *FindData* contains underscore characters in place of characters that could not be converted from Unicode.

Otherwise, the function sets the carry flag and sets the AX register to an error value.

MustMatchAttrs

Additional filter on the attributes specified in *SearchAttrs*. This parameter can be a combination of these values:

FILE_ATTRIBUTE_NORMAL (0000h)

> The file can be read from or written to. This value is valid only if used alone.

FILE_ATTRIBUTE_READONLY (0001h)

> The file can be read from, but not written to.

FILE_ATTRIBUTE_HIDDEN (0002h)

> The file is hidden and does not appear in an ordinary directory listing.

FILE_ATTRIBUTE_SYSTEM (0004h)

> The file is part of the operating system or is used exclusively by it.

FILE_ATTRIBUTE_VOLUME (0008h)

> The name specified by *Filename* is used as the volume label for the current medium.

FILE_ATTRIBUTE_DIRECTORY (0010h)

> The name specified by *Filename* is used as a directory, not a file.

FILE_ATTRIBUTE_ARCHIVE (0020h)

> The file is an archive file. Applications use this value to mark files for backup or removal.

SearchAttrs

> File attributes to search for. This parameter can be a combination of these values:
>
> FILE_ATTRIBUTE_NORMAL (0000h)
>
> FILE_ATTRIBUTE_READONLY (0001h)
>
> FILE_ATTRIBUTE_HIDDEN (0002h)
>
> FILE_ATTRIBUTE_SYSTEM (0004h)
>
> FILE_ATTRIBUTE_VOLUME (0008h)
>
> FILE_ATTRIBUTE_DIRECTORY (0010h)
>
> FILE_ATTRIBUTE_ARCHIVE (0020h)

Filename

> Address of a null-terminated string specifying the name of the file or directory to search for. The name, which must be a valid filename or directory name, can include the "*" and "?" wildcard characters. Long filenames are allowed.

FindData

> Address of a **WIN32_FIND_DATA** structure that receives information about the file.

DateTimeFormat

> Date and time format to be returned. This parameter must be one of these values:

> 0   Returns the date and time in 64-bit file time format.
>
> 1   Returns the MS-DOS date and time values. MS-DOS date and time values are returned in the low doubleword of the **FILETIME** structure. Within the doubleword, the date is returned in the high-order word; the time is in the low-order word.

Find First File and subsequent calls to Find Next File (Interrupt 21h Function 714Fh) use the following algorithm to match the attributes of a file or directory (referred to as *Attributes* in the algorithm) against *MustMatchAttrs* and *SearchAttrs*.

```
if  (((((<MustMatchAttrs> & ~<Attributes>) & 0x3F) == 0)
    && (((~<SearchAttrs> & <Attributes>) & 0x1E) == 0))
    {
        return the file or directory name
    }
    else
    {
        continue searching for the next name
    }
```

The following table lists the *MustMatchAttrs* and *SearchAttrs* values for some common searches where the specified filename is "*.*". In the table, the word normal means that the read only, hidden, or system attributes have not been set. Parentheses are used to indicate that a file or directory has more than one attribute. For example, (hidden and system) indicates that a file or directory has both the hidden attribute and the system attribute.

MustMatchAttrs	SearchAttrs	Find results
10h	10h	All normal directories
10h	12h	All normal and hidden directories
10h	14h	All normal and system directories
10h	16h	All normal, hidden, system and (hidden and system) directories
12h	12h	All hidden directories
14h	14h	All system directories
16h	16h	All (hidden and system) directories
00h	00h	All normal files
00h	01h	All normal and read only files
00h	02h	All normal and hidden files
00h	04h	All normal and system files
00h	06h	All normal, hidden, system, and (hidden and system) files
00h	10h	All normal files and directories
01h	01h	All read only files
02h	02h	All hidden files
02h	06h	All hidden and (hidden and system) files

This function can be used to return the volume label by specifying only FILE_ATTRIBUTE_VOLUME (0008h) in both *MustMatchAttrs* and *SearchAttrs*.

An application may use the handle returned in the AX register in subsequent calls to Find Next File (Interrupt 21h Function 714Fh). It is important to close the handle when it is no longer needed by calling Find Close (Interrupt 21h Function 71A1h).

Wildcard searches are more flexible in Windows 95 than in MS-DOS. For example, *1 finds the filenames (both long filenames and aliases) that end in a *1*, and *mid* finds filenames that contain the characters *mid*. In MS-DOS and in Windows 95 searching on real-mode FAT directories, all characters after the first * are ignored.

Interrupt 21h Function 714Fh Find Next File

```
mov ax, 714Fh            ; Find Next File
mov bx, Handle           ; see below
mov di, seg FindData     ; see below
mov es, di
mov di, offset FindData
mov si, DateTimeFormat   ; see below
int 21h

jc error
mov [ConversionCode], cx  ; Unicode to OEM/ANSI conversion OK?
```

Searches for the next file in a directory, returning information about the file in the given buffer.

- Clears the carry flag, copies information to the specified buffer, and sets the CX register to a combination of these values if successful:

0x0000	All characters in the primary and alternate name member in the structure specified by *FindData* were successfully converted from Unicode.
0x0001	The primary name returned in the structure specified by *FindData* contains underscore characters in place of characters that could not be converted from Unicode.
0x0002	The alternate name returned in the structure specified by *FindData* contains underscore characters in place of characters that could not be converted from Unicode.

Otherwise, the function sets the carry flag and sets the AX register to an error value.

Handle
Search handle. It must have been previously returned from Find First File (Interrupt 21h Function 714Eh).

FindData
Address of a **WIN32_FIND_DATA** structure that receives information about the file.

DateTimeFormat
Date and time format to be returned. This parameter must be one of these values:

0	Returns the date and time in 64-bit file time format.
1	Returns the MS-DOS date and time values. MS-DOS date and time values are returned in the low doubleword of the **FILETIME** structure. Within the doubleword, the date is returned in the high-order word; the time is in the low-order word.

It is important to close the handle when it is no longer needed by calling Find Close (Interrupt 21h Function 71A1h).

Interrupt 21h Function 7156h   Rename File

```
mov ax, 7156h            ; Rename File
mov dx, seg OldName      ; see below
mov ds, dx
mov dx, offset OldName
mov di, seg NewName      ; see below
mov es, di
mov di, offset NewName
int 21h

jc  error
```

Changes the name of the given file or directory to the new name.

- Clears the carry flag if successful. Otherwise, the function sets the carry flag and sets the AX register to an error value.

OldName
    Address of a null-terminated string specifying the original name of the file or the directory to rename. Long filenames are allowed.

NewName
    Address of a null-terminated string specifying the new name for the file or the directory. The function will fail if this parameter specifies an existing file or directory. The new name must not specify a drive different than the original drive. Long filenames are allowed.

Interrupt 21h Function 7160h   Get Full Path Name

```
mov ax, 7160h
mov cl, 0                ; Get Full Path Name
mov ch, SubstExpand      ; see below
mov si, seg SourcePath   ; see below
mov ds, si
mov si, offset SourcePath
mov di, seg DestPath     ; see below
mov es, di
mov di, offset DestPath
int 21h

jc  error
```

Retrieves the full path for the specified file or path.

- Clears the carry flag, modifies the AX register, and returns the full path in the given buffer if successful. Otherwise, the function sets the carry flag and sets the AX register to an error value.

SubstExpand

Flag that indicates whether the returned path should contain a SUBST drive letter or the path associated with the SUBST drive. Zero is specified to indicate that the returned path should contain the path associated with the SUBST drive, and 80h is specified to indicate that the returned path should contain the SUBST drive letter.

SourcePath

Address of a null-terminated string that names the file or path to retrieve the full path for. Either the long filename or the standard 8.3 filename format is acceptable.

DestPath

Address of the buffer that receives the full path. The buffer should be large enough to contain the largest possible Windows 95 path (260 characters, including the drive letter, colon, leading backslash, and terminating null character).

When just a filename is specified, this function merges the name of the current drive and directory with the specified filename to determine the full path. Relative paths containing the characters "." and ".." in *SourcePath* are fully expanded. The function does no validation, so the specified filename or path does not need to exist.

Interrupt 21h Function 7160h Get Short Path Name

```
mov ax, 7160h
mov cl, 1                 ; Get Short Path Name
mov ch, SubstExpand       ; see below
mov si, seg SourcePath    ; see below
mov ds, si
mov si, offset SourcePath
mov di, seg DestPath      ; see below
mov es, di
mov di, offset DestPath
int 21h
jc  error
```

Retrieves the complete path in its short form (the standard 8.3 format) for the specified file or path. The function returns the 8.3 filename for all directories in the path.

- Clears the carry flag, modifies the AX register, and returns the complete short path in the given buffer if successful. Otherwise, the function sets the carry flag and sets the AX register to an error value.

SubstExpand

>   Flag that indicates if the returned path should contain a SUBST drive letter or
>   the path associated with the SUBST drive. Zero is specified to indicate that the
>   returned path should contain the path associated with the SUBST drive, and 80h
>   is specified to indicate that the returned path should contain the SUBST drive
>   letter.

SourcePath

>   Address of a null-terminated string that names the file or path to retrieve the
>   complete short path for. Either the long or short form is acceptable as the source
>   string.

DestPath

>   Address of the buffer that receives the complete path. The buffer should be large
>   enough to contain the largest possible Windows 95 path in the short form (260
>   characters, including the drive letter, colon, leading backslash, and terminating
>   null character).

Relative paths that contain the characters "." and ".." in *SourcePath* are fully
expanded. Since this function performs validation, *SourcePath* must contain either
a valid filename or path.

Interrupt 21h Function 7160h Get Long Path Name

```
mov  ax, 7160h
mov  cl, 2                   ; Get Long Path Name
mov  ch, SubstExpand         ; see below
mov  si, seg SourcePath      ; see below
mov  ds, si
mov  si, offset SourcePath
mov  di, seg DestPath        ; see below
mov  es, di
mov  di, offset DestPath
int  21h
jc   error
```

Retrieves the complete path in its long filename form for the specified file or path.
The function returns the long name for all directories in the path.

*   Clears the carry flag, modifies the AX register, and returns the complete long
    path in the given buffer if successful. Otherwise, the function sets the carry
    flag and sets the AX register to an error value.

SubstExpand

>   Flag that indicates if the returned path should contain a SUBST drive letter or
>   the path associated with the SUBST drive. Zero is specified to indicate that the
>   returned path should contain the path associated with the SUBST drive, and 80h
>   is specified to indicate that the returned path should contain the SUBST drive
>   letter.

SourcePath
> Address of a null-terminated string that names the file or path to retrieve the complete long path for. Either the long filename or the short form is acceptable as the source string.

DestPath
> Address of the buffer that receives the complete path. The buffer should be large enough to contain the largest possible Windows 95 path (260 characters, including the drive letter, colon, leading backslash, and terminating null character).

Relative paths containing the characters "." and ".." in *SourcePath* are fully expanded. Since this function performs validation, *SourcePath* must contain either a valid filename or path.

Interrupt 21h Function 716Ch Create or Open File

```
mov ax, 716Ch          ; Create or Open File
mov bx, ModeAndFlags   ; see below
mov cx, Attributes     ; see below
mov dx, Action         ; see below
mov si, seg Filename   ; see below
mov ds, si
mov si, offset Filename
mov di, AliasHint      ; see below
int 21h

jc error
mov [Handle], ax       ; file handle
mov [ActionTaken], cx  ; action taken to open file
```

Creates or opens a file.

- Clears carry flag, copies the file handle to the AX register, and sets the CX register to one of the following values if successful:

  ACTION_OPENED (0001h)

  ACTION_CREATED_OPENED (0002h)

  ACTION_REPLACED_OPENED (0003h)

  Otherwise, the function sets the carry flag and sets the AX register to an error value.

ModeAndFlags

Combination of access mode, sharing mode, and open flags. This parameter can be one value each from the access and sharing modes and any combination of open flags:

Access mode	Meaning

OPEN_ACCESS_READONLY (0000h)

Opens the file for reading only.

OPEN_ACCESS_WRITEONLY (0001h)

Opens the file for writing only.

OPEN_ACCESS_READWRITE (0002h)

Opens the file for reading and writing.

0003h

Reserved; do not use.

OPEN_ACCESS_RO_NOMODLASTACCESS (0004h)

Opens the file for reading only without modifying the file's last access date.

Sharing mode	Meaning

OPEN_SHARE_COMPATIBLE (0000h)

Opens the file with compatibility mode, allowing any process on a given computer to open the file any number of times.

OPEN_SHARE_DENYREADWRITE (0010h)

Opens the file and denies both read and write access to other processes.

OPEN_SHARE_DENYWRITE (0020h)

Opens the file and denies write access to other processes.

OPEN_SHARE_DENYREAD (0030h)

Opens the file and denies read access to other processes.

OPEN_SHARE_DENYNONE (0040h)

Opens the file without denying read or write access to other processes, but no process may open the file for compatibility access.

Open flags	Meaning

OPEN_FLAGS_NOINHERIT (0080h)

If this flag is set, a child process created with Load and Execute Program (Interrupt 21h Function 4B00h) does not inherit the file handle. If the handle is needed by the child process, the parent process must pass the handle value to the child process. If this flag is not set, child processes inherit the file handle.

OPEN_FLAGS_NO_BUFFERING (0100h)

The file is to be opened with no intermediate buffering or caching done by the system. Read and write operations access the disk directly. All reads and writes to the file must be done at file positions that are multiples of the disk sector size, in bytes, and the number of bytes read or written should also be a multiple of the sector size. Applications can determine the sector size, in bytes, with the Get Disk Free Space function (Interrupt 21h, Function 36h).

OPEN_FLAGS_NO_COMPRESS (0200h)

The file should not be compressed on a volume that performs file compression. If the volume does not perform file compression, this flag is ignored. This flag is valid only on file creation and is ignored on file open.

OPEN_FLAGS_ALIAS_HINT (0400h)

The number in the DI register is to be used as the numeric tail for the alias (short filename). For more information, see *AliasHint* below.

OPEN_FLAGS_NOCRITERR (2000h)

If a critical error occurs while MS-DOS is opening this file, Critical-Error Handler (Interrupt 24h) is not called. Instead, MS-DOS simply returns an error value to the program.

OPEN_FLAGS_COMMIT (4000h)

After each write operation, MS-DOS commits the file (flushes the contents of the cache buffer to disk).

Attributes

Attributes for files that are created or truncated. This parameter may be a combination of these values:

FILE_ATTRIBUTE_NORMAL (0000h)

        The file can be read from or written to. This value is valid only if used alone.

FILE_ATTRIBUTE_READONLY (0001h)

        The file can be read from, but not written to.

FILE_ATTRIBUTE_HIDDEN (0002h)

        The file is hidden and does not appear in an ordinary directory listing.

FILE_ATTRIBUTE_SYSTEM (0004h)

        The file is part of the operating system or is used exclusively by it.

FILE_ATTRIBUTE_VOLUME (0008h)

        The name specified by *Filename* is used as the volume label for the current medium and is restricted to the standard 8.3 format. For information about an alternative way to set the volume label, see Set Media ID (Interrupt 21h Function 440Dh Minor Code 46h) in the *Microsoft MS-DOS Programmer's Reference*.

FILE_ATTRIBUTE_ARCHIVE (0020h)

        The file is an archive file. Applications use this value to mark files for backup or removal.

Action

Action to take it the file exists or if it does not exist. This parameter can be a combination of these values:

FILE_CREATE (0010h)	Creates a new file if it does not already exist. The function fails if the file already exists.
FILE_OPEN (0001h)	Opens the file. The function fails if the file does not exist.
FILE_TRUNCATE (0002h)	Opens the file and truncates it to zero length (replaces the existing file). The function fails if the file does not exist.

The only valid combinations are FILE_CREATE combined with FILE_OPEN or FILE_CREATE combined with FILE_TRUNCATE.

Filename

Address of a null-terminated string specifying the name of the file to be opened or created. The string must be a valid path for the volume associated with the given drive. Long filenames are allowed.

AliasHint

Number that is used in the numeric tail for the alias (short filename).
A numeric tail, which consists of the tilde character (~) followed a number,
is appended to the end of a filename. The system constructs the alias
from the first few characters of the long filename followed by the numeric tail.
The system starts with the number 1 in the numeric tail. If that filename is
in use, it uses the number 2. It continues in this fashion until a unique name
is found. To override the default numbering scheme, you must specify the
OPEN_FLAGS_ALIAS_HINT value when you create the file in addition to
specifying this parameter. If a filename already exists with the specified
numeric tail, the system uses the default numbering scheme. You should
specify a number for this parameter, not the tilde character.

A file on a remote directory—that is, a directory on the network—cannot be
opened, created, or modified, unless the appropriate permissions for the directory
exist.

Interrupt 21h Function 71A0h Get Volume Information

```
mov ax, 71A0h          ; Get Volume Information
mov di, seg Buffer     ; see below
mov es, di
mov di, offset Buffer
mov cx, BufSize        ; see below
mov dx, seg RootName   ; see below
mov ds, dx
mov dx, offset RootName
int 21h

jc  error
mov [Flags], bx        ; file system flags
mov [MaxFilename], cx  ; max. filename length, excluding null
mov [MaxPath], dx      ; max. path length, including null
```

Returns information about the volume associated with the given root directory.

- Clears the carry flag, copies the file system name to the buffer given by the
ES:DI register pair, and sets the BX, CX, and DX registers to the following
values if successful:

BX   File system flags, which can be a combination of these values:

FS_CASE_SENSITIVE (0001h)
Specifies that searches are case-sensitive.

FS_CASE_IS_PRESERVED (0002h)
Preserves case in directory entries.

FS_UNICODE_ON_DISK (0004h)
Uses Unicode characters in file and directory names.

FS_LFN_APIS (4000h)
Supports new long filename functions.

FS_VOLUME_COMPRESSED (8000h)
Specifies that the volume is compressed.

CX   Maximum allowed length, excluding the terminating null
character, of a filename for this volume. For example, on
the protected-mode FAT file system, this value is 255.

DX   Maximum allowed length of a path for this volume, including
the drive letter, colon, leading slash, and terminating null
character. For example, on the protected-mode FAT file system,
this value is 260.

Otherwise, the function sets the carry flag and sets the AX register to an error
value.

Buffer
Address of a buffer that receives a null-terminated string specifying the name of
the file system.

BufSize
Size, in bytes, of the buffer that receives the name. The buffer should include
space for the terminating null character.

RootName
Address of a null-terminated string specifying the name of the root directory of
the volume to check. This parameter must not be NULL, or the function will fail.
The format for this parameter is "C:\".

This function accesses the disk the first time it is called, but subsequent calls do not
access the disk.

Interrupt 21h Function 71A1h Find Close

```
mov ax, 71A1h   ; Find Close
mov bx, Handle  ; see below
int 21h

jc  error
```

Closes the file search identified by the search handle.

- Clears the carry flag if successful. Otherwise, the function sets the carry flag and sets the AX register to an error value.

Handle
> Search handle. It must have been previously returned from Find First File (Interrupt 21h Function 714Eh).

Unlike MS-DOS Find First File (Interrupt 21h Function 4Eh), the long file-name version of Find First File (Interrupt 21h Function 714Eh) allocates internal storage for the search operations and returns a handle that identifies the storage. This handle is used with Find Next File. To make sure this internal storage is freed, you must call Find Close to end the search.

Interrupt 21h Function 71A6h Get File Info By Handle

```
mov ax, 71a6h              ; Get File Info By Handle
mov bx, Handle             ; see below
mov dx, seg lpFileInfo     ; see below
mov ds, dx
mov dx, offset lpFileInfo
stc                        ; must set carry flag
int 21h

jnc success
cmp ax, 7100h
je not_supported
```

Retrieves information about the specified file.

- Clears the carry flag if successful. Otherwise, the function sets the carry flag and sets the AX register to an error value.

Handle

File handle to retrieve information about.

lpFileInfo

Address of a **BY_HANDLE_FILE_INFORMATION** structure that receives the file information. The structure can be used in subsequent calls to Get File Info By Handle to refer to the information about the file.

Note that it is important to explicitly set the carry flag before calling this function.

Interrupt 21h Function 71A7h File Time To DOS Time

```
mov ax, 71A7h          ; date and time format conversion
mov bl, 0              ; File Time To DOS Time
mov si, seg lpft       ; see below
mov ds, si
mov si, offset lpft
int 21h

jc error
mov [DOSTime], cx
mov [DOSDate], dx
mov [MilliSeconds], bh  ; number of 10ms intervals in 2 seconds
```

Converts a 64-bit file time to MS-DOS date and time values.

- Clears the carry flag, and sets the BH, CX, and DX registers to these values if successful:

BH   Number of 10 millisecond intervals in 2 seconds to add to the MS-DOS time. It can be a value in the range 0 to 199.

CX   MS-DOS time. The time is a packed 16-bit value with the following form:

Bits	Contents
0–4	Second divided by 2
5–10	Minute (0–59)
11–15	Hour (0–23 on a 24-hour clock)

DX   MS-DOS date. The date is a packed 16-bit value with the following form:

Bits	Contents
0–4	Day of the month (1–31)
5–8	Month (1 = January, 2 = February, and so on)
9–15	Year offset from 1980 (that is, add 1980 to get the actual year)

Otherwise, the function sets the carry flag and sets the AX register to an error value.

lpft

Address of a **FILETIME** structure containing the 64-bit file time to convert to the MS-DOS date and time format.

The MS-DOS date format can represent only dates between 1/1/1980 and 12/31/2107; this conversion fails if the input file time is outside this range.

The time in **FILETIME** must be Coordinated Universal Time (UTC). The MS-DOS time is local time.

Interrupt 21h Function 71A7h DOS Time To File Time

```
mov ax, 71A7h          ; date and time format conversion
mov bl, 1              ; Dos Time To File Time
mov bh, MilliSeconds   ; see below
mov cx, DOSTime        ; see below
mov dx, DOSDate        ; see below
mov di, seg lpft       ; see below
mov es, di
mov di, offset lpft
int 21h

jc error
```

Converts MS-DOS date and time values to 64-bit file time.

- Clears the carry flag and returns the 64-bit file time in the specified structure if successful. Otherwise, the function sets the carry flag and sets the AX register to an error value.

MilliSeconds

Number of 10 millisecond intervals in 2 seconds to add to the MS-DOS time. The number can be a value in the range 0 to 199.

DOSTime

MS-DOS time to convert. The time is a packed 16-bit value with the following form:

Bits	Contents
0–4	Second divided by 2
5–10	Minute (0–59)
11–15	Hour (0–23 on a 24-hour clock)

DOSDate

MS-DOS date to convert. The date is a packed 16-bit value with the following form:

Bits	Contents
0–4	Day of the month (1–31)
5–8	Month (1 = January, 2 = February, and so on)
9–15	Year offset from 1980 (that is, add 1980 to get the actual year)

lpft

Address of a **FILETIME** structure to receive the converted 64-bit file time.

The time in **FILETIME** must be Coordinated Universal Time (UTC).
The MS-DOS time is local time.

Interrupt 21h Function 71A8h   Generate Short Name

```
mov ax, 71a8h              ; generate short name
mov si, seg LongFilename   ; see below
mov ds, si
mov si, offset LongFilename
mov di, seg ShortFilename  ; see below
mov es, di
mov di, offset ShortFilename
mov dh, ShortNameFormat    ; see below
mov dl, CharSet            ; see below
int 21h
```

Generates an alias (a filename in the 8.3 format) for the specified long filename.

- Returns the generated alias in the specified buffer if successful.

LongFilename

Address of null-terminated string that names the long filename to generate an alias for. This string must contain only a filename, not a path.

ShortFilename

Address of null-terminated string that receives the generated alias.

ShortNameFormat

Format for the returned alias (0 is specified for an 11 character directory entry format or 1 for an 8.3 format).

CharSet

Character set of both the long filename and alias. This parameter is a packed 8-bit value with the following form:

Bits	Contents
0–3	Specifies the character set of the source long filename.
4–7	Specifies the character set of the destination alias.

One of the following values is specified to indicate the character set for the long filename and alias:

BCS_WANSI (0)	Windows ANSI character set
BCS_OEM (1)	Current OEM character set
BCS_UNICODE (2)	Unicode character set

This function generates the alias using the same algorithm that the system uses with the exception that the returned alias will never have a numeric tail. A numeric tail is appended to the end of an alias and consists of the tilde character (~) followed a number. When the system generates an alias, it may attach a numeric tail if the default alias already exists in the current directory. Because this function does not check the current directory to see if the alias already exists, the returned alias will never have a numeric tail. This service is useful for disk utilities that are trying to establish whether the alias, which seems to be associated with a long filename, is correctly associated.

Interrupt 21h Function 71A9h Server Create or Open File

Creates or opens a file. This function is for use by real-mode servers only. It takes the same parameters as Create or Open File (Interrupt 21h Function 716Ch) and returns a global file handle. For more information, see Create or Open File.

Interrupt 21h Function 71AAh Create Subst

```
mov ax, 71aah          ; SUBST
mov bh, 0              ; Create Subst
mov bl, DriveNum       ; see below
mov dx, seg PathName   ; see below
mov ds, dx
mov dx, offset PathName
int 21h

jc error
```

Associates a path with a drive letter.

- Clears the carry flag if successful. Otherwise the function sets the carry flag and returns an error value in the AX register

DriveNum
    Drive to SUBST. This parameter can be 0 for the default drive, 1 for A, 2 for B, and so on.

PathName
    Address of path to associate the drive with.

Interrupt 21h Function 71AAh Terminate Subst

```
mov ax, 71aah            ; SUBST
mov bh, 1                ; Terminate Subst
mov bl, DriveNum         ; see below
int 21h

jc error
```

Terminate the association between a path and a drive letter.

- Clears the carry flag if successful. Otherwise, the function sets the carry flag and returns an error value in the AX register.

DriveNum
    Drive to terminate SUBST. This parameter can 1 for A, 2 for B, and so on. Note that *DriveNum* cannot be 0 to indicate the default drive.

Interrupt 21h Function 71AAh Query Subst

```
mov ax, 71aah            ; SUBST
mov bh, 2                ; Query SUBST
mov bl, DriveNum         ; see below
mov dx, seg PathName     ; see below
mov ds, dx
mov dx, offset PathName
int 21h

jc error
```

Determines if the specified drive is associated with a path and, if it is, retrieves the associated path.

■   Clears the carry flag and retrieves the associated path in the specified buffer if successful. Otherwise, the function sets the carry flag and returns an error value in the AX register.

DriveNum

Drive to SUBST. This parameter can 1 for A, 2 for B, and so on. Note that *DriveNum* cannot be 0 to indicate the default drive.

PathName

Address of buffer that receives the null-terminated string of the path associated with the specified drive. The buffer must be of MAXPATHLEN size.

Structures

The following structures are used with long filenames.

BY_HANDLE_FILE_INFORMATION

```
BY_HANDLE_FILE_INFORMATION struc
    dwFileAttributes      dd ?           ; see below
    ftCreationTime        dd 2 dup(?)    ; see below
    ftLastAccessTime      dd 2 dup(?)    ; see below
    ftLastWriteTime       dd 2 dup(?)    ; see below
    dwVolumeSerialNumber  dd ?           ; see below
    nFileSizeHigh         dd ?           ; see below
    nFileSizeLow          dd ?           ; see below
    nNumberOfLinks        dd ?           ; see below
    nFileIndexHigh        dd ?           ; see below
    nFileIndexLow         dd ?           ; see below
BY_HANDLE_FILE_INFORMATION ends
```

Contains file information retrieved by Get File Info By Handle (Interrupt 21h Function 71A6h).

dwFileAttributes

File attributes. This parameter can be one or more of these values:

FILE_ATTRIBUTE_NORMAL (00000000h)

> The file can be read from or written to. This value is valid only if used alone.

FILE_ATTRIBUTE_READONLY (00000001h)

> The file can be read from, but not written to.

FILE_ATTRIBUTE_HIDDEN (00000002h)

> The file is hidden and does not appear in an ordinary directory listing.

FILE_ATTRIBUTE_SYSTEM (00000004h)

> The file is part of the operating system or is used exclusively by it.

FILE_ATTRIBUTE_DIRECTORY (00000010h)

> The name specifies a directory, not a file.

FILE_ATTRIBUTE_ARCHIVE (00000020h)

> The file is an archive file. Applications use this value to mark files for backup or removal.

ftCreationTime

Time that the file was created in 64-bit file time format. A value of 0,0 indicates that the file system containing the file does not support this member.

ftLastAccessTime

Time that the file was last accessed in 64-bit file time format. A value of 0,0 indicates that the file system containing the file does not support this member.

ftLastWriteTime

Time that the file was last written to in 64-bit file time format. All file systems support this member. If the underlying file system does not support the last write time, this member is the time that the file was created.

dwVolumeSerialNumber
Serial number of the volume that contains the file.

nFileSizeHigh
High-order word of the file size.

nFileSizeLow
Low-order word of the file size.

nNumberOfLinks
Number of links to this file. For FAT and HPFS file systems, this member is always 1. For the NTFS file system, this member may be more than 1.

nFileIndexHigh
High-order word of a unique identifier associated with the file.

nFileIndexLow
Low-order word of a unique identifier associated with the file. This identifier and the volume serial number uniquely identify a file. This number may change when the system is restarted or when the file is opened. After a process opens a file, the identifier is constant until the file is closed. An application can use this identifier and the volume serial number to determine whether two handles refer to the same file.

The value returned by **nFileIndexHigh** and **nFileIndexLow** may be invalid on some file systems, such as real-mode network redirected file systems. In this case, an invalid index value will be returned.

FILETIME

```
FILETIME struc
    dwLowDateTime  dd ?  ; see below
    dwHighDateTime dd ?  ; see below
FILETIME ends
```

Contains a 64-bit value specifying the number of 100-nanosecond intervals that have elapsed since 12:00 A.M. January 1, 1901.

dwLowDateTime
Low-order 32 bits of the file time.

dwHighDateTime
High-order 32 bits of the file time.

WIN32_FIND_DATA

```
WIN32_FIND_DATA struc
    dwFileAttributes    dd ?            ; see below
    ftCreationTime      dd 2 dup(?)     ; see below
    ftLastAccessTime    dd 2 dup(?)     ; see below
    ftLastWriteTime     dd 2 dup(?)     ; see below
    nFileSizeHigh       dd ?            ; high word of file size, in bytes
    nFileSizeLow        dd ?            ; low word of file size, in bytes
    dwReserved0         dd 0            ; reserved; do not use
    dwReserved1         dd 0            ; reserved; do not use
    cFileName           db MAX_PATH dup(?)  ; see below
    cAlternateFileName  db 14 dup(?)        ; see below
WIN32_FIND_DATA ends
```

Describes a file found by Find First File (Interrupt 21h Function 714Eh) or Find
Next File (Interrupt 21h Function 714Fh).

dwFileAttributes

File attributes of the file found. This parameter can be one or more of these
values:

FILE_ATTRIBUTE_NORMAL (00000000h)

> The file can be read from or written to. This value is valid only
> if used alone.

FILE_ATTRIBUTE_READONLY (00000001h)

> The file can be read from, but not written to.

FILE_ATTRIBUTE_HIDDEN (00000002h)

> The file is hidden and does not appear in an ordinary directory
> listing.

FILE_ATTRIBUTE_SYSTEM (00000004h)

> The file is part of the operating system or is used exclusively by it.

FILE_ATTRIBUTE_DIRECTORY (00000010h)

> The name specifies a directory, not a file.

FILE_ATTRIBUTE_ARCHIVE (00000020h)

> The file is an archive file. Applications use this value to mark files
> for backup or removal.

ftCreationTime
Time that the file was created in either MS-DOS date and time format or in 64-bit file time format, depending on the date and time format specified in either Find First File or Find Next File. A value of 0,0 indicates that the file system containing the file does not support this member.

ftLastAccessTime
Time that the file was last accessed in either MS-DOS date and time format or in 64-bit file time format, depending on the date and time format specified in either Find First File or Find Next File. A value of 0,0 indicates that the file system containing the file does not support this member.

ftLastWriteTime
Time that the file was last written to in either MS-DOS date and time format or in 64-bit file time format, depending on the date and time format specified in either Find First File or Find Next File. All file systems support this member.

cFileName
Null-terminated string that is the name of the file. Because long filenames are allowed, the buffer size must be large enough for 256 characters, including the terminating null character.

cAlternateFileName
Null-terminated string, in the standard 8.3 filename format, that is an alternate name of the file. If the **cFileName** member contains an 8.3 format name or the file system does not permit 8.3 format alternates, this member is set to zero.

ARTICLE 25

Exclusive Volume Locking

About Exclusive Volume Locking

Disk utilities and other applications that directly modify file system structures, such as directory entries, must request exclusive volume locking (that is, exclusive use of the volume) before making modifications to the structures. Exclusive use prevents applications from inadvertently changing the file system while a disk utility is trying modify it and ensures that the information on a volume represents the current state of the volume.

This article describes exclusive volume locking and provides guidelines for applications that carry out direct access on volumes while running with Microsoft® Windows® 95. This article also describes the input and output control (IOCTL) functions that applications need for managing exclusive volume locking.

Direct Access

Applications typically use direct access to make changes to the directory entries, paths, and allocation chains in the file allocation table (FAT) of a given volume. The applications access this information by using the Interrupt 13h functions, Absolute Disk Read and Write (Interrupts 25h and 26h), or the Interrupt 21h read, write, and format track IOCTL functions. Some applications may also access the volume using the disk controller input and output (I/O) ports.

As a multitasking operating system, Windows 95 permits any number of applications to access a volume at a given time. Applications that change the file system structures of a volume without regard to other applications risk corruption of that information and subsequent data loss. To prevent data loss, the system manages all requests for direct access. With the exception of floppy disk drives, Windows 95 does not permit direct write operations, unless the volume has been locked by the application. The system returns the ERROR_WRITE_PROTECT error value to functions or interrupts that attempt direct write operations when the volume has not been locked. An application can read directly from a volume, but the system may satisfy the request by reading from internal caches rather than from the medium itself. An application cannot access disk controller I/O ports; the system traps all access.

An application can override the default behavior of the system by requesting exclusive use of the volume using the lock and unlock volume IOCTL functions. An application that has exclusive use of a volume can read and write directly to the medium, and because the system flushes internal caches to the medium, the information there reflects the actual state of the volume. Locking a volume (including the floppy disk drives) ensures consistency of data, because other processes cannot update information about the volume while it is locked.

Exclusive Use Lock

To request exclusive use of a volume, an application use either Lock Logical Volume (Interrupt 21h Function 440Dh Minor Code 4Ah) or Lock Physical Volume (Interrupt 21h Function 440Dh Minor Code 4Bh). Before issuing an Interrupt 13h function, an application must acquire a physical volume lock. An application that only modifies logical volumes should acquire a logical volume lock. The calling interface for both locks is the same except for how the volume to lock is specified; the physical lock requires an Interrupt 13h device unit number, but the logical lock requires a logical drive number. When an application obtains a lock on a physical drive, the system acquires a logical volume lock for each logical volume on the physical drive. Obtaining a lock on a logical volume that is the parent (or host) drive also locks the child drives. For example, a compressed volume is locked when its host drive is locked.

The application that owns the lock can carry out direct disk write operations. Only one application at a time can lock the volume. If an application already owns the volume lock, the system fails subsequent calls to lock the volume.

The volume-locking functions allow the lock owner to control the kind of access that other processes have to the volume. There are three categories of access: *read operations*, which include opening a file as well as reading from a file; *write operations*, which include deleting and renaming a file as well as writing to a file; and *new file mappings*.

When an application calls either of the lock volume functions, it specifies a *lock level* and, depending on the level, passes in additional information known as *permissions*. The lock level and permissions specify what kind of operations the system allows processes other than the lock owner to do on the volume while it is locked.

When another process attempts to access the volume, the file system will *fail* the operation and return the ERROR_WRITE_PROTECT error value or it will block the operation, depending on the lock level and permissions. The system queues a blocked operation and puts the process requesting the operation to sleep until the lock is released and the operation can be performed.

When an application has completed its work, it must unlock the volume. Depending on whether it acquired a logical or physical lock, the application unlocks the volume by calling either Unlock Logical Volume (Interrupt 21h Function 440Dh Minor Code 6Ah) or Unlock Physical Volume (Interrupt 21h Function 440Dh Minor Code 6Bh). Unlocking the volume lets the system perform any blocked operations (in the order that they occurred) and resume normal activity. If an application exits without releasing the lock, the system automatically releases it.

If an application has a lock and the user attempts to close the virtual machine in which the application is running, the system displays a message warning the user that closing the virtual machine could result in damage to the volume. If the user confirms the closing, the system releases the lock and closes the virtual machine.

An application can lock volumes on local drives, but not on network drives or on drives that are not managed by the I/O supervisor, a virtual device driver. Also, the lock and unlock volume IOCTL functions are not available in previous versions of Microsoft® MS-DOS®. If the functions are used with a previous version, they return an error value.

Windows 95 provides 4 levels of exclusive volume locks. The level 0 lock is used alone, and lock levels 1, 2, and 3 form a hierarchy that increasingly restricts access to the file system based on the permissions set when the application obtains the level 1 lock. Although the level 0 lock is not part of the locking hierarchy formed by lock levels 1, 2, and 3, it has a more restrictive sublevel for applications that format volumes. Applications should perform direct disk write operations *only* in either a level 0 or 3 lock.

Level 0 Lock

The level 0 lock cannot be obtained on volumes that have any open files or handles. This restriction includes handles returned by the Windows **FindFirstFile** and **FindFirstChangeNotification** functions. Because the system always has open files, an application cannot take a level 0 lock on the drive that contains the Windows 95 system files. The locking hierarchy can be used on volumes with open files and handles. If the system fails a level 0 lock request because of open files, an application can obtain a list of all the open files on the volume by calling Enumerate Open Files (Interrupt 21h Function 440Dh Minor Code 6Dh).

Before returning from the call to lock the volume, Windows 95 flushes to disk all data from the file system cache. To ensure that the disk and file system remain in a consistent state, the system puts the cache into write-through mode so that it can immediately commit to disk all data from file write operations. If an application has obtained a lock on a child volume, the system does not automatically flush the file system cache after a write operation to the parent volume. To ensure that the cache is flushed when opening files with Open or Create File (Interrupt 21h Function 716Ch), an application should specify the OPEN_FLAGS_NO_BUFFERING (0100h) value. If a file has not been opened with OPEN_FLAGS_NO_BUFFERING or Absolute Disk Write (Interrupt 26h) has been used to write to the parent volume, an application should call Reset Drive (Interrupt 21h Function 710Dh) to flush the cache.

After a process obtains a level 0 lock, the system only allows the lock owner to have access to the volume. The system fails all read operations, write operations, and new file mappings by other processes until the lock owner releases the lock. An application should use a level 0 lock whenever possible, because it guarantees that no other process can access the locked volume.

An application that formats volumes must obtain a more restrictive mode of the level 0 lock. To format a volume, the application should follow these steps:

1. Call the lock volume function to obtain a level 0 lock.

2. Do any needed file system I/O that uses the Interrupt 21h file handle I/O functions while in the level 0 lock.

3. Call the lock volume function a second time to obtain the more restrictive level 0 lock for formatting. When calling the lock volume function the second time, an application should specify 0 as the lock level and specify 4 in the permissions. The application, however, must already own the level 0 lock to obtain this lock.

4. Format the disk using the Interrupt 21h IOCTL functions (such as Read/ Write/Format/Verify Track on Logical Drive or Get/Set Device Parameters). Interrupt 13h will work too, but it is not the preferred method for performance reasons. The system allows direct disk I/O, but it fails all other file system I/O that uses the Interrupt 21h file handle I/O functions while the restrictive level 0 lock is in effect.

5. Release the level 0 lock for formatting. An application is still in a level 0 lock at this point. Before the application releases this lock, the disk must be in a state that would be recognizable as normal FAT media. Otherwise, the functions mentioned in step 6 will not work.

6. Resume normal file system I/O using the Interrupt 21h file handle I/O functions.

7. Release the level 0 lock.

Locking Hierarchy

The locking hierarchy allows an application to obtain a lock in preparation for modifying the file system and yet allows other processes access to the drive. In this way, other processes are only denied access to the volume when absolutely necessary.

An application should perform direct disk write operations only within a level 3 lock. To obtain a level 3 lock, an application must make three calls to the lock volume function—first to obtain a level 1 lock, then a level 2 lock, and finally a level 3 lock. After obtaining the level 3 lock, the application can safely access the volume directly.

To release the lock on a volume, an application must call the appropriate unlock volume function the same number of times that the corresponding lock volume function was called. Each call to the unlock volume function decrements the lock level. For example, a level 3 lock returns to a level 2 lock, and the system processes any blocked read operations. A level 2 lock returns to a level 1 lock, and the system processes any blocked write operations or new file mappings. A call to the unlock volume function on a level 1 lock, however, releases the lock on the volume and allows other processes to obtain the lock.

Exclusive volume locks are owned by a process, not a thread. If necessary, a multithreaded application can obtain a level 1 lock in one thread, a level 2 lock in another, and a level 3 lock in yet another.

Even though the system may block or fail new file mappings, other processes are allowed to write to files through existing file mappings, because file mappings cannot be resized. Writing to an existing file mapping only changes the contents of the memory-mapped file, it does not cause changes to the file system.

Level 1

The level 1 lock acts as a sentinel to guarantee that only one application may obtain the level 2 and 3 locks. An application specifies permissions only when requesting the level 1 lock. The lock level and permissions determine the kind of access that processes other than the lock owner have to the volume while it is locked. Bit 0 of the *Permissions* parameter for the lock volume function determines if the system allows or fails write operations by other processes. Bit 1 of *Permissions* determines if the system allows or fails new file mappings by other processes. Bit 2 of *Permissions* is only used when obtaining the restrictive level 0 lock for formatting and is ignored for a level 1 lock. The following table shows which operations are allowed at each lock level based on the permissions set on the level 1 lock.

Permissions	Level 1	Level 2	Level 3
Bit 0 = 0	Write operations are failed.	Write operations are failed.	Write operations are failed.
Bit 1 = 0	New file mappings are allowed.	New file mappings are allowed.	New file mappings are blocked.
	Read operations are allowed.	Read operations are allowed.	Read operations are blocked.
Bit 0 = 0	Write operations are failed.	Write operations are failed.	Write operations are failed.
Bit 1 = 1	New file mappings are failed.	New file mappings are failed.	New file mappings are failed.
	Read operations are allowed.	Read operations are allowed.	Read operations are blocked.
Bit 0 = 1	Write operations are allowed.	Write operations are blocked.	Write operations are blocked.
Bit 1 = 0	New file mappings are allowed.	New file mappings are allowed.	New file mappings are blocked.
	Read operations are allowed.	Read operations are allowed.	Read operations are blocked.
Bit 0 = 1	Write operations are allowed.	Write operations are blocked.	Write operations are blocked.
Bit 1 = 1	New file mappings are failed.	New file mappings are failed.	New file mappings are failed.
	Read operations are allowed.	Read operations are allowed.	Read operations are blocked.

Calling an unlock physical or logical volume function on a level 1 lock completely releases the lock on the volume.

Level 2

The level 2 lock prevents all processes except the lock owner from writing to the disk, but the lock allows any application to read from it. Depending on the permissions set when the application obtained the level 1 lock, the system will either block or fail write operations and either allow or fail new file mappings. Before obtaining a level 3 lock, an application should call Get Lock Flag State (Interrupt 21h Function 440Dh Minor Code 6Ch) to determine if anything on the disk has changed, such as the swap file growing or shrinking. Calling Get Lock Flag State at this point is an optimization that is done to avoid obtaining the level 3 lock unnecessarily.

Calling an unlock physical or logical volume function on a level 2 lock decrements the lock level to 1 and causes the system to perform previously blocked operations that are allowed at the lower lock level.

Level 3

The level 3 lock prevents all processes except the lock owner from reading or writing to the disk. Read operations are blocked, and write operations and new file mappings are either blocked or failed depending on the permissions set in the level 1 lock. This is the most restrictive lock, not only because it prevents all other processes from accessing the disk but also because the lock owner is limited in what it can do.

Because read operations are blocked in the level 3 lock, an application must not execute any user interface or screen update functions, spawn applications, load dynamic-link libraries (DLLs), or yield to avoid deadlock. For example, if an application yields to a process with a discardable segment that the system has discarded, the system cannot reload the discarded segment because the process cannot read from the disk. This situation results in deadlock. Whenever a process obtains a level 3 lock, it should keep the lock for as short a period as possible to avoid severely degrading system performance. The purpose of the level 3 lock is to write changes to disk, so processes should only call disk I/O functions inside the lock.

After a level 3 lock is obtained, the file system takes several steps to allow a process to write directly to the disk. First, the system flushes all file system buffers and caches. Next, it puts the cache into write-through mode so that changes will be written to disk immediately. Finally, all open files are closed at the file system driver (FSD) level, which is invisible to all processes. While an application is in a level 3 lock, the system does not permit the swap file to grow or shrink, but it can still be read from or written to.

If an application has obtained a lock on a child volume, the system does not automatically flush the file system cache after a write operation to the parent volume. To ensure that the cache is flushed when Open or Create File (Interrupt 21h Function 716Ch) is used, the application should specify the OPEN_FLAGS_NO_BUFFERING (0100h) value. If the file has not been opened with OPEN_FLAGS_NO_BUFFERING or Absolute Disk Write (Interrupt 26h) has been used to write to the parent volume, the application should call Reset Drive (Interrupt 21h Function 710Dh) to flush the cache.

Before releasing the level 3 lock, the process is responsible for putting the file system into a state consistent with what existed before the lock was obtained. The process must be careful to correctly update all file system data, such as the FAT or directory entries. If a file was opened, it must not be deleted, renamed, or moved to a different volume. Otherwise, the system can become very unstable. An application should use Enumerate Open Files (Interrupt 21h Function 440Dh Minor Code 6Dh) to obtain a list of all open files on the volume.

When the level 3 lock is released, the system unblocks all read operations that are pending, reopens closed files on demand, and puts the cache back into write-behind mode. The lock owner returns to a level 2 lock.

Using the Locking Hierarchy

An application should obtain a level 1 lock before beginning an operation, such as a complete defragmentation or compression. The application should release the level 1 lock only after the entire operation is finished. This approach prevents other processes from obtaining a lock on the same disk, which would keep the lock owner from finishing its work.

To minimize the time spent in the level 3 lock, a process should remain in the level 2 lock to perform certain tasks, such as computing disk statistics and preparing data packets to be written before actually writing them in the level 3 lock. As soon as a process enters the level 3 lock, the application must call Get Lock Flag State (Interrupt 21h Function 440Dh Minor Code 6Ch) to determine if anything on the disk has changed, such as the swap file growing or shrinking. If a change has occurred, the process should release the level 3 lock, return to the level 2 lock to recompute any needed information, and then obtain the level 3 lock again. If Get Lock Flag State shows that the disk has not changed, the process should do its writing and then release the level 3 lock.

Swap File

The system pager requires access to the swap file at all times, even when an application has locked the volume containing the file. To ensure access, the system always gives the system pager the opportunity to accept or reject a lock request.

If the system grants a lock to a process, the requesting process must ensure that data for the swap file remains unchanged and that the pager can safely read from or write to the swap file at any time. In particular, the process must *not* change the allocation chain of the swap file, and if it moves the swap file's directory entry, it must ensure that the path to it is always consistent. Failure to observe these guidelines can result in a system crash.

An application can determine the directory entry and allocation chain of the swap file by retrieving the path of the file using Find Swap File (Interrupt 21h Function 440Dh Minor Code 6Eh).

The system permits the swap file to grow or shrink in the level 1 and 2 locks. Because of this, an application should call Get Lock Flag State (Interrupt 21h Function 440Dh Minor Code 6Ch) after obtaining a level 3 lock to determine if anything on the disk has changed as the result of the swap file growing or shrinking.

Virtual Devices

The system broadcasts a message to all virtual devices (VxDs) when an application makes a request for a lock. Any VxD that uses virtual block device and I/O supervisor services to carry out direct I/O on the given volume must check for this message and either accept or reject the request when the message is received.

If the VxD rejects the request, it must return the appropriate error value. In such cases, the system does not grant the lock to the requesting application. If a VxD accepts the request, it must avoid all operations that may affect the consistency of the volume for the duration of the lock.

When the application releases the lock, the system again issues a broadcast message. The VxD can resume normal operation at this point.

Volume-Locking Guidelines

Applications that lock and modify volumes should follow these guidelines to avoid degrading system performance and to prevent data loss:

- If there are no open files on the volume, applications should perform direct disk writes in a level 0 lock. Otherwise, they should use the locking hierarchy and perform disk write operations in a level 3 lock.

- Applications should utilize the locking hierarchy to minimize the time spent in a level 3 lock. They should only call disk I/O functions inside a level 3 lock and drop down to a level 1 or 2 lock whenever possible.

- Applications should neither terminate or relinquish control nor leave a level 0 or 3 lock if the volume information is incomplete or invalid. When applications leave one of these locks, the file system *must* be consistent with what it was when they entered the lock because other applications will regain access to the drive.

- Because the Interrupt 21h file handle I/O functions rely on accurate information about the volume, applications should not use these functions when the volume information is incomplete or invalid.

- Applications should not move the swap file.

- Applications should not move memory-mapped files opened for write access. Read-only memory-mapped files may be moved cluster by cluster.

- Applications may only move 32-bit Windows-based DLLs and executables cluster by cluster.

- Applications may move directory entries for the swap file and open memory-mapped files, but the path to them must always be consistent, even in a level 3 lock.

Because read operations are blocked in the level 3 lock, all applications written for 16-bit Windows, 32-bit Windows, or MS-DOS should follow these guidelines to avoid deadlock while in a level 3 lock:

- Applications should only access the disk by using the low-level disk functions (Interrupt 13h, Interrupt 25h, and Interrupt 26h) or the Interrupt 21h file handle read, write, seek, and IOCTL functions. Other MS-DOS functions are not guaranteed to work. Windows or C run-time library file I/O functions should not be used, because these functions may contain code or call code that is not safe to execute inside the level 3 lock.

- Applications should not yield control, update the screen, execute any user-interface code, or do anything else that could cause Windows 95 to load a new or previously discarded segment, such as by spawning an application or loading a DLL.

- Windows-based applications must have all the code for a level 3 lock contained within the processing for a single message. The application should not process other messages or call any Windows functions.

Special Considerations for 32-bit Windows-Based Applications

32-bit Windows-based applications must call the exclusive volume-locking IOCTL functions indirectly by opening VWIN32.VXD and using its **DeviceIoControl** interface.

In response, VWIN32.VXD issues the low-level disk I/O functions (Interrupt 13h, Interrupt 25h, and Interrupt 26h) as well as the MS-DOS Interrupt 21h file handle read, write, seek, and IOCTL functions in the context of the calling process.

32-bit Windows-based applications may safely call the Windows **ReadFile**, **WriteFile**, **SetFilePointer**, and **DeviceIoControl** functions within a level 3 lock. Other Windows or C run-time library functions should not be used while in the level 3 lock, because these functions may call other functions that are not safe inside a level 3 lock.

Special Considerations for 16-bit Windows-Based Applications

16-bit Windows-based applications may call the exclusive volume-locking IOCTL functions directly using the Interrupt 21h interface, which is described in the reference material. These applications must mark all of the code, data, and resource segments that will be accessed while inside the level 2 and 3 locks as PRELOAD NONDISCARDABLE in the module-definition (.DEF) file. This marking prevents deadlock in case the system needs to load one of the application's segments from the executable file inside a level 3 lock.

Special Considerations for MS-DOS – Based Applications

MS-DOS–based applications may directly call the volume-locking IOCTL functions by using Interrupt 21h, as described in the reference material.

When a windowed MS-DOS–based application obtains a level 3 lock, the system forces it to full screen mode to avoid deadlock with the display driver. When the application releases the level 3 lock, it remains in full screen mode.

Applications must not call the Advanced SCSI Programming Interface (ASPI) functions inside a level 3 lock. These functions bypass the file system, leaving it in an inconsistent state.

When MS-DOS-based applications run in single MS-DOS application mode (real mode), they may issue the volume-locking IOCTL functions and the functions will succeed. However, because there is no multitasking, there is only one lock rather than a hierarchy as when Windows 95 is running. The volume-locking IOCTL functions will fail on down-level versions of MS-DOS.

Functions

The following functions can be used to manage exclusive volume locking.

Lock Logical Volume	Interrupt 21h Function 440Dh Minor Code 4Ah
Lock Physical Volume	Interrupt 21h Function 440Dh Minor Code 4Bh
Unlock Logical Volume	Interrupt 21h Function 440Dh Minor Code 6Ah
Unlock Physical Volume	Interrupt 21h Function 440Dh Minor Code 6Bh
Get Lock Flag State	Interrupt 21h Function 440Dh Minor Code 6Ch
Enumerate Open Files	Interrupt 21h Function 440Dh Minor Code 6Dh
Find Swap File	Interrupt 21h Function 440Dh Minor Code 6Eh
Get Current Lock State	Interrupt 21h Function 440Dh Minor Code 70h
Reset Drive	Interrupt 21h Function 710Dh

The exclusive-volume locking IOCTL functions are similar to other MS-DOS functions. An application must copy function parameters to registers and issue an Interrupt 21h instruction to carry out the call.

Reference

The following functions and structures are associated with exclusive-volume locking IOCTL.

Functions

Interrupt 21h Function 440Dh Minor Code 4Ah Lock Logical Volume

```
mov ax, 440Dh        ; generic IOCTL
mov bh, LockLevel    ; see below
mov bl, DriveNum     ; see below
mov ch, 08h          ; device category (must be 08h)
mov cl, 4Ah          ; Lock Logical Volume
mov dx, Permissions  ; see below
int 21h

jc error
```

Locks the logical volume.

■ Clears the carry flag if successful. Otherwise, the function sets the carry flag and sets the AX register to an error value.

LockLevel
Level of the lock. This parameter must be either 0, 1, 2, or 3.

DriveNum
Drive to lock. This parameter can be 0 for the default drive, 1 for A, 2 for B, and so on.

Permissions
Operations that the system permits while the volume is locked. This parameter is specified only when a level 1 lock is obtained or when a level 0 lock is obtained for the second time for formatting the volume. For other lock levels, this parameter is zero. When a level 1 lock is obtained, bits 0 and 1 of this parameter specify whether the system permits write operations, new file mappings, or both by other processes during a level 1 lock as well as during level 2 and 3 locks. If this parameter specifies that write operations, new file mappings, or both are failed, these operations are failed during level 1, 2, and 3 locks. This parameter has the following form:

Bit	Meaning
0	0 = Write operations are failed (specified when a level 1 lock is obtained).
0	1 = Write operations are allowed (specified when a level 1 lock is obtained).
1	0 = New file mapping are allowed (specified when a level 1 lock is obtained).
1	1 = New file mapping are failed (specified when a level 1 lock is obtained).
2	1 = The volume is locked for formatting (specified when a level 0 lock is obtained for the second time).

The volume must be locked before the application performs direct disk write operations by using Interrupt 26h or the IOCTL control functions. Lock Physical Volume (Interrupt 21h Function 440Dh Minor Code 4Bh) is used instead of this function before a call to an Interrupt 13h function. Unlock Logical Volume (Interrupt 21h Function 440Dh Minor Code 6Ah) should be used to release the lock.

Interrupt 21h Function 440Dh Minor Code 4Bh Lock Physical Volume

```
mov ax, 440Dh        ; generic IOCTL
mov bh, LockLevel    ; see below
mov bl, DriveNum     ; see below
mov ch, 08h          ; device category (must be 08h)
mov cl, 4Bh          ; Lock Physical Volume
mov dx, Permissions  ; see below
int 21h

jc error
```

Locks the physical volume.

- Clears the carry flag if successful. Otherwise, the function sets the carry flag and sets the AX register to an error value.

LockLevel
Level of the lock. This parameter must be either 0, 1, 2, or 3.

DriveNum
Drive to lock. This parameter must be one of these values (same device unit numbers as for Interrupt 13h):

00 - 7Fh	Floppy disk drive (00 for the first floppy drive, 01 for the second, and so on).
80 - FFh	Hard disk drive (80 for the first hard disk drive, 81 for the second, and so on).

Permissions
Operations that the system permits while the volume is locked. This parameter is specified only when a level 1 lock is obtained or when a level 0 lock is obtained for the second time for formatting the volume. For other lock levels, this parameter is zero. When a level 1 lock is obtained, bits 0 and 1 of this parameter specify whether the system permits write operations, new file mappings, or both by other processes during a level 1 lock as well as during level 2 and 3 locks. If this parameter specifies that write operations, new file mappings, or both are failed, these operations are failed during level 1, 2, and 3 locks. This parameter has the following form:

Bit	Meaning
0	0 = Write operations are failed (specified when a level 1 lock is obtained).
0	1 = Write operations are allowed (specified when a level 1 lock is obtained).

Bit	Meaning
1	0 = New file mapping are allowed (specified when a level 1 lock is obtained).
1	1 = New file mapping are failed (specified when a level 1 lock is obtained).
2	1 = The volume is locked for formatting (specified when a level 0 lock is obtained for the second time).

The volume must be locked before the application performs direct disk write operations by using Interrupt 13h, Interrupt 26h, or the Interrupt 21h IOCTL functions. A single physical volume may be divided into more than one logical volume, which is also called a partition. The system automatically takes a logical volume lock on all logical volumes on the specified physical drive.
 If the application performs disk writes only to a logical drive, Lock Logical Volume (Interrupt 21h Function 440Dh Minor Code 4Ah) is used instead of this function. Unlock Physical Volume (Interrupt 21h Function 440Dh Minor Code 6Bh) should be called to release the lock.

Interrupt 21h Function 440Dh Minor Code 6Ah Unlock Logical Volume

```
mov ax, 440Dh        ; generic IOCTL
mov bl, DriveNum     ; see below
mov ch, 08h          ; device category (must be 08h)
mov cl, 6Ah          ; Unlock Logical Volume
int 21h

jc error
```

Unlocks the logical volume or decrements the lock level.

- Clears the carry flag if successful. Otherwise, the function sets the carry flag and sets the AX register to an error value.

DriveNum
   Drive to unlock. This parameter can be 0 for the default drive, 1 for A, 2 for B, and so on.

This function is used to release the lock obtained by using Lock Logical Volume (Interrupt 21h Function 440Dh Minor Code 4Ah). Only the lock owner can release the lock on a volume.

To release the lock on the volume, an application must call Unlock Logical Volume the same number of times that Lock Logical Volume was called.

Interrupt 21h Function 440Dh Minor Code 6Bh Unlock Physical Volume

```
mov ax, 440Dh        ; generic IOCTL
mov bl, DriveNum     ; see below
mov ch, 08h          ; device category (must be 08h)
mov cl, 6Bh          ; Unlock Physical Volume
int 21h

jc enter
```

Unlocks the physical volume or decrements the lock level.

- Clears the carry flag if successful. Otherwise, the function sets the carry flag and sets the AX register to an error value.

DriveNum
   Drive to unlock. This parameter must be one of these values (same device unit numbers as for Interrupt 13h):

00 - 7Fh	Floppy disk drive (00 for the first floppy drive, 01 for the second, and so on).
80 - FFh	Hard disk drive (80 for the first hard disk drive, 81 for the second, and so on).

This function is used to release the lock obtained by using Lock Physical Volume (Interrupt 21h Function 440Dh Minor Code 4Bh). Only the lock owner can release the lock on a volume.

To release the lock on the volume, an application must call Unlock Physical Volume the same number of times that Lock Physical Volume was called.

Interrupt 21h Function 440Dh Minor Code 6Ch Get Lock Flag State

```
mov ax, 440Dh        ; generic IOCTL
mov bl, DriveNum     ; see below
mov ch, 08h          ; device category (must be 08h)
mov cl, 6Ch          ; Get Lock Flag State
int 21h

jc error
mov [AccessFlag], ax  ; state of access flag
```

Polls the state of the access flag on a volume to determine if a write operation (for example, deleting or renaming a file or writing to a file) or a new file mapping has occurred since the last poll.

- Clears the carry flag and sets the AX register to one of the following values if successful:

0   No write operations or file mappings have occurred since the last poll.

1   A write operation has occurred since the last poll (clears the volume access flag).

2   A file mapping has occurred since the last poll, or a 32-bit Windows-based DLL or executable has been opened (clears the volume access flag).

Otherwise, the function sets the carry flag and sets the AX register to an error value.

DriveNum
Drive to poll. This parameter can be 0 for the default drive, 1 for A, 2 for B, and so on.

Only the current lock owner may poll the access flag. The system fails other processes with ERROR_ACCESS_DENIED error value. Write operations performed by the lock owner do not cause a change in the state of the access flag.

When a lock is obtained that allows write operations or new file mappings, the system sets a flag whenever one of these operations happens on the volume. If a write operation or new file mapping has occurred since the last poll, Get Lock Flag State returns 1 or 2 respectively in the AX register and clears the volume access flag. If the swap file has grown or shrunk since the last poll, Get Lock Flag State returns 1. Note that write operations to the swap file that do not cause a change in size do not cause a change in the state of the access flag. If a 32-bit Windows-based DLL or executable has been opened since the last poll, Get Lock Flag State returns 2.

Interrupt 21h Function 440Dh Minor Code 6Dh Enumerate Open Files

```
mov ax, 440Dh            ; generic IOCTL
mov bx, DriveNum         ; see below
mov ch, 08h              ; device category (must be 08h)
mov cl, 6Dh              ; Enumerate Open Files
mov dx, seg PathBuf      ; see below
mov ds, dx
mov dx, offset PathBuf
mov si, FileIndex        ; see below
mov di, EnumType         ; see below
int 21h

jc error
mov [OpenMode], ax       ; mode file was opened in
mov [FileType], cx       ; normal file or memory-mapped file
```

Enumerates open files on the specified drive.

- Clears the carry flag, copies the path of an open file to the given buffer, and sets the AX and CX registers to the following values if successful:

AX	Mode that the file was opened in, which is a combination of access mode, sharing mode, and open flags. It can be one value each from the access and sharing modes and any combination of open flags.

               Access modes

               OPEN_ACCESS_READONLY (0000h)

               OPEN_ACCESS_WRITEONLY (0001h)

               OPEN_ACCESS_READWRITE (0002h)

               OPEN_ACCESS_RO_NOMODLASTACCESS (0004h)

               Share modes

               OPEN_SHARE_COMPATIBLE (0000h)

               OPEN_SHARE_DENYREADWRITE (0010h)

               OPEN_SHARE_DENYWRITE (0020h)

               OPEN_SHARE_DENYREAD (0030h)

               OPEN_SHARE_DENYNONE (0040h)

               Open flags

               OPEN_FLAGS_NOINHERIT (0080h)

               OPEN_FLAGS_NO_BUFFERING (0100h)

               OPEN_FLAGS_NO_COMPRESS (0200h)

               OPEN_FLAGS_ALIAS_HINT (0400h)

               OPEN_FLAGS_NOCRITERR (2000h)

               OPEN_FLAGS_COMMIT (4000h)

CX	File type. It can be one of the following values:

0	For normal files
1	For memory-mapped files (memory-mapped files are unmovable)
2	For any other unmovable files (32-bit Windows-based DLLs and executables)
4	For the swap file

Note that if a memory-mapped file is returned (CX = 1), the value returned in the AX register is limited to the following values:

OPEN_ACCESS_READONLY (0000h)

OPEN_ACCESS_READWRITE (0002h)

Otherwise, the function sets the carry flag and sets the AX register to the following error value:

ERROR_ACCESS_DENIED   The value of *FileIndex* exceeds the number of open files on the drive.

DriveNum
Drive on which to enumerate the files. This parameter can be 0 for the default drive, 1 for A, 2 for B, and so on.

PathBuf
Address of a buffer that receives the path of the open file. The length of the buffer varies depending on the volume. Get Volume Information (Interrupt 21h Function 71A0h) is used to determine the maximum allowed length of a path for the volume.

FileIndex
Index of the file to retrieve the path for.

EnumType
Kind of file to enumerate. This parameter can be 0 to enumerate all open files or 1 to enumerate only open unmovable files, including open memory-mapped files and other open unmovable files (32-bit Windows-based DLLs and executables).

This function returns information about one file at a time. To enumerate all open files, the function must be called repeatedly with *FileIndex* set to a new value for each call. *FileIndex* should be set to zero initially and then incremented by one for each subsequent call. The function returns the ERROR_NO_MORE_FILES error value when all open files on the volume have been enumerated.

This function may return inconsistent results when used to enumerate files on an active volume—that is, on a volume where other processes may be opening and closing files. Applications should use Lock Logical Volume (Interrupt 21h Function 440Dh Minor Code 4Ah) to take a level 3 lock before enumerating open files.

Interrupt 21h Function 440Dh Minor Code 6Eh Find Swap File

```
mov ax, 440Dh          ; generic IOCTL
mov ch, 08h            ; device category (must be 08h)
mov cl, 6Eh            ; Find Swap File
mov dx, seg PathBuf    ; see below
mov ds, dx
mov dx, offset PathBuf
int 21h

jc  error
mov [PagerType], ax            ; pager type
mov WORD PTR [FileSize], bx    ; swap file size in 4K pages
mov WORD PTR [FileSize+2], cx
```

Retrieves information about the swap file.

- Clears the carry flag, copies the swap file path to the given buffer, and sets the following registers if successful:

AX
: Pager type. It can be 1 for no pager, 2 for paging through MS-DOS, and 3 for paging through the protected-mode input and output (I/O) supervisor.

CX:BX
: Current size of the swap file in 4K pages.

Otherwise, this function sets the carry flag and sets the AX register to an error value.

PathBuf
: Address of the buffer that receives the path of the swap file. To determine the maximum allowed length of a path for the volume, call Get Volume Information (Interrupt 21h Function 71A0h).

Interrupt 21h Function 440Dh Minor Code 70h Get Current Lock State

```
mov ax, 440Dh          ; generic IOCTL
mov bl, DriveNum       ; see below
mov ch, 08h            ; device category (must be 08h)
mov cl, 70h            ; Get Current Lock State
int 21h

jc  error
```

Retrieves the current lock level and permissions on the specified drive.

▪ Clears the carry flag and sets the AX and CX registers to these values if successful:

AX   Current lock level. It may be either 0, 1, 2 or 3. If the volume is not locked, AX contains −1

CX   Lock permissions. The bits have the following form:

Bit	Meaning
0	0 = Write operations are failed.
0	1 = Write operations are allowed, unless they are blocked by the lock level.
1	0 = New file mapping are allowed, unless they are blocked by the lock level.
1	1 = New file mapping are failed.
2	1 = The volume is locked for formatting.

DriveNum
Drive to retrieve lock information about. This parameter can be 0 for the default drive, 1 for A, 2 for B, and so on.

The lock level and the permissions determine the kind of access processes other than the lock owner have to the volume while it is locked. The following operations are allowed by processes other than lock owner at each lock level:

Level	Operations
0	Read operations, write operations, and new file mappings are failed.
1	Read operations are allowed. Write operations and new file mappings are either allowed or failed based on permissions.
2	Read operations are allowed. Write operations and new file mappings are either failed or blocked based on permissions.
3	Read operations are blocked. Write operations and new file mappings are either failed or blocked based on permissions.

Interrupt 21h Function 710Dh Reset Drive

```
mov ax, 710Dh      ; Reset Drive
mov cx, Flag       ; see below
mov dx, DriveNum   ; see below
int 21h

jc  error
```

Flushes file system buffers and caches and optionally remounts the drivespace
volume. Any write operations that the system has buffered are performed, and
all waiting data is written to the appropriate drive.

- This function has no return value.

Flag

Flag specifying whether the system should flush and invalidate the data in
the cache as well as the file system buffers. This parameter must be one of
these values:

0000h	Resets the drive and flushes the file system buffers for the given drive.
0001h	Resets the drive, flushes the file system buffers, and flushes and invalidates the cache for the specified drive.
0002h	Remounts the drivespace volume.

The *Flag* value of 0002h is only supported on drivespace volumes. You
should specify this value when the on-media format of the drivespace volume
has changed and you want the file system to reinitialize and read the new
format.

DriveNum

Drive to reset. This parameter can be 0 for the default drive, 1 for A, 2 for B,
and so on.

ARTICLE 26

Program Information File Management

About Program Information File Management

Program information file management lets Microsoft® Windows®–based applications create, examine, and modify program information files (.PIF files). These files contain the detailed information needed by the operating system to prepare virtual machines for running Microsoft® MS-DOS®–based applications. Installation programs and other applications can open the files, retrieve and set information in these files, and display the information to the user for editing. This article describes program information file management and the corresponding functions and structures provided by the dynamic-link library (DLL) called PIFMGR.DLL.

Program Information Files

A .PIF file contains information about the *properties* of an MS-DOS–based application. These properties define how the application uses resources, such as memory, and specify the computer's devices, the virtual machine, and the window that the application is displayed in.

A .PIF file typically has the same filename as the corresponding MS-DOS–based application, but with the .PIF filename extension. Every .PIF file contains one or more sections called *information groups*. Each group has a unique name or ordinal. Applications use the name or ordinal to identify the group to be examined or modified.

Many groups are predefined and have associated structures that define the content of the group. The following predefined groups are listed by their ordinal.

Group ordinal	Information
GROUP_ENV	Environment. This group uses a **PROPENV** structure.
GROUP_FNT	Fonts. This group uses a **PROPFNT** structure.
GROUP_KBD	Keyboard. This group uses a **PROPKBD** structure.
GROUP_MEM	Memory. This group uses a **PROPMEM** structure.
GROUP_MSE	Mouse. This group uses a **PROPMSE** structure.
GROUP_PRG	Program. This group uses a **PROPPRG** structure.
GROUP_TSK	Task. This group uses a **PROPTSK** structure.
GROUP_VID	Video. This group uses a **PROPVID** structure.
GROUP_WIN	Windows. This group uses a **PROPWIN** structure.

The following predefined groups are identified by name (null-terminated string).

Group name	Information
AUTOEXECBAT 4.0	AUTOEXEC.BAT file image used for an application if the application is marked to run in MS-DOS mode.
CONFIG SYS 4.0	CONFIG.SYS file image used for an application if the application is marked to run in MS-DOS mode.
MICROSOFT PIFEX	Windows versions 1.x and 2.x information.
WINDOWS 286 3.0	Windows version 3.x standard mode information. This group uses a **W286PIF30** structure.
WINDOWS 386 3.0	Windows version 3.x enhanced mode information. This group uses a **W386PIF30** structure.
WINDOWS VMM 4.0	Windows 95 information. This group uses a **WENHPIF40** structure.

Applications can also create new groups called *PIF extensions* to store information that is specific to the given MS-DOS–based application. All new groups are identified by name only, and the format of the information is entirely application-defined. If PIF extensions are used to store application-specific information, applications do not need to store the information in .INI files.

Program information file management supports .PIF files in these formats: Windows version 1.x, Windows version 2.x, Windows version 3.x, and Windows 95.

Properties

To access the properties in a .PIF file, you first open the file by using the **OpenProperties** function. You can open a .PIF file directly by supplying the name of the file. Otherwise, you can supply the name of an MS-DOS–based application (that is, a file having the .COM, .EXE, or .BAT filename extension), and the function will open the corresponding .PIF file. If the function does not find the .PIF file in the current directory, it searches the WINDOWS directory, the Windows SYSTEM directory, the Windows PIF directory, and finally the directories on the current path to locate the file.

After opening the .PIF file, **OpenProperties** loads the properties into memory and returns a *properties handle* that you use in subsequent functions to identify the information. If you try to open a .PIF file that does not exist, the function creates a temporary file in memory and initializes it using internal data or data from the _DEFAULT.PIF file. To locate the _DEFAULT.PIF file, the function first searches the PIF directory and then searches for it in the directories on the current path. Unlike Windows version 3.1, Windows 95 does not create the _DEFAULT.PIF file. A system will have a _DEFAULT.PIF file only if it inherited one from a Windows version 3.1 installation, or if one was created manually.

You can retrieve individual properties by using the **GetProperties** function. You specify the property to retrieve by group name or ordinal. The name can be any predefined name, as given in the previous section, or the name of your own group. If you do not know the size of the information group, you can determine it by using the **GetProperties** function, specifying zero as the size. The function copies no data, but it returns the size of the requested group. You use this size in a subsequent call to retrieve the group.

You can change property information by using the **SetProperties** function. You specify the property to change by group name or ordinal and provide a copy of the new information. **SetProperties** typically saves changes to disk as you make the changes. You can direct **SetProperties** to cache the changes in memory by specifying the SETPROPS_CACHE value. Caching the changes lets you use the **FlushProperties** function later to either discard the changes or save them to disk.

You can create your own information group by using the **SetProperties** function, specifying the format for the information in the group. The operating system returns the information in exactly the same format as you create it. You can also use **SetProperties** to remove an information group.

Once you have finished using the properties information from a .PIF file, you must close it by using the **CloseProperties** function. If you make changes to a temporary file, **CloseProperties** will permanently save the property information in a new file on disk.

You can enumerate all loaded .PIF files by using the **EnumProperties** function. Each call to the function retrieves a properties handle, which you can use in the next call to **EnumProperties** to retrieve the next handle. The function returns zero when all open properties have been enumerated.

You can enumerate all named information groups associated with a properties handle by using the **GetProperties** function. The function copies the name of the group that corresponds to a zero-based group index to the specified 16-byte buffer. You can continue to call **GetProperties**, incrementing the index before each call, to retrieve all group names. The function returns zero when all groups have been enumerated. To minimize disk usage, the PIF manager does not store an information group if all settings have default values. This means that **GetProperties** may return the name of a group for which no PIF extension actually exists.

You can let the user edit property information by using the **EditProperties** function. The function displays a property sheet for each group listed in the previous section. When the user chooses a sheet, the function displays all the properties within the group and allows the user to edit the properties. **EditProperties** saves any changes, copying them back to the .PIF file. Some changes may not affect currently running applications, but they will apply to subsequently started applications.

The operating system may associate a given virtual machine or window handle with a specific set of properties. You can determine which handles are associated with a given set by using the **AssociateProperties** function. Generally, only system components should change these associations.

To retrieve a complete copy of the .PIF file, specify the OPENPROPS_RAWIO value when opening the file using the **OpenProperties** function. Reading or writing the entire file requires a thorough understanding of the .PIF file format and is not recommended.

Property Sheets

A *property sheet* is a set of controls that gives users access to the information in an information group. Property sheets are used by the **EditProperties** function to create a dialog box that displays the current values for settings in the information group and lets users edit those values. **EditProperties** uses default property sheets for each of the predefined information groups, but the function requires custom property sheets for any information groups that contain application-specific information.

An application or DLL can add a property sheet to the system by using the **AddPropertySheet** function. Before adding the property sheet, you must fill a **PROPSHEETPAGE** structure with names or values identifying the dialog box template, dialog box procedure, icon resource, and other resources to be used to display and manage the property sheet. Property sheets can be simple or advanced. Simple property sheets typically display a small set of values from the information group, and advanced property sheets display all values. You specify the property sheet type when you add the property sheet to the .PIF file.

You can retrieve information about the property sheets associated with a .PIF file by using the **EnumPropertySheets** function. For each property sheet, the function copies information, such as the name of the dialog box template and dialog box procedure, to a **PROPSHEETPAGE** structure. To use **EnumPropertySheets**, you must first load the property sheets by using the **LoadPropertySheets** function. After retrieving the property sheet information, you should free the loaded sheets by using the **FreePropertySheets** function.

To remove a property sheet from the system, use the **RemovePropertySheet** function.

Property Libraries

A *property library* is a DLL that provides dialog box templates and procedures for displaying property sheets and editing properties. Property libraries let you develop property sheets for information groups that are specific to your MS-DOS –based applications. These libraries ensure that system applications, such as the shell, can display the application-specific information and allow users to edit it.

You can register a property library by using the **LoadPropertyLib** function. The function records the name of the library and returns a handle, but it does not actually load the library. You use the handle when adding property sheets to the .PIF file to identify the library containing the template and dialog box procedure for the property sheet. The system eventually loads the library when the user attempts to access the property sheet. You can enumerate the currently registered property libraries by using the **EnumPropertyLibs** function. When you no longer need a given property library, you should free it by using the **FreePropertyLib** function.

Properties and Virtual Devices

Virtual devices (VxDs) also have access to information in .PIF files. This means that any VxDs you create to support MS-DOS–based applications can use information in the .PIF file. Typically, you add a specific PIF extension for use by the VxD and create corresponding a property sheet to give the user the opportunity to edit the information.

A VxD cannot retrieve property information directly. Instead, it installs a callback procedure using the **SHELL_Hook_Properties** service provided by the Shell virtual device (SHELL.VXD). The system notifies the VxD of changes to the properties by calling the callback procedure. The VxD can install callback procedures as either predefined or customized groups.

Reference

The following functions and structures are associated with program information file management.

Functions

The following functions are used with program information file management.

AddPropertySheet

```
int AddPropertySheet(LPPROPSHEETPAGE lppsi, int iType)
```

Adds a new property sheet.

- Returns a property sheet handle if successful or NULL otherwise.

lppsi
  Address of the **PROPSHEETPAGE** structure containing the property sheet information.

iType
  Sheet type. This parameter can be either the SHEETTYPE_SIMPLE or SHEETTYPE_ADVANCED value.

AssociateProperties

```
long AssociateProperties(int hProps, int iAssociate, long lData)
```

Associates data with the given property information. This function can also return the currently associated data without associating new data.

- Returns the data previously associated with the given index data. If no data was previously associated or an error occurs, the function returns zero.

hProps
  Properties handle. It must have been created previously by using the **OpenProperties** function.

iAssociate
  Association index. This parameter can be the HVM_ASSOCIATION or HWND_ASSOCIATION value.

lData

Data to associate. This parameter can be any 32-bit value or address.

Association of data is reserved exclusively for system components. Applications may use this function to retrieve the associated data, but they must not set the associated data.

If *iAssociate* is negative, the currently associated value is returned, but it is not modified. In other words, *lData* is ignored.

CloseProperties

```
int CloseProperties(int hProps, int flOpt)
```

Closes the property information for the application.

- Returns NULL if successful or the properties handle otherwise.

hProps

Properties handle. It must have been created previously by using the **OpenProperties** function.

flOpt

Operation flag. This parameter can be the CLOSEPROPS_DISCARD value to discard the data or zero to save cached program information data by copying it to the .PIF file on disk.

EditProperties

```
int EditProperties(int hProps, LPSTR lpszTitle, UINT uStartPage,
    HWND hwnd, UINT uMsgPost)
```

Displays the editing dialog box, allowing the user to edit the given property sheet information.

- Returns TRUE if successful or FALSE otherwise.

hProps

Properties handle. It must have been created previously by using the **OpenProperties** function.

lpszTitle

Address of null-terminated string specifying the title of the editing dialog box. If no title is needed, this parameter can be NULL.

uStartPage

Number of the first property sheet to edit.

hwnd

Parent window handle. If no parent window needed, this parameter can be NULL.

uMsgPost

Notification message value. If no notification message is needed, this parameter can be zero. If it is not zero, the function posts a message having this value to the parent window whenever properties change. The *wParam* parameter in the posted message specifies the size of the changed data, and the *lParam* parameter specifies the name or ordinal of the changed group.

EnumProperties

```
int EnumProperties(int hProps)
```

Enumerates all open properties handles.

- Returns a properties handle or zero if all properties have been enumerated.

hProps

Properties handle. It must have been previously returned by **EnumProperties**, or it must be NULL to start enumeration.

EnumPropertyLibs

```
int EnumPropertyLibs(int iLib, LPHANDLE lphDLL, LPSTR lpszDLL,
    int cbszDLL)
```

Enumerates property libraries, filling the variables with the module handle and name of each library.

- Returns a library identifier if successful. If all libraries have been enumerated or an error occurs, the function returns zero.

iLib

Library identifier. It must have been previously returned by the **EnumPropertyLibs** function or must be zero to start enumeration.

lphDLL

Address of the variable that receives the module handle of the library. If the handle is not needed, this parameter can be NULL.

lpszDLL

Address of the buffer that receives the zero-terminated name of the library. If the name is not needed, this parameter can be NULL.

cbszDLL

Size, in bytes, of the buffer pointed to by *lpszDLL*.

EnumPropertySheets

```
int EnumPropertySheets(int hProps, int iType, int iSheet,
    LPPROPSHEETPAGE lppsi)
```

Enumerates property sheets.

- Returns a property sheet handle if successful. If all property sheets have been enumerated or an error occurs, the function returns zero.

hProps
Properties handle. It must have been created previously by using the **Open Properties** function.

iType
Sheet type. This parameter can be either the SHEETTYPE_SIMPLE or SHEETTYPE_ADVANCED value.

iSheet
Property sheet handle. It must have been previously returned by **EnumPropertySheets** or must be zero to start enumeration.

lppsi
Address of the **PROPSHEETPAGE** structure that receives the property sheet information.

FlushProperties

```
int FlushProperties(int hProps, int flOpt)
```

Flushes or discards cached property information. The function flushes data by copying the data to the corresponding .PIF file on disk.

- Returns TRUE if successful or FALSE otherwise.

hProps
Properties handle. It must have been created previously by using the **OpenProperties** function.

flOpt
Operations flag. This parameter can be the FLUSHPROPS_DISCARD value to discard the cached program information data or zero to flush the data to the corresponding .PIF file.

FreePropertyLib

```
BOOL FreePropertyLib(int hLib)
```

Frees an installable property library.

- Returns TRUE if successful or FALSE otherwise.

hLib
   Handle of the property library.

FreePropertySheets

```
int FreePropertySheets(int hProps, int flags)
```

Frees all property sheets for the .PIF file identified by the given properties handle.

- No return value.

hProps
   Properties handle. It must have been created previously by using the **OpenProperties** function.

flags
   Reserved; must be zero.

GetProperties

```
int GetProperties(int hProps, LPSTR lpszGroup, LPVOID lpProps,
    int cbProps, int flOpt)
```

Retrieves property information for the given group; retrieves the size, in bytes, of the property information; or enumerates all named groups in the .PIF file.

- Returns the size, in bytes, of the information retrieved if successful. If the group is not found, all groups have been enumerated, or an error occurred, the function returns zero.

hProps
   Properties handle.

lpszGroup

Group ordinal, address of a null-terminated string specifying the name of the property group, or NULL. If a name is given, it must be the name of a valid PIF extension or one of these predefined group names:

MICROSOFT PIFEX	WINDOWS 386 3.0
WINDOWS 286 3.0	WINDOWS VMM 4.0

If a group ordinal is given, it can be one of these predefined ordinals:

GROUP_ENV	GROUP_PRG
GROUP_KBD	GROUP_TSK
GROUP_MEM	GROUP_VID
GROUP_MSE	GROUP_WIN

The ordinal must be in the low-order word, and zero must be in the high-order word.

If NULL is specified, the function enumerates all named groups. In this case, *cbProps* must be a zero-based group name index, and *lpProps* must be the address of the 16-byte buffer that receives the name of the given group.

lpProps

Address of the buffer that receives the property information. The size of the buffer depends on the type of information retrieved.

cbProps

Size, in bytes, of the buffer pointed to by *lpProps*. If *cbProps* is zero and *lpszGroup* is not NULL, the function returns the size of the corresponding property information without copying that information to the *lpProps* buffer.

flOpt

Operations flag. This parameter can be the GETPROPS_RAWIO value to read the entire .PIF file as a single, unformatted block (that is, *lpszGroup* is ignored) or zero to read the given group.

LoadPropertyLib

```
int LoadPropertyLib(LPSTR lpszDLL, int fLoad)
```

Loads a property library.

- Returns the handle of the property library if successful or FALSE otherwise.

lpszDLL
Address of a null-terminated string specifying the name of a property library.

fLoad
Load flags. This parameter can be zero or the LOADPROPLIB_.DEFER value. Specifying LOADPROPLIB_.DEFER defers loading of the property library until **LoadPropertySheets** is called and automatically unloads the library when **FreePropertySheets** is called. **LoadPropertySheets** and **FreePropertySheets** may be called directly by an application or indirectly when an application calls the **EditProperties** function. When a deferred library is loaded, its initialization handler must call **AddPropertySheet** for all the sheets to be added. When the deferred library is unloaded, its Windows exit procedure (WEP) handler must call **RemovePropertySheet** for all added sheets if it has not already freed them.

LoadPropertySheets

```
int LoadPropertySheets(int hProps, int flags)
```

Loads all property sheets for the .PIF file identified by the given properties handle.

- Returns the number of sheets loaded if successful or zero otherwise.

hProps
Properties handle. It must have been created previously by using the **OpenProperties** function.

flags
Reserved; must be zero.

OpenProperties

```
int OpenProperties(LPSTR lpszApp, LPSTR lpszPIF, int hInf, int flOpt)
```

Opens the .PIF file associated with the given application and returns a properties handle that identifies the property information for the application.

▪   Returns a properties handle if successful. If the .PIF file cannot be opened or there is insufficient memory to load the PIF data, the function returns FALSE.

lpszApp
    Address of a null-terminated string specifying the filename of an MS-DOS– based application.

lpszPIF
    Address of a null-terminated string specifying a new PIF filename to create. If the file is created successfully, the returned properties handle operates on that file. Any .PIF file for the specified MS-DOS–based application that exists in the PIF directory or on the path is still opened and read to obtain the initial set of properties to be stored in the new .PIF file.

hInf
    Information handle. This parameter can be zero if no information handle is needed or −1 to prevent information processing. If zero is specified, the APPS.INF file is used by default.

flOpt
    Operations flag. This parameter can be the OPENPROPS_RAWIO value to open the .PIF file for raw file input and output (I/O) or zero to open the file for standard access.

The function loads the content of the given .PIF file into memory and then closes the file, preserving the contents in memory until the properties handle is closed. If the given .PIF file does not exist, the function allocates memory and loads it with default PIF data. This function fails if there is insufficient memory for the PIF data or the given .PIF file exists but cannot be opened.

RemovePropertySheet

```
BOOL RemovePropertySheet(int hSheet)
```

Removes a property sheet.

- Returns TRUE if successful or FALSE otherwise.

hSheet
> Property sheet handle. It must have been previously created by using the **AddPropertySheet** function.

SetProperties

```
int SetProperties(int hProps, LPSTR lpszGroup, LPVOID lpProps,
    int cbProps, int flOpt)
```

Sets property information for the given group, removes the given group from the .PIF file, or writes raw data to the .PIF file.

- Returns the number of information bytes written to the .PIF file if successful. If the group does not exist or an error occurs, the function returns zero.

hProps
> Properties handle. It must have been previously opened by using the **OpenProperties** function.

lpszGroup
> Group ordinal or address of a null-terminated string specifying the name of the property group. If a name is given, it must be the name of a valid PIF extension or one of these predefined names:

> | | |
> |---|---|
> | MICROSOFT PIFEX | WINDOWS 386 3.0 |
> | WINDOWS 286 3.0 | WINDOWS VMM 4.0 |

> If a group ordinal is given, it can be one of these predefined ordinals:

> | | |
> |---|---|
> | GROUP_ENV | GROUP_PRG |
> | GROUP_KBD | GROUP_TSK |
> | GROUP_MEM | GROUP_VID |
> | GROUP_MSE | GROUP_WIN |

> The ordinal must be in the low-order word, and zero must be in the high-order word.

lpProps

Address of the buffer that contains the property information to write to the .PIF file.

cbProps

Size, in bytes, of the information pointed to by *lpProps*. If *cbProps* is zero and *lpszGroup* is not NULL, the function removes the given group from the .PIF file.

flOpt

Operations flag. This parameter can be one of these values:

0	Writes information to the given group.
SETPROPS_RAWIO	Writes data to the .PIF file as if it were a single, unformatted block. (The *lpszGroup* parameter is ignored).
SETPROPS_CACHE	Caches changes until properties are closed by using the **CloseProperties** function.

Structure

The following structure is used with program information file management.

PROPSHEETPAGE

```
typedef struct _PROPSHEETPAGE {
    DWORD   dwSize;            // size of structure, in bytes
    DWORD   dwFlags;          // see below
    HINSTANCE hInstance;      // instance handle for template
    union {
        LPCSTR  pszTemplate;        // resource name of template
        const VOID FAR *pResource;  // address of resource in memory
    };
    union {
        HICON       hIcon;   // icon handle
        LPCSTR      pszIcon; // icon name or identifier
    };
    LPCSTR      pszTitle;   // string or string identifier
    DLGPROC     pfnDlgProc; // address of dialog box procedure
    LPARAM      lParam;     // user data
    LPFNRELEASEPROPSHEETPAGE pfnRelease; // see below
    UINT FAR * pcRefParent; // address of ref count variable
} PROPSHEETPAGE, FAR *LPPROPSHEETPAGE;
```

Contains information about the property sheet.

dwFlags

Flags identifying which members contain valid values. This member can be a combination of these values:

PSP_DEFAULT	The **pszTemplate** member contains address of resource template name. The **pResource** member is not valid. The **hIcon**, **pszIcon**, **pfnRelease**, and **pcRefParent** members are not used.
PSP_DLGINDIRECT	The **pResource** member contains address of a dialog box template in memory. The **pszTemplate** member is not valid.
PSP_USEICON	The **hIcon** member contains a valid icon handle. The **pszIcon** member is not valid.
PSP_USEICONID	The **pszIcon** member contains the address of a valid resource name or resource identifier. The **hIcon** member is not valid.
PSP_USERELEASEFUNC	The **pfnRelease** member has the address of the function to call before releasing the property sheet.
PSP_USERREFPARENT	The **pcRefParent** member contains the address of the variable to the receive reference count.

pfnRelease

Address of the release function. The operating system calls this function before destroying the given property sheet.

A R T I C L E   2 7

Virtual Machine Services

About Virtual Machine Services

Virtual machine services allow Microsoft® MS-DOS®–based applications to take advantage of features provided by Microsoft® Windows® 95 when the applications run in a window. MS-DOS–based applications can retrieve and, optionally, set the title of the window in which they run.

This article describes the virtual machine services and shows how to use them in MS-DOS–based applications.

Window Title

The window title for an MS-DOS–based application, which is displayed when the application runs in a window, identifies the application and its operating state. The operating system sets the title when an application first starts, but the application can change portions of the title to better communicate its state to the user.

The window title consists of three strings: a virtual machine state, a virtual machine title, and an application title. The system creates the window title by concatenating the three strings, separating the strings with a system-defined separator, typically a hyphen.

The virtual machine state, which can be set by the operating system only, identifies whether the virtual machine is inactive or whether the user is carrying out tasks, such as cut and paste operations. The state is frequently an empty string. The virtual machine title and the application title, which can be set by an application, identify the application and the current document or activity of the application, respectively.

By default, the operating system sets the virtual machine title to the title stored in the corresponding .PIF file or to a title specified by the shell. You can determine the current virtual machine title by using the Get Virtual Machine Title function. You can change the title by using the Set Virtual Machine Title function.

The system typically sets the application title to the name of the application, so the virtual machine title and application title are frequently the same when the application first starts. Many applications change this title to the name of the current document or to an empty string if there is no current document. You can determine the current application title by using the Get Application Title function. You can change the title by using the Set Application Title function.

If you set the virtual machine title or application title, the length of the individual titles must not exceed 30 and 80 characters, respectively.

You can call the window title functions at any time. Furthermore, you can call these functions regardless of whether your application is running with the Windows 95 or MS-DOS operating system. However, not all operating systems support these calls. The functions are not supported if a call to a function leaves the AX register unchanged.

Close-Aware Applications

A close-aware application is any MS-DOS–based application that periodically checks the state of an internal close flag and terminates if the flag is set. Windows 95 sets this flag when the user chooses the Close command from the system menu of the window in which the MS-DOS–based application runs. Close-aware applications enable the Close command, which gives the user an alternate way to exit the application and close the window.

An application enables or disables the Close command by using the Enable or Disable Close Command function. The function takes a flag indicating whether to enable or disable the command. Once the command is enabled, the application must periodically check the close flag by using the Query Close function. The function returns zero in the AX register if the user has chosen the command.

If the Query Close function returns zero in AX, the application should call the Acknowledge Close function to acknowledge the close state of the internal close flag. After the application acknowledges the close state, subsequent calls to the Query Close function will return 1 in AX, indicating that the user has chosen the Close command and the close state has been acknowledged. After acknowledging the close state, an application should take all necessary steps to shut down and eventually exit, or it should cancel the close operation by calling the Cancel Close function.

An application should acknowledge the close state if it needs to perform additional keyboard input before exiting. When the close state has been signaled but has not yet been acknowledged by the application, all keyboard reads will return NULL and buffered line input will return an empty string.

After an application acknowledges the close state, the state changes back to unacknowledged if the application either exits or cancels the close operation. If the application acknowledges the close state and then exits, the parent process will be in an unacknowledged close state. The application must then acknowledge the close state to perform additional keyboard input before exiting or canceling the close operation.

For example, if a text editor receives a positive response from the Query Close function and has some buffers that have not been saved, it should call Acknowledge Close and ask the user if the buffers should be saved with these possible responses: "Yes," "No," or "Cancel."

If the user responds "Yes" or "No," the text editor should save (or not save if the response was "No") the buffers and then exit. The close state remains active, and the parent process (probably the command interpreter) will also receive a positive response from Query Close and will also terminate.

If the response is "Cancel," the application should call the Cancel Close function and not exit. Canceling the close operation informs the system that any attempted shutdown should be abandoned.

This sequence of operations is analogous to the way that Windows-based applications handle the WM_QUERYENDSESSION message.

Depending on the tasking option chosen for the application, there may be some time between when the user chooses the Close command and the application checks the internal close flag. During this time, the system changes the window title of the application, appending the word "Closing" to it, and gives the user the opportunity to cancel the command by changing the command name to Cancel Close. If the user chooses the Cancel Close command, the close flag is reset, preventing the application from closing. If a close-aware application fails to check the close flag within a system-defined amount of time, the system automatically abandons the operation and resets the close flag.

The system tracks the close-awareness and close state for each process. For the virtual machine to close, all applications in the virtual machine must close. When the user chooses the Close command, the operating system detects applications that are not close-aware and displays a dialog box with a warning message, but gives the user the option of forcing the application to exit anyway. If you make an application close-aware, it can shut down cleanly.

Reference

The following functions and commands are associated with virtual machine services.

Window Title Functions

The following window title functions are used with virtual machine services.

Get Application Title

```
mov   ah, 16h            ; Windows multiplex function
mov   al, 8Eh            ; VM Title
mov   di, seg AppTitle   ; see below
mov   es, di
mov   di, offset AppTitle
mov   cx, Size           ; see below
mov   dx, 2              ; Get Application Title
int   2Fh
cmp   ax, 1
je    success
```

Copies the application title to the specified buffer.

- Returns 1 in the AX register if successful or zero otherwise.

AppTitle
Address of a buffer that receives the application title. This parameter must not be zero.

Size
Size, in bytes, of the buffer pointed to by *AppTitle*.

Get Application Title copies as much of the title as possible, but never more than the specified number of bytes. The function always appends a terminating null character to the title in the buffer.

Get Virtual Machine Title

```
mov   ah, 16h           ; Windows multiplex function
mov   al, 8Eh           ; VM Title
mov   di, seg VMTitle   ; see below
mov   es, di
mov   di, offset VMTitle
mov   cx, Size          ; see below
mov   dx, 3             ; Get Virtual Machine Title
int   2Fh
cmp   ax, 1
je    success
```

Copies the virtual machine title to the specified buffer.

- Returns 1 in the AX register if successful or zero otherwise.

VMTitle
    Address of a buffer that receives the virtual machine title. This parameter must not be zero.

Size
    Size, in bytes, of the buffer pointed to by *VMTitle*.

Get Virtual Machine Title copies as much of the title as possible, but never more than the specified number of bytes. The function always appends a terminating null character to the title in the buffer.

Set Application Title

```
mov   ah, 16h           ; Windows multiplex function
mov   al, 8Eh           ; VM Title
mov   di, seg AppTitle  ; see below
mov   es, di
mov   di, offset AppTitle
mov   dx, 0             ; Set Application Title
int   2Fh
cmp   ax, 1
je    success
```

Sets the application title to the given string.

- Returns 1 in the AX register if successful or zero otherwise.

AppTitle

>Address of a null-terminated string specifying the application title. The title must not exceed 80 characters, including the terminating null character. If this parameter is zero or points to an empty string, the function removes the current application title.

Although not common, Set Application Title may return 1 in the AX register even though the title was not changed. In general, applications must not rely on the operating system to keep an accurate copy of the current title.

Set Virtual Machine Title

```
mov   ah, 16h           ; Windows multiplex function
mov   al, 8Eh           ; VM Title
mov   di, seg VMTitle   ; see below
mov   es, di
mov   di, offset VMTitle
mov   dx, 1             ; Set Virtual Machine Title
int   2Fh
cmp   ax, 1
je    success
```

Sets the virtual machine title to the given string. Applications should not change the virtual machine title except under explicit instructions from the user.

- Returns 1 in the AX register if successful or zero otherwise.

VMTitle

>Address of a null-terminated string specifying the virtual machine title. The title must not exceed 30 characters, including the terminating null character. If this parameter is zero or points to an empty string, the function removes the current virtual machine title.

Although not common, Set Virtual Machine Title may return 1 in the AX register even though the title was not changed. In general, applications must not rely on the operating system to keep an accurate copy of the current title.

Close-Aware Application Functions

The following close-aware application functions are used with virtual machine services.

Acknowledge Close

```
mov ah, 16h    ; Windows multiplex function
mov al, 8Fh    ; VM Close
mov dh, 2       ; Acknowledge Close
mov dl, 0       ; always 0
int 2Fh
or ax, ax
jz success
```

Acknowledges the close state of the internal close flag.

- Returns zero in the AX register if successful.

Acknowledging the close state is necessary if an application needs to perform additional keyboard input before exiting. If the close state has been signaled but not yet acknowledged by an application, all keyboard read operations will return NULL and buffered line input will return an empty string.

Cancel Close

```
mov ah, 16h    ; Windows multiplex function
mov al, 8Fh    ; VM Close
mov dh, 3       ; Cancel Close
mov dl, 0       ; always 0
int 2Fh
or ax, ax
jz success
```

Cancels the close operation.

- Returns zero in the AX register if successful.

After acknowledging the close state of the internal close flag, an application should either exit or cancel the close operation by calling Cancel Close.

Enable or Disable Close Command

```
mov ah, 16h     ; Windows multiplex function
mov al, 8Fh     ; VM Close
mov dh, 0       ; Enable or Disable Close Command
mov dl, Flags   ; see below
int 2Fh
or ax, ax
jz success
```

Enables or disables the Close command in the system menu.

- Returns zero in the AX register if successful.

Flags

Close flags. This parameter can be one of these values:

00h   Disables the Close command.

01h   Enables the Close command.

Query Close

```
mov ah, 16h     ; Windows multiplex function
mov al, 8Fh     ; VM Close
mov dh, 1       ; Query Close
mov dl, 0       ; always 0
int 2Fh
```

Indicates whether the user has attempted to close an MS-DOS–based application from Windows by choosing the Close command from the system menu.

- Returns one of the following values in the AX register:

0	The close command was chosen, and the application has not acknowledged the close state.
1	The close command was chosen, and the application has acknowledged the close state.
168Fh	The close command has not been chosen, and the application should continue running.

Query Close returns a nonzero value if the application has not enabled the Close command by using the Enable or Disable Close Command function.

P A R T   6

Applications for International Markets

A R T I C L E   2 8

International Guidelines

About International Guidelines

This article is a reference guide to help developers write modules or applications that can be localized and that take full advantage of the Microsoft® Windows® 95 international environment.

Windows 95 Platform Strategy

Windows 95 is available in many different languages. The languages and the rules associated with them can be divided into these three groups:

- Western/Eastern European languages, such as German, French, and Russian. These languages use an 8-bit character set and are written from left to right. In this article, these languages are called "WE" languages.

- Middle-Eastern languages, such as Hebrew and Arabic. These languages use an 8-bit character set and are written from both left to right and right to left. In this article, these languages are called "ME" languages.

- Far-Eastern languages, such as Japanese and Chinese. These languages use a 16-bit character set (also referred to as a double-byte character set or DBCS) and are written from left to right or top to bottom. In this article, these languages are called "FE" languages.

Windows 95 is a multiple character-set system, which means you can use more than one character set at a time. To accommodate the text management rules associated with WE, ME, and FE languages, Windows 95 uses a three-platform strategy that can be summarized in the following manner.

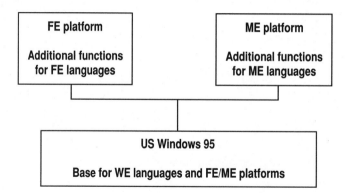

WE Platform

The WE platform (U.S. Windows 95) is the code base of Windows 95. It supports all WE languages and the rules associated with them, and it includes application programming interface (API) elements and other mechanisms for manipulating these languages. The WE platform is also the base on which the ME and FE platforms are built. Applications built for the WE platform can also run on the ME and FE platforms, but they can not take advantage of functions written specifically for those platforms.

The WE platform will be localized in the following languages: German, French, Spanish, Swedish, Dutch, Italian, Norwegian, Danish, Finnish, Portuguese (Brazil), Portuguese (Portugal), Russian, Czech, Polish, Hungarian, Turkish, Greek, and Catalan.

ME Platform

The ME platform is built on the WE platform. It includes the API elements and other mechanisms found in the WE platform. It also includes additional API elements specifically designed to support ME languages. To take full advantage of the ME platform, an application must use the additional API elements and may need to be recompiled.

The ME platform will be localized in the Arabic and Hebrew languages.

FE Platform

The FE platform is built on the WE platform. It includes the API elements and other mechanisms found in the WE platform. It also includes additional API elements specifically designed to support FE languages. To take full advantage of the FE platform, an application must use the additional API elements and may need to be recompiled.

The FE platform will be localized in the Japanese, Chinese (Traditional), Chinese (Simplified), and Korean languages.

International Language Requirements

This section is divided into three subsections: localization, national language support functions, and multilingual content support. Each subsection describes a set of rules that you should follow when writing Windows 95 modules or applications for international audiences.

Localization

Certain rules should be followed so that Windows 95 modules or applications can be translated into different languages. For example, you should use resources for all elements to be localized, including strings, messages, icons, and so on.

General Programming Guidelines

You should follow these general programming guidelines when writing applications for international audiences:

- Do not store handles or identifiers in resources.
- Do not shift resource identifiers when adding resources to a file. Instead, just add an identifier (allowing no duplicate identifiers).
- Do not store user interface elements (strings, messages, menus, and so on) in initialization (.INI) files.
- Use the **FormatMessage** function to dynamically allocate buffer sizes for your Microsoft® Win32®–based applications. For more information, see the description of **FormatMessage**.
- Do not hard code filenames into a binary file. Windows 95 modules or applications may use long filenames, and these filenames appear on the desktop. Because the filenames are visible to the user, they may need to be translated. Windows 95–based modules or applications should be able to be renamed without requiring any code change.

Guidelines for Using Strings

You should follow these guidelines when using strings in applications for international audiences:

- Do not concatenate strings in dialog box controls. Doing so can create a string that crosses a character set boundary. For example, setting a control's text to be the result of "Can not find %s" will create a string that does not make sense if the user types in Greek in an application with English resources. You should use two controls instead of one in this situation.

- Use *%numbers* instead of *%letters* when using a string with variables in case translators and localizers need to invert the variables. The wrong and right approaches follow.

  WRONG   "The file type %s on the drive %s should first be
               copied to the drive %s."

  RIGHT   "The file type %1 on the drive %2 should first be
               copied to the drive %3."

- Do not allow English text strings to use more than 70 percent of the available space in dialog boxes. Providing extra space ensures that a translated string will not exceed the length limit. An English string of 240 characters will sometimes result in a localized string of 300 characters. In a dialog box where the string limit is 256 characters, incomplete and improper localization will appear. In general, if a string that must be localized exceeds 70 percent of the limit, it should be split into two parts.

National Language Support Functions

Windows 95 includes a set of functions that allows Windows 95–based modules or applications to find and use locale-dependent information. A locale is a collection of user-preference information related to the user's language and sublanguage, represented as a list of values. The system has one default locale, but an application can also get locale information that is specific to an application or task. To take advantage of this feature, an application must use the National Language Support (NLS) functions described in the Microsoft Win32 Software Development Kit (SDK).

Multilingual Content Support

Windows 95 includes multilingual content support for documents, which means that Windows 95 applications can mix characters from different character sets in the same document. For example, an application can mix Greek and German in the same document, even though characters for these languages belong to two different character sets. This feature makes Windows 95 a multiple character set (or multiple code page) operating system.

The basic multilingual architecture is based on languages, especially keyboard languages. A user can create a list of keyboard languages from the set of all keyboard languages available. The system can be started with one language active, and the additional selected languages loaded and available. When the user switches from one language to another, a WM_INPUTLANGCHANGE message is sent to the application with the focus to indicate that the language has changed. The message includes the handle of the new keyboard layout (language) and character. The application can then use the information to determine whether the locale has changed and whether the character set has changed.

To take full advantage of multilingual content support, you should not assume that the character set is U.S. ANSI. Many "ANSI" character sets are available today. For example, Russian Windows 95 uses the "Cyrillic ANSI" character set, which is different from the one used by U.S. Windows 95 (U.S. ANSI). In addition, you should always use the Choose Font common dialog box. If that is not possible, you should use the **EnumFontFamiliesEx** function. Finally, you should always save the character set with the font names in documents and process multilingual Windows messages, including WM_INPUTLANGCHANGEREQUEST and WM_INPUTLANGCHANGE. They either request that the keyboard language be changed or indicate that a the keyboard language has changed.

Note   You should store the character set and keyboard layout of the next run of text when your application receives the WM_INPUTLANGCHANGEREQUEST or WM_INPUTLANGCHANGE message. You should also modify your Find or Search dialog boxes or algorithms so that they support multilingual search and replace operations. In addition, any headers, footers, and other peripheral annotations should be able to handle different fonts and languages.

After the keyboard language has changed, you should use the following API elements:

- Determine whether the character set has changed by using the *wParam* parameter from the WM_INPUTLANGCHANGE message.

- Select a new font by using **EnumFontFamiliesEx** function if the character set has changed.

- Use the "Ex" versions of keyboard functions—for example, **ToAsciiEx** instead of **ToAscii**.

- Use the CR_ formats with the **SetClipboardData** function when placing text on the clipboard and with the **GetClipboardData** function when getting text from the clipboard.

- Use the **GetCharacterPlacement** and **GetFontLanguageInfo** functions when drawing text, calculating caret positions, or performing any other action related to a device. The functions provide intermediate information that make caret placement easier and allow the application to take advantage of new features in graphics device interface (GDI). They also ensure the application is compatible across all three platforms. Even if you write your application for non-ME and non-FE platforms, using **GetFontLanguageInfo** allows you to detect when the user tries to use one of the ME or FE fonts and allows you to prevent the user from producing strange text on the screen and printer.

For more information about multilingual content and support, see the reference pages for the functions and messages mentioned in this section.

Using the Far-Eastern Platform

For your Windows 95–based module or application to run on the FE platform, you must enable your module or application to use double-byte characters by using the **CharNext**, **CharPrev**, and **IsDBCSLeadByte** functions. For information about double-byte characters enabling, see Article 29, "Using Double-Byte Characters." You should also enable your module to use the IMM (Input Method Manager) functions and modify your application to interact with an IME (Input Method Editor), so the user will be able to use Far-Eastern characters. For information about FE enabling, see Article 30, "Using Input Method Editors."

Using the Middle-Eastern Platform

You should follow certain guidelines to enable your Windows 95–based module or application to run on the ME platform:

- Use the Windows 95 functions. There are no specific ME functions. All of the functions for writing ME-based software are built into the basic Windows 95 code, and all the items mentioned under "Multilingual Content Support" earlier in this article are also relevant. However, for standard left to right languages, these features are desirable, but not necessary.

- Call the **GetCharacterPlacement** function to provide line layout support for getting the visual orientation, character widths, and character placement required for laying out and displaying any single-byte character text.

- Call the **GetFontLanguageInfo** function to determine which services are required for a particular language. The main difference between ME and WE languages is that the text may be oriented to the right of the page instead of to the left. This means you need some form of user interface for switching direction, and you need the ability to write text from right to left instead of left to right. You can achieve this by using the **SetTextAlign** function.

- Use the ME-specific window styles and common control styles. If you have enabled your application to run using ME resources (for example, right to left menus), you must also modify calls to functions, such as **MessageBox** and **CreateWindow**, to use the ME-specific flags (for example, to allow right to left orientation of menus). If a particular window class has no specific right to left style, like the button class, use extended window styles, such as WS_EX_RTLREADING and WS_EX_RIGHT.

For more information about ME enabling, see Article 31, "Writing Applications for Middle-Eastern Languages."

ARTICLE 29

Using Double-Byte Characters

About Using Double-Byte Characters

String operations in applications running with an operating system that uses a double-byte character set (DBCS) are slightly different from those in applications running with a system that uses a single-byte character set. A DBCS-enabled application allows users to create, edit, print, and save documents in their own languages, even if the user interface has not been localized. DBCS enabling involves adding code to handle DBCS strings, which are made up of a mixture of 1-byte and 2-byte characters. For example, a user could run an English version of a DBCS-enabled application with a Japanese version of Microsoft® Windows®, freely typing in and editing kanji strings without any problem. This article provides guidelines to reduce the work necessary to port an application written for a single-byte character set system (SBCS) to a DBCS system.

DBCS enabling is only one step in internationalizing an application. For more information about DBCS and other internationalization issues, see *Developing International Software for Microsoft Windows* by Nadine Kano, available through Microsoft Press®.

Code Pages

Accented characters are an integral part of many languages. However, the 7-bit ASCII character set does not provide support for accented characters. To compensate, Microsoft® MS-DOS® uses 8-bit *code pages* as a means of providing support for character sets and keyboard layouts used in different countries. Each code page table relates the binary character codes used by an application to keys on the keyboard or to the appearance of characters on the display.

Over the years, support for code pages that include different accented characters has been added to MS-DOS. In each code page, the characters numbered 32 through 127 are the same characters that form the 7-bit ASCII set. The characters above 127, known as extended characters, vary from code page to code page. The set of extended characters, which contains accented characters, determines which languages the code page can support.

Microsoft Windows 95 uses the same type of code pages introduced in Windows version 3.1. These code pages are different from the ones used in MS-DOS. For example, the line-drawing characters that allow MS-DOS–based applications to draw boxes have not been included in Windows code pages and have been replaced with additional publishing characters.

Double-Byte Character Sets

The Chinese language defines more than 10,000 basic *ideographic* characters. Each ideographic character represents a word or syllable, and many of these characters were adapted long ago by other Far-Eastern languages. These characters are called *kanji* in Japanese, *hantsu* or *hanzi* in Chinese, and *hanja* in Korean. Because there are so many ideographic characters, single-byte character sets, which have room for only 256 characters, are too small to accommodate those languages.

The solution used in Windows 95 (and in earlier versions of Windows) has been to encode most characters (primarily ideographs) with 2-byte values, making many more than 256 characters available. However, characters, such as the ASCII set, the Japanese phonetic syllabary known as *katakana*, and some symbols still have single-byte representations. The result is a code page that mixes 1-byte and 2-byte characters. Double-byte character sets typically contain a mixture of 1-byte and 2-byte characters.

The mixing of byte lengths in Far-Eastern versions of Windows leads to more complex string parsing code. Each 2-byte character is composed of a *lead byte* and a *trail byte*, which must be stored together and manipulated as a unit. A lead byte value always falls into one or more ranges above 127. Although 1-byte characters may be defined above 127, they cannot exist in the lead byte ranges. NULL can never be a trail byte, but the range of possible trail bytes can overlap to some degree with the ASCII character set. Lead byte values are frequently indistinguishable from trail byte values; the only way to tell the difference is from the context of the surrounding characters. For that reason, if a trail byte is taken without its lead byte, it can be mistaken for a 1-byte character.

Because 1-byte characters are displayed in half the width of 2-byte characters for most fonts on Far-Eastern versions of Windows, they are sometimes referred to as half-width characters. Most half-width characters also have a full-width (2-byte) representation to make column layout on a display easier. Ideographic characters exist only in full-width form; there is, for example, no such thing as a 1-byte kanji character. In Windows 95, ASCII characters can be drawn with proportional fonts, but ideographic characters, including Japanese kanji, are always monospaced.

Using Double-Byte Characters in an Application

To handle 2-byte characters, you should have any code that searches, selects, edits, moves, replaces, deletes, or inserts text check for double-byte pairs. An application should not split 2-byte characters and should accommodate 2-byte characters in its display operations. Rules of selection, cursor placement, and cursor movement are the same as for alphabetic characters; the cursor should always end up between characters, never in the middle of one.

Because 1- and 2-byte characters can be mixed, it is not safe to use unary operators, such as ++ or - -, which increment or decrement string pointers one byte at a time instead of a character at a time. These operators can be replaced with the Microsoft® Win32® **CharNext** and **CharPrev** functions (or the **AnsiNext** and **AnsiPrev** functions used in Windows version 3.*x*). These functions increment string pointers properly whether the current character is a single byte or a double byte.

In addition, it is not safe to access a string with 2-byte characters randomly in the following manner.

```
Mychar = string[i]
```

Unless a string is searched from the beginning, there is no way of knowing if the byte accessed is a single byte, lead byte, or trail byte.

For string processing, it is often important to determine if a byte is a lead byte. The **IsDBCSLeadByte** function can be used to test whether a particular byte is in the default code page's lead byte range, and the **IsDBCSLeadByteEx** function can be used to check the lead byte range of a specified code page. The following example shows how to search for a backslash ('\') character in a DBCS string by using **IsDBCSLeadByte**.

```
// Returns a pointer to the first '\' in a given string.
char* GetBackSlash( char *pszString)
{
 while(*pszString)
 {
     if (!IsDBCSLeadByte(*pszString))
     {
         if (*pszString == '\\')
             break;
     }
     else // it is a lead byte
     {
         // Increment the pointer 1 byte to point to the trail byte.
         pszString++;
     }
     // Increment the pointer 1 byte to point to the next character.
     pszString++;
 }
 return( pszString);
}
```

Although **IsDBCSLeadByte** and **IsDBCSLeadByteEx** are convenient, calls to these functions may impact performance if you have a large number of bytes to test. As an alternative, you can check the ranges yourself by calling the **GetCPInfo** function, which returns the lead byte ranges in the **LeadByte** member of the **CPINFO** structure. **LeadByte** is an array of bytes. Each range, which consists of two bytes, specifies a starting and ending value for the range. Ranges are inclusive, and there can be a maximum of five ranges. Any unused bytes in **LeadByte** are set to zero.

To further optimize your code, you should only call DBCS functions or special string handling code when using a DBCS code page. There are several methods of doing this. For example, an application can determine whether it is running on a DBCS system at run time by using **GetCPInfo** in its initialization code. **GetCPInfo** returns the maximum number of bytes for a character in the code page in the **MaxCharSize** member of the **CPINFO** structure. The advantage of this method is that it requires having only one executable file.

Another method is to use a DBCS command-line option at compile time and bracket sections of string handling code with **#ifdef** directives. The number of **#ifdef** blocks can be greatly reduced by defining the following macros.

```
#ifndef DBCS
#define CharNext(pc)     ((*pc) ? pc + 1 : pc)
#define CharPrev(pcStart, pc) ((pc > pcStart) ? \
                                    pc - 1 : pcStart)

#ifndef WIN32
#define IsDBCSLeadByte (bByte) (FALSE)
#endif
#endif
```

A R T I C L E   3 0

Using Input Method Editors

About Using Input Method Editors

In Asian versions of Microsoft® Windows® 95, an input method editor (IME) allows users to generate single- and double-byte characters by typing at the keyboard. By default, Windows 95 carries out all actions required to enable the user to generate characters for input to your application. However, you can also customize this process by using input method manager (IMM) functions to carry out actions on your own. This article shows some simple ways to customize the operation of an IME for your application. For more information about the IMM functions, see the documentation included in the Microsoft® Win32® Software Development Kit (SDK).

Handling Character Input

You receive character input from an IME in the form of WM_CHAR or WM_IME_CHAR messages. Windows 95 provides a default IME that automatically displays a status window enabling users to choose the conversion mode and other properties for generating single- and double-byte characters for the current application. (Users can also purchase third-party IMEs that may have additional capabilities.)

Depending on the conversion mode, an IME provides a composition window into which the user types the initial characters and a candidates window from which the user picks the final character(s). Selecting the final character causes the IME to send either one or two WM_CHAR messages to the window procedure for the application.

You can use the **IsDBCSLeadByte** function to determine whether the character in a WM_CHAR message is the first byte of a double-byte character. If it is, the next WM_CHAR message contains the second byte. Once you have both bytes, you can display the character by using a function such as **ExtTextOut**.

In some cases, you may receive WM_IME_CHAR messages from the IME. The *wParam* parameter of this message contains one or two bytes, depending on the user's final selection. To determine the size of the character, you need to use the **IsDBCSLeadByte** function in the following manner.

```
WORD wChar;

case WM_IME_CHAR:
    wChar = (WORD) wParam;
    if (IsDBCSLeadByte(HIBYTE(wChar) == TRUE)
        // wChar is a double-byte character.
    else
        // wChar is a single-byte character.
    break;
```

If you choose not to handle the WM_IME_CHAR message, you can pass it to the **DefWindowProc** function. This function converts the message into one or two WM_CHAR messages and sends them to your window procedure.

Managing the IME

You manage the IME by enabling (opening) it for conversions, setting the conversion modes, and positioning the composition window. By default, the IME opens when the user chooses a conversion mode from the status window, and the IME displays the composition window when the user begins to type. You can change this default behavior by using the **ImmSetOpenStatus**, **ImmSetConversionStatus**, and **ImmSetCompositionWindow** functions.

You open the IME when you want to allow users to enter characters for conversion. You can determine whether the IME is currently open by by using the **ImmGetOpenStatus** function. If it is not, you can open the IME by using the **ImmSetOpenStatus** function as follows.

```
HIMC hIMC;
BOOL bOpen;

if (hIMC = ImmGetContext(hwnd)){
    bOpen = ImmGetOpenStatus(hIMC);
    if (!bOpen)
        ImmSetOpenStatus(hIMC, TRUE);
    ImmReleaseContext(hwnd,hIMC);
}
```

Once you open the IME, the composition window opens as soon as the user begins to type in the window associated with the input context. By default, the composition is displayed as a pop-up window placed near the window having the input focus. You can change this default position and appearance by using the **ImmSetCompositionWindow** function. The following example shows how to embed the composition window into the current line of text (similar to edit controls) by using the CFS_POINT style.

```
HIMC hIMC;
COMPOSITIONFORM cf;

if (hIMC = ImmGetContext(hwnd)){
    cf.dwStyle = CFS_POINT;
    cf.ptCurrentPos.x = ptCurrent.x;
    cf.ptCurrentPos.y = ptCurrent.y;
    ImmSetCompositionWindow(hIMC, &cf);
    ImmReleaseContext(hWnd,hIMC);
}
```

In this example, the **ptCurrent** member contains the coordinates of the caret in the window identified by the *hwnd* parameter. The function places the composition window at that position, and characters that the user types appear there.

Once the user starts typing, the IME converts and displays the characters using the current conversion and sentence modes. The user typically sets the modes through the status window, but you can set them as well by using the **ImmSetConversionStatus** function. In most cases, it is best to retrieve and change the current modes by using both the **ImmGetConversionStatus** and **ImmSetConversionStatus** functions in the following manner.

```
HIMC hIMC;
DWORD dwConvMode, dwSentence;

if (hIMC = ImmGetContext(hWnd)){
    // Get the current modes.
    ImmGetConversionStatus(hIMC, &fdwConversion, &fdwSentence);
    // Change to full shape input mode.
    fdwConversion |= IME_CMODE_FULLSHAPE;
    // Set the new modes.
    ImmSetConversionStatus(hIMC, fdwConversion, fdwSentence);
    ImmReleaseContext(hWnd,hIMC);
}
```

Managing the IME Window

Windows 95 creates an IME window for each thread in an application. The IME window, belonging to the system-defined "IME" window class, creates and owns the status, composition, and candidates windows that give users the means to control the conversion of characters. The IME window carries out default processing for the status, composition, and candidates windows for the application, so changing the IME window changes those windows too.

You can control the position and style of the status, composition, and candidates windows directly by using functions such as **ImmSetStatusWindow**, **ImmSetCompositionWindow**, and **ImmSetCandidateWindow**. You can also control the windows indirectly be sending WM_IME_CONTROL messages to the IME window. You can retrieve the handle of the IME window by using the **ImmGetDefaultIMEWnd** function.

The following example shows how to create an IME window by using the "IME" window class in a call to the **CreateWindowEx** function.

```
hwndIME = CreateWindowEx(
    0,
    "IME",                      // IME class
    NULL,                       // no window title
    WS_DISABLED | WS_POPUP,     // disabled window
    0, 0, 0, 0,                 // no need to set size
    hwnd,                       // owner window
    NULL,
    hinstance,
    NULL);
```

If your application does not process character input from the keyboard, you can close an IME window by retrieving the handle and passing it to the **DestroyWindow** function.

Monitoring the Composition

You can monitor the user's interaction with the status, composition, and candidates windows by processing WM_IME_NOTIFY and WM_IME_COMPOSITION messages. The IME sends these messages to the window having the input focus whenever the user carries out some action in one of the IME windows.

WM_IME_NOTIFY is useful for monitoring changes that the user makes through the status window. For example, the IME sends this message with the IMN_SETCONVERSIONMODE value when the user changes modes in the status window. When you receive this message, you can determine the new conversion and sentence modes by using the **ImmGetConversionStatus** function.

WM_IME_NOTIFY is also useful for monitoring selections made by the user in the candidates window. The IME sends this message with the IMN_CHANGECANDIDATE value when the user changes the selection. When you receive this message, you can use the **ImmGetCandidateList** function to retrieve the list of candidates and the index of the current selection.

WM_IME_COMPOSITION is useful for monitoring input and conversions made in the composition window. The IME sends this message whenever the user types a character. When you receive this message, you can use the **ImmGetCompositionString** function, as shown in the following example, to retrieve the characters typed by the user or the converted characters proposed by the IME.

```
HIMC hIMC;
char szComp[256];
DWORD dwSize;

case WM_IME_COMPOSITION:
    if ((hIMC = ImmGetContext(hwnd)) == NULL)
        break;

    // Get the composition string.
    dwSize = ImmGetCompositionString(hIMC, GCS_COMPSTR, szComp, 256);

    ImmReleaseContext(hWnd,hIMC);
    break;
```

The IME sets the *lParam* parameter in WM_IME_COMPOSITION to the GCS_RESULTSTR value when the user completes the composition. The following example shows how to retrieve the final result of the conversion by using **ImmGetCompositionString**.

```
HIMC hIMC:
LPSTR lpstr;
DWORD dwSize;

case WM_IME_COMPOSITION:
    if (!(lParam & GCS_RESULTSTR))
        break;

    // Get the context.
    if ((hIMC = ImmGetContext(hwnd)) == NULL)
        break;

    // Get the result string size, and add 1 for the terminating
    // null character.
    dwSize = ImmGetCompositionString(hIMC, GCS_RESULTSTR, NULL, 0);
```

```
                    // Allocate memory to receive the string.
                    if ((lpstr = GlobalAlloc(GPTR, dwSize)) == NULL) {
                        MyError();
                        break;
                    }

                    // Get the result string.
                    ImmGetCompositionString(hIMC, GCS_RESULTSTR, lpstr, dwSize);

                    // Release the context when it is no longer needed.
                    ImmReleaseContext(hWnd,hIMC);

                    // Do something with the result string here.

                    // Free the memory now.
                    GlobalFree((HGLOBAL)lpstr);
                    break;
```

When you process WM_IME_COMPOSITION in this manner, you can safely
ignore any WM_IME_CHAR messages sent for the result string.

Customizing the User Interface

You can customize the user interface for the IME by replacing the default IME
window with your own window. In this case, you define your own IME window
class and window procedure and create the IME window for your application
after destroying the default IME window.

Your IME window must provide the same capabilities as the default IME window,
or your application windows must be prepared to provide the same functionality
as the status, composition, and candidates windows. The window also must handle
any WM_IME_CONTROL messages sent to it and send WM_IME_NOTIFY and
other messages in response to any user input to it.

To ensure that your IME window receives all appropriate messages, you must call the **ImmIsUIMessage** function from every window procedure in your application that accepts character input from the keyboard. The following example shows how to restructure your window procedure to process these messages.

```
HWND hwndIME;  // handle of IME window

long CALLBACK WndProc(HWND hwnd, UINT msg, WPARAM wParam, LPARAM lParam)
{

    if (ImmIsUIMessage(hwndIME, msg, wParam, lParam)==TRUE) {
        // Already processed and ready for post-processing.
        switch(msg) {
            // Post-process WM_IME_COMPOSITION and other messages.
        }
        return 0;
    } else {
        // Not processed yet.
        switch(msg) {
        case WM_CREATE:
            // Create your IME window here.
            break;
        case WM_DESTROY:
            // Destroy your IME window here.
            break;
        }
    }
}
```

If you choose not to create an IME window and provide instead the status, composition, and candidates functionality from within the window procedures of your application, your window procedures must handle the following IME messages rather than pass them to the **DefWindowProc** function.

```
COMPOSITIONFORM cf;
POINT ptMyPoint;
LOGFONT lf;

// The message was not handled by the IME window.
switch(uMsg) {
    case WM_CREATE:
        hIMC = ImmCreateContext();
        hOldIMC = ImmAssociateContext(hWnd ,hIMC);
        break;

    case WM_IME_STARTCOMPOSITION:
        // Prepare to receive the WM_IME_COMPOSITION message.
        break;

    case WM_IME_ENDCOMPOSITION:
        // Finish handling the composition string.
        break;

    case WM_IME_COMPOSITION:
        // Get the composition string, the result string,
        // and also the information for displaying the strings.
        break;

    case WM_IME_SETCONTEXT:
        // Remove bits from lParam to indicate that
        // this window can draw the composition string
        // and index 0 candidate list.
        lParam &= ~(ISC_SHOWUICOMPOSITIONWINDOW &
                    ISC_SHOWUICANDIDATEWINDOW);
        return DefWindowProc(hWnd, uMsg, wParam, lParam);

    case WM_IME_NOTIFY:
        // Handle each IMN_ submessage, and display the IME
        // and candidate list status.
        switch (wParam) {
        case IMN_OPENCANDIDATE:
        case IMN_CHANGECANDIDATE:
```

```
                case IMN_CLOSECANDIDATE:
                    // This application can draw only one candidate list
                    //   whose index is 0.
                    if (lParam == 0x01)  // Bit 0 is On, it is index 0.
                        // Draw the candidate list.
                    else
                        return DefWindowProc(hWnd, uMsg, wParam, lParam);
                    break;
                default:
                    // Make a notification to the IME window.
                    return DefWindowProc(hWnd, uMsg, wParam, lParam);
            }
        break;

        case WM_IME_COMPOSITIONFULL:
            // Adjust the size of the window/area to draw the
            // composition string.
            break;

        case WM_DESTROY:
            ImmAssociateContext(hWnd, hOldIMC);
            ImmDestroyContext(hIMC);
            break;
    }
```

To draw the composition string without the default IME window, you need to handle the WM_IME_COMPOSITION, WM_IME_STARTCOMPOSITION, and WM_IME_ENDCOMPOSITION messages. However, if you receive WM_IME_COMPOSITION and the composition is not final, you need to retrieve the attribute information as well as the composition characters to determine how to draw the characters.

```
HIMC hIMC:
LPSTR lpCompStr;
LPBYTE lpbAttr;
LPSTR lpResultStr;
DWORD dwStrSize;
DWORD dwAttrSize;

case WM_IME_COMPOSITION:
    if ((hIMC = ImmGetContext(hwnd)) == NULL)
        break;
```

```
        if (lParam & GCS_RESULTSTR) {
            // Received the final result, so grab it.
            dwSize = ImmGetCompositionString(hIMC, GCS_RESULTSTR,
                NULL, 0);

            // Allocate space for the string and attributes.

            // Draw the result string here.

        } else if (lParam & (GCS_COMPSTR | GCS_COMPATTR)) {

            // Get the size of the composition string and the attribute
            // information.
            dwStrSize = ImmGetCompositionString(hIMC, GCS_COMPSTR, NULL, 0);
            dwAttrSize = ImmGetCompositionString(hIMC, GCS_COMPATTR,
                NULL, 0);

            // Allocate space for the string and attributes.

            // Get the strings and attributes.
            ImmGetCompositionString(hIMC, GCS_COMPSTR, lpCompStr, dwSize);
            ImmGetCompositionString(hIMC, GCS_COMPATTR, lpAttrStr, dwSize);

            // Draw text using attributes to distinguish converted
            // characters from user input.
        }

        // Free the memory for the buffers here.

        ImmReleaseContext(hWnd,hIMC);

    case WM_IME_SETCONTEXT:
        // Remove bits from lParam to indicate that
        // this window can draw the composition string.
        lParam &= ~(ISC_SHOWUICOMPOSITIONWINDOW);
        return DefWindowProc(hWnd, uMsg, wParam, lParam);
```

Setting the IME Context

Applications that use the default IME window must pass the message WM_IME_SETCONTEXT to the **DefWindowProc** or **ImmIsUIMessage** function without modification. This message identifies the current IME context and specifies which window or windows must be shown. If you choose to customize the IME interface by drawing the composition string, candidate lists, guideline string, and soft keyboard on your own, you must process WM_IME_SETCONTEXT before passing the message to **DefWindowProc** or **ImmIsUIMessage** by modifying the *lParam* parameter.

If you draw the composition string in addition to processing the WM_IME_STARTCOMPOSITION, WM_IME_ENDCOMPOSTION, and WM_IME_COMPOSITION messages, you must also clear the ISC_SHOWUICOMPOSITIONWINDOW value in the *lParam* parameter of WM_IME_SETCONTEXT before passing the message to **DefWindowProc** or **ImmIsUIMessage**.

If you draw the candidate lists in addition to processing the IMN_OPENCANDIDATEWINDOW, IMN_CLOSECANDIDATEWINDOW, and IMN_CHANGECANDIDATEWINDOW notification messages (passed with the WM_IME_NOTIFY message), you must clear the ISC_SHOWUICANDIDATEWINDOW values in the *lParam* parameter of WM_IME_SETCONTEXT that correspond to the candidate lists that you can draw. For example, if you draw the second candidate list (index 2), you must clear the corresponding ISC_SHOWUICANDIDATEWINDOW value as follows.

```
lParam &= ~ISC_SHOWUICANDIDATEWINDOW<<2;
```

If you draw all candidate lists, you can clear all values by using the ISC_SHOWUIALLCANDIDATEWINDOW value in the following manner.

```
lParam &= ~ISC_SHOWUIALLCANDIDATEWINDOW;
```

If you draw the guideline string in addition to processing the IMN_GUIDELINE notification message (passed with the WM_IME_NOTIFY message), you must clear the ISC_SHOWUIGUIDEWINDOW value in the *lParam* parameter of WM_IME_SETCONTEXT before passing the message to **DefWindowProc** or **ImmIsUIMessage**.

If you hide the soft keyboard, you must clear the ISC_SHOWUISOFTKBD value in the *lParam* parameter of WM_IME_SETCONTEXT before passing the message to **DefWindowProc** or **ImmIsUIMessage**.

Compatibility

Windows 95 supports IME applications that were written for previous versions of the operating system as long as the applications are compatible with the Windows version 3.1 IME. In addition, Windows 95 supports Windows version 3.1 IMEs and can load and assign any Windows version 3.1 IME to a keyboard layout, making the IME available to applications written for either Windows version 3.1 or Windows 95. Also, because Windows 95 manages the interface with Windows version 3.1 IMEs, applications can use either the Windows 95 or Windows version 3.1 input method management functions to access Windows version 3.1 IMEs. You can retrieve the operating system version number of an IME by using the **ImmGetProperty** function and specifying the IGP_GETIMEVERSION value. (Note, however, that Korean Windows version 3.1 IMEs are not supported by Korean Windows 95.)

Although any application can use a Windows version 3.1 IME, not all functions and messages are available. In particular, the **ImmGetCandidateListCount**, **ImmGetCandidateList**, **ImmGetGuideLine**, and **ImmGetConversionList** functions return an error if called, and the IMC_OPENSTATUSWINDOW, IMC_CLOSESTATUSWINDOW, IMC_GETSTATUSWINDOWPOS, and IMC_SETSTATUSWINDOWPOS messages are not available. Also, the clause information of the result string and the reading information of the composition string are not available.

Windows 95 does not support IME applications written for versions of IME that are earlier than the Windows version 3.1 IME.

A R T I C L E   3 1

Writing Applications for Middle-Eastern Languages

About Writing Applications for Middle-Eastern Languages

Writing applications for the Middle-Eastern languages is relatively simple. The multilingual features of the Microsoft® Win32® application programming interface (API) together with the unified architecture of international versions of Microsoft® Windows® 95 makes it possible to develop these applications just by changing the application resource files. This article describes the process. It is assumed that the reader is familiar with techniques used to write international applications, especially separating resources from code.

Middle-Eastern Language Elements

In Middle-Eastern languages, portions of written text are read right to left and other portions are read left to right. Arabic and Hebrew are two such languages. These languages have the following similarities:

- Both have a right to left orientation of characters within each word.

- Both have a right to left orientation for reading order of words, but both find a left to right reading order acceptable in some cases.

- Both have a left to right order of numbers and characters in foreign (Latin-based) text.

- Both use a left to right reading order for foreign (Latin-based) text.

- Both have diacritics, as most Latin scripts do. A *diacritic* is an accent or phonetic element that modifies another element (for example, ` + A = À).

- Both are single-byte character set languages. In some cases, two or more of their characters may actually represent a single character called a ligature. A *ligature* is two or more letters joined together (for example, A + E = Æ).

Arabic and Hebrew language are different in these ways:

- Arabic has contextual shaping of characters, depending on whether the character is positioned at the beginning, middle, or end of a word or whether it stands alone. (Hebrew has a few characters that change at the end of a sentence, but these are typed as a separate character.)

- Arabic uses kashidas. A *kashida* is a null element that is the extension of the end of a character, either filling empty space or joining two characters.

In general, the languages and cultures of the Middle East have a general right to left orientation just as Latin-based languages and cultures have a left to right orientation. This means that lists, menus, sets of buttons, or anything else that can have an alignment should be designed with a right to left orientation. Although this general right to left orientation and contextual shaping of Arabic may be intimidating at first, Windows 95 provides the resources and functions needed to make handling these language easier.

System Resources and Text Handling

In Windows 95, any string of text is saved in the order typed. This means that what you see on the screen or on the printed page may be in a different order than what you typed in. Obviously, this makes the modification of existing text a little tricky, but the Windows 95 and Win32 functions help make this easier.

Whenever possible, applications should use system edit controls for text input, subclassing them as necessary. If an application edits and displays text, it should use the **GetCharacterPlacement** function to determine the order in which the individual characters in the string are displayed. If the application displays a caret with the text, it should use **GetCharacterPlacement** to determine the caret position for each character in the text. The function also returns information about the order and number of glyphs for the string. This information is useful for determining whether the displayed string contains ligatures or extra characters, such as kashidas.

Everything in the resource file that pertains to country specific information should be thought of as part of the localization process. For the Middle East, this includes the orientation of menu items, buttons, dialog boxes, and so on. All these should be set in the resource file. If an application has menus, dialog boxes, lists, list boxes, and other visual elements that contain text, it must display the text in right to left order. Because Windows 95 allows applications to use the same functions to display text in right to left order as are used to display in left to right order, you can adapt a carefully designed application for the Middle Eastern market simply by changing the text strings, control positions, and text orientation styles in the resource file. In such cases, the application does not need to be recompiled.

In some cases, it may still make sense to modify and recompile your application source code—for example, if you need a highly optimized version of your application to compete successfully in the Middle-Eastern market.

P A R T   7

Advanced Programming

ARTICLE 32

Thunk Compiler

About the Thunk Compiler

Writing applications for the Microsoft® Win32® application programming interface (API) is recommended for these reasons:

- The flat address space—that is, no segments or offsets
- Better performance
- Greater robustness

However, as compelling as arguments are to move to the 32-bit programming model, there may be pragmatic reasons for not making the move all at once. Certain components of an application may lend themselves to the migration to 32 bits, while other components may be more tightly bound to the 16-bit environment. For example, an application developer may want to move the application's user interface code to 32 bits to take advantage of new system features, but may have an existing dynamic-link library (DLL) specifically optimized for the 16-bit architecture. Rather than delay the release of a new version of the application, the developer can decide instead to take advantage of the Microsoft Thunk Compiler to mix 16- and 32-bit components.

Thunking Mechanics

The Thunk Compiler needs to check for these elements in a mixed 16- and 32-bit environment:

- Pointers consist of a selector and a 16-bit offset in a 16-bit Microsoft® Windows® environment. However, in a 32-bit Windows environment, pointers essentially consist of a 32-bit offset; that is, the DS, ES, SS, and CS registers all contain selectors with the same base address. All pointers in this environment are considered to be near 0:32 pointers. Translating a 16:16 pointer to a 0:32 pointer involves determining the segment base for the selector portion of the pointer and adding the offset to it. Translating a 0:32 pointer to a 16:16 pointer involves allocating a selector and calculating the offset from the base of the corresponding segment.

- Both 16- and 32-bit applications pass function parameters on the stack. However, 16-bit applications address the stack using the SS:SP registers, but 32-bit applications use the SS:ESP registers. When thunking from 16 bits to 32 bits (or thunking back in the other direction), the processor's method of addressing the stack must be switched.

- The word size is 32 bits in a 32-bit environment and 16 bits in a 16-bit environment. When an application uses both 16- and 32-bit environments, some piece of software must be able to translate 16-bit words to 32-bit words. The following 16-bit function can be used to illustrate the translation.

```
DWORD Sample(WORD i);
```

If a 32-bit component calls this 16-bit function, it pushes a 32-bit argument on the stack, but the 16-bit function only pops 16 bits off the stack. Later, when the function returns, it places the returned doubleword value in the DX:AX register pair, but the 32-bit calling application expects the return value to be in the EAX register. It is the thunking layer's responsibility to negotiate these translations.

- To correctly handle packing and conversion, the Thunk Compiler translates structure members one at a time. The Thunk Compiler supports structure packing on 1-, 2-, or 4-byte boundaries (corresponding to the /Zp1, /Zp2, and /Zp4 compiler options for Microsoft C language products). However, 8-byte structure alignment is not supported. Structure packing boundaries must be the same on both sides of a thunk.

- Unlike 32-bit code, 16-bit code is usually not reentrant; 16-bit code is typically written with the assumption of a cooperative mulitasking model. The thunk layer must serialize access to 16-bit code. In contrast, 32-bit code must execute without serialization to prevent deadlocks. The thunk layer manages serialization on transitions in both directions.

Thunking Benefits and Drawbacks

If you use thunking to avoid porting all of your code to 32 bits or to take advantage of 16-bit components, you may save development time. In addition, your executable files may have a smaller memory footprint than if they were full 32-bit applications. However, there are some issues related to thunking that may make you choose to avoid it in your application. These issues are described in the following sections.

Thunking Models

Microsoft® Win32s®, Microsoft® Windows NT™, and Windows 95 use different thunking models. Win32s supports "universal thunks," which are not supported by either Windows NT or Windows 95. Window NT supports "generic thunks," which only allow thunking from 16 bits to 32 bits. Although Windows 95 supports generic thunks, it does not support the underlying process model used by Windows NT. Use of the Windows 95 model can lead to serious incompatibilities with the Windows NT generic thunking model. (For more information about generic thunks in Windows 95, see "Generic Thunking Mechanism" later in this article. Windows 95 implements a new thunking model, "flat thunks." Flat thunks allow thunking from 32 bits to 16 bits or vice versa. The flat thunking model requires use of the Thunk Compiler described in this topic.

If you use flat thunks, your application cannot be ported to Windows NT.

Compatibility with Existing 16-Bit DLLs

The Thunk Compiler accepts the following compatibility statement.

```
win31compat = true;
```

You must use this statement if a 16-bit DLL replaces a DLL that is currently used in a Windows version 3.1 environment or if the DLL runs as part of a graphics device interface (GDI) device driver. You should probably use this statement even if your 16-bit DLL does not fit into one of these categories, because it provides extra protection against poorly behaved DLLs that might be used by your thunk DLL.

The compatibility statement causes the unloading of a 32-bit DLL to be deferred until the containing process terminates. Use of this statement ensures that interprocess loading and freeing procedures, which may have worked with a pure 16-bit DLL, will not cause the thunked version of the 32-bit DLL to be freed prematurely. It also allows the 16-bit library to be freed without execution of the 32-bit DLL's notification routine—an occurrence that could cause reentry into 16-bit code.

16- to 32-Bit Thunks and Preemption

Because 16-bit processes multitask cooperatively with respect to each other, 16-bit code is often written with the assumption that it will not be interrupted by another process until it explicitly yields the 16-bit scheduler (typically by calling the **GetMessage** function). In contrast, 32-bit code is written with the expectation that it can wait on Win32 synchronization objects without impeding the progress of other processes. If you mix code written under these different assumptions, you should take care to avoid deadlocks or errors due to unexpected reentrancy.

While a process is executing 32-bit code, it is possible for other processes to enter 16-bit code, possibly reentering the 16-bit code that was thunked from. That is, entering a 16- to 32-bit thunk releases the 16-bit subsystem for use by other processes (under certain conditions noted in the following paragraph). Thus, 16- to 32-bit thunks should not be used if your code cannot be reentered at that time. In addition, you should avoid using 16- to 32-bit thunks inside callback functions passed to a third-party DLL, unless it is documented that the code calling the call-back function is reentrant. (For example, if the callback function is allowed to yield, it is probably reentrant.)

If the process executing the thunk is 32 bits, any other process can reenter 16-bit code inside a 16- to 32-bit thunk. On the other hand, if the process executing the thunk is 16 bits, only 32-bit processes can reenter 16-bit code, because 16-bit processes are cooperatively multitasked with respect to each other. Thus, if your 16-bit code is used only by 16-bit processes, the reentrancy requirement can be relaxed, because other 16-bit processes can get control only if your 16-bit process yields. (A DLL cannot control what applications call it, of course, so guaranteeing that your 16-bit code will be used only by 16-bit processes is difficult.) There are other restrictions on what can be done in 16-bit processes, as described in the following section, "Behavior of Win32 Functions Inside 16-Bit Processes" later in this article.

Behavior of Win32 Functions Inside 16-Bit Processes

In Windows 95, 16- to 32-bit thunks are primarily useful for implementing callback thunks on 32-bit processes. They can also be used to execute 32-bit code in 16-bit processes. Although the latter can improve performance and multitasking, there are important restrictions on what can be done in a 16-bit process.

The "bitness" of a process is determined by the format of the executable file that launched it, and it is a permanent attribute of the process. A 16-bit process executing 32-bit code is not the same as a 32-bit process executing the same code. The following important differences apply:

- The 32-bit code will still execute on the stack reserved by the 16-bit application, which is much smaller than the 1MB stack used by true 32-bit applications.

- 16-bit processes cannot create new threads. Certain Win32 API elements, such as the functions supporting the new common dialog boxes or those supporting console applications, create threads on behalf of the calling application. These functions cannot be used in a 16-bit process.

- Thunking into 32-bit code releases the 16-bit subsystem to other 32-bit processes, but other 16-bit processes will still be blocked, unless your process explicitly yields (typically by calling the **GetMessage** function). In other words, 16-bit applications still multitask cooperatively even when executing 32-bit code. This means that no 16-bit application will get processing time if a 16-bit application blocks for a long time without yielding. A common problem is using the **CreateProcess** function to launch a 16-bit application and then waiting on a synchronization object to do something. If the application does not yield, the new application will never run and signal the object, so deadlock will occur.

  One way to avoid this problem is to use the **MsgWaitForMultipleObjects** function to wait for either messages or synchronization objects. Although this solution is effective when required, it still results in a less efficient blocking operation than that of a 32-bit application.

In general, 32-bit code within 16-bit processes should be limited to code that uses the 32-bit heap functions, memory-mapped file functions, file functions, and functions involving the current process and thread. 32-bit code using GDI, dialog box, message box, and message functions will also work within 16-bit processes. You should avoid using third party libraries, unless you are sure they work safely in a 16 bit-environment.

Globally Fixing Handles

Translating a 16:16 pointer to a 0:32 pointer involves determining the segment base for the selector portion of the pointer and adding the offset to it. The global memory compacter in Windows 95 may move a block of memory at any time, however, making the linear address invalid. When the Thunk Compiler converts pointers from 16 bits to 32 bits, it fixes the segment portion before computing the linear address. If you translate pointers without using the Thunk Compiler, however, you must be aware of the requirement to fix the segment portion. For more information about the functions you can use to translate pointers, see "Translating Pointers Outside Thunks" later in this article.

16- to 32-Bit Thunks in GDI Device Drivers

The following compatibility statement is required for any 16- to 32-bit thunk script that runs as part of a GDI device driver.

```
win31compat = true;
```

You may only thunk using the following control display driver interface (DDI) functions in a GDI device driver.

Control(ABORTDOC)

Control(ENDDOC)

Control(NEWFRAME)

Control(NEXTBAND)

Control(STARTDOC)

If you use thunking, your driver must be reentrant.

You may call the **OpenJob**, **StartSpoolPage**, **EndSpoolPage**, **CloseJob**, and **DeleteJob** functions during the five listed control DDI calls. These calls will go through drivers written for Windows version 3.*x* for the sake of backward compatibility, but they will fail for Windows 95–based drivers.

Generic Thunking Mechanism

Windows 95 supports the Windows NT generic thunk functions and the Windows NT version 3.5 extensions. The Win32s universal thunk mechanism is not supported.

The same limitations apply to generic thunks as to the flat thunks introduced in Windows 95. For more information, see "Thunking Models" earlier in this article.

The following thunking functions are implemented in the Windows 95 KRNL386 and can be called by 16-bit Windows applications.

CallProc32W	**GetProcAddress32W**
CallProcEx32W	**GetVDMPointer32W**
FreeLibrary32W	**LoadLibraryEx32W**

The following WOW32 thunking functions are implemented in Windows 95. Win32 applications can call these functions. (You should avoid using these functions inside shared DLLs.)

WOWCallback16	**WOWGlobalFree16**
WOWCallback16Ex	**WOWGlobalLock16**
WOWGetVDMPointer	**WOWGlobalLockSize16**
WOWGetVDMPointerFix	**WOWGlobalUnlock16**
WOWGetVDMPointerUnfix	**WOWGlobalUnlockFree16**
WOWGlobalAlloc16	**WOWHandle16**
WOWGlobalAllocLock16	**WOWHandle32**

Because of architectural differences between Windows NT and Windows 95, programs using generic thunks may not be portable between the two platforms. In particular, a Win32 function that works with Windows NT in a 16-bit process is not guaranteed to do so with Windows 95 and vice versa. Also, Windows 95 may activate the global memory compacter at times where Windows NT would not and vice versa. Finally, generic thunks work differently in 32-bit processes in Windows 95, and they do not work at all on 32-bit processes in Windows NT.

Because generic thunks are wrappers around flat thunks, they are subject to the same synchronization issues as flat thunks. For more information about synchronization issues, see "Compatibility with Existing 16-Bit DLLs" earlier in this article and "Behavior of Win32 Functions Inside 16-Bit Processes" earlier in this article.

Using the Thunk Compiler

The Microsoft Win32 Software Development Kit (SDK) includes a sample application that illustrates the use of the Thunk Compiler. This application, APP32.EXE, simply thunks some basic types from 32 bits to 16 bits. This sample is an important supplement to the information in this topic.

The thunk compiler's input is a "thunk script," which is a list of C style function prototypes and type definitions. The compiler produces an .ASM file, which is really two .ASM files in one. You can assemble this .ASM file with the **-DIS_16** option to get the 16-bit .OBJ file to link to the 16-bit component and then assemble it with the **-DIS_32** option to get the 32-bit .OBJ file to link to the 32-bit component.

The 16-bit component of the .ASM file contains a jump table containing the 16:16 address of each function named in the thunk scripts. (The linker must be able to resolve these references; the functions must use the Pascal calling convention and either be implemented in the 16-bit DLL or be imported by the DLL.) The 32-bit half of the .ASM file contains a Stdcall function for each thunk, which converts its parameters to 16 bits and then employs some internal processing to call the 16-bit target referenced in the jump table. When a 32-bit application uses a thunked function, it calls these compiler-generated Stdcall functions directly.

For example, a thunk script's declaration for the **LineTo** function might look like this.

```
typedef         int INT;
typedef unsigned int UINT;
typedef UINT        HANDLE;
typedef HANDLE      HDC;

BOOL LineTo(HDC, INT, INT) {
}
```

For more information about thunk script files, see "Script Files" later in this article.

An application would never include the **LineTo** function in a thunk script, of course, because this function already exists in 16- and 32-bit versions. This example (and the assembly language example that follows) are intended to illustrate the process; the assembly language code, in particular, could differ from the actual code that is generated by the current version of the Thunk Compiler.

When the preceding example from a thunk script is processed by the Thunk Compiler, the following assembly language code is generated. On the 16-bit half, there is the following jump table.

```
externDef LineTo:far16

FT_gdiTargetTable label word
    dw      offset LineTo
    dw       seg LineTo
```

The 32-bit half contains the following code.

```
public LineTo@12
LineTo@12:
    mov     cl,0
; LineTo(16) = LineTo(32) {}
;
; dword ptr [ebp+8]:   param1
; dword ptr [ebp+12]:  param2
; dword ptr [ebp+16]:  param3
;
public IILineTo@12
IILineTo@12:
    call    QT_Entry
    push    word ptr [ebp+8]      ;param1: dword->word
    push    word ptr [ebp+12]     ;param2: dword->word
    push    word ptr [ebp+16]     ;param3: dword->word
    call    QT_Target_gdi
    movsx   ebx,ax
    jmp         QT_Exit12
```

When a Win32-based application calls the **LineTo** function, it transfers directly to this routine, which builds a 16-bit call frame and calls a local routine asking it to look up the appropriate address in the jump table and sign-extend the return value. (Each component receives its own set of QT_ routines, which automatically use the correct jump table. The QT_ and FT_ routines are exported by the kernel.)

Script Files

Script files contain descriptions of the functions that are thunked. These files usually have a .THK filename extension. The script files are easily created using function prototypes. For example, a function might be prototyped in the following manner.

```
BOOL WINAPI Sample(int n);
```

The corresponding definition would look like this in the script file.

```
typedef bool BOOL;
typedef int INT;

BOOL Sample(INT n)
{
}
```

Many functions take pointers in their parameter lists. Some pointers are for input only, some are output only, and some are for both input and output. For example, a "ThunkIt" function might take a pointer to an input string, update a second string, and produce a third string as output in the following manner.

```
BOOL WINAPI ThunkIt(LPSTR lpstrInput, LPSTR lpstrInOut, LPSTR Output);
```

The corresponding thunk script declaration for the function follows.

```
typedef char *LPSTR;

BOOL ThunkIt(LPSTR lpstrInput, LPSTR lpstrInOut, LPSTR Output)
{
    pstrInput = input;       // optional, because pointers are input
                             // by default
    lpstrInOut = inout;      // pointer taken in and updated
    lpstrOutput = output;    // pointer returned
}
```

When a pointer is passed from 32-bit to 16-bit code, a single selector with a limit of 64K is allocated in the thunk. If the Win16 code needs to access more than the first 64K of the block, it must change the base address of the selector or allocate additional selectors to access the block.

The thunk compiler supports the following constructions:

- Structures passed by value or reference.
- Structures within structures.
- Pointers within structures, provided that the object pointed to does not require repacking. The object can be another structure.
- Arrays of scalar values embedded in structures.
- The "input", "output," and "inout" qualifiers for pointers, as shown in the preceding example. The default qualifier is "input."
- Returning pointers for 32- to 16-bit thunks, provided that the object pointed to requires no repacking. The object can be a structure. The segment is not globally fixed by the thunk compiler. As a general rule, the Thunk Compiler deallocates the selectors that it allocates.
- The **bool** type. This type is preferred over **int** in situations where an application may use nonzero values other than 1 to represent TRUE.

The Thunk Compiler does not support arrays of pointers, arrays of structures, or floating-point types (such as **float** or **double**).

Procedure for Adding Flat Thunks

You should follow these steps to add flat thunks:

1. Write a thunk script containing thunk declarations and type definitions for the functions that need to be thunked. You should place the following line at the beginning of the script to create 32- to 16-bit thunks.

```
enablemapdirect3216 = true;      // creates 32 to 16 thunks
```

Alternatively, you can use this line to create 16- to 32-bit thunks.

```
enablemapdirect1632 = true;      // creates 16 to 32 thunks
```

2. Compile your thunk script.

```
thunk.exe <inputfile> [-o <outputfile>]
```

The thunk compiler has the following command line.

thunk [{-l/}*options*] *infile*[.*ext*]

?	Displays the help screen.
h	Displays the help screen.
o *name*	Overrides the default output filename.
p *n*	Changes the 16-bit structure alignment (default = 2).
P *n*	Changes the 32-bit structure alignment (default = 4).
t *name*	Overrides the default base name.
N*x name*	Specifies the name segment or class where *x* is either C32 (for 32-bit code segment name) or C16 (for 16-bit code segment name).

3. Assemble the resulting .ASM file to create the 16-bit side of the thunk, and make sure to define the **DIS_16** option. For example, using Microsoft MASM version 6.11, you might use the following command line.

```
ml /DIS_16 /c /W3 /nologo /Fo thk16.obj 32to16.asm
```

4. Make sure to mark your 16-bit DLL as being compatible with subsystem version 4.0 by running the Microsoft Resource Compiler (RC.EXE), which is included in the Win32 SDK, on the DLL.

```
\mstools\bin16\rc -40 <.DLL output file>
```

Important   If the 16-bit DLL is not marked for subsystem version 4.0, the 32-bit DLL will not load. For more information, see "Troubleshooting" later in this article.

---

5. Assemble the resulting .ASM file to create the 32-bit side of the thunk, and make sure to define the **DIS_32** option. For example, using Microsoft MASM version 6.11, you might use the following command line.

```
ml /DIS_32 /c /W3 /nologo /Fo thk32.obj 32to16.asm
```

6. Add the entrypoint functions to the DLLs and the export and import statements to their module-definition (.DEF) files.

7. Compile and link the 16- and 32-bit components.

8. The code generated by the Thunk Compiler links to several Windows 95 entrypoint functions in KRNL386.EXE and KERNEL32.DLL. These entry-point functions are specific to the Thunk Compiler and are not supported in Windows NT.

    The entrypoint functions for KERNEL32.DLL are defined in THUNK32.LIB. You must link your 32-bit DLL with this library file.

    In addition, the following two import statements should be added to the .DEF file for the 16-bit DLL.

```
C16ThkSL01    = KERNEL.631
ThunkConnect16 = KERNEL.651
```

    Once again, these entrypoint functions exist only in Windows 95 and not in Windows NT. Attempts to load DLLs that use these functions will fail in Windows NT.

Implementing a Thunking Layer

The thunking model allows either the 16- or 32-bit thunk component to start first and clean up everything afterward. Follow these steps to implement the thunking layer:

1. Add a procedure named "DllEntryPoint" to your 16-bit DLL. This procedure should look like the following example. (The names of the DLLs are for illustration only.)

```
BOOL FAR PASCAL __export SAMP_ThunkConnect16(LPSTR pszDll16,
    LPSTR pszDll32, WORD hInst, DWORD dwReason);

BOOL FAR PASCAL __export DllEntryPoint(DWORD dwReason, WORD hInst,
        WORD wDS, WORD wHeapSize, DWORD dwReserved1,
        WORD wReserved2) {
```

```
        if (!(SAMP_ThunkConnect16("DLL16.DLL", // name of 16-bit DLL
                "DLL32.DLL",                    // name of 32-bit DLL
                hInst, dwReason))) {
            return FALSE;
        }
        return TRUE;
    }
```

In this example, "SAMP" is the base name—that is, the name of the thunk script file, not including the path and filename extension. If you used the **/t** option with the Thunk Compiler to specify a different base name, you would use the new base name in your procedure. You could, for example, use following command line.

```
THUNK /t MYNAME SAMP.THK
```

The thunk compiler generates the MYNAME_ThunkConnect16 routine, which should then be called in the DllEntryPoint procedure.

2. Add the following import and export statements to your 16-bit DLL's module definition (.DEF) file, picking ordinals that are appropriate for your DLL.

```
EXPORTS
DllEntryPoint       @1 RESIDENTNAME
SAMP_ThunkData16    @2
IMPORTS
C16ThkSL01    = KERNEL.631
ThunkConnect16 = KERNEL.651
```

3. Add the following function to your 32-bit DLL's entrypoint procedure (named DllMain by default). Again, the names of the DLLs are for illustration only.

```
BOOL WINAPI SAMP_ThunkConnect32(LPSTR pszDll16, LPSTR pszDll32,
        DWORD hIinst, DWORD dwReason);
BOOL _stdcall DllMain(DWORD hInst, DWORD dwReason,
            DWORD dwReserved) {
        if (!(SAMP_ThunkConnect32("DLL16.DLL", // name of 16-bit DLL
                "DLL32.DLL",                    // name of 32-bit DLL
                hInst, dwReason))) {
            return FALSE;
        }
        // Process dwReason.
    }
```

4. Add the following export statement to your 32-bit DLL's .DEF file.

```
EXPORT
SAMP_ThunkData32
```

The following implementation rules are very important:

- The 16-bit **DllEntryPoint** function is called each time the module's usage count is incremented or decremented. The *dwReason* parameter is 1 when the usage count is incremented and zero when it is decremented.

- Because the system calls the **DllEntryPoint** function while loading is underway, the value returned by the **GetModuleUsage** function is not reliable if you call it inside your **DllEntryPoint** function.

- Do not call thunks inside the **DllEntryPoint** routines. Do not perform operations that reenter the 16-bit loader, yield the 16-bit scheduler, or release the 16-bit subsystem. These actions could cause unpredictable results and are not guaranteed to work in future versions of the Thunk Compiler.

- You can have multiple **ThunkConnect***XX* calls, so long as they connect to the same DLL. In fact, this is the only way to get both 32- to 16-bit and 16- to 32-bit thunks in one thunk-paired DLL set. The procedure is to have a thunk script for each direction and link both into each DLL. Then each entrypoint function will have two **ThunkConnect** calls.

Translating Pointers Outside Thunks

You may occasionally need to translate 16:16 pointers to 0:32 pointers outside of thunks. The **GetVDMPointer32W**, **WOWGetVDMPointer**, and **WOWGetVDMPointerFix** functions accomplish this. These functions are only required outside of thunks, because when pointers are thunked from 16 to 32 bits by the Thunk Compiler, no special handling is required to fix the segments. Because the Thunk Compiler fixes these segments automatically, 16:16 pointers can be passed to these thunks with no special treatment.

GetVDMPointer32W is a 16-bit function and is portable across Windows NT versions 3.1 and 3.5.

WOWGetVDMPointer is a 32-bit function and is portable across Windows NT version 3.5, but not Windows NT version 3.1.

WOWGetVDMPointerFix is a new 32-bit function. It is similar to **WOWGetVDMPointer**, but ensures that the memory pointed to will not be moved by the global memory compacter until **WOWGetVDMPointerUnfix** has been called. Using **WOWGetVDMPointerFix** and **WOWGetVDMPointerUnfix** is faster and easier than using **WOWGetVDMPointer** or **GetVDMPointer32W**.

If you use **GetVDMPointer32W** or **WOWGetVDMPointer** and the affected segment points to a movable global memory manager block, it is important to call the **GlobalFix** or **GlobalWire** function on the segment portion before computing its linear address. In Windows 95, the global memory compacter can break in at any time when your process is in 32-bit code. If this happens, the block may move and the linear address will become invalid. The debugging version of Windows 95 generates warnings about calls to **GetVDMPointer32W** on unfixed segments.

WOWGetVDMPointerFix converts a 16:16 pointer to a linear address like **WOWGetVDMPointer**. However, it also performs an implicit **GlobalFix** operation on the selector, if necessary. If the selector is allocated as a fixed block or if it is not from the global memory manager, no special action is taken. You should use this function instead of calling **GlobalFix** separately, because it is easier to implement and performance is better.

WOWGetVDMPointerUnfix takes a 16:16 address and undoes the effect of **WOWGetVDMPointerFix** on the segment (the offset portion is ignored). This function should be called once the linear address is no longer needed to avoid bottlenecks in the global memory manager. It is faster than the **GlobalUnfix** function and correctly handles (that is, ignores) selectors that are not from the global memory manager.

Note that the **CallProc32W** and **CallProc32ExW** functions do not call these functions for you. Pointers passed to these functions must be fixed manually.

Late Loading

Windows 95 improves system performance by supporting late loading for thunk DLLs. Loading the 16-bit DLL does not cause the corresponding 32-bit DLL to load immediately. Instead, the thunk subsystem loads the 32-bit DLL when the first 16- to 32-bit thunk is started.

Late loading has the following implications:

- The performance and working set are improved for 16-bit applications that use only the 16-bit portions of thunked DLLs. The 32-bit DLL will not load into those processes.

- The 16-bit DLL must not depend on any action taken by the 32-bit DLL's initialization code until at least one 16- to 32-bit thunk has been called.

- Missing 32-bit DLLs or failed 32-bit loads will not be detected until the first call is made to a 16- to 32-bit thunk. If the 32-bit DLL cannot load or fails to initialize, the 16- to 32-bit thunk call will return a value of zero. This error code may be changed on a thunk by thunk basis by including a **faulterrorcode** = *dword*; line between the curly braces of a function call. For example, the following function instructs the thunk subsytem to return a−1 from the thunk call if it is the first thunk call and the 32-bit DLL cannot finish loading.

```
int Sample(void) {
    faulterrorcode = -1;
}
```

Although late loading is a valuable optimization for a 16-bit DLL that can execute autonomously from its 32-bit partner, it does complicate error recovery. Late loading can be disabled by including the following line in the thunk script.

```
preload32 = true;
```

If you use this option, the 16-bit subsystem will be released during the loading of your 16-bit DLL, possibly causing other 16-bit code to be reentered. For this reason, the **preload32** statement is not available if your thunk script requires the **win31compat** statement. For more information about the **win31compat** statement, see "Compatibility with Existing 16-Bit DLLs" earlier in this article.

Although the thunk compiler supports a "**preload16**" keyword for future expansion, late loading of 16-bit DLLs is neither supported nor planned.

Troubleshooting

This section outlines two common problems when thunking is implemented and describes their likely causes.

- The 32-bit DLL will not load.

  The Windows 95 loader requires that the 16-bit DLL be marked as subsystem version 4.0 or greater for the **DllEntryPoint** function to run. In addition, **DllEntryPoint** must be exported using the name "DllEntryPoint" and must be marked RESIDENTNAME.

  To check the version number, run the Microsoft EXE File Header Utility (EXEHDR), using the following command line.

  ```
  exehdr -v <your-16-bit-DLL>
  ```

  The output should contain the following line.

  ```
  Operating system: Microsoft Windows - version 4.0
  ```

  If the subsystem version number is less than 4.0, you should use RC.EXE from the Win32 SDK to set the version of your 16-bit DLL correctly.

- Loading the 16-bit DLL does not load the 32-bit DLL.

  This is by design. A 32-bit DLL does not load into a process context until that process calls its first 16- to 32-bit thunk. For more information, see "Late Loading" earlier in this article.

  If this feature is incompatible with your DLL design, you may disable it by including the following line in your thunk script.

  ```
  preload32 = true;
  ```

Reference

The following functions are associated with the Thunk Compiler.

16-bit WOW Functions

The functions in this section are 16-bit WOW API elements exported by kernel for use in generic thunks.

CallProc32W

```
DWORD FAR PASCAL CallProc32W(DWORD param1, DWORD param2, ... ,
    LPVOID lpProcAddress32, DWORD fAddressConvert, DWORD nParams);
```

Used by a 16-bit thunk dynamic-link library (DLL) to call an entrypoint function in a 32-bit DLL.

- Returns a 32-bit value if successful. This value is the return value from the 32-bit entrypoint function represented by *lpProcAddress32*. The return value can also be zero if *lpProcAddress32* is zero or if *nParams* is greater than 32.

param1 through *param32*
Parameters for the 32-bit procedure represented by *lpProcAddress32*.

lpProcAddress32
32-bit value corresponding to the procedure to be called, which is returned by the **GetProcAddress32** function.

fAddressConvert
Bit mask representing which parameters will be treated as 16:16 pointers and translated into flat linear pointers before being passed to the 32-bit procedure.

nParams
Number of **DWORD** parameters passed (not counting *fAddressConvert* and *nParams*). For functions that take no parameters, this parameter will be zero.

CallProc32W takes at least three parameters: *lpProcAddress32*, *fAddressConvert*, and *nParams*. In addition, it can take a maximum of 32 optional parameters. These parameters must be **DWORD** types and must match the type that the 32-bit thunk DLL is expecting. If the appropriate bit is set in the *fAddressConvert* mask, the parameter will be translated from a 16:16 pointer to a 32-bit flat linear pointer. Note that the lowest bit in the mask represents *param1*, the second lowest bit represents *param2*, and so on.

This function causes Windows 95 to release the 16-bit subsystem. If this function is used exclusively in 16-bit processes (as in Windows NT), there are no new reentrancy issues. Otherwise, the use of this function can cause 16-bit code to be reentered. For more information about reentrancy issues, see "Behavior of Win32 Functions Inside 16-Bit Processes" earlier in this article.

Unlike the flat thunks, **CallProc32W** and **CallProc32WEx** do not automatically fix global memory handles that are translated to 0:32 pointers. Therefore, you must call the **GlobalFix** or **GlobalWire** function on the handle first. In Windows 95, global compaction can move memory blocks at any time while the current thread is executing 32-bit code. Because of this, certain pointer translation practices that worked in Windows NT may cause small, but undesirable, race conditions in Windows 95.

Note   You should be careful when using this function, because there is no compiler check made on the number and type of parameters, no conversion of types (all parameters are passed as DWORDs and are passed directly to the function called without conversion). No checks of the 16:16 address are made (limit checks, NULL checks, correct ring level, and so on).

CallProcEx32W

```
DWORD FAR CallProcEx32W(DWORD nParams, DWORD fAddressConvert,
    DWORD lpProcAddress, DWORD param1, ...);
```

Used by a 16-bit thunk dynamic-link library (DLL) to call an entrypoint function in a 32-bit DLL.

- Returns a 32-bit value if successful. This value is the return value from the 32-bit entrypoint function represented by *lpProcAddress*. The return value can also be zero if *lpProcAddress* is zero or if *nParams* is greater than 32.

nParams
Number of **DWORD** parameters passed (not counting *fAddressConvert* and *nParams*). For functions that take no parameters, this parameter will be zero.

fAddressConvert
Bit mask representing which parameters will be treated as 16:16 pointers and translated into flat linear pointers before being passed to the 32-bit procedure.

lpProcAddress
32-bit value corresponding to the procedure to be called, which is returned by the **GetProcAddress32** function.

param1 through *param32*
Parameters for the 32-bit procedure represented by *lpProcAddress*

CallProcEx32W is similar to **CallProc32W**, but it uses the C calling convention to allow easier and more flexible prototyping.

This function causes Windows 95 to release the 16-bit subsystem. If this function is used exclusively in 16-bit processes (as in Windows NT), there are no new reentrancy issues. Otherwise, the use of this function can cause 16-bit code to be reentered. For more information about reentrancy issues, see "Behavior of Win32 Functions Inside 16-Bit Processes" earlier in this article.

Unlike the flat thunks, **CallProc32W** and **CallProc32WEx** do not automatically fix global memory handles that are translated to 0:32 pointers. Therefore, you must call the **GlobalFix** or **GlobalWire** function on the handle first. In Windows 95, global compaction can move memory blocks at any time while the current thread is executing 32-bit code. Because of this, certain pointer translation practices that worked in Windows NT may cause small, but undesirable, race conditions in Windows 95.

FreeLibrary32W

```
BOOL FAR PASCAL FreeLibrary32W(DWORD hInst);
```

Allows a 16-bit thunk dynamic-link library (DLL) to free a 32-bit thunk DLL that it had previously loaded by using the **LoadLibraryEx32W** function.

▪ Returns TRUE if successful or FALSE otherwise.

hInst
   This function thunks to the Win32 **FreeLibrary** function. For a complete description of this parameter, see the documentation included in the Win32 SDK.

Note that WOW does not do any cleanup of 32-bit thunk DLLs when the WOW task exits. It is up to the 16-bit thunk DLLs to free the 32-bit thunk DLLs, as necessary.

This function causes Windows 95 to release the 16-bit subsystem. Therefore, your code may be reentered during the call to this function. However, if this function is only used in 16-bit processes (as in Windows NT) and none of the DLL's notification routines yield, this reentrancy will not occur.

GetProcAddress32W

```
DWORD FAR PASCAL GetProcAddress32W(DWORD hModule, LPCSTR lpszProc);
```

Allows a 16-bit thunk dynamic-link library (DLL) to retrieve a value that corresponds to a 32-bit thunk routine.

- Returns a 32-bit value if successful. This value must be passed as a parameter to the **CallProc32W** or **CallProcEx32W** function rather than being used directly.

hModule through *lpszProc*
This function thunks to the Win32 **GetProcAddress** function. For a complete description of these parameters, see the documentation included in the Win32 SDK.

This function causes Windows 95 to release the 16-bit subsystem. Therefore, your code may be reentered during the call to this function. However, if this function is only used in 16-bit processes (as in Windows NT) and none of the DLL's notification routines yield, this reentrancy will not occur.

GetVDMPointer32W

```
DWORD FAR PASCAL GetVDMPointer32W(LPVOID lpAddress, UINT fMode);
```

Allows a 16-bit thunk dynamic-link library (DLL) to translate a 16-bit far pointer into a 32-bit flat pointer for use by a 32-bit thunk DLL.

- Returns a 32-bit linear address if successful or NULL otherwise.

lpAddress
Valid 16:16 address, either in protected or real mode.

fMode
One of the following flags:

1   The address is interpreted as a protected-mode address.

0   The address is interpreted as a real-mode address.

The WOW kernel memory manager moves segments in memory and keeps the selectors the same. However, if you get the linear address, it may not be valid if the memory manager has moved memory. You should assume that global compaction can occur any time that a 16- to 32-bit flat thunk or generic thunk is entered, a function is called, or the current task yields.

LoadLibraryEx32W

```
DWORD FAR PASCAL LoadLibraryEx32W(LPCSTR lpszLibFile, DWORD hFile,
    DWORD dwFlags);
```

Allows a 16-bit thunk dynamic-link library (DLL) to load a 32-bit thunk DLL.

- Returns a 32-bit handle to a DLL instance if successful or NULL otherwise.

lpszLibFile through *dwFlags*
> This function thunks to the Win32 **LoadLibraryEx** function. For a complete description of these parameters, see the documentation included in the Win32 SDK.

After calling this function, the 16-bit thunk DLL can call the **GetProcAddress32W** function to get the address of the 32-bit entrypoint function(s) and then call the thunk(s) by using the **CallProc32W** function.

This function causes Windows 95 to release the 16-bit subsystem. Therefore, your code may be reentered during the call to this function. However, if this function is only used in 16-bit processes (as in Windows NT) and none of the DLL's notification routines yield, this reentrancy will not occur.

32-bit WOW Functions

The functions in this section are 32-bit WOW API elements exported by WOW32.DLL.

WOWCallback16

```
DWORD WINAPI WOWCallback16(DWORD vpfn16, DWORD dwParam);
```

Used in 32-bit code called from 16-bit code (through generic thunks) to call back to the 16-bit side (generic callback).

- The return value comes from the callback routine. If the callback routine returns a **WORD** type instead of a **DWORD** type, the upper 16 bits of the return value are undefined. If the callback routine has no return value, the entire return value of this function is undefined.

vpfn16
> Pointer to 16-bit callback routine, which is passed from the 16-bit side.

dwParam
> Parameter for the 16-bit callback routine.

This function will not work when called in a 32-bit process.

The 16-bit function to be called must be declared with one of the following types.

```
LONG FAR PASCAL CallbackRoutine(DWORD dwParam);
```

```
LONG FAR PASCAL CallbackRoutine(VOID FAR *vp);
```

The type used is determined by whether the parameter is a pointer.

If you are passing a pointer, you will need to get the pointer by using either the **WOWGlobalAlloc16** or **WOWGlobalAllocLock16** function.

WOWCallback16Ex

```
BOOL WINAPI WOWCallback16Ex(DWORD vpfn16, DWORD dwFlags, DWORD cbArgs,
    PVOID pArgs, PDWORD pdwRetCode);
```

Used in 32-bit code called from 16-bit code (through generic thunks) to call back to the 16-bit side (generic callback).

- If *cbArgs* is larger than the WCB16_MAX_ARGS bytes that the system supports, the return value is FALSE and the **GetLastError** function returns the ERROR_INVALID_PARAMETER value. Otherwise, the return value is TRUE and the **DWORD** pointed to by *pdwRetCode* contains the return code from the callback routine. If the callback routine returns a **WORD** type, the upper 16 bits of the return code are undefined and should be ignored by using **LOWORD**(*dwRetCode*).

vpfn16
　　Pointer to 16-bit callback routine, which is passed from the 16-bit side.
dwFlags
　　One of the following flags:

WCB16_CDECL	Calls a **_cdecl** callback routine.
WCB16_PASCAL	Calls a **_pascal** callback routine (default).

cbArgs
　　Count of bytes in arguments (used to properly clean the 16-bit stack).
pArgs
　　Arguments for the callback routine.
pdwRetCode
　　Return code from the callback routine.

This function will not work when called in a 32-bit process.

WOWCallback16Ex allows any combination of arguments up to
WCB16_MAX_CBARGS bytes total to be passed to the 16-bit callback
routine. Regardless of the value of *cbArgs*, WCB16_MAX_CBARGS bytes
will always be copied from *pArgs* to the 16-bit stack. If *pArgs* is less than
WCB16_MAX_CBARGS bytes from the end of a page and the next page is
inaccessible, **WOWCallback16Ex** will incur an access violation.

The arguments pointed to by *pArgs* must be in the correct order for the callback routine's calling convention. For example, to call the Pascal routine
SetWindowText, *pArgs* would point to an array of words.

```
LONG FAR PASCAL SetWindowText(HWND hwnd, LPCSTR lpsz);

WORD SetWindowTextArgs[] = {OFFSETOF(lpsz), SELECTOROF(lpsz), hwnd};
```

In other words, the arguments are placed in the array in reverse order, with the
least significant word first for **DWORD** types and offset first for **FAR** pointers.

To call the **_cdecl** routine **wsprintf**, *pArgs* would also point to an array of words.

```
LPSTR lpszFormat = "%d %s";
int _cdecl wsprintf(lpsz, lpszFormat, nValue. lpszString);

WORD wsprintfArgs[] = {OFFSETOF(lpsz), SELECTOROF(lpsz),
    OFFSETOF(lpszFormat), SELECTOROF(lpszFormat), nValue,
    OFFSETOF(lpszString), SELECTOROF(lpszString)};
```

In other words, the arguments are placed in the array in the order listed in the
function prototype with the least significant word first for **DWORD** types and
offset first for **FAR** pointers.

WOWGetVDMPointer

```
LPVOID WINAPI WOWGetVDMPointer(DWORD vp, DWORD dwBytes,
    BOOL fProtectedMode);
```

Converts a 16:16 address to the equivalent flat address.

- Returns a 32-bit address if successful. If the selector is invalid, the return value
  is NULL.

vp
> Valid 16:16 address.

dwBytes
> Size of the block pointed to by *vp*.

fProtectedMode
> One of the following flags:

> 1   The upper 16 bits are treated as a selector in the local descriptor table.

> 0   The upper 16 bits are treated as a real-mode segment value.

Limit checking is performed only in the checked (debugging) build of the WOW32.DLL file, which will cause NULL to be returned when the limit is exceeded by the supplied offset.

This function should never be used on a 16-bit global memory handle selector that has not been previously fixed in memory by using the **GlobalFix** or **GlobalWire** function. You should assume that global compaction can occur at any time the 16-bit subsystem is not locked by the current thread.

WOWGetVDMPointerFix

```
LPVOID WINAPI WOWGetVDMPointerFix(DWORD vp, DWORD dwBytes,
    BOOL fProtectedMode);
```

Converts a 16:16 address to the equivalent flat address. Unlike the function **WOWGetVDMPointer**, this function calls the **GlobalFix** function before returning the flat address so that the 16-bit memory will not move around in linear space.

- Returns a 32-bit address if successful. If the selector is invalid, the return value is NULL.

vp
> Valid 16:16 address.

dwBytes
> Size of the block pointed to by *vp*.

fProtectedMode
> One of the following flags:

> 1   The upper 16 bits are treated as a selector in the local descriptor table.

> 0   The upper 16 bits are treated as a real-mode segment value.

WOWGetVDMPointerUnfix

```
VOID WINAPI WOWGetVDMPointerUnfix(DWORD vp);
```

Uses the **GlobalUnfix** function to unfix a pointer retrieved by the function **WOWGetVDMPointerFix**.

- No return value.

vp
    Address retrieved by the **WOWGetVDMPointerFix** function.

WOWGlobalAlloc16

```
WORD  WINAPI WOWGlobalAlloc16(WORD wFlags, DWORD cb);
```

Thunks to the 16-bit version of the function with the same name. For more information, see the documentation for the 16-bit versions.

WOWGlobalAllocLock16

```
DWORD WINAPI WOWGlobalAllocLock16(WORD wFlags, DWORD cb, WORD *phMem);
```

Combines the functionality of the **WOWGlobalAlloc16** and **WOWGlobalLock16** functions, thunking to the 16-bit versions of the functions with those names. For more information, see the documentation for the 16-bit versions.

WOWGlobalFree16

```
WORD  WINAPI WOWGlobalFree16(WORD hMem);
```

Thunks to the 16-bit version of the function with the same name. For more information, see the documentation for the 16-bit versions.

WOWGlobalLock16

```
DWORD WINAPI WOWGlobalLock16(WORD hMem);
```

Thunks to the 16-bit version of the function with the same name. For more information, see the documentation for the 16-bit versions.

WOWGlobalLockSize16

```
DWORD WINAPI WOWGlobalLockSize16(WORD hMem, PDWORD pcb);
```

Combines the functionality of the **WOWGlobalLock16** and **GlobalSize** functions, thunking to the 16-bit versions of the functions with those names. For more information, see the documentation for the 16-bit versions.

WOWGlobalUnlock16

```
BOOL  WINAPI WOWGlobalUnlock16(WORD hMem);
```

Thunks to the 16-bit version of the function with the same name. For more information, see the documentation for the 16-bit versions.

WOWGlobalUnlockFree16

```
WORD  WINAPI WOWGlobalUnlockFree16(DWORD vpMem);
```

Combines the functionality of the **WOWGlobalUnlock16** and **WOWGlobalFree16** functions, thunking to the 16-bit versions of the functions with those names. For more information, see the documentation for the 16-bit versions.

WOWHandle16

```
WORD WINAPI WOWHandle16(HANDLE, WOW_HANDLE_TYPE);
```

This function (and the associated macro) is used to map a 32-bit handle to a 16-bit handle. Because the relationship between a Win16 handle and a Win32 handle may change in the future, this function should be used instead of any private knowledge of the relationship between them.

This function uses the *WOW_HANDLE_TYPE* parameter to indicate the type of handle being translated. Types supported include **HWND, HMENU, HDWP, HDROP, HDC, HFONT, HMETAFILE, HRGN, HBITMAP, HBRUSH, HPALETTE, HPEN, HACCEL, HTASK,** and **FULLHWND.**

The *WOW_HANDLE_TYPE* name corresponding to each of these types is of the form WOW_TYPE_*handle* (for example, WOW_TYPE_HWND).

You can use macros to map handles between Win16 and Win32. For example, to map a Win16 **HWND** to a Win32 **HWND,** you would use the **HWND_32** macro.

```
hWnd32 = HWND_32(hWnd16)
```

A "full" hWnd is a hWnd that a Win32-based application would see (and therefore can be used in comparisons with 32-bit hWnds received from Win32 functions.) The other hWnd type has a different value, but is recognized by the system. Do not make assumptions about the relationship between the 16-bit hWnd, the 32-bit Hwnd, and the 32-bit full hWnd. This relationship has changed in the past (for performance reasons), and it may change again in the future.

WOWHandle32

```
HANDLE WINAPI WOWHandle32(WORD, WOW_HANDLE_TYPE);
```

This function (and the associated macro) is used to map a 16-bit handle to a 32-bit handle. Because the relationship between a Win16 handle and a Win32 handle may change in the future, this function should be used instead of any private knowledge of the relationship between them.

This function uses the *WOW_HANDLE_TYPE* parameter to indicate the type of handle being translated. Types supported include **HWND, HMENU, HDWP, HDROP, HDC, HFONT, HMETAFILE, HRGN, HBITMAP, HBRUSH, HPALETTE, HPEN, HACCEL, HTASK,** and **FULLHWND.**

The *WOW_HANDLE_TYPE* name corresponding to each of these types is of the form WOW_TYPE_*handle* (for example, WOW_TYPE_HWND).

You can use macros to map handles between Win16 and Win32. For example, to map a Win16 **HWND** to a Win32 **HWND**, you would use the **HWND_32** macro.

```
hWnd32 = HWND_32(hWnd16)
```

A "full" hWnd is a hWnd that a Win32-based application would see (and therefore can be used in comparisons with 32-bit hWnds received from Win32 functions.) The other hWnd type has a different value, but is recognized by the system. Do not make assumptions about the relationship between the 16-bit hWnd, the 32-bit Hwnd, and the 32-bit full hWnd. This relationship has changed in the past (for performance reasons), and it may change again in the future.

Index

WELCOME TO THE WORLD OF WINDOWS® 95

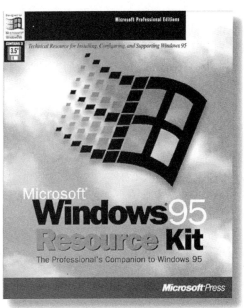

The MICROSOFT® WINDOWS® 95 RESOURCE KIT provides you with all of the information necessary to plan for and implement Windows 95 in your organization.

ISBN 1-55615-678-2
1376 pages, $49.95 ($67.95 Canada)
Three 3.5" disks

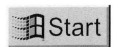

Details on how to install, configure, and support Windows 95 will save you hours of time and help ensure that you get the most from your computing investment. This exclusive Microsoft publication, written in cooperation with the Windows 95 development team, is the perfect technical companion for network administrators, support professionals, systems integrators, and computer professionals.

The MICROSOFT WINDOWS 95 RESOURCE KIT contains important information that will help you get the most out of Windows 95. Whether you support Windows 95 in your company or just want to know more about it, the MICROSOFT WINDOWS 95 RESOURCE KIT is a valuable addition to your reference library.

Microsoft Press® books are available wherever quality books are sold and through CompuServe's Electronic Mall—**GO MSP**.
Call **1-800-MSPRESS** for more information or to place a credit card order.* Please refer to **BBK** when placing your order. Prices subject to change.
*In Canada, contact Macmillan Canada, Attn: Microsoft Press Dept., 164 Commander Blvd., Agincourt, Ontario, Canada M1S 3C7, or call 1-800-667-1115.
Outside the U.S. and Canada, write to International Coordinator, Microsoft Press, One Microsoft Way, Redmond, WA 98052-6399, or fax +1-206-936-7329.

Microsoft®Press

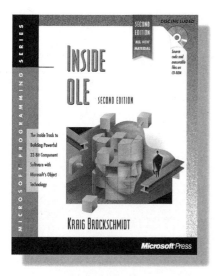

ISBN 1-55615-843-2, 1232 pages, $49.95 ($67.95)

OLE is a unified and extensible environment of object-based services with the overall purpose of enabling rich integration between components. As Microsoft's object technology, it represents major innovations in object-based programming, making it possible to create applications and software components with unprecedented capabilities. But with this power comes additional complexity and new programming paradigms.

INSIDE OLE provides both a clear tutorial and a strong set of example programs, giving you the tools to incorporate OLE into your own development projects. Written by a member of the Microsoft® OLE team, this book truly gives you the insider's perspective on the power of OLE for creating the next generation of innovative software.

INSIDE OLE provides detailed coverage and reference material on:

- **OLE and object fundamentals:** Objects and interfaces, connectable objects, custom components and the Component Object Model, and Local/Remote Transparency

- **Storage and naming technologies:** Structured storage and compound files, persistent objects, and naming and binding

- **Data transfer, viewing, and caching:** Uniform Data Transfer, viewable objects, data caching, OLE Clipboard, and OLE Drag and Drop

- **OLE Automation and OLE Property:** Automation controllers; property pages, changes, and persistence

- **OLE Documents:** OLE Documents and embedding containers; OLE Documents and local embedding servers; in-process object handlers and servers; linking containers; and in-place activation (visual editing) for containers and objects

- **OLE Controls and the future of OLE:** OLE Controls, future enhancements, and component software

VALUABLE INFORMATION INCLUDED ON CD!

CD includes 75 source code examples (more than 100,000 lines of code) that demonstrate how to create components and how to integrate OLE features into applications.

System Requirements

32-Bit Platforms: Windows® 95 or Windows NT™ 3.51 and Visual C++™ 2.0 or later (Win32® SDK required for some samples). 16-Bit Platforms: Windows 3.1 or later and Visual C++ 1.51 or later (some samples are 32-bit only and will not work with 16-bit Windows).

If you're interested in fully exploring and understanding OLE and component software, there's no better source than INSIDE OLE.

Microsoft Press® books are available wherever quality books are sold and through CompuServe's Electronic Mall—**GO MSP**.
Call **1-800-MSPRESS** for more information or to place a credit card order.* Please refer to **BBK** when placing your order. Prices subject to change.
*In Canada, contact Macmillan Canada, Attn: Microsoft Press Dept., 164 Commander Blvd., Agincourt, Ontario, Canada M1S 3C7, or call 1-800-667-1115.
Outside the U.S. and Canada, write to International Coordinator, Microsoft Press, One Microsoft Way, Redmond, WA 98052-6399, or fax +1-206-936-7329.

Microsoft Press

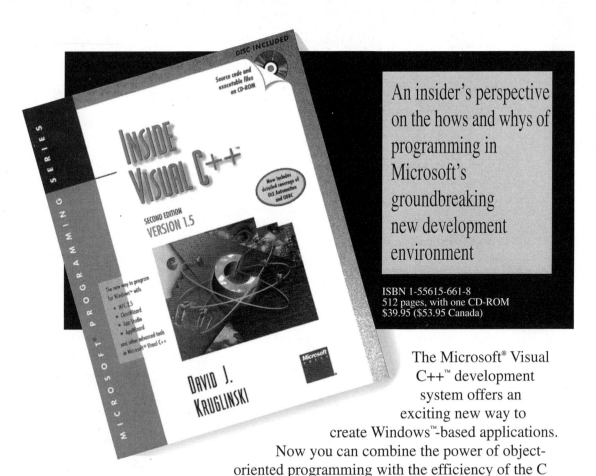

An insider's perspective
on the hows and whys of
programming in
Microsoft's
groundbreaking
new development
environment

ISBN 1-55615-661-8
512 pages, with one CD-ROM
$39.95 ($53.95 Canada)

The Microsoft® Visual C++™ development system offers an exciting new way to create Windows™-based applications. Now you can combine the power of object-oriented programming with the efficiency of the C language. The application framework approach in Visual C++ version 1.5—centering on the Microsoft Foundation Class Library version 2.5—enables programmers to simplify and streamline the process of creating robust, professional applications for Windows.

INSIDE VISUAL C++ takes you one step at a time through the process of creating real-world applications for Windows—the Visual C++ way. Using ample source code examples, this book explores MFC 2.5, App Studio, and the product's nifty "wizards"—AppWizard and ClassWizard—in action. The book also provides a good explanation of application framework theory, along with tips for exploiting hidden features of the MFC library.

Whether you are relatively new to programming for Windows or you are an old dog ready for new tricks, Kruglinski's insider expertise makes INSIDE VISUAL C++ the fastest route to mastering this powerful development system.

Microsoft Press